OXFORD DICTIONARY OF

BUSINESS ENGLISH

FOR LEARNERS OF ENGLISH

Edited by Allene Tuck

Phonetics Editor
Michael Ashby

OXFORD UNIVERSITY PRESS

Oxford University Press, Walton Street, Oxford OX2 6DP

Oxford New York Toronto Madrid Delhi Bombay Calcutta Madras
Karachi Kuala Lumpur Singapore Hong Kong Tokyo Nairobi Dar es Salaam
Cape Town Melbourne Auckland

and associated companies in Berlin Ibadan

OXFORD and OXFORD ENGLISH are
trade marks of Oxford University Press

First published 1993
Fourth impression 1994

ISBN 0 19 431440 5

Cover illustration by David Loftus
Typeset in Great Britain by Tradespools Limited, Frome, Somerset
Printed and bound in Great Britain

Preface

This is the first dictionary of Business English written especially for learners of English to be published by Oxford University Press.

In researching and writing this dictionary it has been necessary to draw on the combined expertise of people in the world of business and those involved in the teaching of English as a foreign language. The result is a dictionary that is comprehensive and up-to-date in its coverage of business words and phrases, clear and helpful in its explanations of the meanings and grammar of these words, and authentic in its choice of example of their use.

I should like to thank the following lexicographers for their careful and committed work in writing the dictionary: Judy Colbeck, John Mahood, James Matson, Michael Nash, Kathryn Phillips-Miles, Joe Rimmer, Mary Shields, Peter Snook and Tony Thorne. I am very grateful to Simon Deefholts for his advisory work on the banking and financial terms. I should also like to acknowledge the work of the large team of people involved in the production of the dictionary once the text was complete.

Oxford, 1993 Allene Tuck

User's Guide to the Dictionary

This dictionary is intended for learners of English of intermediate to advanced level who need to speak, read and write English for business. Business words and phrases are presented clearly and simply, but in enough detail to make this dictionary a valuable resource for students of business and experienced business people alike. The dictionary provides extensive coverage of terms commonly used in accounting, banking, computing, international trade, law, marketing, sales, shipping and the stock exchange, reflecting the many areas with which business people and their advisers need to be familiar. (A complete list of the subject areas covered can be found on the inside front cover.)

To ensure that the material included is authentic and up-to-date, this dictionary has been compiled with the help of the Oxford Corpus. This is a collection of contemporary written and spoken English taken from a variety of sources and stored on computer. Many examples in this dictionary are corpus-based.

As time is so very important to business people, this dictionary has been specially designed for quick and easy access. If you just want to look up a word to find its meaning and see how it is used in an example phrase or sentence, you need only look at the left-hand column of the dictionary. If you want to know more about the word, for example how to pronounce it, how the plural is formed, what words are commonly used with it, you can look at the specially designed *language column* on the right-hand side of the page. In this column you will also find cross-references to other related words, and words with the same or opposite meaning.

The key to entries on the following pages will show you just how many different types of information are contained in a dictionary entry, and exactly where to look to find the information you require.

KEY TO ENTRIES

headword (headwords are listed in a strictly letter-by-letter alphabetical order, ignoring hyphens, spaces and other punctuation)

geographical label

part of speech label

number of definition

letters to show closely related meanings

compound of the headword

alternative form of the headword used in a particular case

advert *abbr* (advertising)

(*UK informal*) an advertisement: *a soap powder advert/an advert for soap powder* ○ *place a full-page advert in the Times.*

/ˈædvɜːt/

pl adverts

▶ **advertisement, commercial**

---

adjourn *verb*

1 **(a)** to stop (a court case, a meeting, etc) for a time before beginning again: *The chairman adjourned the meeting until the following day.* ○ *The conference was adjourned to allow the participants to contact their companies.* **(b)** to come to a stop for a time before beginning again: *The committee adjourned for lunch.* ○ *Let's adjourn and reconvene at 2 o'clock.* **2** to move to another place, esp to continue a discussion, etc: *Let's adjourn to my office where we can have some privacy.*

/əˈdʒɜːn/

adjourn, adjourning, adjourned

1a note transitive verb

⋈ **adjourn** a court case, meeting, talk, trial

1b note intransitive verb

⋈ **adjourn** *for* something

▶ **resume**

2 note intransitive verb

⋈ **adjourn** *to* (a place)

---

aptitude *noun*

natural ability: *She has an aptitude for figures.*

aptitude test an examination to find out what kind of work a person is most suited to: *Most school-leavers should take an aptitude test.*

/ˈæptɪtjuːd/

pl aptitudes

⋈ an **aptitude** *for* (something)

---

associate[1] *noun* (management)

1 a person connected with another or others in an organization; a colleague or partner: *business associates* ○ *an associate in an insurance firm* **2** **Associates** used in the name of an organization to show there are a number of professional partners: *David Irvine Associates*

/əˈsəʊʃiət/

pl associates

abbr assoc

▶ **colleague, Lloyd's associate, partner**

subject label

register label

start of cross-reference section

cross-reference to other headwords with related meanings

definition of the headword

parts of the verb

reference to the number of the definition in the left-hand column

reference to the letter of the definition in the left-hand column

examples of different uses of the headword

note on transitivity of the verb

preposition used with the headword

continued on page 492

A1 *adjective*
1 (*shipping*) (of a ship described in LLOYD'S REGISTER OF SHIPPING) in excellent condition; first class: *an A1 ship* **2** (*insurance*) written on a form used by life assurance companies to describe someone in perfect health: *an A1 life*

/ˌeɪ ˈwʌn/
1 ▶ **Lloyd's Register of Shipping**
2 ▶ **life assurance**

AA *abbr* (advertising)
Advertising Association: *be a member of the AA*

/ˌeɪ ˈeɪ /

AAR *abbr* (insurance/shipping)
against all risks

/ˌeɪ eɪ ˈɑː(r)/
note pronounced as individual letters

---

abandon *verb*
1 (*insurance*) to give up ownership of something (eg a ship or cargo) in exchange for an insurance payment, esp when the cost of repair is greater than the total value of the item: *The company decided to abandon the ship to the insurance company.* **2** (*law*) to withdraw from making a claim in a court of law: *The claim was abandoned with the permission of the court.* **3** (*shipping*) to leave a ship because it is sinking, on fire, etc: *a call to abandon ship*

/əˈbændən/
abandon, abandoning, abandoned
note transitive verb
1 ⧓ **abandon** cargo, a ship
2 ⧓ **abandon** an appeal, a claim
3 ⧓ **abandon** ship

---

abandonment *noun*
1 giving up something, eg the ownership of goods or the right to manufacture a certain product: *the abandonment of property rights* **2** (*insurance*) giving up ownership of something (eg a ship or cargo) in exchange for an insurance payment, especially when the cost of repair is greater than the total value of the item: *After the storm the shipowners decided on abandonment in return for an insurance payment.*

/əˈbændənmənt/
note not used with *a* or *an*. No plural and used with a singular verb only.
1 ⧓ product **abandonment**
2 ⧓ announce, declare **abandonment**
▶ **loss 3, partial loss, total loss**

---

abandonment clause *noun* (insurance/shipping)
part of a marine insurance policy that allows the owners to give up a damaged ship to an insurance company in return for an insurance payment, esp when the cost of repair is greater than the total value of the item: *include an abandonment clause in an insurance policy*

/əˈbændənmənt klɔːz/
pl abandonment clauses
⧓ accept, agree to, include an **abandonment clause**
▶ **assignment clause, clause, loss 3, partial loss, total loss**

---

abbreviation *noun*
a short form of a word or phrase: *Wed is an abbreviation of Wednesday.* ○ *Don't use abbreviations that no one understands.*

/əˌbriːviˈeɪʃn/
pl abbreviations
abbr abbr, abbrev
⧓ use an **abbreviation**
▶ **acronym**

ABC *abbr* (advertising)
the Audit Bureau of Circulation: *The ABC figures have been falling for the last two months.*

/ˌeɪ biː ˈsiː/

---

above par *adjective* (stock exchange)
(of the price of a fixed-interest security) higher than the price at which it was first issued (the NOMINAL PRICE): *The gilts achieved a price above par.* ○ *above par securities*

/əˌbʌv ˈpɑː(r)/
⧓ rise **above par**
▶ **at par, below par, nominal price**

---

above-the-line *adjective*

/əˌbʌv ðə ˈlaɪn/
(also **above the line**)

1 (*accounting*) relating to part of a PROFIT AND LOSS ACCOUNT or budget that records everyday income and expenditure rather than unusual items: *record above-the-line transactions* **2** (*advertising*) relating to the part of an advertising budget that includes paying a fee to an advertising agency: *allow for above-the-line costs in an advertising budget* **3** (*finance*) of financial transactions concerning income rather than capital: *make an above-the-line transaction* **4** (*personnel*) directly involved in the important parts of a business activity: *We really depend on above-the-line people.*

1 ⋈ **above-the-line** costs, entries, funds
▶ **below-the-line 1**
2 ⋈ **above-the-line** activities, costs, expenditure
▶ **below-the-line 2**
3 ⋈ **above-the-line** deals, transactions
▶ **below-the-line 3**

---

absenteeism *noun* (personnel)

/ˌæbsənˈtiːɪzəm/

staying away from work, esp often and without good reason: *Absenteeism has cost the organization thousands of working days this year.* ○ *Improvements in working conditions helped to reduce levels of absenteeism.*

note not used with *a* or *an*. No plural and used with a singular verb only.
⋈ the amount of, a case of, the rate of **absenteeism**

---

absenteeism rate *noun* (personnel)

/ˌæbsənˈtiːɪzəm reɪt/

1 the percentage of days that were not worked during a stated period: *There was an absenteeism rate of 25% in the office during the heatwave.* **2** the number of absentees per 100 workers on a particular working day: *an absenteeism rate of 2%*

pl absenteeism rates
⋈ calculate the **absenteeism rate**
▶ **rate 2**

---

absolute interest *noun* (law)

/ˌæbsəluːt ˈɪntrest/

the total possession or ownership of property: *The company has an absolute interest in the building.*

note usually singular
⋈ hold an **absolute interest**
syn absolute title
▶ **interest 3**

---

absolute monopoly *noun* (economics)

/ˌæbsəluːt məˈnɒpəli/

a situation in which one producer controls the production and supply of a particular product or service: *Absolute monopolies rarely exist.*

pl absolute monopolies
⋈ have an **absolute monopoly**
syn perfect monopoly, pure monopoly
▶ **monopoly, perfect market**

---

absorption costing *noun* (accounting)

/əbˈsɔːpʃn ˌkɒstɪŋ/

a way of pricing goods by allowing for all costs relating to production (eg a percentage of the factory rent) in the sale price: *Absorption costing usually prevents underpricing.*

note not used with *a* or *an*. No plural and used with a singular verb only.
syn full costing
▶ **costing, marginal costing, overhead**

---

abstract *noun*

/ˈæbstrækt/

a short account of the contents of a longer piece of writing: *include an abstract at the top of the report* ○ *An abstract of each talk is printed in the conference programme.*

pl abstracts
⋈ print, publish, write an **abstract**
▶ **summary**

---

abstract of title *noun* (law)
a legal document that lists all deeds, claims, mortgages, etc relating to a property: *Ownership was verified by reference to the abstract of title.*

/ˌæbstrækt əv ˈtaɪtl/
pl abstracts of title
▶ **assent, deed, deeds of transfer, title, title deeds**

a/c *abbr* (accounting/banking)
account: *a/c no. 01157293*

(also **A/C**, **A/c**)
note used in written English only

à.c. *abbr* (accounting)
(*French*) à compte; in part: *The sum was paid à.c.*

note used in written English only

ACAS *abbr* (industrial relations)
(*UK*) the Advisory Conciliatory and Arbitration Service: *The union decided to refer the dispute to ACAS.*

/ˈeɪkæs/
note pronounced as a word

a/c bks. *abbr* (accounting)
account books: *The transactions are recorded in the a/c bks.*

note used in written English only

acc *abbr* (banking)
accepted. Written on a bill of exchange (with a signature) to show that someone agrees to pay it.

note used in written English only

accelerated cost recovery system *noun* (tax)
▶ **accelerated depreciation**

/əkˌseləreɪtɪd ˈkɒst rɪˌkʌvəri ˌsɪstəm/

accelerated depreciation *noun* (tax)
a form of TAX RELIEF where a high proportion of the cost of new machinery is subtracted from the company's annual taxable profit, to help a business to develop and expand: *The machinery was written off as accelerated depreciation.*

/əkˌseləreɪtɪd dɪˌpriːʃiˈeɪʃn/
note not used with *a* or *an*. No plural and used with a singular verb only.
syn accelerated cost recovery system
▶ **accumulated depreciation, depreciation, reducing-balance method of depreciation, straight line depreciation**

acceleration clause *noun* (finance)
a condition in a bond that states that if one party fails to make a payment then all future payments immediately become due: *The whole of the loan was recalled under the acceleration clause.*

/əkˌseləˈreɪʃn klɔːz/
pl acceleration clauses
⧓ include an acceleration clause
▶ **clause**

acceleration premium *noun* (personnel)
a pay rate that increases as productivity increases: *An acceleration premium has been introduced to stimulate productivity.*

/əkˌseləˈreɪʃn ˌpriːmiəm/
pl acceleration premiums
⧓ pay an **acceleration premium**
▶ **premium 2**

accept *verb*
1 to take or agree to something that is offered: *accept a bid, deal, delivery, price, etc* ○ *The unions voted to accept the latest pay offer.* ○ *I'll accept £100 if you give me cash.* **2** to agree to undertake (responsibility for) something: *The manufacturers will not accept responsibility for damage caused by misuse.* **3** (*banking*) to sign a bill of exchange to say that you promise to pay it: *The bill of exchange was accepted for payment.* **4** (*law*) to agree to an offer made as part

/əkˈsept/
accept, accepting, accepted
note transitive verb
opp reject
▶ **offer**[2]
2 abbr acc

of the negotiations in a contract: *He accepted my offer.* **5** (*insurance*) to agree to provide insurance payments if a claim for loss, damages, etc is made: *Will your insurance company accept the claim?* **6** to receive someone/something as adequate or suitable: *Will you accept a cheque?*

3 ▶ **dishonour, honour**

---

acceptance *noun*

/ək'septəns/

note not used with *a* or *an*. No plural and used with a singular verb only.

⋈ **acceptance** *of* something

▶ **bank acceptance, non-acceptance, offer[1] 1**

1 agreement of a bid, deal, delivery, price, proposal, etc: *They indicated their acceptance by raising their hands.* **2** (*banking*) (**a**) the words (including a signature) written on a bill of exchange to say that a person agrees to pay it (**b**) the act of signing a bill of exchange to say that you promise to pay it (**c**) a bill of exchange that has been signed to show that a person agrees to pay it **3** (*law*) agreement to an offer made as part of the negotiations in a contract: *Please confirm your acceptance of this proposal by signing the attached letter.* **4** (*insurance*) agreement to provide insurance payments if a claim for loss or damage is made: *The insurance plan provides immediate cover and guaranteed acceptance.* **5** (*marketing*) the willingness of consumers to buy a particular product or service: *monitor the degree of consumer acceptance of a new product*

partial acceptance agreeing to pay only part of the value of a bill of exchange. The rest is paid by another acceptor.

---

acceptance bank *noun* (banking)

/ək'septəns bæŋk/

(*US*) ▶ **accepting house**

---

accepting house *noun* (banking)

/ək'septɪŋ haʊs/

pl accepting houses

syn (*US*) acceptance bank

▶ **accept 3, acceptance 2, discount house**

an organization, often a merchant bank, that promises to pay a bill of exchange in return for a fee

---

acceptor *noun* (banking)

/ək'septə(r)/

pl acceptors

▶ **accept 3, acceptance 2, drawee 2**

the person who signs a bill of exchange and promises to pay it: *The bill of exchange was signed by the acceptor.*

---

access *verb* (computing)

/'ækses/

access, accessing, accessed

note transitive verb

⋈ **access** data, information; **access** a computer, a database

▶ **input[2], output[2]**

to get information from or put information into a computer: *I am unable to access your file.* ○ *Use the password to access the database.*

---

accident frequency rate *noun* (health and safety)

/ˌæksɪdənt 'fri:kwənsi reɪt/

abbr AFR

⋈ cut down, reduce the **accident frequency rate**

▶ **health and safety, rate 2**

the number of accidents in which employees are killed or injured per million working hours: *Steps are being taken to cut down the accident frequency rate.*

---

accommodation *noun*

/əˌkɒmə'deɪʃn/

1 note (*UK*) not used with *a* or *an*. No plural and used with a singular verb only. (*US*) can be

1 a place to live, work or stay: *hotel, office, tourist, etc accommodation* ○ *temporary, long-term accommodation* ○ *There's always a shortage of accommodation in the capital.* ○ (*US*) *The*

vacation packages include hotel accommodations and tours but not meals. **2** arrangements or provision for someone/something: (*US*) *Legislation requires employers to make reasonable accommodations for the handicapped in hiring and other ways.* **3** (*banking*) money lent for a short time, esp to meet urgent needs: *We're going to request a short-term accommodation from the bank to cover these payments until we can find other funds.* **4** (*formal*) an agreement or a convenient arrangement: *The two sides hoped to reach some sort of accommodation on the pay issue.*

used in plural (accommodations)

2 note (*UK*) used in singular only. (*US*) can be used in plural (accommodations)

3 note usually singular

⋈ a **bank** accommodation

▶ **bridging loan, day-to-day loan, loan[1]**

4 note usually singular

---

accommodation address *noun*

an address that is used by someone to receive letters, messages, etc although the person does not live there: *Please write to my accommodation address.*

/əˌkɒməˈdeɪʃn əˌdres/

pl accommodation addresses

⋈ use, write to an **accommodation address**

▶ **address[1] 1, box number 1, poste restante**

---

accommodation bill *noun* (banking)

a bill of exchange that is signed by someone (the ACCOMMODATION PARTY) who promises to pay it to help another person to raise money

/əˌkɒməˈdeɪʃn bɪl/

pl accommodation bills

⋈ sign an **accommodation bill**

syn accommodation note

▶ **kite, kite-flying**

---

accommodation endorsement *noun* (banking)

▶ **endorsement**

/əˌkɒməˈdeɪʃn ɪnˌdɔːsmənt/

---

accommodation paper *noun* (banking)

a bill of exchange, a cheque, etc that has an accommodation endorsement: *He was asked to sign the accommodation paper.*

/əˌkɒməˈdeɪʃn ˌpeɪpə(r)/

note usually singular

⋈ sign an **accommodation paper**

▶ accommodation endorsement *under* **endorsement**

---

accommodation party *noun* (banking)

a person with a good financial reputation who signs a bill of exchange, cheque, etc to make it easier to exchange: *She acted as an accommodation party.*

/əˌkɒməˈdeɪʃn ˌpɑːti/

pl accommodation parties

▶ **guarantor, party**

---

accord and satisfaction *noun* (law)

an agreement between two people who have signed a contract that allows one of them to withdraw from the conditions of the contract by paying a sum of money: *Accord and satisfaction was reached on the contract after the payment of a small sum.*

/əˌkɔːd ənd ˌsætɪsˈfækʃn/

note not used with *a* or *an*. No plural and used with a singular verb only.

⋈ reach **accord and satisfaction**

▶ **adoption of contract, breach of contract, contract[1]**

---

account[1] *noun*

1 (*finance*) a statement of money paid or owed for goods or services: *Have you kept an account of expenses?* ○ *Put it on my account.* **2** (*banking*) an arrangement with a bank or firm that allows credit for financial and commercial payments: *open an account with the bank* ○ *have an account with a supplier* ○ *Please*

/əˈkaʊnt/

pl accounts

abbr A/C, a/c, acct.

1 ⋈ an itemized **account**

charge it to my account. **3** (*commerce*) a trader, esp the owner or manager of a shop, who has an arrangement to buy from a particular supplier: *The salesman was visiting one of his most important accounts.* **4** a spoken or written report: *Please give me a detailed account of the meeting.* **5** (*stock exchange*) the period (usually two weeks) during which trading takes place on the stock exchange; the period between one ACCOUNT DAY and the next

on account to be paid for later: *buy goods on account*

take (something) into account consider, allow for: *You must take inflation into account when fixing prices.* ○ *take into account the quality as well as the quantity of goods produced*

▶ **accounts, appropriation account, capital account, expense account, income and expenditure account, nominal account, profit and loss account, revenue account, statement of account, suspense account, trading account**

2 ⧓ close, open, settle an **account**

▶ **approved account 1, bank account, budget account, credit account, current account 1, deposit account, joint account 1, loro account, nostro account, vostro account**

4 ⧓ an accurate, a brief, a detailed, a long, a short **account**

▶ **report[1]**

5 ▶ **contango**

---

account[2] *verb*

to explain or give a reason for something: *account for all expenses on a business trip* ○ *Exports account for 42% of sales.*

/əˈkaʊnt/

account, accounting, accounted

note intransitive verb

1 ⧓ **account** *for* something

▶ **unaccounted for**

---

accountable *adjective*

required or expected to give an explanation to someone for something; responsible for something: *The manager is accountable to investors for losses.* ○ *Government officials in control of public money should be accountable (to the public).* ○ *The sales manager is accountable for meeting the sales targets.*

/əˈkaʊntəbl/

⧓ be **accountable** *to* someone; be **accountable** *for* something

---

accountancy *noun* (accounting)

1 the profession of or work done by an accountant: *Accountancy is an expanding profession.* ○ *a career in accountancy* ○ *We provide a range of accountancy services.* **2** the study of this: *a degree in accountancy*

/əˈkaʊntənsi/

note not used with *a* or *an*. No plural and used with a singular verb only.

⧓ an **accountancy** degree, firm

▶ **accounting**

---

accountant *noun* (accounting)

a professionally trained person whose job is to keep and check the financial records of an organization, or to advise people on income, spending, tax, etc: *a firm of accountants* ○ *The Chief Accountant prepares the company's annual accounts.* ○ *My accountant advised me to become self-employed.*

/əˈkaʊntənt/

pl accountants

▶ **auditor, certified accountant, chartered accountant, cost accountant, financial accountant, management accountant, public finance accountant**

---

account books *noun* (accounting)

▶ **books**

/əˈkaʊnt bʊks/

Account Day *noun* (stock exchange)
the last day of the trading period at the stock exchange when payments are made: *Payment was received before Account Day.*

/əˈkaʊnt deɪ/
syn pay-day
▶ **account 5, last trading day, new time buying, prompt day, settlement day**

accounting *noun* (accounting)
the work of keeping or checking accounts; accountancy: *She works in accounting.*

/əˈkaʊntɪŋ/
note not used with *a* or *an*. No plural and used with a singular verb only.
⧓ an **accounting** method, service, system
▶ **creative accounting, current cost accounting, historic cost accounting**

accounting period *noun* (accounting)
a period at the end of which the totals for the money coming into and money going out of a business (the ACCOUNTS) are calculated: *The payment will be carried over to the next accounting period.* ○ *calculate the total profit at the end of the accounting period*

/əˈkaʊntɪŋ ˌpɪəriəd/
pl accounting periods
⧓ the current, next, preceding **accounting period**
▶ **account[1] 5, Account Day, financial year**

accounting rate of return *noun* (accounting)
the net profit expected from money invested in an asset, a project or a business, expressed as a percentage: *We expect a high accounting rate of return from the new computer system.*

/əˌkaʊntɪŋ ˌreɪt əv rɪˈtɜːn/
pl accounting rates of return
abbr ARR
⧓ calculate, estimate the **accounting rate of return**
▶ **annual return, net present value, rate of return, return[1]**

accounting summary *noun* (accounting)
a short statement that forms part of the final accounts or financial report of a business at the end of an accounting period: *The total profits and earnings are shown in the accounting summary.*

/əˈkaʊntɪŋ ˌsʌməri/
pl accounting summaries
▶ **annual report**

account of profits *noun* (law)
a request for details of how money has been spent when a person or an organization is suspected of obtaining or using it illegally; compensation for money lost in this way: *The author sued for account of profits when the copyright agreement was broken.*

/əˌkaʊnt əv ˈprɒfɪts/
note no plural
⧓ demand an **account of profits**
▶ **profit[1]**

account payable *noun* (accounting)
a sum of money owed by a company; an invoice received but not paid: *What name is given on that account payable?*

/əˌkaʊnt ˈpeɪəbl/
note no plural
▶ **account receivable, accounts payable**

account payee *noun* (banking)
words written across a cheque so that it can only be paid into the bank account of the person named on the cheque: *account payee only*

/əˌkaʊnt peɪˈiː/
note no plural
abbr a/c payee
▶ **crossed cheque, non-negotiable 2**

account receivable *noun* (accounting)
a sum of money owed to a company; an invoice sent but not paid: *file an account receivable*

/əˌkaʊnt rɪˈsiːvəbl/
note no plural
▶ **account payable, accounts receivable**

account rendered *noun* (accounting)
an unpaid amount recorded in a statement of account, details of which were in a previous statement: *The unpaid sums were marked account rendered.*

/əˌkaʊnt ˈrendəd/
pl accounts rendered
⋈ listed under **accounts rendered**
▶ **render**

accounts *noun* (accounting)
1 a set of accounting records for a business over a particular period, showing the total amount of profit made: *The auditor has finished checking the company accounts.* ○ *The director presented the annual report and accounts.* ○ *The financial director was accused of falsifying the company accounts.* **2** the department in a company where money spent and owed is recorded: *She works in accounts.*

/əˈkaʊnts/
note plural noun, used with a plural verb
1 ⋈ annual, monthly, quarterly **accounts**
▶ **approved account 2, balance sheet, books, current account 2, final accounts, profit and loss account, revenue accounts**
2 ⋈ the **accounts** department

account sale *noun* (accounting/commerce)
a statement given by a person who sells goods for someone else (an AGENT) to the owner (the PRINCIPAL) giving details of the goods sold, amounts received and agent's fees: *The account sale shows the sale less commission.*

/əˈkaʊnt seɪl/
pl account sales
▶ **sale**

accounts payable *noun* (accounting)
(the heading on) a list of amounts owed by a business to suppliers of goods and services: *add an entry to accounts payable*

/əˌkaʊnts ˈpeɪəbl/
note plural noun, used with a plural verb
▶ **account payable, accounts receivable, bought ledger**

accounts receivable *noun* (accounting)
(the heading on) a list of amounts owed to a business by suppliers of goods and services: *Such a large accounts receivable could force the small firm out of business.*

/əˌkaʊnts rɪˈsiːvəbl/
note plural noun, used with a plural verb
▶ **account receivable, accounts payable, receivables, sales ledger**

account terms *noun* (commerce)
written on a bill or invoice, etc to show that the amount will be charged to the customer's account and payment will be required at the end of the agreed period: *invoice marked 'account terms'*

/əˈkaʊnt tɜːmz/
note plural noun, used with a plural verb
▶ **terms 2**

accredited *adjective* (commerce)
officially recognized: *our accredited representative* ○ *obtain an accredited training qualification* ○ *The agent was accredited by the company.*

/əˈkredɪtɪd/
abbr accred
⋈ **accredited** *by* someone or something

accrual *noun*
1 (*finance*) a gradual and/or automatic increase: *the accrual of interest* ○ *the accrual of debt* ○ *accruals of taxes* ○ *Accrual has been allowed for.* **2** (*accounting*) accrued charge

/əˈkruːəl/
pl accruals
▶ **accrued charges, accrued costs, accrued expenses,**

accrued income, accrued interest

---

accrue *verb* (finance)
to come (to somebody or something) as a gradual and/or automatic increase: *Interest accrues from the first of the month.* ○ *accrued interest* ○ *All charges accruing are payable at the end of the year.*

/əˈkruː/
accrue, accruing, accrued
note intransitive verb
⧓ income, interest, wealth **accrues**

---

accrued benefits *noun* (finance)
the money owed to an employee in the form of a pension: *She left the firm with substantial accrued benefits.*

/əˌkruːd ˈbenɪfɪts/
note usually plural
⧓ receive **accrued benefits**

---

accrued charges *noun* (accounting)
an amount owed but not yet paid and therefore added to the next list of charges: *There are still several outstanding accrued charges.*

/əˌkruːd ˈtʃɑːdʒɪz/
note plural noun, used with a plural verb
⧓ add up the **accrued charges**
syn accruals
▶ **accounting period**

---

accrued costs *noun* (accounting)
the money paid or owed for goods or services used during a particular ACCOUNTING PERIOD: *The costs shown in the balance are total accrued costs.*

/əˌkruːd ˈkɒsts/
note plural noun, used with a plural verb
▶ **cost**[1]

---

accrued expenses *noun* (accounting)
the money paid or owed for heating, lighting, staff wages, etc (OVERHEADS) during a particular ACCOUNTING PERIOD: *The firm has reduced its accrued expenses.*

/əˌkruːd ɪkˈspensɪz /
note usually plural
⧓ increase, reduce **accrued expenses**

---

accrued income *noun* (accounting)
the total amount earned by a company during a particular ACCOUNTING PERIOD, whether paid or not: *Earnings have been calculated on accrued income.*

/əˌkruːd ˈɪŋkʌm/
note not used with *a* or *an*. No plural and used with a singular verb only.
⧓ calculate **accrued income**
▶ **income**

---

accrued interest *noun* (accounting)
interest earned during a particular period that has not yet been received: *The statement shows all accrued interest.*

/əˌkruːd ˈɪntrest/
note not used with *a* or *an*. No plural and used with a singular verb only.
⧓ calculate, receive **accrued interest**

---

acct. *abbr* (accounting)
account

note used in written English only

---

accumulate *verb* (finance)
to grow through regular additions: *My savings are accumulating interest.* ○ *calculate losses accumulated over the past six months*

/əˈkjuːmjəleɪt/
accumulate, accumulating, accumulated
note transitive and intransitive verb
⧓ **accumulate** debts, losses, wealth
▶ **accrue**

---

accumulated depreciation *noun* (accounting)
the total amount taken off the value of an asset to allow for wear and tear: *The accumulated depreciation is the sum of the yearly instalments of depreciation.*

/əˌkjuːmjəleɪtɪd dɪˌpriːʃiˈeɪʃn/
note not used with *a* or *an*. No plural and used with a singular verb only.
⧓ calculate the **accumulated depreciation**
▶ **accelerated depreciation, depreciation, reducing-balance method of depreciation, straight line depreciation**

accumulated dividends *noun* (finance)
part of a company's profit owed but not yet paid to shareholders: *Accumulated dividends are shown as liabilities in the accounts.*

/əˌkjuːmjəleɪtɪd ˈdɪvɪdendz/
note plural noun, used with a plural verb
▶ **dividend, accumulated profit**

accumulated profit *noun* (finance)
the remaining profit after paying taxes and dividends to shareholders: *The accumulated profit has been carried forward to next year.*

/əˌkjuːmjəleɪtɪd ˈprɒfɪt/
note usually singular
▶ **accumulated dividends, profit[1]**

accumulation unit *noun* (finance)
an amount invested in an INVESTMENT TRUST that does not pay regular dividends, but adds the amount earned to the original value of the investment: *He has a life assurance policy linked to accumulation units.*

/əˌkjuːmjəˈleɪʃn ˌjuːnɪt/
pl accumulation units
⧓ hold, invest in an **accumulation unit**
▶ **dividend, income unit**

acid test *noun*
a test that proves the true value of someone/something: *The acid test is whether or not somebody will actually buy the product.*

/ˌæsɪd ˈtest/
pl acid tests
⧓ the **acid test** *for*; the **acid test** *of* someone/something

acid test ratio *noun* (finance/accounting)
a measure of a company's liquidity by comparing its LIQUID ASSETS to its CURRENT LIABILITIES: *The acid test ratio shows that the company is unable to pay its debts on time.*

/ˈæsɪd test ˌreɪʃiəʊ/
pl acid test ratios
⧓ calculate the **acid test ratio**
▶ **ratio**

acknowledge *verb*
to say that you have received something: *acknowledge receipt of a letter*

/əkˈnɒlɪdʒ/
acknowledge, acknowledging, acknowledged
note transitive verb
⧓ **acknowledge** a letter

acknowledgement *noun*
a letter stating that something has been received: *I didn't receive an acknowledgement of my application.*

/əkˈnɒlɪdʒmənt/
pl acknowledgements
⧓ receive, send an **acknowledgement**; an **acknowledgement** *of* something

acknowledgement of debt *noun* (commerce/law)
a written statement by someone to say that he/she owes money: *We have received their acknowledgement of debt.*

/ək,nɒlɪdʒmənt əv 'det/
pl acknowledgements of debt
⧓ receive an **acknowledgement of debt**

à compte *noun* (accounting)
(*French*) in part; a part payment: *payment received à compte*

/æ 'kɔ:mt/
abbr à.c.

---

a/c payee *abbr* (banking)
account payee: *a/c payee only*

note used in written English only

---

acquire *verb*
1 to buy or take possession of something: *Madison Plc is hoping to acquire Rosewall Holdings.* **2** to get or gain something by your efforts or actions: *We seem to be acquiring a reputation for efficiency.* ○ *Trainees will be expected to acquire word processing skills.*

/ə'kwaɪə/
acquire, acquiring, acquired
note transitive verb
1 ⧓ **acquire** a company, property
2 ⧓ **acquire** a reputation, skill

---

acquired surplus *noun* (finance)
an amount of money that has been gained by a company other than by normal trading: *The takeover gave rise to an acquired surplus.*

/ə,kwaɪəd 'sɜ:pləs/
pl acquired surpluses
⧓ result in an **acquired surplus**

---

acquisition *noun*
1 the act of obtaining something: *The acquisition of wealth usually takes time.* ○ *the acquisition of Williams plc by Mangrove properties* **2** something obtained, esp a company that has been bought or taken over: *The recession forced Fitzroy to sell some of his recent acquisitions.*

/,ækwɪ'zɪʃn/
pl acquisitions
1 ⧓ an **acquisition** *of* something
2 ⧓ the latest, a new, a recent **acquisition**
▶ **merger, requisition, takeover**

---

acronym *noun*
a word formed from the first letters of a group of words: *ALGOL is an acronym for algorithmic oriented language.*

/'ækrənɪm/
pl acronyms
▶ **abbreviation**

---

across-the-board *adjective, adverb*
including or affecting all members of a group (of workers, jobs, products, etc): *The drop in sales applies across-the-board.* ○ *an across-the-board pay increase of 7%* ○ *They have decided to increase prices by 4% across-the-board.*

/ə,krɒs ðə 'bɔ:d/
⧓ an **across-the-board** agreement, decision, increase

---

action[1] *noun* (law)
a legal process; a lawsuit: *She has decided to take legal action.* ○ *The company is trying to avoid a court action.*

/'ækʃn/
pl actions
⧓ a court **action**; legal **action**
▶ **lawsuit, litigation, right of action**

---

action[2] *verb*
(*informal*) to do something; to put something into effect: *Matters decided today will be actioned next week.* ○ *He actioned the report.*

/'ækʃn/
action, actioning, actioned
note transitive verb

---

active capital *noun* (finance)
money or items of value (ASSETS) that can be easily converted to money: *calculate the amount of active capital*

/ˌæktɪv ˈkæpɪtl/
note not used with *a* or *an*. No plural and used with a singular verb only.
► **capital, dead capital**

active circulation *noun* (banking)
the money that is being used by the public as opposed to the money held by the bank in reserve: *Efforts are being made to reduce active circulation by 10%.*

/ˌæktɪv sɜːkjəˈleɪʃn/
note not used with *a* or *an*. No plural and used with a singular verb only.
⋈ increase, reduce **active circulation**
► **circulation 1**

active market *noun* (stock exchange)
1 a situation where stocks and shares that are always in demand are frequently bought and sold: *The company's stocks are being traded in an active market.* **2** any market where there is a lot of buying and selling: *Property owners gain when prices rise in an active market.*

/ˌæktɪv ˈmɑːkɪt/
note usually singular
1 ► **thin market**
2 opp depressed market
► **heavy market**

active money *noun* (banking)
money that is being used by the public as opposed to money left in bank accounts: *The recession has reduced the amount of active money.*

/ˌæktɪv ˈmʌni/
note not used with *a* or *an*. No plural and used with a singular verb only.
⋈ increase, reduce the amount of **active money**
► **money**

active partner *noun* (management)
a person who invests money in a business, has a right to a share of the profits, and controls some of the business activities: *Both active partners were present at the meeting.*

/ˌæktɪv ˈpɑːtnə(r)/
pl active partners
► **partner, sleeping partner**

act of God *noun* (insurance/law)
an unexpected or unavoidable event such as a storm, a flood, an earthquake, etc mentioned in some insurance contracts as a cause of loss or damage: *The insurance policy does not cover acts of God.*

/ˌækt əv ˈgɒd/
pl acts of God
(also **Act of God**)
► **force majeure, riot and civil commotion**

actual *adjective*
real, true, genuine: *The actual cost was much higher than our predictions. What is the actual date on the document?*

/ˈæktʃuəl/
► **current, present**[1]

actual loss *noun* (finance)
the real cost of something as opposed to a sum of money stated on paper: *The plaintiff sustained an actual loss when she had to make mortgage repayments without any tax relief.*

/ˌæktʃuəl ˈlɒs/
pl actual losses
⋈ calculate, carry, sustain an **actual loss**
► **loss 1, paper loss**

actuals *noun*
1 (*commerce/stock exchange*) goods that can be purchased and used, as opposed to goods traded on a futures contract that are represented by documents **2** (*finance*) real figures, costs, etc rather than estimated ones: *These are the actuals for last year's turnover.*

/ˈæktʃuəlz/
note plural noun, used with a plural verb
1 syn physicals

▶ **fungibles, futures, spot goods**
2 ▶ **estimate[1]**

---

actuarial *adjective* (insurance)
relating to the information used or the work done by an ACTUARY: *She is involved in actuarial work.* ○ *carry out an actuarial valuation*

/ˌæktʃuˈeəriəl/
⋈ **actuarial** data, services, work

---

actuarial tables *noun* (insurance)
lists of figures that show, for example, how many years people of certain ages are likely to live, used to calculate insurance risks: *make a calculation based on actuarial tables*

/ˌæktʃuˈeəriəl ˌteɪblz/
note usually plural
▶ **life expectancy, mortality tables, risk[1]**

---

actuary *noun* (insurance)
a person employed by an insurance company or pension fund to calculate insurance risks and payments by studying death rates and the number of (possible) accidents, fires, thefts, etc: *Actuaries spend their time working out whether or not an accident will happen and how much it will cost if it does.*

/ˈæktʃuəri/
pl actuaries
▶ **risk[1]**

---

ad *abbr* (advertising)
(*informal*) **1** an advertisement: *Are there any interesting job ads in the paper this week?* **2** advertising: *Our ad budget has been cut this year.*

/æd/
pl ads
⋈ **ad** columns, features, pages
▶ **classified advertisement, commercial[2] 1**

A/D *abbr* (banking)
after date

note used in written English only

---

addendum *noun*
an extra section that is attached to, or follows, a letter, report, etc: *send an addendum to a letter*

/əˈdendəm/
pl addenda
⋈ attach an **addendum**
▶ **allonge, annex, appendix, rider**

---

add-on *noun* (computing)
1 a piece of (HARDWARE or SOFTWARE) equipment that can be joined to a computer system to improve or increase its functions: *use a computer with an add-on* **2** any extra part, section or service that can be joined to a machine, system, contract, etc to improve or expand it: *Various add-ons can be purchased to increase the output of the machine.*

/ˈæd ɒn/
pl add-ons
⋈ **add-on** features, functions
▶ **component**

---

address[1] *noun*
1 the details of where a person or an organization can be found and where letters can be delivered: *Please write your postal address in full.* ○ *Is this your correct home address?* **2** (*computing*) part of a computer instruction that specifies where a piece of information is stored in the computer memory: *Once the correct address is found, the computer can retrieve the record directly from the disk storage.* **3** a formal speech made to a group of people: *The Chairman made his annual address to the staff.*

/əˈdres/
pl addresses
1 ⋈ complete, full **address**
▶ **accommodation address, telegraphic address**
2 ⋈ memory **address**
▶ **memory**
3 ⋈ deliver, give an **address**

---

address² *verb*
1 to write the name and place of the receiver on an envelope or parcel: *Have you addressed the letter correctly?* **2** to make a speech to a person or a group: *The chairman addressed the meeting.* **3** to direct a remark or a written statement to a person or an organization: *Please address all complaints to the manager.*

/ə'dres/
address, addressing, addressed
note transitive verb
1 ⋈ **address** an envelope, a letter
2 ⋈ **address** an audience, a meeting
3 ⋈ **address** a complaint, remark *to* (someone or something)

---

addressee *noun*
the person or organization to whom a letter, parcel, etc is sent and whose name and address appears on it: ○ *This letter should only be opened by the addressee.*

/ˌædre'siː/
pl addressees
▶ **recipient**

---

adjourn *verb*
1 (**a**) to stop (a court case, a meeting, etc) for a time before beginning again: *The chairman adjourned the meeting until the following day.* ○ *The conference was adjourned to allow the participants to contact their companies.* (**b**) to come to a stop for a time before beginning again: *The committee adjourned for lunch.* ○ *Let's adjourn and reconvene at 2 o'clock.* **2** to move to another place, esp to continue a discussion, etc: *Let's adjourn to my office where we can have some privacy.*

/ə'dʒɜːn/
adjourn, adjourning, adjourned
1a note transitive verb
⋈ **adjourn** a court case, meeting, talk, trial
1b note intransitive verb
⋈ **adjourn** *for* something
▶ **resume**
2 note intransitive verb
⋈ **adjourn** *to* (a place)

---

adjust *verb*
1 to alter or correct something: *The sales figures have been adjusted slightly.* **2** (*insurance*) to settle an insurance claim: *The claim is being adjusted.*

/ə'dʒʌst/
adjust, adjusting, adjusted
note transitive verb
1 ⋈ **adjust** a figure
▶ **amend**
2 ⋈ **adjust** a claim
▶ **claims assessor, loss adjuster**

---

adjuster *noun* (insurance)
▶ **claims assessor, loss adjuster**

/ə'dʒʌstə(r)/

---

adjustment *noun* (insurance)
1 the settlement between an insurance company and the person insured over the amount of a claim: *Adjustment has been reached on our claim.* **2** the actual amount due to the person insured: *The insurance company has paid the adjustment*

/ə'dʒʌstmənt/
pl adjustments
1 ⋈ discuss, reach (an) **adjustment**
2 ⋈ pay an **adjustment**

---

ad man *abbr* (advertising)
(*informal*) advertising manager: *work as an ad man for a television company*

/'ædmæn/

---

admin *abbr* (administration)
(*informal*) administration: *She works in admin.* ○ *the admin department*

/'ædmɪn/

abbr abbreviation **pl** plural ⋈ collocate (*word often used with the headword*)

administration *noun* (administration)
the control or routine organization of a company or particular business activity: *We must reduce the amount of time and money spent on administration.* ○ *The administration of employees' expense accounts is very time-consuming.*

/əd,mɪnɪ'streɪʃn/
note not used with *a* or *an*. No plural and used with a singular verb only.
abbr admin
⧓ **administration** costs, fees; an **administration** department
▶ **organization 2, paperwork**

administrative *adjective* (administration)
relating to the control or routine organization of a company or particular business activity: *calculate administrative costs*

/əd'mɪnɪstrətɪv/
⧓ **administrative** costs, details, duties, problems, staff

administrator *noun*
1 (*law*) a person who is involved in the control or routine organization of a company or a particular business activity: *a hospital administrator* **2** (*finance*) a person named by the courts to manage an organization that is in debt: *an independent administrator appointed by the courts*

/əd'mɪnɪstreɪtə(r)/
pl administrators
2 ⧓ appoint, be in the hands of, call in an **administrator**
▶ **official receiver, liquidator**

adoption *noun* (sales)
1 the acceptance of a new idea, plan or proposal: *At the meeting they discussed the proposals up for adoption.* **2** the acceptance or purchase of a new product; a new product that is accepted: *We have had a number of adoptions in most of our major markets.*

/ə'dɒpʃn/
1 note not used with *a* or *an*. No plural and used with a singular verb only.
2 pl adoptions
⧓ get an **adoption**

adoption of contract *noun* (law)
the acceptance of a contract by one party even though the right to be relieved from duties is part of the contract: *Our client agrees to adoption of contract.*

/ə,dɒpʃn əv 'kɒntrækt/
note not used with *a* or *an*. No plural and used with a singular verb only.
▶ **accord and satisfaction, breach of contract, contract**

ad valorem *adjective* (tax)
(*Latin*) of tax that is calculated as a percentage of the value of the goods: *VAT is an ad valorem tax.*

/,æd væ'lɔ:rem/
abbr ad val, a/v
▶ **tax[1], value added tax**

advance[1] *noun* (finance)
money paid before it is due, or for work only partially completed; a loan: *I asked for an advance on my wages.* ○ *The author was given an advance on royalties.*

/əd'vɑ:ns/
pl advances
⧓ to make, pay, receive an **advance**

advance[2] *verb*
1 to increase; to move forward: *Shares advanced today.* **2** to pay something before it is due: *Can you advance me £100?*

/əd'vɑ:ns/
advance, advancing, advanced
1 note intransitive verb
2 note transitive verb
⧓ **advance** money, pay

advance bill *noun* (banking/commerce)
a bill of exchange that has been written before the goods have been sent off: *The advance bill has already been sent.*

/əd'vɑ:ns bɪl/
pl advance bills
⧓ accept, draw, sign an **advance bill**
▶ **time bill**

advances ratio *noun* (banking)
the relationship between the amount of money lent by a bank to individuals and companies and the total amount it holds in deposits and investments: *The Treasury keeps control of the overall advances ratio.*

/ədˈvɑːnsɪz ˌreɪʃiəʊ/
note no plural
⋈ have, keep, maintain an **advances ratio**
▶ **cash ratio, ratio**

adverse balance *noun* (banking)
an amount of debt shown on an account; a deficit: *Our bankers have advised us of our adverse balance.*

/ˌædvɜːs ˈbæləns/
pl adverse balances
syn unfavourable balance
▶ **balance, deficit**

advert *abbr* (advertising)
(*UK informal*) an advertisement: *a soap powder advert/an advert for soap powder ○ place a full-page advert in the Times.*

/ˈædvɜːt/
pl adverts
▶ **advertisement, commercial**

advertise *verb* (advertising)
1 to make a product, a service, a job vacancy, an event, etc known to people: *The new sales job was advertised this week. ○ She advertised her second-hand car in the local paper. ○ an advertised film, price, speaker, etc* **2** to ask for someone or something by putting a notice in a newspaper, on a notice-board, etc: *We'll have to advertise for a new secretary.*

/ˈædvətaɪz/
advertise, advertising, advertised
1 note transitive verb
▶ **promote 1, publicize**
2 note intransitive verb
⋈ **advertise** *for* someone or something

advertisement *noun* (advertising)
a notice or message in a newspaper, or on a poster in a public place, or an announcement on television or on the radio offering or asking for a product or service, or a person to do a certain job: *The best way to sell your car is to put an advertisement in the local paper. ○ an advertisement for a washing powder/a washing powder advertisement ○ a full-page advertisement ○ an advertisement for a sales manager*

/ədˈvɜːtɪsmənt/
pl advertisements
abbr ad, advert
⋈ place, put, take out an **advertisement** (in a newspaper); an **advertisement** *for* someone or something
▶ **classified advertisement, commercial 1, keyed advertisement**

advertising *noun* (advertising)
1 the act of making a product, a service, a job vacancy, an event, etc publicly known; advertisements collectively: *Cigarette advertising has now been banned on television. ○ Advertising is often aimed at the young. ○ How easily are you persuaded by advertising?* **2** (related to) the business that deals with making, distributing and selling advertisements: *She works in advertising. ○ draw up an advertising budget*

/ˈædvətaɪzɪŋ/
note not used with *a* or *an*. No plural and used with a singular verb only.
⋈ an **advertising** agency, campaign, manager, slogan
▶ **promotion 1, publicity 1**

Advertising Association *noun* (advertising)
an organization set up in the UK to maintain high standards in advertising and to protect the interests of advertisers and advertising agencies: *The Advertising Association predicts no real growth in advertising next year.*

/ˈædvətaɪzɪŋ əˌsəʊsiˌeɪʃn/
abbr AA

the Advertising Standards Authority *noun* (advertising)
an organization set up in the UK to protect the public from advertisements that contain misleading or false information: *The Advertising Standards Authority monitors over 850 advertisements a week.*

/ðə ˈædvətaɪzɪŋ ˌstændədz ɔːˌθɒrəti /
abbr ASA

advice note *noun* (transport)
a note to the receiver of goods from the sender that gives details of the quantity and description of goods and when and how they will be transported: *We have received an advice note for the goods we ordered.*

/ədˈvaɪs nəʊt/
pl advice notes
⧓ receive, send an **advice note**
▶ **arrival notice, despatch note**

the Advisory Conciliation and Arbitration Service *noun* (industrial relations)
an organization set up in the UK to advise on relations between management and workers, and to help settle industrial disputes between trade unions and employers: *Management has agreed to refer the dispute to the Advisory Conciliation and Arbitration Service.*

/ði ədˌvaɪzəri kənsɪliˌeɪʃn ənd ɑːbɪˈtreɪʃn ˌsɜːvɪs/
abbr ACAS
note the abbreviation is more commonly used than the full term
⧓ refer, take (a dispute) to **the Advisory Conciliation and Arbitration Service**
▶ **industrial dispute, industrial relations, tribunal**

advisory service *noun*
part of an organization that provides specialist information on a particular subject: *He decided to consult a careers advisory service.* ○ *The bank provides a financial advisory service for all its clients.*

/ədˈvaɪzəri ˌsɜːvɪs/
pl advisory services
⧓ offer, provide an **advisory service**

advocate *noun* (law)
(*Scottish*) ▶ **barrister**

/ˈædvəkət/

affidavit *noun* (law)
a written and signed statement of facts to be produced as evidence in a court of law: *He signed an affidavit saying that he did not know about the fraud.*

/ˌæfɪˈdeɪvɪt/
pl affidavits
⧓ make, sign, swear an **affidavit**

affiliate[1] *noun*
a person or an organization that is attached to a larger organization (eg a firm completely or partly owned by another company): *The organization has 46 affiliates and 500 000 members.* ○ *an affiliate of the holding company*

/əˈfɪliət/
pl affiliates
⧓ an **affiliate** bank, company, society, trade union

affiliate[2] *verb*
to attach (a person or an organization) to a larger organization: *The Oxford Chamber of Commerce is affiliated to the Association of British Chambers of Commerce.*

/əˈfɪlieɪt/
affiliate, affiliating, affiliated
note transitive verb

affiliation *noun*
attaching or being attached to a larger organization; the connection made by this: *We have a number of affiliations throughout the country.* ○ *Please put your name, address and affiliation* (ie the organization that you work for or represent) *on the form.*

/əˌfɪliˈeɪʃn/
pl affiliations
⧓ **affiliation** *to, with* something

affirmative action *noun* (personnel) /əˌfɜːmətɪv ˈækʃn/

(*US*) ▶ **equal opportunity**

---

affluence *noun* /ˈæfluəns/

a lot of goods, money or property: *a society with a high level of affluence*

note not used with *a* or *an*. No plural and used with a singular verb only.

⋈ great, relative **affluence**

▶ **wealth**

---

affluent *adjective* /ˈæfluənt/

having a lot of money; able to afford a high standard of living: *He has a highly-paid job and an affluent life-style.*

⋈ an **affluent** country, family, life-style, society

▶ **wealthy**

---

afford *verb* /əˈfɔːd/

1 to have enough money to buy or pay for something: *We really can't afford a new car/to buy a new car.* ○ *Surely he can afford £2 000?* **2** to be able to do something without risk to yourself: *I can't afford to lose the goodwill of our customers.* ○ *We cannot afford further stoppages in the production plant.*

afford, affording, afforded

note transitive verb

⋈ able to, can, can't, could **afford** something/to do something

---

afmd *abbr*

aforementioned: *Please note afmd names.*

note used in written English only

---

aforementioned *adjective* /əˌfɔːˈmenʃənd/

of things that have already been spoken of in a document, report, etc: *with reference to the aforementioned points*

abbr afmd

⋈ **aforementioned** items, names, points

▶ **undermentioned**

---

after date *adjective*, *adverb* (banking) /ˌɑːftə ˈdeɪt/

written on a bill of exchange to show that payment will be made at a specified time after the date given on the bill: *six months after date* ○ *an after-date bill*

abbr A/D, a.d.

note used with a hyphen before a noun

syn from date

▶ **after sight, at sight, on demand**

---

after-hours dealing *noun* (stock exchange) /ˌɑːftər aʊəz ˈdiːlɪŋ/

trading between members of a stock exchange after the official trading hours are over: *The security was sold in after-hours dealing.*

note not used with *a* or *an*. No plural and used with a singular verb only.

syn street dealing

---

after-hours price *noun* (stock exchange) /ˌɑːftər aʊəz ˈpraɪs/

the price of a security that has been traded in after-hours dealing: *sell at a low after-hours price*

⋈ sell at an **after-hours price**

syn street price

---

aftermarket *noun* (stock exchange) /ˈɑːftə ˌmɑːkɪt/

a situation where a newly issued security is traded before its real price has been established in the stock market: *Demand for the shares from City institutions and the general public should ensure a healthy aftermarket.*

pl aftermarkets

(also **after-market**)

⋈ buy, sell, trade on the **aftermarket**

▶ **flotation, market**[1]

after-sales service *noun* (retail)
the care of a product provided by the supplier after it has been sold. It usually applies to CONSUMER DURABLES, eg cars, computers, washing machines, etc and may include testing for faults, repairs and advice: *We offer a free after-sales service for the first twelve months after purchase.*

/ˈɑːftə seɪlz ˌsɜːvɪs/
note usually singular
⧓ offer, provide an **after-sales service**
▶ **service agreement, service charge**

after sight *adverb* (banking/finance)
written on a bill of exchange to show that the bill should be paid within a specified time after the payer (the DRAWEE) is presented with it: *The bill was accepted for payment at 30 days after sight.*

/ˌɑːftə ˈsaɪt/
abbr AS, A/S, a/s
▶ **after date, at sight, on demand**

against all risks *adverb* (insurance/shipping)
(of a marine insurance policy) providing insurance for all types of loss or damage: *goods insured against all risks*

/əˌgenst ɔːl ˈrɪsks/
abbr AAR
▶ **all-risks policy, average[1] 3, risk[1]**

agcy *abbr*
agency: *ad agcy*

note used in written English only

agency *noun* (commerce)
1 the work carried out by a person (the AGENT) chosen to act on behalf of another (the PRINCIPAL): *The contract will be negotiated under the agency of my representative.* **2** a business that provides a particular service: *find a job at an employment agency* ○ *work for an advertising agency*

/ˈeɪdʒənsi/
pl agencies
abbr agcy, agy
1 ⧓ under the **agency** (of a person or an organization)
2 ⧓ use an **agency**

agenda *noun*
(a list of) items to be discussed at a meeting: *The agenda will be sent out in advance of the meeting.* ○ *What is the next item on the agenda?*

/əˈdʒendə/
pl agendas
⧓ draft, draw up, set an **agenda**

agent *noun* (commerce)
1 a person or an organization that is appointed to act on behalf of another (the PRINCIPAL), esp when negotiating a contract: *The agent is not normally liable on the contract.* **2** a person or an organization that buys or sells goods for someone else: *our agents in the Middle East* **3** a person or an organization that provides a particular service: *book a holiday through a travel agent* ○ *buy a house from an estate agent*

/ˈeɪdʒənt/
pl agents
abbr agt
1, 2 ⧓ act as, appoint, go through an **agent**
syn business agent
▶ **broker, dealer, del credere agent, estate agent, factor, forwarding agent, go-between, land agent, Lloyd's agent, representative 2, shipping and forwarding agent, sole agent, sub-agent, transfer agent, travel agent**

agent of necessity *noun* (law)
a person who acts for another in an emergency but does not have a formal right to do so: *The captain of the ship acted as the agent of necessity in order to save what was left of the cargo.*

/ˌeɪdʒənt əv nəˈsesəti/
pl agents of necessity
⧓ act as an **agent of necessity**

aggregate planning *noun* (industry)
estimating sales figures and using these to plan the amount of time and resources needed to produce the right amount of

/ˈægrɪgət ˌplænɪŋ/
note not used with *a* or *an*. No plural and used with a singular verb only.

goods: *The factory uses aggregate planning to prevent a surplus from being produced.*

▶ **planning 1**

---

agio *noun* (banking)
the charge a dealer makes for changing money from one currency to another: *The dealer charged 1% agio.* ○ *an agio of 1%*

/ˈædʒiəʊ/
note no plural

---

agiotage *noun* (finance)
the business of buying and then later selling foreign currencies: *Agiotage involves some risk but can be profitable.*

/ˈædʒiətɪdʒ/
note not used with *a* or *an*. No plural and used with a singular verb only.
▶ **arbitrage, averaging**

AGM *abbr*
annual general meeting: *The Society's AGM will be held next Wednesday.* ○ *The annual report was given at the AGM.*

/ˌeɪ dʒiː ˈem/

---

agreement *noun*
1 a state of understanding between people, organizations, countries, etc: *If all parties are in agreement we shall move to the next point on the agenda.* ○ *The two sides failed to reach (an) agreement.* **2** (*law*) an arrangement, promise or contract made with a person or an organization: *The supermarket chain has signed an agreement with a Japanese trading company.* ○ *an agreement made between two major oil companies*

/əˈgriːmənt/
1 note no plural
⧓ be in **agreement**; reach (an) **agreement**
2 pl agreements
⧓ enter into, make, sign an **agreement**
▶ **contract**[1]

---

agribusiness *noun* (agriculture)
1 agriculture that is run like an industry, using modern technology to produce high profits: *new developments in agribusiness* **2** an organization that is involved in this: *work for an agribusiness company*

/ˈægrɪbɪznəs/
1 note not used with *a* or *an*. No plural and used with a singular verb only.
2 ⧓ an **agribusiness** company, group

---

agricultural bank *noun* (agriculture)
a bank that helps farmers, esp by providing loans that do not have to be repaid quickly: *The farmer got the development loan from an agricultural bank.*

/ˌægrɪˌkʌltʃərəl ˈbæŋk/
pl agricultural banks
▶ **land bank**

---

agt *abbr* (commerce)
agent

note used in written English only

---

agy *abbr*
agency: *ad agy*

note used in written English only

---

airline *noun* (transport)
a business that operates regular flights for passengers and cargo: *Which airline did you fly with?*

/ˈeəlaɪn/
pl airlines
⧓ an international **airline**; an **airline** passenger

---

airmail *noun* (transport)
the transport of letters and parcels by aeroplane: *send a package (by) airmail* ○ *Airmail is the most expensive way to send something.*

/ˈeəmeɪl/
note not used with *a* or *an*. No plural and used with a singular verb only.
abbr A.M.
⧓ an **airmail** envelope, service
▶ **mail**[1] **2, surface mail**

ALGOL *abbr* (computing)
an acronym for AlGorithmic Oriented Language, used in computer programming: *The program has been written in ALGOL.*

/ˈælgɒl/
▶ **BASIC, COBOL, FORTRAN, PASCAL**

---

allocate *verb*
to set something aside for a particular purpose; to share or give something: *to allocate money for the advertising budget* ○ *We have allocated costs equally among all members of the department.* ○ *New staff have all been allocated jobs./Jobs have been allocated to new staff.*

/ˈæləkeɪt/
allocate, allocating, allocated
note transitive verb
⧓ **allocate** costs, jobs, money, resources

---

allocation *noun*
1 the setting aside of money, materials, etc for a particular purpose: *plan the most efficient allocation of resources* **2** the amount set aside: *We've already spent our allocation for the year.*

/ˌæləˈkeɪʃn/
1 note no plural
⧓ the **allocation** of costs, jobs, money, resources
2 pl allocations
▶ **allowance 1**

---

allonge *noun* (international trade)
a piece of paper attached to a bill of exchange that can be written on when there is no room left on the bill: *write something on an allonge*

/æˈlɒnʒ/
pl allonges
⧓ attach an **allonge**
▶ **addendum, annex, appendix, rider**

---

allotment *noun* (stock exchange)
the distribution of new company shares to the people who have applied for them: *Allotment has been made by random draw because of oversubscription.*

/əˈlɒtmənt/
note not used with *a* or *an*. No plural and used with a singular verb only.
▶ **issue[1], letter of allotment**

---

allotment letter *noun* (stock exchange)
▶ **letter of allotment**

/əˈlɒtmənt ˌletə(r)/
pl allotment letters

---

allotment money *noun* (stock exchange)
the money that a person who has been allotted new shares owes to the issuing company: *Shares will be made over on receipt of allotment money owed.*

/əˈlɒtmənt ˌmʌni/
note no plural
⧓ owe, pay **allotment money**
▶ **allotment, issue[1], money**

---

allowance *noun*
1 money given to a person for a particular purpose: *a petrol allowance of 30p per mile* **2** (*commerce*) money taken off a price for a specified purpose, eg for substandard goods or a late delivery: *The carriers made an allowance of 5% for late delivery.* **3** (*tax*) an amount taken off a sum of money earned before tax is calculated: *a single person's allowance*

/əˈlaʊəns/
1 pl allowances
⧓ a car, clothing, petrol, subsistence **allowance**
▶ **allocation 2, budget[1] 2, entertainment allowance, expenses 2, travel allowance**
2 ⧓ make an **allowance**
3 ▶ **capital allowance, tax allowance**

---

all-risks policy *noun* (insurance)
an insurance policy that pays for damage or loss of personal possessions for any reason except those listed: *We have taken out an all-risks policy on the electronic equipment.*

/ˌɔːl ˈrɪsks ˌpɒləsi/
pl all-risks policies
⧓ take out an **all-risks policy**
▶ **against all risks, risk[1]**

alphanumeric *adjective* (computing)
having both letters and numbers: *an alphanumeric code*

/ˌælfənju:ˈmerɪk/

---

alpha stocks *noun* (stock exchange)
the securities of the largest companies that are most actively traded on the STOCK EXCHANGE AUTOMATED QUOTATIONS SYSTEM of the International Stock Exchange: *trade alpha stocks in the banking and insurance sectors*

/ˈælfə stɒks/
note plural noun, used with a plural verb
▶ **Financial Times 100 Share Index**

---

alteration of share capital *noun* (commerce/finance)
an increase, a reduction or any other change in the amount of money a company can raise in shares (the AUTHORIZED SHARE CAPITAL): *An alteration of share capital is permitted in the Articles of Association of the company.*

/ˌɔ:ltəˌreɪʃn əv ˈʃeə ˌkæpɪtl/
note not used with *a* or *an*. No plural and used with a singular verb only.
▶ **share capital**

---

alternate director *noun* (commerce)
a person allowed to replace a named director of a company who is ill, absent, etc: *An alternate director was appointed to attend the meeting in his place.*

/ɔ:lˌtɜ:nət dəˈrektə(r)/
pl alternate directors
⧓ appoint an **alternate director**
▶ **director 1**

A.M. *abbr* (transport)
airmail

/ˌeɪ ˈem/
note pronounced as individual letters

---

amalgamate *verb* (industry)
to join together two or more organizations: *Several companies have been amalgamated to make one large corporation.* ○ *The two firms are amalgamating to increase productivity and save running costs.*

/əˈmælgəmeɪt/
amalgamate, amalgamating, amalgamated
note transitive and intransitive verb
⧓ **amalgamate** something *with* something
▶ **merge, take over**

---

amalgamator *noun* (management)
a person, usually an accountant, qualified in the work of amalgamating companies: *use a firm of external amalgamators*

/əˈmælgəmeɪtə(r)/
pl amalgamators
⧓ appoint, use an **amalgamator**

---

amend *verb*
to correct or change something: *The report will be amended to include the latest information.* ○ *Please amend these sales figures.*

/əˈmend/
amend, amending, amended
note transitive verb
⧓ **amend** a document, law, report, will
▶ **adjust 1, draft**[2]

---

amendment *noun*
a change or correction to something: *The committee are voting on the amendments to the proposal.* ○ *Have you included the amendments?*

/əˈmendmənt/
pl amendments
⧓ add, include, propose an **amendment**

American selling price *noun* (commerce)
(*US*) a charge made by US customs on an imported product to make it the same price as a similar product produced in the US: *The customs adjust the value of goods to the American selling price.*

/əˌmerɪkən ˈselɪŋ praɪs/
abbr ASP
▶ **price**[1]

American Stock Exchange *noun* (stock exchange)
(*US*) the second biggest stock exchange in the US after the New York Stock Exchange. It is based in New York and deals in the stocks of new and smaller companies and many foreign organizations: *The shares will be floated on the American Stock Exchange.*

/əˌmerɪkən ˈstɒk ɪksˌtʃeɪndʒ/
abbr Amex
▶ **International Stock Exchange, New York Stock Exchange, stock exchange**

---

amortization *noun* (finance)
the process of repaying a debt by making regular payments of part of the original amount and interest: *the amortization of a debt* ○ *pay £30 000 in amortization*

/əˌmɔːtɪˈzeɪʃn/
(also **amortisation**)
note not used with *a* or *an*. No plural and used with a singular verb only.

---

amortize *verb* (finance)
to repay a debt by making regular payments of part of the original amount and interest: *I intend to amortize the total cost of the car over three years.*

/əˈmɔːtaɪz/
amortize, amortizing, amortized
(also **amortise**)
note transitive verb
⧓ **amortize** the cost, a debt, a loan
▶ pay something off *under* **pay**[1]

---

amount *noun*
a sum or quantity of something: *charge the maximum amount for something* ○ *repay the money at a fixed monthly amount* ○ *calculate the total amount of interest* ○ *order the same amount each time*

/əˈmaʊnt/
pl amounts
⧓ a fixed, maximum, minimum **amount**; the total, whole **amount**

---

amounts differ *noun* (banking)
the words written on a cheque to show that the amount in words differs from that in figures: *The cheque was sent back stamped 'amounts differ'.*

/əˌmaʊnts ˈdɪfə(r)/
▶ **words and figures do not agree**

---

analysis *noun*
a detailed examination or report: *Close analysis of the sales figures shows the regional variations.* ○ *carry out an analysis of our overseas markets*

/əˈnæləsɪs/
pl analyses
⧓ carry out, do, make an **analysis**; an **analysis** *of* something; market, sales **analysis**
▶ **cost benefit analysis, econometrics, job analysis, systems analysis, value analysis**

---

analyst *noun*
a person who makes a close examination of something: *employ an analyst to look at the financial results*

/ˈænəlɪst/
pl analysts
⧓ a business, financial **analyst**
▶ **investment analyst, systems analyst**

---

annex *noun* (administration)
a section attached to the end of a document or report: *The information is given in annex B of the report.* ○ *No names are mentioned in the report, although they are listed in the annex which has been circulated privately.*

/ˈæneks/
pl annexes
(also **annexe**)
⧓ add, attach an **annex**
▶ **addendum, allonge, appendix, rider**

annual general meeting *noun* (management)
1 a meeting of the members, shareholders and directors of a company, held by law once a year, at which the company's ACCOUNTS are presented, DIVIDENDS are decided and AUDITORS chosen: *The financial results will be announced at the annual general meeting.* **2** a meeting of members held once a year by any organization to discuss and plan activities

/ˌænjuəl ˌdʒenrəl ˈmiːtɪŋ/
pl annual general meetings
abbr AGM
⧓ attend, be present at an **annual general meeting**
▶ **extraordinary general meeting**

---

annual percentage rate *noun* (finance)
the amount of interest and commission charged on a loan or received from an investment, calculated as a yearly rate: *When asking for credit, check that the interest quoted is the annual percentage rate.* ○ *a loan with an annual percentage rate of 15.4%*

/ˌænjuəl pəˈsentɪdʒ reɪt/
pl annual percentage rates
abbr APR
▶ **base rate, flat rate, rate 2, rate of return**

---

annual report *noun* (law/management)
a report, containing financial results, presented each year by the directors to the members and shareholders of a company. It must be produced by law: *The directors have published their annual report.*

/ˌænjuəl rɪˈpɔːt/
pl annual reports
⧓ present, produce, publish an **annual report**
▶ **accounting summary, report[1], results**

---

annual return *noun* (law/management)
a formal statement which, by law, must be made once a year, signed by a director and secretary of a limited company and sent to the Registrar of Companies, giving details of share capital and assets: *We are in the middle of making our annual return.*

/ˌænjuəl rɪˈtɜːn/
pl annual returns
⧓ compile, draw up the **annual return**
▶ **return[1], tax return**

---

annuitant *noun* (insurance)
a person who receives a fixed sum of money (an ANNUITY) paid on regular dates: *The insurance company has decreased the figure paid to the annuitant.*

/əˈnjuːɪtənt/
pl annuitants

---

annuity *noun* (finance)
1 a fixed sum of money paid to someone (the ANNUITANT) yearly: *receive an annuity for life* ○ *get a disability annuity* **2** an insurance contract or pension that pays someone a sum of money regularly for life, usually in return for a large payment: *an annuity that gives tax-free payments*

/əˈnjuːəti/
annuities
⧓ receive an **annuity**; **annuity** income, rates
▶ **reversionary annuity**

---

annul *verb*
to cancel something or stop it from being legally effective: *The contract was annulled.*

/əˈnʌl/
annul, annulling, annulled
note transitive verb
▶ **nullify, invalid, valid**

---

annulment *noun*
the act of cancelling something or stopping it from being legally effective: *The annulment of the contract has come through.*

/əˈnʌlmənt/
pl annulments
⧓ obtain an **annulment**
▶ **invalid, valid**

---

answerphone *noun* (office practice)
a device that automatically answers telephone calls and records any message left by the caller: *If I'm out leave a message on the answerphone.*

/ˈɑːnsəfəʊn/
pl answerphones
(also **ansaphone**)
⧓ install, switch on, use an **answerphone**
▶ **dictaphone**

antedate *verb*
to put an earlier date (on a document, letter, cheque, etc) than the date at the time of writing: *antedate the report by three days*

/ˌæntiˈdeɪt/
antedate, antedating, antedated
note transitive verb
⋈ **antedate** a cheque, an invoice
▶ **backdate, date[2] 1, post-date**

---

anti-dumping *adjective* (economics)
of ways in which a country protects its economy by preventing other countries from DUMPING in it, ie selling goods there at unfairly low prices: *pass anti-dumping laws against other countries*

/ˌænti ˈdʌmpɪŋ/
⋈ **anti-dumping** legislation, rules, strategies
▶ **protectionism**

---

any other business *noun*
an item on a list (an AGENDA) or part of a meeting (usually at the end) when any subject can be discussed: *bring an item up under any other business.* ○ *Is there any other business?*

/ˌenɪ ˌʌðə ˈbɪznəs/
abbr AOB

AOB *abbr*
any other business: *Any AOB?*

/ˌeɪ əʊ ˈbiː/

---

append *verb*
to add or attach (something written): *Would you append your signature to this document?* ○ *We'll append a clause concerning the amended delivery dates to the contract.*

/əˈpend/
append, appending, appended
note transitive verb
⋈ **append** (something) *to* (something)
▶ **attach 1, enclose**

---

appendix *noun*
a section attached to the end of a document, report or book: *The up-to-date information has been put in an appendix.* ○ *See appendix 1 for more information.*

/əˈpendɪks/
pl appendices
abbr app
⋈ add, include an **appendix**
▶ **addendum, allonge, annex, rider**

---

applicant *noun*
1 a person who asks for a job, usually by answering an advertisement and attending an interview: *We had over 200 applicants for the sales job.* **2** (*stock exchange*) a person or an organization that applies to buy shares: *the applicant company* **3** a person or an organization that applies to an authority for permission to do something: *Applicants for export licences should contact the Ministry of Foreign Trade.*

/ˈæplɪkənt/
pl applicants
⋈ a successful, an unsuccessful **applicant**
1 ▶ **appointee, candidate, interviewee, referee 1**

---

application *noun*
a formal request for something: *Shares are available on application.* ○ *There were lots of applications for the manager's job.* ○ *draw up a planning application for a new leisure centre*

/ˌæplɪˈkeɪʃn/
pl applications
⋈ a job, share **application**; deal with, receive, send in an **application**
▶ **letter of application**

---

application form *noun* (management)
a piece of printed paper, sent out by an organization to whom a formal request is made: *Applications should be made on the official application form.* ○ *fill in an application form for a job*

/ˌæplɪˈkeɪʃn fɔːm/
pl application forms
⋈ complete, fill in, send off, send out an **application form**

application for quotation *noun* (stock exchange)
a request by a PUBLIC LIMITED COMPANY to be listed on the International Stock Exchange: *The company has made its application for quotation to the Stock Exchange.*

/ˌæplɪˌkeɪʃn fə kwəʊˈteɪʃn/
pl applications for quotation
⋈ make an **application for quotation**
► **listed company, quotation 2, Stock Exchange Daily Official List**

application money *noun* (stock exchange)
the money paid by someone who asks for shares in a new share issue: *Application money must be returned with the application form.*

/ˌæplɪˈkeɪʃn ˌmʌni/
note no plural
► **allotment money, letter of application, money**

appoint *verb*
1 (*personnel*) to choose a person or a group of people for a job or position of responsibility: *She was appointed to the post of sales director.* ○ *They appointed him as chairman.* ○ *We must appoint a new committee.* **2** to arrange or decide on something: *Their representative failed to turn up on the appointed day/day appointed.*

/əˈpɔɪnt/
appoint, appointing, appointed
note transitive verb
1 ⋈ **appoint** someone *as* something; **appoint** someone *to* something
► **recruitment**
2 ⋈ the date, day, time **appointed**

appointee *noun* (personnel)
the person chosen for a job or position: *The appointee will be expected to familiarize himself/herself with the company rules.*

/əpɔɪnˈtiː/
pl appointees
⋈ a new **appointee**
► **applicant 1, candidate, interviewee**

appointment *noun*
1 an arrangement to meet someone at a particular time: *The appointment was made for 9.30.* ○ *Please make an appointment with my secretary.* **2** (*personnel*) a job or position of responsibility: *There has been a new appointment to the board.* ○ *appointments vacant*, ie as a heading in a newspaper advertisement

/əˈpɔɪntmənt/
pl appointments
1 ⋈ cancel, fix, keep, make an **appointment**; an **appointments** book
2 ⋈ a permanent, temporary, vacant **appointment**
► **engagement, letter of appointment**

appraisal *noun* (personnel)
a meeting between an employee and a manager to assess the quality of the employee's work and to plan future tasks: *I've got an appraisal with my boss tomorrow.* ○ *conduct a staff appraisal* ○ *This company has an annual appraisal system.*

/əˈpreɪzl/
pl appraisals
⋈ staff **appraisal**
syn performance appraisal

appraiser *noun* (commerce)
(*US*) ► **valuer**

/əˈpreɪzə(r)/

appreciate *verb*
1 to be aware of the value of something: *We appreciate all you have done for the firm.* **2** (*finance*) to increase in value: *My shares have appreciated by 10% over one year.* ○ *The pound is appreciating.*

/əˈpriːʃieɪt/
appreciate, appreciating, appreciated
1 note transitive verb
2 note intransitive verb
⋈ **appreciate** in value
opp depreciate

appreciation *noun* (finance)
1 an increase in the value of an asset: *The company's balance sheets do not show appreciation of land values.* **2** an increase in the value of currency in comparison with other currencies: *The table shows appreciation of the mark against the lira.*

/əˌpriːʃiˈeɪʃn/
note not used with *a* or *an*. No plural and used with a singular verb only.
⋈ capital **appreciation**
opp depreciation

apprentice *noun* (personnel)
a person (usually young) who learns a skill or trade by working at it for a fixed time while supervised by an experienced worker: *an engineering apprentice* ○ *an apprentice engineer* ○ *Apprentice wages are very low.*

/əˈprentɪs/
pl apprentices
⋈ **apprentice** labour, work
▶ **trainee**

apprenticeship *noun* (personnel)
a fixed time spent by a (young) person learning a skill or trade while supervised by an experienced worker or workers: *a four-year apprenticeship in engineering*

/əˈprentɪʃɪp/
pl apprenticeships
⋈ complete, get, obtain, serve an **apprenticeship**

appro *abbr*
▶ **approval**

/ˈæprəʊ/

appropriate *verb* (accounting)
to set aside money for a special purpose: *£5 000 has been appropriated for a new training scheme.*

/əˈprəʊprieɪt/
appropriate, appropriating, appropriated
note transitive verb

appropriation *noun* (finance)
1 (**a**) setting aside an amount of money for a particular purpose in the company accounts: *Appropriation for advertising has been increased.* (**b**) an instance of this **2** the money set aside: *An appropriation of £5 000 has been made for staff training.* **3** taking legal possession of money or property, usually if it is not claimed by the owner: *The bank had the right to appropriation in the case of unclaimed deposits.*

/əˌprəʊpriˈeɪʃn/
1a note not used with *a* or *an*. No plural and used with a singular verb only.
1b pl appropriations
2 pl appropriations
⋈ make an **appropriation**
3 note not used with *a* or *an*. No plural and used with a singular verb only.

appropriation account *noun* (accounting)
a section of a PROFIT AND LOSS ACCOUNT that shows how profits have been used: *The appropriation account itemizes the uses profit was put to.*

/əˌprəʊpriˈeɪʃn əˌkaʊnt/
pl appropriation accounts
syn outlay account
▶ **account[1] 1**

approval *noun*
acceptance of something: *They sought approval for the budget.* ○ *Do the plans meet with your approval?*

on approval of goods sent or given to possible customers to look at or use before buying them: *I got the computer on approval.* ○ *send goods on approval* ○ *On approval goods must be returned within 14 days if they are not satisfactory.*

/əˈpruːvl/
abbr appro
note not used with *a* or *an*. No plural and used with a singular verb only.
⋈ meet with, seek **approval**

approve *verb*
to accept something; to find something good or satisfactory: *The minutes of the last meeting have been approved.* ○ *The managing director has approved the sales budget for next year.*

/əˈpruːv/
approve, approving, approved
note transitive verb

⧓ **approve** a budget, minutes
▶ **pass**[2]

approved account *noun*
1 (*retail*) a CREDIT ACCOUNT held by a customer who has shown that he/she is able to pay for the goods: *I have an approved account here.* **2** (*accounting*) financial records that have been formally accepted by a company and are therefore legally binding: *According to the approved accounts those figures are inaccurate.*

/əˌpruːvd əˈkaʊnt/
pl approved accounts
1 ⧓ hold an **approved account**
▶ **account**[1] **2**
2 ▶ **accounts**

approx *abbr*
approximate; approximately: *The office space is approx 15 square metres.*

/əˈprɒks/

approximate *adjective*
almost correct or exact but not completely so: *Can you give me an approximate price?*

/əˈprɒksɪmət/
abbr approx
⧓ an **approximate** amount, figure

approximately *adverb*
not exactly but nearly: *The journey takes approximately 45 minutes.*

/əˈprɒksɪmətli/
abbr approx

approximation *noun*
an amount that is not exact but nearly so; an estimate: *These sales figures are just approximations.* ○ *If you don't know exactly, just give me an approximation.*

/əˌprɒksɪˈmeɪʃn/
pl approximations
▶ **actuals 2, ballpark figure, estimate**[1] **1**

APR *abbr* (finance)
annual percentage rate: *APR is 26.9%.*

/ˌeɪ piː ˈɑː(r)/

aptitude *noun*
natural ability: *She has an aptitude for figures.*

aptitude test an examination to find out what kind of work a person is most suited to: *Most school-leavers should take an aptitude test.*

/ˈæptɪtjuːd/
pl aptitudes
⧓ an **aptitude** *for* (something)

arbitrage *noun* (stock exchange)
the buying and selling of shares, goods, currencies, etc in two different markets at almost the same time to make a profit from price differences: *The difference in prices between the two markets was reduced by arbitrage.*

/ˈɑːbɪtrɪdʒ/
note not used with *a* or *an*. No plural and used with a singular verb only.
⧓ an **arbitrage** dealer, position, trader
▶ **agiotage, averaging**

arbitrageur *noun* (stock exchange)
1 a person who carries out ARBITRAGE **2** a person who hopes to make a profit by buying and selling stock when a takeover bid is expected, or by encouraging others to think that one is expected: *The arbitrageur was accused of manipulating stock prices.*

/ˌɑːbɪtrɑːˈʒɜː(r)/
pl arbitrageurs
▶ **insider dealing**

arbitration *noun* (industrial relations)
the settling of a dispute by means of a neutral third party rather than by a court of law: *The issue has been taken to arbitration.* ○ *They decided to settle the dispute by arbitration.* ○ *The management refused to agree to arbitration.*

/ˌɑːbɪˈtreɪʃn/
note not used with *a* or *an*. No plural and used with a singular verb only.
⧓ an **arbitration** board, decision, hearing, panel,

tribunal; to go to, to refer (something) to, to take (something) to **arbitration**

▶ **Advisory Conciliation and Arbitration Service, industrial dispute, mediation**

---

arbitrator *noun* (industrial relations)
a person who is appointed to settle a dispute: *Both sides have agreed to abide by the decision of the arbitrator.*

/ˈɑːbɪtreɪtə(r)/
pl arbitrators
⧓ act as (an) **arbitrator**; appoint an **arbitrator**
▶ **industrial dispute, referee 3, umpire**

---

area manager *noun* (management)
▶ **manager**

/ˌeəriə ˈmænɪdʒə(r)/

ARR *abbr* (accounting)
accounting rate of return

/ˌeɪ ɑːr ˈɑː(r)/

---

arrears *noun* (finance)
money that is owed and should have been paid earlier: *Local authorities have reported an increase in rent arrears.* ○ *arrears of interest*

in arrears be late in paying money that is owed: *I'm in arrears with the rent.* ○ *The rent is in arrears.*

/əˈrɪəz/
note plural noun, used with a plural verb
⧓ mortgage, rent, salary **arrears**

---

arrival *noun* (transport)
1 the act of reaching a place: *Please contact head office on arrival.*
2 a person or thing that has reached a destination: *New arrivals will be welcomed at the conference dinner.* ○ *I'll meet you in the arrivals lounge at the airport.*

/əˈraɪvl/
1 note not used with *a* or *an*. No plural and used with a singular verb only.
⧓ on **arrival**
2 pl arrivals
▶ **departure**

---

arrival notice *noun* (transport)
a note sent by a carrier to the receiver (the CONSIGNEE) saying that goods have arrived: *We have not yet received the carrier's arrival notice.*

/əˈraɪvl ˌnəʊtɪs/
pl arrival notices
⧓ receive, send an **arrival notice**
▶ **advice note, despatch note**

---

articled clerk *noun* (law)
▶ **trainee solicitor**

/ˌɑːtɪkld ˈklɑːk/

---

articles *noun* (law)
period spent in a legal firm by someone training to be a solicitor: *She's doing her articles with a firm in London.*

/ˈɑːtɪklz/
note plural noun, used with a plural verb
⧓ do, take **articles**
▶ **trainee solicitor**

Articles of Association *noun* (law)
1 the rules and regulations for running a UK company, drawn up when the company is formed. The Articles of Association show shareholders' rights, the powers of directors, how to conduct formal meetings, etc: *Under the Articles of Association the*

/ˌɑːtɪklz əv əˌsəʊsiˈeɪʃn/
note plural noun, used with a plural verb
⧓ amend, change, draw up the **Articles of Association**

company is not allowed to engage in property speculation. **2** the legal document containing the Articles of Association, a copy of which is placed with the Registrar of Companies at Companies House

▶ **authorized share capital, Memorandum of Association**

---

artificial person *noun* (law)
a company considered as having a separate legal identity from the people who work for it, although some of these people will represent the will of the company: *The corporation was treated legally as an artificial person.*

/ˌɑːtɪˌfɪʃl ˈpɜːsn/
note usually singular
syn fictitious person, juristic person
▶ **company, corporation, legal person, natural person**

---

artisan *noun* (industry)
a person who is skilled in a manufacturing or industrial trade: *We employ only trained artisans.* ○ *an artisan trade such as plumbing*

/ˌɑːtɪˈzæn/
pl artisans
▶ **craftsman, labourer**

AS *abbr* (banking/finance)
after sight

/ˌeɪ ˈes/
note pronounced as individual letters

ASA *abbr* (advertising)
the Advertising Standards Authority: *The ASA has no power to vet advertisements before they are printed.*

/ˌeɪ es ˈeɪ/
note pronounced as individual letters

---

asap *abbr*
as soon as possible: *The boss needs that report asap.*

/ˌeɪ es eɪ ˈpiː, ˈæsæp/
note can be pronounced as a word or as individual letters

A share *noun* (stock exchange)
an ORDINARY SHARE that does not give the owner the right to vote on company issues: *A shares do not dilute the control of a company.*

/ˈeɪ ʃeə(r)/
pl A shares
⧓ issue **A shares**
▶ **share, voting rights**

---

as is *adjective* (commerce)
a description of goods that are for sale in their existing condition and present place: *The goods are to be sold as is.*

/ˌæz ˈɪz/
▶ **as seen**

---

asking price *noun* (sales)
the price at which something is offered for sale: *I managed to get the full asking price of £2000 for my car.* ○ *Always negotiate, never pay the full asking price.*

/ˈɑːskɪŋ praɪs/
pl asking prices
⧓ increase, pay, reduce the **asking price**; less than, more than the **asking price**
▶ **price**[1]

ASP *abbr* (commerce)
(*US*) American Selling Price

/ˌeɪ es ˈpiː/
note pronounced as individual letters

---

as per *adverb*
according to: *as per your letter*

as per advice (*banking*) the words written on a bill of exchange to show that the bank (the DRAWEE) knows the bill is being written and will have to be paid: *The bill is marked as per advice.*

as per contra (*accounting*) relating to an entry on the opposite side of an account: *The entry is as per contra.*

/æz pɜː(r)/

as seen *adjective, adverb* (sales)
(of something offered for sale) in the condition in which the buyer sees it, ie the seller cannot guarantee or improve its quality: *If you buy at a car auction you take the vehicle as seen.*

/æz ˈsiːn/
▶ **as is**

---

assembly *noun*
1 (*industry*) fitting together the parts of something: *The furniture is designed for easy assembly.* ○ *The checks are done at assembly.* ○ *The assembly instructions are quite clear.* **2** a gathering of people for a particular purpose: *He addressed the assembly.* ○ *an assembly of over 200 people*

/əˈsembli/
1 note not used with *a* or *an*. No plural and used with a singular verb only.
⋈ **assembly** instructions, manual
▶ **assembly line, assembly plant**
2 pl assemblies
⋈ a general, national **assembly**
▶ **business meeting, committee, conference, meeting**

---

assembly language *noun* (computing)
a system of codes used in computer programming. The assembly language codes, which are easy to learn, are then converted into machine codes which can be read by the computer.

/əˈsembli ˌlæŋgwɪdʒ/
note no plural
▶ **programming language**

---

assembly line *noun* (industry)
a production system in a factory where items are put together by workers who add parts as the items pass along a slow moving line: *He works on an assembly line in a car factory.* ○ *Finished goods come off the assembly line ready for delivery.*

/əˈsembli laɪn/
pl assembly lines
⋈ work on an **assembly line**
▶ **production line**

---

assembly plant *noun* (industry)
a place, eg a factory, where machines and other manufactured goods are put together: *a car assembly plant*

/əˈsembli plɑːnt/
pl assembly plants
▶ **plant 2**

---

assembly point *noun* (health and safety)
a place where people should gather in an emergency: *By law, the assembly point in case of fire must be clearly marked.*

/əˈsembli pɔɪnt/
pl assembly points
⋈ gather at, meet at, go to an **assembly point**

---

assent *noun* (law)
a document that transfers the ownership of property, etc from the relatives of a dead person to the person named in the will: *We have received the assent on the property.*

/əˈsent/
pl assents
▶ **deed, deed of transfer, title, title deeds**

---

assented stock *noun* (stock exchange)
an item of financial value, eg an ordinary share, that belongs to someone who has agreed to the conditions of a TAKEOVER BID: *20% of the total is already assented stock.*

/əˌsentɪd ˈstɒk/
note usually singular
⋈ quote (a price) for **assented stock**
▶ **stock²**

---

assess *verb*
to work out the amount, value or quality of something: *The damage was assessed at £2 500.* ○ *The damaged goods were assessed for insurance.* ○ *The overall cost is difficult to assess.*

/əˈses/
assess, assessing, assessed
note transitive verb

⧓ **assess** costs, damage, insurance, quality, value
▶ **loss assessor, value**[1]

---

assessment *noun*
1 a calculation of the amount, value or quality of something: *The insurance company carried out an assessment of damages.* **2** (*tax*) a calculation of the amount of tax a person has to pay; the document that shows this: *Tax assessments have been sent out to all self-employed taxpayers.*

/əˈsesmənt/
pl assessments
⧓ carry out, make an **assessment**
▶ **loss assessor, valuation**

---

asset *noun*
an item of value belonging to a person or a company, such as a share, a piece of land, a building or a machine, esp if it can be sold to pay a debt: *The factory is the most valuable asset.* ○ *The company was forced to sell off its assets.*

/ˈæset/
pl assets
⧓ chief, financial, foreign, main, principal **asset**
▶ **bankable asset, capital asset, current assets, illiquid assets, intangible asset, liability 2, liquid assets, tangible asset, wasting asset**

---

asset backing *noun* (accounting)
the total value of the assets of a company divided by the number of ordinary shares issued: *The company's asset backing is 340p a share.*

/ˈæset ˌbækɪŋ/
note not used with *a* or *an*. No plural and used with a singular verb only.
⧓ a solid, strong **asset backing**
▶ **net asset value, net asset value per share**

---

asset stripping *noun* (finance)
buying an unsuccessful company and selling some or all of its assets: *Asset stripping can both help and destroy industry.* ○ *Many employees lose their jobs as a result of asset stripping.*

/ˈæset strɪpɪŋ/
(also **asset-stripping**)
note not used with *a* or *an*. No plural and used with a singular verb only.
▶ **poison pill, unbundling**

---

asset value *noun* (accounting)
▶ **net asset value**

/ˈæset ˌvælju:/

---

assign *verb*
1 (*personnel*) to share out work or duties: *We are assigning the task to a team of experts.* ○ *The factory supervisors plan schedules, assign work and monitor progress.* **2** (*personnel*) to choose someone for a job or position: *She has been assigned to a new post.* **3** (*law*) to give property or legal rights to someone: *The writer assigned the copyright to the publisher.* ○ *The lease was assigned to a new tenant.*

/əˈsaɪn/
assign, assigning, assigned
note transitive verb
1 ⧓ **assign** something *to* someone
2 ⧓ **assign** someone *to* something
▶ **appoint 1**
3 ⧓ **assign** something *to* someone

---

assignee in bankruptcy *noun* (law)
▶ **trustee in bankruptcy**

/ˌæsaɪˌni: ɪn ˈbæŋkrəpsi/

---

assignment *noun*
1 (*management*) a task or duty that is given to someone: *I was sent overseas on a special assignment.* ○ *She was given a very difficult assignment.* **2** (*law*) the transfer of a legal right to someone: *The deed of assignment has been signed.* **3** the transfer of the whole or part of the terms of a LEASE to someone: *assignment of a lease to a new tenant*

/əˈsaɪnmənt/
pl assignments
1 ⧓ give someone, work on an **assignment**
► **appointment 2**
2 ⧓ a legal, statutory **assignment**

---

assignment clause *noun* (insurance/shipping)
part of a marine insurance policy that allows the insured person to transfer the rights stated in the policy: *He transferred the policy to the bank under an assignment clause.*

/əˈsaɪnmənt klɔːz/
pl assignment clauses
⧓ accept, agree to, include an **assignment clause**
► **abandonment clause, clause**

---

assistant *noun* (personnel)
1 a person who helps in a business, usually by doing general, not very skilled work: *We are taking on an extra assistant over Christmas.* **2** a person who helps with a particular job or activity: *an administrative, a laboratory, a research, a technical assistant* **3** a person who sells goods in a shop or store: *Ask one of the assistants if you can try the suit on.* **4** a person who helps a more senior employee, and may do his/her work if necessary: *The manager is ill, so the assistant manager is in charge today.*

/əˈsɪstənt/
pl assistants
abbr asst
1 ⧓ a general, temporary **assistant**
2 ► **clerical assistant, personal assistant**
3 syn (*US*) clerk
⧓ a sales, shop **assistant**
4 ⧓ an **assistant** director, editor, manager, professor

Assoc. *abbr*
1 association: *a bankers' assoc* ○ *the Consumers' Assoc.* **2** associates: *David Irvine Assoc.*

(also **assoc**)
note used in written English only

---

associate[1] *noun* (management)
1 a person connected with another or others in an organization; a colleague or partner: *business associates* ○ *an associate in an insurance firm* **2 Associates** used in the name of an organization to show there are a number of professional partners: *David Irvine Associates*

/əˈsəʊʃiət/
pl associates
abbr assoc
► **colleague, Lloyd's associate, partner**

---

associate[2] *adjective*
linked with a person or an organization: *Four associate members were elected to sit on the management committee.* ○ *apply for associate membership of an organization*

/əˈsəʊʃiət/
⧓ an **associate** banker, director, member; **associate** membership

---

associate company *noun* (commerce/finance)
a company of which more than 20%, but less than 51% of the share capital is held by another company: *The company has a subsidiary in France and an associate company in the United States.*

/əˈsəʊʃiət ˌkʌmpəni/
pl associate companies
► **group, holding company, subsidiary company**

---

association *noun* (management)
1 a group of people, departments or institutions joined together for a common purpose; an organization: *Do you belong to any professional associations?* ○ *the British Bankers Association* **2** the act of being linked with a person or a company: *Mr Smith has had a long and successful association with the firm.* ○ *We are working in association with a company based overseas for this project.*

/əˌsəʊsiˈeɪʃn/
1 pl associations
abbr Assoc.
⧓ a national, political, professional, regional **association**
► **business 3, company,**

federation, group, organization 1

2 note usually singular

⧓ form, have an **association** *with* (someone/something); work in **association** *with* (someone/something)

---

asst *abbr*
assistant: *admin asst*

note used in written English only

---

assurance *noun* (insurance)
(*UK*) insurance, esp on someone's life: *What is the number of your assurance policy?* ○ *take out life assurance*

/əˈʃʊərəns/

note not used with *a* or *an*. No plural and used with a singular verb only.

⧓ an **assurance** company, policy

▶ **insurance**

---

at call *adverb* (banking)
of money that has been lent but must be repaid on demand: *The sum will be lent at call.*

/æt ˈkɔːl/

▶ **call money, money at call and short notice**

---

at cost *adverb* (commerce)
selling something at the price of manufacture or the wholesale cost: *We were forced to sell at cost to get rid of the stock.*

/æt ˈkɒst/

▶ **cost price**

---

at date *adjective*
at the time or day mentioned: *The balance at date below has increased.*

/æt ˈdeɪt/

ATM *abbr* (banking)
automatic teller machine: *withdraw money from a bank account using an ATM*

/ˌeɪ tiː ˈem/

---

at par *adjective, adverb* (stock exchange)
of a share or other security that has the same value in the market as the value written on the share itself: *Gilt-edged securities are always repaid at par.* ○ *sell at par* ○ *The shares are currently at par.*

/æt ˈpɑː(r)/

▶ **above par, below par, nominal price**

---

at sight *adverb* (banking/international trade)
written on a bill of exchange to show that it must be paid as soon as it is presented for payment: *pay a bill at sight*

/æt ˈsaɪt/

▶ **after date, sight bill, after sight, on demand**

---

attach *verb*
1 to join or fix something to something: *attach an invoice to a letter* ○ *Please read the attached document/the document attached.* **2** (of a person) to be linked to something: *She has been temporarily attached to this department.* ○ *Are you attached to the project?*

/əˈtætʃ/

attach, attaching, attached

note transitive verb

1 ⧓ **attach** something *to* something

▶ **append, enclose**

2 ⧓ **attach** someone *to* (someone/something)

▶ **assign 2**

---

attention of *noun*
▶ **for the attention of**

/əˈtenʃn ɒv/

abbr attn

attest *verb* (law)
to state formally that something is true or genuine: *He was asked to attest the signature.*

/ə'test/
attest, attesting, attested
note transitive verb
⋈ **attest** a signature, will
▶ **authenticate, certify, validate, witness**[2] **2**

---

attested copy *noun* (law)
▶ **certified copy**

/əˌtestɪd 'kɒpi/

---

attitude research *noun* (marketing)
an examination of people's feelings towards an organization or its products: *The results of the attitude research show a strong brand loyalty.*

/'ætɪtju:d rɪˌsɜ:tʃ, ˌri:sɜ:tʃ/
note not used with *a* or *an*. No plural and used with a singular verb only.
⋈ carry out **attitude research**
▶ **market research**

---

attn *abbr*
for the attention of: *Attn Ms Howard*

note used in written English only

---

attorney *noun* (law)
1 a person who has the right to represent another in legal matters: *I appointed him attorney in the case.* **2** (*US*) a barrister

/ə'tɜ:ni/
pl attorneys
1 ▶ **power of attorney**
2 ▶ **lawyer, solicitor**

---

attributable profit *noun* (accounting/finance)
an amount of money that belongs to, or is produced by, a particular division, department, period, organization, area, etc: *90% of the total is attributable profit.*

/ə'trɪbjʊtəbl 'prɒfɪt/
note usually singular
▶ **profit**[1] **1**

---

at warehouse *adjective* (distribution)
of the price of goods which includes delivery and loading: *All prices given are at warehouse.* ○ *an at warehouse price*

/æt 'weəhaʊs/
▶ **ex warehouse**

---

auction[1] *noun* (sales)
1 a way of selling in which each item is sold at an open meeting to the person who makes the highest bid, ie offers the most money: *The house will be sold by auction.* ○ *The painting should fetch £2 000 at auction.* **2 auction sale** an event where this way of selling takes place: *go to a car auction*

up for auction offered for sale in an auction: *The house is up for auction.*

/'ɔ:kʃn/
1 note not used with *a* or *an*. No plural and used with a singular verb only.
2 pl auctions
⋈ buy, sell something in an **auction**; sell something by **auction**

---

auction[2] *verb* (sales)
to sell something to the person who makes the highest offer; sell something by auction: *The house was auctioned last week.*

/'ɔ:kʃn/
auction, auctioning, auctioned
note transitive verb

---

auctioneer *noun* (sales)
a person who organizes and sells goods at an AUCTION, and acts for the seller until the goods are sold: *The auctioneer is paid by commission.*

/ˌɔ:kʃə'nɪə(r)/
pl auctioneers

audio conference *noun* (management)
a meeting with people who cannot all be together at the same time, using audio (telephone) equipment: *hold an audio-conference with delegates from all over the world*

/ˌɔːdiəʊ ˈkɒnfərəns/
pl audio conferences
⋈ conduct, hold an **audio conference**
▶ **conference, video conference**

---

audio-typist *noun*
a person who types letters, etc that have been spoken onto a tape recorder (a DICTATING MACHINE): *work as an audio-typist*

/ˈɔːdiəʊ taɪpɪst/
pl audio-typists
▶ **copy-typist, keyboarder, shorthand typist, typist**

---

audit[1] *noun* (accounting)
a detailed inspection, usually once a year, of the accounts of an organization by a professionally trained person (an AUDITOR): *carry out an annual audit of the company accounts*

external audit an audit carried out by a person not employed by the company to check that the accounts are accurate and honest: *An external audit is required for tax purposes.*

/ˈɔːdɪt/
pl audits
⋈ carry out an **audit**
▶ **annual report, environmental audit, marketing audit, qualified report, store audit, true and fair view, value for money audit**

---

audit[2] *verb* (accounting)
to examine the accounts of an organization to check that they are true and correct: *The accounts have not yet been audited.*

/ˈɔːdɪt/
audit, auditing, audited
note transitive verb
⋈ **audited** accounts, figures, profit
▶ **unaudited**

---

the Audit Bureau of Circulation *noun* (sales)
an organization in the UK that regularly records and publishes the number of copies of newspapers and magazines sold in a particular period: *The circulation figures were certified by the Audit Bureau of Circulation.*

/ðiˌɔːdɪt ˌbjʊərəʊ əv ˌsɜːkjuˈleɪʃn/
abbr ABC
⋈ calculated, certified, published by the **Audit Bureau of Circulation**
▶ **circulation 2**

---

auditor *noun* (sales)
a professionally trained person who examines the accounts of an organization to check that they are true and correct: *The auditors were called in to inspect the accounts.*

/ˈɔːdɪtə(r)/
pl auditors
⋈ examined, inspected by an **auditor**
▶ **accountant, audit, true and fair view**

---

authenticate *verb* (law)
to provide proof that something is true or real: *Extra documentation was required to authenticate the signature.* ○ *Has the document been authenticated?*

/ɔːˈθentɪkeɪt/
authenticate, authenticating, authenticated
note transitive verb
▶ **attest, certify, validate, witness**[2] **2**

---

authentication *noun*
proof that something is real or true; the act of providing this proof: *The signature was sent to the solicitor for authentication.*

/ɔːˌθentɪˈkeɪʃn/
note not used with *a* or *an*. No plural and used with a singular verb only.

⧓ a letter of **authentication**; provide, require **authentication**

▶ **proof 1**

---

authority *noun*

1 (**a**) the (official) power to give orders, make decisions, etc: *I have no authority to change decisions taken by the management.* ○ *Who's in authority here?* ○ *She's now in a position of authority.* (**b**) the right or permission to do something: *Do you have legal authority to build here?* **2** a natural ability to control and influence people: *The new manager lacks/is lacking in authority.* **3** (**a**) a government or other body that has the power to make and carry out regulations: *the water, health, education, etc authority* ○ *local, tax, etc authorities* (**b**) **the authorities** organizations with powers that are often unspecified or unknown: *Do the authorities know about this?*

/ɔːˈθɒrəti/

1, 2 note not used with *a* or *an*. No plural and used with a singular verb only.

⧓ legal, official **authority**

▶ **permission, power 3**

3 pl authorities

---

authority to negotiate *noun* (banking)

the power given by an importer's bank to a bank in the exporter's country to allow a bill of exchange to be drawn on the importer: *give your bank authority to negotiate*

/ɔːˌθɒrəti tə nɪˈɡəʊʃieɪt/

note no plural

▶ **authority to pay**

---

authority to pay *noun* (banking)

the power given to the importer's bank to pay the bill of exchange presented by the exporter: *When the bill of exchange was presented for payment the bank exercised its authority to pay.*

/ɔːˌθɒrəti tə ˈpeɪ/

note no plural

▶ **authority to negotiate**

---

authorization *noun*

1 (**a**) the (official) power or permission given to a person or an organization: *The committee has no authorization to change company policy.* (**b**) the act of giving this power or permission: *I didn't agree with the authorization of these payments.* **2** a document that gives or proves official power: *I had to show them my (letter of) authorization before they let me into the building.*

/ˌɔːθəraɪˈzeɪʃn/

(also **authorisation**)

note not used with *a* or *an*. No plural and used with a singular verb only.

⧓ give, grant, receive, refuse **authorization**

---

authorization code *noun* (computing)

▶ **password**

/ˌɔːθəraɪˈzeɪʃn kəʊd/

---

authorize *verb*

1 to give (official) permission for something: *Only the director can authorize payment of this cheque.* ○ *Payment was authorized by the bank.* ○ *Has your visit been authorized?* **2** to give (official) power to someone: *My secretary is authorized to accept payments on my behalf.* ○ *I'm afraid I can't authorize you to act for us overseas.*

/ˈɔːθəraɪz/

authorize, authorizing, authorized

(also **authorise**)

note transitive verb

1 ⧓ **authorized** *by* someone/something

2 ⧓ **authorize** someone *to* do something

▶ **permit**[2]

---

authorized fund *noun* (tax)

a fund of money (an INVESTMENT TRUST) that has been registered for tax purposes: *The money is in an authorized fund and tax will be deducted.*

/ˌɔːθəraɪzd ˈfʌnd/

(also **authorised fund**)

pl authorized funds

⧓ invest in, manage an **authorized fund**

▶ **fund**[1] **1**

---

authorized share capital *noun* (stock exchange)
the amount of money that a company is allowed to raise from the issue of shares, according to its ARTICLES OF ASSOCIATION: *The company has not yet issued all its authorized share capital.*

/ˌɔːθəraɪzd ˈʃeə ˌkæpɪtl/
(also **authorised share capital**)
note not used with *a* or *an*. No plural and used with a singular verb only.
syn nominal capital, registered capital
▶ **issued capital, share, share capital**

auto-financing *adjective* (finance)
▶ **self-financing**

/ˌɔːtəʊ ˈfaɪnænsɪŋ/

automate *verb* (technology)
to use machines that need little or no human control (to make work more efficient or replace people): *This part of the factory is now fully automated.* ○ *We're in the process of automating the production department.*

/ˈɔːtəmeɪt/
automate, automating, automated
note transitive verb
▶ **computerize, mechanize**

automatic pilot *noun* (transport)
▶ **pilot**[1]

/ˌɔːtəˌmætɪk ˈpaɪlət/

automatic teller machine *noun* (banking)
▶ **cashpoint**

/ˌɔːtəˈmætɪk ˈtelə məˌʃiːn/
pl automatic teller machines
abbr ATM

automation *noun* (technology)
the use of machines, computer systems, etc to do work previously done by people: *Some people feared that automation would lead to job losses.*

/ˌɔːtəˈmeɪʃn/
note not used with *a* or *an*. No plural and used with a singular verb only.
⋈ introduce **automation**
▶ **computerization, mechanization**

a/v *abbr* (tax)
ad valorem

note used in written English only

average[1] *noun*
1 an amount calculated by adding together several figures and dividing by the number of figures added: *Add up these prices and find the average.* **2** something that is standard or usual: *Her qualifications were above average.* ○ *Sales for this month were well below average.* **3** (*insurance/shipping*) (**a**) a loss or damage arising from an event at sea: *The shipowners paid the average.* (**b**) the way that the cost of replacing a ship or cargo damaged at sea is shared between owners and insurers: *All marine insurance policies are subject to average.*

on average usually; the result after the average has been calculated: *We sell on average about 500 a month.*

/ˈævərɪdʒ/
1 pl averages
⋈ **average** age, cost, price, quality, size, etc
2 note no plural
⋈ above, below **average**
3 note no plural
▶ **free of all average, free of particular average, general average, with average**

average[2] *verb*
to do or amount to something as an average: *The pay rises averaged 10% over all.*

/ˈævərɪdʒ/
average, averaging, averaged

average out (at something) to result in an average amount of something: *The conference dinner averages out at £15 per head.*

average (something) out to share out an amount of something over a period of time: *We are averaging out the cost over the whole year.*

note transitive verb

---

average adjuster *noun* (insurance/shipping)
a qualified person who studies marine insurance claims to calculate how much money should be paid by the insurer: *The claim is in the hands of the average adjuster.*

/ˈævərɪdʒ əˌdʒʌstə(r)/
pl average adjusters
▶ **average[1] 3, loss adjuster**

---

average bond *noun* (insurance/shipping)
an insurance agreement taken out by someone receiving cargo that allows insurance payments, rather than a replacement of the cargo, to be used to share the cost of loss or damages at sea: *The cargo owners decided to take out an average bond with an insurance company.*

/ˈævərɪdʒ bɒnd/
pl average bonds
⧓ take out an **average bond**
▶ **average[1] 3, free of all average, free of particular average, general average, with average**

---

average clause *noun* (insurance)
a condition in an insurance policy stating that the sum paid for loss or damages will not be more than the proportion of the amount insured to the real value of the item. If, for example, goods worth £1 000 are insured for £500, in the event of a fire only £250 will be paid: *Because of the average clause we made sure that everything was insured to its full value.*

/ˈævərɪdʒ klɔːz/
pl average clauses
⧓ agree to, include an **average clause**

---

average cost *noun* (manufacturing)
the total cost of producing a number of items divided by the number of items produced: *The new production methods have reduced the average cost.*

/ˌævərɪdʒ ˈkɒst/
note usually singular
⧓ calculate, increase, reduce the **average cost**
▶ **cost[1], unit cost**

---

average due date *noun* (finance)
the date when several payments, due to the same person on different dates, are combined and paid together: *An average due date has been selected for the payment of the sums owed.*

/ˌævərɪdʒ ˈdjuː deɪt/
pl average due dates
⧓ agree, select, set an **average due date**

---

average revenue *noun* (sales)
the total cost received from the sale of goods divided by the total number of items sold: *The best price can be found by calculating the average revenue.*

/ˌævərɪdʒ ˈrevənjuː/
pl average revenues
⧓ calculate, increase, reduce the **average revenue**
▶ **revenue 1**

---

average stock *noun* (commerce/accounting)
a method of calculating the value of goods held during a specific period where the AVERAGE COST of goods coming in is assumed to be the same as the average cost of goods sold: *We needed to know the average stock to make a comparison with last year.*

/ˌævərɪdʒ ˈstɒk/
note not used with *a* or *an*. No plural and used with a singular verb only.
▶ **first in first out, last in first out, stock control**

---

averaging *noun* (stock exchange)
trading shares from the same company at different prices at the same time: *Averaging can maintain the price of a security.*

averaging down buying more shares when the price is falling, thus reducing average cost but increasing potential overall loss: *Averaging down is a very risky strategy.*

/ˈævərɪdʒɪŋ/
note not used with *a* or *an*. No plural and used with a singular verb only.
▶ **agiotage, arbitrage**

averaging in buying shares at various price levels in order to build up investments: *An investor averaging in will not go below a pre-set limit.*

averaging out selling only when the price rises above a pre-set figure: *The investor started averaging out after building up a small holding.*

averaging up buying more of a share issue when the market price is rising: *By averaging up he was able to increase his profit.*

---

award *verb* (law)
to make an official decision to pay someone for something: *The court awarded him damages of £5 000.* ○ *She was awarded compensation after the accident.*

/ə'wɔːd/
award, awarding, awarded
note transitive verb
⧓ **award** compensation, damages

---

awareness *noun* (advertising)
the degree to which a consumer knows of the existence of a product: *The advertising campaign has been planned to raise awareness of the product amongst the public.*

/ə'weənəs/
note not used with *a* or *an*. No plural and used with a singular verb only.
⧓ consumer **awareness**; increase **awareness**

---

axe *verb*
1 (*personnel*) to remove something or someone: *Her job has been axed.* **2** (*finance*) suddenly to reduce services or money spent: *The government has axed public spending.*

the axe (*informal*) removal or dismissal: *1 000 workers will come under/face/get the axe.*

/æks/
axe, axing, axed
(*US* **ax**)
note transitive verb

Bb

BA *abbr* (banking)
bank acceptance

/ˌbiː 'eɪ/

---

back *verb*
to give help or support, esp financial, to something: *The bank agreed to back the company's expansion plans.* ○ *They are expecting high returns after backing the new business.*

/bæk/
back, backing, backed
note transitive verb
⧓ **back** an idea, a merger, a plan, a proposal, a scheme

---

backdate *verb*
1 to put a date on a document that is earlier than the real date, so that it is valid from that earlier date: *The loan agreement was backdated to April.* ○ *She backdated the invoice to November for tax purposes.* **2** to make salary increases or other payments effective from a previous date: *Your salary increase will be backdated to January.*

/'bækdeɪt/
backdate, backdating, backdated
note transitive verb
1 ⧓ **backdate** a bill, cheque, contract, document
▶ **antedate, date² 1, post-date**
2 ⧓ **backdate** a pay, salary, wages increase; **backdate** pay
▶ **antedate, date² 1, post-date**

---

backer *noun* (finance)
a person or company that gives help or support, esp financial, to another person or company: *The backers gave the company a loan secured on its assets.*

/ˈbækə(r)/
⋈ a commercial, a financial, an important, a major **backer**

backhander *noun*
▶ **bribe**

/ˈbækhændə(r)/

backing *noun* (finance)
help or support, esp financial: *The new business received government backing in the form of a grant.*

/ˈbækɪŋ/
note not used with *a* or *an*. No plural and used with a singular verb only.
⋈ have, receive, request **backing**; commercial, financial, full **backing**
▶ **asset backing**

backloading *noun* (finance)
a method of arranging a loan in which the interest, fees and major repayments are higher towards the end of the loan period

/ˈbækˌləʊdɪŋ/
note not used with *a* or *an*. No plural and used with a singular verb only.
syn back-end loading
▶ **front loading, loading**

backlog *noun*
a number of jobs waiting to be done that were not done at the proper time, resulting in a lot of extra work: *There is a backlog of orders waiting to be processed.* ○ *Extra staff were employed to clear the backlog.*

/ˈbæklɒg/
pl backlogs
⋈ clear, get through, get rid of the **backlog**; an enormous, a large, a massive **backlog**

back office *noun* (stock exchange)
the department of a bank or stockbroking firm that provides administrative support for the buying and selling of shares: *Confirmation of all deals must be processed by the back office.*

/ˈbæk ˌɒfɪs/
pl back offices
⋈ **back office** activities, functions, procedures; an automated, a computerized **back office**
▶ **office 2**

back orders *noun* (commerce)
an order for goods that have not yet been produced or supplied: *The company has over 1 000 back orders for the new model.*

/ˈbæk ˌɔːdəz/
pl back orders
⋈ pending, uncompleted **back orders**
▶ **order[1] 1**

back out *verb*
to give up or not do something after agreeing to do it: *They backed out of the deal at the last moment.* ○ *Now that the contract is signed, it's too late to back out.*

/ˌbæk ˈaʊt/
back out, backing out, backed out
note intransitive verb
⋈ **back out** *of* an agreement, a contract, a deal
▶ **withdraw 2**

back pay *noun* (personnel)
money that is paid to an employee for work already done. It is usually paid to cover an increase in wages set for a date in the past: *She received 6 months' back pay in her July pay packet.*

/ˈbæk peɪ/
(also **backpay**)
note no plural

⧓ award, demand, receive **back pay**
▶ **pay**[2]

---

back-to-back loan *noun* (finance)
a loan in one currency made to a company in exchange for a loan in another currency. This is done to avoid currency restrictions and allows each company to raise money in the currency available to it and to obtain the currency it needs.

/ˌbæk tə bæk ˈləʊn/
pl back-to-back loans
⧓ arrange, negotiate, organize a **back-to-back loan**
▶ **swap, loan**[1]

---

backup *noun* (computing)
a copy of a disk, file, program, etc for use in case the original is lost or destroyed: *do a/the backup* ○ *make a backup copy*

/ˈbækʌp/
pl backups
(also **back-up**)
⧓ do, make a **backup**; start, finish the **backup**

---

back up *verb* (computing)
to make a copy of a disk, file, program, etc for use in case the original is lost or destroyed: *Don't use the computer, we're backing up at the moment.* ○ *Always remember to back up your work at the end of the day.*

/ˌbæk ˈʌp/
back up, backing up, backed up
note transitive verb
⧓ **back up** a disk, a file, a program, work
▶ **save 3**

---

backwardation *noun* (stock exchange)
a situation that may exist on the FUTURES MARKET when prices for goods that will be delivered in the future are lower than prices for goods that will be delivered immediately: *A shortage of supplies for immediate delivery has caused a state of backwardation on the coffee futures market.*

/ˌbækwəˈdeɪʃn/
note not used with *a* or *an*. No plural and used with a singular verb only.
⧓ **backwardation** charges
▶ **contango 2, futures, spot price**

---

backward integration *noun* (industry)
a situation where a company buys other companies which supply it with raw materials or necessary products: *The company followed a strategy of backward integration to ensure a continuity of supplies.*

/ˌbækwəd ɪntɪˈgreɪʃn/
note not used with *a* or *an*. No plural and used with a singular verb only.
⧓ a policy, strategy of **backward integration**
▶ **diversification, forward integration, integration, horizontal integration, vertical integration**

BACS *abbr* (banking)
Bankers' Automated Clearing Services: *Most of our employees are paid through BACS.*

/bæks/
note the abbreviation is pronounced as a word and is used more often than the full term
⧓ pay through, pay via, use **BACS**
▶ **CHAPS**

---

bad debt *noun* (banking)
an unpaid debt that is not likely to be paid in future: *Because of the recession, the company was forced to increase its provision for bad debts.* ○ *The bank wrote off one million pounds in bad debts.*

/ˌbæd ˈdet/
pl bad debts
⧓ make provision for, write off a **bad debt**

▶ **secured debt, unsecured debt**

bad faith *noun* (commerce)
dishonesty; having a dishonest intention: *Each dealer accused the other of bad faith.*

in bad faith with the intention to deceive or be dishonest: *It was discovered that the goods had been sold in bad faith.*

/ˌbæd ˈfeɪθ/

note not used with *a* or *an*. No plural and used with a singular verb only.

⋈ act in **bad faith**

▶ **bona fide, good faith, mala fide, misrepresentation**

bail *noun* (law)
money paid to a court by or for a defendant as a guarantee that someone will return for trial: *The judge set bail at £10 000.* ○ *He was released on bail.* ○ *The judge refused to grant bail for the accused.*

/beɪl/

note not used with *a* or *an*. No plural and used with a singular verb only.

⋈ allow, grant, put up, refuse, release on, remand on, stand **bail**

bail-out *noun* (commerce)
money given to a person or company to help them out of financial difficulties: *The parent company organized a bail-out of its subsidiary.*

/ˈbeɪlaʊt/

pl bail-outs

⋈ mount, organize a **bail-out**

bail out *verb*
1 (*commerce*) to help a person or company out of difficulties by providing money: *The parent company bailed out its subsidiary after it suffered severe losses last year.* **2** (*law*) to pay money (BAIL) to a court as a guarantee that a prisoner will return for trial: *His company had to bail him out when he was arrested.*

/ˌbeɪl ˈaʊt/

bail out, bailing out, bailed out

note transitive verb

1 ⋈ **bail out** a bank, business, company, venture

2 ⋈ **bail out** a defendant, prisoner

balance[1] *noun*
1 (*accounting/banking*) the difference between the totals of money coming into (CREDITS) and money going out of (DEBITS) an account; the amount needed to make these totals correspond: *My bank statement shows a balance of £150.* ○ *Please work out the balance for me.* **2** (*accounting/banking*) the amount of money still owed after some has been paid: *We have received your deposit, please send us the balance by the end of the month.* **3** (*commerce*) the remainder of something after part of it has been used or taken: *The balance of your order will be supplied when we have new stock.*

/ˈbæləns/

note usually singular

1 ⋈ **balance** of account; a bank **balance**

▶ **balance sheet, credit balance, debit balance**

2 ⋈ **balance** outstanding; pay the **balance**

3 ⋈ receive, send the **balance**

balance[2] *verb* (accounting)
1 to compare the totals of money coming into (CREDITS) and money going out of (DEBITS) an account and calculate the amount needed to make them equal: *She spent hours trying to balance the company's accounts.* ○ *At the end of each day I have to balance the books.* **2** to show that the difference between the total credits and total debits is the same as the real amount that remains or is lost: *These figures don't balance. Either I've added them up wrong or I've left something out.* ○ *Do the books balance?*

/ˈbæləns/

balance, balancing, balanced

1 note transitive verb

⋈ **balance** the accounts, books, figures

▶ **books**

2 note intransitive verb

⋈ (the books) *don't* **balance**

balanced economy *noun* (economics)
the control of a money supply in which the total income is equal

/ˌbælənst ɪˈkɒnəmi/

⋈ achieve, establish, maintain a **balanced economy**

to the total expenditure: *The government was blamed for not achieving a balanced economy.*

▶ **economy 2**

---

balance of payments *noun* (economics)
the difference between the amount of money coming into a country from the goods and services it exports, and the amount of money going out for the goods and services it imports: *Britain's balance of payments is up this month because of increased exports.*

/ˌbæləns əv ˈpeɪmənts/
note singular noun, used with a singular verb
⋈ a **balance of payments** deficit, surplus; a drop, a rise, a fall, an increase in the **balance of payments**; **balance of payments** figures

---

balance of trade *noun* (economics)
the difference in value between the visible exports (goods and services) and visible imports of a country: *The country has had a balance of trade deficit since 1982.*

/ˌbæləns əv ˈtreɪd/
note singular noun, used with a singular verb
⋈ a **balance of trade** deficit, surplus; **balance of trade** figures, statistics
▶ **terms of trade, trade deficit, trade gap, trade surplus**

---

balance sheet *noun* (accounting)
a document that shows the totals of money received (CREDITS) and money paid out (DEBITS) by a company and the difference between them: *The company's balance sheet for the end of the year showed a sharp rise in borrowings.* ○ *The bank carefully examined the company's balance sheet before deciding to approve the loan.*

/ˈbæləns ʃi:t/
⋈ a company, monthly, yearly **balance sheet**
▶ **balance[1] 1, group balance sheet**

---

ballast[1] *noun* (shipping)
heavy material carried by a ship, esp one without cargo, to keep it steady: *The ship was filled with ballast before it set sail.*

/ˈbæləst/
note not used with *a* or *an*. No plural and used with a singular verb only.
⋈ sand, stone, water **ballast**; **ballast** tank

---

ballast[2] *verb* (shipping)
to fill a ship with heavy material to keep it steady: *We'll ballast the ship with stones before we set sail.*

/ˈbæləst/
ballast, ballasting, ballasted
note transitive verb
⋈ **ballast** a ship, a tanker

---

ballot[1] *noun*
1 an occasion when people can vote: *The members held a ballot for the position of General Secretary of the union.* ○ *The committee decided to put the motion to the ballot.* **2** a system of secret voting: *Members will be allowed to vote by ballot.* **3** (*stock exchange*) a method of choosing shareholders when there are too many applications: *hold a ballot for an oversubscribed share issue*

/ˈbælət/
pl ballots
⋈ demand, have, hold a **ballot**; a postal, a secret, a strike, a union **ballot**; a **ballot** box, paper
▶ **poll**

---

ballot[2] *verb*
1 to vote: *They balloted for the new union president.* **2** to find out the opinions of people by having a vote: *The members must be balloted before a strike can be declared.* **3** (*stock exchange*) to choose which share applications to accept when there are too many of them: *The issue was oversubscribed and all share applications were balloted.*

/ˈbælət/
ballot, balloting, balloted
1 note intransitive verb
⋈ **ballot** *for* something
2 note transitive verb
3 note intransitive verb
▶ **strike**

---

ballot rigging *noun*
a dishonest way of arranging voting so that a particular person or group wins: *Ballot rigging was suspected so a second election was held.*

/ˈbælət ˌrɪgɪŋ/
note singular noun, used with a singular verb
⧓ a case of, to suspect **ballot rigging**

ballpark figure *noun*
an approximate figure: *If we take 1 000 as a ballpark figure, we can come up with some costs.*

/ˈbɔːlpɑːk ˌfɪgə(r)/
pl ballpark figures
▶ **actuals 2, approximation, estimate[1] 1**

the Baltic Exchange *noun* (international trade)
an international exchange for freight and shipping in London

/ðə ˌbɔːltɪk ɪksˈtʃeɪndʒ/
note the full name is *The Baltic Mercantile and Shipping Exchange*, but this is rarely used
▶ **commodity market, exchange[1] 2, futures, freight[1], London Fox, London International Financial Futures and Options Exchange, London Metal Exchange**

the Baltic International Freight and Futures Exchange *noun* (international trade/shipping)
an international exchange for agricultural and commodity futures that operates from the Baltic Exchange in London

/ðə ˌbɔːltɪk ɪntəˌnæʃnəl ˌfreɪt ənd ˈfjuːtʃəz ɪksˌtʃeɪndʒ/
abbr BIFFEX
▶ **commodity market, exchange[1] 2, futures, London Fox, London International Financial Futures and Options Exchange, London Metal Exchange**

ban[1] *verb*
to forbid something; to forbid someone to do something: *The government will ban tobacco advertising on television.* ○ *Employees are banned from using company telephones for personal calls.*

/bæn/
ban, banning, banned
⧓ **ban** someone *from* something/doing something
note transitive verb

ban[2] *noun*
an official order or law that forbids something: *a ban on overtime, smoking, drugs, etc*

/bæn/
⧓ impose, introduce, lift, remove a **ban**
▶ **economic sanctions, embargo, sanction**

banco *noun* (banking)
the unit of currency in which a bank keeps its accounts, which may differ from that of the country where it is doing business: *Our banco is US dollars and not francs.*

/ˈbæŋkəʊ/
note not used with *a* or *an*. No plural and used with a singular verb only.

bank[1] *noun* (banking)
an organization that holds money, important documents and other valuables in safe keeping, and lends money at interest. It may also arrange mortgages and insurance, and be involved in a number of financial trading activities: *My salary is paid into the*

/bæŋk/
pl banks
⧓ deposit (money) with, pay (money) into, withdraw (money) from a **bank**
▶ **the Bank of England,**

bank. ○ arrange a mortgage with the bank ○ keep a copy of the will at the bank

clearing bank, commercial bank, databank, discount house, federal reserve system, investment bank, merchant bank, private bank, World Bank

---

bank² *verb* (banking)
1 to deposit something in a bank: *We need to bank that cheque today to avoid being overdrawn.* **2** to have an account with a bank: *Do you bank with National Westminster?*

/bæŋk/
bank, banking, banked
1 note transitive verb
2 note intranstive verb
⋈ **bank** at/with (a particular bank)

---

bankable *adjective* (banking/finance)
acceptable by the bank as security for a loan

/ˈbæŋkəbl/
⋈ a **bankable** security

---

bankable asset *noun* (banking/finance)
buildings, land, machinery, stock, etc that can be used as security for a bank loan: *We must ensure that we have enough bankable assets before we apply for this loan.*

/ˌbæŋkəbl ˈæset/
pl bankable assets
⋈ assess, calculate a **bankable asset**
► **asset, tangible asset, intangible asset**

---

bank acceptance *noun* (banking)
a bill of exchange that is accepted by a bank for a fee: *We can finance this purchase by a bank acceptance.*

/ˈbæŋk əkˌseptəns/
pl bank acceptances
abbr BA
⋈ discount, dishonour, draw, honour, issue a **bank acceptance**
syn (*UK*) bank bill, bank paper
► **acceptance 2 c, bank draft**

---

bank account *noun* (banking)
an arrangement with a bank that allows the customer to pay in and take out money, settle bills, etc. The bank keeps a record of all these payments (TRANSACTIONS) in the customer's name: *Do you have a bank account?*

/ˈbæŋk əˌkaʊnt/
pl bank accounts
syn (*US*) banking account
⋈ close, hold, open a **bank account**; pay (money) into, take (money) out of, withdraw (money) from a **bank account**
syn account
► **budget account, current account 1, deposit account, savings account**

---

bank bill *noun* (banking)
1 (*UK*) bank acceptance **2** (*US*) banknote

/ˈbæŋk bɪl/
pl bank bills

---

bank book *noun* (banking)
a book that lists all payments into and withdrawals from a customer's bank account: *My bank book shows that I made a deposit of £100 last week.*

/ˈbæŋk bʊk/
⋈ update a **bank book**
► **bank statement, passbook, paying-in book**

---

bank card *noun* (banking)
► **cheque card**

/ˈbæŋk kɑːd/

---

bank certificate *noun* (banking)
a formal document, signed by a bank manager, that states the amount of money (CREDIT) that a company has on a specific date: *The auditors require a bank certificate for the end of the financial year.*

/ˈbæŋk səˌtɪfɪkət/
pl bank certificates
⧓ request, require a **bank certificate**
▶ **bank statement**

bank charge *noun* (banking)
the amount of money paid by a customer to the bank for its services, esp when the account is not in credit: *There will be a small increase in bank charges next year.*

/ˈbæŋk ˌtʃɑːdʒ/
pl bank charges
⧓ incur, waive **bank charges**

bank cheque *noun* (banking)
▶ **bank draft**

/ˈbæŋk tʃek/

bank clerk *noun* (banking)
a person who serves customers, keeps accounts and does other administrative work in a bank: *I asked the bank clerk to find out how much I had in my account.*

/ˈbæŋk klɑːk; *US* ˈbæŋk klɜːk/
syn bank teller, teller
▶ **bank manager, clerk**

bank credit *noun* (banking)
money made available by banks in the form of overdrafts or loans: *Attempts to restrict bank credit in the 1980s led to a recession.*

/ˈbæŋk ˌkredɪt/
note not used with *a* or *an*. No plural and used with a singular verb only.
▶ **credit[1] 2, bank loan, overdraft**

bank deposit *noun* (banking)
a sum of money left with a bank for safe keeping or to earn interest. It can be repaid after an agreed length of time: *Bank deposits for this month were the highest this year.*

/ˈbæŋk dɪˌpɒzɪt/
pl bank deposits
⧓ make a **bank deposit**
▶ **deposit[1] 1, safe deposit**

bank draft *noun* (banking)
a cheque that guarantees payment by a bank. It can be bought from the bank by a customer and used to pay someone else: *Ask for a bank draft to make sure you get paid.*

/ˈbæŋk drɑːft; *US* ˈbæŋk dræft/
pl bank drafts
⧓ accept, arrange, issue a **bank draft**; pay by **bank draft**
syn (*US*) bank check, bank cheque, banker's cheque, banker's draft, draft
▶ **bank acceptance**

banker *noun* (banking)
1 a person or an organization that lends money or provides the services of a bank: *A banker will advise you on the best method of payment for these goods.* **2** a person who has an important job in a bank, eg a bank manager: *She's a banker by profession.*

/ˈbæŋkə(r)/
pl bankers
1 ⧓ act as a **banker**
▶ **paying banker**
2 ▶ **bank manager**

the Banker's Automated Clearing System *noun* (banking)
a computerized system through which banks or building societies can make payments, such as a DIRECT DEBIT or STANDING ORDER to customers of other member banks or building societies

/ðə ˌbæŋkəz ˌɔːtəmeɪtəd ˈklɪərɪŋ ˌsɪstəm/
abbr BACS
note the abbreviation is pronounced as a word and is used more often than the full term
▶ **Clearing House Automated Payment System**

banker's card *noun* (banking)
▶ **cheque card**

/ˈbæŋkəz kɑːd/

banker's cheque *noun* (banking)
▶ **bank draft**

/ˈbæŋkəz tʃek/

banker's draft *noun* (banking)
▶ **bank draft**

/ˈbæŋkəz drɑːft; *US* ˈbæŋkəz dræft/

banker's order *noun* (banking)
▶ **standing order**

/ˈbæŋkəz ˌɔːdə(r)/

the Bank for International Settlements *noun* (banking)
an international bank, established in Basle in 1930. It is now a centre for co-operation between the central banks of Europe, the USA and Japan, although many of its original functions are carried out by the International Monetary Fund.

/ðə ˌbæŋk fər ˌɪntənæʃnəl ˈsetlmənts/
abbr BIS
▶ **International Monetary Fund, World Bank**

bank holiday *noun*
(*UK*) a day, not a Saturday or Sunday, when banks are closed and which is also a general holiday: *The London office will be closed next Monday because it is a bank holiday.*

/ˌbæŋk ˈhɒlədeɪ/
pl bank holidays
▶ **holiday, public holiday**

banking *noun* (banking)
the business of running or working in a bank: *She works in banking.* ○ *Banking hours are now from 9.30 to 5 pm.*

/ˈbæŋkɪŋ/
⋈ **banking** facilities, hours, services, system
▶ **bank**[1]

banking account *noun* (banking)
(*US*) ▶ **bank account**

/ˈbæŋkɪŋ əˌkaʊnt/

bank loan *noun* (banking)
money that has been lent by a bank to a customer for a fixed period, often at a fixed level of interest: *I'll have to get a bank loan to buy a new car.*

/ˈbæŋk ləʊn/
pl bank loans
⋈ apply for, arrange, ask for, organize, take out a **bank loan**
▶ **bank credit, loan**[1]**, overdraft**

bank manager *noun* (banking)
a person employed by a bank to control a particular branch or department: *To open a new account you have to see the bank manager.*

/ˈbæŋk ˌmænɪdʒə(r)/
▶ **bank clerk,** branch manager *under* **branch, manager**

banknote *noun* (banking)
a piece of paper money issued by a bank: *The clerk counted up the used banknotes.*

/ˈbæŋknəʊt/
⋈ accept, change, count, issue, pay in **banknotes**
syn (*US*) bank bill, note
▶ **cash**[1]

the Bank of America *noun* (banking)
a commercial bank that is based in the state of California. The Federal Reserve System and not the Bank of America is the country's central banking system.

/ðə ˌbæŋk əv əˈmerɪkə/
▶ **the Bank of England, Federal Reserve System**

the Bank of England *noun* (banking)
the central bank of the UK that provides banking facilities for the government and the other banks. It issues banknotes in England and Wales and manages the NATIONAL DEBT.

/ðə ˌbæŋk əv ˈɪŋglənd/
abbr BE, B/E, B of E
▶ **Federal Reserve Bank, treasury 1**

---

bank order *noun* (banking)
▶ **standing order**

/ˈbæŋk ˌɔːdə(r)/

---

bank paper *noun* (banking)
▶ **bank acceptance**

/ˈbæŋk ˌpeɪpə(r)/

---

bank rate *noun* (banking)
▶ **minimum lending rate**

/ˈbæŋk reɪt/

---

bank reference *noun* (banking)
▶ **reference 3**

/ˈbæŋk ˌrefərəns/

---

bankrupt[1] *noun* (finance)
a person or a company that has been judged by a court of law to be unable to pay debts: *The court declared him a bankrupt.*

/ˈbæŋkrʌpt/
pl bankrupts
⋈ certify (someone) as, declare (someone) a **bankrupt**
▶ **debtor, judgment debtor, undischarged bankrupt**

---

bankrupt[2] *verb* (finance)
to put a person or company into a position where they have no money left to pay their debts: *Replacing those machines now will bankrupt us.*

/ˈbæŋkrʌpt/
bankrupt, bankrupting, bankrupted
note transitive verb

---

bankrupt[3] *adjective* (finance)
having no money; unable to pay your debts: *The court declared him bankrupt.* ○ *Several local companies have gone bankrupt.*

/ˈbæŋkrʌpt/
⋈ be, become, be declared, go **bankrupt**
▶ **insolvent**

---

bankruptcy *noun* (finance)
the state of being unable to pay your debts: *The firm I work for is facing bankruptcy.* ○ *make a declaration of bankruptcy*, ie announce in a court of law that a person is bankrupt

/ˈbæŋkrəpsi/
⋈ face, head for **bankruptcy**
▶ **insolvency, liquidation, receivership**

---

bank statement *noun* (banking)
a printed report that shows all the money paid into and out of a customer's bank account within a certain period and the total amount left in the account: *receive a bank statement once a month*

/ˈbæŋk ˌsteɪtmənt/
pl bank statements
⋈ ask for, receive, request, send out a **bank statement**
▶ **bank account, bank book, bank certificate, cash statement, statement of account**

---

bank teller *noun* (banking)
▶ **bank clerk**

/ˈbæŋk ˌtelə(r)/

bank transfer *noun* (banking)
the removal of money from one bank or bank account to another; a document that allows this: *We have arranged to pay our overseas staff by bank transfer.* ○ *A bank transfer will be needed for such a large amount.*

/ˌbæŋk ˈtrænsfɜː(r)/
pl bank transfers
⋈ arrange, obtain, organize a **bank transfer**; pay by **bank transfer**
▶ **telegraphic transfer**

the bar *noun* (law)
(*UK*) **1** the profession of a barrister: *She is training for the bar.* **2** barristers collectively
to be called to the Bar to become a barrister

/ðə bɑː(r)/
(also **the Bar**)
note not used with *a* or *an*. No plural and used with a singular verb only.
▶ **barrister, lawyer, solicitor**

bar chart *noun*
a diagram where quantities are displayed in columns of varying heights: *Last year's sales figures for all our markets are shown on this bar chart.*

/ˈbɑː tʃɑːt/
⋈ compile, draw, produce a **bar chart**
syn histogram
▶ **block diagram, chart[1] 1, diagram, flow chart, graph, pictogram, pie chart**

bar code *noun* (retail)
a series of lines printed on a product that can be read by a machine connected to a computer system to give a price or reference number: *The shop assistant scanned the bar code to check the price.*

/ˈbɑː kəʊd/
pl bar codes
⋈ read, scan, use a **bar code**
▶ **machine-readable, serial number**

bargain[1] *noun*
1 (*sales*) something that is cheaper than usual: *These coats are a bargain — they're being sold at half-price.* **2** (*sales*) an agreement between two or more people on the price of something: *After lengthy discussions they managed to strike a bargain.* **3** a promise or an agreement to do something: *As part of the bargain staff were allowed to take an extra day's holiday.* **4** (*stock exchange*) a single buying or selling transaction on the stock exchange: *The bargains made during the day are recorded in the Daily Official List.*

/ˈbɑːɡən/
pl bargains
1 ⋈ a **bargain** counter, price, store
2 ⋈ strike a **bargain**
3, 4 ⋈ make a **bargain**
▶ **matched bargain**

bargain[2] *verb*
1 (*sales*) to discuss or argue the price of something: *The dealers bargained over the share price.* **2** (*industrial relations*) to discuss or argue the terms and conditions of something: *The union bargained for better pay and working conditions.*

/ˈbɑːɡən/
bargain, bargaining, bargained
note intransitive verb
⋈ **bargain** *for* (something), *over* (something)
▶ **haggle, negotiate**

bargaining power *noun* (industrial relations)
the strength or position of a person or group when discussing or asking for something, esp a wage increase: *The creation of a trade union increased the employees' bargaining power.*

/ˈbɑːɡənɪŋ ˌpaʊə(r)/
note not used with *a* or *an*.
⋈ decrease, gain, increase, lose **bargaining power**
▶ **collective bargaining, trade union**

barge *noun* (shipping) a large flat-bottomed boat used for transporting heavy loads, esp on canals and rivers: *The goods were taken by barge.* ○ *a Thames barge*	/bɑːdʒ/ ⋈ hire, load, use a **barge** ▶ **lighter**
barratry *noun* (shipping) an act committed by the captain and/or crew of a ship which is harmful to the owner or charterer: *The crew committed barratry by destroying some of the cargo.* ○ *Barratry can include smuggling drugs aboard a ship.*	/ˈbærətri/ (also **barretry**) **note** not used with *a* or *an*. No plural and used with a singular verb only. ⋈ an act of, to commit **barratry**
barrister *noun* (law) (in English law) a person who is qualified to speak in a higher court of law: *a barrister specializing in employment law*	/ˈbærɪstə(r)/ **syn** (*Scottish*) advocate, (*US*) attorney **pl** barristers ⋈ a **barrister** for the defence ▶ **counsel, lawyer, solicitor**
base rate *noun* (banking) **1** the rate of interest on which rates charged by banks to borrowers are based: *The interest charged was 10% above the base rate.* ○ *The base rate is low so more people are borrowing.* **2** the rate of interest charged by the Bank of England when lending to the discount houses: *The base rate controls the lending rate throughout the banking system.*	/ˈbeɪs reɪt/ ⋈ above, below the **base rate**; control, establish, set the **base rate** **1 syn** (*US*) prime rate, (*US*) prime lending rate ▶ **annual percentage rate, discount rate, rate 2**
BASIC *abbr* (computing) Beginner's All-Purpose Symbolic Instruction Code: *BASIC is a computing language that is easy to learn.*	/ˈbeɪsɪk/ ⋈ know, learn, use **BASIC** **note** the abbreviation is more commonly used than the full term ▶ **ALGOL, BASIC, FORTRAN, PASCAL**
basic wage *noun* (personnel) normal amount paid weekly or monthly to a worker without extra payments: *The basic wage is low, but you can earn more with overtime.*	/ˌbeɪsɪk ˈweɪdʒ/ **note** usually singular ⋈ earn, pay, receive a **basic wage** ▶ **wage**
batch *noun* (manufacturing) **1** a group of similar items that are made together or within a certain period: *This is the batch of watches that all have the same fault.* **2** a group of similar items that are put or dealt with together: *a batch of letters, orders, invoices*	/bætʃ/ **pl** batches ⋈ **batch** number, production ▶ **job lot**
batch costing *noun* (manufacturing) pricing articles in a group rather than individually: *Batch costing will show us the most economic number of items to produce in one batch.*	/ˈbætʃ ˌkɒstɪŋ/ **note** not used with *a* or *an*. No plural and used with a singular verb only. ⋈ carry out, use **batch costing** ▶ **costing, job costing, unit cost**

BCE *abbr* (import)
Board of Customs and Excise

/ˌbiː siː ˈiː/

b/d *abbr* (industry)
barrels per day: *Oil was produced at a rate of 1 000 b/d.*

note used in written English only

BE *abbr* (banking)
the Bank of England

note used in written English only

b/e *abbr* (banking/international trade)
bill of exchange

note used in written English only
(also **B/E**, **b.e.**)

bearer *noun* (finance)
a person who presents a document, such as a cheque or bill of exchange, for payment: *Ten pound notes from the Bank of England have the words 'I promise to pay the bearer on demand the sum of ten pounds' printed on them.*

/ˈbeərə(r)/
pl bearers
⋈ notify, pay the **bearer**
▶ **holder**

bear market *noun* (stock exchange)
a situation in a stock market or currency market where prices are falling because lots of shareholders are selling: *Sterling has now moved into a major bear market.*

/ˈbeə ˌmɑːkɪt/
note usually singular
⋈ **bear market** dealing, prices
▶ **bull market, market**[1]

bear position *noun* (stock exchange)
a situation in which a dealer of commodities or securities does not actually have all the items he has arranged to sell for an agreed price, but hopes to obtain the necessary items at a cheaper price before the delivery date: *The dealer was in a bear position until he found more stock to buy.*

/ˈbeə pəˌzɪʃn/
note usually singular
syn short position
▶ **bull position, short covering, shorts**

bed and breakfasting *noun* (stock exchange)
(*slang*) selling shares just before the end of the financial year and buying them back at the beginning of the next to register a loss for tax purposes: *Bed and breakfasting is a means of avoiding tax.*

/ˌbed ənd ˈbrekfəstɪŋ/
note not used with *a* or *an*. No plural and used with a singular verb only.

Beginner's All-Purpose Symbolic Instruction Code *noun* (computing)
a simple and easy to learn computer language: *The program was written in Beginner's All-Purpose Symbolic Instruction Code.*

/bɪˌɡɪnəz ˌɔːl pɜːpəs sɪmˌbɒlɪk ɪnˈstrʌkʃn kəʊd/
abbr BASIC
⋈ learn, use the **Beginner's All-Purpose Symbolic Instruction Code**
note the abbreviation is used more often than the full term

below par *adjective* (stock exchange)
(of the price of a fixed-interest security) lower than the price at which it was first issued (the NOMINAL PRICE): *The gilts had fallen below par.* ○ *below par securities*

/bɪˌləʊ ˈpɑː(r)/
⋈ drop, fall **below par**
▶ **above par, at par, nominal price**

below-the-line *adjective*
1 (*accounting*) relating to part of a PROFIT AND LOSS ACCOUNT or budget that records unusual receipts and payments, rather than everyday income and expenditure: *below-the-line payments* **2** (*advertising*) relating to the part of an advertising budget that does not involve paying a fee to an advertising agency: *Free samples are below-the-line advertising.* **3** (*finance*) of financial

/bɪˌləʊ ðə ˈlaɪn/
(also **below the line**)
1 ⋈ **below-the-line** costs, entries, funds
▶ **above-the-line 1**
2 ▶ **above-the-line 2**

transactions concerning capital rather than income: *a below-the-line transaction.*

3 ⧓ deals, transactions
▶ **above-the-line 3**

---

benchmark *noun*
1 a reference point or standard amount against which other things can be measured and compared: *These prices will act as a benchmark for other firms.* **2** (*computing*) a program used to test how quickly and accurately a computer can perform certain tasks: *test a computer using a benchmark program*

/ˈbentʃmɑːk/
pl benchmarks
1 ⧓ above, below the **benchmark**
▶ **average¹ 2**
2 ⧓ a **benchmark** program, test

---

beneficiary *noun*
a person who receives something, esp money or property, from a trust or will: *My sister was the only beneficiary of my uncle's will.* ○ *Third world countries were the beneficiaries of the aid.*

/ˌbenɪˈfɪʃəri/
pl beneficiaries
⧓ the only, sole **beneficiary**; a joint **beneficiary**; **beneficiary** *of* (a will)
▶ **bequest, estate 3, executor, will**

---

benefit¹ *noun* (personnel)
1 money that the government gives to people who are ill, disabled or unemployed: *Are you entitled to claim benefit?* **2** money, goods, etc given to an employee in addition to his/her normal salary: *a job with a good salary and a range of benefits*

/ˈbenɪfɪt/
pl benefits
⧓ **benefit** cheque, payment; child, housing, unemployment **benefit**
▶ **dole, maternity pay, income support, National Insurance, sickness benefit**
2 syn fringe benefit
▶ **perk**

---

benefit² *verb*
1 to help or improve something: *Better working conditions will benefit the staff.* **2** to gain help from or to be helped by something: *People in the town have benefited from the new transport system.*

/ˈbenɪfɪt/
benefit, benefiting, benefited
1 note transitive verb
2 note intransitive verb
⧓ **benefit** *from* (something)

---

bequeath *verb* (law)
to leave money or property to someone in a will: *She bequeathed £1 000 to her nephew.*

/bɪˈkwiːð/
bequeath, bequeathing, bequeathed
note transitive verb
▶ **beneficiary**

---

bequest *noun* (law)
something, usually money or property, that is given to someone in a will: *He made a number of valuable bequests to charity.*

/bɪˈkwest/
⧓ make, receive a **bequest**
▶ **beneficiary, endowment, estate 3, gift 2, legacy, trust**

---

berth¹ *noun* (shipping)
1 a position in a dock or harbour for a ship to be tied up or anchored **2** a place to sleep on a ship: *book two berths on an ocean liner*

/bɜːθ/
pl berths
1 ⧓ find, request a **berth**
2 ⧓ book a **berth**

berth² *verb* (shipping)
to tie up or anchor a ship in a harbour: *We have berthed the ship and are now unloading the cargo.* ○ *We should be able to berth at Southampton tomorrow.*

/bɜːθ/
berth, berthing, berthed
note transitive and intransitive verb
▶ **dock² 1, moor**

best price *noun* (commerce)
the lowest price for goods or services that the seller will accept: *What is your best* (ie lowest) *price?* ○ *The company's best price is still higher than all the others.*

/ˌbest ˈpraɪs/
▶ **discount, price¹**

b/f *abbr* (accounting)
brought forward

note used in written English only

bid¹ *noun* (sales)
a price offered in order to buy something, esp at an auction: *make a bid for £5 000*

/bɪd/
pl bids
⧓ make a **bid**; a high, low **bid**
▶ **auction**

bid² *verb* (sales)
to make an offer to buy something: *She bid £3 000 for the car.* ○ *The auctioneer asked 'What am I bid for this furniture?'*

/bɪd/
bid, bidding, bid
note transitive and intransitive verb
⧓ **bid** *for* (something)
▶ **auction, outbid, underbid**

BIFFEX *abbr* (international trade/shipping)
the Baltic International Freight and Futures Exchange

/ˈbɪfeks/

Big Bang *noun* (stock exchange)
the major changes that occurred in the UK Stock Exchange on 27 October 1986, including computerization. The previous distinction between jobbers and brokers, where jobbers could not deal directly with the public, was abolished. Companies as well as individuals could become members of the stock market and fees obtained from the buying and selling of shares were no longer fixed: *Big Bang resulted in modernization for many companies.* ○ *He has worked for us since Big Bang.*

/ˌbɪg ˈbæŋ/
⧓ after, as a result of, before, since **Big Bang**

Big Board *noun* (stock exchange)
(*US informal*) the New York Stock Exchange: *She works for the Big Board.* ○ *Prices fell on the Big Board.*

/ˌbɪg ˈbɔːd/
⧓ **Big Board** prices, stocks, trading
▶ **Amex, New York Stock Exchange**

bilateral *adjective*
of two sides, eg two people or two organizations: *The two countries signed a bilateral trade agreement.* ○ *bilateral trading*

/baɪˈlætərl/
⧓ **a bilateral** agreement, decision, treaty
▶ bilateral monopoly *under* **monopoly, multilateral, unilateral**

bilateral credit *noun* (banking)
an arrangement between two parties to allow time for debts to

/baɪˌlætərl ˈkredɪt/
note no plural
⧓ a **bilateral credit** agreement, arrangement, union

be paid: *Most banks use bilateral credit to allow cheques to be cleared.*

▶ **credit[1] 3**

---

bilateral monopoly *noun* (economics)
▶ **monopoly**

/baɪˌlætərl məˈnɒpəli/

---

bill[1] *noun*
1 (*commerce*) a written or printed list of charges or money owed for goods and services: *a telephone, an electricity, a gas bill* **2** (*banking*) (*US*) a banknote **3** (*banking/international trade*) a bill of exchange **4** (*law*) (*UK*) a proposal for a new law to be discussed by parliament: *The opposition is trying to stop the bill being passed.*

/bɪl/
pl bills
1 ⋈ pay, receive, send (out) a **bill**
▶ **invoice[1]**
2 ▶ **bank acceptance**
3 ⋈ accept, discount, dishonour, draw, endorse, sign a **bill**
▶ **bill of exchange**
4 ⋈ discuss, draw up, pass a **bill**

---

bill[2] *verb*
to prepare and send out statements of money owed; invoice: *Will you bill me for the materials later?*

/bɪl/
bill, billing, billed
note transitive verb
⋈ **bill** someone *for* something
▶ **invoice[2]**

---

bill of entry *noun* (export/import)
a detailed list of goods prepared by the exporter or importer for examination by customs: *prepare a bill of entry for customs*

/ˌbɪl əv ˈentri/
pl bills of entry
⋈ check, draw up, prepare a **bill of entry**
▶ **Board of Customs and Excise, bill of sight, bond note, entry 1, export licence, import licence**

---

bill of exchange *noun* (banking/international trade)
a signed document, such as a cheque, that orders a person or an organization, such as a bank, to pay a fixed sum of money on demand or on a certain date to the person specified: *Bills of exchange are a convenient way of collecting payments from overseas customers, but we prefer an irrevocable letter of credit.* ○ *You may obtain a cash advance from the bank, using a bill of exchange as security.*

/ˌbɪl əv ɪksˈtʃeɪndʒ/
pl bills of exchange
abbr B/E, b.e., b/e
⋈ accept, discount, dishonour, draw, endorse, sign a **bill of exchange**
▶ **accommodation bill, discounted bill, documentary bill, documents-against-acceptance bill, documents-against-payments bill, exchange[2], foreign bill, inland bill, letter of credit, promissory note, short bill, sight bill, time bill, trade bill**

---

bill of lading *noun* (shipping)
a document that shows details of goods (a CONSIGNMENT) being transported. It is a receipt from the transporter to the sender (the CONSIGNOR) and entitles the receiver (the CONSIGNEE) to collect the goods on arrival: *The shipping company will only release the goods against a signed original of the bill of lading.*

/ˌbɪl əv ˈleɪdɪŋ/
pl bills of lading
abbr B/L, b/l, b.l.
⋈ hold, issue, surrender a **bill of lading**
▶ **consignment note,**

clean bill of lading a bill of lading that states that the goods sent were received by the shipping agent in good condition

dirty bill of lading a bill of lading that states that the goods sent were damaged when they were received by the shipping agent

manifest, shipping documents, way-bill

---

bill of materials *noun* (manufacturing)

a list that shows the quantities and costs of the substances and parts used in manufacturing a product: *prepare a bill of materials for inspection*

/ˌbɪl əv məˈtɪəriəlz/

pl bills of materials

abbr BOM, B.O.M, b.o.m

⋈ draw up, prepare a **bill of materials**

► **material**

---

bill of quantities *noun* (industry)

a list of the materials, labour and costs necessary for a building project: *A bill of quantities was drawn up by the quantity surveyor.*

/ˌbɪl əv ˈkwɒntɪtiz/

pl bills of quantities

⋈ draw up, prepare a **bill of quantities**

► **quantity surveyor**

---

bill of sale *noun*

1 (*commerce*) a document that shows the transfer of goods from the owner to another person. It is often used as security for a loan and gives the buyer a legal right to the goods, but not the goods themselves: *A bill of sale is used when mortgaging goods.* **2** (*shipping*) a document that records the sale of a ship and is used by the buyer as proof of legal ownership: *Details of the bill of sale were recorded in the shipping register.*

absolute bill of sale a bill of sale that states that the original owner gives up all legal right to the goods

conditional bill of sale a bill of sale that allows the original owner to reclaim the goods when the debt is repaid

/ˌbɪl əv ˈseɪl/

pl bills of sale

abbr B.S., B/S, b.s., b/s

⋈ draw up, sign a **bill of sale**

► **sale**

---

bill of sight *noun* (international trade)

a document given to customs by an importer who cannot give a detailed description of the goods until they have been unloaded and inspected. When the missing information is provided by the importer, this is known as perfecting the sight: *prepare a bill of sight for inspection*

/ˌbɪl əv ˈsaɪt/

pl bills of sight

⋈ check, draw up, prepare a **bill of sight**

► **bill of entry, bond note, sight bill**

---

bill rate *noun* (banking)

► **discount rate**

/ˈbɪl reɪt/

---

bills in a set *noun* (finance)

a foreign bill of exchange in three identical parts (in TRIPLICATE). Two parts are sent (separately for security reasons) to the importer, the third is kept by the exporter. When one part is presented for payment, the others are immediately cancelled: *one part of the bills in a set was presented for payment*

/ˌbɪlz ɪn ə ˈset/

note plural noun, used with a plural verb

abbr B/ST

⋈ draw up **bills in a set**

► **bill of exchange**

---

bills payable *noun* (accounting)

an item in the accounts of a company that shows a list of bills of exchange that a company will have to pay at a later date: *add an entry to bills payable*

/ˌbɪlz ˈpeɪəbl/

note plural noun, used with a plural verb

► **current liabilities**

---

bills receivable *noun* (accounting)
an item in the accounts of a company that shows a list of bills of exchange that will be paid to a company at a later date: *add an entry to bills receivable*

/ˌbɪlz rɪˈsiːvəbl/
note plural noun, used with a plural verb
▶ **current assets**

BIM *abbr* (management)
British Institute of Management

/ˌbiː aɪ ˈem/
note pronounced as individual letters
(also **B.I.M.**)

binary digit *noun* (computing)
either of the numbers 0 or 1 used in the BINARY SYSTEM. Binary digits represent units, twos, fours and eights as written in columns from the right: *The number 13 is written as 1101 in binary digits.*

/ˌbaɪnəri ˈdɪdʒɪt/
pl binary digits
note The shortened version of binary digit is bit, and in computing this is used more often than the full term.
▶ **bit, byte, digit**

binary system *noun* (computing)
a way of counting using only 0 and 1: *The code is based on the binary system.*

/ˈbaɪnəri ˌsɪstəm/
note usually singular
syn binary code
⋈ base something on, use the **binary system**
▶ **binary digit, bit, byte**

biotechnology *noun* (technology)
the use of biological processes in industrial and engineering systems (especially food, drugs, agriculture and pollution control): *Biotechnology is used to develop crops that have an in-built resistance to pests.*

/ˌbaɪəʊtekˈnɒlədʒi/
note not used with *a* or *an*. No plural and used with a singular verb only.
⋈ develop, introduce, use **biotechnology**

BIS *abbr* (banking)
the Bank for International Settlements

/ˌbiː aɪ ˈes/
note pronounced as individual letters

bit *noun* (computing)
either of the numbers 0 or 1 used in the BINARY SYSTEM. Bits are used in computing because digital computers represent numbers (and therefore information) in terms of the presence (1) or absence (0) of an electrical impulse: *Pictorial information can be stored in binary form, using as many as one million bits to code one picture that appears on screen.*

/bɪt/
pl bits
note The shortened version of binary digit is bit, and in computing this is used more often than the full term.
⋈ store, use **bits**
▶ **binary digit, byte**

black, in the *adjective*
1 (*banking*) having money in your bank account; not having an overdraft: *We can afford a new car, we're in the black at the moment.* ○ *My account is in the black.* **2** (*accounting*) operating at a profit; having income exceeding expenditure: *The company should end the financial year in the black.*

/ɪn ðə ˈblæk/
⋈ be **in the black**
opp in the red
▶ in credit *under* **credit**

black economy *noun* (economics)
the part of a country's money supply, trade and industry that is outside legal controls, eg where taxes are not paid, or stolen or

/ˌblæk ɪˈkɒnəmi/
note usually singular
⋈ work in the **black economy**; a

illegally imported goods are sold: *The true size of the black economy can never be known.* ○ *find work in the black economy*

declining, flourishing, thriving **black economy**

▶ **black market, economy 1**

---

black knight *noun* (stock exchange)

(*informal*) a person or company that tries to buy (TAKE OVER) another company that does not want to sell: *A black knight has made an unwanted takeover bid.*

/ˌblæk ˈnaɪt/

pl black knights

▶ **grey knight, takeover, white knight**

---

blackleg *noun* (industrial relations)

(*informal*) a person who continues to work when the people he/she works with are on strike, or who takes the job of someone on strike: *Fighting broke out between strikers and blacklegs.* ○ *blackleg miners*

/ˈblækleg/

note the word blackleg is used as an insult

⧓ **blackleg** labour, worker

syn scab, strikebreaker

▶ **strike**

---

blacklist[1] *noun*

a list of people or organizations whom it is best not to deal with because they cannot be trusted: *Don't release the goods until the cheque has been cleared, Mr Smith is on our blacklist of slow payers.* ○ *Trade unions have blacklists of bad employers.*

/ˈblæklɪst/

pl blacklists

⧓ be on a/the **blacklist**

▶ **bad debt**

---

blacklist[2] *verb*

to put the name of a person or company on a list of customers, suppliers, etc that cannot be trusted or should not be dealt with: *She hasn't got a credit card because she's been blacklisted by the bank.* ○ *He was blacklisted for leading a strike.*

/ˈblæklɪst/

blacklist, blacklisting, blacklisted

note transitive verb

⧓ be **blacklisted** *by* (a company), *for* something/doing something

---

black market *noun* (commerce)

a situation of illegal trading in goods, currencies or services: *the black market in illegal drugs* ○ *He sells stolen goods on the black market.*

/ˌblæk ˈmɑːkɪt/

note usually singular

⧓ **black market** dealing, goods, prices, trading; on the **black market**; organize, run a/the **black market**

▶ **black economy, grey market, market[1]**

Black Monday *noun* (stock exchange)

Monday 19 October, 1987 when stock exchanges all over the world crashed suddenly and heavily: *In the 1987 crash the index fell 249.6 points to 2052.3 on Black Monday.*

/ˌblæk ˈmʌndeɪ/

▶ **crash[1] 1**

---

blank cheque *noun* (banking)

a cheque that is signed but without the amount of money written in. This is added later by the person to whom the cheque is paid (the PAYEE) when the amount is known: *I'll give you a blank cheque to buy this list of books.*

/ˌblæŋk ˈtʃek/

pl blank cheques

⧓ draw up, make out, sign, write a **blank cheque**

▶ **cheque, crossed cheque, open cheque**

---

blanket agreement *noun* (commerce)

a contract or statement of agreed terms in which similar conditions apply to a number of different situations: *We have a blanket agreement with a retailer of imperfect goods; they take all our rejects.*

/ˈblæŋkɪt əˌgriːmənt/

pl blanket agreements

⧓ draw up, have, make, sign a **blanket agreement**

blanket cover *noun* (insurance)
a form of insurance that covers all items insured against all losses or accidents, ie rather than having separate policies for buildings, contents, fire, theft, etc: *an insurance policy with blanket cover*

/ˈblæŋkɪt ˌkʌvə(r)/
note not used with *a* or *an*. No plural and used with a singular verb only.
► **insurance**

blank transfer *noun* (finance)
a document that records the change of ownership of shares which is signed by the present owner, but does not have the name of the new owner or the date of the change written in: *As she was using her shares to guarantee a loan, she left a blank transfer with the bank.*

/ˌblæŋk ˈtrænsfɜː(r)/
pl blank transfers
⧓ fill in, make out, sign a **blank transfer**
► **deed of transfer, transfer**[1] **1**

block diagram *noun*
a drawing that shows how the different parts of a machine, system or process are linked to each other. The different parts are shown simply as squares: *a block diagram of the electronic system*

/ˌblɒk ˈdaɪəgræm/
pl block diagrams
⧓ a **block diagram** illustrates, represents, shows
► **bar chart, chart**[1] **1, diagram, flow chart, graph, pictogram, pie chart**

block release *noun* (personnel)
a form of training in which an employee is given a week or several weeks off work to study at a college: *We're short-staffed at the moment as two of our team are on block release.*

/ˌblɒk rɪˈliːs/
note not used with *a* or *an*. No plural and used with a singular verb only.
⧓ a **block release** course; be *on* **block release**
► **day release, sandwich course, training**

blue chip *noun* (stock exchange)
a share in a reliable company with very little risk of losing its value: *She put her money into blue chips.*

/ˌbluː ˈtʃɪp/
pl blue chips
⧓ invest in, put money into **blue chips**; a **blue chip** company, investment, portfolio, share, stock
► **chip 2**

blue-collar worker *noun* (personnel)
an employee who does unskilled work, usually in a factory. The blue collar refers to the blue overalls traditionally worn by some manual workers: *The jobs of many blue-collar workers are now done by machines.*

/ˌbluː ˈkɒlə ˌwɜːkə(r)/
pl blue-collar workers
► **artisan, craftsman, labourer, manual worker, white-collar worker**

blueprint *noun*
1 (*industry*) a photographic copy of a technical drawing or engineering design coloured white on a blue background: *Here's the blueprint of my new design.* **2** (*figurative*) any detailed plan, esp in the early stages of a project: *It's not finished yet, we're only at blueprint stage.*

/ˈbluːprɪnt/
pl blueprints
⧓ make, produce a **blueprint**
► **diagram**

board *noun* (management)
1 a group of directors who are responsible for running a company and usually have legal responsibilities to it. They are elected by the shareholders: *She has been elected to the board.* ○ *He has been on the board for ten years.* ○ *The board is/are discussing the*

/bɔːd/
pl boards
note used with a singular or plural verb
⧓ be, have a seat, sit *on* the **board**; appoint, elect someone

annual pay rise. **2** a group of people who meet regularly for a particular purpose; a committee: *The board of educational advisers.*

to the **board**; dismiss, remove someone *from* the **board**; a **board** member, room

syn board of directors

▶ **director, commission[1] 2, committee, council**

---

board meeting *noun* (management)

a gathering of the directors of a company to discuss important company business: *The takeover will be discussed at the next board meeting.*

/ˈbɔːd ˌmiːtɪŋ/

pl board meetings

⋈ arrange, chair, conduct, hold a **board meeting**

▶ **business meeting**

Board of Customs and Excise *noun* (import/export/tax)

the department of the British Government responsible for collecting certain taxes on goods and for preventing smuggling. It also produces statistics of Britain's imports and exports: *import regulations imposed by the Board of Customs and Excise*

/ˌbɔːd əv ˌkʌstəmz ənd ˈeksaɪz/

abbr BCE

syn Customs and Excise, (*informal*) customs

▶ **customs duty, excise duty, import duty, tariff 1**

---

board of directors *noun* (management)

▶ **board 1**

/ˌbɔːd əv daɪˈrektəz/

Board of Inland Revenue *noun* (tax)

▶ **Inland Revenue**

/ˌbɔːd əv ˌɪnlənd ˈrevənjuː/

---

bom *abbr* (industry)

bill of materials

/ˌbiː əʊ ˈem/

note pronounced as individual letters

---

bona fide *adjective*

(*Latin*) **1** genuine: *This is a bona fide reduction in price.* ○ *The deal is all quite bona fide.* **2** (*law*) honest; having an honest intention: *The bona fide purchaser did not know that the seller was not the legal owner of the goods.*

/ˌbəʊnə ˈfaɪdi/

1 ⋈ a **bona fide** bargain, deal, offer

2 ⋈ a **bona fide** contract, purchaser

▶ **bad faith, good faith, mala fide**

---

bond *noun*

1 (*stock exchange*) a document from a government or a company that states that money borrowed from an investor will be repaid. Bonds are usually for long-term loans that earn a fixed rate of interest: *Government bonds are usually considered to be a safe investment.* **2** (*law*) a legal promise made by one person to another to do or not do something; the document that shows this

/bɒnd/

pl bonds

1 ⋈ cash in, hold, redeem a **bond**

▶ **debenture, Eurobond, fixed interest security, government bond**

2 ⋈ make, sign a **bond**

▶ **contract[1]**

---

bonded goods *noun* (import/export)

imported items on which customs duties must be paid before they can be collected by the importer or exported again: *We need permission to release these bonded goods to the importer.*

/ˌbɒndɪd ˈɡʊdz/

note plural noun, used with a plural verb

⋈ release **bonded goods**

▶ **customs duty, duty-free, excise duty, import duty**

---

bonded warehouse *noun* (export/import)
a building where BONDED GOODS are kept until the customs duty has been paid and they can be collected by the importer or exported again: *The goods were released from the bonded warehouse.*

/ˌbɒndɪd ˈweəhaʊs/
pl bonded warehouses
⋈ collect goods from, store goods in a **bonded warehouse**
▶ **customs duty, warehouse**

bond note *noun* (import/export)
a document signed by a customs officer that allows BONDED GOODS to be collected by the importer or exported again: *The goods can be collected as soon as the bond note has been signed by customs.*

/ˈbɒnd nəʊt/
⋈ approve, check, sign a **bond note**
▶ **bill of entry, bill of sight, export licence, import licence, landing order**

bonus *noun*
1 (*personnel*) an extra payment given to employees in addition to their normal wages: *All staff received a Christmas bonus of £100.* **2** (*insurance*) an extra payment made by a life assurance company to policy holders from the company's profits: *Bonuses are paid on the 31st of January of each year.* **3** (*finance/stock exchange*) an extra payment or share given by a company to its shareholders: *a bonus share, dividend*

/ˈbəʊnəs/
pl bonuses
1 ⋈ be eligible for, be entitled to, get, give, receive a **bonus**
▶ **danger money**
2 ▶ **no-claims bonus, loading**
3 ⋈ a **bonus** dividend, share

bonus issue *noun* (stock exchange)
▶ **scrip issue**

/ˈbəʊnəs ˌɪʃuː/

bookkeeping *noun* (accounting)
the recording of all money received into and paid out of a company in a book or on a computer file: *I do all my own bookkeeping.*

/ˈbʊkkiːpɪŋ/
note not used with *a* or *an*. No plural and used with a singular verb only.
▶ **double-entry bookkeeping**

book of prime entry *noun* (accounting)
▶ **prime entry book**

/ˌbʊk əv praɪm ˈentri/

books *noun* (accounting)
the books, files or computer records where a company's accounts are kept: *The tax inspector wants to examine the books.*

close the books to add up the totals of income and expenditure at the end of the financial year: *We've closed the books for last year now.*

cook the books (*slang*) to put false information onto a company's financial records: *The accountant was putting money into his own bank account and cooking the books.*

/bʊks/
note plural noun, used with a plural verb
⋈ balance, do, keep the **books**
syn account books
▶ **accounts 1, balance[2], day book, ledger, prime entry book**

book value *noun* (accounting)
the worth of an item of value (an ASSET) as recorded in the account books of a company: *The old photocopier is still useful, although its book value is almost nothing.*

/ˈbʊk ˌvæljuː/
abbr bv
▶ **depreciation, market value, net book value, value[2] 2**

boom[1] *noun* (economics/industry)
a rapid increase in sales, profits, production, etc; a time of prosperity: *Our company is enjoying a sales boom at the moment.* ○ *The country was in the middle of an economic boom.*

/buːm/
pl booms
⋈ an economic, an industrial, a sales, a trade **boom**, a **boom** period, year
opp recession

▶ **depressed market, depression, slump[1]**

---

boom² *verb* (economics/industry)
(of trade and business activity) to do well; to increase or expand rapidly: *The computer industry is booming.* ○ *Sales boomed last year.*

/buːm/
boom, booming, boomed
note intransitive verb
⋈ business, industry, trade is **booming**; sales are **booming**
▶ **slump²**

---

boost¹ *noun* (economics)
something that helps, increases or encourages: *The cut in interest rates will give a boost to the economy/give the economy a boost.*

/buːst/
⋈ give (something) a **boost**; give a **boost** to something; a **boost** in prices, production, sales

---

boost² *verb* (economics)
to increase the strength or value of something; to help and encourage something: *The channel tunnel should boost European trade.* ○ *Lower prices are boosting sales.*

/buːst/
boost, boosting, boosted
note transitive verb
⋈ **boost** business, the economy, prices, sales, trade

---

borrow *verb* (banking/finance)
to receive money from a person, a bank or other financial organization and agree to pay it back later, usually with interest: *I have borrowed £5 000 from the bank.* ○ *They borrowed against their house* (ie used their house as security).

/ˈbɒrəʊ/
borrow, borrowing, borrowed
note transitive and intransitive verb
⋈ **borrow** from someone/something; **borrow** against something; **borrow** at a high/low rate of interest
▶ **lend, loan²**

---

borrowing *noun* (banking/finance)
1 receiving money from a person, a bank, or other financial organization and agreeing to pay it back later, usually with interest: *Banks reported a high level of borrowings this month.* **2** money that is received in this way: *We must not increase our borrowing(s) at the moment.*

/ˈbɒrəʊɪŋ/
pl borrowings
⋈ level, rate of **borrowing**; **borrowing** power, requirements
▶ **loan¹**

---

boss *noun* (personnel)
(*informal*) a person who is responsible for the work of a company, a department or at least one other person: *I have weekly meetings with my boss.* ○ *If you need time off you'll have to ask the boss.*

/bɒs/
pl bosses
▶ **foreman, manager, supervisor**

---

bought ledger *noun* (accounting)
a book or computer file in which the money a company spends on goods and services is recorded: *make an entry in the bought ledger*

/ˈbɔːt ˌledʒə(r)/
pl bought ledgers
⋈ a **bought ledger** clerk, department
syn purchase ledger
▶ **accounts payable, ledger, nominal ledger, sales ledger**

---

bounce[1] *verb*

(*informal*) **1** (*banking*) (of a cheque) to be refused as payment by a bank because there is not enough money in the account: *The bank bounced the cheque.* ○ *You'd better ask him to pay cash, his cheques always bounce.* **2** (*stock exchange*) (**a**) (of a stock exchange) to suddenly become very active, causing share prices to rise: *The Hong Kong market bounced as confidence grew.* (**b**) (of securities, etc) to rise suddenly: *The company's share prices bounced at the end of last week.*

to bounce back to recover well, to rise again: *Car sales bounced back after a poor July.*

/baʊns/

bounce, bouncing, bounced

1 note usually intransitive, but can be a transitive verb

⧓ **bounce** a cheque

▶ **dishonour**

2a note intransitive verb

⧓ the market, the stock exchange, the stock market **bounced**

2b ⧓ equities, share prices, shares **bounced**

▶ **jump**[1]

---

bounce[2] *noun* (stock exchange/sales)

(of securities, prices, sales, etc) a sudden rise: *Tokyo was preparing for a sudden bounce today.* ○ *There was a sharp 14.5% bounce in exports.*

/baʊns/

pl bounces

⧓ a **bounce** in equities, exports, sales, shares, share prices

▶ **jump**[2]

---

box file *noun*

a container for letters, documents, invoices, etc in the shape of a box: *It's in the box file marked 'invoices'.*

/ˈbɒks faɪl/

pl box files

⧓ close, go through, open, sort out a **box file**

---

box number *noun*

1 a number that is given as part of a temporary address to which letters should be sent: *You can contact her through Box Number 62, American Express, Rome.* **2** a number that is given in a newspaper advertisement as part of the address to which replies should be sent: *All replies should be sent to the box number given at the bottom of the advertisement.*

/ˈbɒks ˌnʌmbə(r)/

pl box numbers

(also **Box Number**)

abbr Box No

1 ⧓ reply, write to a **box number**

2 ⧓ apply, reply, write to a **box number**

▶ **accommodation address, poste restante**

---

brainstorming *noun*

a method of solving problems or planning activities in which all the members of a group make suggestions which are then discussed: *Brainstorming can produce a lot of ideas very quickly.* ○ *We're holding a brainstorming session on our new product next Tuesday.*

/ˈbreɪnstɔːmɪŋ/

note not used with *a* or *an*. No plural and used with a singular verb only.

⧓ arrange, hold, organize, set up a **brainstorming** meeting, session, etc

---

branch *noun* (commerce)

a local office, shop or group that is part of a larger organization with a main office elsewhere: *The company now has branches in all major towns in the UK.* ○ *Is there a branch of Barclays bank near here?* ○ *I'll be working in an overseas branch/a branch overseas for a while.*

branch manager (*personnel*) a person in control of a local office, esp a bank, that is part of a larger organization: *Applications for major loans are dealt with by the branch manager.*

/brɑːntʃ/

pl branches

⧓ close, establish, open, set up a **branch**; a large, a local, a main, an overseas, a small **branch**; a **branch** network, office

▶ **head office, headquarters**

branch out *verb* (industry)
to develop or expand into new areas or business activities: *The television and radio shop has branched out into computers.* ○ *I'm going to leave my job and branch out on my own.*

/ˌbrɑːntʃ ˈaʊt/
branch out, branching out, branched out
note intransitive verb
⋈ **branch out** *into* something
▶ **diversification**

brand[1] *noun* (manufacturing)
a product or group of products or a service, with a particular name, that usually forms part of an easily recognizable design on packaging or advertising material: *I always buy the same brand of toothpaste.* ○ *Most supermarkets have their own brands of tea and coffee, etc now.*

branded goods products or services that have a brand name: *The shop sells low-priced branded goods.*

/brænd/
pl brands
⋈ buy, develop, launch, sell, test a (particular) **brand**
▶ **make**[1], **model**

brand[2] *verb* (manufacturing)
to give a product, a group of products or a service a particular name: *We'll have to brand the product differently in different markets.*

/brænd/
brand, branding, branded
note transitive verb
⋈ **brand** goods

brand image *noun* (advertising/manufacturing)
the feelings and opinions that a buyer has about a particular named product. These can be created and influenced by advertising and packaging: *Mercedes cars have a quality brand image.*

/ˈbrænd ˌɪmɪdʒ/
note usually singular
⋈ alter, create, cultivate, develop, establish, improve, project a **brand image**
▶ **corporate image**

brand leader *noun* (manufacturing)
the product with a particular BRAND NAME that is bought by the greatest number of people: *We are doing a survey to find out which is the brand leader in the coffee market.*

/ˈbrænd ˌliːdə(r)/
pl brand leaders
⋈ be, become a **brand leader**
▶ **market leader**

brand loyalty *noun* (advertising/manufacturing)
the willingness of a customer to keep buying the same named product or group of products: *Every manufacturer wants to encourage brand loyalty.*

/ˈbrænd ˌlɔɪəlti/
⋈ develop, encourage, establish **brand loyalty**; high, low, strong, weak **brand loyalty**

brand name *noun* (manufacturing)
the name of a particular product or group of products, or a service that is recognized by customers. If the name is registered no other company may use it: *St Michael is the brand name of Marks and Spencer.*

/ˈbrænd neɪm/
pl brand names
⋈ buy, register, sell, use a **brand name**
▶ **household name, own brand,** proprietary name *under* **proprietary, trade name**

breach of contract *noun* (law)
a situation where one person who has signed a contract ignores or fails to keep the conditions agreed in it: *By giving information to our competitors he is in breach of contract.* ○ *We're claiming damages for breach of contract.*

/ˌbriːtʃ əv ˈkɒntrækt/
note usually singular
⋈ be guilty of, be in, sue for **breach of contract**
▶ **accord and satisfaction, adoption of contract, contract, default, illegal contract, lapse of time**

break even *verb* (commerce)

1 (*UK*) to be in a situation where income from sales equals costs: *After six months of trading the company broke even.* ○ *You'll be lucky to break even on that project.* **2** (*US*) to make a small profit: *The film didn't make a fortune but it broke even.*

/ˌbreɪk ˈiːvn/

break even, broke even, broken even

⧓ fail, manage to **break even**

break-even point *noun* (commerce)

the postion where income from sales equals costs: *We estimate it will take a year to reach break-even point.*

/breɪk ˈiːvn pɔɪnt/

pl break-even points

⧓ reach **break-even point**

bribe[1] *noun*

money or goods offered to someone to persuade them to do something, esp something dishonest: *It is illegal to offer a bribe to a judge.*

/braɪb/

pl bribes

⧓ accept, offer, take a **bribe**

syn backhander

▶ **gift 1, gratuity 1, kickback, rake-off, slush fund, tip**[1]

bribe[2] *verb*

to give someone money or goods to persuade them to do something: *He was bribed to give them confidential information.* ○ *The employee tried to bribe her boss.*

/braɪb/

bribe, bribing, bribed

note transitive verb

⧓ attempt, intend, manage to **bribe** someone

▶ **tip**[2]

bribery *noun*

giving or taking bribes: *Two members of the jury were accused of bribery.*

/ˈbraɪbəri/

note not used with *a* or *an*. No plural and used with a singular verb only.

⧓ accuse, convict someone of **bribery**

▶ **corruption 1**

bridging loan *noun* (banking/finance)

money borrowed for a short time, to cover the period between buying one thing, esp a house, and selling another: *She arranged a bridging loan with the local bank.*

/ˈbrɪdʒɪŋ ləʊn/

pl bridging loans

syn (*US*) bridge loan

⧓ arrange, negotiate, offer, pay back, pay off, secure a **bridging loan**

▶ **accommodation 3, day-to-day loan, loan**[1]

bring forward *verb*

1 (*accounting*) to carry (copy) a figure from the previous page or period of accounts to the next: *an amount brought forward* **2** to move something to an earlier time or date: *We'll bring forward the board meeting to 10 October.* ○ *Did you forget the time of the meeting was brought forward to 2 pm?*

/ˌbrɪŋ ˈfɔːwəd/

bring forward, bringing forward, brought forward

note transitive verb

1 ⧓ **bring forward** an amount, a balance, a figure

▶ **brought forward, carried forward**

2 ⧓ **bring forward** a date, an event, a meeting, a time

British Institute of Management *noun* (management)

the main professional organization for managers in the UK, providing advice and information and promoting management

/ˌbrɪtɪʃ ˌɪnstɪtjuːt əv ˈmænɪdʒmənt/

abbr BIM, B.I.M

studies and education: *become a member of the British Institute of Management*

⧓ an associate member, a fellow, a member of the **British Institute of Management**

▶ **management, manager**

British Standards Institution *noun* (manufacturing)
an organization formed in the UK to set and test quality and safety standards in the building, engineering, chemical industries and of consumer products: *safety belts approved by the British Standards Institution*

/ˌbrɪtɪʃ ˈstændədz ɪnstɪtjuːʃn/

abbr BSI

⧓ approved by the **British Standards Institution**

▶ **International Standards Organization, kite mark**

---

broker *noun* (finance)
a person or organization that buys and sells, esp shares or insurance, for others: *He works as an insurance broker/for a firm of insurance brokers.* ○ *I must ring my broker this afternoon.*

/ˈbrəʊkə(r)/

pl brokers

⧓ act as (a) **broker** *to* someone; a finance, an insurance, a mortgage **broker**

▶ **agent, commodity broker, dealer, factor, merger broker, middleman, money broker, shipbroker, stockbroker**

---

brokerage *noun* (finance)
1 the fee charged by a BROKER for buying or selling shares, insurance, etc for another person: *Brokerage on this deal is 2%.* **2** the business done by a BROKER: *The firm aims to provide further brokerage services to companies and individuals.*

/ˈbrəʊkərɪdʒ/

1 ⧓ charge, levy, pay, receive **brokerage**

2 ⧓ a **brokerage** firm, house; **brokerage** services

---

brought forward *adjective, adverb* (accounting)
the words written at the top of an account to show an amount that has had to be carried (copied) from a previous period or page of accounts: *Put that figure in the brought forward column.* ○ *£550 is the amount brought forward.*

/ˌbrɔːt ˈfɔːwəd/

abbr B/f, b/f, bt.fwd, bt/fwd

note usually written in abbreviated form

⧓ an amount, a balance, a credit, a debit, a figure **brought forward**

▶ **account 1, bring forward, carried forward**

---

brown goods *noun* (commerce)
items such as television sets and radios that are sold in cabinets made of wood or similar materials: *Manufacturers of brown goods have to face competition from Japan.*

/ˈbraʊn gʊdz/

note plural noun, used with a plural verb

⧓ buy, order, sell, stock, trade in **brown goods**

▶ **white goods**

BS *abbr* (manufacturing)
British Standard. Used on product labels to show the British Standards Institution specification number: *The designer specified a printing ink colour of BS 70326.* ○ *Manufactured to BS 10083.*

/ˌbiː ˈes/

▶ **British Standards Institution**

---

b/s *abbr* (sales)
bill of sale

note used in written English only

(also **B.S.**, **B/S**, **b.s.**)

---

abbr abbreviation **pl** plural ⧓ collocate (*word often used with the headword*)

BSI *abbr* (manufacturing)
British Standards Institution

/ˌbiː es ˈaɪ/

bt/fwd *abbr* (accounting)
brought forward

note used in written English only
(also **B/f**, **b/f**, **bt.fwd**)

budget[1] *noun* (finance)
1 a plan of income and expenditure for a particular period of time: *an annual, a departmental, a sales budget* ○ *The financial director is responsible for the firm's budgets.* **2** an amount of money to be spent on particular business activities or equipment: *She was given a budget of £25 000 to launch the magazine.* **3 the Budget** (*UK*) the annual plan of income and expenditure produced by the government: *The Budget is announced in April.*

/ˈbʌdʒɪt/
pl budgets
1 ⋈ do, draw up, plan a **budget**
▶ **allowance 1, budget account, business plan, variable budget**
2 ⋈ cut, increase, overshoot, reduce, set a **budget**

budget[2] *verb* (finance)
1 to save or allocate money for a particular purpose: *Business is bad so we'll have to budget carefully.* ○ *We're budgeting for a new van.* **2** to make a plan of future income and expenditure for a particular period of time: *The company budgeted for a 5% increase in sales.*

/ˈbʌdʒɪt/
budget, budgeting, budgeted
note transitive and intransitive verb
⋈ **budget** *for* (something)
▶ **estimate**[2] **1**

budget account *noun* (banking)
a bank account designed to help customers pay large annual expenses by transferring an equal amount of money each month from the customer's current account to a separate budget account: *I have a budget account for bills and insurance.*

/ˈbʌdʒɪt əˌkaʊnt/
pl budget accounts
⋈ open, pay bills through, transfer money into a **budget account**
▶ **account**[1] **2, bank account, instalment**

budgetary *adjective* (finance/sales)
relating to a budget: *What are your budgetary requirements for this year* (ie how much money do you need)*?*

/ˈbʌdʒɪtəri/
⋈ **budgetary** arrangements, control, requirements
▶ **budget**[1], **2, 3**

bug *noun* (computing)
a problem or defect that appears or is deliberately introduced into a computer program: *Someone has put a bug in the system.*

/bʌg/
pl bugs
⋈ introduce, put a **bug** (into a computer program/system); discover, eliminate, remove, sort out a **bug**
▶ **virus**

building society *noun* (finance)
an organization, similar to a bank, with which people can save money and get interest on it, and that lends money, in the form of a MORTGAGE, to people who want to buy houses or flats: *Do you have a building society account?*

/ˈbɪldɪŋ səˌsaɪəti/
pl building societies
⋈ invest in, open an account with, save with a **building society**
▶ **bank**[1], **mortgage**[1], **savings account, savings bank**

built-in obsolescence *noun* (manufacturing)
▶ **planned obsolescence**

/ˌbɪlt ɪn ˌɒbsəˈlesns/

bulk *noun* (commerce)
large size, volume or quantity: *Because of their bulk these filing cabinets are very difficult to move.*

in bulk 1 in large amounts: *buy something in bulk* **2** unpacked; loose: *Grain is often transported in bulk.*

/bʌlk/
note not used with *a* or *an*. No plural and used with a singular verb only.
⧓ **bulk** cargo, goods; **bulk** buying
▶ **wholesale**[1]

bulk carrier *noun* (shipping)
a ship designed to carry BULK GOODS: *The goods will be transported by bulk carrier.*

/ˈbʌlk ˌkæriə(r)/
pl bulk carriers
⧓ load, unload a **bulk carrier**

bulk goods *noun* (commerce)
items usually carried in large amounts and without packaging: *Coal, grain and sand are bulk goods.*

/ˈbʌlk gʊdz/
note plural noun, used with a plural verb
⧓ carry, transport **bulk goods**

bulk shipment *noun* (shipping)
a delivery of BULK GOODS

/ˈbʌlk ˌʃɪpmənt/
⧓ receive, send off a **bulk shipment**
▶ **shipment**

bullion *noun* (finance)
gold or silver in large bars, not coins: *The train is carrying £100 000 pounds worth of gold bullion.* ○ *the bullion market*

/ˈbʊliən/
note not used with *a* or *an*. No plural and used with a singular verb only.
⧓ buy, deal in, sell, trade in **bullion**
▶ **gold**

bull market *noun* (stock exchange)
a situation in a stock market or currency market where prices are rising and lots of shareholders are buying: *a bull market for the US dollar*

/ˈbʊl ˌmɑːkɪt/
note usually singular
⧓ **bull market** dealing, prices
▶ **bear market, market**[1]

bull position *noun* (stock exchange)
a situation in which a dealer of securities or commodities keeps hold of a particular stock or share because he/she expects a rise in price: *remain in a bull position until the market changes*

/ˈbʊl pəˌzɪʃn/
note usually singular
syn long position
▶ **bear position, longs**

bureaucracy *noun*
1 a system of government by a large number of officials in various departments **2** (often used in a critical way) the system of official rules that an organization has for doing something, that people often think are too complicated: *It took ages to get this visa because of all the bureaucracy involved.*

/bjʊəˈrɒkrəsi/
1 pl bureaucracies
2 note not used with *a* or *an*. No plural and used with a singular verb only.
▶ **red tape**

business *noun* (commerce)
1 (**a**) a line of work; a profession: *What business are you in?* ○ *Banking has always been my business.* (**b**) work as opposed to leisure: *She always puts business before pleasure.* ○ *You've been talking business all evening.* **2** commercial activities in general, such as trading, buying and selling, manufacturing, arranging deals: *We're in business to make a profit.* ○ *He wants to work in the world of business.* ○ *a business deal* ○ *a business appointment* **3** a

/ˈbɪznəs/
1a note usually singular
▶ **job 1, occupation, trade**[1] **5**
2 note not used with *a* or *an*. No plural and used with a singular verb only.
▶ **commerce, industry, trade**[1] **1**

person or group of people making, distributing, buying or selling goods or providing services; a firm or company: *a furniture, an insurance, a dry-cleaning business ○ a small, family, one-man, one-woman business ○ The business started 100 years ago.* **4** the level of commercial activity: *How's business? ○ Business is good/bad/slow/booming at the moment.* **5** something that needs to be discussed or dealt with: *If there's no more business, I'll close the meeting. ○ The business of the enquiry is to hear opinions on the new power station. ○ I have important business to attend to today.*

do business (with someone) to buy from or sell to someone; to meet and discuss commercial activities with a client: *It's been a pleasure to do business with you.*

(have) a head for business be skilful at commercial activities: *He'll get a good price for your car, he's got a real head for business.*

(be) in business 1 to work in or own a commercial company: *My wife is a doctor, but I'm in business.* **2** to have lots of customers; be trading successfully: *We've received three big orders already, now we're in business!*

(be) on business to do something or be in a certain place for work: *He's gone to Germany on business. ○ I'm here on business.*

get down to business to start work seriously: *I know you're busy, so let's get down to business.*

go into business to start or go to work for a commercial firm: *She's gone into business on her own. ○ My son wants to go into business when he leaves college.*

go out of business to become bankrupt; stop trading: *Small shops go out of business very quickly.*

(be) open for business (be) ready for work or to receive customers: *The sign on the door says 'open for business'.*

set up in business to start a new firm, shop, etc: *He has just set up in business as a grocer.*

3 pl businesses

⋈ close (down), establish, run, start a **business**

▶ **association 1, company, corporation, federation, firm, group, organization 1**

4 note not used with *a* or *an*. No plural and used with a singular verb only.

5 note not used with *a* or *an*. No plural and used with a singular verb only.

⋈ important, pressing, urgent **business**

---

business agent *noun* (commerce)

▶ **agent**

/ˈbɪznəs ˌeɪdʒənt/

---

business card *noun* (commerce/management)

a small card showing a person's name, his/her position in the company and the company's address, that is handed out to clients: *Make sure you give a business card to every customer you meet. ○ I think I have a business card in my wallet.*

/ˈbɪznəs kɑ:d/

▶ **business cards**

⋈ carry, give, hand out, leave a **business card**

---

business hours *noun* (commerce)

the time during the day when shops, offices, banks, etc are open for work: *Please call at any time during business hours. ○ Normal business hours are between 9 am and 5 pm.*

/ˈbɪznəs ˌaʊəz/

note plural noun, used with a plural verb

syn working hours

▶ **office hours**

---

businesslike *adjective*

well-organized, efficient: *He was always a businesslike chairman. ○ She is usually prompt and businesslike. ○ You must take a more businesslike approach to your job.*

/ˈbɪznəslaɪk/

⋈ a **businesslike** approach, attitude, manner, method, person, way

▶ **professional**[1]

---

business lunch *noun* (commerce)

a meeting with lunch to talk about work or to entertain clients:

/ˌbɪznəs ˈlʌntʃ/

pl business lunches

I've had three business lunches this week. ○ *The new Italian restaurant is a good place to go for a business lunch.*

⋈ attend, go to, hold a **business lunch**

---

businessman, businesswoman, business person *noun* (commerce)

1 a person who owns or has an important position in a company: *The company is owned by an American businessman.* **2** a man who is skilful in financial matters: *She set up her own company and proved to be a very good businesswoman.*

/ˈbɪznəsmən, ˈbɪznəswʊmən, ˈbɪznəspɜːsn/

pl businessmen, businesswomen, business people

2 ⋈ an astute, a successful, a wealthy **businessman, businesswoman, business person**

---

business meeting *noun* (commerce)

a gathering of people to discuss work topics: *Some business meetings are much too long.* ○ *There's an important business meeting after lunch.*

/ˈbɪznəs ˌmiːtɪŋ/

pl business meetings

⋈ attend, go to, hold a **business meeting**

▶ **board meeting, meeting**

---

business plan *noun* (finance/management)

a written report that states what a company (or part of a company) aims to do to increase sales, develop new products, etc within a certain period, and how it will obtain the necessary finances and resources: *The bank manager wants to see a business plan before agreeing to lend money.* ○ *I've just finished writing the three-year business plan.*

/ˈbɪznəs plæn/

pl business plans

⋈ discuss, draw up, present a **business plan**

▶ **budget[1] 1, corporate planning, mission statement**

---

business school *noun* (commerce)

a college or part of a college, university or polytechnic where students attend courses in BUSINESS STUDIES: *She's doing a course at Manchester business school.*

/ˈbɪznəs skuːl/

pl business schools

⋈ attend, go to, study at a **business school**

---

business sense *noun* (commerce)

a knowledge of commercial procedures; the ability to encourage or predict commercial activity: *We need to employ someone with (a) good business sense.*

/ˈbɪznəs sens/

note singular noun, used with a singular verb

▶ a head for business *under* **business**

---

business studies *noun* (commerce)

economics, management, commerce, etc as subjects studied at a college or university; the course consisting of such subjects: *She's doing business studies at university.*

/ˈbɪznəs ˌstʌdiz/

note not used with *a* or *an*. No plural and used with a singular verb only.

⋈ do, take **business studies**; a course in, a degree in **business studies**

---

business trip *noun* (commerce)

a journey, usually involving at least one overnight stay, undertaken to meet clients to discuss work topics: *She's gone to Paris on a business trip.* ○ *Did you have a successful business trip?*

/ˈbɪznəs trɪp/

pl business trips

⋈ be/go on, make a **business trip**

---

buy[1] *noun*

act of buying something; a thing bought: *National Savings are a good buy for cautious investors.* ○ *You won't find a better buy than this freezer.*

/baɪ/

pl buys

⋈ bad, better, good **buy**

▶ **purchase[1] 1**

---

buy[2] *verb* (commerce/retail)

to obtain something by giving money for it; purchase: *buy a ticket, a newspaper, a box of chocolates* ○ *They are planning to buy an American company.* ○ *I have just bought some gas shares.* ○ *Prices are low, it's a good time to buy.*

buy in to obtain goods or materials for stock or storage: *Our customers are buying in lots of coal for the winter.*

buy into to pay money in exchange for a share in a business: *She was advised to buy into smaller companies.*

buy out to pay someone in exchange for their financial share of a business or property: *He bought out the other director/bought the other director out. Now he's the sole owner.* ○ *She bought out his share of the firm.*

buy up to buy all or nearly all of what is available of something: *He bought up all the milk in the shop.*

/baɪ/
buy, buying, bought
note usually transitive
▶ **purchase**[2], **sell**[1] **1**

---

buyer *noun*

1 a person who buys something: *Have you found a buyer for the house yet?* ○ *a first-time buyer*, ie someone who has not bought a house before **2** (*commerce/retail*) a person who buys stock, materials, equipment, etc for a company: *She's a buyer for a large department store.* ○ *a senior buyer for a firm*

/ˈbaɪə(r)/
pl buyers
1 ⋈ a cash, a potential, a ready **buyer**
syn vendee
▶ **consumer, purchaser, seller**
2 ⋈ clothes, fashion, materials **buyer**
▶ **materials buyer**

---

buyer's market *noun* (commerce)

a situation where certain products are in plentiful supply, resulting in low prices and good credit terms for buyers: *An unusually good summer created a buyer's market in tomatoes.*

/ˌbaɪəz ˈmɑːkɪt/
pl buyer's markets
⋈ create, result in a **buyer's market**
▶ **easy market, market**[1], **sellers' market**

---

buyout *noun* (management)

▶ **employees' buyout, leveraged buyout, management buyout**

/ˈbaɪ aʊt/

---

bv *abbr* (accounting)

book value

/ˌbiː ˈviː/

---

by-product *noun* (industry)

a substance produced as the result of making something else: *Skimmed milk powder is a by-product of butter production.*

/ˈbaɪ prɒdʌkt/
pl by-products
⋈ produce, sell, use a **by-product**
▶ **end-product, spin-off, waste product**

---

byte *noun* (computing)

a unit of computer information consisting of a number of BITS or binary digits: *One byte is used to represent one letter or one number.*

/baɪt/
pl bytes
▶ **kilobyte, megabyte**

c/a *abbr* (banking)
1 capital account **2** credit account **3** current account

note used in written English only

---

cable address *noun* (international trade)
► **telegraphic address**

/ˈkeɪbl əˌdres/

---

cable television *noun* (technology)
a system of broadcasting television programmes by cable instead of radio signals: *Have you subscribed to* (ie paid to get) *cable television?*

/ˌkeɪbl ˈtelɪvɪʒn/
note no plural
⧓ a **cable television** channel, company, network, system

---

cable transfer *noun* (banking/international trade)
► **telegraphic transfer**

/ˌkeɪbl ˈtrænsfɜː(r)/
abbr CT

---

cabotage *noun*
1 (*shipping*) the movements of ships from port to port along the coast of a country for trade purposes: *Most of the small ships in the Arabian Gulf are employed in cabotage.* **2** (*transport*) the laws allowing a ship, an aircraft, a lorry, etc to pick up goods from one country and transport them to another for trade: *Free access to the airports and seaports of that country is now restricted by its government's laws of cabotage.*

/ˈkæbətaːʒ/
note not used with *a* or *an*. No plural and used with a singular verb only.
⧓ aircraft, lorry, shipping **cabotage**; **cabotage** restrictions
► **trade restriction**

CAD *noun* (banking/shipping)
cash against documents

/ˌsiː eɪ ˈdiː/
note pronounced as individual letters

---

calculator *noun* (office practice)
a small electronic instrument for making mathematical calculations: *She used a calculator to add up the sales figures.* ○ *I can't work this out without a calculator.* ○ *a pocket calculator*

/ˈkælkjəleɪtə(r)/
pl calculators
⧓ use a **calculator**
► **computer**

---

call *noun*
1 (*banking*) a request for the immediate withdrawal of money from a bank account for which no advance warning need be given: *have money on call* **2** (*stock exchange*) a demand from a company to a shareholder to pay for the shares he/she has been allotted: *Shares in the privatized industry have now been allotted and the shareholders will soon have to meet the first call.* **3** (*commerce*) a short visit by a salesman to a potential customer: *Our representatives made a number of calls on shops in the eastern region.*

/kɔːl/
pl calls
2 ► **call money, call option**
3 ⧓ **call** *at* (a place), *on* (someone)

---

called-up capital *noun* (stock exchange)
the amount of money that a company has when shareholders have bought only part of the total share capital that has been issued: *Called-up capital now forms 79% of the total share capital.*

/ˌkɔːld ʌp ˈkæpɪtəl/
note not used with *a* or *an*. No plural and used with a singular verb only.
► **authorized share capital, issued capital, paid-up capital**

---

call money *noun* (banking)
money lent on condition that it must be repaid immediately if necessary: *Last month the bank advanced very large sums of call money to the money market.*

/ˈkɔːl ˌmʌni/
note no plural
⧓ borrow, lend **call money**
► **at call, money**

---

call option *noun* (stock exchange)
the right to buy a fixed quantity of a commodity, currency or security at a certain price and on a certain date: *make a call option agreement*

/ˈkɔːl ˌɒpʃn/
pl call options
⋈ a **call option** agreement, contract, deal, market
▶ **option, put option, time option, traded option**

---

campaign[1] *noun* (advertising/marketing)
a series of planned activities with a particular commercial, political or social aim: *plan a new campaign to increase sales* ○ *The Ministry of Health is conducting a campaign to show the dangers of smoking.*

/kæmˈpeɪn/
pl campaigns
⋈ conduct, launch, lead, mount, plan a **campaign**; a **campaign** for, against (something)
▶ **promotion 1, sales campaign**

---

campaign[2] *verb*
to lead or take part in a series of planned activities with a particular commercial, political or social aim: *to campaign for better working conditions* ○ *They were campaigning against racial discrimination at work.*

/kæmˈpeɪn/
campaign, campaigning, campaigned
note intransitive verb
⋈ to **campaign** for, against (something)
▶ **advertise 1, promote 1, publicize**

---

cancel *verb* (commerce)
to stop an arrangement already made; to make something invalid: *Owing to a strike by railway workers all train journeys have been cancelled.* ○ *I'm afraid the meeting has been cancelled.* ○ *If you are dissatisfied with the goods you have a right to cancel the order and receive a full refund.*

/ˈkænsl/
cancel, cancelling, cancelled
(*US* **cancel, canceling, canceled**)
note transitive verb
⋈ to **cancel** an appointment, a holiday, a meeting, an order, a payment, a reservation, a visit
▶ **countermand**

---

cancellation *noun* (commerce)
the stopping of an arrangement already made: *The bad weather has resulted in many holiday cancellations.* ○ *If you cancel the booking within six weeks of departure, you will have to pay a cancellation charge.*

/ˌkænsəˈleɪʃn/
pl cancellations
⋈ announce, make a **cancellation**; a **cancellation** charge, fee

---

candidate *noun* (commerce)
a person offering to take up a post or job: *There are six candidates for the post of senior clerk.* ○ *It is important to choose the best candidate for the job.* ○ *an internal candidate*, ie a person who asks for another job in the organization where he/she already works

/ˈkændɪdət/
pl candidates
⋈ choose, elect, select a **candidate**
▶ **applicant 1, appointee, interviewee**

---

c and f *abbr* (shipping)
cost and freight

/ˌsiː ənd ˈef/

---

c and i *abbr* (shipping)
cost and insurance

/ˌsiː ənd ˈaɪ/

canteen *noun* (industry)
a place in a factory, office, etc where workers may obtain food and drink: *The canteen serves meals between 12 noon and 2 pm.*

/kænˈtiːn/
pl canteens
⋈ eat at, eat in, go to the **canteen**; a factory, an office, a staff, a works **canteen**; **canteen** food, meals

CAP *abbr* (agriculture)
Common Agricultural Policy

/ˌsiː eɪ ˈpiː/
note pronounced as individual letters

capital *noun* (finance)
1 the total value of the land, buildings, machinery, etc (ASSETS) belonging to a business less the sum of any debts it has: *The company has grown rapidly but needs more capital to obtain further growth.* **2** money that is used to start a business: *They set up in business with a starting capital of £200 000.* **3** money that is lent or borrowed with interest charged on it: *How much capital do you need to borrow?* **4** (*economics*) wealth which can be used to produce further wealth: *the free movement of goods, labour and capital*

/ˈkæpɪtl/
note no plural
1 ▶ **authorized share capital, called-up capital, current capital, equity capital, issued capital, loan capital, paid-up capital, physical capital, share capital, venture capital**
2 ⋈ initial, starting, start-up **capital**
▶ **seed capital**
3 ⋈ borrow, invest, lend **capital**
4 ⋈ **capital** accumulates, grows
▶ **factor of production**

capital account *noun* (accounting)
a record of the amount of money a company spends on land, buildings, machinery, etc: *The capital account shows that the company invested heavily in new machine tools.*

/ˈkæpɪtl əˌkaʊnt/
pl capital accounts
abbr c/a
⋈ audit, keep a **capital account**
▶ **account[1] 1, capital expenditure**

capital allowance *noun* (tax)
a tax reduction granted to the owners of certain CAPITAL ASSETS (eg machinery, vehicles, etc) as compensation for the declining value of those assets as time goes by: *To encourage greater capital investment the government has announced higher capital allowances in the coming year.*

/ˌkæpɪtl əˈlaʊəns/
pl capital allowances
syn investment allowance
⋈ grant, offer a **capital allowance**
▶ **allowance 3, tax allowance**

capital asset *noun* (accounting)
an item such as land, a machine, a building or a vehicle belonging to a business and expected to last a long time: *The company is badly managed but its capital assets are of great value.* ○ *The company has capital assets worth £3 million.*

/ˌkæpɪtl ˈæset/
pl capital assets
⋈ maintain, register, replace, sell a **capital asset**
syn fixed asset, permanent asset
▶ **current asset, wasting asset**

capital charges *noun* (finance)
the costs a business must meet, eg for repairing and replacing machines, buildings, vehicles, etc, and repaying loans with interest: *The company has had a very profitable year but large sums have had to be put aside to meet capital charges.*

/ˈkæpɪtl ˌtʃɑːdʒɪz/
note plural noun, used with a plural verb
⋈ incur, pay **capital charges**

capital expenditure *noun* (finance)
money spent on land, buildings, machinery, vehicles and materials, etc to be used for producing goods: *A great amount of capital expenditure will be required before we see any profit from this business.*

/ˌkæpɪtl ɪkˈspendɪtʃə(r)/
note not used with *a* or *an*. No plural and used with a singular verb only.
syn capital outlay
▶ **capital account, capital investment, expenditure**

capital gains tax *noun* (tax)
a tax imposed, usually with some exemptions, on any profit made when an asset is sold (eg a building, land, shares in a business): *pay capital gains tax on the sale of a factory*

/ˌkæpɪtl ˈgeɪnz tæks/
abbr CGT, C.G.T.
⧓ pay **capital gains tax**
▶ **tax[1]**

capital good *noun* (manufacturing)
an item such as a machine, a building, or a raw material that is used to manufacture products for sale to consumers: *Petrol is a consumer good to a pleasure motorist but a capital good to a transport company.*

/ˈkæpɪtl gʊd/
pl capital goods
⧓ buy, make, produce **capital goods**
syn investment good, producer good
▶ **consumer goods**

capital growth *noun* (finance)
an increase in the value of investments, eg shares in a business: *An investment in shares with a low income may be acceptable if the chances of capital growth look good.*

/ˌkæpɪtl ˈgrəʊθ/
note not used with *a* or *an*. No plural and used with a singular verb only.
⧓ provide **capital growth**; high, long-term **capital growth**

capital investment *noun* (finance)
spending money on items needed to produce goods in the future, eg machinery, factories, etc; the money invested in this way: *an initial capital investment of £66 million* ○ *raise money for capital investment*

/ˌkæpɪtl ɪnˈvestmənt/
pl capital investments
⧓ (a) heavy, high, low **capital investment**; a **capital investment** plan, programme
▶ **capital account, capital expenditure, financial investment, investment 1**

capitalization issue *noun* (stock exchange)
▶ **scrip issue**

/ˌkæpɪtəlaɪˈzeɪʃn ˌɪʃuː/

capital market *noun* (finance)
a place where deals are made relating to the long-term investment needed by businesses and public authorities. The money is obtained from private investors, banks, insurance companies, pension funds, etc: *Needing a long-term loan, the company has again turned to the capital market.*

/ˈkæpɪtl mɑːkɪt/
pl capital markets
⧓ borrow from, invest in the **capital market**
▶ **loan market, money market**

capital sum *noun* (insurance)
a lump sum of money paid by an insurance company to an insured person on a specified date, eg when the insured person reaches a certain age: *When the insurance policy matures, the insured person will receive the capital sum agreed.*

/ˌkæpɪtl ˈsʌm/
pl capital sums
⧓ receive a **capital sum**
▶ **premium, terminal bonus**

captive market *noun* (commerce)
a situation where buyers have no choice of goods or have to deal with only one seller: *The water company which supplies the region, having no competitors, enjoys a captive market.*

/ˌkæptɪv ˈmɑːkɪt/
▶ **absolute monopoly, buyers' market, market[1],**

monopoly, perfect market, sellers' market

---

carbon copy *noun* (office practice)
a copy of a typed or handwritten document made by putting a sheet of carbon paper between the sheets of writing paper: *The clerk who typed the letter kept two carbon copies for the files.*

/ˌkɑːbən ˈkɒpi/
pl carbon copies
abbr cc
⋈ make a **carbon copy**
► **copy[1], master 1, original, top copy**

---

card index *noun* (office practice)
a system of recording information on cards which fit into a drawer or box, usually in alphabetical order: *keep addresses on a card index system*

/ˈkɑːd ˌɪndeks/
pl card indexes *or* card indices
⋈ use a **card index**; a **card index** system

---

caretaker *noun* (health and safety)
a person whose job is to keep a building clean, protect it and check that its services (eg telephones, water, heating and electrical supply) are kept working: *The caretaker locks the building at 8 pm every evening.*

/ˈkeəteɪkə(r)/
pl caretakers
⋈ an office **caretaker**
syn (*US*) janitor

---

cargo *noun* (shipping/transport)
goods carried by a plane or ship: *The ship arrived in Karachi with a cargo of electrical goods.*

/ˈkɑːgəʊ/
abbr cgo
pl cargoes
⋈ carry, handle, load, unload (a) **cargo**; a **cargo** plane, ship, vessel
► **deck cargo, freight[1] 2**

---

carriage *noun* (transport)
(the cost of) transporting goods from one place to another: *Carriage of the goods ordered can be arranged by sea or air.* ○ *The price does not include carriage or insurance.*

/ˈkærɪdʒ/
abbr cge
note not used with *a* or *an*. No plural and used with a singular verb only.
► **haulage, transportation**

---

carr. fwd. *abbr* (commerce/transport)
carriage forward

note used in written English only

---

carriage forward *noun* (commerce/transport)
a condition of sale where the cost of transporting goods is paid by the receiver

/ˌkærɪdʒ ˈfɔːwəd/
abbr CF, carr. fwd.

---

carriage paid *noun* (commerce/transport)
a condition of sale where the cost of transporting goods is paid by the sender

/ˌkærɪdʒ ˈpeɪd/
abbr CP

---

carried down *adjective* (accounting)
► **carried forward**

/ˌkærɪd ˈdaʊn/
abbr c/d

---

carried forward *adjective* (accounting)
the words written at the bottom of an account to show an amount that has to be carried (copied) to a next period or page of accounts: *Put that figure in the carried forward column.* ○ *£550 is the amount carried forward.*

/ˌkærɪd ˈfɔːwəd/
abbr c/f, cd.fwd
note usually written in abbreviated form
⋈ an amount, a balance, a credit, a debit, a figure **carried forward**

▶ **account 1, brought forward**

---

carrier *noun* (transport)

a person or business that transports goods for commercial purposes: *A carrier can be hired to transport the goods from the railway station to your factory.*

/ˈkæriə(r)/
pl carriers
⧓ hire, use a **carrier**
syn haulier

---

case study *noun* (management)

a detailed study of a real person or event over a period of time for training or educational purposes: *a case study of a real work situation*

/ˈkeɪs ˌstʌdi/
pl case studies
⧓ conduct, present, provide a **case study**

---

cash[1] *noun* (banking)

1 money in the form of banknotes and coins: *Small amounts are usually paid in cash rather than by cheque.* ○ *Please do not send cash with your order.* **2** money or finance generally, esp if it is immediately available: *The company is short of cash at the moment.*

/kæʃ/
note not used with *a* or *an*. No plural and used with a singular verb only.
1 ⧓ pay (in), use **cash**; a **cash** payment, refund
▶ **banknote, cheque, credit card**
2 ▶ **prompt cash**

---

cash[2] *verb* (banking)

to exchange a cheque or money order for banknotes and coins: *cash traveller's cheques on holiday*

cash in (something) to give up bonds, certificates, vouchers, etc in return for the amount of money (plus interest) stated on them: *I've decided to cash in my share certificates as they don't bring me much money.*

cash in on (something) to take advantage of or profit from something: *Rank cinemas have managed to cash in on the video boom.*

cash up to add up the amount of money taken by a shop in a day, so that it can be checked against the till receipts and put in the bank: *Don't forget to cash up at the end of the day.*

/kæʃ/
cash, cashing, cashed
note transitive verb
⧓ **cash** a cheque
syn encash
▶ **uncashed**

---

cash against documents *noun* (banking/shipping)

an arrangement made between an exporter, a bank and a person receiving goods (the CONSIGNEE), in which the shipping documents are sent to the bank with instructions to hold them until the goods are paid for: *The exporter agreed to send the goods cash against documents.*

/ˌkæʃ əgenst ˈdɒkjəmənts/
abbr CAD
syn documents against cash
▶ **documents against acceptance bill, documents against payment bill, shipping documents**

---

cashcard *noun* (banking)

a plastic card issued by a bank to its customers for use in a CASHPOINT machine. Each card has a code that the owner taps into the machine to get money out: *Never tell anyone the number of your cashcard.*

/ˈkæʃkɑːd/
pl cashcards
(also **cash card**)
⧓ use a **cashcard**

---

cash crop *noun* (agriculture)

the produce grown by farmers who intend to sell it rather than use it themselves: *grow coffee, potatoes, tomatoes, etc as a cash crop*

/ˈkæʃ krɒp/
pl cash crops
⧓ grow (something) as a **cash crop**
▶ **main crop, produce**[1]

---

cash deal *noun* (stock exchange)
▶ **cash settlement**

/ˈkæʃ diːl/

cash-deposit ratio *noun* (banking)
▶ **cash ratio**

/ˌkæʃ dɪˈpɒzɪt ˌreɪʃiəʊ/

cash discount *noun* (commerce)
a price reduction given if a buyer pays immediately or before a certain date: *Our prices are already low, but we also offer a 5% cash discount for prompt payment.*

/ˌkæʃ ˈdɪskaʊnt/
pl cash discounts
⧓ give, offer a **cash discount**
▶ **discount[1] 1**

cash dispenser *noun* (banking)
▶ **cashpoint**

/ˈkæʃ dɪˌspensə(r)/

cash flow *noun* (accounting)
the amount of money moving into and out of a business at a particular point in time: *Problems of cash flow are causing businesses to delay payments during the recession.* ○ *It is important to plan your cash flow carefully.*

/ˈkæʃ fləʊ/
note no plural
⧓ **cash flow** problems; a high, low, strong **cash flow**
▶ **discounted cash flow**

cash market *noun* (stock exchange)
▶ **spot market**

/ˈkæʃ ˌmɑːkɪt/

cash on delivery *noun* (commerce)
an arrangement by which goods are sent to a buyer on condition that they are paid for when they arrive: *The conditions of payment are cash on delivery.*

/ˌkæʃ ɒn dɪˈlɪvəri/
abbr COD, C.O.D., cod
note no plural
⧓ pay **cash on delivery**
syn (*US*) collect on delivery
▶ **cash with order**

cashpoint *noun* (banking)
a place inside or outside a bank where customers may get money out of their accounts by putting a card into a cash machine: *The bank was closed so I got some money out of the cashpoint.*

/ˈkæʃpɔɪnt/
pl cashpoints
⧓ get money from, get money out of, use the **cashpoint**
syn cash dispenser, automatic teller machine
▶ **cash card**

cash price *noun* (commerce)
the price a seller will accept if payment is made immediately: *By paying the cash price I was able to buy the furniture for less than if I'd bought on credit.* ○ *a cash price of $500*

/ˌkæʃ ˈpraɪs/
pl cash prices
▶ **cost price, price[1]**

cash ratio *noun* (banking)
the relationship between the amount of money a bank holds in cash and the total amount it holds in deposits and investments: *The bank maintains a cash ratio of 10%.*

/ˈkæʃ ˌreɪʃiəʊ/
pl cash ratios
⧓ have, keep, maintain a **cash ratio**
syn cash-deposit ratio, liquidity ratio
▶ **advances ratio, ratio**

cash register *noun* (commerce)
▶ **till**

/ˈkæʃ ˌredʒɪstə(r)/

cash sale *noun* (commerce)
a sale where payment is made immediately in banknotes or coins: *The customer paid at once and was given a receipt for a cash sale. ○ cash sales of records and cassettes*

/ˌkæʃ ˈseɪl/
pl cash sales
⧓ make a **cash sale**
▶ **credit sale, sale**

---

cash settlement *noun* (stock exchange)
a stock exchange transaction where payment is required immediately, instead of payment on the next ACCOUNT DAY: *The dealer in gilts required a cash settlement for the investment we made.*

/ˈkæʃ ˌsetlmənt/
pl cash settlements
⧓ offer a **cash settlement**
syn cash deal
▶ **settlement 2, settlement day**

---

cash statement *noun* (accounting)
a record made by a cashier at the end of a day's business to show details of money kept rather than put in the bank: *When the last customer had gone the cashier prepared the cash statement.*

/ˈkæʃ ˌsteɪtmənt/
pl cash statements
⧓ prepare, write out a **cash statement**
▶ **bank statement,** cash up *under* **cash**[2]

---

cash surrender value *noun* (insurance)
▶ **surrender value**

/ˌkæʃ səˈrendə ˌvæljuː/

---

cash voucher *noun* (commerce)
1 a document showing that goods or services have been paid for: *The plumber signed a cash voucher to show that payment had been made for the repair work.* **2** a coupon that gives someone a reduction in the price of certain specified goods: *a cash voucher for 20p off a packet of soap powder*

/ˈkæʃ ˌvaʊtʃə(r)/
pl cash vouchers
1 ⧓ ask for, receive, sign a **cash voucher**
▶ **receipt 1**
2 ⧓ exchange, use a **cash voucher**
▶ **gift voucher, voucher**

---

cash with order *noun* (commerce)
a statement by a supplier saying that requests for goods or services must be accompanied by payment: *Please do not ask for credit as our terms are strictly cash with order.*

/ˌkæʃ wɪð ˈɔːdə(r)/
abbr CWO
⧓ pay, send **cash with order**
syn payment with order
▶ **cash on delivery**

---

casting vote *noun* (administration)
a deciding vote, usually given by the chairperson when votes for and against something are equal: *We couldn't proceed until the director used his casting vote in favour of the proposal.*

/ˌkɑːstɪŋ ˈvəʊt/
pl casting votes
⧓ give, have, use a **casting vote**
▶ **vote**[1]

---

casual *adjective* (personnel)
(of work, workers, etc) temporary or irregular: *earn a living doing casual labour ○ Men waited near the building site, hoping to be taken on as casual labour.*

/ˈkæʒuəl/
⧓ a **casual** labourer, worker; **casual** labour, work
▶ **labour, manual**[1]**, temp**[1]

---

catalog *noun*
(*US*) ▶ **catalogue**

/ˈkætəlɒg/
pl catalogues

catalogue[1] *noun* (commerce)
a list, usually in a special order, of items for sale or on display. It is often in the form of a book or booklet and gives a description (and sometimes a picture and the price) of each item: *After studying the catalogue, we decided to order a set of furniture.* ○ *Please send for our free catalogue.*

/ˈkætəlɒɡ/
pl catalogues
abbr cat.
⋈ an exhibition, an illustrated, a mail order **catalogue**; mail, produce, send out a **catalogue**
(*US* **catalog**)
▶ **prospectus**

---

catalogue[2] *verb* (office practice)
to make a list of items, usually in alphabetical or some other logical order: *The company librarian has just catalogued all our training manuals.*

/ˈkætəlɒɡ/
catalogue, cataloguing, catalogued
(*US* **catalog, cataloging, cataloged**)
note transitive verb
⋈ **catalogue** books, pictures, records

---

catch a cold *verb* (commerce)
to lose money in a business deal: *The price of shares has fallen heavily today and many recent investors are likely to catch a cold.*

/ˌkætʃ ə ˈkəʊld/
catch, catching, caught
⋈ investors, shareholders **catch a cold**

---

catching bargain *noun* (law)
▶ **unconscionable bargain**

/ˌkætʃɪŋ ˈbɑːɡən/

---

caterer *noun* (commerce)
a person or business that supplies and serves food and drink at a large event: *The caterers arrived early to set up their tables before the guests appeared.*

/ˈkeɪtərə(r)/
pl caterers
⋈ hire a **caterer**

---

catering *noun* (commerce)
the business of supplying food and drink to be consumed at a particular place or event: *Catering at major sports events is becoming increasingly profitable.*

/ˈkeɪtərɪŋ /
note not used with *a* or *an*. No plural and used with a singular verb only.
⋈ the **catering** business, industry, trade; hotel, office, restaurant **catering**; a **catering** manager; **catering** staff

---

caution money *noun* (commerce)
money offered by someone to show that he/she is honest and truthful and will keep to all agreed terms and conditions: *Members of the association must deposit caution money before being allowed to use the association's facilities.*

/ˈkɔːʃn ˌmʌni/
note not used with *a* or *an*. No plural and used with a singular verb only.
⋈ deposit, pay **caution money**
▶ **money**

---

caveat *noun* (law)
a warning given to parties to a contract or legal procedure that there may be problems or restrictions they do not know about: *The solicitor drew his client's attention to a caveat in the contract regarding planning permission.*

/ˈkæviæt/
pl caveats
⋈ enter, issue, put in a **caveat**
▶ **contract 1**

CBA *abbr* (accounting)
cost-benefit analysis

/ˌsiː biː ˈeɪ/

CBI *abbr* (industry)
Confederation of British Industry

/ˌsiː biː ˈaɪ/

cc *abbr* (office practice)
carbon copy

/ˌsiː ˈsiː/

CCA *abbr* (accounting)
current cost accounting

/ˌsiː siː ˈeɪ/

CD *abbr* (banking)
Certificate of Deposit

/ˌsiː ˈdiː/

c/d *abbr*
1 (*accounting*) carried down **2** (*stock exchange*) cum dividend

note used in written English only

cd/fwd *abbr* (accounting)
carried forward

note used in written English only

CEEFAX *noun* (computing)
(in the UK) a service provided by the BBC (British Broadcasting Corporation) allowing people to obtain news, information about market prices, the weather, etc on their television screens: *We can consult CEEFAX for the latest news reports.*

/ˈsiːfæks/
⋈ consult, use **CEEFAX**
▶ **Prestel, Teletext, Videotex, Viewdata**

ceiling *noun* (commerce)
an upper limit: *The OPEC members have tried to put a ceiling on oil production.* ○ *raise the ceiling on tax-free earnings*

/ˈsiːlɪŋ/
pl ceilings
⋈ impose, put a **ceiling (on something)**
▶ **maximum**

center *noun*
(*US*) ▶ **centre**

/ˈsentə(r)/

central bank *noun* (banking)
the most important bank in a country because it issues and manages currency, influences the base lending rate and helps to carry out the government's financial policy: *The central bank's lead in raising the base lending rate has been followed by the commercial banks.*

/ˌsentrəl ˈbæŋk/
pl central banks
▶ **bank[1], Bank of England, Federal Reserve Bank, base rate 2**

centralization *noun* (administration)
the control of all the parts of an organization by the staff of one main office, where all major decisions are made: *The company is moving towards greater centralization with a head office in London.*

/ˌsentrəlaɪˈzeɪʃn/
note not used with *a* or *an*. No plural and used with a singular verb only.
⋈ greater, increased **centralization**

central processing unit *noun* (computing)
the part of a computer that controls all the other parts of the system: *The central processing unit of our computer is faulty and we are unable to complete the salary statements today.*

/ˌsentrəl ˈprəʊsesɪŋ ˌjuːnɪt/
abbr CPU, C.P.U.
pl central processing units
▶ **computer, mainframe, terminal 1**

centre *noun* (commerce)
a place where certain activities or facilities are concentrated: *New York is the financial centre of the USA.* ○ *build a new shopping centre*

/ˈsentə(r)/
pl centres
(*US* **center**)
⋈ a business, a commercial, an industrial, a shopping **centre**

---

cert. *abbr* (administration)
certificate

/sɜːt/

---

certificate *noun* (administration)
a written or printed paper issued by an authority as proof of something: *a certificate of ownership* ○ *She received a certificate to show that she had attended the training course.*

/səˈtɪfɪkət/
pl certificates
abbr cert.
⋈ be awarded, issue, receive a **certificate**
► **document, share certificate**

---

certificate of damage *noun* (insurance/shipping)
► **damage certificate**

/səˌtɪfɪkət əv ˈdæmɪdʒ/

---

certificate of deposit *noun* (banking)
a transferable document issued by a bank as evidence that a large sum of money has been lent to the bank for a fixed period: *Certificates of deposit have proved attractive to investors because they offer good rates of interest.*

/səˈtɪfɪkət əv dɪˈpɒzɪt/
pl certificates of deposit
abbr CD
⋈ issue, negotiate a **certificate of deposit**
► **deposit[1] 1, memorandum of deposit**

Certificate of Incorporation *noun* (law)
a document issued by the Registrar of Companies to the shareholders of a company, legalizing the existence of the company: *The company has received its Certificate of Incorporation and may now start trading.*

/səˌtɪfɪkət əv ɪnˌkɔːpəˈreɪʃn/
pl Certificates of Incorporation
syn (*US*) corporation charter
► **declaration of compliance, Registrar of Companies**

---

certificate of insurance *noun* (insurance)
a document issued by an insurance company as proof of the existence of an insurance contract and summarizing the details of it: *The driver of the crashed car was asked by the police to show them his certificate of insurance.*

/səˌtɪfɪkət əv ɪnˈʃʊərəns/
pl certificates of insurance
abbr C of I
⋈ issue, require, show a **certificate of insurance**
► **insurance**

---

certificate of origin *noun* (international trade)
a document that shows where goods were made: *Before we could clear the goods through customs we had to show the certificate of origin.*

/səˌtɪfɪkət əv ˈɒrɪdʒɪn/
pl certificates of origin
abbr c/o
⋈ issue, require, show a **certificate of origin**
► **negative certificate of origin**

---

certificate of ownership *noun* (shipping)
► **ship's certificate of registry**

/səˌtɪfɪkət əv ˈəʊnəʃɪp/

---

certified accountant *noun* (accounting)
(*UK*) a person who is a member of the Association of Certified Accountants and is therefore qualified to keep books of account

/ˌsɜːtɪfaɪd əˈkaʊntənt/
pl certified accountants

and to audit accounts: *The company's accounts are now being audited by a certified accountant.*

▶ **accountant, chartered accountant**

---

certified cheque *noun* (banking)
a cheque marked by the bank it is drawn on as 'Good for payment': *The seller will only accept a certified cheque.*

/ˌsɜːtɪfaɪd ˈtʃek/
pl certified cheques
(*US* **certified check**)
⋈ accept a **certified cheque**
syn (*UK*) marked cheque
▶ **cheque**

---

certified copy *noun* (law)
an exact copy of a document with an official declaration that it is authentic: *a certified copy of a birth certificate, a death certificate, an insurance policy, etc*

/ˌsɜːtɪfaɪd ˈkɒpi/
pl certified copies
⋈ issue, make, produce a **certified copy**
syn attested copy
▶ **copy[1] 1**

---

certify *verb* (law)
to state formally, usually in writing, that something is true and genuine: *The student asked the college to certify a copy of the examination results.* ○ *The doctor certified that the patient was unfit for work.*

/ˈsɜːtɪfaɪ/
certify, certifying, certified
note transitive verb
▶ **attest, authenticate, validate, witness[2] 2**

CF *abbr* (transport)
carriage forward

/ˌsiː ˈef/

---

cf *abbr*
compare: *A bill of exchange (cf promissory note) is negotiable.*

note used in written English only

---

c/f *abbr* (commerce)
cost and freight

note used in written English only

---

cge *abbr* (transport)
carriage

note used in written English only

---

cgo *abbr* (transport)
cargo

note used in written English only

CGT *abbr* (tax)
capital gains tax

/ˌsiː dʒiː ˈtiː/

---

chain store *noun* (retail)
one of a number of similar shops belonging to the same company: *It's a chain store, so you will be able to change the shirt in your town if it does not fit.* ○ *Marks and Spencers is a chain store.*

/ˈtʃeɪn stɔː(r)/
pl chain stores
▶ **department store, store[1] 2**

---

chair[1] *noun* (administration)
1 the chair (**a**) a chairperson: *The chair has the deciding vote.* ○ *Please address your comments to the chair.* (**b**) the seat occupied by the person conducting a meeting: *Who is in the chair today?* ○ *Who is going to take the chair?* **2** the post held by a university professor: *He was offered the chair in economics.* ○ *Who holds the chair in sociology?*

/tʃeə(r)/
1 note singular noun, used with a singular verb
⋈ address, leave, take, vacate the **chair**

---

chair² *verb* (administration)
to act as a chairperson; to preside over a meeting or gathering: *They haven't yet decided who is to chair the meeting.* ○ *Who chaired the meeting last week?*

/tʃeə(r)/
chair, chairing, chaired
note transitive verb
⋈ **chair** a debate, meeting

---

chairman, chairperson, chairwoman
noun (administration)
1 (*UK*) the chief officer of a company who is responsible for deciding and carrying out company policy: *become chairman of an international company* **2** the man or woman who presides over a meeting: *The chairperson of the society is elected annually.*

/ˈtʃeəmən, ˈtʃeəˌpɜːsn, ˈtʃeəˌwʊmən/
pl chairmen, chairwomen, chairpersons
note Chairperson is used to avoid sexual bias, but when addressing the chair it is usual to say 'Mr Chairman' or 'Madam Chair' as appropriate.
1 syn (*US*) president
▶ **managing director**

---

chamber of commerce *noun* (commerce)
an association of local business people, formed to promote and protect their interests: *The local chamber of commerce decided to protest against plans to pedestrianize the shopping centre.*

/ˌtʃeɪmbər əv ˈkɒmɜːs/
▶ **International Chamber of Commerce, London Chamber of Commerce**

---

the Channel Tunnel *noun* (transport)
a railway tunnel under the English Channel joining England and France: *The Channel Tunnel could have as big an impact as the first railways in the nineteenth century.*

/ðə ˌtʃænl ˈtʌnl/
syn (*informal*) Chunnel
⋈ the **Channel Tunnel** link; **Channel Tunnel** links, services

---

CHAPS *abbr* (banking)
Clearing House Automated Payment System

/tʃæps/
note pronounced as a word. The abbreviation is used more often than the full term.

---

charge¹ *noun*
1 (*commerce*) a price asked for goods or services: *What is the charge for left luggage?* ○ *Cheques may now be cashed at most hotels for a small charge.* ○ *Our advice is free of charge* (ie you do not have to pay for it). **2** (*law*) a formal accusation that someone has committed a crime: *The treasurer is facing a charge of theft.* ○ *bring a charge against someone* ○ *deny charges of fraud* **3** (*law*) a legal right over assets belonging to another person: *The bank took a charge on the company's inventory.*

(be) in charge of someone/something be in control of or responsible for someone/something

take charge of someone/something to take control of or responsibility for someone/something

/tʃɑːdʒ/
pl charges
1 ⋈ an annual, a maximum, a minimum, a monthly, a standard, a weekly **charge**
▶ **dues 1, fee, landing charge, service charge, surcharge**
2 ⋈ a **charge** *of* (something), *against* (someone); a criminal **charge**
3 ⋈ take a **charge**
▶ **fixed charge, floating charge, lien, mortage, pledge**

---

charge² *verb*
1 (*commerce*) to ask for payment for goods or services: *The bank charges 1% for changing traveller's cheques.* ○ *What do you charge for car hire?* **2** (*accounting*) to record a debit in an account: *Interest on the overdraft is charged to the current account.* **3** (*law*) to accuse someone of a crime: *The police have charged them with fraud.*

/tʃɑːdʒ/
charge, charging, charged
note transitive verb
2 syn debit
3 ⋈ to **charge** (someone) *with* (something)

charge account *noun* (retail)
▶ **credit account**

/ˈtʃɑːdʒ əˌkaʊnt/
pl charge accounts

charge card *noun* (retail)
a plastic card issued by a shop and produced by a customer when buying something that they will pay for later: *To save time at the supermarket checkout I always pay by charge card.*

/ˈtʃɑːdʒ kɑːd/
(also **chargecard**)
pl charge cards
▶ **cheque card, credit card, debit card**

charitable trust *noun* (law)
an organization formed to raise money for people in need or to finance cultural, educational or sports activities. In the UK registration with the Charity Commissioners is required: *scholarship money provided by a charitable trust*

/ˌtʃærətəbl ˈtrʌst/
pl charitable trusts
⋈ form, set up a **charitable trust**
▶ **trust**

chart[1] *noun*
1 (*administration*) a map, graph, diagram or table giving clear information, esp about something that changes over a period of time: *The chart shows how our sales figures have improved over the last six months.* **2** (*shipping*) a map of the sea, coasts and rivers, used to find your way by ship: *The chart shows shallow water in the estuary.*

/tʃɑːt/
pl charts
1 an organization, a progress, a sales **chart**
▶ **bar chart, flow chart, pie chart, table**
2 a navigation **chart**

chart[2] *verb*
1 (*administration*) to record information on a graph, diagram or map: *Production figures for last month are now being charted.* **2** (*shipping*) to make a map of the sea, coasts and rivers: *The survey ship has returned from charting the western coastline.*

/tʃɑːt/
chart, charting, charted
note transitive verb
1 ⋈ **chart** figures, information

charter[1] *noun*
1 (*law*) a document, issued by the ruling authority in a country, that formally accepts the existence of a town, a university or other organization: *A charter was granted to the town many years ago.* **2** (*law*) a set of rules and guidelines showing how an organization should function: *Under the new charter all employees must sign a contract of employment.* **3** (*transport*) (the hiring of) a ship, plane, train or coach for business or holiday transport: *The next plane due to arrive is a charter from Bombay.*

/ˈtʃɑːtə(r)/
pl charters
2 syn constitution
3 ⋈ **charter** airline, company, fee, flight
▶ **time charter, voyage charter**

charter[2] *verb*
1 (*law*) to grant a charter to a person or an organization **2** (*transport*) to hire a ship, plane, train or coach for business or holiday transport: *The travel agency is going to charter a plane to bring the holidaymakers home.*

/ˈtʃɑːtə(r)/
charter, chartering, chartered
note transitive verb
2 ⋈ **charter** a boat, plane, ship
▶ **charter**[1] **2, 3, hire**[2]

chartered accountant *noun* (accounting)
in the UK, a person who is a member of the Institute of Chartered Accountants and is therefore qualified to keep books of account: *A chartered accountant is auditing the company's annual accounts.*

/ˌtʃɑːtəd əˈkaʊntənt/
pl chartered accountants
▶ **accountant, certified accountant**

cheap *adjective*
1 low in price: *If you want to buy cheap food go to the supermarket.* **2** worth more than it costs; good value: *If that's all you paid for it, it was very cheap.* **3** of poor quality: *These cheap shoes are wearing out already.*

/tʃiːp/
1 syn inexpensive
opp expensive
2 ▶ **bargain**[1] **1**

cheap money *noun* (finance)
money easily available on loan and at a low rate of interest: *During a period of cheap money some borrowers took on loans they now find difficult to pay back.*

/ˌtʃiːp ˈmʌni/
note not used with *a* or *an*. No plural and used with a singular verb only.
⋈ a **cheap money** policy
opp dear money
► **easy money, money**

check[1] *noun*
1 (*banking*) (*US*) cheque **2** a slowing down or stopping: *Public spending has been held in check.* **3** an inspection or examination of the condition of something: *All our machines are given regular checks.* **4** (*US*) a bill issued in a restaurant: *Ask the waiter for the check.*

check-in 1 the act of registering arrival at a hotel, an airport or a place of work: *What time is check-in?* **2** the area where this takes place: *the check-in desk*

check-out 1 the act of departing from a hotel, an airport, a place of work **2** the place where customers pay for goods in a supermarket: *Please pay at the check-out.*

/tʃek/
pl checks
1 ► **cheque**
3 ⋈ a regular, routine, security **check**

check[2] *verb*
1 to slow down or stop the progress of something: *The rise in unemployment has been checked.* **2** to examine the state of something: *I'll just check if there are any more in the storeroom.* ○ *You should have your car brakes checked regularly.*

check in to register arrival at a hotel, an airport or a place of work: *We arrived at the hotel and checked in.* ○ *Office staff are expected to check in before eight-thirty.*

check out to register departure from a hotel or place of work: *Departing guests are asked to check out by noon.*

/tʃek/
check, checking, checked
note transitive verb
► **clock on, clock off**

check card *noun* (banking)
(*US*) ► **cheque card**

/ˈtʃek kɑːd/

checking account *noun*
(*US*) (*banking*) ► **current account**

/ˈtʃekɪŋ əˌkaʊnt/

checklist *noun*
a list of names or items to be marked as present or as having been dealt with: *Before starting the machine, the operator referred to the checklist to be sure that all safety precautions had been followed.* ○ *a checklist of things to take on the business trip*

/ˈtʃek lɪst/
pl checklists
⋈ add something to, go through, refer to, tick something off a **checklist**
► **list**

cheque *noun* (banking)
a special printed form filled in and signed by a person (the DRAWER) asking a bank (the DRAWEE) to pay a sum of money to someone (the PAYEE): *The electricity bill may be paid in cash or by cheque.* ○ *write a cheque for £50*

/tʃek/
pl cheques
(*US* **check**)
⋈ cross, endorse, honour, issue, sign, stop, write a **cheque**
► **blank cheque, certified cheque, crossed cheque, open cheque, stale cheque, stopped cheque, traveller's cheque**

cheque card *noun* (banking)
a card issued by a bank to an account holder, showing the holder's signature. It guarantees that the bank will HONOUR any cheque written by the holder up to a pre-arranged limit: *Cheques will only be accepted if accompanied by a cheque card.*

/ˈtʃek kɑːd/
pl cheque cards
syn (*US*) check card, bank card, banker's card, cheque guarantee card
▶ **charge card, credit card, debit card**

---

chip *noun*
1 (*computing*) a very small piece of silicon material with a complex electrical circuit, used in computers: *The use of chips in constructing computers has made pocket-size computers a reality.* **2** (*stock exchange*) (*informal*) a share in a business: *Small investors were allocated only a hundred chips maximum.*

/tʃɪp/
pl chips
1 syn microchip
2 ▶ **blue chip**

CHIPS *abbr* (banking)
(*US*) Clearing House Inter-bank Payment System

/tʃɪps/
note pronounced as a word. The abbreviation is used more often than the full term.

---

chunnel *noun* (transport)
(*informal*) ▶ **the Channel Tunnel**

/ˈtʃʌnl/

CIF *abbr* (commerce)
cost insurance freight

/ˌsiː aɪ ˈef/
note pronounced as individual letters

---

circuit *noun*
1 (*technology*) a path along which an electric current flows: *There is a break in the circuit and the light has gone out.* **2** (*technology*) the apparatus through which an electric current passes: *build an electrical circuit*

/ˈsɜːkɪt/
pl circuits
⧓ a **circuit** board, breaker

---

circular *noun* (administration)
a printed letter, notice or advertisement sent to a large number of people: *The circular was sent to everyone in the company.*

/ˈsɜːkjələ(r)/
pl circulars
⧓ distribute, send a **circular**
▶ **mailshot**

---

circular letter of credit *noun* (banking/commerce)
▶ **letter of credit**

/ˌsɜːkjələ ˌletər əv ˈkredɪt/
pl circular letters of credit

---

circulating capital *noun* (finance)
▶ **current capital**

/ˌsɜːkjəleɪtɪŋ ˈkæpɪtl/

---

circulation *noun*
1 the distribution and movement of goods, money, etc: *The old banknotes are being withdrawn from circulation.* ○ *There aren't many of these old machines in circulation now.* **2** the number of copies of a newspaper, magazine, etc sold to the public: *a newspaper with a daily circulation of one million*

/ˌsɜːkjəˈleɪʃn/
1 ⧓ come into, go out of **circulation**
▶ **active circulation, income velocity of circulation, transactions velocity of circulation, velocity of circulation**
2 ⧓ a limited, small, wide **circulation**; **circulation** figures
▶ **Audit Bureau of Circulation, readership**

the City *noun* (finance)
the oldest part of London, the financial centre of the UK, where the International Stock Exchange, the major banks and insurance companies are: *He works in the City.* ○ *Reports from the City show a general fall in share prices.*

/ðə ˈsɪti/
▶ **Wall Street**

City Code on Takeovers and Mergers *noun* (stock exchange)
a set of regulations, agreed by the International Stock Exchange, ensuring that companies act fairly and honestly when attempting to buy or combine with other companies: *Failure by some dealers to observe the City Code on Takeovers and Mergers has led to demands for the government to step in with tough legislation.*

/ˌsɪti ˌkəʊd ɒn ˌteɪkəʊvəz ənd ˈmɜːdʒəz/
▶ **acquisition, merger, Monopolies and Mergers Commission, takeover**

---

the Civil Service *noun* (administration)
all government departments apart from the armed forces: *The government has announced pay rises for members of the Civil Service.* ○ *She works in the Civil Service.*

/ðə ˌsɪvl ˈsɜːvɪs/
abbr CS
⋈ a **Civil Service** job, position, post

---

claim[1] *noun*
1 (*insurance*) a demand for a sum of money from an insurance company: *He made an insurance claim after the car accident.* **2** (*law*) a demand for something that is legally due: *a claim for a share in an inheritance* ○ *a claim to the right to mine land and extract minerals* **3** (*industrial relations*) a demand for higher wages or better working conditions: *The trade union put in a claim for a shorter working week.*

/kleɪm/
pl claims
1 ⋈ make, submit a **claim**
▶ **compensation, insurance, no-claims bonus**
2 ⋈ have a **claim**
▶ **small claims**
3 ⋈ put in a **claim**; a pay, wage **claim**

---

claim[2] *verb*
1 (*insurance*) to demand a sum of money from an insurance company: *He's claiming £2 000 from the insurance company.* ○ *Have you claimed yet?* **2** (*law*) to demand something as a legal right: *After the bank's failure many people claimed compensation.* ○ *Are you able to claim unemployment benefit?* **3** (*industrial relations*) to demand higher wages or better working conditions: *The oil-rig workers are claiming a 12% pay rise.*

/kleɪm/
claim, claiming, claimed
note usually transitive but can be an intransitive verb
1 ⋈ **claim** compensation, insurance
2 ⋈ **claim** benefit
3 ⋈ **claim** a pay rise, higher pay, higher wages

---

claimant *noun*
1 (*insurance*) a person who demands a sum of money from an insurance company: *The maximum that the claimant is entitled to is £10 000.* **2** (*law*) a person who demands something that is legally due: *The deceased person left no will and now several relatives have come forward as claimants to the estate.*

/ˈkleɪmənt/
pl claimants
2 ⋈ an illegal, a legal, a rival, a sole **claimant**

---

claims assessor *noun* (insurance)
an expert who may be consulted when assessing the amount of money to be paid by an insurer to the person insured: *The claims assessor was called in to assess the claim.*

/ˈkleɪmz əˌsesə(r)/
pl claims assessors
▶ **loss adjuster**

---

classified advertisement *noun* (advertising)
short advertisements in a newspaper or magazine placed by people offering or asking for a product or service, or who are offering or looking for employment: *You can phone the newspaper and place a classified advertisement quite cheaply.* ○ *look at the classified advertisements in the situations vacant column*

/ˌklæsɪfaɪd ədˈvɜːtɪsmənt/
pl classified advertisements
abbr classified ad
⋈ insert, place, read, reply to a **classified advertisement**

syn (*informal*) small ad
▶ **advertisement**

---

clause *noun* (law)
part of a legal document, eg a contract, that deals with a particular item or condition in it: *Clause 3 in the contract specifies the method of transportation.* ○ *There is a clause in the insurance policy excluding damage caused by negligence.*

/klɔːz/
pl clauses
abbr cl
⧓ add, include, insert a **clause**
▶ **abandonment clause, acceleration clause, assignment clause, escalation clause, escape clause**, payback clause *under* **payback**, penalty clause *under* **penalty**

---

clawback *noun* (finance)
money that has been paid out and taken back by another agency: *The new benefit will be paid to all over the age of 70, but clawback from taxation will much reduce the value of the benefit to the better-off.*

/ˈklɔːbæk/
note singular noun, used with a singular verb

---

claw back *verb* (finance)
to recover money paid out by getting it back from another agency: *Through taxation the government will claw back a quarter of the cost of increasing retirement pensions.*

/ˌklɔː ˈbæk/
claw back, clawing back, clawed back
note transitive verb

---

clean bill of health *noun*
1 a report stating that a person or an organization is fit and in good condition: *The auditors gave the company a clean bill of health.* ○ *The patient quickly recovered and was given a clean bill of health.* **2** (*shipping*) a certificate issued by a port authority stating that a ship and the port it is leaving from are free from infectious disease: *Owing to an epidemic in the port locality, the ship left without a clean bill of health.*

/ˌkliːn ˌbɪl əv ˈhelθ/
pl clean bills of health
2 ▶ **suspect bill of health**

---

clean bill of lading *noun* (shipping)
▶ **bill of lading**

/ˌkliːn ˌbɪl əv ˈleɪdɪŋ/

---

clear[1] *adjective*
1 easy to understand: *The instructions are clear.* **2** relating to an amount of money left after all expenses have been paid: *a clear profit of 60%* **3** complete: *Please allow four clear days for delivery.*

/klɪə(r)/

---

clear[2] *verb*
1 (*commerce*) to dispose of goods: *The sale is intended to clear old stock.* **2** (*banking*) to pass a cheque through the banking system so that the transaction is completed: *The bank requires a minimum of four days to clear personal cheques.* **3** (*export/import*) to pass goods through customs: *Your baggage has been cleared through customs.* **4** (*computing*) to remove unwanted information from the memory of a computer: *Clear the screen and start again.*

/klɪə(r)/
clear, clearing, cleared
note transitive verb
2 (*UK*) ▶ **Clearing House Automatic Payments System**
(*US*) ▶ **Clearing House Inter-Bank Payment Systems**

---

clearance sale *noun* (commerce)
an event held by a trader to dispose of old stock, usually at reduced prices, to make way for new stock: *The department store is holding its end-of-season clearance sale.*

/ˈklɪərəns seɪl/
pl clearance sales
▶ **closing-down sale, sale**

clearing *noun* (banking)
a process by which cheques and other payments are passed through the banking system until the transactions are completed: *The bank has received the cheque but a few days must be allowed for clearing.*

/ˈklɪərɪŋ/
note singular noun, used with a singular verb

clearing bank *noun* (banking)
a bank that belongs to a clearing house where cheques and bills from member banks are exchanged: *The four main clearing banks in the UK are Barclays, Lloyd's, Midland and National Westminster.*

/ˈklɪərɪŋ bæŋks/
pl clearing banks
► **bank**[1], **commercial bank, merchant bank, private bank**

Clearing House Automated Payment System *noun* (banking)
(*UK*) a computerized system through which details of high value cheques and credit transfers are sent between banks to be paid

/ˌklɪərɪŋ haʊs ˌɔːtəmeɪtəd ˈpeɪmənt ˌsɪstəm/
abbr CHAPS
syn (*US*) Clearing House Interbank Payment System
abbr CHIPS
note the abbreviation is pronounced as a word and is usually used in place of the full term
► **Banker's Automated Clearing System**

clerical *adjective* (administration)
relating to office staff and their work: *The company's clerical staff were given a 5% salary increase.* ○ *We need a new clerical assistant to help with the typing and filing.* ○ *Owing to a clerical error the document was wrongly filed.*

/ˈklerɪkl/
⋈ a **clerical** assistant, job, position, worker; **clerical** staff, work
► **manual**[1]

clerical assistant *noun* (administration)
a person employed in an office to do typing, filing, etc: *work as a clerical assistant*

/ˌklerɪkl əˈsɪstənt/
pl clerical assistants
► **assistant, personal assistant, secretary**

clerk *noun*
1 a person in an office whose work is to keep records and accounts: *The clerk at the reception desk dealt with the enquiry.* **2** a person in charge of the records of a town council or a court: *The Town Clerk offered legal advice to the Council.* **3** (*US*) a sales assistant in a shop or store: *Ask the sales clerk if they have a larger size.*

/klɑːk/
pl clerks
1 ⋈ a filing, shipping, wages **clerk**
► **bank clerk**
2 ⋈ Town, Magistrate's **Clerk**
3 ⋈ a sales, shop **clerk**
► **assistant 3**

client *noun*
1 a person who buys goods or services in a shop: *A good hairdresser never lacks clients.* **2** a person who uses the services of a professional such as an accountant, a solicitor, an estate agent: *The architect is meeting a client this morning.*

/ˈklaɪənt/
pl clients
1 ► **customer**
2 ⋈ receive, work for, work on behalf of a **client**

clientele *noun*
all the people who use the services of a particular firm: *The business has built up a very large clientele.*

/ˌkliːənˈtel/
note singular noun, used with a singular verb

clock on *verb* (personnel)
to register the time of your arrival at work, usually by putting a card into a time-recording machine; to start work: *The factory workers were queuing to clock on.*

/ˌklɒk ˈɒn/
clock on, clocking on, clocked on
note intransitive verb
syn clock in, (*US*) check in
opp clock off, (*US*) check out

---

clock off *verb* (personnel)
to register the time of leaving work, usually by putting a card into a time-recording machine; to stop work: *What time do you clock off tonight?*

/ˌklɒk ˈɒf/
clock off, clocking off, clocked off
note transitive verb
syn clock out, (*US*) check out
opp clock in, (*US*) check in
► **knock off**

---

closed indent *noun* (international trade)
an order given to an overseas agent to buy goods that states the name of a particular supplier: *The principal gave his agent a closed indent for the goods.*

/ˌkləʊzd ˈɪndent/
pl closed indents
⋈ give, receive a **closed indent**
opp open indent

---

closed shop *noun* (industrial relations)
a workplace where only members of a particular trade union are allowed to work: *The trade union would not call off the strike until the management agreed to operate a closed shop.*

/ˌkləʊzd ˈʃɒp/
pl closed shops
⋈ abolish, establish, form a **closed shop**; a **closed shop** agreement, policy
► **open shop**

---

closing down sale *noun* (commerce)
an event arranged by a trader to dispose of all stock, usually at low prices, before going out of business: *People crowded into the closing down sale looking for bargains.*

/ˌkləʊzɪŋ ˈdaʊn seɪl/
pl closing down sales
⋈ hold a **closing down sale**
syn winding-up sale
► **clearance sale, sale**

---

closure *noun*
the act of bringing something to an end: *A slump in business has led to the closure of many factories.*

/ˈkləʊʒə(r)/
pl closures
⋈ face, result in **closure**; factory, pit, shop **closures**

Co *abbr* (industry)
1 company: *Jenkins & Co, furniture-makers* **2** county: *Co Down, Northern Ireland*

/kəʊ/
2 note used in written English only

---

c/o *abbr*
1 care of; used to address a letter to someone staying at someone else's house: *Mr Brown, c/o Mr and Mrs Phillips* **2** (*international trade*) certificate of origin

note used in written English only

---

co- *prefix*
together with (someone or something). It is often used to describe someone who shares a job with another person: *co-director, co-driver*

/kəʊ/

COBOL *abbr* (computing)
an acronym for Common Business Oriented Language, used to write computer programs: *Most data processing programs are written in COBOL.*

/ˈkəʊbɒl/
note pronounced as a word
▶ **ALGOL, BASIC, FORTRAN, PASCAL**

COD *abbr* (commerce)
(*UK*) cash on delivery

/ˌsiː əʊ ˈdiː/
note pronounced as individual letters

C of I *abbr* (insurance)
certificate of insurance

note used in written English only

---

collateral *noun* (banking/finance)
property or an item of value (an ASSET) that can be claimed by a person, bank or other organization if a loan is not repaid: *The bank is holding the deeds of our house as collateral for the loan.*

/kəˈlætərəl/
note singular noun, used with a singular verb
⋈ ask for, offer, use something as **collateral**
syn collateral security
▶ **guarantee[1] 3, security 3**

---

colleague *noun*
a person that you work with in a profession or business: *I had lunch with two of my colleagues.* ○ *I'd like you to meet my colleague David Smith.*

/ˈkɒliːg/
pl colleagues
⋈ a professional **colleague**
▶ **associate[1] 1, counterpart, partner**

---

collective bargaining *noun* (industrial relations)
negotiation between an employer and a trade union about pay and working conditions: *Management wanted to replace collective bargaining with individual discussion.*

/kəˌlektɪv ˈbɑːgənɪŋ/
note not used with *a* or *an*. No plural and used with a singular verb only.
▶ **bargain[2] 2, bargaining power, trade union**

---

collect on delivery *noun* (commerce)
(*US*) ▶ **cash on delivery**

/kəˌlekt ɒn dɪˈlɪvəri/

COMECON *abbr* (international trade)
an acronym for Council for Mutual Economic Assistance, an organization set up in Moscow in 1949 to promote trade and development in its member countries: *Members of COMECON attended a meeting in Moscow.*

/ˈkɒmikɒn/
note pronounced as a word
⋈ a **COMECON** country, member

---

command economy *noun* (economics)
▶ **planned economy**

/kəˈmɑːnd ɪˌkɒnəmi/

---

commerce *noun* (commerce)
the buying and selling of goods and services between people, businesses and countries and the activities of banks, insurers and other organizations that contribute to this: *The growth of commerce between member states in the Community is remarkable.*

/ˈkɒmɜːs/
note not used with *a* or *an*. No plural and used with a singular verb only.
▶ **Chamber of Commerce, business 2, trade**

---

commercial[1] *adjective* (commerce)
1 relating to the buying and selling of goods and services: *Commercial activity is expected to intensify towards Christmas.* **2** relating to the possibility of making a profit: *Gold has been*

/kəˈmɜːʃl/
1 ⋈ **commercial** activity
▶ **mercantile**
2 ⋈ a **commercial** failure, success

discovered by the prospectors but not in commercial quantities. ○ *He has a commercial interest in the project.*

► **industrial**

---

commercial[2] *noun*

/kəˈmɜːʃl/

pl commercials

1 (*advertising*) an advertisement on television, radio or in a cinema: *Every fifteen minutes the programme was interrupted for the showing of commercials.* **2** (*stock exchange*) a share in a company dealing in consumer goods: *In the City today commercials rose slightly but there was little interest in industrials.*

1 ⧓ a **commercial** break

► **advertisement**

⧓ **commercial** radio

---

commercial bank *noun* (banking)

/kəˌmɜːʃl ˈbæŋk/

pl commercial banks

a bank that provides many different services for its customers, eg providing bank accounts and credit cards, arranging loans, etc and acts as a profit-making company. In the UK, most of the banks seen in the high street and used by the public are commercial banks: *The commercial banks have announced a cut in lending rates.* ○ *Lloyd's is one of the major commercial banks in the UK.*

syn high street bank, joint-stock bank

► **bank[1], clearing bank, merchant bank, private bank, state bank**

---

commercial bill *noun* (commerce)

/kəˈmɜːʃl bɪl/

► **trade bill**

---

commercial law *noun* (law)

/kəˌmɜːʃl ˈlɔː/

pl commercial laws

a group of laws relating to banking, insurance, buying and selling, making contracts, establishing and running a business, etc: *a solicitor specializing in commercial law*

syn mercantile law

► **company law, law**

---

commercial monopoly *noun* (economics)

/kəˌmɜːʃl məˈnɒpəli/

► **monopoly**

---

commercial traveller *noun* (commerce)

/kəˌmɜːʃl ˈtrævlə(r)/

pl commercial travellers

(*UK dated*) a person who travels around an area selling goods or showing samples to try to obtain orders: *Our commercial travellers have visited every shop in the eastern region.*

► **door-to-door salesman, representative 3, salesman, sales representative, travelling salesman**

---

commission[1] *noun*

/kəˈmɪʃn/

pl commissions

1 (*commerce*) a payment made to someone for providing a service or goods. The amount is usually a percentage of the total value of the deal: *The estate agent required 2% commission on the proceeds from the sale of the house.* ○ *The bank charges a commission for exchanging foreign currency.* ○ *He's on commission* (ie the amount he gets paid depends on how much he sells). **2** (*law*) (**a**) a group of people, organizations or countries who come together for a particular purpose: *the European Commission* ○ *the Forestry Commission* (**b**) a group of people brought together to investigate a problem and report on it: *a Royal Commission on environmental pollution* **3** a task given to someone to do: *a commission to design new stationery for the company*

1 ⧓ get a **commission**

► **fee**

2 ► **Monopolies and Mergers Commission**

3 ⧓ accept, offer someone a **commission**

---

commission[2] *verb*

/kəˈmɪʃn/

commission, commissioning, commissioned

to give a person or an organization a task to do; to bring something into operation: *The artist was commissioned to design a new logo.* ○ *The oil company has commissioned a new tanker.*

note transitive verb

---

committee *noun*
a group of people chosen to represent others in organizing affairs that concern them all: *She sits on* (ie is a member of) *the finance committee.* ○ *The committee is/are meeting now.*

/kəˈmɪti/
pl committees
note used with a singular or plural verb
⋈ appoint, elect, form, set up a **committee**; a **committee** meeting, member
▶ **board, commission[1] 2, council, meeting, selection committee, working party**

commodity *noun* (commerce/economics)
a raw material or manufactured product made available for use or sale: *The country exports such commodities as coffee and tea.* ○ *Cotton is no longer a cheap commodity.*

/kəˈmɒdəti/
pl commodities
⋈ a cheap, an expensive, a plentiful, a scarce **commodity**
▶ **goods, product**

commodity broker *noun* (commerce)
a person who buys and sells raw materials or manufactured products for a fee in a commodities market: *Commodity brokers in the Corn Exchange reacted swiftly to news about crop failure in N. America.*

/kəˈmɒdəti ˌbrəʊkə(r)/
pl commodity brokers
▶ **broker**

commodity market *noun* (commerce)
a place where raw materials and some manufactured goods are bought and sold for immediate or future delivery: *buy coffee on the commodity market*

/kəˈmɒdəti ˌmɑːkɪt/
pl commodity markets
syn commodities market, commodity exchange
▶ **Baltic Exchange, Baltic International Freight and Futures Exchange, exchange[1] 2, London Commmodity Exchange, London FOX, London International Financial Futures and Options Exchange, London Metal Exchange, market[1]**

Common Agricultural Policy *noun* (agriculture/international trade)
an agreement between members of the European Community to support free trade in agricultural products within the Community, and to protect their farmers against outside competition by imposing import tariffs, fixing prices and paying subsidies: *Producers outside the European Community complain that the Common Agricultural Policy discriminates against them.*

/ˌkɒmən ˌægrɪˈkʌltʃərəl ˌpɒləsi/
abbr CAP
▶ **General Agreement on Tariffs and Trade, subsidy, threshold price**

Common Market *noun* (international trade)
the European Community: *France is a member of the Common Market.*

/ˌkɒmən ˈmɑːkɪt /
▶ **European Community**

common stock *noun* (stock exchange)
(*US*) ▶ **ordinary share**

/ˌkɒmən ˈstɒk/

communication *noun*
1 exchanging information verbally or by means of a letter, telephone call, memo, fax, etc: *The tourists found communication with their hosts difficult.* **2** the letters, etc that do this: *This letter is*

/kəˌmjuːnɪˈkeɪʃn/
1 note not used with *a* or *an*. No plural and used with a singular verb only.

to confirm our recent telephone communication. **3 communications** the road, rail, aircraft, river, sea, canal, postal, radio and television systems which allow goods and passengers to be transported and information to be exchanged; the technology connected with this: *The area has been devastated by the earthquake but communications are now being restored.*

2 pl communications
⧓ a verbal, written **communication**
▶ **correspondence**
3 ⧓ a **communications** network, services, system

---

community charge *noun* (tax)
▶ **poll tax**

/kəˈmju:nəti tʃɑ:dʒ/

---

community investment *noun* (finance)
▶ **real investment**

/kəˌmju:nəti ɪnˈvestmənt/

---

commute *verb* (transport)
to travel regularly by train, bus or car between home and the place where you work: *I commute from Oxford to London each day.* ○ *Commuting a long way to work is very tiring.*

/kəˈmju:t/
commute, commuting, commuted
note intransitive verb
⧓ **commute** *by* train, bus, etc. *in* (from somewhere)

---

commuter *noun* (transport)
a person who travels regularly by train, bus or car between home and a place of work: *During the rush hour the trains are crowded with commuters.*

/kəˈmju:tə(r)/
pl commuters
⧓ **commuter** services, travel; a **commuter** train

Companies House *noun* (law/commerce)
an office in Cardiff, Wales where by law all private and public UK companies must register their names and details of their directors, shareholders, and accounts: *The newly-formed company could not lawfully begin trading until it had been registered at Companies House.*

/ˌkʌmpəniz ˈhaʊs/
syn Companies Registration Office
▶ **private limited company, public limited company**

---

company *noun* (commerce)
a legally recognized organization that makes, buys or sells goods or provides services for a profit: *They work for an engineering company.* ○ *Company profits have risen in the last two years.*

/ˈkʌmpəni/
pl companies
abbr Co
syn corporation
⧓ to form, register, set up a **company**
▶ **associate company, association 1, business 3, corporation, federation, firm, group, holding company, joint-stock company, limited company, listed company, organization 1, private limited company, public limited company, subsidiary company, unlisted company**

---

company law *noun* (law)
the group of laws that relate to the formation, conduct and control of companies: *Accountants need to be familiar with company law.*

/ˌkʌmpəni ˈlɔ:/
pl company laws
▶ **commercial law, law**

---

company secretary *noun* (management)
a person appointed by the directors of a company to keep company records as required by law and to carry out other important administrative duties: *The company secretary prepared the agenda for a meeting of the board of directors.*

/ˌkʌmpəni ˈsekrətri/
pl company secretaries
note often known as 'the Secretary'
▶ **secretary**

compensation *noun*
a payment made to help someone who is injured or whose property has been lost or damaged: *The airline passenger demanded compensation for the loss of all her luggage.* ○ *She was given £3 000 in compensation.*

/ˌkɒmpenˈseɪʃn/
note usually singular
⧓ ask for, demand, get, receive **compensation**
▶ **claim[1] 1, damages, indemnity, redundancy pay**

competitor *noun* (commerce)
a person or company that offers the same or better goods and services as another and therefore competes for the same customers: *Competitors in the book trade did their best to undercut each other's prices.* ○ *This firm is one of our biggest competitors.*

/kəmˈpetɪtə(r)/
pl competitors
⧓ a leading, major **competitor**
▶ **rival**

complainant *noun* (law)
▶ **plaintiff**

/kəmˈpleɪnənt/

complementary supply *noun* (industry)
▶ **joint supply**

/ˌkɒmplɪˌmentri səˈplaɪ/

component *noun*
any of the parts of which something is made: *a factory supplying components for the car industry* ○ *make washing machine components*

/kəmˈpəʊnənt/
pl components
⧓ an electrical **component**; make, manufacture, supply **components**
▶ **part, replacement 2**

computer *noun* (computing)
an electronic machine that can organize, store, and display information, do calculations and control other machines and processes: *All the information is stored on computer.* ○ *I use a computer most of the time at work.* ○ *The movement of goods into and out of the warehouse is controlled by computer.*

/kəmˈpjuːtə(r)/
pl computers
⧓ controlled by, stored on **computer**
▶ **central processing unit, database, hardware, mainframe, personal computer, peripheral, software, terminal, word processor**

computer analyst *noun* (computing)
▶ **systems analyst**

/kəmˈpjuːtər ˌænəlɪst/

computerate *adjective* (computing)
(*informal*) having a good knowledge of and able to understand computers: *Applicants for the position of accounts clerk must be computerate.*

/kəmˈpjuːtərət/
note formed from the words computer+literate

computerization *noun* (computing)
the use of computers to do work previously done by people: *Warehouse distribution has become far more efficient since computerization.*

/kəmˌpjuːtəraɪˈzeɪʃn/
(also **computerisation**)
note not used with *a* or *an*. No plural and used with a singular verb only.

⋈ introduce **computerization**
► **automation, mechanization**

---

computerize *verb* (computing)
to use computers to do work formerly done by people: *Stock control in the factory is now computerized.* ○ *The library is going to computerize its system of cataloguing.*

/kəmˈpjuːtəraɪz/
computerize, computerizing, computerized
(also **computerise**)
note transitive verb
⋈ a **computerized** factory, office
► **automate, mechanize**

---

computer program *noun* (computing)
a list of instructions written in a language understood by a computer and used to perform a specific task or function: *We had to write a special computer program to analyse the data.*

/kəmˈpjuːtə ˌprəʊgræm/
pl computer programs
syn program
⋈ design, write a **computer program**

---

computer programmer *noun* (computing)
a person who writes or designs computer programs: *He is a computer programmer.* ○ *She works as a computer programmer.*

/kəmˈpjuːtə ˌprəʊgræmə(r)/
pl computer programmers
syn programmer

---

concession *noun*
1 a thing granted or yielded, esp after discusssion: *After lengthy pay talks employers finally granted some concessions to staff.* **2** (*commerce*) a right given or sold to someone by the owner allowing him/her to use or operate something: *A private company now has the catering concession in the state hospital.* ○ *The oil company asked the government for a drilling concession.* **3** (*tax*) a special price or tax reduction for certain groups of people: *As a concession, taxpayers over the age of 75 have been given additional tax relief.* ○ *Student concessions/concessions for students are available.*

/kənˈseʃn/
pl concessions
1, 2 ⋈ grant, make, offer a **concession**
3 ► **tax relief**

---

condition *noun*
1 the state of something or someone: *a car in poor condition* **2** a thing needed to make something else possible: *One of the conditions of the job is that you must be able to drive.* **3** (*law*) an item in a contract or agreement that must be adhered to if it is to remain valid: *We ask for immediate delivery as one of the conditions of the sales agreement.*

/kənˈdɪʃn/
pl conditions
1 ⋈ in bad, excellent, good **condition**
► **working conditions**
2 ► **requirement**
3 ► **implied term, proviso**

---

conditional takeover bid *noun* (stock exchange)
► **takeover bid**

/kənˌdɪʃnəl ˈteɪkəʊvə bɪd/
pl conditional takeover bids

Confederation of British Industry *noun* (industry)
an association of industrial and commercial employers formed to promote British industry and represent its interests to the government: *The Confederation of British Industry appealed to the government to help small businesses.*

/kənˌfedəˌreɪʃn əv ˌbrɪtɪʃ ˈɪndəstri/
abbr CBI

---

conference *noun*
a meeting or series of meetings for people with a common interest to exchange information and make plans for the future:

/ˈkɒnfrəns/
pl conferences
⋈ a party, press, staff, trade union **conference**;

The company holds its annual conference in January each year.

in conference (with someone) having a discussion (with someone): *The manager is in conference with a customer at the moment.*

a **conference** delegate, dinner, hall, meeting, member

▶ **audio conference, sales conference, video conference**

---

confidential *adjective*

/ˌkɒnfɪˈdenʃl/

to be kept secret; not to be shared by other people: *This letter is confidential and should only be opened by the person it is addressed to.* ○ *Mark this file 'Confidential'.*

⧓ a **confidential** file, letter, memo

▶ **private 2**

---

confidentiality agreement *noun* (personnel)

/ˌkɒnfɪˌdenʃiˈæləti əˌgriːmənt/

pl confidentiality agreements

a document signed by an employee stating that he/she will not reveal any secret company information to a rival organization: *All new employees must sign a confidentiality agreement.*

⧓ abide by, break a **confidentiality agreement**

▶ **trade secret**

---

confirmed letter of credit *noun* (banking/commerce)

/kənˌfɜːmd ˌletər əv ˈkredɪt/

pl confirmed letters of credit

▶ **letter of credit**

---

conglomerate *noun* (commerce)

/kənˈglɒmərət/

pl conglomerates

a number of companies, sometimes involved with different products, joined together and run as one large company: *One of the oldest breweries has now joined an international conglomerate of drinks manufacturers.*

⧓ a chemical, construction, mining **conglomerate**; become part of, create, form, join a **conglomerate**

▶ **corporation, group, multinational**

---

conman *noun*

/ˈkɒnmæn/

pl conmen

(*informal*) a person who obtains money from someone by promising to do or provide something and then does not do it: *Have nothing to do with that company; they're a bunch of conmen.*

---

consign *verb* (distribution)

/kənˈsaɪn/

consign, consigning, consigned

note transitive verb

to send goods for delivery to a buyer: *The goods are to be consigned by air freight.*

⧓ **consign** (goods) by air, rail, sea, ship

▶ **despatch**[2]**, deliver, distribute, transport**[2]

---

consignee *noun* (distribution)

/ˌkɒnsaɪˈniː/

pl consignees

a person or an organization intended to receive goods sent: *We have informed the consignee of the delivery date.*

▶ **receiver 1, recipient**

---

consignment *noun* (distribution)

/kənˈsaɪnmənt/

pl consignments

a load of goods sent to supply a customer's order or to provide an agent with goods to sell for the owner: *The consignment of books left the airport on time.* ○ *When is the next (furniture) consignment due?*

⧓ a **consignment** *of* (goods)

▶ **shipment**

---

consignment note *noun* (distribution)

/kənˈsaɪnmənt nəʊt/

pl consignment notes

a document sent with goods, giving details of the goods and the

▶ **bill of lading, manifest, way-**

sender. It is signed by the person who receives the goods (the CONSIGNEE) to show that they have arrived.

bill, weight note

---

consignor *noun* (commerce/transport)
a person or organization that sends goods to supply a customer's order or to provide an agent with goods to sell for the owner: *The consignor has arranged delivery by air freight.*

/kənˈsaɪnə(r)/
pl consignors

---

consolidate *verb*
1 (*commerce*) to cause something to become stronger and more firmly established: *The country is now consolidating its position as a leading producer of textiles.* **2** (*finance*) to bring together the financial resources and accounts of a holding company and its subsidiaries so that the strength of the whole group is revealed: *We need to study the consolidated accounts to understand this group.*

/kənˈsɒlɪdeɪt/
consolidate, consolidating, consolidated
note transitive verb
1 ⋈ a **consolidated** position
2 ⋈ **consolidated** accounts, profit, stock

---

consortium *noun* (industry)
a temporary association of two or more companies for a major project that is too complex for any of them to do alone: *The contract was awarded to a consortium of construction and electrical generator companies.* ○ *the Channel Tunnel consortium*

/kənˈsɔːtiəm/
pl consortia *or* consortiums
⋈ become part of, enter, form, join a **consortium**
▶ **syndicate 1**

---

constitution *noun* (law)
▶ **charter[1] 2**

/ˌkɒnstɪˈtjuːʃn/

---

construction *noun* (industry)
the action of building or making something: *construction of a new road*

the construction industry the industry concerned with building houses, shops, factories, roads, bridges, tunnels, etc: *They work in/for the construction industry.* ○ *stone quarried for the construction industry*

under construction being built: *The bridge is under construction.*

/kənˈstrʌkʃn/
pl constructions
⋈ a **construction** site, worker

---

consultant *noun*
an expert who charges a fee for advice or work on a particular subject, eg management, manpower, medicine: *The company called in a tax consultant to advise them.* ○ *a firm of management consultants* ○ *a consultant to a firm, project, etc*

/kənˈsʌltənt/
pl consultants
⋈ a business, a design, an employment, a financial, a management **consultant**

---

consumer *noun* (economics)
a person who buys goods and services for her/his own use and not for resale: *Consumers have the right to return faulty goods and demand a refund from the supplier.*

/kənˈsjuːmə(r)/
pl consumers
⋈ electricity, gas **consumers**; **consumer** choice, industry, products, protection, spending
syn end user
opp producer
▶ **end-user 1, ultimate consumer**

---

consumer credit *noun* (finance)
loans made to the public by banks, shops or finance houses for the purchase of everyday items: *The latest consumer credit figures show a decline in spending.*

/kən,sju:mə 'kredɪt/
note not used with *a* or *an*. No plural and used with a singular verb only.
▶ **credit[1] 1, credit account, credit sale, hire purchase**

consumer disposables *noun* (manufacturing)
▶ **consumer non-durables**

/kən,sju:mə dɪ'spəʊzəblz/

consumer durables *noun* (manufacturing)
goods such as cars, furniture, refrigerators, televisions, etc, that last for a fairly long time: *Sales of consumer durables have increased this month.*

/kən,sju:mə 'djʊərəblz/
note plural noun, used with a plural verb
opp consumer non-durables
syn durables
▶ **household goods**

consumer good *noun* (commerce)
an item created to be used in everyday life, eg food, clothes, drinks, magazines, bicycles, toys. Services such as hairdressing and dentistry are also included as consumer goods: *Prices of consumer goods have risen by an average of 3% in the last 3 months.*

/kən'sju:mə gʊd/
pl consumer goods
syn consumption good
▶ **capital good, fast-moving consumer goods, goods, luxury goods**

consumer market *noun* (commerce)
1 the situation of buying and selling goods for personal use, not for resale: *Sales in the consumer market are beginning to improve.* **2** the buying and selling of a particular consumer product or service: *an expanding consumer market for leisure goods.*

/kən'sju:mə ,mɑ:kɪt/
note usually singular
▶ **market[1]**

consumer non-durables *noun* (manufacturing)
goods such as foods, drinks, newspapers, etc that have a short life and need to be replaced often: *Supermarkets have a fast turnover in consumer non-durables.*

/kən,sju:mə nɒn'djʊərəblz/
note usually plural
syn consumer disposables, disposables, non-durables
opp consumer durables
▶ **perishables**

Consumer Price Index *noun* (commerce)
(*US*) a set of figures showing the movement of prices of everyday goods and services bought by the public over a period of time: *Unions seeking wage increases have pointed to upward trends in the Consumer Price Index.*

/kən,sju:mə 'praɪs ,ɪndeks/
(also **consumer price index**)
abbr CPI
▶ **Cost of Living Index, Producer Price Index, Retail Price Index**

consumption *noun* (economics)
the using up of food, goods, energy and resources by people, organizations and countries: *an increase in fuel consumption* ○ *The meat was found to be unfit for human consumption.*

/kən'sʌmpʃn/
note not used with *a* or *an*. No plural and used with a singular verb only.

consumption good *noun* (commerce)
▶ **consumer good**

/kən'sʌmpʃn gʊd/

contact[1] *noun*
a person you have met or will meet, esp one who is useful: *It is important to build up a few contacts before you start your own business.* ○ *Give him a ring, he could be a useful contact.*

/'kɒntækt/
pl contacts
⋈ a business, an important, a useful **contact**

contact² *verb*
to reach someone by letter, telephone, fax, etc: *Can you be contacted by phone?* ○ *Contact me at my new address.*

/ˈkɒntækt/
contact, contacting, contacted
note transitive verb
⋈ **contact** someone *by* phone, letter, fax, etc; **contact** someone *at* (a place); a **contact** number
▶ **correspond**

---

container *noun*
1 a box, bottle or can, etc in which goods can be sold and transported: *Milk is sold in returnable bottles and disposable containers.* **2** (*transport/shipping*) a very large wooden or metal box into which a number of goods may be packed before being transported by road, rail or ship: *A variety of goods may be packed into the container before it is ready for shipment.*

/kənˈteɪnə(r)/
pl containers
⋈ empty, fill a **container**
2 ⋈ a **container** depot, lorry, port, ship, train, truck; **container** traffic; load, move, pack, shift a **container**
▶ **pallet**

---

contango *noun*
1 (*stock exchange*) the interest which a buyer pays to a seller to obtain postponement of payment until the next SETTLEMENT DAY: *The rate of interest for contango is fixed on Contango Day.* ○ *contango charges* **2** (*commerce*) the amount by which the price of a commodity for sale with immediate delivery is lower than its price for future delivery: *Brokers studied the contango before bidding for the spices.*

/kənˈtæŋgəʊ/
1 pl contangos
▶ **backwardation**
2 ⋈ **futures, new time buying, spot price**

---

contract¹ *noun* (law)
a legally binding agreement made between two or more people: *Both parties agreed to the contract.* ○ *Under the contract the building work must be completed within eighteen months.* ○ *The contract was signed on 23 January 1992.*

(be) under contract have made a binding agreement to work for a person or an organization: *I can't leave now, I'm still under contract.*

put something out to contract to offer work to someone who will sign an agreement to do it for an agreed price and within an agreed time: *This job is too big for us, we'll put it out to contract.*

tender for a contract to offer to carry out work for someone at an agreed price and within an agreed time: *We've had several tenders for the contract already.*

/ˈkɒntrækt/
pl contracts
⋈ draw up, enter into, sign, witness a **contract**; a **contract** builder, firm, worker
▶ **accord and satisfaction, adoption of contract, bond 2, breach of contract, exchange of contracts, fixed term contract, futures contract, illegal contract, leveraged currency contract, quasi-contract, subcontract**

---

contract² *verb* (law)
to make a legally binding agreement with a person or an organization: *The construction company has contracted to build a new airport terminal.* ○ *We have contracted a builder to do the work for us.*

contract out of something to withdraw from or not enter into an agreement or scheme: *The employees were allowed to contract out of the pension scheme if they wished.*

/ˈkɒntrækt, kənˈtrækt/
contract, contracting, contracted
note transitive and intransitive verb

---

contract of employment *noun* (law/personnel)
a legally binding agreement made between an employer and an employee, giving details of salary, holidays, hours of work, etc:

/ˌkɒntrækt əv ɪmˈplɔɪmənt/
pl contracts of employment
syn employment contract

The Personnel Manager went through the contract of employment with each new employee to make sure that it was fully understood before signing.

⋈ draw up, enter into, sign a **contract of employment**

► **employment**

---

control[1] *noun*

1 the power to manage, direct or command something: *Her son now has control of the business.* **2** the switches, levers, etc used to operate a machine: *The television may be operated by (a) remote control.* ○ *Where are the controls of this machine?*

be in control (of something) have the power to manage, direct or regulate something: *Who's in control of the project?* ○ *Can I speak to the person in control, please?*

be/get out of control be no longer manageable: *Inflation has got out of control.*

be under control being dealt with: *The problem of the missing orders is now under control.*

/kən'trəʊl/

pl controls

1 ⋈ gain, keep, take **control**; be in, out of, under **control**

2 ⋈ a **control** board, button, lever, panel, switch

► **exchange control, quality control, stock control**

---

control[2] *verb*

to have power to manage, direct or regulate: *The government is determined to control inflation.* ○ *A computer controls the operation of the fuel pumps.*

/kən'trəʊl/

control, controlling, controlled

note transitive verb

► **manage, run[1] 1**

---

controlling interest *noun* (finance)

a situation where a person or an organization owns enough shares (usually more than 50%) in a company to say how it should be run. The owner of fewer shares may have a controlling interest if the remaining shares are owned by a large number of people: *After buying more shares we now have a controlling interest in the company.*

/kənˌtrəʊlɪŋ 'ɪntrəst/

pl controlling interests

⋈ acquire, hold, retain, take a **controlling interest**

syn majority interest

► **holding, minority interest**

---

convenience food *noun* (commerce)

food specially made and packed so that it can be cooked quickly and easily: *Supermarkets are meeting a growing demand for convenience foods.*

/kən'vi:niəns fu:d/

pl convenience foods

⋈ buy, use **convenience food**

► **fast food**

---

convertible currency *noun* (finance)

money that can be exchanged for the currency of another country: *We only deal in convertible currency.*

/kənˌvɜ:təbl 'kʌrənsi/

pl convertible currencies

► **currency 1, foreign exchange**

---

convertible security *noun* (stock exchange)

an investment that can be exchanged for an ORDINARY SHARE in a company: *holders of convertible securities*

/kənˌvɜ:təbl sɪ'kjʊərəti/

pl convertible securities

syn convertible loan stock

► **security 1**

---

conveyancing *noun* (law)

the work done, usually by a lawyer, in legally transferring the ownership of land and property from one person to another: *The solicitor is proceeding with the conveyancing.*

/kən'veɪənsɪŋ/

note no plural

---

co-operative *noun* (commerce)

a business society owned and run by its members who work together and share the profits: *The poultry farmers formed a co-*

/kəʊ'ɒpərətɪv/

pl co-operatives

(also **cooperative**)

abbr co-op

operative to market their produce and buy poultry feed in bulk. ○ *set up a workers' co-operative*

⋈ a **co-operative** association, bank, organization, society

▶ **joint-stock company**

---

co-owner *noun* (law)

▶ **joint owner**

/ˌkəʊˈəʊnə(r)/

pl co-owners

---

co-ownership *noun* (law)

▶ **joint ownership**

/ˌkəʊˈəʊnəʃɪp/

---

co-partner *noun* (commerce)

a person who works with another, or others, as a partner in a business: *The co-partners in the business have reached agreement on how duties are to be allocated and profits shared.*

/ˌkəʊˈpɑːtnə(r)/

pl co-partners

⋈ a **co-partner** *in* (something)

▶ **partner**

---

copier *noun* (office practice)

▶ **photocopier**

/ˈkɒpiə(r)/

---

copy[1] *noun*

1 (**a**) a thing made to look like another; a photocopy: *make a copy of a letter* ○ *Send him a copy of the memo and keep the original.* (**b**) one of a number of books, newspapers, etc that have been produced: *sell 2 000 copies of a book* ○ *How many copies have been printed?* ○ *I enclose a copy of our price list.* ○ *send for a free copy of a holiday brochure* **2** (*office practice/advertising*) written or typed material that is to be printed: *The printers are ready for more copy.* ○ *Please check the proof against the copy.* ○ *write advertising copy*

/ˈkɒpi/

1 pl copies

▶ **carbon copy, certified copy, duplicate**[1]**, hard copy, master 1, original, photocopy 1, top copy**

2 note not used with *a* or *an*. No plural and used with a singular verb only.

▶ **copywriter, knocking copy, proof 2**

---

copy[2] *verb*

to make another letter, document, etc the same as the original: *copy the letter to Mr Jackson* (ie give or send him a copy) ○ *copy documents on a photocopier* ○ *copy* (ie write) *down this information*

/ˈkɒpi/

copy, copying, copied

note transitive verb

▶ **duplicate**[2] **1, photocopy**[2]

---

copyright *noun* (law)

an exclusive legal right, for a certain number of years, to print, publish, record, perform, sell an original text, work of art or design or part of it. The creator of the work may keep the copyright or sell it to someone else: *Who holds/owns the copyright?* ○ *make a copyright agreement with a publisher* ○ *After fifty years the book goes out of copyright.*

/ˈkɒpiraɪt/

note singular noun, used with a singular verb

⋈ a breach, an infringement of **copyright**; be in, out of, under **copyright**

▶ **intangible asset, intellectual property, patent, piracy 2, royalty, trade mark**

---

copy-typist *noun* (office practice)

a person who types out written material: *work as a copy-typist* ○ *give a letter to a copy-typist to type up*

/ˈkɒpi taɪpɪst/

pl copy-typists

▶ **audio-typist, keyboarder, shorthand typist, typist**

---

copywriter *noun* (advertising)

a person who writes advertising or publicity material: *She works in an advertising agency as a copywriter.* ○ *We need a really good copywriter for our new catalogue.*

/ˈkɒpiraɪtə(r)/

pl copywriters

▶ **copy**[1] **2**

---

corporate *adjective* (management)
relating to a company or group (CORPORATION): *concern for the environment is an important part of our corporate policy*

/ˈkɔːpərət/
⧓ a **corporate** decision, plan, structure

---

corporate identity *noun* (management)
the qualities of a company that distinguish it from others and are often expressed in its name, or in the design of its packaging and publicity materials: *The company is unsuccessful because it lacks a corporate identity.*

/ˌkɔːpərət aɪˈdentəti/
pl corporate identities
⧓ establish, introduce, project, promote a **corporate identity**
▶ **logo, slogan**

---

corporate image *noun* (management)
the impression that a company tries to present to the public through advertising and publicity: *After the accident on the oil-rig, the company tried to restore its corporate image.*

/ˌkɔːpərət ˈɪmɪdʒ/
⧓ alter, create, develop, establish, improve, project, promote a **corporate image**
▶ **brand image**

---

corporate planning *noun* (management)
deciding and making a formal report on the future activities of a company for a certain period, usually several years. The aim is to increase sales and profits, develop new products and enter new markets: *Corporate planning is increasingly important, especially in the computer and electronics industries.*

/ˌkɔːpərət ˈplænɪŋ/
⧓ a **corporate planning** department, meeting, officer
syn strategic planning
▶ **business plan, mission statement, planning 1**

---

corporate sector *noun* (economics)
the part of a country's economy that is made up of public and privately owned companies, as opposed to government authorities: *Representatives from the corporate sector complained to the government about currency exchange rates.*

/ˈkɔːpərət ˌsektə(r)/
pl corporate sectors
▶ **private sector, public sector, sector**

---

corporation *noun* (law)
1 (*UK*) an organization that has legal recognition and is made up of people whose rights and responsibilities within the corporation are separate from their rights as individuals; a large group of companies: *The city corporation is responsible for parks and gardens within its boundaries.* ○ *the British Broadcasting Corporation* ○ *a banking corporation* **2** (*US*) a limited company

/ˌkɔːpəˈreɪʃn/
pl corporations
1 ▶ **association 1, business 3, company, federation, group, organization 1, public corporation**

---

corporation charter *noun*
(*US*) (*law*) ▶ **certificate of incorporation**

/ˌkɔːpəˈreɪʃn ˌtʃɑːtə(r)/

---

corporation tax *noun* (tax)
money taken by a government from the profits made by companies and corporations: *Small businesses have been granted further relief from corporation tax.*

/ˌkɔːpəˈreɪʃn tæks/
pl corporation taxes
▶ **franked income, tax[1], unfranked income**

---

correspond *verb*
1 to have contact with someone by means of a letter, memo, etc: *correspond regularly with overseas staff* **2** to be the same as or in agreement with something: *Do the notes taken during the meeting correspond to the account given in the report?* ○ *The totals given in the balance sheet and those in the statement don't correspond.*

/ˌkɒrɪˈspɒnd/
correspond, corresponding, corresponded
1 note intransitive verb
⧓ **correspond** *with* (someone)
2 ⧓ **correspond** *to, with* (something)
▶ **contact[2]**

---

correspondence *noun*

exchanging information in the form of letters, cables, faxes, telexes, etc; the letters, etc themselves: *We have employed a new secretary to do the correspondence.* ○ *All correspondence received in the office has the date stamped on it immediately.*

in correspondence (with someone) in contact with a person by letter, fax, etc

/ˌkɒrɪˈspɒndəns/

note not used with *a* or *an*. No plural and used with a singular verb only.

⋈ business, personal, private **correspondence**

▶ **communication 1, 2**

---

correspondent *noun*

1 a person who communicates with others by letter, etc: *We have been correspondents for years.* **2** a reporter who sends news and comments to newspapers and radio and television stations: *a sports correspondent* ○ *a foreign news correspondent* ○ **3** (*banking*) a bank which acts as an agent for another bank: *The bank has no branch in that place but we can arrange for you to deal with its correspondent there.*

/ˌkɒrɪˈspɒndənt/

pl correspondents

3 ⋈ a **correspondent** bank; **correspondent** banking

---

corruption *noun*

1 (*law*) dishonesty in business or official dealings, especially by giving or accepting a BRIBE: *The police are investigating allegations of corruption in an international bank.* **2** (*computing*) defects in data stored, received and transmitted, often owing to electrical interference: *Bad storage of the magnetic tapes has led to significant corruption of the data they hold.*

/kəˈrʌpʃn/

note not used with *a* or *an*. No plural and used with a singular verb only.

▶ **bribery, fraud**

---

cost[1] *noun*

1 (*commerce*) the amount of money paid or charged for goods or services: *the cost of a new computer* ○ *the high cost of building a factory* ○ *The machine was repaired at a total cost of £500.* **2** (*finance*) the amount of money spent on running a business or part of it: *We had to increase prices this year just to cover our costs.* ○ *labour, storage, transport costs* **3 costs** (*law*) legal expenses, esp those resulting from a case heard in a court: *The employer was ordered to pay costs.*

/kɒst/

1 pl costs

⋈ cover, meet, pay the **cost**; assess, calculate, estimate, work out the **cost**

▶ **price**[1]

2 pl costs

▶ **accrued costs, at cost, average cost, direct cost, distributive costs, fixed cost, oncost, overhead, running costs, selling costs, unabsorbed cost, unit cost, variable cost**

3 note plural noun, used with a plural verb

⋈ legal **costs**

▶ **damages**

---

cost[2] *verb*

1 to be the price of something: *Local telephone calls cost 5p per minute.* ○ *How much did it cost to repair the machine?* ○ *Each item is costing £20 to produce.* **2** to result in the loss of something: *His inefficiency will cost him his job.* ○ *This is costing us an extra three weeks' work.* **3** (*commerce*) to calculate or set the price for goods or services: *We've planned the research and now we must cost it.* ○ *The project hasn't been costed yet.* ○ *The accountants are costing the production process.*

/kɒst/

1, 2 cost, costing, cost

note intransitive verb

3 cost, costing, costed

note transitive verb

▶ **price**[2]

---

cost accountant *noun* (accounting)

a person employed by a company to analyse the cost of producing goods, and other expenses, and to advise managers

/ˈkɒst əˌkaʊntənt/

pl cost accountants

▶ **accountant, financial**

on how to increase profits: *The company decided to accept the advice of their cost accountant and abandon the project.*

▶ **accountant, management accountant**

---

cost and freight *noun* (international trade)
a condition of sale for goods carried by sea where the seller pays for loading and transporting goods but the buyer pays the insurance costs once the goods have been loaded: *The buyer ordered the goods on a cost and freight basis, preferring to make insurance arrangements personally.*

/ˌkɒst ənd ˈfreɪt/
note no plural
abbr c/f, c and f
▶ **cost, insurance, freight**

---

cost benefit analysis *noun* (management/accounting)
finding out the price and resources needed for an important business activity and comparing them with the profit and advantages to be gained: *Before building the new hotel, the company carried out a cost benefit analysis.* ○ *Cost benefit analysis is necessary for a major business venture.*

/ˈkɒst ˌbenɪfɪt əˌnæləsɪs/
pl cost benefit analyses
abbr CBA
⋈ carry out, do, perform a **cost benefit analysis**
▶ **analysis, feasibility study, value analysis**

---

cost-effective *adjective* (management/accounting)
giving enough profit or gain compared with the amount of money spent: *producing goods in such small quantities would not be cost-effective* ○ *find a more cost-effective method of production*

/ˌkɒst ɪˈfektɪv/
⋈ less, more **cost-effective**; a **cost-effective** process, way
▶ **efficient, profitable**

---

costing *noun* (accounting)
estimating the cost of making goods or fixing the prices they should be sold at to make a profit: *A team of consultants are doing the costing for us.* ○ *She works in the costing department.*

/ˈkɒstɪŋ/
note no plural
⋈ long-term, short-term **costing**
▶ **absorption costing, batch costing, life-cycle costing, marginal costing**

---

cost insurance freight *noun* (international trade)
a condition of sale for goods carried by sea where the seller pays for loading and transporting the goods and arranges marine insurance

/ˌkɒst ɪnˌʃʊərəns ˈfreɪt/
abbr CIF, cif
▶ **cost and freight**

---

cost of living *noun* (economics)
the average amount of money each person spends on everyday items such as accommodation, food, heating, transport, clothes, etc: *People complained about alarming increases in the cost of living.* ○ *The government is trying to bring the cost of living down.*

/ˌkɒst əv ˈlɪvɪŋ/
note no plural
⋈ an increase, a rise, a decrease in the **cost of living**; a high, low **cost of living**
▶ **standard of living, living**

Cost of Living Index *noun* (economics)
a list showing the movement of prices of basic goods and services compared with prices given in a previous list and expressed as a percentage: *This month's Cost of Living Index shows that the rate of price increases is slowing down.*

/ˌkɒst əv ˈlɪvɪŋ ˌɪndeks/
(also **cost of living index**)
▶ **Consumer Price Index, Producer Price Index, Retail Price Index, threshold agreement**

---

cost price *noun*
1 (*commerce*) the price paid by a trader for goods bought to be resold: *The shop sold off old stock at cost price, making no profit but creating space for new stock.* **2** (*manufacturing*) the price of producing goods: *Higher prices of raw materials have added to the manufacturer's cost price.*

/ˌkɒst ˈpraɪs/
pl cost prices
▶ **at cost, cash price, price[1]**

---

cottage industry *noun* (industry)
a method of producing goods by employing workers to make them in their homes: *The use of personal computers has resulted in a new form of cottage industry.*

/ˌkɒtɪdʒ ˈɪndəstri/
pl cottage industries
▶ **freelance, self-employed**

council *noun*
a group of people chosen to give advice, make rules or control things: *The Design Council gives awards for good industrial designs.* ○ *The city council has/have decided to privatize the buses.*

/ˈkaʊnsl/
pl councils
note used with a singular or plural verb
⋈ a **council** member; be elected to, have a seat on, sit on the **council**
▶ **board, commission[1] 2, committee, working party**

counsel *noun* (law)
a barrister, or group of barristers, in a UK court of law (not Scotland): *counsel for the defence/prosecution* ○ *Counsel is to be consulted.*

/ˈkaʊnsl/
pl counsel
▶ **barrister, court 2, jury**

counter[1] *noun*
a table or desk in a shop or bank which separates customers from staff and upon which goods are displayed and money is counted: *Purchases are paid for at the counter.* ○ *buy something from the the cheese counter* ○ *long queues at the Post Office counter* ○ *goods kept under/behind the counter*

/ˈkaʊntə(r)/
pl counters
⋈ behind, on, over, under the **counter**

counter[2] *verb*
to oppose something: *Some of the company directors supported the idea of a merger but others countered it.* ○ *counter the manager's decision*

/ˈkaʊntə(r)/
counter, countering, countered
note transitive verb
▶ **oppose**

counterfeit[1] *noun*
an illegal copy of something: *This twenty-pound note is a counterfeit.*

/ˈkaʊntəfɪt/
pl counterfeits
⋈ **counterfeit** banknotes, coins, documents, money
syn fake
▶ **forgery**

counterfeit[2] *verb*
to make copies of money, documents, paintings and goods with the intention of deceiving people: *He was charged with counterfeiting banknotes.* ○ *These goods have been counterfeited.*

/ˈkaʊntəfɪt/
counterfeit, counterfeiting, counterfeited
note transitive verb
▶ **forge**

counterfoil *noun*
a part of a receipt, ticket, cheque, invoice, etc, which can be detached and is kept as a record of the date, amount, etc: *When writing a cheque, remember to complete the counterfoil in your cheque book.*

/ˈkaʊntəfɔɪl/
pl counterfoils
⋈ complete, detach, fill in, keep, retain, tear off the **counterfoil**
syn stub
▶ **remittance slip**

countermand *verb*
to cancel an order or give a new order that changes the first one: *Before the suppliers could meet the order it was countermanded.* ○ *The drawer of the cheque has countermanded it, so payment cannot be made.*

/ˌkaʊntəˈmɑːnd/
countermand, countermanding, countermanded
note transitive verb
▶ **cancel**

counterpart *noun*
1 (*management*) a person with the same status and duties as another in a business organization: *The sales manager phoned her counterpart in another company,* ie the other company's sales manager. **2** (*law*) a copy of a contract or other document: *The original deed is deposited at a bank but a counterpart is kept in the office.*

/ˈkaʊntəpɑːt/
pl counterparts
1 syn opposite number
▶ **colleague**

counter-productive *adjective*
having the opposite effect to the one intended: *Instead of encouraging industrial effort, the new tax concession is proving to be counter-productive.*

/ˌkaʊntəprəˈdʌktɪv/
⋈ entirely, totally, utterly **counter-productive**
▶ **productive**

countersign *verb* (commerce/banking)
to sign a document already signed by another person: *For security reasons all the Society's cheques must be signed by the Treasurer and countersigned by the Chairman.*

/ˈkaʊntəsaɪn/
countersign, countersigning, countersigned
note transitive verb
⋈ **countersign** a certificate, cheque, document

courier *noun*
1 (*tourism*) a person who accompanies a group of tourists as a guide and helper: *A courier will meet the plane and arrange transport to the hotel.* **2** (*commerce*) a person or an organization employed to carry important papers and packages: *The parcel will be delivered by courier.*

/ˈkʊriə(r)/
pl couriers
1 ⋈ act as **courier**
2 ⋈ send (something) by **courier**; a motorcycle **courier**

court *noun* (law)
1 a place where trials are held and law cases heard; a courtroom: *The accused person was brought to court for trial.* ○ *She has to appear in court to give evidence.* **2 the court** the judge, lawyers and officials who listen to cases in a court: *The court adjourned for lunch.* ○ *Each witness appeared before the court.*

go to court (over something) to ask to have a case heard and decided by a court

settle out of court to resolve a dispute without discussing it in court

take someone to court to make an accusation against someone to be settled in a court: *I took him to court for repayment of the debt.*

/kɔːt/
pl courts
1 ⋈ an appeal, a civil, a criminal, a high, a law, a magistrate's **court**; a **court** case
syn court of law, lawcourt
▶ **hearing**
2 ▶ **counsel, jury**

court order *noun* (law)
an instruction given by a court of law to ensure that a person or an organization acts as the court requires: *People living near the factory have obtained a court order prohibiting factory noise after 6 pm.*

/ˌkɔːt ˈɔːdə(r)/
pl court orders
⋈ apply for, issue, obtain a **court order**
▶ **garnishee order, injunction, subpoena[1], summons, writ**

cover[1] *noun*

/ˈkʌvə(r)/

1 an envelope or a wrapper: *The letter was sent under registered cover.* ○ *Further information will be sent under separate cover.* **2** the pages on the outside of a book, catalogue, etc: *Look at the picture on the cover.* ○ *a cover design* **3** (*personnel*) the act of doing someone else's job when he/she is not there: *One of the staff is ill today so the others will have to provide cover.* **4** (*insurance*) insurance against loss or injury: *a policy that gives cover against fire* **5** (*finance*) a sum of money or item of value given to show that a loan will be repaid: *The bank manager asked what cover could be offered to secure the loan.* **6** (*banking*) the amount of money a bank keeps available for the immediate use of its customers: *A run on the bank caused anxiety about the amount of cover being held.*

1, 2 pl covers

3, 4, 5, 6 note not used with *a* or *an*. No plural and used with a singular verb only.

▶ **collateral, guarantee**[1] **3, indemnity, security 3**

cover[2] *verb*

/ˈkʌvə(r)/

1 to put a protective sheet over something: *Cover the machine when it's not in use.* **2** to include someone or something: *The staff instructions cover everyone.* ○ *The telephone directory doesn't cover addresses outside the city.* ○ *The report covers the whole conference.* **3** to be enough for a particular purpose: *The allowance covers all of the expenses incurred.* **4** (*personnel*) to do someone else's job when he/she is away: *Staff complained that they couldn't cover for so many absent colleagues.* **5** (*insurance*) to provide insurance money for something: *The policy covers fire and theft risks.*

cover, covering, covered

note transitive verb

4 ⋈ **cover** *for* someone

covering letter *noun* (office practice)

/ˌkʌvərɪŋ ˈletə(r)/

a letter sent with a document or goods explaining the contents: *The customer sent the faulty radio back to the shop, with a covering letter.* ○ *Please include a covering letter with your job application form.*

pl covering letters

⋈ accompanied by, include, send, write a **covering letter**

syn covering note

cover note *noun* (insurance)

/ˈkʌvə(r) nəʊt/

a document from an insurance company showing that insurance has been arranged and full details of the policy will be sent later: *Before a vehicle licence could be issued, the motorist had to show a cover note to prove that insurance had been arranged.*

pl cover notes

▶ **insurance**

CP *abbr* (transport)

/ˌsiː ˈpiː/

carriage paid

CPI *abbr* (commerce)

/ˌsiː piː ˈaɪ/

(*US*) Consumer Price Index

CPU *abbr* (computing)

/ˌsiː piː ˈjuː/

Central Processing Unit

craftsman, craftswoman *noun* (manufacturing/personnel)

/ˈkrɑːftsmən, ˈkrɑːftswʊmən/

a skilled worker, esp one who makes things by hand: *The furniture is not mass-produced but made by craftsmen.* ○ *handmade by a craftswoman*

pl craftsmen, craftswomen

⋈ a skilled, trained **craftsman, craftswoman**; a **craftsman, craftswoman** *in* (wood, etc)

▶ **artisan, labourer**

craftsmanship *noun* (manufacturing/personnel)

/ˈkrɑːftsmənʃɪp/

skilled workmanship: *Industry needs good craftsmanship.* ○ *This wooden table is an example of fine craftsmanship.*

note not used with *a* or *an*. No plural and used with a singular verb only. Craftsmanship is used to describe the work of women as well as men.

⋈ fine, skilled **craftsmanship**

► **workmanship**

---

crash[1] *noun*

1 (*stock exchange*) a loss of confidence by investors in a stock market or in investment generally, resulting in a big and sudden fall in share prices: *In the City, share prices fell heavily today amid fears of an impending crash.* ○ *the Wall Street crash* **2** (*computing*) a breakdown in a computer system: *We did no work this afternoon because of the computer crash.*

/kræʃ/

pl crashes

1 ⋈ a share price, stock market **crash**

► **Black Monday**

---

crash[2] *verb*

1 (*stock exchange*) (of a stock market) to suffer a large and sudden loss of value: *The stock market crashed in October 1987.* **2** (*banking*) (of a bank) to fail suddenly: *The international bank has crashed, with enormous debts and thousands of angry depositors.* **3** (*computing*) to stop working suddenly and completely: *Using too many programs at once may cause the system to crash.*

/kræʃ/

crash, crashing, crashed

note intransitive verb

⋈ **crash** heavily, suddenly, unexpectedly

---

credentials *noun* (personnel)

achievements or qualifications that make someone suitable for a job; documents that prove this: *The applicants' credentials were studied before the job interviews began.* ○ *Do you think she has the right credentials for this job?* ○ *Give him time to establish his credentials.*

/krɪˈdenʃlz/

note plural noun, used with a plural verb

⋈ perfect, strong, weak **credentials**

► **curriculum vitae**

---

credit[1] *noun*

1 (*commerce*) an arrangement where goods and services can be received now and paid for later, within an agreed period: *Buy now on credit and pay later!* ○ *I'm sorry but we don't accept credit, please pay now in cash.* ○ *We're offering six months' interest-free credit* (ie you can pay for the goods within six months, without any extra charge for interest). ○ *Credit terms are 30 days* (ie payment must be made within that time). **2** (*banking*) a sum of money paid into a bank account: *The bank statement shows several credits to the account.* **3** (*accounting*) a sum of money gained by a business, shown on the right-hand side of a list of accounts: *The account doesn't balance because a credit has been wrongly entered in the books.* ○ *total the credits at the end of the day*

in credit having money in an account; not owing money

/ˈkredɪt/

1 note not used with *a* or *an*. No plural and used with a singular verb only.

⋈ a **credit** agreement, arrangement; obtain, offer **credit**

► **consumer credit, hire purchase**

2 pl credits

► **bank credit, debit[1] 1, deposit[1] 1, revolving credit**

3 pl credits

► **bilateral credit, debit[1] 2, debt 1, letter of credit, tax credit**

---

credit[2] *verb* (accounting/banking)

to record the payment of a sum of money into an account: *Please acknowledge receipt of the enclosed cheque and credit our account accordingly.* ○ *A sum of £500 has been credited to your account.*

/ˈkredɪt/

credit, crediting, credited

note transitive verb

► **debit[2]**

---

credit account *noun* (retail)

an arrangement with a shop that allows customers to take goods and pay for them within a certain period by putting a specified amount into the account at regular intervals. The customer shows a CHARGE CARD when obtaining goods and the account is debited accordingly: *I asked for the goods to be charged to my credit account.*

/ˈkredɪt əˌkaʊnt/

pl credit accounts

abbr c/a

syn charge account

⋈ charge to, open, settle a **credit account**

▶ account[1] 2, approved account

---

credit balance *noun* (accounting)
the sum of money needed to equalize the totals of money paid or owed (DEBITS) and money received (CREDITS) when the total of the credits is greater than the total of the debits in an account: *When a credit balance shows on your account you will be paid an attractive rate of interest.* ○ *a credit balance of £200*

/ˈkredɪt ˌbæləns/
pl credit balances
▶ **balance[1] 1, debit balance**

---

credit card *noun* (commerce)
a plastic card, issued by a bank or finance company, which guarantees that payment for goods or services will be made to the seller by the card issuer. The cardholder then makes payment to the card issuer at a later date: *pay by credit card* ○ *make a credit card payment*

/ˈkredɪt kɑːd/
pl credit cards
⋈ show, use a **credit card**; a **credit card** holder, number
▶ **charge card, cheque card, debit card**

---

credit column *noun* (accounting)
the right-hand list of entries in a statement of account, showing amounts paid in or still owed: *make an entry in the credit column* ○ *add up the figures in the credit column*

/ˈkredɪt ˌkɒləm/
pl debit columns
▶ **debit column, credit[1] 3**

---

credit control *noun*
1 (*finance*) a system used in a business to check that people who owe money (DEBTORS) do not owe more than the amount allowed (the CREDIT LIMIT) and that they pay within the agreed time: *The company's manager of credit control reported that payments were delayed.* **2** (*finance*) government restrictions on the amount of money lent by banks and finance houses and the arrangements made for paying it back: *introduce credit controls to contain borrowing* ○ *Credit control is not always the cure for inflation.*

/ˈkredɪt kənˌtrəʊl/
1 note not used with *a* or *an*. No plural and used with a singular verb only.
2 pl credit controls
⋈ impose, introduce **credit controls**

---

credit limit *noun* (banking/commerce)
the total amount that a customer is allowed to owe to a bank or business, and the length of time allowed for payment: *Falling sales and rising overheads have obliged the company to review each customer's credit limit.* ○ *a credit limit of £1 000*

/ˈkredɪt ˌlɪmɪt/
syn (US) credit line
pl credit limits
⋈ establish, impose, set a **credit limit**

---

credit note *noun* (commerce)
a document that informs a customer of money owed by a company for faulty or returned goods. It can only be used to buy goods from that company: *We can't give you your money back, but we can issue you a credit note.*

/ˈkredɪt nəʊt/
pl credit notes
⋈ issue, pay by, receive, use a **credit note**
▶ **debit note**

---

creditor *noun* (finance)
a person or an organization that you owe money to: *His main creditor is demanding payment.* ○ *The company has gone bankrupt and can't pay its creditors.*

/ˈkredɪtə(r)/
pl creditors
⋈ owe (money to), pay, pay off, settle with a **creditor**
▶ **debtor, judgment creditor, preferential creditor, secured creditor, trade creditor, unsecured creditor**

---

credit sale *noun* (commerce)
an arrangement where a buyer takes goods that he/she will pay for by an agreed date in the future: *To encourage buyers, the dealer offered credit sales with no interest.*

/ˈkredɪt seɪl/
pl credit sales
▶ **cash sale, hire purchase, sale**

credit slip *noun* (banking)
▶ **paying-in slip**

/ˈkredɪt slɪp/

critical path analysis *noun* (management)
the study of the stages in a complex operation (eg organizing a conference) to decide the quickest and most efficient order in which to do them: *Critical path analysis showed that building materials must not arrive before the site had been cleared and levelled.*

/ˌkrɪtɪkl ˈpɑːθ əˌnæləsɪs/
abbr CPA
pl critical path analyses
⧓ carry out, do a **critical path analysis**

cross-cultural *adjective*
relating to the cultures of different countries and societies: *Business people may be exposed to cross-cultural differences when negotiating with an overseas company.* ○ *It is important for language teachers to undertake cross-cultural studies.*

/ˌkrɒs ˈkʌltʃərəl/
⧓ **cross-cultural** differences, issues, similarities

crossed cheque *noun* (banking)
a cheque that has two lines drawn across it to show that it can only be paid into a bank account and not exchanged for cash: *Crossed cheques only, please.*

/ˌkrɒst ˈtʃek/
pl crossed cheques
▶ **blank cheque, cheque, open cheque**

cross-holding *noun* (stock exchange)
▶ **reciprocal shareholding**

/ˈkrɒs həʊldɪŋ/

cum div *abbr* (stock exchange)
▶ **cum dividend** ***under*** **dividend**

/ˌkʌm ˈdɪv/

cum rights *adjective* (stock exchange)
of a share offered for sale with the right to take up a rights issue

/ˌkʌm ˈraɪts/
▶ **ex-rights, rights issue**

currency *noun*
1 the coins and banknotes that belong to a particular country: *The tourist changed a traveller's cheque into local currency.* **2** coins, banknotes, cheques, bills of exchange, promissory notes, etc that have financial value and can be exchanged for goods: *These old coins are no longer accepted as valid currency.* **3** the period of time that can pass before a bill of exchange becomes payable: *This bill of exchange has a 60-day currency.*

/ˈkʌrənsi/
1 pl currencies
▶ **convertible currency, Eurocurrency, foreign exchange, hard currency, legal tender, local currency, managed currency, paper money**
2, 3 note no plural
▶ **medium of exchange**

currency swap *noun* (finance)
▶ **swap**

/ˈkʌrənsi swɒp/

current *adjective*
in the present time; happening now: *Can you give me a list of current prices?* ○ *the current issue of a magazine*

/ˈkʌrənt/
⧓ the **current** issue, price, year
▶ **actual, present[1], up-to-date**

current account *noun*
1 (*banking*) an arrangement with a bank that allows the customer to pay in money and, by writing cheques, draw it out without giving notice: *pay money into a current account* ○ *a current*

/ˈkʌrənt əˌkaʊnt/
pl current accounts
abbr c/a
1 ⧓ pay (money) into, take

account holder **2** (*accounting*) an account that shows money going into and out of a business for goods and services: *The company's current account shows a healthy credit balance this month.*

(money) out of, withdraw (money) from a **current account**

syn account, (*US*) checking account

▶ **bank account, deposit account, savings account**

2 ▶ **accounts, capital account**

---

current assets *noun* (finance)

cash and other assets which a company can convert quickly into cash, usually stock and BILLS RECEIVABLE falling due within one year: *Current assets are less than current liabilities, which means the company may not be able to pay its debts on time.*

/ˌkʌrənt ˈæsets/

▶ **asset, capital asset, bills receivable, current liabilities**

---

current capital *noun* (finance/commerce)

(*US*) the money and stock of goods held by a business and used to produce and sell more goods, ie to continue trading: *Current capital changes from money into goods, which are sold to produce money to change into more goods.* ○ *have a healthy current capital*

/ˌkʌrənt ˈkæpɪtl/

note singular noun, used with a singular verb

syn circulating capital

⋈ spend, use **current capital**

▶ **capital, fixed capital**

---

current cost accounting *noun* (accounting)

a method of keeping accounts that allows for rising prices. An item of worth (an ASSET) is valued at the amount it would cost to replace it now rather than at its original cost, with an amount taken off for wear and tear: *In times of high inflation, companies are well advised to adopt current cost accounting.*

/ˌkʌrənt kɒst əˈkaʊntɪŋ/

abbr CCA

note not used with *a* or *an*. No plural and used with a singular verb only.

syn inflation accounting

▶ **accounting, depreciation, historic cost accounting**

---

current liabilities *noun* (accounting)

debts that are payable on demand or within one year: *The suppliers are demanding payment of all current liabilities.*

/ˌkʌrənt ˌlaɪəˈbɪlətiz/

note plural noun, used with a plural verb

syn short-term liabilities

▶ **current assets, bills payable, liability 2**

---

curriculum vitae *noun*

(*Latin*) (*personnel*) an account of a person's qualifications, interests and work experience, usually sent with an application for a job: *All job applicants are required to submit a curriculum vitae.*

/kəˌrɪkjələm ˈviːtaɪ/

pl curricula vitae

abbr cv

syn (*US*) résumé

⋈ compile, update, write a **curriculum vitae**

▶ **credentials**

---

cursor *noun* (computing)

a movable symbol on a computer screen that shows where the next item to be typed in will appear: *Move the cursor up to the next line.* ○ *Use the cursor to find where you are on the screen.*

/ˈkɜːsə(r)/

pl cursors

▶ **keyboard, mouse**

---

customer *noun* (commerce)

a person who buys something from a shop, pays for a service or orders something from a company: *Please serve the next customer before answering the phone.* ○ *a bank, a garage, a supermarket customer* ○ *deal with a customer's order*

/ˈkʌstəmə(r)/

pl customers

⋈ an important, a regular **customer**

▶ **client**

---

customize *verb* (commerce)
to alter a standard product to suit the special needs or taste of a customer: *The car was a standard model which had been customized to provide greater luxury and performance.*

/ˈkʌstəmaɪz/
customize, customizing, customized
note transitive verb
⋈ a **customized** car, edition, machine
▶ **mass produce, ready-made, standardize**

---

customs *noun* (tax)
1 a government department responsible for collecting payments on certain imports and exports, and preventing smuggling: *a consignment of stolen goods seized by customs* **2** the tax paid on certain imports and exports: *Only a limited quantity of wine may be imported free of customs.* **3** a place, esp at a port or airport, where government officers examine goods for import or export, or inspect baggage carried by ship or aircraft passengers: *The goods have arrived and are now in customs waiting to be examined.* ○ *take your luggage through customs*

/ˈkʌstəmz/
note plural noun, used with a plural verb
1 ⋈ clear, declare something to, go through, pass through **customs**; **customs** officers, officials
▶ **Board of Customs and Excise**
2 ▶ **excise duty, import duty, tariff 1**

---

customs duty *noun* (tax)
a government tax paid on certain imports and exports, collected at ports and airports: *pay customs duty on imported jewellery*

/ˈkʌstəmz ˌdju:ti/
pl customs duties
⋈ impose, increase, levy, lift, reduce **customs duties**
▶ **duty 1, duty-free, excise duty, import duty**

---

cut-back *noun* (finance)
a reduction in the amount of money, staff and other resources available for a project or an organization: *Local governments have been ordered to make further financial cut-backs.* ○ *A cut-back in staff has slowed down production.*

/ˈkʌtbæk/
pl cut-backs
(also **cutback**)
⋈ announce, make **cut-backs**; a **cut-back** in spending, staff

---

cut back *verb* (finance)
to reduce the amount of money, staff or other resources available for a project or an organization: *Now the project is finished we have to cut back some of our staff.* ○ *The government is cutting back on grants for industrial training.*

/ˌkʌt ˈbæk/
cut back, cutting back, cut back
note transitive verb
⋈ **cut back** on (someone or something)

---

cut-price *adjective* (commerce)
relating to a large reduction in the price of goods or services: *All washing machines are cut-price for one week only!*

/ˌkʌt ˈpraɪs/
▶ **price**[1]

CWO *abbr* (commerce)
cash with order

/ˌsi: dʌblju: ˈəʊ/

---

cv *abbr* (personnel)
curriculum vitae

/ˌsi: ˈvi:/

---

cybernetics *noun* (industry)
the science of communication and control, esp in comparing human abilities with those of machines: *In industry, cybernetics is used to design and improve automated systems of production.*

/ˌsaɪbəˈnetɪks/
note singular noun, used with a singular verb
▶ **automation, computerization, robotics**

D/A *abbr* (banking)
1 deposit account **2** documents against acceptance

/ˌdiː ˈeɪ/
pl D/As
note pronounced as individual letters

D/A bill *abbr* (banking)
documents against acceptance bill

/ˌdiː ˈeɪ bɪl/

Daily Official List *noun* (stock exchange)
▶ **Stock Exchange Daily Official List**

/ˌdeɪli əˌfɪʃl ˈlɪst/

daisywheel *noun* (office practice)
a device used for printing from a typewriter. Each wheel has a number of spokes with letters on the end. The wheel is changed to produce letters from a different typeface: *The daisywheel printer has six different daisywheels offering an excellent choice of print style.*

/ˈdeɪziwiːl/
pl daisywheels
⋈ a **daisy wheel** printer, typewriter
▶ **dot matrix printer, laser printer**

damage certificate *noun* (shipping/insurance)
a document issued by a port official to show that goods have arrived damaged: *An insurance claim for goods damaged in transit must be accompanied by a damage certificate issued by the port authority.*

/ˈdæmɪdʒ səˌtɪfɪkət/
pl damage certificates
syn certificate of damage
▶ **bill of lading**

damage claim *noun* (insurance)
a demand made to an insurance company to pay money under the terms of a policy for goods or property partially destroyed: *After the storm the insurance company received damage claims from householders whose property had been affected.*

/ˈdæmɪdʒ kleɪm/
pl damage claims
⋈ make a **damage claim**
▶ **claim, insurance**

damages *noun* (law)
money given by a court to someone who has suffered a wrong, an injury or loss: *The court awarded damages to the injured person.*

/ˈdæmɪdʒɪz/
note plural noun, used with a plural verb
⋈ award, be awarded, be liable for, claim, win **damages**
▶ **cost**[1] **3, court order**

danger money *noun* (industry)
extra money or high wages paid to people working in hazardous conditions: *The workers unloading explosives were paid danger money in addition to their wages.*

/ˈdeɪndʒə ˌmʌni/
note not used with *a* or *an*. No plural and used with a singular verb only.
⋈ pay, receive **danger money**
▶ **bonus, money**

data *noun*
1 information, facts or statistics: *collect data for market research* ○ *We have insufficient data to reach any firm conclusions.* **2** (*computing*) information put into, or stored and processed by, a computer: *feed data into a computer* ○ *How long will it take to retrieve the data?*

/ˈdeɪtə/
note plural noun but often used with a singular verb. The singular *datum* is rarely used.
1 ⋈ analyse, collect, examine, record, use **data**
2 ⋈ access, feed in, process, retrieve, store **data**
▶ **computer**

databank *noun* (computing)
a centre where information is kept on computer: *A database listing customers' addresses has been added to the databank.*

/ˈdeɪtəbæŋk/
pl databanks
▶ **computer**

database *noun* (computing)
a store of facts and information logically arranged and held ready for use in a computer: *add the names and addresses of new customers to the database* ○ *The database must be updated as new information is received.*

/ˈdeɪtəbeɪs/
pl databases
⧓ manage, update, use a **database**; a central, a computer, an information, an on-line **database**
▶ **computer**

database management *noun* (computing)
a computer facility that allows information to be arranged and stored in a DATABASE: *The new system provides efficient database management and desk top publishing.*

/ˌdeɪtəbeɪs ˈmænɪdʒmənt/
note not used with *a* or *an*. No plural and used with a singular verb only.
⧓ **database management** functions, systems

data capture *noun* (computing)
the process of putting information into a computer: *We need a more efficient means of data capture.* ○ *use data capture at the point of sale*, ie key information about goods sold into a computer in a shop

/ˈdeɪtə ˌkæptʃə(r)/
note not used with *a* or *an*. No plural and used with a singular verb only.
⧓ a **data capture** system

data processing *noun* (computing)
using a computer to analyse and classify information stored in a DATABASE: *Data processing which used to take hours of tedious labour, can now be achieved by computers in a matter of minutes.*

/ˈdeɪtə ˌprəʊsesɪŋ/
note not used with *a* or *an*. No plural and used with a singular verb only.
abbr DP
⧓ a **data processing** program, system
▶ **computer**

date[1] *noun*
a specific numbered day of the month and year: *What's the date today? It's May the 16th.* ○ *All incoming mail is stamped with today's date.* ○ *There's no date on this cheque.* ○ *What is the date of the invoice?* ○ *The closing date of the share offer is 27 April.*

to date up to the present time: *calculate the number of sales to date*

/deɪt/
pl dates
⧓ today's, tomorrow's, yesterday's **date**
▶ **up to date**

date[2] *verb*
1 to write the number of the day, month and year on something: *Don't forget to date the cheque.* ○ *This letter is dated the 5th of January 1992.* **2** to guess or decide the time when something was made or happened: *Is it possible to date these documents?*

/deɪt/
date, dating, dated
note transitive verb
▶ **antedate, post-date, update**

date-stamp[1] *noun*
1 the date printed on a letter, document, etc: *The date-stamp on the envelope shows that the letter was posted yesterday.* **2** (*office practice*) a device that prints the date on documents: *Each morning in the office a clerk changes the date on the date-stamp.*

/ˈdeɪt stæmp/
pl date-stamps
2 ⧓ change, use the **date-stamp**

date-stamp[2] *verb*
1 (*office practice*) to print the date on a letter, document, etc: *All incoming mail is date-stamped before it is circulated.* **2**

/ˈdeɪt stæmp/
date-stamp, date-stamping, date-stamped

(*manufacturing*) to print a date on an item to show when it was made, should be sold or used by: *The cartons of yoghurt are date-stamped before delivery to the retailers.*

note transitive verb

---

daughter company *noun* (stock exchange)
▶ **subsidiary company**

/ˈdɔːtə ˌkʌmpəni/

---

dawn raid *noun* (stock exchange)
a surprise attempt to buy a large number of shares in a company in the first minutes of a day's business on the stock exchange, before dealers can react by raising prices: *mount a dawn raid on the shares of an international company*

/ˌdɔːn ˈreɪd/
pl dawn raids
⋈ carry out, mount a **dawn raid**
▶ **City Code on Takeovers and Mergers, raider, stock exchange, takeover**

---

day book *noun* (accounting)
a book containing records of invoices, credit notes, etc. The information is then used to update the company's accounts record: *enter the invoice number in the day book*

purchase day book a book where details of invoices received by a company from its suppliers are recorded

sales day book a book where details of invoices sent by a company to its customers are recorded

/ˈdeɪ bʊk/
pl day books
abbr DB
⋈ make an entry in, update, write something in the **day book**
▶ **accounts 1, bookkeeping, books, ledger, prime entry book**

---

day off *noun* (industry)
a 24-hour break from work: *How many days off do you get a year?* ○ *a day off in lieu*, eg in return for working during a holiday

/ˌdeɪ ˈɒf/
pl days off
⋈ be due for, be owed, take a **day off**
▶ **holiday, leave, working day**

---

day order *noun* (stock exchange)
an instruction to a dealer to buy or sell something on a specified date: *The dealer was unable to complete the day order and it was no longer valid after the close of business on that day.*

/ˈdeɪ ˌɔːdə(r)/
pl day orders
⋈ give, issue, receive a **day order**
▶ **good till cancelled order, limit order, market order, order[1] 1**

---

day release *noun* (personnel)
a form of training in which an employee is given a regular day off work to study at a college: *The apprentices are on day release today and have gone to the technical college.*

/ˌdeɪ rɪˈliːs/
note not used with *a* or *an*. No plural and used with a singular verb only.
⋈ a **day release** course; be *on* **day release**
▶ **block release, sandwich course, training**

---

day-to-day loan *noun* (banking)
money that is lent by a bank for one day only but the loan agreement can be renewed each day: *As we needed the finance urgently we arranged a day-to-day loan with the bank.*

/ˌdeɪ tə ˌdeɪ ˈləʊn/
pl day-to-day loans
syn day-to-day accommodation
▶ **accommodation 3, bridging loan, loan[1]**

DB *abbr* (accounting)
day book

/ˌdiː ˈbiː/

DCF *abbr* (accounting/finance)
discounted cash flow

/ˌdiː siː ˈef/

DD *abbr* (banking)
direct debit

/ˌdiː ˈdiː/

dead capital *noun* (accounting)
money that is not invested, or not invested profitably: *Unless you invest wisely you will end up with too much money as dead capital.*

/ˌded ˈkæpɪtl/
note not used with *a* or *an*. No plural and used with a singular verb only.
syn dead money
▶ **active capital, capital, idle money, money**

dead cat bounce *noun* (stock exchange)
an upward, but possibly misleading, movement in share prices after a significant fall: *Analysts in the City noted a slight recovery in share prices today, but some referred to it as a dead cat bounce.*

/ˌded ˌkæt ˈbaʊns/
note singular noun, used with a singular verb

deadline *noun*
a time and date by which something must be achieved or completed: *The builders worked through the night in order to meet the deadline for completing the contract.* ○ *When is the deadline for advertising copy?*

/ˈdedlaɪn/
pl deadlines
⋈ meet, miss, set a **deadline**
▶ **schedule**

dead weight[1] *noun* (transport)
the weight of an unloaded vehicle: *The car's dead weight is 1 350 kg.* ○ *a dead weight of 3 tons*

/ˌded ˈweɪt/
pl dead weights
▶ **tare**

deal[1] *noun* (commerce)
a business agreement to buy or sell goods or provide a service: *After lengthy negotiations we finally made a deal.* ○ *The deal fell through*, ie no agreement was reached.

/diːl/
pl deals
⋈ arrange, clinch, conclude, do, finalize, get, make, sign a **deal**
▶ **package deal, transaction**

deal[2] *verb* (sales)
deal in something to buy or sell something; trade in something: *The company deals in textiles.*

deal with someone/something 1 to do business with a person or an organization: *deal with an overseas company* ○ *I usually deal with the sales manager.* **2** attend to a task or problem: *I've finished dealing with the correspondence.* ○ *In this job you have to deal with a lot of angry customers.* ○ *Your order was dealt with yesterday.* ○ *Some complaints are very difficult to deal with.* **3** discuss or be concerned with a subject: *This report deals with our sales prospects for the coming year.*

/diːl/
deal, dealing, dealt
note transitive and intransitive verb
1 ⋈ **deal with** a client, a company, a customer, an organization
2 ⋈ **deal with** a complaint, an enquiry, an order, a problem
▶ **insider dealing, negotiate 1, trade**

dealer *noun*
1 (*commerce*) a person who buys and sells goods or services to make a profit: *a dealer in antiques* ○ *dealers in building materials* ○ *a used-car dealer* **2** (*banking*) a bank employee who specializes in buying and selling securities or foreign currency on behalf of the bank: *The bank's foreign exchange dealer can quote a rate for*

/ˈdiːlə(r)/
pl dealers
1 ⋈ a **dealer** *in* something
▶ **merchant, trader**

changing traveller's cheques. **3** (*stock exchange*) a person in a stock or commodity exchange who buys and sells without the services of a broker or an agent: *Stock exchange dealers reacted sharply today to news of a takeover bid.*

---

dealings *noun* (commerce)
business done between people or organizations: *The two companies have had dealings with each other over many years.* ○ *I've had dealings with him before and he's not to be trusted.*

/ˈdiːlɪŋz/
note plural noun, used with a plural verb
⋈ have **dealings** *with* (a person or an organization); business, financial, property, share **dealings**
▶ **business, transaction**

---

dear money *noun* (finance/banking)
money that is difficult to borrow because of high interest rates. Governments use a policy of dear money to limit spending: *Many small firms are feeling the impact of dear money and are being forced out of business.*

/ˌdɪə ˈmʌni/
note not used with *a* or *an*. No plural and used with a singular verb only.
⋈ a **dear money** policy
syn tight money
opp cheap money
▶ **easy money**

---

deb *abbr*
1 (*stock exchange*) debenture **2** (*banking*) debit

/deb/

---

debenture *noun* (stock exchange)
a form of long-term loan, with a fixed rate of interest and usually repaid at a fixed date. In the UK, a debenture raised by a company is secured by its ASSETS. In the US, debentures are usually unsecured: *The company increased funding through the sale of debentures.*

/dɪˈbentʃə(r)/
pl debentures
abbr deb
⋈ a **debenture** holder, issue, scheme; buy, issue, sell **debentures**
▶ **bond 1, secured debenture, unsecured debenture**

---

debenture bond *noun* (stock exchange)
a document given to a debenture holder that states the conditions of a loan and when it will be repaid: *Holders of debenture bonds received repayment of their loans on the due date.*

/dɪˈbentʃə bɒnd/
pl debenture bonds
⋈ issue a **debenture bond**

---

debenture capital *noun* (stock exchange)
the part of a company's money that has been borrowed in the form of DEBENTURES: *The company decided to raise further debenture capital in order to finance expansion.*

/dɪˈbentʃə ˌkæpɪtl/
note not used with *a* or *an*. No plural and used with a singular verb only.

---

debenture stock *noun* (stock exchange)
money lent to a company, usually in small amounts by large numbers of people, in the form of DEBENTURES. Some debentures may be converted to ORDINARY SHARES at a fixed price on a fixed date: *The company has debenture stock worth £238 million.* ○ *sell debenture stock on the Stock Exchange*

/dɪˈbentʃə ˌstɒk/
note not used with *a* or *an*. No plural and used with a singular verb only.
syn loan stock
▶ **secured debenture, unsecured debenture**

---

debit[1] *noun*

1 (*banking*) a record of money paid out of a bank account or still owed by an account holder: *The cheques issued have been cashed and the amounts now appear as debits in the statement of account.* **2** (*accounting*) a sum of money paid or owed by a business, shown on the left-hand side of a list of accounts: *add up the debits in the left-hand column*

/ˈdebɪt/
pl debits
abbr deb
1 ▶ **credit**[1] **2, direct debit**
2 ▶ **credit**[1] **3, double-entry bookkeeping**

---

debit[2] *verb* (accounting/banking)

to record in an account a sum of money paid out or still owed: *Bank charges for handling the transaction have been debited to the account.* ○ *Please supply the goods as soon as possible and debit our account.*

/ˈdebɪt/
debit, debiting, debited
note transitive verb
⋈ **debit** an account
▶ **credit**[2]

---

debit balance *noun* (accounting)

the sum of money needed to equalize the totals of money paid or owed (DEBITS) and money received (CREDITS) when the total of the debits is greater than the total of the credits in an account: *Your account shows a debit balance which we would like you to settle by sending payment without delay.*

/ˈdebɪt ˌbæləns/
pl debit balances
▶ **balance**[1] **1, credit balance**

---

debit card *noun* (commerce/banking)

a plastic card, issued by a bank and used to buy goods and services. Payment is automatically taken from the cardholder's bank account: *pay by debit card*

/ˈdebɪt ˌkɑːd/
pl debit cards
⋈ issue, use a **debit card**; pay by **debit card**; a **debit card** payment, transaction
▶ **charge card, cheque card, credit card, direct debit**

---

debit column *noun* (accounting)

the left-hand list of entries in a statement of account, showing amounts paid out or still owed: *make an entry in the debit column*

/ˈdebɪt ˌkɒləm/
pl debit columns
▶ **credit column, debit**[1] **2**

---

debit note *noun* (commerce)

a document that informs a customer of money owed to a company for goods or services supplied: *We enclose a debit note showing the amount due and look forward to the settlement of your account.*

/ˈdebɪt nəʊt/
pl debit notes
abbr DN, D/N
⋈ issue, receive, send a **debit note**
▶ **credit note**

---

debt *noun* (finance)

1 money owed by one person or an organization to another: *It took him years to pay off all his debts.* ○ *have debts amounting to over £5 000* **2** owing money, esp when you cannot pay: *The firm was hit by the recession and soon ran into debt.* ○ *The business is heavily in debt.* ○ *She is wanted for debt.*

in debt owing money

/det/
1 pl debts
⋈ clear, incur, pay back, pay off, repay, write off a **debt**
2 note not used with *a* or *an*. No plural and used with a singular verb only.
⋈ be in, get into, get out of, run into **debt**
▶ **acknowledgement of debt, bad debt, default, liability, national debt, public debts, receivables, secured debt, unsecured debt**

---

abbr abbreviation **pl** plural ⋈ collocate (*word often used with the headword*)

debt capital *noun* (accounting)
▶ **loan capital**

/ˈdet ˌkæpɪtl/

---

debt collector *noun* (commerce)
a person employed to recover money owed by a person or an organization (a DEBTOR): *employ a debt collector to recover the money*

/ˈdet kəˌlektə(r)/
pl debt collectors
▶ **debt**

---

debtor *noun* (commerce/finance)
a person or an organization that owes money to another: *After 30 days the debtor was warned that unless payment was made at once, legal action would follow.*

/ˈdetə(r)/
pl debtors
⧓ sue, take action against a **debtor**
▶ **bankrupt, creditor, judgment debtor**

---

debt ratio *noun* (finance/accounting)
the relationship between the total amount of money owed by a company and the company's own funds (SHAREHOLDERS' FUNDS): *Although the business has had a good trading year, investors are uneasy about its debt ratio.*

/ˈdet ˌreɪʃiəʊ/
pl debt ratios
▶ **debt² 1, ratio**

---

debug *verb*
1 (*computing*) to correct faults in a computer or a computer program: *Before the program can be used, it will have to be debugged and then re-tested.* **2** (*technology*) to find and remove any microphones hidden illegally in a conference room or an office: *Before the boardroom meeting began, electronics experts searched the room, ready to debug it if necessary.*

/ˌdiːˈbʌɡ/
debug, debugging, debugged
note transitive verb
1 ▶ **bug¹ 1, program**
2 ▶ **bug² 2**

---

decision-making *noun* (management)
a process of discussion by which an organization determines its policy and resolves any problems and issues: *The managing director called a meeting of senior executives for a session of collective decision-making.* ○ *A top manager must be good at decision-making.*

/dɪˈsɪʒn ˌmeɪkɪŋ/
note not used with *a* or *an*. No plural and used with a singular verb only.
⧓ centralized, collective **decision-making**

---

declaration of compliance *noun* (law)
(*UK*) a document that must be given to the Registrar of Companies in the UK by people who form a company, to show that all of the conditions specified in the Companies Act have been met: *The declaration of compliance was signed by the company's director and then sent to the Registrar of Companies.*

/ˌdekləˌreɪʃn əv kəmˈplaɪəns/
pl declarations of compliance
⧓ draft, sign a **declaration of compliance**
▶ **Certificate of Incorporation**

---

declaration of income *noun* (tax)
a statement, sent to a tax office, that gives a detailed account of all money received during the year by a person liable for income tax: *The tax officer demanded that a declaration of income be submitted within 30 days.*

/ˌdekləˌreɪʃn əv ˈɪŋkʌm/
pl declarations of income
⧓ fill in, sign a **declaration of income**
▶ **income, tax, tax return, tax year**

---

declaration of solvency *noun* (law)
a statement made by the directors of a company that is closing down to show that all money owed will be paid by a specified date: *The directors decided to wind-up the company and publish a declaration of solvency, with a copy to the Registrar of Companies.*

/ˌdekləˌreɪʃn əv ˈsɒlvənsi/
pl declarations of solvency
⧓ make, publish, sign a **declaration of solvency**
▶ **insolvency, liquidation, receivership**

declining-balance method *noun* (accounting)
▶ **reducing-balance method of depreciation**

/dɪˌklaɪnɪŋ ˈbæləns ˌmeθəd/

---

deduct *verb*
to take an amount or a part of something away from another: *Tax will be deducted automatically from your monthly salary.* ○ *For prompt payment of the bill, 5% will be deducted from the total.*

/dɪˈdʌkt/
deduct, deducting, deducted
note transitive verb
⧓ **deduct** National Insurance, tax

---

deductible *adjective*
1 (*tax*) of an amount that may be subtracted or excluded when tax is assessed: *When income tax is assessed, certain business expenses are deductible.* ○ *tax deductible at source*, ie automatically subtracted before payment is received **2** (*insurance*) of an amount, eg the first £50 of repair costs, that cannot be claimed from an insurance policy: *The first £50 of all claims on this policy is deductible, so only claims above that figure will be considered.*

/dɪˈdʌktəbl/
1 ▶ **tax deductible, tax exempt**

---

deed *noun* (law)
a signed agreement, esp about the ownership of property or legal rights: *When the house was sold, the deeds were transferred to the new owner.*

/diːd/
pl deeds
⧓ sign, transfer a **deed**; a debenture, mortgage **deed**
▶ **title deeds, transfer deed, trust deed**

---

deed of partnership *noun* (law)
a document, signed by two or more people who agree to run a business together, that gives details of the rights and duties of each: *A solicitor witnessed the signing of the deed of partnership.*

/ˌdiːd əv ˈpɑːtnəʃɪp/
pl deeds of partnership
⧓ draw up, sign a **deed of partnership**
▶ **partnership**

---

deed of transfer *noun* (law)
a legal document that changes the ownership of shares or property. In the UK, some companies require that their shares are transferred by deed; for others, the simpler TRANSFER FORM is used: *The new owners of the property deposited the deed of transfer at a bank for safe-keeping.*

/ˌdiːd əv ˈtrænsfɜː(r)/
pl deeds of transfer
syn transfer deed
⧓ sign a **deed of transfer**
▶ **blank transfer, title deeds, transfer[1] 1**

---

default[1] *noun*
1 (*law*) failure to do something that is required by law, esp to keep to the terms of a contract or to repay money owed: *The defendant failed to appear in court, so lost the case by default.* ○ *The seller was in default because he failed to supply the goods at the time he was contracted to do so.* ○ *The company is in default of several loan agreements.* **2** (*computing*) an instruction carried out by a computer program when no alternative is specified by the user: *If you don't specify the type size the computer will automatically use the default size.*

/dɪˈfɔːlt/
1 note not used with *a* or *an*. No plural and used with a singular verb only.
⧓ *by, in* **default**
▶ **breach of contract, debt**
2 note singular noun, used with a singular verb
⧓ change, set, use the **default**; a **default** layout, size, style

---

default[2] *verb* (law)
to fail to do something that is required by law, esp to keep to the terms of a contract or to repay money borrowed: *The goods have not arrived because the suppliers have defaulted on the contract.*

/dɪˈfɔːlt/
default, defaulting, defaulted
note intransitive verb
⧓ **default** *on* a credit arrangement, a loan

defaulter *noun* (law/finance)
a person who fails to do something that is required by law, or fails to repay money on a specified date: *Legal action was taken to force the defaulter to repay the loan.*

/dɪˈfɔːltə(r)/
pl defaulters
▶ **debt, judgment debtor**

---

defendant *noun* (law)
a person against whom a legal action has been brought in a court of law: *The case against the defendant was dismissed by the court when the plaintiff failed to appear.* ○ *The defendant was cross-examined* (ie questioned) *by the barrister.*

/dɪˈfendənt/
pl defendants
⧓ acquit, convict, cross-examine a **defendant**
▶ **plaintiff**

---

defer *verb*
to put off something, such as a decision or a payment, until a later time: *To stimulate sales, buyers were allowed to defer payment for up to 90 days.* ○ *Judgment in the law case has been deferred until the court meets again.*

/dɪˈfɜː(r)/
defer, deferring, deferred
note transitive verb
⧓ **defer** something *for, until* (a time); **defer** payment, tax

---

deferred liabilities *noun* (accounting)
money owed that does not have to be repaid until some future date: *set money aside for deferred liabilities*

/dɪˌfɜːd ˌlaɪəˈbɪlətiz/
note plural noun, used with a plural verb
syn long-term liabilities, non-current liabilities
▶ **liability 2**

---

deferred ordinary share *noun* (stock exchange)
1 an ordinary share, that does not provide a dividend until the dividends of all other ordinary shares have been paid. It may provide a larger share of the profit: *distribute the remaining profit among holders of deferred ordinary shares* **2** an ordinary share that receives no dividend until after a specified number of years

/dɪˌfɜːd ˌɔːdənri ˈʃeə(r)/
pl deferred shares
▶ **ordinary share, share**

---

deficit *noun* (accounting)
the amount by which expenditure is greater than income over a particular period: *Last year's sales figures show a deficit of £2.2 million.*

/ˈdefɪsɪt/
pl deficits
⧓ result in, show a **deficit**
opp surplus
▶ **adverse balance, loss 1, shortfall, trade deficit**

---

deflation *noun* (economics/finance)
a reduction in the amount of money circulating in a country's economy, so that prices fall or remain steady: *The government introduced a policy of deflation.*

/ˌdiːˈfleɪʃn/
note not used with *a* or *an*. No plural and used with a singular verb only.
▶ **disinflation, inflation, reflation**

---

defraud *verb* (law)
to deceive someone in order to obtain money, goods, etc dishonestly: *The court ordered the chairman to repay the £11 million pounds to the company he defrauded.* ○ *She was defrauded of £5 000 by a dishonest accountant.*

/dɪˈfrɔːd/
defraud, defrauding, defrauded
note transitive verb
⧓ **defraud** someone *of* something; be **defrauded** *by* someone
▶ **fraud**

degearing *noun* (finance)
a change in the method of raising money in a company by selling more shares and borrowing less money from the bank: *High interest rates have forced the company to consider further degearing.*

/ˌdiːˈɡɪərɪŋ/
note not used with *a* or *an*. No plural and used with a singular verb only.
⧓ carry out, a process of **degearing**
► **gearing, highly geared, ungeared**

del credere agent *noun* (commerce)
a person who sells goods for another and who agrees to pay for them if the customers fail to do so: *For carrying the risk of non-payment by customers, the del credere agent receives extra commission on sales.*

/ˌdel kredˌeəreɪ ˈeɪdʒənt/
pl del credere agents
► **agent, factor**

delegate[1] *noun*
a person who represents others and acts for them, usually at a conference or meeting: *a list of conference delegates* ○ *Each company may send a maximum of three delegates.*

/ˈdelɪɡət/
pl delegates
⧓ a company, a conference, an official **delegate**
► **agent, representative**

delegate[2] *verb*
1 to choose or send someone to act for others at a conference or meeting: *The manager delegated an assistant to represent him at the meeting.* **2** to choose someone to carry out a task: *The accounts manager was delegated to reorganize the finance department.* **3** to give a job to someone in a lower position: *A good manager must know when to delegate (work).*

/ˈdelɪɡeɪt/
delegate, delegating, delegated
1, 2 note transitive verb
3 note transitive and intransitive verb
⧓ **delegate** a job, a task, work

delete *verb*
1 to cross out or remove words from a passage of writing or print: *The written summary was too long, so several sentences had to be deleted.* **2** (*computing*) to remove information, a file, etc from a computer: *Don't delete the wrong file.* ○ *Names and addresses of customers who haven't bought anything for five years have been deleted.* **3** (*manufacturing*) to stop making or selling a particular item: *This model has been deleted and is no longer available.*

/dɪˈliːt/
delete, deleting, deleted
note transitive verb
1 ⧓ **delete** a letter, paragraph, word
2 ⧓ **delete** data, a file, information, a record

deliver *verb*
to take letters, messages, goods, etc to the places or people they are addressed to: *The goods were transported from the factory and delivered to the store.* ○ *We deliver to your door.* ○ *Has the post been delivered yet?*

/dɪˈlɪvə(r)/
deliver, delivering, delivered
note transitive and intransitive verb
⧓ **deliver** goods, a letter, mail, a message, an order, a parcel, post
► **consign, despatch**[2]**, distribute, transport**[2]

delivery *noun* (commerce)
1 taking letters, messages, goods, etc to the places or people they are addressed to: *The suppliers of spare parts promised delivery within 10 days.* **2** (**a**) an instance of this: *How many deliveries do you make in a week?* (**b**) the letters, goods, etc delivered: *We had a large delivery of spare parts today.*

/dɪˈlɪvəri/
1 note not used with *a* or *an*. No plural and used with a singular verb only.
⧓ cash on, daily, express, free, recorded **delivery**; take **delivery** of something
2 pl deliveries

⧓ a **delivery** date, order, point, service

▶ **drop shipment**

---

delivery note *noun* (commerce)

a document sent with goods to a customer, that gives details of the goods. The customer signs the delivery note to say that he/she has received the goods: *The van driver handed over the goods and asked the customer to sign the delivery note.*

/dɪˈlɪvəri ˌnəʊt/

pl delivery notes

abbr d/o

⧓ enclose, sign, write out a **delivery note**

---

demand[1] *noun*

1 (*commerce*) a firm request for payment: *The customer was sent a demand for immediate payment of the bill.* **2** (*economics*) the desire of consumers to obtain goods and services: *an increased demand for luxury goods* ○ *Factory workers are working overtime to keep up with demand.*

market demand the desire of consumers to obtain goods and services of a particular kind or in a particular area: *The market demand for a product is affected by its price.*

/dɪˈmɑːnd/

1 pl demands

▶ **final demand, on demand**

2 note not used with *a* or *an*. No plural and used with a singular verb only.

▶ **excess demand, supply and demand**

---

demand[2] *verb*

1 to ask for something forcefully: *The workers demanded higher wages.* **2** to need or require something: *The work is highly skilled and demands long training.*

/dɪˈmɑːnd/

demand, demanding, demanded

note transitive verb

---

demand bill *noun* (banking)

▶ **sight bill**

/dɪˈmɑːnd bɪl/

pl demand bills

---

demand-led *adjective* (economics)

relating to intensified economic activity caused by a rise in consumers' disposable incomes and a desire by consumers to obtain more goods and services: *The government reduced income tax in order to encourage a demand-led upturn in economic activity.*

/dɪˈmɑːnd led/

⧓ **demand-led** economic activity, inflation

▶ **market orientation, product orientation**

---

demand note *noun* (banking)

a document stating that a specified amount of money will be paid immediately it is asked for: *The buyer gave the seller a demand note as a deposit for goods ordered.*

/dɪˈmɑːnd nəʊt/

pl demand notes

⧓ sign, write out a **demand note**

▶ **sight bill**

---

demarcation dispute *noun* (industrial relations)

an argument between trade unions or members of one trade union about the job or type of work each worker should do: *a demarcation dispute between engine maintenance workers and electricians*

/ˌdiːmɑːˈkeɪʃn dɪˌspjuːt/

pl demarcation disputes

⧓ be involved in, settle a **demarcation dispute**

▶ **industrial dispute**

---

demonstrate *verb*

1 to explain and show how something works or is done: *The salesman demonstrated the use of the photocopier.* **2** (*industrial relations*) to put on a show of protest against, or support for, something: *Workers demonstrated against the low pay offer.* ○ *demonstrate for higher wages*

/ˈdemənstreɪt/

demonstrate, demonstrating, demonstrated

1 note transitive verb

⧓ **demonstrate** how something works, the use of something

2 note intransitive verb

⧓ **demonstrate** *against, for* something

---

demonstration *noun*

1 (**a**) showing and explaining how something works or how something is done: *It's easier to learn by demonstration than by reading a manual.* (**b**) an instance of this: *The systems manager gave a demonstration of the new computer system.* **2** (*industrial relations*) a show of support for, or protest against, something: *Steel workers held a demonstration against proposed job losses.*

/ˌdemənˈstreɪʃn/
abbr demo
1a note not used with *a* or *an*. No plural and used with a singular verb only.
1b pl demonstrations
⋈ give a **demonstration** *of* something
2 pl demonstrations
⋈ hold, organize a **demonstration**

---

denationalization *noun* (industry)

the process or result of putting a government-owned company or industry back into private ownership; privatization: *propose denationalization of the railways*

/ˌdiːˌnæʃənəlaɪˈzeɪʃn/
(also **denationalisation**)
note not used with *a* or *an*. No plural and used with a singular verb only.
⋈ oppose, propose **denationalization**
▶ **nationalization, privatization**

---

denationalize *verb* (industry)

to put a government-owned company or industry back into private ownership; to privatize: *Investors were eager to buy shares in the water industry when it was denationalized.* ○ *make plans to denationalize the aircraft industry*

/ˌdiːˈnæʃənəlaɪz/
denationalize, denationalizing, denationalized
(also **denationalise**)
note transitive verb
⋈ **denationalize** an industry
▶ **nationalize, private sector, privatize, public sector**

---

dep *abbr*

1 departure **2** deposit **3** depot **4** deputy

note used in written English only
(also **Dep**)

---

department *noun*

a section of a large business, organization or shop: *New staff should report to the personnel department.* ○ *work in the accounts, finance, sales, etc department* ○ *The furniture department is on the third floor.*

/dɪˈpɑːtmənt/
pl departments
abbr Dept, dept, dpt
⋈ a **department** manager, meeting; be in charge of, run a **department**
▶ **division**

---

department manager *noun* (management)

▶ **manager**

/dɪˌpɑːtmənt ˈmænɪdʒə(r)/

---

the Department of Employment *noun* (industry)

(*UK*) the government department responsible for reducing unemployment, providing training for industry and improving working conditions: *The Department of Employment has released figures showing a rise in the number of people unemployed.*

/ðə dɪˌpɑːtmənt əv ɪmˈplɔɪmənt/

---

the Department of the Environment *noun*
(*UK*) the government department responsible for controlling pollution and monitoring the effects of building, industrial and leisure activities on towns, villages and the countryside: *The Department of the Environment is giving awards to companies who introduce the most successful waste-recycling schemes.*

/ðə dɪˌpɑːtmənt əv ði ɪnˈvaɪərənmənt/
abbr DoE

the Department of Trade and Industry *noun* (industry)
(*UK*) the government department responsible for controlling international trade, regulating certain industries and protecting consumers and traders from unfair practices: *guidelines on takeovers and mergers issued by the Department of Trade and Industry*

/ðə dɪˌpɑːtmənt əv ˌtreɪd ənd ˈɪndəstri/
abbr DTI
▶ **Monopolies and Mergers Commission, Office of Fair Trading, trade[1] 1, Trading Standards Department**

department store *noun* (retail)
a large shop where many kinds of goods are sold in different departments: *buy clothes from a leading department store*

/dɪˈpɑːtmənt stɔː(r)/
pl department stores
⋈ open, run a **department store**
▶ **chain store, store[1] 2**

departure *noun*
1 the act of leaving a place: *Please remember to return your visitor's badge before departure.* ○ *The flight is scheduled for departure at 16.20.* ○ *an airport departure lounge* **2** an instance of this: *a notice showing arrivals and departures of trains*

/dɪˈpɑːtʃə(r)/
1 note not used with *a* or *an*. No plural and used with a singular verb only.
⋈ before, on **departure**
2 pl departures
▶ **arrival**

deposit[1] *noun*
1 (*banking*) a sum of money paid into a bank or savings account: *make a regular deposit of £100 per month* **2** (*finance*) (**a**) a payment of part of a larger sum to be paid later, esp to prevent the goods being sold to someone else: *pay a 10% deposit to secure the goods* (**b**) a sum of money paid when borrowing or hiring something and given back if the item is returned undamaged: *He returned the hired car and claimed back his deposit.*

/dɪˈpɒzɪt/
pl deposits
abbr Dep, dep
1 ⋈ make a **deposit**
▶ **bank deposit, certificate of deposit, credit[1] 2, public deposits, safe deposit**
opp withdrawal
2 ⋈ ask for, pay, require a **deposit**; a cash, non-returnable, returnable **deposit**
▶ **down payment, instalment**

deposit[2] *verb* (banking)
to put money, securities or valuables into a bank for safety: *The money was deposited with a building society.* ○ *The title deeds of the house are deposited at a bank.*

/dɪˈpɒzɪt/
deposit, depositing, deposited
note transitive verb
opp withdraw

deposit account *noun* (banking)
money invested in a bank account that pays interest and for which the bank needs advance warning of a specified number of days (NOTICE) if the money is to be taken out: *save money in a deposit account* ○ *The deposit account offers a high rate of interest but withdrawals require 90 days' notice.*

/dɪˈpɒzɪt əˌkaʊnt/
pl deposit accounts
abbr D/A
syn account, (*US*) time account, time deposit
⋈ put (money) into, take (money) out of, withdraw (money) from a **deposit account**

▶ **bank account, current account 1, savings account**

---

deposit slip *noun* (banking)
▶ **paying-in slip**

/dɪˈpɒzɪt ˌslɪp/
pl deposit slips

---

depot *noun*
1 (*commerce*) a place where goods are stored, esp before being sent elsewhere: *All supplies were sent to the depot to await shipment.* **2** (*transport*) (**a**) (*UK*) a place where vehicles are parked, cleaned and serviced when not in use: *The bus broke down and had to be towed to the depot for repair.* (**b**) (*US*) a railway or bus station: *The train left the depot on time.*

/ˈdepəʊ/
pl depots
abbr Dep, dep, dpt
1 ⋈ a goods **depot**
▶ **warehouse**
2 ⋈ a bus, lorry, maintenance **depot**

---

depreciate *verb* (finance)
1 to lose value over a period of time: *The pound has depreciated a lot since I was a child.* **2** (*accounting*) to reduce the value of an asset in a company's books: *Fixed assets are depreciated over four years.*

/dɪˈpriːʃieɪt/
depreciate, depreciating, depreciated
1 note intransitive verb
⋈ **depreciate** in value
opp appreciate
2 note transitive verb

---

depreciation *noun*
1 (*finance/banking*) a fall in the value of a country's currency: *The dollar suffered a 5% depreciation against the pound.* **2** (*accounting*) a gradual loss in the value of something, such as a vehicle, a machine or any ASSET that wears out with use and age: *allow for depreciation when calculating the value of the equipment* ○ *a sharp rate of depreciation*

/dɪˌpriːʃiˈeɪʃn/
note no plural
1 ⋈ rate of **depreciation**
▶ **accelerated depreciation, accumulated depreciation, current cost accounting, devaluation, reducing-balance method of depreciation, straight line depreciation, wear and tear**
2 ⋈ currency **depreciation**
opp appreciation

---

depreciation allowance *noun* (tax)
a form of TAX RELIEF that allows the cost of new machinery, etc to be taken off the amount of tax due for the period until the machine is too old to use: *The government has increased depreciation allowances on new plant to encourage investment.*

/dɪˌpriːʃiˈeɪʃn əˌlaʊəns/
pl depreciation allowances
▶ **tax relief**

---

depressed market *noun* (commerce)
a market where there is little demand for the products and services offered for sale: *Many traders are suffering because of the depressed market.*

/dɪˌprest ˈmɑːkɪt/
pl depressed markets
opp active market
▶ **market[1], recession, slump[1]**

---

depression *noun* (economics)
a period with very little economic activity, resulting in mass unemployment and the failure of many businesses: *The depression is resulting in factories closing down and thousands of workers losing their jobs.*

/ˌdɪˈpreʃn/
pl depressions
⋈ an agricultural, economic, industrial **depression**
▶ **boom[1], recession, slump**

Dept *abbr*
department

note used in written English only
(also **dept, dpt**)

---

deputy *noun* (management)
1 a person who is given work, authority, etc when someone more senior is absent: *The chairman is away today, but I'm acting as his deputy.* **2** a person who is immediately below the head of an organization, a department, etc: *a deputy director*

/ˈdepjəti/
pl deputies
abbr Dep, dep
1 ⋈ act as a **deputy** *for* someone; act as someone's **deputy**
2 ⋈ the **deputy** editor, leader, secretary
▶ **vice-**

---

deputy manager *noun* (management)
▶ **manager**

/ˈdepjəti ˈmænɪdʒə(r)/

---

deregulate *verb* (law)
to free an industry, an organization, etc from price control, especially by a government: *The European Commission is trying to deregulate the European airline market.* ○ *deregulate oil prices*

/ˌdiːˈregjuleɪt/
deregulate, deregulating, deregulated
note transitive verb
opp regulate

---

deregulation *noun* (law)
freeing an industry, an organization, etc from control, esp by a government: *deregulation of food prices* ○ *deregulation of the airline industry*

/diːˌregjuˈleɪʃn/
note not used with *a* or *an*. No plural and used with a singular verb only.
⋈ a policy of **deregulation**
opp regulation

---

design[1] *noun* (industry)
1 a plan, drawing or model used to decide how something will look or work: *We have asked the architect to come up with a new design.* **2** the art of making such plans, etc: *Environmental issues will have an important effect on future car design.* ○ *Many design engineers work with computer-aided design* (ie use computers to produce accurate models, do calculations, etc). **3** the shape, form and characteristics of something made, built or manufactured: *I like the design, but is the car expensive to run?* ○ *Damage to the machine was caused by a faulty design.*

/dɪˈzaɪn/
1 pl designs
⋈ a modern, a new, an original, a traditional **design**
2 note no plural
⋈ a **design** fault, feature
3 pl designs
⋈ a bad, complex, good, faulty, simple **design**

---

design[2] *verb* (industry)
to decide how something will look or work by making plans, drawings or models of it: *A graphic artist is designing our new company logo.*

/dɪˈzaɪn/
design, designing, designed
note transitive verb
⋈ **design** a book, building, car, dress, machine, etc

---

designer *noun* (industry)
a person whose job is to decide how something will look or work by making plans, drawings or models of it: *The car designer is still working on our latest saloon model.* ○ *employ a freelance graphic designer to produce a promotions leaflet*

/dɪˈzaɪnə(r)/
pl designers
⋈ a fashion, a graphic, an industrial, an interior, a product **designer**

---

deskilling *noun*
1 (*economics*) the losing of skills by workers through unemployment, lack of training, etc: *The introduction of new technology may have a deskilling effect on the workforce.* **2** (*industry*) reorganizing an industrial process so that it can be done by unskilled workers: *High labour costs have forced the industry to adopt a policy of deskilling.*

/ˌdiːˈskɪlɪŋ/
note no plural

desk research *noun* (marketing)
a form of MARKET RESEARCH using existing information, eg company records, published facts and figures: *The advertising agency spent many hours in desk research before going out to interview people.*

/ˈdesk rɪˌsɜːtʃ/
note not used with *a* or *an*. No plural and used with a singular verb only.
⋈ carry out, do **desk research**
▶ **market research**

desktop *noun* (office practice)
the area on top of a desk or table where work is done: *This small computer is designed to fit on the desktop.*

/ˈdesktɒp/
note usually singular
▶ **workstation**

desktop computer *noun* (computing)
a small computer that can fit on the top of a desk or table: *Desktop computers are now a feature of any modern office.*

/ˌdesktɒp kəmˈpjuːtə(r)/
pl desktop computers
⋈ install, use a **desktop computer**

desktop publishing *noun* (computing)
the producing of good quality printed matter, such as catalogues and magazines, by computer equipment small enough to be used on a desk or table: *Desktop publishing is reducing the company's need to use the services of outside printers.*

/ˌdesktɒp ˈpʌblɪʃɪŋ/
note not used with *a* or *an*. No plural and used with a singular verb only.
abbr DTP

despatch[1] *noun* (distribution)
1 the sending of goods, a letter, a message, etc to a destination: *Despatch of the goods will be within 14 days of receiving the order.*
2 a letter, message or report, etc sent urgently by a news agency or an official: *A despatch just received from the disaster area speaks of heavy casualties.*

/dɪˈspætʃ/
(also **dispatch**)
1 note not used with *a* or *an*. No plural and used with a singular verb only.
⋈ a **despatch** clerk, office
2 pl despatches
⋈ send a **despatch**

despatch[2] *verb* (distribution)
to send goods, letters, messages, reports, etc to their destination: *The goods ordered have been despatched and should arrive shortly.* ○ *When was the parcel despatched?*

/dɪˈspætʃ/
despatch, despatching, despatched
(also **dispatch**)
note transitive verb
⋈ **despatch** goods, a letter, a message, a report
▶ **consign, deliver, distribute, transport**[2]

despatch note *noun* (transport)
a note sent with goods that gives details of the goods and any missing items that will be sent later: *check the despatch note for missing items*

/dɪˈspætʃ ˌnəʊt/
pl despatch notes
▶ **advice note, arrival notice**

despatch rider *noun* (distribution)
a person who carries letters, messages, parcels, etc to their destination, usually on a motor cycle: *The parcel will be delivered by a despatch rider.*

/dɪˈspætʃ ˌraɪdə(r)/
pl despatch riders
⋈ collected, delivered, picked up by a **despatch rider**

destination *noun* (transport)
a place where people or goods are going to or being sent: *Tokyo is the plane's final destination.* ○ *The goods were sent by sea and reached their destination on time.*

/ˌdestɪˈneɪʃn/
pl destinations
⋈ arrive at, reach a **destination**

devaluation *noun* (finance)
1 reducing a currency to a lower value in relation to other currencies: *The government is not willing to resort to devaluation.* **2** an instance of this: *a devaluation of 13% against the Deutschmark*

/ˌdiːvæljuˈeɪʃn/
1 note not used with *a* or *an*. No plural and used with a singular verb only.
2 pl devaluations
▶ **depreciation, exchange rate, floating rate**
opp revaluation

devalue *verb* (finance)
to reduce the value of a currency relative to other currencies: *The government denied any plans to devalue the currency.* ○ *The pound was devalued.*

/ˌdiːˈvæljuː/
devalue, devaluing, devalued
note transitive verb
▶ **exchange rate, floating rate, value**[1]

develop *verb*
1 (**a**) to grow slowly and become more advanced or organized; to make someone or something do this: *The business began in a small way and has developed into a multinational.* ○ *The product is still being developed.* ○ *develop a new idea* (**b**) to begin to happen or be noticeable: *A fault has developed in the computer system.* ○ *The machine is old and is developing problems.* **2** to build houses, factories, shops, etc on a piece of land, esp to increase its economic value: *The property company has been given permission to develop the site.*

/dɪˈveləp/
develop, developing, developed
1 note transitive and intransitive verb
⋈ **develop** *into* something
2 note transitive verb
⋈ **develop** an area, a region, a site

development *noun*
1 developing or being developed: *development from a small business into a multinational company* **2** a new event: *There has been a development in the industrial dispute.* **3** a new product or the act of making a new product: *the latest development in computer software* **4** a piece of land on which houses, shops, factories have been built: *a 65-acre site set aside for an industrial development*

/dɪˈveləpmənt/
1 note not used with *a* or *an*. No plural and used with a singular verb only.
2 pl developments
⋈ an interesting, a major, a minor, a new **development**
3 pl developments
⋈ a technological **development**
▶ **economic development, management development, product development, research and development**
4 pl developments
⋈ an economic, a housing, an industrial **development**

diagram *noun*
a drawing or plan that uses simple lines to show how a machine, a structure or a process works: *Use the diagrams in the instruction manual to help you to assemble the machine.* ○ *a diagram of a computer network*

/ˈdaɪəgræm/
pl diagrams
⋈ draw a **diagram**; a **diagram** *of* something; a **diagram** shows (how something works)
▶ **bar chart, block diagram, chart, graph, pictogram**

dictaphone *noun* (office practice)
a machine for recording words spoken into it, so that the message can be played back and typed: *record a message on the dictaphone*

/ˈdɪktəfəʊn/
pl dictaphones
▶ **answerphone, audio-typist**

dictate *verb* (office practice)
to say or read aloud words to be recorded or written in SHORTHAND and typed later: *She dictated a letter to her secretary.*

/dɪkˈteɪt/
pl dictate, dictating, dictated
note transitive verb
⋈ **dictate** a letter, message, report
▶ **audio-typist, shorthand typist**

dictating machine *noun* (office practice)
a machine used to record a message that can be played back later and typed: *record a letter on the dictating machine*

/dɪkˈteɪtɪŋ məˌʃiːn/
pl dictating machines
▶ **audio-typist, dictaphone, shorthand typist**

differential *noun*
1 (*personnel*) the difference in rates of pay between different types of work, or of different workers doing the same work: *a dispute about the pay differential between skilled and unskilled workers*
2 (*sales*) the difference in prices charged for the same product in different shops, or for different products in a range: *the price differential of petrol among various petrol stations*

/ˌdɪfəˈrenʃl/
pl differentials
1 ⋈ a pay, salary, wage **differential**
2 ⋈ a price **differential**
▶ **multiple pricing, pricing policy**

differentiation *noun* (sales)
distinguishing products from those of a rival company and making them attractive to buyers through differences in price, packaging, advertising, etc: *Firms making similar products compete through a combination of price and product differentiation.*

/ˌdɪfərenʃiˈeɪʃn/
note not used with *a* or *an*. No plural and used with a singular verb only.
⋈ **differentiation** *between* prices, products, services; increase, introduce **differentiation**
▶ **marketing mix, market segmentation, undifferentiated marketing**

digit *noun*
any one of the ten Arabic numbers 0 to 9: *a seven-digit telephone number* ○ *count the number of digits*

/ˈdɪdʒɪt/
pl digits
▶ **binary digit, number**

digital *adjective*
1 relating to electronic equipment that displays information such as time, date, temperature, speed, etc, using the digits 1 to 9 and 0: *set the time on a digital clock* ○ *a watch with a digital display* **2** (*computing*) relating to computers and electronic equipment that process information coded in digits: *a digital computer* ○ *digital electronics*

/ˈdɪdʒɪtl/
⋈ a **digital** clock, radio, thermometer

diminishing-balance method *noun* (accounting)
▶ **reducing-balance method of depreciation**

/dɪˌmɪnɪʃɪŋ ˈbæləns ˌmeθəd/

direct access *noun* (computing)
a system of finding information stored in a computer memory by going straight to the item required, without having to search through each item in order: *a direct access storage device* ○ *direct access processing*

/dɪˌrekt ˈækses/
note not used with *a* or *an*. No plural and used with a singular verb only.
▶ **Random Access Memory, sequential access**

direct cost *noun* (industry)
the cost of materials, labour, etc involved in making a product: *Direct costs grow as output increases.*

/ˌdɪrekt ˈkɒst/
pl direct costs
note usually plural
▶ **cost[1], fixed cost, oncost, overhead, variable cost**

direct debit *noun* (banking)
(*UK*) a system of paying bills, etc by having money automatically transferred from a bank account. The amount paid is not specified in advance as it is in a STANDING ORDER: *arrange to pay insurance by direct debit* ○ *The bank charges for processing cheques, standing orders and direct debits.*

/dɪˌrekt ˈdebɪt/
pl direct debits
abbr DD
⧓ pay by **direct debit**
▶ **debit, debit card, standing order**

direct export *noun* (commerce)
a way of selling goods straight to a customer overseas without using an agent; an item sold in this way: *sell by direct export to former tourists* ○ *an increase in the number of direct exports*

/dɪˌrekt ˈekspɔːt/
pl direct exports
⧓ sell by **direct export**
▶ **export[1]**

direct letter of credit *noun* (banking/commerce)
▶ **letter of credit**

/dɪˌrekt ˌletər əv ˈkredɪt/
pl direct letters of credit

direct mail *noun* (sales)
a method of selling by sending information about goods and services straight to possible customers: *sell goods by direct mail* ○ *a direct mail campaign*

/dɪˌrekt ˈmeɪl/
note not used with *a* or *an*. No plural and used with a singular verb only.
⧓ **direct mail** advertising, selling; advertise by, sell by, use **direct mail**
▶ **mailing list, mailshot, telesales**

direct marketing *noun* (marketing)
selling goods or services without using shops but by using postal and telephone services or calling at customers' homes to obtain orders: *Direct marketing cuts out the costs of supplying shops and enables customers to buy at lower prices.*

/dɪˌrekt ˈmɑːkɪtɪŋ/
note not used with *a* or *an*. No plural and used with a singular verb only.
▶ **mail shot, marketing, telesales**

director *noun*
1 (*law*) a person appointed by the shareholders of a company to help run it and to see that the company follows the rules and regulations stated in the ARTICLES OF ASSOCIATION: *After ten years with the company he was made a director.* **2** (*administration*) a person in charge of a project or a department: *the Director of Studies* ○ *a finance, marketing, sales director*

/dɪˈrektə(r)/
pl directors
⧓ appoint a **director**
▶ **alternate director, board, company, executive, executive director, manager, managing director, shareholder, worker director**

direct sale *noun* (sales)
a way of selling goods or services straight to the customer, without using a shop or agent; an item sold in this way: *Many farmers now sell produce at the farm, a method of direct sale which increases their profits.* ○ *The car was a direct sale from the factory.*

/dɪˌrekt ˈseɪl/
pl direct sales
⧓ make a **direct sale**
▶ **mail order, sale**

direct tax *noun* (tax)
a tax, eg INCOME TAX, that is paid straight to the government as distinct from tax that forms part of the payment for goods and services: *Government policy has been to reduce direct tax, but increase indirect taxes such as value added tax.*

/dɪˌrekt ˈtæks/
pl direct taxes
⧓ cut, impose, levy, pay a **direct tax**
▶ **indirect tax, tax**[1]

dirty bill of lading *noun* (shipping)
▶ **bill of lading**

/ˌdɜːti ˌbɪl əv ˈleɪdɪŋ/
pl dirty bills of lading

disc *noun* (computing)
▶ **disk**

/dɪsk/
pl discs

disciplinary *adjective* (management)
of the way of enforcing the rules, regulations and codes of behaviour of an organization, a profession, etc: *take disciplinary action against an employee who is always late for work* ○ *The director will face disciplinary procedures for stealing company funds.*

/ˈdɪsɪplɪnəri/
⧓ **disciplinary** action, procedures; a **disciplinary** hearing, tribunal

disclaimer *noun* (law)
a formal statement in which someone says he/she is not responsible for something or does not know about something: *The owners of the supermarket issued a disclaimer about damage to cars left in their car park.*

/dɪsˈkleɪmə(r)/
pl disclaimers
⧓ issue, make, publish, send a **disclaimer**

disclosed factoring *noun* (commerce)
the purchasing of the trade debts of a manufacturer, in which the role of the buyer of the debts (the FACTOR) is revealed

/dɪsˈkləʊzd ˈfæktə(r)ɪŋ/
note not used with *a* or *an*. No plural and used with a singular verb only.
⧓ be involved in, carry out **disclosed factoring**
opp undisclosed factoring
▶ **factoring**

discontinue *verb*
to stop making or doing something: *This particular make of washing machine has been discontinued.* ○ *The bus service will be discontinued as from next week.*

/ˌdɪskənˈtɪnjuː/
discontinue, discontinuing, discontinued
note transitive verb
⧓ a **discontinued** make, model

discount[1] *noun*
1 (*commerce*) a reduction in the selling price of something: *get a 10% discount for paying cash* ○ *offer a discount to customers buying large quantities* **2** (*banking*) the amount by which the value of a bill of exchange is reduced if bought before it is due for payment: *The bill of exchange was bought at a discount.* **3** (*stock exchange*) the amount by which the selling price of a security is less than its original price (the NOMINAL PRICE): *The gilts were offered at a discount of 10%.*

/ˈdɪskaʊnt/
pl discounts
⧓ get, offer a **discount**; sell (something) at a **discount**
▶ **best price, cash discount, discount house, discounting, rebate, refund**[1]**, trade discount**

discount[2] *verb*
1 to reduce the selling price of something: *The tour company claimed they do not add surcharges, nor do they discount.* ○ *The original price was discounted by 10%.* **2** to buy a bill of exchange at a reduced price before it is due for payment: *The discounted bill had a month to run before its maturity date.*

/dɪsˈkaʊnt/
discount, discounting, discounted
note transitive verb
1 ⧓ **discount** a price
2 ⧓ **discount** a bill of exchange

discounted bill *noun* (banking)
a bill of exchange bought at a reduced price before it is due for payment: *The discounted bill had a month to run before its maturity date.*

/dɪsˌkaʊntɪd ˈbɪl/
pl discounted bills

discounted cash flow *noun* (accounting/finance)
a method of calculating how profitable an investment will be by looking at the amount paid out, the interest earned and the degree of risk: *The discounted cash flow showed the project to be not worth investing in.*

/dɪsˌkaʊntɪd ˈkæʃ fləʊ/
pl discounted cash flows
abbr DCF
► **cash flow**

discount house *noun* (banking/finance)
a bank that specializes in DISCOUNTING bills of exchange and promotes a flow of short-term loans between the government and the banks: *Discount houses usually lose money when interest rates rise unexpectedly.*

/ˈdɪskaʊnt haʊs/
pl discount houses
► **accepting house, bank[1], merchant bank**

discount rate *noun* (banking)
the percentage rate used by banks when discounting bills of exchange

/ˈdɪskaʊnt reɪt/
note usually singular
⧓ current **discount rate**
syn bill rate
► **base rate, rate 2**

discrimination *noun* (personnel)
treating a person or a group differently, usually worse, than others: *The employer was accused of racial discrimination.*

/dɪˌskrɪmɪˈneɪʃn/
note not used with *a* or *an*. No plural and used with a singular verb only.
⧓ political, racial, sexual **discrimination**
► **equality, equal opportunity, equal pay, price discrimination**

disembark *verb* (transport)
(of people) to leave a ship or an aircraft: *Forty passengers disembarked at Southampton.* ○ *Remember to take everything with you when you disembark.*

/ˌdɪsɪmˈbɑːk/
disembark, disembarking, disembarked
note intransitive verb
⧓ **disembark** *at* (a port or an airport), *from* (an aircraft, a ferry, a ship)

disembarkation *noun* (transport)
the landing of passengers from a ship or an aircraft: *Please have your passports ready for disembarkation.*

/ˌdɪsembɑːˈkeɪʃn/
note not used with *a* or *an*. No plural and used with a singular verb only.
opp embarkation

dishonour *verb* (banking)
1 (of a bank) to refuse to pay a cheque or a bill of exchange because there is not enough money in the account: *The cheque was dishonoured and marked 'refer to drawer'.* **2** (of a drawee) to fail to accept or fail to pay a bill of exchange

/dɪsˈɒnə(r)/
dishonour, dishonouring, dishonoured
(*US* **dishonor**)
note transitive verb, usually passive
► **accept 3, bounce[1] 1, honour 1**

disinflation *noun* (economics)
a gradual reduction in consumers' spending power brought about by a government wanting to control INFLATION: *The government's policy of disinflation is intended to reduce inflation without causing economic hardship.*

/ˌdɪsɪnˈfleɪʃn/
note not used with *a* or *an*. No plural and used with a singular verb only.
▶ **deflation, inflation, reflation**

---

disintegration *noun* (industry)
the breaking up of a company or group of companies: *The company's long-established corporate identity is now facing disintegration.* ○ *Disintegration of the publishing empire brought share prices crashing.*

/dɪsˌɪntɪˈgreɪʃn/
note not used with *a* or *an*. No plural and used with a singular verb only.
⧓ face, result in **disintegration**
▶ **integration**

---

disinvest *verb* (finance/stock exchange)
to stop investing money in a company or country with the aim of making a future profit; to reduce the amount of money invested: *Many governments have disinvested from the developing country because of political unrest.* ○ *The recession has caused many companies to disinvest.*

/ˌdɪsɪnˈvest/
disinvest, disinvesting, disinvested
note intransitive verb
⧓ **disinvest** *from* a country, an organization
▶ **invest**

---

disinvestment *noun* (finance/stock exchange)
the reducing or ending of investment in a company or country: *The country's economy has suffered because of war and disinvestment.*

/ˌdɪsɪnˈvestmənt/
note not used with *a* or *an*. No plural and used with a singular verb only.
▶ **investment**

---

disk *noun* (computing)
a computer storage device, usually with magnetic surfaces, that records information received electronically: *All our customer records are stored on disk.* ○ *insert a disk into the computer*

/dɪsk/
pl disks
(also **disc**)
⧓ save, store information on **disk**; copy (on) to **disk**
syn magnetic disk
▶ **floppy disk, hard disk, laser disk, Winchester disk**

---

disk drive *noun* (computing)
part of a computer that contains a HARD DISK on which information is stored: *a computer unit with a separate disk drive*

/ˈdɪsk draɪv/
pl disk drives

---

dismiss *verb*
1 (*personnel*) to remove an employee from a job or position: *The bank clerk was dismissed for dishonesty.* ○ *Three car workers were dismissed from their jobs.* **2** (*law*) to reject a case or an appeal in a law court: *The case was dismissed.*

/dɪsˈmɪs/
dismiss, dismissing, dismissed
note transitive verb
1 ⧓ be **dismissed** *by* (someone), *for* (something), *from* (a job)
▶ **sack**[2]
2 ⧓ **dismiss** an appeal, a case

---

dismissal *noun*
1 (*personnel*) (**a**) the act of removing an employee from a job or position: *The employee protested against the reason for his dismissal.*

/dɪsˈmɪsl/
1a, b pl dismissals
⧓ wrongful **dismissal**

(**b**) an employee who is dismissed: *Trade union members are concerned about the increasing number of dismissals.* **2** (*law*) the rejection of a case or an appeal: *Newspapers harshly criticized the Judge's dismissal of the appeal.*

► **unfair dismissal**

2 note not used with *a* or *an*. No plural and used with a singular verb only.

---

dispatch *noun, verb*

► **despatch**

/dɪˈspætʃ/

---

dispatch rider *noun* (distribution)

► **despatch rider**

/dɪˈspætʃ ˌraɪdə(r)/

---

display[1] *noun*

1 (*sales*) an arrangement of goods for people to see: *a shop window display* ○ *a display of new cars* **2** the act of putting something on show for people to see: *These items are not for public display.* **3** (*computing*) words, pictures, etc that can be seen on a computer screen: *study the display before making corrections*

on display in a place where people can see it: *All items for sale are on display in the window.*

/dɪˈspleɪ/

1 pl displays

⧓ put on a **display**; a **display** *of* (goods)

► **exhibition**

2 note not used with *a* or *an*. No plural and used with a singular verb only.

3 pl displays

► **visual display unit**

---

display[2] *verb*

1 (*sales*) to put something where people can see it; to show or exhibit something: *The goods were displayed in the shop window.* **2** (*computing*) to show something on a computer screen: *The text will be displayed on screen.*

/dɪˈspleɪ/

display, displaying, displayed

note transitive verb

⧓ **display** *in, on* (something)

---

disposables *noun*

articles meant to be thrown away after use: *The paper cups and plates are disposables.*

/dɪˈspəʊzəblz/

note usually plural

► **consumer non-durables**

---

disposal *noun*

the act of getting rid of something: *Disposal of industrial waste is a serious problem.*

at someone's disposal available for someone to use freely: *The services of the courier are at your disposal throughout the holiday.*

/dɪˈspəʊzl/

note not used with *a* or *an*. No plural and used with a singular verb only.

⧓ refuse, rubbish, (US) trash, waste **disposal**

---

dispute[1] *noun* (industrial relations)

a disagreement or quarrel: *a dispute between workers and employers over pay* ○ *Trade union leaders and employers are meeting to settle the pay dispute.*

in dispute involved in an argument with someone: *We're in dispute with management about overtime rates.*

/dɪˈspjuːt/

pl disputes

⧓ a **dispute** *about, over* something; settle a **dispute**

► **demarcation dispute, industrial dispute**

---

dispute[2] *verb*

to argue or disagree about something: *Ambulance drivers are disputing the low pay offer.* ○ *A great deal of time was wasted disputing with the supplier over a late delivery.*

/dɪˈspjuːt/

dispute, disputing, disputed

note transitive and intransitive verb

⧓ **dispute** *over* something, *with* someone

---

dissolve *verb*
(of a business, etc) to come to or be brought to an end: *Following the death of one of the partners, the partnership was dissolved.* ○ *The planning committee dissolves tomorrow.*

/dɪˈzɒlv/
dissolve, dissolving, dissolved
note transitive and intransitive verb
▶ **liquidate, wind up 1**

---

distribute *verb* (distribution)
to move goods to places where they can be sold: *Goods are distributed to our major customers first.* ○ *We distribute world-wide.*

/dɪˈstrɪbju:t/
distribute, distributing, distributed
note transitive and intransitive verb
⋈ **distribute** *to* (a customer, shop, etc)
▶ **consign, deliver, despatch**[2]**, transport**[2]

---

distribution *noun* (distribution)
the movement of goods to places where they can be sold; the arrangements made for this: *The cost of distribution is high because of the poor transport system.* ○ *The company's main activities are manufacturing, marketing and distribution.*

/ˌdɪstrɪˈbju:ʃn/
note not used with *a* or *an*. No plural and used with a singular verb only.
⋈ limited, wide **distribution**; **distribution** channels, costs; a **distribution** company, network, system
▶ **transportation**

---

distributive costs *noun* (commerce)
the costs of moving goods and materials from place to place: *High distributive costs have added significantly to the prices paid by consumers.*

/dɪˈstrɪbjʊtɪv ˌkɒsts/
note usually plural
▶ **cost**[1] **2**

---

distributive trades *noun* (commerce)
the organizations involved in moving goods and materials, eg from a factory to a shop: *A survey of distributive trades shows that retail sales increased last month.*

/dɪˈstrɪbjʊtɪv ˌtreɪdz/
note usually plural

---

distributor *noun* (commerce)
a person or an organization that supplies goods for a producer or manufacturer to shops, etc: *Please place your order with our local distributor.* ○ *offer a large discount to a major distributor*

exclusive distributor the only distributor used by a particular company to sell its goods in a particular area or country: *We use an exclusive distributor in Japan.*

/dɪˈstrɪbjʊtə(r)/
⋈ a local, an overseas **distributor**; use a **distributor**
▶ **factor 1, sole agent, supplier**

---

div *abbr*
1 dividend **2** divide **3** division

note used in written English only

---

diversification *noun* (industry)
movement by a company into producing or selling a wider range of products or services: *To increase profits we are considering diversification by acquiring a number of smaller businesses.*

/daɪˌvɜ:sɪfɪˈkeɪʃn/
note not used with *a* or *an*. No plural and used with a singular verb only.
⋈ a policy, strategy of **diversification**
▶ **backward integration, forward integration,**

horizontal integration, vertical integration

---

dividend *noun* (stock exchange)

a sum of money paid to shareholders as their part of the company's profit: *receive a dividend of 3p per share* ○ *These shares should pay high dividends.*

cum dividend relating to a share sold with the right to the next dividend due

ex dividend relating to a share sold without the right to the next dividend

final dividend a dividend paid at the end of a year during which an interim dividend was paid: *pay a final dividend of 5p per share*

interim dividend a dividend paid part-way through the year: *receive an interim dividend of 2p per share*

/ˈdɪvɪdend/

pl dividends

abbr Div, div

⋈ offer, pay, receive a **dividend**; a **dividend** payment

▶ **accumulated dividends**

---

dividend per share *noun* (stock exchange)

the amount of money paid by a company to its shareholders divided by the total number of shares issued: *The company paid a dividend per share of 5p.*

/ˌdɪvɪdend pə ˈʃeə(r)/

pl dividends per share

abbr DPS

⋈ a drop, a fall, an increase, a jump, a rise in **dividends per share**

▶ **earnings per (ordinary) share, share**

---

dividend yield *noun* (stock exchange)

the amount received from an investment before tax is taken off, expressed as a percentage of the price of the share: *The shares had an average dividend yield of 8%.*

/ˈdɪvɪdend jiːld/

pl dividend yields

⋈ a high, low **dividend yield**

▶ **yield¹**

---

division *noun* (management)

a major section of an organization: *work in the finance, marketing, services, sales, etc division* ○ *reorganize the company into six major divisions*

/dɪˈvɪʒn/

pl divisions

abbr Div, div

⋈ amalgamate, join, split a **division**

▶ **department**

DN *abbr* (commerce)

debit note

note used in written English only

---

d/o *abbr* (commerce)

delivery note

/ˌdiː ˈəʊ/

note pronounced as individual letters

---

dock¹ *noun* (shipping)

1 part of a port where ships go to be loaded, unloaded and repaired: *Which dock does the ferry leave from?* ○ *The ship is now in dock waiting to be unloaded.* **2 docks** a group of docks with sheds, warehouses, etc: *work at the docks*

/dɒk/

pl docks

⋈ *in* **dock**; a **dock** gate, worker

▶ **wharf**

---

dock² *verb*

1 (of a ship) to sail into a port: *The ferry docked/was docked at Piraeus.* ○ *The ship is anchored in the estuary, waiting to dock.* **2** to take away part of the wages of an employee: *He had his wages docked for arriving late for work.*

/dɒk/

dock, docking, docked

1 note transitive and intransitive verb

▶ **berth²**

2 note transitive verb

⋈ **dock** money, pay, wages

---

doctor's certificate *noun* (management)

/ˈdɒktəz səˌtɪfɪkət/

► **medical certificate**

---

document *noun* (law)

/ˈdɒkjumənt/

pl documents

a written or printed paper that records an event or agreement, or acts as proof of ownership or identification: *Please sign the enclosed document.* ○ *When we receive the money we will hand over the official documents of ownership.*

⋈ a formal, a legal, an official **document**; draw up, issue, sign a **document**

► **certificate**

---

documentary bill *noun* (banking/shipping)

/ˌdɒkjuˈmentri bɪl/

pl documentary bills

a bill of exchange attached to shipping documents such as bills of lading, invoices, etc: *The shipping clerk checked the documents accompanying the packages, including a documentary bill.*

► **bill of exchange**

---

documentary letter of credit *noun* (banking/commerce)

/ˌdɒkjuˈmentri ˌletər əv ˈkredɪt/

pl documentary letters of credit

► **letter of credit**

---

documents against acceptance bill *noun* (banking/shipping)

/ˌdɒkjumənts əˌgenst əkˈseptəns bɪl/

pl documents against acceptance bills

abbr D/A, D/A bill

a bill of exchange sent by an exporter with other shipping documents to an agent who will not release the documents until the bill of exchange has been signed (ACCEPTED) by the person receiving the goods. This is used when the bill of exchange is a PERIOD BILL and must be paid by a specified date: *The documents against acceptance bill was signed by the consignee.*

► **bill of exchange, cash against documents**

---

documents against cash *noun* (banking/shipping)

/ˌdɒkjumənts əˌgenst ˈkæʃ/

► **cash against documents**

---

documents against payment bill *noun* (banking/shipping)

/ˌdɒkjumənts əˌgenst ˈpeɪmənt bɪl/

pl documents against payments bills

abbr D/P bill

a bill of exchange sent by an exporter with other shipping documents to an agent who will not release the documents until the bill of exchange has been signed (ACCEPTED) by the person receiving the goods. This is used when the bill of exchange is a SIGHT BILL and must be paid immediately: *The documents against payment bill was paid by the consignee.*

► **accept 3, bill of exchange, cash against documents, shipping documents**

---

document of title *noun* (law)

/ˌdɒkjumənt əv ˈtaɪtl/

pl documents of title

a document that allows someone to claim the goods specified on it. A BILL OF LADING is a document of title: *The consignee's agent presented the documents of title at the airport.*

DoE *abbr*

/ˌdiː əʊ ˈiː/

note pronounced as individual letters

(*UK*) the Department of the Environment

---

dole *noun* (personnel)

/dəʊl/

note singular noun, used with a singular verb

(*UK informal*) **the dole** a weekly payment made by the

government to people who are unemployed: *He was on the dole for six months before he found another job.*

⋈ be on, draw, go on the **dole**
▶ **benefit[1] 1, income support**

---

domestic *adjective*
1 of or inside a particular country: *Oil exports have decreased, but domestic consumption is increasing.* ○ *There is a need to regulate foreign ownership of domestic airlines.* **2** of the home, house or family: *domestic water supplies* ○ *sell domestic goods, eg televisions, washing machines, soap powders, etc*

/dəˈmestɪk/
1 ⋈ **domestic** courts, laws, markets, sales, spending, trade
▶ **global, internal, international**
2 ⋈ **domestic** appliances, goods, products, services, work

---

domestic bill *noun* (international trade)
▶ **inland bill**

/dəˈmestɪk bɪl/

---

door-to-door salesman, salesperson, saleswoman *noun* (sales)
a person who calls at people's houses to sell goods or services: *The door-to-door salesman showed some samples to the householder.* ○ *Some homeowners don't like dealing with door-to-door salespeople.*

/ˌdɔː tə ˌdɔː ˈseɪlzmən, ˌdɔː tə ˌdɔː ˈseɪlzˌpɜːsn, ˌdɔː tə ˌdɔː ˈseɪlzˌwʊmən/
pl door-to-door salesmen, saleswomen, salespeople
▶ **commercial traveller, salesman, sales representative, travelling salesman**

---

dossier *noun*
a set of documents about a person or an event: *The police are building up a dossier on the suspected conman.* ○ *a dossier of complaints from dissatisfied customers*

/ˈdɒsieɪ/
pl dossiers
⋈ to build a **dossier** (on someone)
▶ **file[1] 2**

---

dot matrix printer *noun* (computing)
a machine that prints letters, numbers, etc formed by a group of dots close together: *The dot matrix printer is cheap but the print quality is not very good.*

/ˌdɒt ˈmeɪtrɪks ˌprɪntə(r)/
pl dot matrix printers
▶ **daisywheel, laser printer, letter quality printer, near letter quality printer**

---

double-entry bookkeeping *noun* (accounting)
a system of recording accounts where each sale or purchase is shown as having an effect on both the DEBIT COLUMN and the CREDIT COLUMN of an account: *Double-entry bookkeeping helps an accountant to check accounts quickly by seeing whether they balance.*

/ˌdʌbl ˌentri ˈbʊkkiːpɪŋ/
note not used with *a* or *an*. No plural and used with a singular verb only.
▶ **entry 2**

---

double time *noun* (industrial relations)
an amount paid for extra work done, ie if normal pay is £10 per hour, double time is £20 per hour: *I get paid double time for working on Sundays.*

/ˌdʌbl ˈtaɪm/
note not used with *a* or *an*. No plural and used with a singular verb only.
⋈ get, pay **double time**
▶ **overtime, time and a half**

Dow Jones Industrial Average *noun* (stock exchange)
an index of the share prices quoted on the New York Stock Exchange for a group of 30 leading industrial companies: *The Dow Jones Industrial Average was up 8.96 points at 2 761.09 by the close.*

/ˌdaʊ ˌdʒəʊnz ɪnˌdʌstriəl ˈævərɪdʒ/
(also **Dow Jones Average**)
▶ **Nikkei Index, the Financial Times-Stock Exchange 100 Share Index**

download *verb* (computing)
to transfer information (DATA) from one computer to another: *At the end of the day's work, the data held by the computer was downloaded.*

/ˌdaʊnˈləʊd/
download, downloading, downloaded
note transitive verb
⋈ **download** data, a font, a program

downmarket *adjective, adverb* (sales)
of something that is cheap and not very high quality or is designed for less wealthy consumers: *The company is trying to get rid of its downmarket image.* ○ *This holiday resort has gone downmarket.*

/ˌdaʊnˈmɑːkɪt/
⋈ **downmarket** goods, restaurants, shops; go, move **downmarket**
opp upmarket

down payment *noun* (finance)
a payment of part of a larger sum, the balance to be paid later: *The seller insisted on a down payment of 10% of the full price before accepting the order.*

/ˌdaʊn ˈpeɪmənt/
⋈ ask for, make, require a **down payment**
► **deposit**[1] **2, payment 2**

down time *noun* (industry)
time lost in industry because, for example, materials have not arrived or a machine, esp a computer, has broken down: *Down time must be included in the cost of production.*

/ˈdaʊn ˌtaɪm/
note not used with *a* or *an*. No plural and used with a singular verb only.
⋈ computer, machine **down time**

downturn *noun* (sales)
a fall in sales or profits: *Our sales figures are undergoing a downturn this month.*

/ˈdaʊntɜːn/
note usually singular
⋈ receive, see, undergo a **downturn**; a **downturn** in profit, sales; an economic, a market **downturn**
opp upturn

DP *abbr*
1 data processing **2** delivery point

/ˌdiː ˈpiː/

D/P bill *abbr*
documents against payment bill

/ˌdiː ˈpiː bɪl/
pl D/P bills

DPS *abbr* (stock exchange)
dividend per share

/ˌdiː piː ˈes/

dpt *abbr*
1 department **2** depot

note used in written English only
pl dpts

draft[1] *noun*
1 an early, rough version of a letter, a report, a speech, an agreement, or any piece of writing: *edit the first draft of a report* ○ *This is only a rough draft, the final copy will be typed.* **2** (*banking*) bank draft

/drɑːft; *US* dræft/
pl drafts
1 ⋈ amend, make, prepare, write a **draft**; a first, second, etc, final **draft**; a **draft** copy

draft[2] *verb*
to prepare an early, rough version of a letter, report, speech, etc: *The managing director is drafting the annual report.*

/drɑːft; *US* dræft/
draft, drafting, drafted
note transitive verb
► **redraft**

draw *verb* (banking)
1 to write a cheque or bank order that instructs a bank to make a payment to another person or organization: *The person who drew the cheque forgot to sign it.* ○ *Which bank was the cheque drawn on?* **2** to write a bill of exchange demanding payment from a person or an organization (the DRAWEE): *The shipper drew a bill on the consignee.* **3** to take money out of a bank account: *I'd like to draw £500 out of my account.*

draw (something) up to prepare, to write out an agreement, a budget, a plan, etc: *I'll draw up a list of charges for you.*

/drɔː/
draw, drawing, drawn
note transitive verb
2 ⧓ **draw** *out*
► **withdraw 1**

---

drawee *noun* (banking)
1 the bank holding the account of the person who has written a cheque and is therefore instructed to make a payment to another person or organization: *The drawee refused to accept the cheque because the drawer had not signed it.* **2** the person named on a bill of exchange who promises to pay (ACCEPT) it

/ˌdrɔːˈiː/
pl drawees
► **endorsee, payee**
2 ► **accept 3, acceptor**

---

drawer *noun* (banking)
a person who writes a cheque, a bank order, etc and therefore instructs a bank to make a payment to another person or organization: *The cheque was returned to the drawer because there was no money in the account.*

/ˈdrɔːə(r)/
pl drawers
► **drawee, payee, refer to drawer**

---

drop shipment *noun* (commerce)
sending a large quantity of goods or materials from the producer directly to a customer, without using a DISTRIBUTOR ; the goods sent in this way: *The distributor's charges were too high so the goods were sent as a drop shipment.*

/ˈdrɒp ˌʃɪpmənt/
pl drop shipments
⧓ make, send a **drop shipment**
► **delivery, shipment**

---

dry goods *noun* (commerce)
goods such as cloth, coffee, grain and sugar, as distinct from goods that are liquid: *The carrier is suitable for transporting dry goods only.*

/ˈdraɪ gʊdz/
note plural noun, used with a plural verb
⧓ store, transport **dry goods**
► **wet goods**

DTI *abbr*
(*UK*) Department of Trade and Industry

/ˌdiː tiː ˈaɪ/

DTP *abbr* (computing)
desk top publishing

/ˌdiː tiː ˈpiː/

---

dues *noun*
1 an official payment or fee, esp one paid to become a member of an organization: *pay trade union dues* **2** (*shipping*) money to be paid for using port and harbour services: *Vessels must not leave port until all dues have been paid.* **3** (*commerce*) orders accepted for goods that cannot be supplied immediately: *When the new stock arrives all dues will be given priority.*

/djuːz/
1 note plural noun, used with a plural verb
⧓ membership **dues**; pay **dues**
► **charge[1] 1, fee**
2 ⧓ harbour **dues**; pay **dues**
3 ⧓ receive **dues**

---

dump bin *noun* (commerce)
a large box placed in a shop to hold goods, esp those at a reduced price: *Customers turned over the articles in the dump bin, looking for bargains.*

/ˈdʌmp bɪn/
pl dump bins

dumping *noun* (commerce) /ˈdʌmpɪŋ/
selling goods in a foreign market at very low prices: *Manufacturers complained that the dumping of foreign goods was driving the home industry out of business.*

note not used with *a* or *an*. No plural and used with a singular verb only.
▶ **anti-dumping**

duplicate[1] *noun* /ˈdju:plɪkət/
an exact copy of a document such as letter, a report, a receipt, an invoice, etc: *Send the original letter but keep a duplicate of it for our own file.* ○ *Type the letter in duplicate.*

pl duplicates
⧓ a **duplicate** certificate, document, key
▶ **copy**[1] **1**, **master 1**, **original**, **photocopy**[1], **triplicate**

duplicate[2] *verb* /ˈdju:plɪkeɪt/
1 to make an exact copy of something: *The report was typed, duplicated and sent to each member of the committee.* **2** to do something again in exactly the same way: *The research was done originally in Europe but it has been duplicated in America.* ○ *There's no point in duplicating work.*

duplicate, duplicating, duplicated
note transitive verb
▶ **copy**[2], **photocopy**[2]

duplicating machine *noun* (office practice) /ˈdju:plɪkeɪtɪŋ məˌʃi:n/
▶ **duplicator**

duplicator *noun* (office practice) /ˈdju:plɪˌkeɪtə(r)/
a machine that can make copies of letters, documents, etc: *Use the duplicator to make fifty copies of this letter.*

syn duplicating machine
▶ **photocopier**

durables *noun* (manufacturing) /ˈdjʊərəblz/
▶ **consumer durables**

duty *noun* /ˈdju:ti/
1 (*tax*) a government tax paid on certain goods and services: *Duty must be paid on all imported wines and spirits.* **2** (*personnel*) a job or task that someone must do: *I'm on night duty this week.* ○ *perform routine duties* ○ *be released from normal duties*

be on/off duty (esp of doctors, the police, etc) be working/not working: *The porter is on duty from 10 till 6.* ○ *What time do you go off duty?*

pl duties
1 ▶ **customs duty**, **excise duty**, **import duty**, **stamp duty**, **transfer duty**
2 ⧓ be off, be on, do your **duty**; carry out, perform, take on a **duty**; extra, normal, special **duties**

duty-free *adjective, adverb* (tax) /ˌdju:ti ˈfri:/
of goods that can be imported, usually in limited quantities, without customs duties: *During the flight, passengers were able to buy duty-free wines, spirits and perfumes.* ○ *Up to 200 cigarettes per person may be imported duty-free.*

⧓ **duty-free** goods, sales, shopping; a **duty-free** allowance, bar, shop
▶ **customs duty**, **free list**, **import duty**, **tax-free**

ea *abbr*
each

note used in written English only

E. & O.E. *abbr* (accounting)
errors and omissions excepted

note used in written English only

earn *verb* (finance)
1 to get money by working: *He earns his living as an architect.* ○ *She earns £20 000 a year.* **2** to produce financial gain: *The money is earning a high rate of interest.* ○ *How much profit did the company earn last year?*

/ɜːn/
earn, earning, earned *or* **earnt**
note transitive verb
1 ⋈ **earn** a living, money, a salary
2 ⋈ **earn** a dividend, interest, a profit
▶ **yield**[2]

earned income *noun* (tax)
(*UK*) money received for work done, rather than from investments or property owned: *enter the amount of earned income on a tax form*

/ˌɜːnd ˈɪŋkʌm/
note no plural
⋈ be taxed on, calculate, live on **earned income**
opp unearned income

earnings *noun* (finance)
payment received for work done or from money invested by a person or an organization: *He received compensation for loss of earnings after the accident.* ○ *Earnings are often lower in rural areas.*

gross earnings the total amount of money received before tax and insurance payments are taken off

/ˈɜːnɪŋz/
note plural noun, used with a plural verb
▶ **price earnings ratio**
⋈ high, increased, low, reduced **earnings**

earnings per (ordinary) share *noun* (stock exchange)
the total amount of money paid by a company to its shareholders in DIVIDENDS and transferred to reserves in any one year, divided by the total number of shares issued: *Earnings per share increased 16% to 10.4p.*

/ˌɜːnɪŋz pə(r) (ˌɔːdənri) ˈʃeə(r)/
note plural noun, used with a plural verb
abbr eps
⋈ a drop, a fall, an increase, a jump, a rise in **earnings per share**
▶ **dividend per share, ordinary share, price earnings ratio, share**

Eastern Standard Time *noun*
the standard time used in the eastern states of the USA and eastern Canada. It is five hours behind GREENWICH MEAN TIME and one hour ahead of Central Time: *The meeting is at 11.30 am Eastern Standard Time.*

/ˌiːstən ˈstændəd taɪm/
abbr EST
syn Eastern Time

easy market *noun* (stock exchange)
a market where certain securities are plentiful and prices are low because there are few buyers: *It was an easy market today.*

/ˌiːzi ˈmɑːkɪt/
⋈ create, result in an **easy market**
▶ **buyer's market, market**[1]**, seller's market**

easy money *noun* (finance)
money that is earned without difficulties: *A vending machine could bring us some easy money.*

/ˌiːzi ˈmʌni/
note not used with *a* or *an*. No plural and used with a singular verb only.

⧓ bring, earn, make **easy money**
▶ **cheap money, dear money, money**

EC *abbr* (international trade)
the European Community

/ˌiː ˈsiː/
note pronounced as individual letters

---

econ *abbr*
economics

note used in written English only

---

econometrics *noun* (economics)
the study of economic problems and events using financial facts and figures: *use econometrics to predict consumer trends*

/ɪˌkɒnəˈmetrɪks/
note singular noun, used with a singular verb
⧓ use **econometrics**
▶ **analysis, statistics**

---

economic *adjective* (economics/finance)
1 cheap: *It is more economic to transport a full lorry load.* ○ *This machine is no longer economic to run.* **2** of an economy; of producing, distributing and using goods: *The country is in a state of economic crisis.* **3** of the science of economics: *We value his knowledge of economic theory.*

/ˌiːkəˈnɒmɪk, ˌekəˈnɒmɪk/
1 ⧓ an **economic** method, price, process
opp uneconomic
2 ⧓ an **economic** boom, crisis, depression, plan, system; **economic** policy, power, trends

---

economical *adjective* (economics)
careful with money or resources; not wasteful: *The new heating system proved economical to use.* ○ *We are looking for more economical production methods.*

/ˌiːkəˈnɒmɪkl, ˌekəˈnɒmɪkl/
⧓ **economical** to run, to use; an **economical** method

---

economic development *noun* (economics)
increasing and expanding industry and employment in a country or a region: *We are attempting to encourage economic development in the area.* ○ *a policy of economic development*

/ˌiːkəˌnɒmɪk dɪˈveləpmənt, ˌekəˌnɒmɪk dɪˈveləpmənt/
note not used with *a* or *an*. No plural and used with a singular verb only.
⧓ an **economic development** area, plan, programme, region, scheme

---

economic growth *noun* (economics)
the rate of increase of the money received by a country from industry and trade. It is usually measured by dividing the GROSS NATIONAL PRODUCT by the number of people in the country: *The country has maintained a high level of economic growth.*

/ˌiːkəˌnɒmɪk ˈgrəʊθ, ˌekəˌnɒmɪk ˈgrəʊθ/
note no plural
⧓ high, low, rapid, slow, steady **economic growth**

---

economic indicators *noun* (economics)
statistics that show the strength or weakness of a country's economy. These may include the rate of inflation, the amount of foreign investment, interest rates, employment figures, etc: *The government's index of economic indicators for May dropped sharply.*

/ˌiːkəˌnɒmɪk ˈɪndɪkeɪtə(r), ˌekəˌnɒmɪk ˈɪndɪkeɪtə(r)/
note usually plural

Economic and Monetary Union *noun* (economics)
the central control of financial affairs planned by the European Community, which includes a single European currency and a single central bank: *work towards Economic and Monetary Union*

/ˌiːkəˌnɒmɪk ənd ˌmʌnɪtri ˈjuːniən, ˌekənɒmɪk ənd ˌmʌnɪtri ˈjuːniən/
abbr EMU

▶ **European Currency Unit, Exchange Rate Mechanism**

---

economics *noun* (economics)

1 (**a**) the study of the processes involved in the production, distribution and consumption of goods, esp in relation to cost: *study economics at university* (**b**) the application of this to a particular activity, industry, etc: *the economics of the tourist industry* ○ *the economics of producing new products* **2** the financial conditions of a country: *third world economics*

/ˌiːkəˈnɒmɪks, ˌekəˈnɒmɪks/

note singular noun, used with a singular verb

abbr econ

⋈ an **economics** adviser, course, editor, lecturer, student

---

economic sanctions *noun* (international trade)

measures taken to force a country to obey international law, by stopping or reducing trade with that country: *impose economic sanctions on a country*

/ˌiːkəˌnɒmɪk ˈsæŋkʃnz, ˌekəˌnɒmɪk ˈsæŋkʃnz/

note plural noun, used with a plural verb

⋈ apply, enforce, impose, lift, maintain, oppose **economic sanctions**

▶ **ban²**, **embargo**, **sanction**

---

economies of scale *noun* (economics)

the reductions in UNIT COST and increase in profit obtained when goods are produced in large quantities: *Companies that sell world-wide have benefited from economies of scale.*

/ɪˌkɒnəmiz əv ˈskeɪl/

note plural noun, used with a plural verb

---

economist *noun* (economics)

a student of or an expert in ECONOMICS: *Statistics of consumer spending were analysed by the economist.*

/ɪˈkɒnəmɪst/

pl economists

---

economize *verb*

to save money, time, resources, etc; to spend less than before: *We must economize on fuel.* ○ *economize by reducing the number of staff* ○ *make plans to economize*

/ɪˈkɒnəmaɪz/

economize, economizing, economized

(also **economise**)

note intransitive verb

⋈ **economize** *on* costs, manpower, space, etc

---

economy *noun* (economics)

1 the economy a country's money supply, trade and industry: *The government is attempting to reduce inflation and strengthen the economy.* ○ *Industrial production has slowed down in all the world's major economies, with the UK and US worst hit.* ○ *send money to help the struggling economies of the developing world* **2** the control and management of money, resources, etc of an organization, a society, a country, etc: *an industrial, a rural, a market economy* **3** the act of saving money, time, resources: *We will have to practise a little economy if we are to survive the recession.* ○ *make some important economies in the promotions department*

economy class the cheapest form of air travel: *travel economy class*

economy pack a collection of goods that costs less than buying the goods separately: *The economy pack has three cartons of orange juice for the price of two.*

economy size one large packet, box, etc of goods that costs less than two smaller packets: *Buy the economy size, it's cheaper.*

/ɪˈkɒnəmi/

pl economies

1 ⋈ improve, stabilize, strengthen the **economy**

▶ **black economy**

2 ⋈ a capitalist, a centralized, an industrial, a market, a rural, a socialist **economy**

▶ **balanced economy, mixed economy, planned economy**

3 ⋈ to make **economies**

---

economy drive *noun* (finance/accounting)
an organized effort to save money, time and resources: *Cutting back on advertising is all part of the economy drive.*

/ɪˈkɒnəmi draɪv/
pl economy drives
⋈ launch, mount, organize, plan an **economy drive**
▶ **sales drive**

economy measure *noun* (accounting)
an action taken to save money, time or resources: *We need to introduce some economy measures in this department.*

/ɪˈkɒnəmi ˌmeʒə(r)/
pl economy measures
⋈ carry out, introduce an **economy measure**

ECU *abbr* (finance)
European Currency Unit

/ˈekju:/
(also **ecu**)
note pronounced as a word

EEC *abbr* (economics/finance)
European Economic Community

/ˌi: i: ˈsi:/
note pronounced as individual letters

EET *abbr*
Eastern European Time

/ˌi: i: ˈti:/
note pronounced as individual letters

efficiency *noun*
the ability to produce a good result without wasting time or energy: *Regular training will improve staff efficiency.* ○ *The introduction of new technology has increased the efficiency of our distribution system.*

/ɪˈfɪʃnsi/
note not used with *a* or *an*. No plural and used with a singular verb only.
⋈ economic, energy, fuel, machine, staff, technical **efficiency**; improve, increase, reduce **efficiency**
opp inefficiency

efficient *adjective*
1 (of people) able to work well without making mistakes or wasting time: *a very efficient secretary* **2** (of machines, systems, etc) able to produce a good result without wasting time or energy: *We need to make our production process more efficient.* ○ *We must find a more efficient way of advertising our products.*

/ɪˈfɪʃnt/
⋈ highly, less, more **efficient**; an **efficient** method, service, system
opp inefficient
▶ **cost-effective**

EFTA *abbr* (international trade)
European Free Trade Association

/ˈeftə/
note pronounced as a word

EFTPOS *abbr* (banking/retail)
electronic funds transfer at point of sale

/ˈeftpɒs/
note pronounced as a word

eg *abbr*
for example

/ˌi: ˈdʒi:/
note pronounced as individual letters

electronic funds transfer at point of sale *noun* (banking/retail)
a system that allows shoppers to pay for goods using a CREDIT CARD or CHARGE CARD to transfer money automatically from the buyer's bank account to that of the shop: *We are experimenting with electronic funds transfer at point of sale in some branches.*

/ɪlekˌtrɒnɪk ˌfʌndz ˌtrænsfɜ:r ət ˌpɔɪnt əv ˈseɪl/
abbr EFTPOS
note not used with *a* or *an*. No plural and used with a singular verb only.

electronic mail *noun* (computing)
a system of sending messages and information from one computer terminal to another, using a computer network or telephone lines: *send a message by electronic mail*

/ˌɪlektrɒnɪk ˈmeɪl/
note not used with *a* or *an*. No plural and used with a singular verb only.
⧓ an **electronic mail** service, system
syn e-mail
► **fax**[1], **mail**[1] **2**, **modem**, **telex**[1]

---

e-mail *noun* (computing)
electronic mail

/ˈiː meɪl/

---

embargo *noun* (international trade)
a government order to stop trade with another country: *The government hopes to lift the embargo on trade when the peace treaty is signed.*

/ɪmˈbɑːgəʊ/
pl embargoes
⧓ impose, lift, remove an **embargo**; an **embargo** *against* (a country); an **embargo** *on* coal, oil, etc
► **ban**[2], **economic sanctions**, **sanction**

---

embark *verb* (transport)
to go or be taken onto a ship or an aircraft: *Passengers with cars must embark first.* ○ *embark passengers and cargo at Bilbao*

/ɪmˈbɑːk/
embark, embarking, embarked
note transitive and intransitive verb
⧓ **embark** *on* a ship or an aircraft

---

embarkation *noun* (shipping)
getting onto a ship or an aircraft: *Embarkation will be at 11 am.*

/ˌembɑːˈkeɪʃn/
note not used with *a* or *an*. No plural and used with a singular verb only.
⧓ port of **embarkation**
opp disembarkation

---

embezzle *verb*
to steal money that you are responsible for: *An employee was embezzling the company pension fund.* ○ *The solicitor embezzled money from his clients.*

/ɪmˈbezl/
embezzle, embezzling, embezzled
note transitive verb
⧓ **embezzle** funds, money

---

embezzlement *noun* (law)
stealing money that you are responsible for: *The director was charged with the embezzlement of company funds.* ○ *She was found guilty of embezzlement.*

/ɪmˈbezlmənt/
note not used with *a* or *an*. No plural and used with a singular verb only.
⧓ **embezzlement** *of* funds, money
► **fraud**

---

employ *verb* (industry)
1 to give someone work, especially for payment: *They hope to employ ten people.* ○ *He is employed as an accountant.* ○ *She is employed by Midland Bank.* **2** to make use of someone/something: *A general assistant could be better employed elsewhere.*

/ɪmˈplɔɪ/
employ, employing, employed
note transitive verb
1 ⧓ **employ** someone *as*

something: be **employed** *by* a person or an organization
▶ **hire[1] 2**

---

employee *noun* (personnel)
a person who works for another person or an organization in return for wages: *take on three new employees* ○ *bank, hotel, railway, etc employees* ○ *the company has 1 200 employees*

/ɪmˈplɔɪiː/
pl employees
⋈ hire, pay, take on an **employee**
▶ **personnel 1**, **staff[1]**, **workforce**

---

employee participation *noun* (industry)
▶ **worker participation**

/ɪmˌplɔɪiː pɑːˌtɪsɪˈpeɪʃn/

---

employees' buyout *noun* (finance)
a situation in which the employees obtain control of a company by buying the majority of shares: *It was hoped that the employees' buyout would prevent the closure and save jobs.*

/ɪmˌplɔɪiːz ˈbaɪaʊt/
pl employees' buyouts
▶ **leveraged buyout**, **management buyout**

---

employer *noun* (personnel)
a person or an organization with regular paid workers: *She asked her employer for a pay rise.* ○ *The steel works used to be the largest employer in the town.*

/ɪmˈplɔɪə(r)/
pl employers
⋈ a bad, good, large, small **employer**

---

employment *noun* (personnel)
1 regular paid work: *find employment in a bank* **2** the state of having a job: *Are you in full-time employment?* **3** the act of giving someone a paid job: *the employment of skilled workers*

seasonal employment work that is available at certain times of the year: *There is plenty of seasonal employment in the tourist industry.*

/ɪmˈplɔɪmənt/
note not used with *a* or *an*. No plural and used with a singular verb only.
⋈ full-time, part-time, permanent, regular, seasonal, secure, temporary **employment**
opp unemployment
▶ **contract of employment**

---

employment agency *noun* (personnel)
an organization that provides information about available jobs and finds employees for companies. The agency is paid a fee by the employer: *contact the employment agency to find a temporary secretary*

/ɪmˈplɔɪmənt ˌeɪdʒənsi/
pl employment agencies
⋈ contact, use an **employment agency**
▶ **job centre**

---

employment protection *noun* (law)
a group of laws that aim to stop employers from dismissing employees unfairly, and to ensure that employees are given the legal amount of sick pay, maternity pay, etc: *guarantee employment protection for part-time workers*

/ɪmˈplɔɪmənt prəˌtekʃn/
note not used with *a* or *an*. No plural and used with a singular verb only.
⋈ **employment protection** laws, legislation
▶ **unfair dismissal**

EMS *abbr* (finance)
European Monetary System

/ˌiː em ˈes/
note pronounced as individual letters

EMU *abbr* (economics)
Economic and Monetary Union

/ˌiː em ˈjuː/
note pronounced as individual letters

---

encash *verb* (banking)
▶ **cash**[2]

/ɪnˈkæʃ/

encashment *noun* (banking)
exchanging a cheque for cash: *We can arrange for the cheque's encashment next Thursday.*

/ɪnˈkæʃmənt/
note not used with *a* or *an*. No plural and used with a singular verb only.

enc *abbr* (office practice)
enclosure; written on a letter to show that another document is in the envelope with the letter

note used in written English only

enclose *verb* (office practice)
to put something in an envelope, usually as well as a letter: *I enclose a stamped addressed envelope.* ○ *A copy of the invoice is enclosed.*

/ɪnˈkləʊz/
enclose, enclosing, enclosed
note transitive verb
⋈ **enclose** a copy of (a document, brochure, etc), instructions, an invoice, a map, a stamped addressed envelope
▶ **append, attach 1**

end-consumer *noun* (retail)
▶ **end-user 1**

/ˈend kənˌsjuːmə(r)/

endorse *verb*
1 (*banking*) to sign the back of a bill of exchange or cheque to make it payable to another person: *The bank asked him to endorse the cheque.* ○ *She endorsed the cheque to my order.* **2** (*advertising*) to say in an advertisement that you use and approve of a product: *Well-known sportspeople can earn lots of money by endorsing sports clothes and equipment.* **3** (*law*) to record details of a motoring offence on a driving licence: *He's had his licence endorsed twice for dangerous driving.*

/ɪnˈdɔːs/
endorse, endorsing, endorsed
(also **indorse**)
note transitive verb
1 ⋈ **endorse** a bill of exchange, bill of lading, cheque, document of title

endorsee *noun* (banking)
the person named on a bill of exchange or cheque as having the right to cash it: *The cheque was cashed by the person named as the endorsee.*

/ɪnˌdɔːsˈiː/
pl endorsees
(also **indorsee**)
▶ **drawee, endorser, payee**

endorsement *noun*
1 (*law*) a signature needed on a document to make it legal
2 (*banking*) a signature on the back of a bill of exchange or cheque by the payee, making it payable to another person **3** (*insurance*) a note on an insurance policy that records a change in the conditions of insurance: *The endorsement states that all our drivers must be over twenty-five.* **4** (*law*) (*UK*) a note on a driving licence recording the driver's conviction for a motoring offence: *She has had two endorsements for speeding.*

accommodation endorsement the name and signature written on the back of an accepted bill of exchange as a guarantee that payment will be made on the date given

blank endorsement a signature on a bill of exchange or cheque, by the payee, making it payable to any other person

restrictive endorsement a signature on a bill of exchange or cheque, by the payee, making it payable only to a named person or account. It is no longer a NEGOTIABLE INSTRUMENT.

/ɪnˈdɔːsmənt/
pl endorsements
(also **indorsement**)
⋈ add, give, include, make an **endorsement**
▶ **payable**

special endorsement a signature on a bill of exchange or cheque, by the payee, making it payable to another person

---

endorser *noun* (banking)
a person who signs the back of a bill of exchange, a cheque, etc to make it payable to someone else: *Has the bill been signed by the endorser?*

/ɪnˈdɔːsə(r)/
pl endorsers
► **endorsee**

---

endow *verb* (finance)
to give money or property to a person or an organization to provide a regular income: *The chemical company used some of its profit to endow a research centre.*

/ɪnˈdaʊ/
endow, endowing, endowed
note transitive verb
⋈ **endow** money, property
► **bequeath**

---

endowment *noun* (law/finance)
money or property given to provide a regular income for a person or an organization: *The charity is funded largely by endowments.*

/ɪnˈdaʊmənt/
pl endowments
⋈ provide, receive an **endowment**; an **endowment** fund, loan, mortgage
► **bequest, trust**

---

endowment policy *noun* (insurance)
a life assurance policy that pays the sum insured on an agreed date or on the death of the person insured: *The endowment policy is payable in 2004.*

/ɪnˈdaʊmənt ˌpɒləsi/
pl endowment policies
⋈ claim on, draw up, take out an **endowment policy**

---

end-product *noun* (industry)
the final article produced by the manufacturing process: *The end-product is produced from a variety of raw materials.*

/ˈend ˌprɒdʌkt/
pl end-products
⋈ buy, make, manufacture, market, produce, sell, use an **end-product**
► **by-product, product, waste product**

---

end-user *noun* (retail)
1 the person who actually uses a product: *The end-user likes our product.* ○ *We want to identify our end-users for marketing purposes.* **2** (*computing*) the person who uses a computer: *design a program specially for the end-user*

/ˈend ˌjuːzə(r)/
pl end-users
⋈ appeal to, ask, identify, reach, target the **end-user**; **end-user** price
syn end-consumer
► **consumer, ultimate consumer**

---

engage *verb* (personnel)
to employ someone: *We have engaged a surveyor to inspect the site.* ○ *Watson's have engaged ten new staff.* ○ *She was engaged as an editor.*

/ɪnˈgeɪdʒ/
engage, engaging, engaged
note transitive verb
⋈ **engage** someone *as* something, someone *to* do something

---

engaged *adjective*
1 (of a person) busy; occupied: *I can't go to the meeting, I'm otherwise engaged this afternoon.* **2** (of a telephone line) in use: *The number is engaged at the moment.* ○ *I rang earlier, but you were engaged.*

/ɪnˈgeɪdʒd/
2 ⋈ the **engaged** tone

---

engagement *noun* (management)
an arrangement to meet someone or to do something; an appointment: *Do you have many engagements on Tuesday?* ○ *I'm sorry, but I have a prior* (ie I already have an) *engagement.*

/ɪnˈgeɪdʒmənt/
pl engagements
⧓ have an **engagement**; a prior **engagement**; an **engagement** *at* (a certain time), *on* (a certain day); an **engagements** diary

---

enter *verb*
1 to begin something: *enter into a contract with another firm*
2 (*banking/accounting*) to write figures in a book of accounts: *She entered the amount in the account book.*

/ˈentə(r)/
enter, entering, entered
1 note intransitive verb
⧓ **enter** *into* an agreement, a contract, negotiations, a partnership
2 note transitive verb
⧓ **enter** an amount, a figure *in* (a book)

---

enterprise *noun* (commerce)
1 a company or business project: *start up a new enterprise* **2** the courage and willingness to undertake business projects: *She has great enterprise and is sure to make the business work.* **3** business activity: *an economy based on free enterprise*, ie companies owned by people rather than the state

/ˈentəpraɪz/
1 pl enterprises
⧓ a large, a small, a successful, an unsuccessful **enterprise**
▶ **venture**[1]
2 note not used with *a* or *an*. No plural and used with a singular verb only.
⧓ considerable, great **enterprise**
3 note not used with *a* or *an*. No plural and used with a singular verb only.
▶ **free enterprise, private enterprise**

---

enterprise zone *noun* (commerce)
(*UK*) an area chosen by the government as being in need of new business activity. Government grants and tax benefits are used to attract organizations to the area: *The government plans to make the city into an enterprise zone.*

/ˈentəpraɪz zəʊn/
pl enterprise zones
⧓ create, designate an **enterprise zone**

---

entertainment allowance *noun*
money given to employees, esp sales staff, to buy meals, drinks, etc for customers, agents, etc: *I spent most of my entertainment alllowance on my last overseas trip.*

/ˌentəˈteɪnment əˌlaʊəns/
note usually singular
syn entertainment expenses

---

entrepôt *noun* (international trade)
(*French*) a warehouse at an airport or a port where goods are stored before they are sent elsewhere: *store goods at an entrepôt*

entrepôt trade the buying and selling of goods that pass through a port, an airport or a district before they are sent elsewhere: *Rotterdam and Singapore are centres for entrepôt trade.*

/ˈɒntrəpəʊ/
pl entrepôts

---

entrepreneur *noun* (commerce)
a person who starts or runs a business activity, esp one that involves financial risk: *He would not have succeeded in such a risky business if he had not been such a clever entrepreneur.*

/ˌɒntrəprəˈnɜː(r)/
pl entrepreneurs
⧓ a fashion, an oil, a publishing, etc **entrepreneur**

---

entrepreneurial *adjective* (economics/management)
willing or able to take risks in business: *use your entrepreneurial skills to expand the business*

/ˌɒntrəprəˈnɜːriəl/
⧓ **entrepreneurial** qualities, skills

entry *noun*
1 the right to enter a place: *The sign says 'No Entry'.* ○ *obtain an entry visa* ○ *We were refused entry to the building.* **2** (*accounting*) an item written in a list, a diary, an accounts book, etc: *I'll have to check the entries in the ledger.* ○ *There are no entries in her diary for today.* **3** (*computing*) the act of putting information into a computer: *We need to reduce the cost and error rate of data entry.*

/ˈentri/
1 note no plural
⧓ an **entry** charge, point, visa
2 pl entries
► **bill of entry, double-entry bookkeeping, prime entry book**
3 note not used with *a* or *an*. No plural and used with a singular verb only.
⧓ a **data entry** clerk, system, technique, terminal

environment *noun*
1 the conditions in which people live, work, etc: *These new offices should improve our working environment.* **2 the environment** the natural world, eg land, air, water, etc in which people, animals and plants live: *Manufacturing companies are becoming more aware of how toxic waste can damage the environment.*

/ɪnˈvaɪərənmənt/
1 pl environments
⧓ a healthy, a rural, an unhealthy, an urban, a working **environment**
2 note singular noun, used with a singular verb
⧓ conserve, damage, harm, pollute, protect the **environment**
► **green**

environmental *adjective*
of the natural world, eg land, air, water, etc in which people, animals and plants live: *environmental damage from mining and oil spills* ○ *The company is working to reduce environmental pollution.*

/ɪnˌvaɪərənˈmentl/
⧓ **environmental** conditions, issues, pollution, pressures, problems
► **green**

environmental audit *noun*
a report on the way natural resources, eg fuel, water, etc are used by an organization, the amount of pollution caused by its activities and how this can be improved: *All businesses will be encouraged to carry out environmental audits.*

/ɪnˌvaɪərənˌmentl ˈɔːdɪt/
pl environmental audits
⧓ carry out an **environmental audit**
► **audit**[1]

environmentalist *noun*
a person who wants to protect the environment: *Environmentalists are protesting against chemical pollution of rivers.*

/ɪnˌvaɪərənˈmentəlɪst/
pl environmentalists
► **green**

environmentally-friendly *adjective*
of activities, products, production processes, etc that do not harm the environment: *buy environmentally-friendly washing powder* ○ *Are all your products environmentally-friendly?*

/ɪnˌvaɪərənˌmentəli ˈfrendli/
► **green**

eps *abbr* (stock exchange)
earnings per share

/ˌiː piː ˈes/
note pronounced as individual letters

equality *noun*
the state of being the same as someone or something else: *campaign for racial and sexual equality in all professions* ○ *equality between men and women at work*

/ɪˈkwɒləti/
note not used with *a* or *an*. No plural and used with a singular verb only.
⧓ economic, financial **equality**
▶ **discrimination, parity**

equal opportunity *noun* (personnel)
the idea that people should be treated the same at work or in education, etc regardless of age, sex, race, etc: *The company believes in equal opportunity for all its staff.*

/ˌiːkwəl ˌɒpəˈtjuːnəti/
pl equal opportunities
syn (*US*) affirmative action
⧓ **equal opportunity** laws, legislation, policies; an **equal opportunity** employer
▶ **discrimination**

equal pay *noun* (personnel)
the idea stated in the Equal Pay Act (1970) that men and women should receive the same rate of pay for doing the same work: *The company guarantees equal pay for work of the same value.*

/ˌiːkwəl ˈpeɪ/
note not used with *a* or *an*. No plural and used with a singular verb only.
⧓ demand, offer, provide, seek **equal pay**
▶ **discrimination, pay²**

equities *noun* (stock exchange)
the ORDINARY SHARES of a company: *Investing in equities carries a fairly high risk.* ○ *a fall in the value of UK equities*

/ˈekwətiz/
note plural noun, used with a plural verb
⧓ buy, issue, purchase, sell, trade **equities**
▶ **share**

equity capital *noun* (stock exchange)
the part of a company's money owned by shareholders, who have the right to a share in the company's profits and to any other assets if the company is closed down: *The company wants to attract more equity capital from investors.*

/ˌekwəti ˈkæpɪtl/
note not used with *a* or *an*. No plural and used with a singular verb only.
▶ **ordinary share, preference share**

equity *noun* (stock exchange)
the part of a company's money that is raised by selling ORDINARY SHARES: *The company is planning to issue more equity.*

/ˈekwəti/
note singular noun, used with a singular verb
1 ⧓ issue, raise **equity**
2 ⧓ **equity** investment, market, shareholder
▶ **equities, share capital**

equity share *noun* (stock exchange)
▶ **equities**

/ˈekwəti ʃeə(r)/

ERM *abbr* (finance)
Exchange Rate Mechanism

/ˌiː ɑːr ˈem/
note pronounced as individual letters

errors and omissions excepted *noun* (accounting)
words printed on an invoice to show that mistakes may be corrected at a later date

/ˌerəz ənd əˌmɪʃnz ɪkˈseptɪd/
abbr E. & O.E.

escalation clause *noun* (commerce)
a condition in a contract that allows a price to be changed, eg because of unexpected manufacturing costs: *Labour costs have increased but thankfully we included an escalation clause.*

/ˌeskəˈleɪʃn klɔːz/
pl escalation clauses
⋈ add, include an **escalation clause**
▶ **clause**

---

escape clause *noun* (commerce)
a condition in a contract that frees one of the parties from carrying out the terms of the contract in certain specified circumstances: *Make sure you include an escape clause.*

/ɪˈskeɪp klɔːz/
pl escape clauses
⋈ add, include, use an **escape clause**
▶ **clause**

---

escrow *noun* (law)
a contract, deed or other written agreement held until a specified duty is performed; the act of keeping such documents: *The bonds were held in escrow by the solicitor.*

escrow account (*US*) an account in which money is held until a specified duty is performed, eg a document is signed or goods are delivered: *The money was held in an escrow account.*

/ˈeskrəʊ/
pl escrows

EST *abbr*
Eastern Standard Time

/ˌiː es ˈtiː/
note pronounced as individual letters

---

estate *noun* (law)
1 a large area of land developed for a specific purpose, eg for houses or factories: *The industrial estate is located just outside town.* **2** a large area of land in the country that is owned by one person or family: *The family own a large estate in Scotland.* **3** the money and property that someone leaves when he/she dies: *The estate was worth £600 000.*

/ɪˈsteɪt/
pl estates
1 ⋈ a housing, an industrial **estate**
▶ **trading estate**
2 ⋈ farm, manage an **estate**; an **estate** worker
▶ **real estate**
3 ▶ **beneficiary, bequest, life estate, will**

---

estate agent *noun*
a person whose job is to buy and sell houses, offices, land, etc for others: *Most people sell their homes through an estate agent.*

/ɪˈsteɪt ˌeɪdʒənt/
pl estate agents
⋈ use an **estate agent**
syn real estate agent, (*US*) realtor
▶ **agent**

---

estate manager *noun* (agriculture)
▶ **land agent 2**

/ɪˈsteɪt ˌmænɪdʒə(r)/

---

estimate[1] *noun* (industry)
1 a calculation of the cost, size, value, etc of something: *I can give you a rough estimate of the number of staff needed to work on the project.* ○ *I suspect that £30 000 for the work is a conservative estimate* (ie it will cost more than that). **2** a price given for work to be done or a service to be provided: *prepare an estimate for printing the brochures.* ○ *Your estimate was for more than we want to pay.*

/ˈestɪmət/
pl estimates
1 ⋈ an accurate, an approximate, a careful, a conservative, a rough **estimate**
▶ **actuals 2, approximation, ballpark figure**

2 ⋈ agree to, ask for, prepare, receive, send, write an **estimate**

▶ **quotation 1**

---

estimate² *verb* (industry)

1 to calculate the approximate cost, size, value, etc of something: *We estimated that it would take two years to complete the job.* ○ *The building societies estimate a 10% reduction in property values.* **2** to give a price for a job to be done or a service to be provided: *You must ask three companies to estimate for the job.*

/ˈestɪmeɪt/

estimate, estimating, estimated

1 note transitive verb

⋈ **estimate** the cost, price, value (of something)

2 note intransitive verb

⋈ **estimate** for a job

▶ **budget² 2, quote 1**

ETA *abbr* (transport)

estimated time of arrival: *ETA is 10 am tomorrow.*

/ˌiː tiː ˈeɪ/

note pronounced as individual letters

Euro- *abbr, combining form*

European; of Europe or the European Community: *Eurodollar* ○ *a Euro bank, election, MP*

/ˈjʊərəʊ/

---

eurobond *noun* (stock exchange)

a bond issued in a EUROCURRENCY by a government or organization and sold internationally: *Eurobonds are usually issued in London through syndicates of banks.*

/ˈjʊərəʊbɒnd/

pl eurobonds

⋈ buy, hold, issue, sell **eurobonds**; the **eurobond** market

▶ **bond 1**

---

eurocard *noun* (finance/banking)

a CHEQUE CARD for use with eurocheques: *I can't accept this cheque without a eurocard.*

/ˈjʊərəʊkɑːd/

pl eurocards

(also **Eurocard**)

⋈ issue, use a **eurocard**

▶ **eurocheque**

---

eurocheque *noun* (banking)

a cheque from a European bank that can be cashed at any bank in the world that displays a eurocheque sign. It can also be used in shops or hotels with a EUROCARD: *Do you accept eurocheques?*

/ˈjʊərəʊtʃek/

pl eurocheques

(also **Eurocheque**)

⋈ accept, cash, issue, sign, write a **eurocheque**

▶ **cheque, traveller's cheque**

---

eurocurrency *noun* (banking/international trade)

a currency held in a country other than its country of origin. It is used by banks and large companies as a convenient way of financing international trade and investment because interest rates are often lower and taxes can sometimes be avoided: *Interest rates were favourable on the eurocurrency market.*

/ˈjʊərəʊˌkʌrənsi/

pl eurocurrencies

⋈ a **eurocurrency** loan, market

▶ **currency 1**

---

eurodollar *noun* (banking/finance)

a dollar kept in a bank outside the USA: *Eurodollar loans and deposits are used to finance international trade.*

/ˈjʊərəʊdɒlə(r)/

pl eurodollars

⋈ the **eurodollar** market

▶ **eurocurrency**

---

euromarket *noun* (banking/international trade)
a market in which commercial banks and large organizations finance international trade, usually with eurobonds issued in a eurocurrency: *eurobonds traded on the euromarket*

/ˈjʊərəʊˌmɑːkɪt/
pl euromarkets
⋈ buy, sell, trade in a **euromarket**
► **foreign exchange market, market**[1]

the European Bank for Reconstruction and Development *noun* (banking)
a bank set up in 1991 to provide loans and financial services for formerly state-controlled economies to become free market economies

/ðə ˌjʊərəˌpiːən ˌbæŋk fə ˌriːkənˌstrʌkʃn ənd dɪˈveləpmənt/
⋈ financed by the **European Bank for Reconstruction and Development**
► **International Bank for Reconstruction and Development, International Development Agency, International Finance Corporation, International Monetary Fund, the Overseas Development Administration, the World Bank**

European Commission *noun* (law)
a group of people chosen by the European Community to make routine decisions and propose new laws: *The European Commission is trying to establish closer links between small businesses throughout Europe.*

/ˌjʊərəˌpiːən kəˈmɪʃn/
⋈ the **European Commission** accepts, imposes, introduces, plans, proposes (new laws, directives, etc)

European Community *noun* (economics/international trade)
an organization of twelve Western European Countries that developed from the European Economic Community. It aims to allow money, goods, services and people to move freely within the community without political or trade barriers: *Does the product meet European Community safety standards?*

/ˌjʊərəˌpiːən kəˈmjuːnəti/
abbr EC
⋈ a member of the **European Community**; **European Community** plans, policies, regulations, requirements, standards
syn the common Market

European Currency Unit *noun* (finance)
a unit of money in the EUROPEAN MONETARY SYSTEM. Its value is calculated as an average of specified amounts of a group of European currencies. It is used for transactions between the governments of European Community countries and may eventually replace national currencies: *The deal was completed in the European Currency Unit to be sure of a steady exchange rate.* ○ *A European Currency Unit is made up of a 'basket' of ten European currencies including sterling.*

/ˌjʊərəˌpiːən ˈkʌrənsi ˌjuːnɪt/
pl European Currency Units
abbr ECU
pl ECUs
► **monetary unit, Economic and Monetary Union, Exchange Rate Mechanism**

European Free Trade Association *noun* (finance/international trade/economics)
an organization formed in 1959 with the aim of removing trade restrictions between member countries. Member countries are: Austria, Finland, Iceland, Norway, Sweden and Switzerland: *talks between ministers of the European Free Trade Association and the European Community*

/ˌjʊərəˌpiːən ˌfriː ˈtreɪd əsəʊsiˌeɪʃn/
abbr EFTA
► **free trade, trade association, trade bloc**

European Monetary System *noun* (finance)
a system of money set up by the European Community to keep the currency exchange rates of member countries steady. Each currency must be kept within agreed limits on a PARITY GRID, and is given a value in EUROPEAN CURRENCY UNITS.

/ˌjʊərəˌpiːən ˈmʌnɪtri ˈsɪstəm/
abbr EMS
▶ **European Currency Unit, Exchange Rate Mechanism, monetary system**

---

ex-bonus *noun* (stock exchange)
▶ **ex-scrip**

/ˌeks ˈbəʊnəs/

---

ex-cap *noun* (stock exchange)
▶ **ex-scrip**

/ˌeks ˈkæp/

---

excess *noun*
1 the amount by which one quantity is more than another: *We note an excess of expenditure over revenue.* ○ *The final cost will be well in excess of $5 000.* **2** an amount that is more than allowed: *Luggage in excess of 100 kg will be charged extra.* **3** (*insurance*) an amount of money that an insured person agrees to pay each time a claim is made: *It isn't worth making a small claim as we have an excess of £100.*

/ˈekses/
1 note usually singular
abbr XS
⧓ an **excess** *of* (an amount)
2 note no plural
⧓ **excess** baggage, fare, postage, weight
3 pl excesses

---

excess capacity *noun* (industry)
machines, resources, etc not being used: *We have some excess capacity in the machine shop at present.*

/ˈekses kəˈpæsəti/
note no plural
⧓ to find a use for, to have **excess capacity**

---

excess demand *noun* (economics)
a situation in which more of a product is wanted by buyers than can be supplied by the industry: *price increases resulting from excess demand*

/ˈekses dɪˈmɑːnd/
note not used with *a* or *an*. No plural and used with a singular verb only.
⧓ meet, remove **excess demand**
▶ **demand[1] 2, supply and demand**

---

excess supply *noun* (economics)
1 a situation in which industry provides more of a product than buyers want: *Prices have fallen as a result of excess supply.* **2** the goods available in this way: *reduce prices to get rid of excess supplies*

/ˈekses səˈplaɪ/
1 note not used with *a* or *an*. No plural and used with a singular verb only.
2 pl excess supplies
▶ **supply[1]**

---

exchange[1] *noun*
1 (**a**) giving or receiving something in return for something else: *be given a higher salary in exchange for doing a more responsible job* (**b**) an instance of this: *We had a useful exchange of views.* **2** (*stock exchange*) a place where goods and services are traded: *futures traded on the commodity exchange*

part-exchange a method of buying something in which an old item is given as part of the payment of a new one: *They took the old van in part-exchange.*

/ɪksˈtʃeɪndʒ/
1a note not used with *a* or *an*. No plural and used with a singular verb only.
1b pl exchanges
⧓ an **exchange** of ideas, information, views
2 pl exchanges
▶ **the Baltic Exchange, the Baltic International Freight and Futures Exchange, commodity exchange, foreign exchange, London FOX, London International Financial Futures and**

▶ **Options Exchange, London Metal Exchange, stock exchange**

---

exchange[2] *verb* (commerce)

1 to give or receive goods, money, etc in return for something of the same value: *Sale goods cannot be exchanged.* ○ *Can I exchange these shoes for a larger size?* **2** to give something and receive something (from another person) in return: *The sales conference is a good place to exchange information.* ○ *exchange contracts with a buyer* **3** (*banking*) to change one currency for another: *They exchanged their dollars for pounds.*

/ɪksˈtʃeɪndʒ/

exchange, exchanging, exchanged

note transitive verb

1 ⋈ **exchange** something *for* something; **exchange** something *with* someone

▶ **bill of exchange, long exchange, medium of exchange, stock exchange**

2 ⋈ **exchange** addresses, contracts, correspondence, ideas, information, views

▶ **exchange of contracts**

3 ▶ **exchange rate, foreign exchange**

---

exchange control *noun* (finance)

a set of restrictions imposed by a government on buying and selling foreign currencies: *The United Kingdom removed all exchange controls in 1979.*

/ɪksˈtʃeɪndʒ kənˌtrəʊl/

note usually plural

▶ **control[1] 1, foreign exchange**

---

exchange of contracts *noun* (law)

the time when a person buying a house, land, etc signs the sale contract and exchanges it for an exact copy signed by the seller. The sale is now legal: *The date for the exchange of contracts is 20 May 1992.*

/ɪksˌtʃeɪndʒ əv ˈkɒntrækts/

note singular noun, used with a singular verb

⋈ set a date for the **exchange of contracts**

▶ **contract[1], exchange[2] 2**

---

exchange rate *noun* (banking)

the amount of one currency that can be bought with another: *The exchange rate is 9.74 francs to the pound sterling.*

/ɪksˈtʃeɪndʒ reɪt/

pl exchange rates

⋈ alter, change, fix, increase lower, the **exchange rate**; a bad, fluctuating, good, high, low **exchange rate**

syn rate of exchange

▶ **devaluation, European Monetary System, floating rate, rate 2, revaluation**

Exchange Rate Mechanism *noun* (finance)

the scheme used by countries in the EUROPEAN MONETARY SYSTEM to keep the relative values of their currencies within agreed limits: *The aim of the Exchange Rate Mechanism is to stabilize exchange rate fluctuations.*

/ɪksˈtʃeɪndʒ reɪt ˌmekənɪzəm/

abbr ERM

⋈ enter, join the **Exchange Rate Mechanism**

▶ **Economic and Monetary Union, European Currency Unit, European Monetary System, parity grid**

---

excise duty *noun* (tax)

a tax on certain goods and services sold within a country, such as alcohol and tobacco: *reduce the excise duty on lead-free petrol*

/ˈeksaɪz ˌdjuːti/

⋈ increase, levy, pay, reduce an **excise duty**

▶ **customs duty, duty 1, duty-free, import duty**

---

ex-claim *adjective* (stock exchange)
▶ **ex-new**

/ˌeks ˈkleɪm/

---

exclusive *adjective* (sales/commerce)
1 not including: *The price is exclusive of tax.* **2** expensive; intended for a few select customers: *The store has an exclusive range of designs.* ○ *an exclusive shop, hotel, restaurant* ○ *The clothes in this shop are really exclusive.* **3** limited to a particular organization, group or place: *an exclusive offer to customers with credit accounts* ○ *sign an exclusive sales agreement with a local trader*

/ɪkˈskluːsɪv/

1 **exclusive** *of* (something)

3 ▶ exclusive distributor *under* **distributor, sole agent**

---

ex div *abbr* (stock exchange)
▶ **ex dividend *under* dividend**

/ˌeks ˈdɪv/

---

ex dock *adjective* (shipping)
▶ **ex quay**

/ˌeks ˈdɒk/

---

exec *abbr* (management)
executive

/ɪgˈzek/

---

executive *noun* (management)
1 a person who makes and carries out important decisions in a company; a senior business person: *a policy decision taken by the chief executive* ○ *be appointed marketing executive* **2** the part of an organization that takes important decisions: *The Health and Safety Executive has issued new guidelines on safety at work.*

/ɪgˈzekjʊtɪv/

abbr exec

1 pl executives

⧓ an advertising, a chief, a marketing, a sales, a senior **executive**

2 note singular noun, used with a singular verb

⧓ an **executive** board, body, committee

▶ **director, manager**

---

executive director *noun* (management)
a full-time employee of a company who is also a member of the board of directors: *The sales manager has been invited to join us as an executive director.*

/ɪgˌzekjʊtɪv dɪˈrektə(r)/

▶ **director**

---

executor *noun* (law)
a person appointed by the maker of a will to carry out the terms of the will: *appoint a close relative to act as executor for the will*

/ɪgˈzekjʊtə(r)/

pl executors

⧓ act as **executor**; appoint an **executor**

▶ **beneficiary, will**

---

exempt *adjective* (law/tax)
free from a duty or payment: *Books are still exempt from value added tax in the United Kingdom.* ○ *People with very low incomes will be exempt.*

/ɪgˈzempt/

⧓ **exempt** *from* a tax, payment, etc

▶ **tax exempt**

---

exempt gilts *noun* (stock exchange)
▶ **gilts**

/ɪgˌzempt ˈgɪlts/

---

exemption *noun* (tax)
1 freedom from a duty, tax, etc: *apply for tax exemption* ○ *be granted exemption from overtime duties* **2** an instance of this: *qualify for an exemption*

/ɪɡˈzempʃn/
1 note not used with *a* or *an*. No plural and used with a singular verb only.
⋈ apply for, grant, qualify for, seek **exemption**; **exemption** *from* a duty, tax, etc
2 pl exemptions
▶ **tax exemption**

ex factory *adjective* (commerce)
▶ **ex works**

/eks ˈfæktəri/

ex growth *adjective* (stock exchange)
(of a share or company) that has risen in importance or value in the past, but is not likely to do so again in the near future: *It is now an ex growth company* ○ *try to sell ex growth shares*

/ˌeks ˈɡrəʊθ/

exhibition *noun* (advertising)
a collection of objects that are shown to the public; an event when such objects are shown: *an exhibition of microcomputers* ○ *Join us on our stand at the local industry exhibition.* ○ *The exhibition was organized by the Chamber of Commerce.*

/ˌeksɪˈbɪʃn/
pl exhibitions
⋈ arrange, have a stand at, hold, organize, put on, set up, visit an **exhibition**; an **exhibition** catalogue, centre, hall, stand
▶ **display[1] 1, trade fair**

exhibitor *noun* (advertising)
a person or company that displays goods or services at an exhibition: *There were 350 exhibitors at the trade fair.*

/ɪɡˈzɪbɪtə(r)/
pl exhibitors

ex-new *adjective* (stock exchange)
of a share that is offered for sale without the right to take up a RIGHTS ISSUE or a SCRIP ISSUE

/ˌeks ˈnjuː/
syn ex-claim
▶ **ex-rights, ex-scrip**

ex officio *adjective, adverb*
because of a position or office held: *present at the meeting ex officio* ○ *an ex officio member of the planning committee*

/ˌeks əˈfɪʃiəʊ/

expenditure *noun* (finance)
1 action of spending money or using time and resources: *Expenditure on heat and lighting was too high last year.* **2** an amount of money spent: *Updating these machines will increase our expenditure this year.* ○ *an expenditure of £20 000 on new computer equipment*

/ɪkˈspendɪtʃə(r)/
1 note not used with *a* or *an*. No plural and used with a singular verb only.
⋈ high, low **expenditure**; increase, reduce **expenditure**
2 note singular noun, used with a singular verb
▶ **capital expenditure, income, income and expenditure account, outlay, revenue expenditure**

expense account *noun* (finance)
a record of money spent by an employee on work activities and later paid by the employer: *The hotel bill was charged to his expense account.* ○ *I'll put the cost of the petrol on my expense account.*

/ɪkˈspens əˌkaʊnt/
pl expense accounts
⋈ charge something to, put

something on an **expense account**

▶ **account[1] 1**

---

expenses *noun* (finance/accounting)

1 sums of money spent by a company on goods and services that do not become part of a company's ASSETS, eg rent, wages, insurance, etc: *We earn enough to cover our fixed expenses, but have nothing left to invest in new machinery.* **2** money spent by an employee while doing his/her job and later paid by the employer: *Your salary will be £25 000 plus expenses.* ○ *I need the receipt in order to claim travel expenses.*

/ɪkˈspensɪz/

note plural noun, used with a plural verb

1 ⋈ business, fixed, handling, legal **expenses**

▶ **overhead**

2 ⋈ charge something to, claim, put something on **expenses**

---

expensive *adjective*

high in price; not cheap: *This method of production is too expensive.* ○ *This is the most expensive restaurant in the town.*

/ɪkˈspensɪv/

opp cheap

---

expert *noun* (management)

a person with special knowledge, skill, or training in a particular subject: *We need a tax expert to sort out this problem.* ○ *a business, a computer, an economics, a financial, etc expert*

/ˈekspɜːt/

pl experts

⋈ an **expert** *at, in, on* (something); a body, panel, team of **experts**

---

expertise *noun* (management)

specialist knowledge or skill: *employ someone with a high level of expertise* ○ *a job that allows you to acquire technical expertise*

/ˌekspɜːˈtiːz/

note not used with *a* or *an*. No plural and used with a singular verb only.

⋈ acquire, gain, have **expertise**; managerial, professional, scientific, technical **expertise**

▶ **know-how**

---

export[1] *noun* (international trade)

1 an item, a service, an idea or a person that is sent from one country to another to be sold: *There is a ban on the export of ivory.* ○ *Exports have fallen this year.* **2** the action of exporting goods: *This size is made specifically for export.*

/ˈekspɔːt/

1 pl exports

⋈ control, restrict **exports**

2 note not used with *a* or *an*. No plural and used with a singular verb only.

⋈ goods for **export**

▶ **direct export, import[1], invisible exports, re-exports, reimports, visible exports**

---

export[2] *verb* (export)

to send goods, services, ideas or people to other countries: *Most of these products are exported to Spain.* ○ *export medical knowledge to developing countries*

/ɪkˈspɔːt/

export, exporting, exported

note transitive verb

⋈ **export** (something) *to* (a country)

▶ **import[2]**

---

export documents *noun* (international trade/shipping)

▶ **shipping documents**

/ˈekspɔːt ˌdɒkjumənts/

note plural noun, used with a plural verb

---

exporter *noun* (export)
a person, an organization or a country that sends goods or services to other countries for sale: *Japan, not Switzerland, is now the world's biggest watch exporter.* ○ *a car, food, oil, etc exporter* ○ *shipping documents prepared by an exporter*

/ɪkˈspɔːtə(r)/
pl exporters
⋈ an **exporter** *of* (something)
▶ **importer**

export licence *noun* (import/tax)
a document that must be obtained by an exporter before certain goods are sent out of the country: *Some works of art require export licences before they are sent abroad.*

/ˈekspɔːt ˌlaɪsns/
pl export licences
⋈ apply for, grant, issue, obtain, refuse an **export licence**
syn export permit
▶ **bill of entry, bill of sight, bond note, import licence**

export quota *noun* (export)
a limit on the number or type of goods sent out of a country: *introduce export quotas on coffee to balance supply with demand in the export market*

/ˈekspɔːt ˌkwəʊtə/
pl export quotas
⋈ abolish, raise, reduce, remove the **export quota**; impose an **export quota**
▶ **import quota, quota**

ex quay *adjective* (shipping)
of a price for goods where the seller pays all the costs for delivery to a named port, including unloading onto the quay and onto road or rail vehicles

/ˌeks ˈkiː/
syn ex dock, ex wharf
▶ **ex ship**

ex-rights *adjective* (stock exchange)
of a share that is offered for sale without the right to take up a rights issue

/ˌeks ˈraɪts/
▶ **cum rights, ex-new, rights issue**

ex-scrip *adjective* (stock exchange)
of a share that is offered for sale without the right to take up a scrip-issue

/ˌeks ˈskrɪp/
syn ex-bonus, ex-cap
▶ **ex-new, ex-rights**

ex ship *adjective* (shipping)
of a price for goods where the seller pays for all costs up to delivery at a named port, but the buyer pays for unloading the goods and transporting them from the port

/ˌeks ˈʃɪp/
abbr x shp
▶ **ex quay**

ex stock *adjective* (commerce)
of a price for goods that applies to present supplies. The price of future supplies may change.

/ˌeks ˈstɒk/
abbr x stk
▶ **stock**[1]

ex store *adjective* (commerce)
of a price for goods that includes delivery to a store, but the buyer pays for transporting goods away from the store

/ˌeks ˈstɔː(r)/
abbr x store

external *adjective*
outside (a country, an area, a region, etc): *profit from external trade* ○ *hold an external bank account*

/ɪkˈstɜːnl/
⋈ **external** finance, funding, investment, trade
▶ **internal**

external audit *noun* (accounting)
▶ **audit**[1]

/ɪkˌstɜːnl ˈɔːdɪt/
pl external audits

external liabilities *noun* (accounting)
the debts owed by a company to organizations other than its ordinary shareholders: *The company's debt to the Inland Revenue makes up most of its external liabilities.*

/ɪkˌstɜːnl ˌlaɪəˈbɪlətiz/
note plural noun, used with a plural verb
▶ **liability 2**

extortion *noun* (law)
1 obtaining money from someone by the use of threats or violence: *We would need more evidence to prove extortion.* **2** an instance of this: *an increase in the number of extortions*

/ɪkˈstɔːʃn/
1 note not used with *a* or *an*. No plural and used with a singular verb only.
⋈ attempt, prove, use **extortion**
2 pl extortions
▶ **blackmail, bribery**

extra *noun* (commerce)
an additional item, esp one not included in a price: *Any delivery charges or postage and package will be charged as extras.* ○ *The price does not include extras.*

/ˈekstrə/
pl extras
⋈ charged as an **extra**; **extras** included, not included

extraordinary general meeting *noun* (management)
a special meeting of the members, shareholders and directors of a company, called to discuss matters that cannot wait until the next ANNUAL GENERAL MEETING: *The directors called an extraordinary general meeting to discuss the effect of the budget on the business.*

/ɪkˌstrɔːdnri ˌdʒenrəl ˈmiːtɪŋ/
abbr EGM
⋈ attend, be present at, call an **extraordinary general meeting**

ex warehouse *adjective* (commerce)
of a price where the buyer pays for transporting the goods away from the warehouse

/ˌeks ˈweəhaʊs/

ex wharf *adjective* (shipping)
▶ **ex quay**

/ˌeks ˈwɔːf/

ex works *adjective* (commerce)
of a price where the buyer pays for transporting the goods away from the factory

/ˌeks ˈwɜːks/
abbr x wks
syn ex factory
▶ **works**

Ff

faa *abbr* (insurance/shipping)
free of all average

note used in written English only

face value *noun* (finance)
the amount printed on a coin, banknote or other financial document: *Currency will only be exchanged at face value.*

/ˌfeɪs ˈvæljuː/
note singular noun, used with a singular verb
▶ **nominal price**

factor *noun*
1 (*commerce*) a person who buys and sells for another organization for a fee. The factor is responsible for holding and transferring the document proving ownership of the goods and, unlike a broker, acts in his/her own name: *We asked a motor*

/ˈfæktə(r)/
pl factors
⋈ act as, employ, use a **factor**
1 syn mercantile agent
▶ **agent, broker, dealer, del**

trade factor to sell our cars for us. **2** (*international trade*) a person who buys the right to manage the debts of an export company by paying for goods as soon as they are supplied, charging the company a fee, and collecting payment from the customers

credere agent, distributor, middleman

---

factoring (international trade) *noun*
a process where an export company sells the right to collect payment from its customers to an agent (a FACTOR). The factor, who charges the company a fee, pays for the goods as soon as they are supplied and must then recover the money from the customers: *Many firms used factoring services in the development of their business last year.*

/ˈfæktərɪŋ/
⋈ a **factoring** business, company, firm; the **factoring** industry
► **disclosed factoring, undisclosed factoring**

---

factor of production *noun* (economics)
one of the elements that contribute to the production of goods. These elements are usually listed as land, labour and capital: *In an agricultural community, land is a very important factor of production.*

/ˌfæktər əv prəˈdʌkʃn/
pl factors of production
⋈ a chief, key, main, major, vital **factor of production**
► **capital 4, labour, land[1] 1**

---

factory *noun* (industry)
a building or group of buildings containing machinery where people make goods for sale: *He has a job in a factory/a factory job.* ○ *She works in a textiles factory.*

factory floor the area of the factory where the manual work is done: *It is on the factory floor, not at company headquarters, that the economic war will be won.*

/ˈfæktəri/
pl factories
⋈ a **factory** building, manager, worker; a car, chocolate, plastics **factory**
► **assembly line, production line, works**

---

fair average quality *noun*
(international trade/shipping)
a way of classifying goods, eg wheat, where the quality of goods supplied equals the average quality of the goods in a number of shipments, rather than exactly matching a particular sample: *The contract was for goods of fair average quality.*

/ˌfeər ˌævərɪdʒ ˈkwɒləti/
note no plural
abbr f.a.q.
⋈ of **fair average quality**
► **quality**

---

fair trading *noun*
1 (*commerce*) buying and selling activities that are honest and do not restrict the rights of the buyer, seller or consumer: *The company is committed to a policy of fair trading.* **2** (*international trade*) a system of international trade where the countries involved agree not to impose duties on certain items they import from each other: *Some state subsidies could pose a threat to fair trading conditions.*

/ˌfeə ˈtreɪdɪŋ/
note not used with *a* or *an*. No plural and used with a singular verb only.
1 ⋈ a **fair trading** agreement, policy, system
► **Office of Fair Trading**
2 ► **free trade 2**

---

fair wage *noun* (personnel)
an amount of money paid which is equivalent to the work done: *The workers have gone on strike for a fair wage.*

/ˌfeə ˈweɪdʒ/
pl fair wages
⋈ demand, earn, pay, receive a **fair wage**
► **wage**

---

fake *noun*
► **counterfeit**

/feɪk/

---

f.a.o. *abbr* (office practice)
for the attention of

note used in written English only

---

f.a.q. (international trade/shipping)
fair average quality

/ˌef eɪ ˈkjuː/
note pronounced as individual letters

FAS *abbr* (transport)
free alongside ship

/ˌef eɪ ˈes/
note pronounced as individual letters

fast food *noun* (commerce)
food such as hamburgers, chips that can be cooked easily and is sold by restaurants to be eaten quickly or taken away: *He owns a chain of fast food restaurants.*

/ˌfɑːst ˈfuːd/
note usually singular
⧓ a **fast food** counter, restaurant, take-away
▶ **convenience food**

fast-moving consumer goods *noun* (marketing/sales)
cheap, everyday items that are bought and used up quickly: *Soap, toothpaste, batteries and light bulbs are all fast-moving consumer goods.*

/ˌfɑːst ˌmuːvɪŋ kənˈsjuːmə gʊdz/
note usually plural
abbr FMCG
⧓ manufacture, process, produce, sell, stock **fast-moving consumer goods**
▶ **consumer goods, low involvement product**

faulty goods *noun* (commerce)
damaged or imperfect articles. The buyer can usually claim a new article or have his/her money returned: *New legislation will give consumers the right to have faulty goods repaired or replaced within five days.*

/ˌfɔːlti ˈgʊdz/
note plural noun, used with a plural verb
⧓ change, refund, replace, return, take back **faulty goods**

favoured nation status *noun* (international trade)
a condition in an international trade agreement where the countries involved promise to give each other the same or better trading terms than they would offer to any other country they trade with: *The countries have given each other favoured nation staus.*

/ˌfeɪvəd ˈneɪʃn ˌsteɪtəs/
note no plural
⧓ exchange, offer, request **favoured nation status**

fax[1] *noun* (administration)
1 a copy of a document, an illustration, etc sent by an electronic system using telephone lines: *Has that fax arrived yet?* **2** (**a**) a machine for sending documents, etc in this way: *Is there a fax (machine) on this floor?* ○ *What is your fax code/number?* (**b**) a system for sending documents, etc in this way: *To save time, we'll send it by fax.*

/fæks/
pl faxes
⧓ get, receive, send a **fax**
▶ **electronic mail, modem, telex**[1]

fax[2] *verb* (administration/office practice)
to send copies of a document, an illustration, etc by an electronic system using telephone lines: *Can you fax me tomorrow?* ○ *I'll fax the report to you as soon as I've finished it.* ○ *Fax it through to the New York office.*

/fæks/
fax, faxing, faxed
note transitive verb
⧓ **fax** a copy, document, report
▶ **telex**[2]

feasibility study *noun* (finance/industry)
an examination of the costs, benefits, risks, etc involved in starting a new commercial activity to see if it will be successful: *A feasibility study is being carried out before we invest in the new leisure centre.*

/ˌfiːzəˈbɪləti ˌstʌdi/
pl feasibility studies
⧓ carry out, conduct, draw up, prepare a **feasibility study**
▶ **cost benefit analysis**

FED *abbr* (banking)
(*US*) **1** Federal Reserve Board **2** Federal Reserve System

/fed/
(also **Fed**)
note pronounced as a word

---

fed *abbr*
federation

/fed/
note pronounced as a word

Federal Reserve Bank *noun* (banking)
(*US*) a bank that is part of the FEDERAL RESERVE SYSTEM and provides banking facilities for all the other state and national banks: *an increase in interest rates offered by the Federal Reserve Banks*

/ˌfedərəl rɪˈzɜːv bæŋk/
abbr FRB
▶ **the Bank of America, the Bank of England, national bank**

Federal Reserve Board *noun* (banking)
(*US*) the organization based in Washington that controls the central banking system (the FEDERAL RESERVE SYSTEM) of the USA: *The Federal Reserve Board plans to cut interest rates.*

/ˌfedərəl rɪˈzɜːv bɔːd/
abbr FED, Fed
note FED or Fed is used for Federal Reserve Board and Federal Reserve System.
▶ **the Bank of America, the Bank of England**

Federal Reserve System *noun* (banking)
(*US*) the central banking system of the USA that provides banking facilities for the government and other banks and issues banknotes and coins: *changes in monetary policy adopted by the Federal Reserve System*

/ˌfedərəl rɪˈzɜːv ˌsɪstəm/
abbr FED, Fed
note FED or Fed is used for Federal Reserve System and Federal Reserve Board.
▶ **the Bank of America, the Bank of England, reserve**

---

federation *noun*
a group of companies, societies or trade unions with a common interest and controlled by a central organization: *a federation of local industries* ○ *He belongs to the Engineering Employers Federation.*

/ˌfedəˈreɪʃn/
pl federations
abbr fed
⧓ belong to, establish, form a **federation**
▶ **association 1, business 3, company, corporation, group, organization 1**

---

fee *noun*
an amount paid for a professional service or advice: *How much is the fee?* ○ *The fees will be about 30% of the total cost.* ○ *charge an administration/a consultancy fee*

/fiː/
pl fees
⧓ ask for, charge, command, demand, pay, receive a **fee**
▶ **charge[1] 1, commission[1] 1, dues 1, service charge**

---

feedback *noun*
information about a product, service, etc that the user gives to the supplier or organizer: *Feedback from customers helps us to improve our products.* ○ *Did you get any useful feedback from the sales conference?*

/ˈfiːdbæk/
note not used with *a* or *an*. No plural and used with a singular verb only.
⧓ important, interesting, useful **feedback**; ask for, get, need, receive **feedback**

---

fictitious person *noun* (law)
▶ **artificial person**

/fɪkˌtɪʃəs ˈpɜːsn/
pl fictitious people

---

fiduciary[1] *noun* (law)
a person who holds a position of trust and honesty when dealing with the affairs of others: *The solicitor acted as fiduciary.*

/fɪˈdjuːʃəri/
pl fiduciaries
⧓ act as **fiduciary**
▶ **trustee**

fiduciary[2] *adjective* (law)
relating to a position of trust and honesty when dealing with the affairs of others: *Solicitors have a fiduciary relationship with their clients.*

/fɪˈdjuːʃəri/
⧓ a **fiduciary** position, relationship

fiduciary issue *noun* (banking)
an issue of paper money not supported by gold: *The limit of the fiduciary issue has been steadily raised.*

/fɪˌdjuːʃəri ˈɪʃuː/
note usually singular
⧓ fix, raise, reduce the **fiduciary issue**
▶ **gold standard**

FIFO *abbr* (commerce)
first in, first out

/ˈfaɪːfəʊ/
note pronounced as a word

file[1] *noun*
1 a box or cover that is used for keeping papers together or in order: *Put that letter in the file marked 'urgent'.* **2** a collection of papers or information kept in a file: *I can't remember exactly what I said in the letter. I need to look at the file.* ○ *We keep a file on each member of staff.* **3** (*computing*) a collection of information on one subject kept in a file: *open the file called 'miscellaneous'*
on file kept in a file: *We have all the information you need on file.*

/faɪl/
pl files
1 ⧓ put (a letter) in a **file**
2 ⧓ consult, refer to a **file**
▶ **dossier**
3 ⧓ close, create, name, open a **file**

file[2] *verb*
to put a document, a letter, etc in a file: *File these letters under 'Job Applications', please.* ○ *What name were they filed under?*

/faɪl/
file, filing, filed
note transitive verb
⧓ **file** a document, a letter

FIMBRA *abbr* (finance/stock exchange)
Financial Intermediaries, Managers and Brokers Regulatory Association

/ˈfɪmbrə/
note pronounced as a word

final accounts *noun* (accounting)
the finished version of a firm's PROFIT AND LOSS ACCOUNT, showing all money received and spent in a year: *The balance sheet of a company is worked out from the final accounts.*

/ˌfaɪnl əˈkaʊnts/
note usually plural
⧓ check, compile, do, put together the **final accounts**
▶ **accounts 1, profit and loss account**

final demand *noun* (finance)
the last request for payment of a debt before court action is taken; the document that states this: *She received a final demand for her gas bill.*

/ˌfaɪnl dɪˈmɑːnd/
pl final demands
⧓ get a, issue a, pay on, receive a **final demand**
▶ **demand[1] 1, on demand, ultimatum**

finance[1] *noun* (finance)
1 money as a resource for business and other activities: *The company agreed to provide finance for the purchase of the property.* **2** the management of money for business and other activities:

/ˈfaɪnæns, faɪˈnæns/
1, 2 note not used with *a* or *an*. No plural and used with a singular verb only.

Finance can be arranged for first-time home buyers. **3 finances** money available to a person, an organization or a country: *Are the company's finances sound* (ie do they have enough money for their business activities)*?*

⋈ apply for, arrange, provide, supply **finance**; a **finance** clerk, committee, department, director

3 note plural noun, used with a plural verb

► **capital, public finance**

---

finance² *verb* (finance)

to obtain or supply money for a business or other activity: *The oil deal was financed by 12 international banks.* ○ *The company has agreed to finance a day nursery for children of its employees.*

/ˈfaɪnæns/

finance, financing, financed

note transitive verb

► **fund²**

---

finance bill *noun* (public finance)

► **Treasury bill**

/ˈfaɪnæns bɪl/

---

finance house *noun* (finance)

an organization that lends money to individuals or businesses to enable them to buy goods. Repayment, with interest, is made in instalments, but the goods remain the property of the finance company until all or most of the debt is repaid: *a loan from a finance company* ○ *The finance house asked the director for a personal guarantee against the money lent.*

/ˈfaɪnæns haʊs/

pl finance houses

⋈ a **finance house** arranges, provides (a loan)

syn finance company

► **hire purchase, investment bank**

---

financial *adjective* (finance)

of money and finance: *The company is in financial difficulties.*

/faɪˈnænʃl/

⋈ a **financial** arrangement, benefit, problem, resource

► **fiscal, monetary**

---

financial accountant *noun* (accounting)

an accountant who manages the money of a company and who prepares the accounts: *appoint a financial accountant* ○ *act as financial accountant*

/faɪˌnænʃl əˈkaʊntənt/

pl financial accountants

⋈ appoint, consult a **financial accountant**

► **accountant, cost accountant, management accountant**

---

financial adviser *noun* (finance)

1 a person who offers financial advice to a company or an individual, esp on investments: *I need to consult a financial adviser before buying any shares.* **2** an organization, such as a bank, that advises a company during a takeover: *The bank is acting as financial adviser in the deal.*

/faɪˌnænʃl ədˈvaɪzə(r)/

pl financial advisers

(also **financial advisor**)

⋈ call upon, consult, employ, engage a **financial adviser**

► **analyst, investment analyst**

---

financial instrument *noun* (finance)

any stock, share, money or other financial security: *In the city there are banks which trade in all types of financial instruments.*

/faɪˌnænʃl ˈɪnstrəmənt/

pl financial instruments

⋈ deliver, receive a **financial instrument**

► **security 1, share, stock², tradeable instrument**

Financial Intermediaries, Managers and Brokers Regulatory Association

noun (finance/stock exchange)

a SELF-REGULATORY ORGANIZATION that draws up and enforces codes

/faɪˌnænʃl ɪntəˌmiːdiəriz ˌmænɪdʒəz ənd ˌbrəʊkəz ˈregjələtri əsəʊsiˌeɪʃn/

abbr FIMBRA

of conduct for the control of independent financial advisers: *Independent financial advisers are registered at the Financial Intermediaries, Managers and Brokers Regulatory Association.*

⧓ be ruled by, consult, refer to the **Financial Intermediaries, Managers and Brokers Regulatory Association**

► **Investment Management Regulatory Organization, Life Assurance and Unit Trust Regulatory Organization, Securities and Futures Authority, Securities and Investment Board, self-regulatory organization**

---

financial investment *noun* (finance)

buying shares, securities, etc to make a profit in the form of interest or dividends or by selling them again at a higher price; the item bought in this way: *make a sound financial investment* ○ *a financial investment worth £5 000*

/faɪˌnænʃl ɪnˈvestmənt/

pl financial investments

⧓ a bad, good, poor, profitable **financial investment**

► **capital investment, investment**

---

the Financial Times-Actuaries All-Share Index *noun* (stock exchange)

(*UK*) a list published daily by the Financial Times based on the prices of more than 700 companies quoted on the International Stock Exchange

/ðə faɪˌnænʃl ˌtaɪmz ˌæktʃuəriz ˌɔːl ʃeər ˈɪndeks/

---

the Financial Times-Ordinary Share Index *noun* (stock exchange)

(*UK*) a list published hourly by the Financial Times based on the share prices of 30 major industrial companies: *The Financial Times-Ordinary Share Index closed at 1 876.9.* ○ *The Financial Times-Ordinary Share Index gained 19.7 points to 1 721.4.*

/ðə faɪˌnænʃl ˌtaɪmz ˌɔːdənri ˈʃeər ˌɪndeks/

abbr FT Index, FT 30 Share Index

syn Thirty Share Index

⧓ **the Financial Times-Ordinary Share Index** climbed, closed, ended, fell, finished, plunged, rose, soared

► **Dow Jones Industrial Average, Nikkei Index**

---

the Financial Times-Stock Exchange 100 Share Index *noun* (stock exchange)

(*UK*) a list published by the Financial Times newspaper based on the prices of 100 specially selected shares: *The Financial Times-Stock Exchange 100 Share Index closed 15.7 points up at 2273.7.*

/ðə faɪˌnænʃl ˌtaɪmz ˌstɒk ɪksˌtʃeɪndʒ ˌwʌn ˌhʌndrəd ˈʃeər ˌɪndeks/

abbr FT-SE 100 Index, Footsie

⧓ **the Financial Times-Stock Exchange 100 Share Index** climbed, closed, ended, fell, finished, plunged, rose, soared

► **Dow Jones Industrial Average, Nikkei Index, stock exchange**

---

financial year *noun* (accounting)

the period used by companies and governments for accounting and tax purposes: *The aim is to meet the target projected for the current financial year.* ○ *In the UK, the government's financial year runs from 6 April to the following 5 April.*

/faɪˌnænʃl ˈjɪə(r)/

pl financial years

⧓ current, last, next, previous **financial year**

syn fiscal year

► **accounting period, tax year**

fine rate *noun* (banking)
▶ **prime rate**

/ˈfaɪn reɪt/
pl fine rates

fine trade bill *noun* (banking)
a bill of exchange that is accepted by the Bank of England as security for a loan

/ˌfaɪn ˈtreɪd bɪl/
pl fine trade bills
⋈ accept, endorse a **fine trade bill**
▶ **bill of exchange**

fire *verb* (personnel)
▶ **sack**[2]

/ˈfaɪə(r)/

firm[1] *noun* (commerce)
two or more people in business to make a profit by selling goods or services: *an engineering, an accountancy, a mail order firm* ○ *John was invited to join the family firm.*

/fɜːm/
pl firms
⋈ go into, set up a **firm**
▶ **association 1, business 3, company, corporation, organization 1**

firm[2] *adjective* (stock exchange)
(of prices) steady; rising steadily: *Oil shares remained firm yesterday.* ○ *Commercial Union remained firm, up 2p at 521p.*

/fɜːm/
⋈ remain, stay **firm**

firm[3] *verb* (stock exchange)
(of prices) to steady or rise steadily: *Gold shares closed sharply higher as the gold price firmed to over 384 dollars an ounce.*

/fɜːm/
firm, firming, firmed
note transitive and intransitive verb
⋈ **firm** at, to, up

first in, first out *adjective* (commerce)
a method of stock control where the items first taken into stock are also the first sold or used for production. For accounting purposes existing stock is therefore costed at the most recent prices.

/ˌfɜːst ˌɪn ˌfɜːst ˈaʊt/
abbr FIFO
▶ **last in first out, stock control**

first officer *noun* (shipping)
▶ **mate**

/fɜːst ˈɒfɪsə(r)/

fiscal *adjective* (finance)
relating to public or government money, esp taxation: *Many business people want sweeping changes in the government fiscal policy to ease the tax burden on business.*

/ˈfɪskl/
▶ **financial, monetary, taxation**

fiscal year *noun* (finance)
▶ **financial year**

/ˌfɪskl ˈjɪə(r)/
pl fiscal years

fixed asset *noun* (accounting)
▶ **capital asset**

/ˌfɪkst ˈæset/
pl fixed assets

fixed charge *noun* (commerce/finance)
1 an arrangement where specific items of a business (ASSETS), such as buildings or machinery, can be claimed or sold if a loan is not repaid: *The bank took a fixed charge on the company's head office.* **2** a pre-arranged price: *There is a fixed charge for installing a new phone.*

/ˌfɪkst ˈtʃɑːdʒ/
pl fixed charges
1 ▶ **floating charge**
2 ⋈ introduce, make a **fixed charge**
syn fixed rate, set price

fixed cost *noun* (industry)
a sum of money needed to run a business (part of the OVERHEADS) that does not change: *Fixed costs include rent.*

/ˌfɪkst ˈkɒst/
pl fixed costs
▶ **direct cost, oncost, overhead, unit cost, variable cost**

fixed-interest securities *noun* (stock exchange)
financial instruments which pay an agreed rate of interest, which does not change, at regular intervals: *The safest fixed-interest securities are gilts.*

/ˌfɪkst ˌɪntrest sɪˈkjʊərətiz/
note plural noun, used with a plural verb
⋈ buy, issue, sell, trade-in **fixed-interest securities**
▶ **guilts, security 1**

fixed rate *noun* (commerce/finance)
▶ **fixed charge**

/ˌfɪkst ˈreɪt/
pl fixed rates

fixed term contract *noun* (personnel)
an agreement to employ someone for a limited period only: *be given a fixed term contract* ○ *be employed under a fixed term contract*

/ˌfɪkst tɜːm ˈkɒntrækt/
pl fixed term contracts
▶ **contract[1]**

flat rate *noun* (finance)
1 a fixed amount of interest which is calculated on the original value of a loan over the full period of the loan, even though the loan is repaid in instalments: *be charged a flat rate of interest* ○ *The true rate of interest may be twice as much as the flat rate.* **2** the same amount paid or charged to all people: *The workforce received a flat rate pay rise this year.*

/ˌflæt ˈreɪt/
note usually singular
1 ⋈ charge a **flat rate**
▶ **annual percentage rate, rate 1**

flat yield *noun* (finance)
the amount of interest obtained from an investment expressed as a percentage of the original price: *a flat yield of 8%*

/ˌflæt ˈjiːld/
note no plural
▶ **dividend yield, redemption yield**

flexible budget *noun* (finance)
▶ **variable budget**

/ˌfleksɪbl ˈbʌdʒɪt/

flexitime *noun* (personnel)
a system where employees can start and finish work at different times each day, provided they work a certain number of hours in a week or month: *The company has just introduced flexitime.* ○ *Staff are allowed to work flexitime.*

/ˈfleksitaɪm/
(also **flexi-time**)
note not used with *a* or *an*. No plural and used with a singular verb only.
⋈ work **flexitime**

flip-chart *noun*
large sheets of paper fixed onto a stand so that one can be used and turned over to reveal the next one. It is used to present information to a group of people: *I'll use the flip-chart for the presentation.*

/ˈflɪp tʃɑːt/
pl flip-charts
⋈ draw on, use, write on a **flip-chart**

float[1] *verb* (commerce)
to offer company shares for sale on a stock exchange for the first time: *Seventy per cent of the workforce bought shares when the company was floated on the stock exchange.*

/fləʊt/
float, floating, floated
note transitive verb
⋈ **float** a business, company, firm
▶ **launch[2] 2, flotation**

float[2] *noun* (finance)
a small sum of money used for changing larger sums: *There isn't enough money in the float to change a twenty-pound note.*

/fləʊt/
pl floats
⧓ add up, increase, take money out of the **float**
► **kitty, petty cash**

floating charge *noun* (finance)
an arrangement where all items of value of a business (ASSETS) can be claimed or sold if a loan is not repaid: *A floating charge creates an immediate security interest.*

/ˌfləʊtɪŋ ˈtʃɑːdʒ/
pl floating charges
⧓ demand, require a **floating charge**
► **fixed charge**

floating rate *noun* (finance)
1 the rate of exchange between one currency and another that is allowed to rise and fall according to market forces: *exchange currency at a floating rate* **2** a percentage of interest that varies according to market forces: *The company's debts are all at floating rates of interest.*

/ˌfləʊtɪŋ ˈreɪt/
pl floating rates
1 syn floating exchange rate
► **exchange rate, rate 2**

floppy disk *noun* (computing)
a removable piece of plastic and magnetic material, used with computers to store information: *Make a copy of your report and store it on (a) floppy disk.* ○ *a floppy disk copy*

/ˌflɒpi ˈdɪsk/
pl floppy disks
⧓ copy onto, eject, insert, store on, use a **floppy disk**
syn floppy
► **disk, hard disk**

flotation *noun* (stock exchange)
offering company shares for sale to the public or on a stock exchange for the first time: *The company has had a difficult time since its flotation in 1989.* ○ *The stock market flotations of Eurodisney have caused a lot of publicity.*

/fləʊˈteɪʃn/
pl flotations
⧓ **flotation** plans, price, shares; announce, prepare for (a) **flotation**
► **issue[1], offer by prospectus, offer for sale**

flow chart *noun* (administration)
a diagram showing the progress of something through various stages. It is used to plan a business activity efficiently and see how long it will take: *I won't be able to finish it by the date on your flow chart.*

/ˈfləʊ tʃɑːt/
pl flow charts
syn flow diagram
⧓ design, follow, refer to, use a **flow chart**
► **bar chart, block diagram, chart[1] 1, diagram, graph, pictogram, pie chart**

fluctuate *verb*
(of prices, numbers, rates, amounts) to rise and fall or change suddenly: *Our sales figures have fluctuated over the past year.* ○ *The shares fluctuated between 251p and 124p.*

/ˈflʌktʃueɪt/
fluctuate, fluctuating, fluctuated
note intransitive verb
⧓ **fluctuate** *from* (something to something), *between* (something and something)

fluctuation *noun*
the rising and falling or changing of prices, numbers, rates or amounts: *major fluctuations of share prices on the stock market* ○ *The government is attempting to control currency fluctuation.*

/ˌflʌktʃuˈeɪʃn/
pl fluctuations
⧓ (a) **fluctuation** *in*

(something), *of* (something); cause, expect, predict a **fluctuation**

FMCG *abbr* (commerce)
fast-moving consumer goods

/ˌef em siː ˈdʒiː/

FOB *abbr* (shipping)
free on board

/ˌef əʊˈbiː/
(also **f.o.b.**)
note pronounced as individual letters

Footsie *noun* (stock exchange)
(*informal*) Financial Times-Stock Exchange 100 Share Index

/ˈfʊtsi/
▶ **Dow Jones Industrial Average, the Financial Times Ordinary Share Index**

FOR *abbr* (transport)
free on rail

/ˌef əʊ ˈɑː(r)/
note pronounced as individual letters

---

force majeure *noun* (law)
(*French*) an unexpected and unavoidable event that causes or allows a contract to be changed or cancelled if it has a force majeure clause: *As a result of force majeure the transaction was not completed.*

/ˌfɔːs mæˈʒɜː/
note no plural
⧓ accept, challenge, declare **force majeure**
▶ **act of God**

---

foreclose *verb* (law)
(of a bank or building society) to take possession of the property of someone after a court order (a foreclosure nisi) because the money borrowed (the MORTGAGE) has not been repaid: *The bank foreclosed (on the mortgage).* ○ *How can we prevent the bank foreclosing?*

/fɔːˈkləʊz/
foreclose, foreclosing, foreclosed
note transitive and intransitive verb
⧓ **foreclose** *on* (someone/something)

---

foreclosure *noun* (law)
the legal right of a lender of money if the borrower does not repay the debt on the agreed date. The lender may apply to a court to sell or reclaim property held as security for the loan, eg a building society may repossess a house if the mortgage payments are not met: *The mortgagor applied for foreclosure when the mortgagee failed to pay the instalments of the loan.* ○ *There are an increasing number of foreclosures for mortgage debt.*

/fɔːˈkləʊʒə(r)/
pl foreclosures
⧓ apply for, right of **foreclosure**

---

foreign bill *noun* (banking/international trade)
a bill of exchange that is drawn or payable in another country: *The foreign bill was drawn up in the Netherlands,*

/ˈfɒrən bɪl/
pl foreign bills
⧓ draw up, pay a **foreign bill**
▶ **bill of exchange, inland bill**

---

foreign exchange *noun* (banking/international trade)
money in a foreign currency: *The country earns one third of its foreign exchange from the sale of grain.* ○ *Tourism used to be a major source of foreign exchange.*

/ˌfɒrən ɪksˈtʃeɪndʒ/
note not used with *a* or *an*. No plural and used with a singular verb only.
⧓ deal in, earn, trade **foreign exchange**
syn foreign currency
▶ **currency 1, exchange[1],2,**

exchange rate, local currency

---

foreign exchange market *noun* (international trade)
a market where foreign currencies are traded: *The pound was stronger than the dollar on the foreign exchange market yesterday.*

/ˌfɒrən ɪksˈtʃeɪndʒ ˌmɑːkɪt/
pl foreign exchange markets
⋈ dealing, trading on the **foreign exchange markets**
▶ **leveraged currency contract, market**[1]**, money market**

---

foreign sales *noun* (sales)
the value or number of goods sold abroad: *Foreign sales have improved this year.*

/ˌfɒrən ˈseɪlz/
note plural noun, used with a plural verb
syn overseas sales
opp home sales
▶ **sales**

---

foreman *noun* (personnel)
an experienced worker who supervises and directs other workers: *a foreman on a building site*

/ˈfɔːmən/
pl foremen
⋈ a factory **foreman**
▶ **boss, manager, supervisor,** works manager *under* **works**

---

forge *verb*
to make an illegal copy of something: *The signature on the cheque was forged.* ○ *a forged document*

/fɔːdʒ/
forge, forging, forged
note transitive verb
⋈ **forge** a banknote, document, signature, will
▶ **counterfeit**[2]

---

forgery *noun*
an illegal copy of a banknote, a signature, a will, etc: *We can't accept the cheque, that signature is a forgery.*

/ˈfɔːdʒəri/
pl forgeries
⋈ detect, discover a **forgery**
▶ **counterfeit**[1]

---

for the attention of *noun*
written on a letter to show that it must be read and dealt with by the person named: *for the attention of Mr Brown*

/fə ði əˈtenʃn əv/
abbr f.a.o., attn

FORTRAN *abbr* (computing)
an acronym for *For*mula *Tran*slation, a language used in computer programming: *The programme has been written in FORTRAN.*

/ˈfɔːtræn/
▶ **ALGOL, BASIC, COBOL, PASCAL**

---

forwarding agent *noun* (shipping)
▶ **freight forwarder**

/ˈfɔːwədɪŋ ˌeɪdʒənt/
pl forwarding agents

---

forward integration *noun* (industry)
a situation where a company buys other companies that provide the next stage in the production process: *Forward integration will allow us to produce goods more cheaply.*

/ˌfɔːwəd ɪntɪˈgreɪʃn/
note not used with *a* or *an*. No plural and used with a singular verb only.
⋈ a policy, strategy of **forward integration**
▶ **backward integration, diversification, integration,**

horizontal integration, vertical integration

FOT *abbr* (transport)
free on truck

/ˌef əʊ ˈtiː/
note pronounced as individual letters

---

fpa *abbr* (insurance/shipping)
free of particular average

/ˌef piː ˈeɪ/

---

franchise[1] *noun* (commerce)
authorization given by a company for others to use its name and sell its goods; a business selling named goods in this way: *start a new business by obtaining a franchise* ○ *Most of the shops are run as franchises.*

/ˈfræntʃaɪz/
pl franchises
⋈ apply for, buy, grant, purchase, sell, win a **franchise**
▶ **outlet**

---

franchise[2] *verb* (commerce)
to authorize others to use a company's name and sell its goods: *The company has franchised over 50% of its fast food outlets.*

/ˈfræntʃaɪz/
franchise, franchising, franchised
note transitive verb
⋈ **franchise** something *to* someone

---

franco *adjective, adverb* (international trade)
a term in an export sales contract to show that goods will be delivered free of transport costs to a place specified by the buyer: *The goods will be delivered franco to your warehouse.*

/ˈfræŋkəʊ/
▶ **free on board, free on rail, free alongside ship**

---

franked income *noun* (commerce)
money earned, such as dividends from shares, on which CORPORATION TAX has already been paid: *receive £20 000 in franked income*

/ˌfræŋkt ˈɪŋkʌm/
note no plural
syn franked investment income
▶ **unfranked income**

---

fraud *noun*
1 deceiving someone in order to obtain money, goods or other benefits dishonestly: *Thousands of frauds are committed in business every year.* ○ *My boss was charged with fraud.* **2** a person who pretends to be someone or something he/she is not: *Don't trust him, he's a fraud.* ○ *She's not really a lawyer, she's a fraud.*

/frɔːd/
1 pl frauds
⋈ be charged with, be guilty of, commit (a) **fraud**
▶ **defraud, embezzlement**
2 pl frauds
▶ **conman**

FRB *abbr* (banking)
(*US*) Federal Reserve Bank

/ˌef ɑː ˈbiː/

FRC *abbr* (transport)
free carrier

/ˌef ɑː ˈsiː/

---

free alongside ship *adverb* (shipping)
a condition of sale where the seller pays for transportation and insurance of the goods until they have arrived at the ship. The buyer is then responsible for the actual loading of the goods.

/ˌfriː əˌlɒŋsaɪd ˈʃɪp/
abbr FAS
▶ **free on board, free on rail, free on truck**

---

free carrier *noun* (shipping)
a condition of sale where the seller pays for transportation and insurance of the goods until they have been loaded onto a container at a specified place

/ˌfriː ˈkæriə(r)/
abbr FRC
▶ **free on board, free on rail, free on truck**

free enterprise *noun* (economics)
an economic system that allows businesses to compete for profit without much government control: *operate a system of free enterprise*

/ˌfriː ˈentəpraɪz/
note not used with *a* or *an*. No plural and used with a singular verb only.
⋈ a **free enterprise** economy
▶ **enterprise, mixed economy, private enterprise**

free gift *noun* (advertising/marketing)
an extra item given free with a purchase to encourage sales: *Buy one today and claim your free gift!* ○ *receive a free gift with a magazine*

/ˌfriː ˈɡɪft/
pl free gifts
⋈ claim, receive a **free gift**
▶ **free offer, free sample**

freehold *noun* (law)
the right of complete ownership of property or land for an unlimited period of time: *The landlord is selling the freehold to one of the tenants.*

/ˈfriːhəʊld/
pl freeholds
⋈ acquire, buy, own, pass on, retain, sell, share the **freehold; freehold** land, ownership, property, tenure
▶ **leasehold**

free issue *noun* (stock exchange)
▶ **scrip issue**

/ˌfriː ˈɪʃuː/

freelance[1] *adjective, adverb* (personnel)
of work that is done (usually at home) for a number of different organizations; of a person who works in this way: *She works freelance.* ○ *What are the rates for doing the job freelance?* ○ *work as a freelance designer*

/ˈfriːlɑːns/
⋈ a **freelance** architect, designer, journalist, writer; **freelance** rates, work
▶ **cottage industry, self-employed**

freelance[2] *verb* (personnel)
to work independently (usually at home) and sell work to several organizations: *She's freelancing/she freelances for a publisher.*

/ˈfriːlɑːns/
freelance, freelancing, freelanced
note intransitive verb
▶ **self-employed**

free list *noun* (export)
a list produced by the BOARD OF CUSTOMS AND EXCISE of goods that may be imported into the UK without payment: *We were given a free list as we went through customs.*

/ˈfriː lɪst/
pl free lists
⋈ issue, produce a **free list**
▶ **duty-free**

free market *noun* (economics)
a market where prices are allowed to rise and fall according to supply and demand, without prices being fixed by governments: *compete for buyers in a free market*

/ˌfriː ˈmɑːkɪt/
note usually singular
⋈ buy, sell, trade *in* a **free market**; a **free market** economy
▶ **market[1], open market, planned economy, single market**

free of all average *adverb* (insurance/shipping)
a form of marine insurance that covers only total loss of a ship's cargo, eg if the ship sinks

/ˌfriː əv ˌɔːl ˈævərɪdʒ/
abbr faa
note no plural
▶ **average[1] 3, free of particular average, with average**

free offer *noun* (advertising/marketing)
an extra item obtained free with a purchase, usually by sending a number of product labels, tokens, etc as a way of encouraging sales: *Send off today for your free offer!*

/ˌfriː ˈɒfə(r)/
pl free offers
⋈ receive, send off for a **free offer**
▶ **free gift, free sample**

free of particular average *adverb* (insurance/shipping)
a form of marine insurance that covers total and partial loss of a ship's cargo

/ˌfriː əv pəˌtɪkjələr ˈævərɪdʒ/
abbr fpa
▶ **average[1] 3, free of all average, general average, with average**

free on board *adverb* (shipping)
a condition of sale where the seller pays for transportation and insurance of the goods until they are loaded onto the ship

/ˌfriː ɒn ˈbɔːd/
abbr FOB, f.o.b.
▶ **cost and freight, cost, insurance, freight, landed**

free on rail *adverb* (transport)
a condition of sale where the seller pays to deliver the goods to a specified railway station and ensures that they are loaded onto wagons ready for transportation

/ˌfriː ɒn ˈreɪl/
abbr FOR
▶ **free alongside ship, free on board**

free on truck *adverb* (transport)
a condition of sale where the seller pays to deliver the goods to a specified transport depot and ensures that they are loaded onto trucks or lorries ready for transportation

/ˌfriː ɒn ˈtrʌk/
abbr FOT

free sample *noun* (advertising/marketing)
a single item or part of a whole product given free to encourage people to buy more: *receive a free sample of shampoo*

/ˌfriː ˈsɑːmpl/
pl free samples
⋈ give (away), include, receive, send off for a **free sample**
▶ **free gift, free offer, sample[1] 1**

free trade *noun* (economics)
a situation where there are no restrictions (TARIFFS) on the import and export of goods: *adopt a system of free trade*

free trade zone an area where there are no trade restrictions: *While on board this ship we are in a free trade zone.*

/ˌfriː ˈtreɪd/
note not used with *a* or *an*. No plural and used with a singular verb only.
⋈ **free trade** areas; a **free trade** agreement
▶ **European Free Trade Association, fair trading 2, General Agreement on Tariffs and Trade, the Grain and Free Trade Association, restrictive trade practices, single market, trade[1]**

freight[1] *noun* (transport)
/freɪt/
1 the transport of goods by sea or air: *Freight was organized by our distributor.* **2** the goods transported: *loading/unloading freight* **3** the cost of transporting goods: *Freight is usually paid when the goods are delivered for shipment.*

note not used with *a* or *an*. No plural and used with a singular verb only.

⋈ air, rail, sea **freight**; **freight** charges, costs

► **cargo**

freight[2] *verb* (transport)
/freɪt/
to transport goods by sea or air: *The goods were freighted by air at great expense.*

freight, freighting, freighted

note transitive verb

freight car *noun* (transport)
/ˈfreɪt kɑː(r)/
(*US*) ► **wagon**

freight forwarder *noun* (shipping)
/ˈfreɪt ˌfɔːwədə(r)/
a person or an organization that sends goods to their destination: *The goods were handed over to the freight forwarder by the airline company.*

pl freight forwarders

syn forwarding agent

⋈ hand goods over to, use a **forwarding agent**

from date *adjective, adverb* (banking)
/ˈfrɒm deɪt/
► **after date**

front loading *noun* (finance)
/ˌfrʌnt ˈləʊdɪŋ/
a system of structuring a loan in which the interest, fees and principal repayments are higher at the beginning of the loan period

note not used with *a* or *an*. No plural and used with a singular verb only.

syn front end loading

► **back loading, loading**

full costing *noun* (accounting)
/ˌfʊl ˈkɒstɪŋ/
► **absorption costing**

full-time *adjective, adverb*
/ˌfʊl ˈtaɪm/
for the whole of the normal working day or week: *She applied for a full-time job.* ○ *He still works full-time in the bank.*

⋈ a **full-time** employee, job, worker; **full-time** employment, staff, work

► **part-time**

fully paid capital *noun* (finance)
/ˌfʊli ˌpeɪd ˈkæpɪtl/
► **paid-up capital**

function[1] *noun*
/ˈfʌŋkʃn/
the purpose or special duty of a person or thing: *One of the most important functions of my job is to see that goods are delivered on time.*

pl functions

⋈ carry out a **function**; an important, a major, a minor **function**

► **performance, work**[1] **1, 3**

function[2] *verb*
/ˈfʌŋkʃn/
to work; to be in action: *Only one engine is still functioning.* ○ *The new computer system doesn't seem to function very well.*

function, functioning, functioned

note intransitive verb

▸◂ **function** badly, well
▸ **perform, work² 2**

---

fund¹ *noun* (finance)
1 money or assets collected for a specific purpose. The money is usually invested to provide further income: *contribute towards a pension fund ○ put money in an investment fund ○ a fund set up to provide training for industry* **2 funds** money; financial resources: *The company is short of funds at the moment. ○ The training scheme was abandoned through lack of funds.*

/fʌnd/
1 pl funds
▸◂ invest in, manage a **fund**
▸ **authorized fund, investment trust, life fund, managed fund, offshore fund, pension fund, reserve fund, revolving fund, sinking fund, slush fund, trust fund, umbrella fund, unit trust**
2 note plural noun, used with a plural verb
▸◂ company, government **funds**

---

fund² *verb* (finance)
to provide money for a specific purpose: *The company will fund a new training programme. ○ The research was funded by a pharmaceutical company.*

/fʌnd/
fund, funding, funded
note transitive verb
▸◂ **funded** *by* someone or something
▸ **finance²**

---

funding *noun* (finance)
1 providing money for a specific purpose: *The funding of the project will be the biggest problem.* **2** the money for this: *Funding is now available for a new computer system. ○ It is difficult to obtain adequate funding for new projects during the recession.*

/ˈfʌndɪŋ/
note not used with *a* or *an*. No plural and used with a singular verb only.
2 ask for, obtain, receive, request **funding**; adequate, insufficient, sufficient **funding**

---

fund management *noun* (finance/management)
the organized investment of money provided by individuals or companies and their shareholders: *Most large companies make use of fund management. ○ Many merchant banks have fund management operations.*

/ˈfʌnd ˌmænɪdʒmənt/
note not used with *a* or *an*. No plural and used with a singular verb only.
▸◂ a **fund management** business, company, group
syn investment management
▸ **investment trust, managed fund, portfolio management, unit trust**

---

fund manager *noun* (finance/management)
a person or a company that, for a fee, invests money on behalf of a number of individuals or companies: *Fund managers must obtain the best possible deal for their clients.*

/ˈfʌnd ˌmænɪdʒə(r)/
pl fund managers
syn investment manager
▸ **managed fund**

---

funds flow statement *noun* (accounting)
(*US*) ▸ **source and application of funds**

/ˈfʌndz fləʊ ˌsteɪtmənt/

---

fungibles *noun*
1 (*commerce*) goods that are usually valued by number, measurement and weight: *Grain and flour are fungibles.* **2** (*stock exchange*) financial instruments, eg shares, which are traded on more than one exchange and are freely interchangeable:

/ˈfʌndʒəblz/
1 note plural noun, used with a plural verb
▸◂ measure, number, value,

Fungibles have been issued by several multinational companies to raise funds from different markets at the same time.

weigh **fungibles**
► **actuals 1**
2 syn fungible securities

---

futures *noun* (commerce/stock exchange)
goods, currency or securities that will be supplied or exchanged on an agreed future date and for a price fixed in advance: *copper, commodity, financial, stock-index, etc futures* ○ *trade in futures* ○ *Coffee futures fell at midday.*

/ˈfjuːtʃəz/
note plural noun, used with a plural verb
⋈ acquire, buy, sell **futures**
► **spot goods, time bargain**

---

futures contract *noun* (commerce/stock exchange)
an agreement to buy or sell goods, currency or securities on an agreed future date and for a price fixed in advance: *draw up a crude oil futures contract*

/ˈfjuːtʃəz ˌkɒntrækt/
pl futures contracts
⋈ arrange, draw up, sign a **futures contract**
► **contract**[1]

---

futures market *noun* (commerce/stock exchange)
the buying and selling of goods, currency or securities (FUTURES) for delivery at a future date and for a price fixed in advance: *London FOX is a futures market for coffee, cocoa and other food products.*

/ˈfjuːtʃəz ˌmɑːkɪt/
pl futures markets
⋈ buy, sell, trade on the **futures market**
► **market**[1], **spot market**

Gg

GA *abbr* (insurance)
general average

/ˌdʒiː ˈeɪ/
note pronounced as individual letters

GAFTA *noun* (agriculture)
Grain and Free Trade Association

/ˈgæftə/
note pronounced as a word

---

gain[1] *noun*
1 increase in wealth; profit: *We hope for some gain from our investment.* **2** an increase in amount: *Shares prices ended unchanged at 2 212.8 after swinging from a gain of 13.7 points to a loss of 5.5 points.*

/geɪn/
1 note not used with *a* or *an*. No plural and used with a singular verb only.
⋈ commercial, financial **gain**
2 pl gains
► **loss, profit**[1]

---

gain[2] *verb*
to obtain or get more of something: *The shares gained 29p to close at 785p.*

/geɪn/
gain, gaining, gained
note transitive verb

---

gain and loss account *noun* (accounting)
► **profit and loss account**

/ˌgeɪn ənd ˈlɒs əˌkaʊnt/

---

garnishee order *noun* (banking/finance)
a court order used to prevent someone who owes money (the JUDGMENT DEBTOR) from having free access to his/her bank account. It is obtained by a person the court names (the JUDGMENT CREDITOR) and sent to anyone who owes money to the judgment debtor or the debtor's bank (the GARNISHEE). Money that is owed must go directly to the judgment creditor.

/ˌgɑːnɪˈʃiː ˌɔːdə(r)/
pl garnishee orders
⋈ issue, place, serve a **garnishee order**
► **bankrupt, court order, creditor, debtor**

GATT *abbr* (international trade)
the General Agreement on Tariffs and Trade: *GATT talks, members, negotiations, etc*

/gæt/
(also **Gatt**)
note pronounced as a word

---

gazump *verb* (sales)
to raise the price of, or accept a higher offer for, property after the price has been agreed, but before written contracts have been exchanged: *We were gazumped twice before buying this house.* ○ *Someone else must have offered more money and gazumped us.*

/gəˈzʌmp/
gazump, gazumping, gazumped
note transitive verb

---

gazumping *noun* (sales)
the practice of raising the price of or accepting a higher offer for property after the price has been agreed, but before written contracts have been exchanged: *Gazumping increases during a property boom.*

/gəˈzʌmpɪŋ/
note not used with *a* or *an*. No plural and used with a singular verb only.
▶ **exchange of contracts**

GDP *abbr* (economics)
▶ **gross domestic product**

/ˌdʒiː diː ˈpiː/

---

gearing *noun* (finance/stock exchange)
the ratio between the amount of money provided by shareholders and the amount of money a company owes to its banks: *The company is concentrating on repaying its loans to reduce gearing.* ○ *Gearing fell from 0.66:1 to 0.52:1.*

high gearing the situation of a company which has large bank borrowings in proportion to shareholders' funds: *a high gearing of 2:1*

low gearing the situation of a company which has low bank borrowings in proportion to shareholders' funds: *a low gearing of 0.23:1*

/ˈgɪərɪŋ/
note not used with *a* or *an*. No plural and used with a singular verb only.
⧓ cut, increase, reduce **gearing**
syn (*US*) leverage
▶ **degearing, highly geared, ungeared**

General Agreement on Tariffs and Trade *noun* (international trade)
an agreement drawn up in 1947 in Geneva with the aim of reducing trade restrictions and problems worldwide: *trade restrictions removed by the General Agreement on Tariffs and Trade*

/ˌdʒenrəl əˌgriːmənt ɒn ˌtærɪfs ən ˈtreɪd/
abbr GATT, Gatt
▶ **Common Agricultural Policy, tariff, trade[1]**

---

general average *noun* (insurance/shipping)
a loss arising from action taken at sea to save a ship or its cargo for which insurance can be claimed. The loss is shared between the ship and cargo owners: *claim general average* ○ *a general average policy*

/ˌdʒenrəl ˈævərɪdʒ/
note not used with *a* or *an*. No plural and used with a singular verb only.
abbr GA
▶ **average[1] 3, free of all average, free of particular average, general average, with average**

---

general lien *noun* (law)
▶ **lien**

/ˌdʒenrəl ˈliːən/

---

general partner *noun* (management)
▶ **partner**

/ˌdʒenrəl ˈpɑːtnə(r)/

gift *noun*

1 a thing that is given willingly and without payment; a present. In business it may be used (sometimes unfairly) to encourage people to give priority treatment in return: *A bank manager was accused of accepting gifts in return for granting loans.* **2** (*law*) property or money given as a legally recognized present that may be taxed: *leave money in a will as a gift*

/gɪft/
pl gifts
1 ⋈ accept, offer, receive, refuse a **gift**; a **gift** pack, shop; **gift** wrapping
▶ **bribe[1], free gift, gratuity 1**
2 ⋈ donate, make, receive a **gift**
▶ **bequest**

---

gift voucher *noun* (sales)

a card that can be exchanged for goods up to the value stated: *a gift voucher for £10* ○ *buy clothes with a gift voucher*

/ˈgɪft ˌvaʊtʃə(r)/
pl gift vouchers
⋈ pay with, use a **gift voucher**
syn gift token
▶ **voucher**

---

gilts *noun* (stock exchange)

government securities with a fixed interest payable at regular intervals, usually each six months: *Normally the value of gilts falls as interest rates rise.* ○ *buy gilts as a secure investment*

exempt gilts gilts on which interest is paid in full, without any money taken off as income tax: *Exempt gilts are popular with overseas investors who do not pay UK income tax.*

/gɪlts/
note plural noun, used with a plural verb
⋈ buy, issue, sell, trade (in) **gilts**
syn gilt-edged securities, gilt-edged stocks
▶ **fixed-interest securities, government bonds, security 1, tap issue, tap stocks**

---

giro *noun* (banking)

(*UK*) **1** a system for transferring money from one bank to another: *pay through bank giro credit* ○ *pay bills by giro* **2** a cheque that is given by the government to people who are ill, unemployed, etc: *cash a giro at the post office*

/ˈdʒaɪrəʊ/
(also **Giro**)
1 note not used with *a* or *an*. No plural and used with a singular verb only.
⋈ pay *by*, *through* **giro**; a **giro** account
2 pl giros
⋈ cash a **giro**

---

global *adjective*

1 of or affecting the whole world; worldwide: *Companies and markets are becoming more global*, ie are trading throughout the world. ○ *Environmental pollution is a global problem.* ○ *a 6% increase in the global grain harvest* ○ *trading in global markets* **2** of or affecting the whole of something; total: *make global changes to the database* ○ *change company policy at a global level*

/ˈgləʊbl/
⋈ a **global** agreement, economy, situation
▶ **domestic 1, international**

---

glut[1] *noun* (commerce)

a situation where supply exceeds demand: *Prices fell because of the glut of timber on the market.*

/glʌt/
⋈ a **glut** *of* something
note usually singular
▶ **shortage, surplus**

---

glut[2] *verb* (commerce)

to supply something with much more than needed: *to glut the market with cheap goods from abroad* ○ *a glutted coffee market*

/glʌt/
glut, glutting, glutted
note transitive verb
⋈ **glut** (the market) *with* something
▶ **saturate**

GNP *abbr* (economics)
▶ **gross national product**

/ˌdʒiː en ˈpiː/

go-between *noun*
a person or an organization that acts as a messenger or negotiator between two parties that cannot or do not want to meet: *An American firm acted as go-between in the deal.* ○ *He was appointed as the official go-between for the negotiations.*

/ˈɡəʊ bɪtwiːn/
pl go-betweens
⋈ act as (a) **go-between**
▶ **agent, middleman**

gold *noun* (finance)
precious metal, formerly used as a monetary standard: *Gold is bought as an investment, particularly at times of financial uncertainty.* ○ *gold-plated jewellery* ○ *a watch made of 18-carat gold*

/ˈɡəʊld/
note not used with *a* or *an*. No plural and used with a singular verb only.
⋈ buy, deal in, invest in **gold**
▶ **bullion**

gold standard *noun* (finance)
a system of currency where the value of money is based on that of gold and can be exchanged for gold: *The gold standard is no longer used in global markets.*

/ˈɡəʊld ˌstændəd/
note singular noun, used with a singular verb
⋈ be on, return to, withdraw from the **gold standard**
▶ **fiduciary issue**

good faith *noun* (commerce)
honesty; honest intention: *Like all trade agreements, its success depends ultimately on the good faith of the parties involved.*

in good faith with honest intentions; believing something to be true and honest: *He accepted the cheque in good faith.* ○ *All holidays described in our brochure are advertised by us in good faith and every care is taken to ensure their accuracy.*

/ˌɡʊd ˈfeɪθ/
note not used with *a* or *an*. No plural and used with a singular verb only.
⋈ act in, buy in, sell in, show **good faith**; a **good faith** payment, settlement
▶ **bad faith, bona fide 2, true and fair view, utmost good faith**

goods *noun* (commerce)
manufactured items, eg fridges, prepared items, eg flour, or raw materials, eg coal that are for sale: *manufacture electrical goods* ○ *luxury goods imported from France* ○ *All goods arriving at the warehouse are automatically checked by the computer system.*

/ɡʊdz/
note usually plural
⋈ buy, export, import, manufacture, sell, transport **goods**; a **goods** train, van, vehicle, wagon, warehouse
▶ **capital goods, commodity, consumer good, fast moving consumer goods, luxury goods, product**

good till cancelled order *noun* (stock exchange)
an order (to buy or sell) given by an investor in the FUTURES MARKET to a broker that applies until the deal is made or the order withdrawn: *issue a good till cancelled order to a broker*

/ˌɡʊd tɪl ˈkænsld ˌɔːdə(r)/
pl good till cancelled orders
⋈ issue, receive a **good till cancelled order**
▶ **day order, order[1] 1**

goodwill *noun* (commerce/finance)
items such as knowledge, contacts or reputation that can have a financial effect on a business and are therefore measured in financial terms: *Much of the cost was written off as goodwill.* ○ *A company cannot afford to lose its goodwill.*

/ˌɡʊdˈwɪl/
note no plural
⋈ keep, measure, write off **goodwill**
▶ **intangible asset, tangible assets**

go-slow *noun* (industrial relations)
working more slowly than usual as a protest: *The union called a go-slow when two union members were sacked.*

/ˌgəʊ ˈsləʊ/
note usually singular
⧓ call, organize a **go-slow**
▶ **industrial action, strike**[1], **walk-out, work-to-rule**

government bonds *noun* (finance/stock exchange)
securities issued by a government in the form of DEBENTURE STOCKS with a fixed interest that is paid at regular intervals

/ˈgʌvənmənt bɒndz/
note usually plural
⧓ buy, deal in, issue, trade in **government bonds**
▶ **bond 1, fixed-interest securities, gilts, security 1**

Gp *abbr* (stock exchange)
group

note used in written English only

grace period *noun* (commerce)
▶ **period of grace**

/ˈgreɪs ˌpɪəriəd/

the Grain and Free Trade Association *noun* (agriculture)
an association that controls dealings in grain, potatoes, etc and operates from the Baltic Exchange in London

/ðə ˌgreɪn ənd ˌfriː ˈtreɪd əˌsəʊsiˌeɪʃn/
abbr GAFTA
▶ **Baltic Exchange, free trade**

graph *noun*
a diagram used to show the relationship between two variable quantities: *a graph showing that costs were reduced when materials were purchased in bulk ○ plot figures on a graph ○ draw a graph for each month of the project*

graph paper paper with small squares of equal size used for drawing graphs: *draw a curve on graph paper*

/grɑːf; *US* græf/
pl graphs
⧓ draw a **graph**; **graph** paper
▶ **bar chart, block diagram, chart**[1] **1, diagram, flow chart, pie chart, pictogram, table**

gratis *adverb*
free; without payment: *receive a gratis copy of a book ○ coffee will be supplied gratis throughout the conference*

/ˈgrætɪs/
▶ **free gift**

gratuity *noun* (personnel)
1 (*formal*) an extra payment given to someone who has provided good service; a tip: *Federal employees must not accept gratuities.*
2 money given to someone when he/she retires, or on a special occasion: *There were no gratuities for staff this Christmas.*

/grəˈtjuːəti/
pl gratuities
⧓ accept, offer, pay, receive, refuse a **gratuity**
▶ **bribe**[1], **gift 1**

green *adjective*
connected with or caring about the environment and the natural world: *The cosmetics company is trying to develop a green image. ○ A green car is one that runs on unleaded petrol.*

go green to produce or use products that do not harm the environment: *The chemical company is being forced to go green.*

/griːn/
⧓ **green** issues, measures, policies, products
▶ **environment, environmentally-friendly**

Greenwich Mean Time *noun*
▶ **Western European Time**

/ˌgrenɪtʃ ˈmiːn taɪm/

grey knight *noun* (stock exchange)
(*informal*) a person or company that tries to buy (TAKE OVER) another company and does not reveal any plans for the

/ˌgreɪ ˈnaɪt/
pl grey knights

company's future: *An unknown bidder appeared as a grey knight at a late stage in the takeover proceedings.*

▶ **black knight, takeover, white knight**

---

grey market *noun* (stock exchange)

/ˌgreɪ ˈmɑːkɪt/

note usually singular

1 a situation where goods are in short supply, but are traded legally: *buy and sell on the grey market* ○ *pay grey market prices* **2** a situation where shares are traded before they are officially issued: *Water company shares gained up to 24p in grey market trading.* ○ *quote grey market prices*

1 ⋈ buy, sell something on the **grey market**

▶ **black market, market[1]**

2 ⋈ **grey market** dealing, prices, trading

▶ **share issue**

---

gross[1] *adjective* (finance)

/grəʊs/

total, without anything taken off: *His gross pay was £15 000* (ie before amounts for tax and insurance were taken off). ○ *Your salary will be £32 000 gross.* ○ *calculate the gross weight of the goods*

⋈ **gross** earnings, income, interest, revenue, sales, wages

▶ **net[1]**

---

gross[2] *verb* (finance)

/grəʊs/

gross, grossing, grossed

note transitive verb

to produce or earn as a total amount: *The film grossed over 60 million dollars in the United States.*

▶ **net[2]**

---

gross domestic product *noun* (economics)

/ˌgrəʊs dəˌmestɪk ˈprɒdʌkt/

note no plural

abbr GDP

the annual total value of goods produced and services provided by a country: *In 1990 gross domestic product rose by 7%.* ○ *Manufacturing industries aim to increase their share of gross domestic product.*

⋈ calculate, contribute to, increase, reduce the **gross domestic product**

▶ **gross national product**

---

gross income *noun* (accounting)

/ˌgrəʊs ˈɪŋkʌm/

note usually singular

the amount of money received by a person or an organization in the form of wages, profit or interest before tax, etc has been taken off: *receive a gross income of £67 000 a year* ○ *Tax is deducted from a person's gross income.*

⋈ an annual, a monthly **gross income**

▶ **income, net income, take-home pay**

---

gross interest *noun* (finance/stock exchange)

/ˌgrəʊs ˈɪntrest/

note not used with *a* or *an*. No plural and used with a singular verb only.

the amount charged for money borrowed or paid in return for money invested before tax, etc has been taken off: *receive gross interest from a savings account*

⋈ earn, pay, receive **gross interest**

▶ **interest 1, 2**

---

gross loss *noun* (accounting)

/ˌgrəʊs ˈlɒs/

▶ **trading loss**

---

gross margin *noun* (accounting/retail)

/ˈgrəʊs ˌmɑːdʒɪn/

pl gross margins

the difference between the price of goods paid by a shopkeeper (the TRADE PRICE) and the price paid by the customer (the RETAIL PRICE): *produce a gross margin of 10%* ○ *The gross margin for fresh foods increased from 21% to 28% in four years.*

⋈ a **gross margin** *of* (15%)

▶ **margin 1, mark-down, mark-up**

---

gross misconduct *noun* (personnel)
very bad behaviour, eg theft or violence, by an employee while at work: *In the case of gross misconduct employees will be dismissed immediately.* ○ *be suspended without pay for gross misconduct*

/ˌgrəʊs mɪsˈkɒndʌkt/
note not used with *a* or *an*. No plural and used with a singular verb only.
⋈ be accused of, a case of **gross misconduct**

---

gross national product *noun* (economics)
the annual total value of goods produced and services provided by a country, plus the total income from abroad: *Foreign investment produces about 5% of the gross national product.*

/ˌgrəʊs ˌnæʃnəl ˈprɒdʌkt/
note no plural
abbr GNP
⋈ calculate, contribute to, increase, reduce the **gross national product**
► **gross domestic product, net national product**

---

gross profit *noun* (accounting)
► **trading profit**

/ˌgrəʊs ˈprɒfɪt/

---

gross yield *noun* (stock exchange)
the amount received from an investment before tax is taken off: *The initial gross yield of each share is 8.1%.*

/ˌgrəʊs ˈjiːld/
note usually singular
⋈ a **gross yield** *of* (a certain percentage)
► **yield 2**

---

group *noun* (stock exchange)
a HOLDING COMPANY together with any subsidiary companies in which it owns more than half of the share capital: *Over 200 jobs were lost in the group's petrochemical divisions.* ○ *a clothing, an engineering, an insurance, etc group*

/gruːp/
pl groups
abbr Gp
⋈ **group** profits, shares
syn group of companies
► **association 1, business 3, company, conglomerate, federation, group balance sheet, organization 1**

---

groupage *noun* (transport/shipping)
the listing of several small cargoes sent from different owners, but bound for the same destination on the same document (a BILL OF LADING): *Groupage was carried out by the forwarding agent.*

/ˈgruːpɪdʒ/
note not used with *a* or *an*. No plural and used with a singular verb only.
► **bill of lading**

---

group balance sheet *noun* (accounting)
a document that shows the financial position of a group of companies at the end of the financial year: *These recent acquisitions will strengthen the group balance sheet.*

/ˌgruːp ˈbæləns ʃiːt/
pl group balance sheets
⋈ appear in/on, compile, include in/on, prepare, present, show a **group balance sheet**
► **balance sheet, group**

---

growth industry *noun* (industry)
► **industry**

/ˈgrəʊθ ɪndəstri/

---

guarantee[1] *noun* (banking/commerce)
1 (**a**) a promise to do or provide something: *Included in your holiday guarantee is a choice of another resort if your original holiday is cancelled by the travel company.* (**b**) a document that states that such a promise has been made: *The watch comes with a year's*

/ˌgærənˈtiː/
pl guarantees
1a ⋈ offer a **guarantee**
► **indemnity**

guarantee, ie it will be replaced or repaired free if it stops working within a year. **2** a promise to pay another's debt: *provide a guarantee for a loan* **3** money, goods or property or a person's good name that supports a promise to repay a loan or do something: *How much (money) can you offer as guarantee?*

1b ⧓ show a **guarantee**
▶ **warranty 1**
2 ⧓ provide a **guarantee**
3 ▶ **collateral, security 3, surety**

---

guarantee[2] *verb* (banking/commerce)
1 to promise to do, provide or replace something: ○ *All the products we sell are guaranteed by the manufacturer*, ie the manufacturer promises to replace or repair them if they break down. *The watch is guaranteed for one year.* ○ *If you are not satisfied with your purchase, we guarantee to refund your money in full.* ○ *We guarantee that the price will not increase.* **2** to promise to pay another's debt: *The bank guaranteed the loan.*

/ˌɡærənˈtiː/
guarantee, guaranteeing, guaranteed
note transitive verb
⧓ **guarantee** something *for* (a period of time); **guarantee** *that* (something will happen)
2 ▶ **indemnify**

---

guaranteed income bond *noun* (insurance)
▶ **single premium policy**

/ˌɡærəntiːd ˈɪŋkʌm bɒnd/

---

guaranteed wage *noun* (personnel)
an agreement between employers and employees that wages will still be paid even if there is no work to do: *A guaranteed wage gives workers security.*

/ˌɡærəntiːd ˈweɪdʒ/
pl guaranteed wages
⧓ offer, provide, receive a **guaranteed wage**
▶ **wage**

---

guarantor *noun* (banking/commerce)
a person who promises to be responsible for or to repay another's debt: *The bank will give us a loan, but we have to find a guarantor first.*

/ˌɡærənˈtɔː(r)/
pl guarantors
⧓ act as **guarantor**
▶ **accommodation party, warrantor**

Hh

haggle *verb* (sales)
to argue about the price for something before buying or selling: *It's not worth haggling over such a small amount.* ○ *He always haggles over the price.*

/ˈhæɡl/
haggle, haggling, haggled
note intransitive verb
⧓ **haggle** *over* (a price)
▶ **bargain**[1] **1, negotiate**

---

handbook *noun*
a book giving useful information and advice about something: *The user's handbook should tell you how it works.* ○ *look it up in the staff handbook* ○ *a handbook of office procedures*

/ˈhændbʊk/
pl handbooks
⧓ consult, refer to, use a **handbook**
▶ **manual**[2]

---

handle *verb* (commerce)
1 to deal in or with: *We handle all our own distribution.* ○ *We can't handle orders for less than 500.* **2** to store, pack or move goods: *Handling of fragile items has been reduced to a minimum.* ○ *There is a 5% handling charge on all orders.* **3** to organize or manage: *I'll get my solicitor to handle this.* ○ *Who handles your affairs?*

/ˈhændl/
handle, handling, handled
note transitive verb
1 ⧓ **handle** claims, enquiries, orders, (telephone) calls
2 ⧓ **handle** equipment, goods

handout *noun*
a sheet of paper with written or typed information on it, given to people at a meeting, conference, etc: *You'll find further details in the handout.* ○ *I've brought some handouts to distribute.*

/ˈhændaʊt/
pl handouts
⋈ circulate, pass round, print **handouts**

---

hard copy *noun* (computing)
information obtained from a computer and printed on paper: *The corrections were made on (the) hard copy.* ○ *Keep a hard copy in case the disk is lost or damaged.*

/ˌhɑːd ˈkɒpi/
pl hard copies
⋈ print to **hard copy**; **hard copy** output
► **copy[1] 1, hard disk**

---

hard currency *noun* (finance)
1 a national money system that has a fairly stable or rising value in other countries: *The country now has a hard currency and a strong economy.* **2** any foreign currency: *Cash crops such as cocoa and coffee are often grown in developing countries to earn hard currency.*

/ˌhɑːd ˈkʌrənsi/
pl hard currencies
⋈ buy with, earn, exchange for, sell in, trade in **hard currency**
► **currency 1**

---

hard disk *noun* (computing)
a rigid magnetic disk sealed in a box (a DISK DRIVE) on which information is stored. A hard disk stores more information and retrieves it more quickly than a floppy disk: *Save the data on hard disk.* ○ *All the files are held on (the) hard disk.*

/ˌhɑːd ˈdɪsk/
pl hard disks
⋈ use, work on the **hard disk**
► **disk, floppy disk**

---

hard loan *noun* (finance)
a loan from one country to another made on the condition that it is repaid in the lender's currency: *a hard loan to be repaid in dollars in two years' time*

/ˌhɑːd ˈləʊn/
pl hard loans
⋈ make, repay a **hard loan**
► **soft loan**

---

hard sell *noun* (advertising/sales)
a forceful way of getting people to buy things: *The presentation turned out to be a hard sell for time-share holidays.*

/ˌhɑːd ˈsel/
note no plural
⋈ a **hard sell** approach, method
opp soft sell
► **sell 2**

---

hardware *noun* (computing)
the mechanical and electronic parts of a computer, including the screen, the keyboard and the hard disk: *New hardware was installed in the office.* ○ *Will this computer program run on different hardware?*

/ˈhɑːdweə(r)/
note not used with *a* or *an*. No plural and used with a singular verb only.
⋈ a **hardware** component, manufacturer
► **peripheral, software**

---

haulage *noun* (transport)
(the cost of) moving goods by road, rail or canal: *There is no charge for haulage.* ○ *run a road haulage business*

/ˈhɔːlɪdʒ/
note not used with *a* or *an*. No plural and used with a singular verb only.
⋈ a **haulage** company, contractor, firm
► **carriage, road haulage, transportation**

---

haulier *noun* (transport)
► **carrier**

/ˈhɔːliə(r)/

headed paper *noun* (office practice)
writing paper with the name, address and telephone number of an organization printed at the top: *type the letter on headed paper*

/ˌhedɪd ˈpeɪpə(r)/
note no plural
⋈ use **headed paper**
syn headed notepaper
► **letterhead**

---

headhunt *verb* (personnel)
(*informal*) to look for someone for a job or position, esp someone from another firm: *She was headhunted by a rival firm.* ○ *Some of our best managers have been headhunted from larger companies.*

/ˈhedhʌnt/
headhunt, headhunting, headhunted
note transitive verb
⋈ be **headhunted** *by, from* (a company)

---

head office *noun* (management)
the central office of an organization that controls all the regional offices: *He was promoted and now works at head office.* ○ *go up to head office for a meeting*

/ˌhed ˈɒfɪs/
pl head offices
abbr HO
► **branch, office 3, registered office**

---

headquarters *noun* (management)
the place from which an organization is controlled: *The company's headquarters is/are in London.*

/ˌhedˈkwɔːtəz/
note used with a singular or plural verb
abbr HQ
⋈ be based, work at **headquarters**
► **branch**

---

health and safety *noun* (personnel)
an essential part of laws concerning the workplace. Health and safety regulations must be followed by employers and employees to prevent accidents and protect the health of people at work: *The European Community has already set basic health and safety standards for most machines and manufactured products.*

/ˌhelθ ənd ˈseɪfti/
note no plural
abbr H & S
note In the UK, these regulations are based on the Health and Safety at Work Act of 1974 and are an important part of an employee's contract of employment.
⋈ **health and safety** regulations, requirements, rules, standards
► **accident frequency rate, industrial injury, safety**

---

heavy industry *noun* (industry)
► **industry**

/ˌhevi ˈɪndəstri/
pl heavy industries

---

heavy market *noun* (stock exchange)
1 (*UK*) a situation where prices are falling and buyers are slow to buy: *trade in a heavy market* **2** (*US*) a situation where there is a lot of buying and selling but prices do not change: *buy in a heavy market*

/ˌhevi ˈmɑːkɪt/
pl heavy markets
⋈ buy, sell, trade in a **heavy market**; **heavy market** dealing, trading
► **active market, light 2, market**[1]

---

hedge *verb* (stock exchange)
to buy a commodity, share or other investment at a fixed price for future delivery to protect oneself against loss caused by a

/hedʒ/
hedge, hedging, hedged
note intransitive verb

possible change in price: *hedge against rising prices*

⋈ **hedge** *against* inflation, fluctuating exchange rates, rising prices

▶ **futures market**

---

hedging *noun* (stock exchange)

buying a commodity, share or other investment at a fixed price for future delivery to protect yourself against loss caused by a possible change in price: *Hedging is a way of protecting yourself against unexpected price increases.*

/ˈhedʒɪŋ/

note not used with *a* or *an*. No plural and used with a singular verb only.

⋈ a **hedging** deal, transaction

▶ **futures market**

---

highly geared *adjective* (finance/stock exchange)

(of a company) that has borrowed a lot of money in relation to the amount of money provided by its shareholders: *An economic recession is a very bad time for a highly geared company/for a company that is highly geared.*

/ˌhaɪli ˈɡɪəd/

⋈ a **highly geared** business, company, organization

▶ **degearing, gearing, ungeared**

---

high priority *noun*

▶ **priority 2**

/ˌhaɪ praɪˈɒrəti/

pl high priorities

---

highs and lows *noun* (stock exchange)

a list of securities in a stock exchange index showing the highest and lowest prices in a given period: *In just over six trading days, the highs and lows showed the dollar had plunged 4.6% against the yen.*

/ˌhaɪz ənd ˈləʊz/

note plural noun, used with a plural verb

⋈ calculate, estimate **highs and lows**

---

high street bank *noun* (banking)

▶ **commercial bank**

/ˌhaɪ striːt ˈbæŋk/

---

hire[1] *verb*

1 to borrow or lend a car, tools, machinery, a service, etc for a fixed time and payment: *You can hire cars locally for £20 a day.*
2 (*personnel*) to employ someone: *The company hired three new people last week.*

hire something out (to someone) to lend something to someone for a fixed time and payment: *We hire out computers to local firms.*

/ˈhaɪə(r)/

hire, hiring, hired

note transitive verb

1 ⋈ **hire** a car, a van; **hire** equipment, machinery

▶ **lease[2], rent[2]**

2 ⋈ **hire** someone to do something

▶ **employ**

---

hire[2] *noun*

borrowing or lending a car, tools, machinery, etc for a fixed time and payment: *The hire of equipment will add considerable expense to the project.* ○ *a car hire firm*

/ˈhaɪə(r)/

note not used with *a* or *an*. No plural and used with a singular verb only.

⋈ a **hire** company, firm, shop; (available) for **hire**

▶ **charter[2] 2, finance lease, lease[1]**

---

hire purchase *noun* (sales)

a way of buying goods where the buyer takes the goods and pays for them in regular instalments over a fixed period of time. The goods can be reclaimed if the payments are not made, but at the end of the fixed period or after a certain number of payments the goods legally belong to the buyer: *buy a computer on hire purchase* ○ *He failed to keep up the hire purchase payments.*

/ˌhaɪə ˈpɜːtʃəs/

note no plural

abbr HP, hp

⋈ a **hire purchase** agreement, company, repayment; buy (something) on **hire purchase**

syn instalment plan

▶ **consumer credit, credit account, credit sale**

---

histogram *noun*
▶ **bar chart**

/ˈhɪstəgræm/
pl histograms

---

historic cost accounting *noun* (accounting)
a method of accounting where an item (an ASSET) is valued in terms of its original cost not its replacement cost: *Historic cost accounting can be misleading in times of high inflation.*

/hɪˌstɒrɪk ˈkɒst əˌkaʊntɪŋ/
note not used with *a* or *an*. No plural and used with a singular verb only.
⧓ use **historic cost accounting**
syn historical cost accounting
▶ **accounting, current cost accounting**

HO *abbr* (management)
head office

/ˌeɪtʃ ˈəʊ/
note pronounced as individual letters

---

holder *noun* (finance)
the person who legally possesses a document, esp a bill of exchange: *remind the holder that payment is now due*

/ˈhəʊldə(r)/
pl holders
▶ **bearer, endorsee, payee**

---

holder for value *noun* (banking/commerce)
a person who takes a bill of exchange for which goods have already been supplied

/ˌhəʊldə fə ˈvælju:/
pl holders for value
▶ **holder in due course, value² 2**

---

holder in due course *noun* (banking/commerce)
a person who takes a bill of exchange before payment is required and who has sole claim to the value of the bill

/ˌhəʊldər ɪn ˌdju: ˈkɔ:s/
pl holders in due course
▶ **holder for value**

---

holding *noun* (stock exchange)
the amount of financial investment a person or group of people has in a company: *The family still has a majority holding in the company.* ○ *Shareholders should be informed of company activities whatever the size of their holding.*

/ˈhəʊldɪŋ/
pl holdings
▶ **controlling interest, minority interest, nominee holding**

---

holding company *noun* (stock exchange)
the leading company of a group that holds all or more than half of the shares of the other companies: *We had better refer this matter to the holding company.*

immediate holding company a company that has control over a subsidiary company because of the number of shares that it owns, but is itself under the control of a holding company: *The immediate holding company is registered in the UK, but the ultimate parent company is based in Liechtenstein.*

/ˈhəʊldɪŋ ˌkʌmpəni/
pl holding companies
⧓ form, set up a **holding company**
syn parent company
▶ **associate company, group, subsidiary company**

---

holiday *noun* (personnel)
time off work, that in full-time employment is usually paid. A contract of employment states how much holiday an employee may take in a year: *I'll have to ask my boss for an extra day's holiday this year.* ○ *I'm sorry I can't make that meeting, I'm going to be on holiday then.* ○ *What is your holiday entitlement* (ie how much holiday do you get a year)*?*

/ˈhɒlədeɪ/
pl holidays
⧓ annual, paid, unpaid **holiday**; go on **holiday**; **holiday** pay
▶ **bank holiday, contract of employment, day off, leave, public holiday, tax holiday**

home sales *noun* (sales)
the value or number of goods sold in the seller's own country: *The car industry should try to improve home sales as well as increasing exports.* ○ *Home sales are down on last year.*

/ˈhəʊm seɪlz/
note plural noun, used with a plural verb
opp foreign sales
▶ **sales**

honour *verb*
1 (*banking*) to accept and pay a cheque or a bill of exchange when it is due: *The bank refused to honour the cheque because there was no money in the account.* ○ *When you use this cheque card any cheque you write up to £50 will be honoured.* **2** to keep or carry out a promise: *The company was forced to honour all existing contracts.*

/ˈɒnə(r)/
honour, honouring, honoured
note transitive verb
1 ⋈ **honour** a bill, cheque, draft
▶ **accept**[3], **bounce**[1] **1, dishonour, re-present**
2 ⋈ **honour** an agreement, a contract, a deal
▶ **breach of contract**

horizontal integration *noun* (industry)
a situation where two or more organizations that produce similar goods or carry out the same stage of the production process are combined and controlled by one company: *The aim of horizontal integration is to eliminate competition.*

/hɒrɪˌzɒntl ɪntɪˈgreɪʃn/
note not used with *a* or *an*. No plural and used with a singular verb only.
syn lateral integration
▶ **backward integration, diversification, forward integration, integration, vertical integration**

hot money *noun* (finance/stock exchange)
money that is passed quickly from country to country to take advantage of differences in interest rates and exchange rates: *This month's balance of payments has been distorted by hot money.*

/ˌhɒt ˈmʌni/
note not used with *a* or *an*. No plural and used with a singular verb only.
⋈ financed by **hot money**
▶ **money**

hourly rate *noun* (personnel)
the amount paid for each hour worked: *be paid on an hourly rate* ○ *The hourly rate has gone up.* ○ *an hourly rate of £7.50*

/ˌaʊəli ˈreɪt/
pl hourly rates
⋈ increase, reduce the **hourly rate**
▶ **rate 1, time rate**

household goods *noun* (industry)
items such as washing machines, china, cutlery, etc that are used regularly in a house: *a shop selling household goods* ○ *a firm manufacturing household goods*

/ˈhaʊshəʊld gʊdz/
note plural noun, used with a plural verb
▶ **consumer durables**

household name *noun* (advertising)
the name of a product, an organization, etc that is very well known: *If you advertise often enough your goods may become household names.*

/ˌhaʊshəʊld ˈneɪm/
pl household names
▶ **brand name, trade name**

household policy *noun* (insurance)
a contract that provides insurance for loss or damage to buildings or their contents: *The household policy does not include damage caused by nuclear waste.*

/ˈhaʊshəʊld ˌpɒləsi/
pl household policies
⋈ take out a **household policy**
▶ **insurance policy**

house journal *noun*
a magazine produced by a large organization for its staff that contains company news: *She is editor of the house journal.* ○ *an article in the house journal*

/haʊs ˈdʒɜːnl/
pl house journals
⋈ contribute to, feature in, publish, write for a **house journal**
▶ **journal, magazine, periodical, trade journal**

HP *abbr* (finance)
hire purchase

/ˌeɪtʃ ˈpiː/
(also **hp**)

HQ *abbr* (management)
headquarters

/ˌeɪtʃ ˈkjuː/

HRM *abbr* (management)
human resource management

/ˌeɪtʃ ɑːr ˈem/

---

human resource management *noun* (management)
the control of the skills, knowledge and ability of people and how they contribute to an organization: *take a course in human resource management*

/ˌhjuːmən rɪˈsɔːs ˌmænɪdʒmənt/
abbr HRM
note not used with *a* or *an*. No plural and used with a singular verb only.
▶ **management 1**

Ii

IBRD *abbr* (banking)
▶ **The International Bank for Reconstruction and Development**

/ˌaɪ biː ɑː ˈdiː/

ICC *abbr* (commerce)
the International Chamber of Commerce: *The European Commission set up information offices using the network of the ICC.*

/ˌaɪ siː ˈsiː/

IDA *abbr* (banking)
the International Development Agency

/ˌaɪ diː ˈeɪ/
note pronounced as individual letters
▶ **the World Bank**

---

idle money *noun* (finance/economics)
money that is not circulated or invested and does not earn interest: *calculate the amount of idle money in personal bank accounts*

/ˌaɪdl ˈmʌni/
note not used with *a* or *an*. No plural and used with a singular verb only.
⋈ cause, create **idle money**
syn inactive money
opp active money
▶ **dead capital**

IFC *abbr* (finance/law)
the International Finance Corporation

/ˌaɪ ef ˈsiː/

illegal *adjective* (law)
not allowed by law; unlawful: *It is illegal to forge a signature on a cheque.*

/ɪˌliːgl/
opp legal
⋈ an **illegal** act
opp legal

---

illegal contract *noun* (commerce/law)
a contract that includes a dishonest or immoral act, or any crime against the state in which it is made, and therefore has no legal force: *A contract which offends the laws of a friendly foreign state is against public policy, and therefore an illegal contract.*

/ɪˌliːgl ˈkɒntrækt/
pl illegal contracts
⋈ disown, reject, sever an **illegal contract**
► **contract**[1]

---

illegal partnership *noun* (law/management)
an arrangement between two or more people that is formed to carry out unlawful acts, or formed in an unlawful way, and therefore has no legal force: *The illegal partnership was dissolved because it was not recognized by the courts.*

/ɪˌliːgl ˈpɑːtnəʃɪp/
pl illegal partnerships
⋈ dissolve, draw up, sever an **illegal partnership**
► **partnership**

---

illiquid assets *noun* (accounting)
items that cannot easily be converted into money at short notice: *Illiquid assets won't help us to raise more cash in a hurry.*

/ɪˌlɪkwɪd ˈæsets/
note usually plural
opp liquid assets
► **asset**

ILO *abbr* (industrial relations)
the International Labour Organization

/ˌaɪ el ˈəʊ/
note pronounced as individual letters

IMF *abbr* (finance/international trade)
the International Monetary Fund

/ˌaɪ em ˈef/

---

immediate holding company *noun* (stock exchange)
► **holding company**

/ɪˌmiːdiət ˈhəʊldɪŋ ˌkʌmpəni/

---

impact day *noun* (stock exchange/finance)
the day on which the terms of a new issue of shares are announced to the public: *The share price was not revealed until impact day.* ○ *Impact day for the new share issue will be 22 November.*

/ˈɪmpækt deɪ/
pl impact days
► **issue**[1]

---

imperfect market *noun* (economics/sales)
a trading situation in which not enough goods are produced, or goods are priced too highly because of lack of competition or knowledge about market conditions: *be forced to buy goods from a single producer in an imperfect market*

/ɪmˌpɜːfɪkt ˈmɑːkɪt/
note usually singular
⋈ buy, sell, trade in an **imperfect market**
► **market**[1], **perfect market**

---

impersonal account *noun* (accounting)
► **nominal account**

/ɪmˌpɜːsənl əˈkaʊnt/

---

impersonal ledger *noun* (accounting)
► **nominal ledger**

/ɪmˌpɜːsənəl ˈledʒə(r)/

---

implied term *noun* (commerce/law)
a condition in a contract that is not stated directly but can be assumed because it is laid down by statute and is necessary for the contract to be legal: *It was an implied term that the bulk of the goods would correspond to the sample.*

/ɪmˌplaɪd ˈtɜːm/
pl implied terms
⋈ assume, introduce, presume, regard an **implied term**
syn implied condition
► **contract**[1]

import[1] *noun* (international trade)
1 an item, a service, an idea or a person that is brought into one country from another: *an increase in food imports* **2** the action of importing goods: *increase tariffs on the import of manufactured goods*

/ˈɪmpɔːt/
1 pl imports
⧓ control, restrict **imports**
2 note not used with *a* or *an*. No plural and used with a singular verb only.
⧓ **import** goods
► **export**[1], **invisible imports, re-exports, reimports, visible imports**

---

import[2] *verb* (import)
to bring goods, services, ideas or people from one country into another: *This wine is imported from France.* ○ *importing raw materials from abroad to manufacture goods at home* ○ *rely on imported technical expertise*

/ɪmˈpɔːt/
import, importing, imported
note transitive verb
⧓ **import** (something) *from* (a country)
► **export**[2]

---

import duty *noun* (import/tax)
a tax on goods brought into a country from another country: *The import duty on all goods between member states in the European Community will be abolished by the end of 1992 (or when the single market is achieved).*

/ˈɪmpɔːt ˌdjuːti/
pl import duties
⧓ levy, impose, raise, reduce an **import duty**
► **customs duty, duty 1, duty-free, excise duty**

---

importer *noun* (import/export)
a person, an organization or a country that brings in goods or services from another country: *the world's largest importer of oil* ○ *The documents must be signed by the importer.* ○ *a tea importer*

/ɪmˈpɔːtə(r)/
pl importers
⧓ an **importer** *of* (something)
► **exporter**

---

import licence *noun* (import/tax)
a document that must be obtained by an importer for certain goods brought into a country from abroad: *Some toxic chemicals require an import licence before they can be brought into the country.*

/ˈɪmpɔːt ˌlaɪsns/
pl import licences
⧓ grant, issue, obtain, refuse an **import licence**
► **bill of entry, bill of sight, bond note, export licence**

---

import quota *noun* (import)
a limit on the number or type of goods brought into a country: *Japanese car manufacturers want an increase in the UK import quota.* ○ *goods protected by import quotas*

/ˈɪmpɔːt ˌkwəʊtə/
pl import quotas
⧓ abolish, impose, raise, reduce, remove the **import quota**
► **export quota, quota**

---

import restrictions *noun* (export/international trade)
regulations that control the import of goods or currencies from other countries: *impose import restrictions on toxic waste*

/ˈɪmpɔːt rɪˌstrɪkʃnz/
note usually plural
⧓ abolish, impose, increase, reduce **import restrictions**
► **embargo, protectionism, tariff 1, trade restriction**

---

impulse buying *noun* (sales/commerce)
the sudden purchase of an item without thinking about it first: *An exciting display of new stock encourages impulse buying.* ○ *Impulse buying increases at Christmas time.*

/ˈɪmpʌls ˌbaɪɪŋ/
note not used with *a* or *an*. No plural and used with a singular verb only.

⧓ encourage **impulse buying**

► **brand loyalty, fast-moving consumer goods, low involvement product**

IMRO *abbr* (finance/stock exchange)
Investment Management Regulatory Organization

/ˈɪmrəʊ/
note pronounced as a word

---

inactive money *noun* (finance)
► **idle money**

/ɪnˌæktɪv ˈmʌni/

---

incentive wage *noun* (personnel)
a sum of money paid to a worker that depends on the amount of work done: *The company has introduced an incentive wage to increase productivity.*

/ɪnˈsentɪv ˌweɪdʒ/
pl incentive wages
⧓ introduce, offer, receive an **incentive wage**
► **wage**

---

inclusive *adjective* (tax/sales)
including; with nothing to be added: *The bill was inclusive of VAT* ○ *Prices are inclusive* (ie with no extra charges added).

/ɪnˈkluːsɪv/
⧓ **inclusive** *of* something; **inclusive** charges, prices, terms
► **exclusive 1**

---

income *noun* (finance/tax)
money (in the form of WAGES or a SALARY or PROFIT) received from work done, or (as INTEREST) from money invested or (as RENT) from property owned: *earn a regular income* ○ *receive an annual income of £20 000* ○ *Tax is payable on all income over £2 000.*

/ˈɪŋkʌm/
pl incomes
⧓ an annual, a high, a low, a monthly, a regular **income**
► **accrued income, declaration of income, earned income, expenditure, franked income, gross income, net income, taxable income, total income, transfer income, unearned income, unfranked income**

---

income and expenditure account *noun* (accounting/finance)
an account prepared by an organization, eg a charity or an educational institution, that does not aim to make a profit: *Oxfam presented an income and expenditure account.*

/ˌɪŋkʌm ənd ɪkˈspendɪtʃər əˌkaʊnt/
pl income and expenditure accounts
⧓ draw up, prepare, present an **income and expenditure account**
► **account[1] 1, expenditure, profit and loss account**

---

income support *noun* (finance/tax)
money provided by the government to help people who are unemployed, disabled or cannot work because they are caring for relatives: *People who bring up a child on their own receive income support.* ○ *He is on income support.*

/ˈɪŋkʌm səˌpɔːt/
note not used with *a* or *an*. No plural and used with a singular verb only.
⧓ be eligible for, claim, get, qualify for, receive **income support**
► **benefit[1] 1, dole, social security**

---

income tax *noun* (tax/finance)
tax payable on the total amount of money received from work done and from investments: *pay income tax on your earnings*

/ˈɪŋkʌm ˌtæks/
note not used with *a* or *an*. No plural and used with a singular verb only.
⧓ evade, increase, levy, pay, reduce **income tax**
▶ **negative income tax, standard rate, tax[1], taxable income, tax allowance**

income velocity of circulation *noun* (economics)
the number of times one particular unit of currency forms part of a person's income within a given period: *income velocity of circulation is obtained by dividing the gross national product by the total amount of money in circulation.*

/ˌɪŋkʌm vəˌlɒsəti əv ˌsɜːkjəˈleɪʃn/
note no plural
⧓ decrease, increase the **income velocity of circulation**; a high, low **income velocity of circulation**
▶ **circulation 1, transactions velocity of circulation, velocity of circulation**

incoterm *noun* (commerce/international trade)
one of a number of terms concerning transport and insurance costs issued by the International Chamber of Commerce for use in international trade contracts: *Free on board (FOB) and cost, insurance, freight (CIF) are incoterms.*

/ˈɪŋkəʊtɜːm/
pl incoterms
▶ **carriage forward, carriage paid, cost and freight, cost insurance and freight, ex quay, ex ship, ex works, free alongside ship, free carrier, free on board, free on rail, free on truck**

increment *noun* (finance/personnel)
an increase, esp in money paid as a salary: *a salary of £30 000 with annual increments of £1 000*

/ˈɪŋkrəmənt/
pl increments
⧓ receive an **increment**

indemnify *verb* (finance/commerce)
1 to repay someone for money spent or goods lost or damaged: *You will be indemnified for costs incurred on the company's behalf.*
2 to promise to protect someone from money lost or goods damaged: *The water companies were indemnified by the government against legal action.*

/ɪnˈdemnɪfaɪ/
indemnify, indemnifying, indemnified
note transitive verb
⧓ **indemnify** someone *for* something; **indemnify** someone *against* something
▶ **guarantee[2] 2**

indemnity *noun* (finance/commerce)
a promise to protect someone from money lost or goods damaged; repayment for this. An insurance contract that promises to pay for the replacement or repair of lost or damaged goods is a form of indemnity: *arrange an indemnity against loss* ○ *demand an indemnity for the delayed payment* ○ *The courts have allowed the company directors to seek indemnity following the unwelcome takeover.*

/ɪnˈdemnəti/
pl indemnities
⧓ an **indemnity** agreement, arrangement
▶ **compensation, cover[1] 3, guarantee[1] 2, insurance, letter of indemnity**

indexation *noun* (finance/stock exchange)
the policy of connecting income with an index such as the RETAIL PRICE INDEX to combat inflation: *Civil Service pensions are calculated by indexation.*

/ˌɪndekˈseɪʃn/
note not used with *a* or *an*. No plural and used with a singular verb only.
syn index linking

⧓ adopt, demand, use **indexation**

▶ **threshold**

---

index-linked *adjective* (finance)
of savings, pensions, taxes, wages, etc whose value changes in relation to rising prices as recorded in the RETAIL PRICE INDEX: *take out an index-linked pension so that it keeps up with inflation*

/ˌɪndeks ˈlɪŋkt/

⧓ an **index-linked** bond, payment, pension, savings certificate

---

indirect cost *noun* (finance/industry)
▶ **overhead**

/ˌɪndɪrekt ˈkɒst/

---

indirect tax *noun* (tax)
a tax that is paid by producers and traders but is added to the cost of goods or services so that it is finally paid by the person (the CONSUMER) who buys the finished item: *VAT is the standard form of indirect tax paid throughout the European Community.* ○ *pay the indirect tax on petrol*

/ˌɪndɪrekt ˈtæks/

pl indirect taxes

⧓ increase, pay, reduce **indirect tax**

▶ **direct tax, tax[1], value added tax**

---

industrial *adjective* (industry)
1 of or involved in making goods or providing a service: *use electricity to provide energy for an industrial process* ○ *provide money for industrial development* ○ *More money is needed for industrial training.* **2** having a lot of industries: *The Ruhr in Germany is an industrial area.*

/ɪnˈdʌstriəl/

1 ⧓ an **industrial** building, worker

2 ⧓ an **industrial** city, country, nation, town

▶ **commercial**

---

industrial action *noun* (industrial relations)
any organized action, such as stopping work or refusing to work normally, that aims to obtain better pay and working conditions: *The workers threatened industrial action if they were not given a pay rise.*

/ɪnˌdʌstriəl ˈækʃn/

note not used with *a* or *an*. No plural and used with a singular verb only.

⧓ call for, call off, prepare for, take, threaten **industrial action**

▶ **go-slow, strike[1], walk-out, work-to-rule**

---

industrial dispute *noun* (industrial relations)
a disagreement between workers and employers, usually about pay or working conditions: *Air traffic control staff are involved in an industrial dispute over working hours.* ○ *Managers and trade union officials are meeting to try to settle an industrial dispute.*

/ɪnˌdʌstriəl dɪˈspjuːt/

pl industrial disputes

⧓ an **industrial dispute** *over* something; settle an **industrial dispute**

syn trade dispute

▶ **Advisory Conciliation and Arbitration Service, arbitration, demarcation dispute, dispute, lock-out, mediation, tribunal**

---

industrial estate *noun* (commerce)
▶ **trading estate**

/ɪnˌdʌstriəl ɪˈsteɪt/

---

industrial injury *noun* (industrial relations/industry)
an injury received by someone at work who may receive compensation, esp if the workplace was unsafe: *He received £5 000 in compensation for an industrial injury.* ○ *Are you insured against industrial injury?*

/ɪnˌdʌstriəl ˈɪndʒəri/

pl industrial injuries

⧓ claim for, insure against **industrial injuries**

▶ **accident frequency rate, health and safety**

---

industrial park *noun* (commerce)
▶ **trading estate**

/ɪnˌdʌstriəl ˈpɑːk/

industrial relations *noun* (industry)
the relationship between employers and workers: *Good industrial relations are necessary for a happy working environment.* ○ *The company is attempting to improve its industrial relations.*

/ɪnˌdʌstriəl rɪˈleɪʃnz/
note plural noun, used with a plural verb
⋈ bad, good, poor **industrial relations**
▶ **Advisory Conciliation and Arbitration Service**

industrial tribunal *noun* (industrial relations)
a body that hears and attempts to settle disputes between employers and employees: *The redundant worker decided to take his case to an industrial tribunal.* ○ *The industrial tribunal instructed the company to re-employ the sacked worker.*

/ɪnˌdʌstriəl traɪˈbjuːnl/
pl industrial tribunals
⋈ go to, refer to, take a case to an **industrial tribunal**
▶ **Advisory Conciliation and Arbitration Service, arbitration, mediation**

industry *noun* (industry)
an organized activity in which money (CAPITAL) and work (LABOUR) are used to produce goods or services to sell: *the car, construction, electronics, tourist industry* ○ *The computer industry needs more people with advanced technical skills.*

growth industry an industry that produces goods or services for an increasing demand: *The disposal of toxic waste has become a growth industry.*

heavy industry an industry that obtains, produces or uses heavy materials, eg coal or steel, or produces large goods, eg cars

light industry an industry concerned with producing small goods, eg watches

primary industry an industry that is concerned with obtaining and using raw materials, eg mining

secondary industry an industry that uses raw materials to produce consumer goods or makes the machines, etc used by manufacturing companies to produce consumer goods

/ˈɪndəstri/
pl industries
⋈ close down, develop, finance an **industry**
▶ **business 2, commerce, leisure industry, manufacture**[1]**, production, trade**[1]

inefficiency *noun*
the wasting of effort, time and money when working or producing something: *We aim to eliminate inefficiency in our production system.* ○ *The fault was due to staff inefficiency.*

/ɪnɪˈfɪʃnsi/
note not used with *a* or *an*. No plural and used with a singular verb only.
⋈ machine, staff, technical **inefficiency**; eliminate, reduce **inefficiency**
opp efficiency

inefficient *adjective*
not working or producing results in the best way, so that time and money are wasted: *The new manager is very nice, but he's very inefficient.* ○ *an inefficient way of working*

/ˌɪnɪˈfɪʃnt/
⋈ an **inefficient** method, service, system
opp efficient

inertia selling *noun* (sales/marketing)
a type of selling where goods are sent to someone who has not asked for them in the hope that he/she will decide to buy them.

/ɪˈnɜːʃə ˌselɪŋ/
note not used with *a* or *an*. No plural and used with a singular verb only.

If unwanted, the goods can be returned: *The video club used inertia selling.*

⧓ adopt, use **inertia selling**

▶ **sale or return**

---

inexpensive *abbr*

▶ **cheap 1**

/ˌɪnɪk'spensɪv/

---

inflation *noun* (finance)

the rise in prices resulting from an increase in demand for goods and services (which may be connected with an increase in the money supply): *The government is trying to control inflation.* ○ *Inflation now stands at 8%.* ○ *bring wages in line with inflation* ○ *measure the rate of inflation* ○ *reduce inflation by 2%*

/ɪn'fleɪʃn/

note not used with *a* or *an*. No plural and used with a singular verb only.

⧓ control, curb, reduce **inflation**; above, below, high, low, rising **inflation**

▶ **deflation, disinflation, reflation**

---

inflation accounting *noun* (accounting)

▶ **current cost accounting**

/ɪn'fleɪʃn əˌkaʊntɪŋ/

---

information technology *noun* (computing)

the study or use of electronic equipment, esp computers, to store, obtain or send information: *use information technology to speed up the production process* ○ *advances in information technology*

/ˌɪnfə'meɪʃn tekˌnɒlədʒi/

note not used with *a* or *an*. No plural and used with a singular verb only.

abbr IT

⧓ apply, introduce, use **information technology**

▶ **management information system, technology, telecommunications**

---

infrastructure *noun* (economics/transport)

the system of goods and services needed for a country, a city or an organization to function efficiently: *develop the transport infrastructure of the city.* ○ *Ports, roads, railways are part of a country's infrastructure.* ○ *invest money in improving the infrastructure.*

/'ɪnfrəˌstrʌktʃə(r)/

pl infrastructures

⧓ a road, a transport **infrastructure**; an international, a local, a national **infrastructure**

▶ **network[1] 1 b**

---

injunction *noun* (law)

a legal order that forbids or forces someone to do something: *The court granted him an injunction to prevent the document being published.* ○ *take out an injunction against someone* ○ *apply for an injunction to stop the building work*

/ɪn'dʒʌŋkʃn/

pl injunctions

⧓ apply for, grant, issue, obtain, seek an **injunction**

▶ **court order, subpoena[1], summons, writ**

---

inland bill *noun* (international trade/transport)

a bill of exchange that is payable in the country in which it is drawn up: *draw up an inland bill in the UK*

/'ɪnlænd bɪl/

pl inland bills

⧓ accept, draw up, pay, sign an **inland bill**

syn domestic bill

▶ **bill of exchange, foreign bill**

Inland Revenue *noun* (tax)

in the UK, the government organization responsible for collecting direct taxes such as income tax and corporation tax, but not indirect taxes such as VAT: *be prosecuted by the Inland Revenue for not paying tax*

/ˌɪnlənd 'revənjuː/

⧓ declare earnings to, defraud, owe tax to the **Inland Revenue** syn Board of Inland Revenue

▶ **revenue 2, tax**

---

input¹ *noun*

1 (*industry*) something that is put into a business, a system or a process and has an effect on it: *The business needs more financial input.* ○ *encourage maximum input from the work-force* ○ *increase profits without increasing input* **2** (*computing*) information that is put into a computer; the action of putting data into a computer: *control the accuracy of the data input* ○ *prepare information for input*

/ˈɪnpʊt/

note not used with *a* or *an*. No plural and used with a singular verb only.

1 ⋈ capital, cash, financial, human, worker **input**

▶ **output¹ 1**

2 ⋈ data **input**

▶ **output¹ 2**

---

input² *verb* (computing)

to put information into a computer: *When did you last input new data?*

/ˈɪnpʊt/

input, inputting, input *or* **inputted**

note transitive verb

⋈ **input** data

▶ **access, load² 2, output² 2**

---

insider dealing *noun* (stock exchange)

the trading of company shares to make a profit by using confidential information that could affect the share price: *insider dealing in Eurotunnel shares* ○ *The director was charged with insider dealing.*

/ɪnˌsaɪdə ˈdiːlɪŋ/

note not used with *a* or *an*. No plural and used with a singular verb only.

⋈ be accused of, be found guilty of, prohibit, suspect **insider dealing**

syn insider trading

▶ **City Code on Takeovers and Mergers, deal²**

---

insolvency *noun* (finance)

a state of being unable to pay your debts: *face the risk of insolvency* ○ *sell off assets in an attempt to prevent insolvency*

/ɪnˈsɒlvənsi/

note not used with *a* or *an*. No plural and used with a singular verb only.

⋈ admit, avoid, declare **insolvency**

▶ **bankruptcy, declaration of solvency, liquidation, receivership**

---

insolvent *adjective* (finance)

to have no money; to be unable to pay your debts: *The owner of the small business became insolvent during the recession.*

/ɪnˈsɒlvənt/

⋈ become, be declared **insolvent**

▶ **bankrupt**

Inspector of weights and measures *noun* (commerce)

a government official who checks that the correct quantities of goods are sold: *The Inspector of weights and measures discovered that the shop was giving short weight.*

/ɪnˌspektər əv ˌweɪts ənd ˈmeʒəz/

---

instalment *noun* (sales/finance)

one of a series of payments, usually as a means of buying goods: *Would you prefer to pay the full amount now or pay in instalments?* ○ *pay insurance by instalments* ○ *Each instalment is due on the first of the month.*

/ɪnˈstɔːlmənt/

pl instalments

⋈ fall behind in, pay by, pay in **instalments**

▶ **lump sum, part-payment**

instalment plan *noun* (sales)
/ɪnˈstɔːlmənt plæn/
▶ **hire purchase**

instrument of transfer *noun* (finance)
/ˌɪnstrʊmənt əv ˈtrænsfɜː(r)/
▶ **deed of transfer**

insurance *noun* (finance/insurance)
/ɪnˈʃʊərəns/
1 a method of guarding against injury, loss or damage to property by paying a sum of money (a PREMIUM) to an insurance company that agrees to provide money to repair or replace the property in the case of a fire, theft, etc: *take out insurance on a house* ○ *Car insurance is compulsory in the UK.* **2** the business of providing insurance: *He works in insurance.* **3** the payment made to or by an insurance company: *After the car accident she received £5 000 in insurance.*

note not used with *a* or *an*. No plural and used with a singular verb only.

⋈ an **insurance** claim, company, contract, firm, payment, risk; accident, fire, holiday, medical, travel **insurance**

▶ **assurance, blanket cover, certificate of insurance, claim[1] 1, cover note, Lloyd's of London, motor insurance, mutual insurance company, products liability insurance, reinsurance, renewal notice, third party insurance, time policy**

insurance broker *noun* (insurance)
/ɪnˈʃʊərəns ˌbrəʊkə(r)/
a person who advises on insurance policies from different companies and arranges insurance contracts for clients with an insurer who pays the broker a fee: *arrange cover through an insurance broker*

pl insurance brokers
▶ **broker**

insurance policy *noun* (insurance)
/ɪnˈʃʊərəns ˌpɒləsi/
an agreement between an insurance company and the person insured. In return for regular payments the insurance company agrees to pay money only for the particular losses or damage specified in the policy: *take out an insurance policy on a house* ○ *What are the terms of your insurance policy?*

pl insurance policies
▶ **act of God, household policy, policy, riot and civil commotion**

insurance premium *noun* (insurance)
/ɪnˈʃʊərəns ˌpriːmiəm/
a payment made to an insurance company in return for a contract that insurance will be paid for loss or damage to the property and up to the amount specified: *My insurance premium has been increased this year.* ○ *pay an insurance premium in monthly instalments*

pl insurance premiums
⋈ an annual, a monthly **insurance premium**
▶ **premium**

insure *verb* (insurance)
/ɪnˈʃʊə(r)/
to guard against injury, loss or damage to property by paying a regular sum of money (a PREMIUM) to an insurance company that provides money to repair or replace the property in the case of a fire, theft, etc: *insure your house against fire* ○ *Are you insured?* ○ *be insured against sickness, accident or redundancy*

insure, insuring, insured
note transitive verb
⋈ **insure** someone/something *against* something

intangible asset *noun* (accounting/finance)
/ɪnˌtændʒəbl ˈæsets/
something owned by a person or company that does not have a physical substance, eg goodwill, a patent or a trade mark: *A trade mark is one of the most important intangible assets.*

pl intangible assets
⋈ assess, measure, value **intangible assets**
syn intangibles, invisible asset

▶ **copyright, goodwill, intellectual property, patent, tangible asset, trade mark**

---

integration *noun* (industry)
a situation where two or more companies work together for their mutual benefit: *decide on integration to save costs and share resources*

/ˌɪntɪˈgreɪʃn/
note not used with *a* or *an*. No plural and used with a singular verb only.
▶ **backward integration, disintegration, diversification, forward integration, horizontal integration, vertical integration**

---

intellectual property *noun* (law)
an idea, a design, a piece of writing, etc that belongs to a person or an organization and cannot be sold or copied without the owner's permission: *If you copy this design you will be infringing* (ie encroaching) *on intellectual property rights.* ○ *It is important to protect the company's intellectual property.*

/ˌɪntəˌlektʃuəl ˈprɒpəti/
note not used with *a* or *an*. No plural and used with a singular verb only.
▶ **copyright, intangible asset, patent, royalty, trade mark**

---

interest *noun* (stock exchange/finance)
1 an amount charged for money borrowed: *a loan with a 10% interest* , ie if you borrow £100, the interest will be £10 ○ *an interest-free loan* ○ *Most major banks charge the same rate of interest.* ○ *Interest rates have gone up again.* **2** an amount paid in return for money invested: *My building society pays 13% interest.* ○ *These gas shares earn a lot of interest.* **3** a right in or over land or property or a company: *hold an interest in agricultural land*

/ˈɪntrest/
note not used with *a* or *an*. No plural and used with a singular verb only.
1 ⋈ charge, levy **interest**
2 ⋈ earn, pay **interest**
▶ **dividend, yield[1] 2**
3 ⋈ have an **interest** *in* (property)
▶ **absolute interest, controlling interest, life interest, minority interest**

---

interest rate *noun* (finance)
the cost of borrowing money expressed as a percentage of the capital borrowed: *The new interest rate is 11.5%.* ○ *Borrowers are encouraged to take out loans while interest rates are low.*

/ˈɪntrest reɪt/
pl interest rates
⋈ current, fixed, high, low **interest rate**
syn rate of interest
▶ **annual percentage rate, base rate, flat rate, rate 2**

---

interest rate swap *noun* (finance)
▶ **swap**

/ˈɪntrest reɪt swɒp/

---

interface *noun* (computing)
the part of a computer, usually consisting of a screen and keyboard, where the user can read or add information: *A large, clear screen is an important part of the user interface.*

/ˈɪntəfeɪs/
pl interfaces
⋈ man-machine, user **interface**
▶ **terminal**

---

internal *adjective*
inside (a country, an area, a region, etc): *We are getting more internal competition for our products.*

/ɪnˈtɜːnl/
⋈ **internal** investment, market, trade
▶ **external**

international *adjective*
involving two or more countries: *set up an international company* ○ *an increase in international trade*

/ˌɪntəˈnæʃnəl/
⋈ an **international** agreement; **international** law, trade
▶ **domestic 1, global**

the International Bank for Reconstruction and Development *noun* (banking)
the central bank, controlled by the United Nations, that lends money to member states. Together with the International Development Association it is commonly known as the World Bank: *apply to the International Bank for Reconstruction and Development for financial assistance*

/ðiː ˌɪntəˌnæʃnəl ˌbæŋk fə ˌriːkənˌstrʌkʃn ənd dɪˈveləpmənt/
abbr IBRD
⋈ financed by **the International Bank for Reconstruction and Development**
▶ **the European Bank for Reconstruction and Development, International Development Association, International Finance Corporation, International Monetary Fund, the Overseas Development Administration, the World Bank**

International Chamber of Commerce *noun* (commerce)
an international association of business people formed to promote and protect their business interests in international affairs. It is based in Paris: *The International Chamber of Commerce has published a number of guidelines for world industry about the care of the environment.*

/ˌɪntəˌnæʃnəl ˈtʃeɪmbər əv ˈkɒmɜːs/
abbr ICC
▶ **chamber of commerce, London Chamber of Commerce**

International Development Association *noun* (banking)
an organization set up by the United Nations that together with the International Bank for Reconstruction and Development is commonly known as the World Bank. It provides money for economic growth in developing countries: *funds provided by the International Development Association*

/ˌɪntəˌnæʃnəl dɪˈveləpmənt əˌsəʊsiˌeɪʃn/
abbr IDA
▶ **European Bank for Reconstruction and Development, International Bank for Reconstruction and Development, International Finance Corporation, International Monetary Fund, Overseas Development Administration, World Bank**

International Finance Corporation *noun* (banking)
an agency of the INTERNATIONAL BANK FOR RECONSTRUCTION AND DEVELOPMENT, set up in 1956, to provide money for privately-owned businesses in developing countries

/ˌɪntəˌnæʃnəl ˈfaɪnæns ˌkɔːpəˌreɪʃn/
abbr IFC
▶ **European Bank for Reconstruction and Development, International Bank for Reconstruction and Development, International Development Association, International Finance Corporation, International Monetary Fund, the Overseas**

Development Administration, World Bank

International Labour Organization *noun*
(industrial relations)
an organization set up by the United Nations to improve working conditions throughout the world: *The trade union is seeking advice from the International Labour Organization.*

/ˌɪntəˌnæʃnəl ˈleɪbər ˌɔːɡənaɪˌzeɪʃn/
abbr ILO
⧓ apply to, consult the **International Labour Organization**
► **trade union**

International Monetary Fund *noun*
(finance/international trade)
an agency of the United Nations that lends money to encourage trade and economic development in poor countries: *The third world country was advised to seek a loan through the International Monetary Fund.*

/ˌɪntəˌnæʃnəl ˈmʌnɪtri fʌnd/
abbr IMF
⧓ apply to, financed by, use the **International Monetary Fund**
► **European Bank for Reconstruction and Development, fund[1] 2, International Bank for Reconstruction and Development, International Development Association, International Finance Corporation, the Overseas Development Administration, the World Bank**

---

international reply coupon *noun*
a printed form enclosed with a letter that can be exchanged for the cost of the minimum airmail postage back from the country to which it is sent: *I enclose an international reply coupon for your reply.*

/ˌɪntəˌnæʃnəl rɪˈplaɪ ˌkuːpɒn/
pl international reply coupons
⧓ enclose, send, use an **international reply coupon**
► **reply coupon**

International Standards Organization *noun*
(manufacturing)
an organization formed to standardize measurements and to set quality and safety standards for manufacturing and industy

/ˌɪntəˌnæʃnəl ˈstændədz ɔːɡənaɪˌzeɪʃn/
abbr ISO
⧓ approved, set by the **International Standards Organization**
► **British Standards Institution**

---

the International Stock Exchange *noun*
(stock exchange)
the market for the buying and selling of securities, based in London: *a company with shares listed on the International Stock Exchange*

/ˌɪntəˌnæʃnəl ˈstɒk ɪksˌtʃeɪndʒ/
abbr ISE
note the official name is the *International Stock Exchange of the United Kingdom and the Republic of Ireland Limited.* It is still also known as the *London Stock Exchange.*
⧓ buy, deal, sell, trade on the **International Stock Exchange**
► **foreign exchange market, main market, New York**

Stock Exchange, stock exchange, third market, unlisted securities market**

---

intervention price *noun* (law/economics)
the price paid by the European Community under its COMMON AGRICULTURAL POLICY to farmers who are unable to sell their produce: *The Council of the European Community determined the intervention price on wheat.*

/ˌɪntəˈvenʃn praɪs/
pl intervention prices
⋈ cut, decide on, fix, pay an **intervention price**; the **intervention price** for (maize, beef, eggs, etc)
▶ **price[1], subsidy, target price, threshold price**

---

interview[1] *noun* (personnel)
a meeting at which someone, esp a person applying for a job, is asked questions about his/her work experience, interests and abilities to see if he/she is suitable: *Interviews for the job of sales manager will be held next week.* ○ *I've got an interview with an accountancy firm.* ○ *Ten candidates were called for interview.*

/ˈɪntəvjuː/
pl interviews
⋈ attend, conduct, go to, hold an **interview**
▶ **recruitment, selection procedure**

---

interview[2] *verb* (personnel)
to ask someone, esp a person who has applied for a job, questions about his/her work experience, interests and abilities to see if he/she is suitable: *Ten people were interviewed for the manager's job.* ○ *She was interviewed by the managing director.* ○ *I'm interviewing all afternoon.*

/ˈɪntəvjuː/
interview, interviewing, interviewed
note transitive and intransitive verb
⋈ be **interviewed** *by* someone; be **interviewed** *for* something

---

interviewee *noun* (personnel)
a person who is interviewed, esp for a job: *ask the interviewee about his/her work experience*

/ˌɪntəvjuːˈiː/
pl interviewees
▶ **applicant 1, appointee, candidate**

---

interviewer *noun* (personnel)
a person who carries out an interview: *The interviewer asked him some awkward questions.*

/ˈɪntəvjuːə/
pl interviewers

---

intestate *adjective* (law)
without having left a legal will at death: *She died intestate.*

/ɪnˈtesteɪt/
⋈ an intestate **person**
opp testate
▶ **will**

---

invalid *adjective*
not legally effective or acceptable or legally recognized: *an out-of-date passport is invalid.* ○ *The licence is invalid unless it has your correct address on it.* ○ *refuse to sign an invalid contract*

/ɪnˈvælɪd/
⋈ an **invalid** contract, document, driving licence, passport, receipt, ticket, will
opp valid
▶ **null and void**

---

inventory *noun* (manufacturing/retail)
▶ **stock-in-trade**

/ˈɪnvəntri/

---

inventory control *noun* (manufacturing/retail)
▶ **stock control**

/ˈɪnvəntri kənˌtrəʊl/

---

invest *verb* (stock exchange/finance)
to buy property, shares, securities, etc to sell again to make a profit or to receive money in the form of INTEREST: *He invested in government bonds because they are considered safe.* ○ *invest money in a business* ○ *The more you invest the more interest you earn.*

/ɪnˈvest/
invest, investing, invested
note transitive and intransitive verb
⧓ **invest** (money) *in* something
▶ **disinvest**

investment *noun* (finance/stock exchange)
1 the purchase of materials, machines, etc to produce goods to sell: *make a profit by careful investment* ○ *This new computer system is a major investment for us.* **2** the purchase of property, shares, securities, etc to sell again to make a profit or to receive money in the form of INTEREST or DIVIDENDS: *buy shares in a gas company as an investment* ○ *These oil shares were a good investment*, ie were profitable ○ *Government bonds are considered to be a safe investment.* **3** the money invested: *an investment of £3 000/a £3 000 investment*

/ɪnˈvestmənt/
pl investments
⧓ a bad, good, poor, safe, secure, shaky, sound **investment**
▶ **capital investment, disinvestment, financial investment, joint investment, real investment, trade investment**

investment allowance *noun* (tax)
▶ **capital allowance**

/ɪnˈvestmənt əˌlaʊəns/

investment analyst *noun* (finance/stock exchange)
a person employed by an organization to study and advise on stock market conditions and the rise or fall of company shares: *The investment analyst predicted that the price of metals such as copper would rise again.*

/ɪnˈvestmənt ˌænəlɪst/
pl investment analysts
⧓ consult an **investment analyst**
▶ **analyst, financial adviser**

investment bank *noun* (finance/stock exchange)
a bank that provides finance for companies, esp by buying stocks and securities and selling them in smaller units to members of the public. It also advises on takeovers and mergers and ways of raising money: *an investment bank dealing in corporate finance*

/ɪnˈvestmənt bæŋk/
pl investment banks
▶ **bank[1], finance house**

investment goods *noun* (manufacturing)
▶ **capital goods**

/ɪnˈvestmənt gʊdz/

investment income *noun* (tax)
▶ **unearned income**

/ɪnˈvestmənt ˌɪŋkʌm /

investment management *noun* (stock exchange)
▶ **fund management**

/ɪnˈvestmənt ˌmænɪdʒmənt/

Investment Management Regulatory Organization *noun* (finance/stock exchange)
a SELF-REGULATORY ORGANIZATION that draws up and enforces codes of conduct for the control of investment companies: *The Investment Management Regulatory Organization has proposed rules for unit trust accounting.*

/ɪnˌvestmənt ˌmænɪdʒmənt ˌregjələtəri ɔːgənaɪˌzeɪʃn/
abbr IMRO
⧓ be ruled by, consult, refer to the **Investment Management Regulatory Organization**
▶ **Financial Intermediaries, Managers and Brokers Regulatory Association, Life Assurance and Unit Trust Regulatory Organization, self-regulatory organization, Securities and Futures Authority,**

Securities and Investment Board

---

investment manager *noun* (management)
▶ **fund manager**

/ɪnˈvestmənt ˌmænɪdʒə(r)/

---

investment trust *noun* (finance/stock exchange)
a limited company that uses its shareholders' money to buy securities on the stock exchange. The securities provide interest, dividends and capital gains when they are sold. The company uses its knowledge to limit the risk of investment: *an investment trust that provides a high income* ○ *hold shares in an investment trust*

/ɪnˈvestmənt trʌst/
pl investment trusts
⧓ launch, manage, set up an **investment trust**
▶ **managed fund, trust, unit trust**

---

investor *noun* (finance/stock exchange)
a person or an organization that buys property, shares, securities, etc in order to sell again to make a profit or to receive money in the form of INTEREST or DIVIDENDS: *a major investor in an overseas company* ○ *There are an increasing number of private investors* (ie people who invest for themselves, not for a company).

/ɪnˈvestə(r)/
pl investors
⧓ a big, major, small **investor**
▶ **private investor**

---

invisible assets *noun* (finance)
▶ **intangible assets**

/ɪnˌvɪzɪbl ˈæsets/

---

invisible exports *noun* (international trade)
services such as banking, insurance and tourism that are sent from one country to another: *an increase in the amount of invisible exports*

/ɪnˌvɪzəbl ˈekspɔːts/
note usually plural
syn invisibles
opp visible exports
▶ **export**[1]

---

invisible imports *noun* (international trade)
services such as banking, insurance and tourism that are brought from other countries: *Invisible imports have decreased this year.*

/ɪnˌvɪzəbl ˈɪmpɔːts/
note usually plural
syn invisibles
opp visible exports

---

invoice[1] *noun* (commerce)
a list of goods sold or services received that states how much you must pay for them: *We haven't received payment for our invoice dated 3 September.*

/ˈɪnvɔɪs/
pl invoices
⧓ pay, receive, send (out) an **invoice**
▶ **bill**[1] **1**, **proforma invoice**

---

invoice[2] *verb* (commerce)
1 to make a list of goods sold or services received with their prices **2** to send a list of goods sold or services received as a request for payment: *Please invoice me for the goods.*

/ˈɪnvɔɪs/
invoice, invoicing, invoiced
note transitive verb
⧓ **invoice** someone *for* something; **invoice** someone *on* (a certain date)
▶ **bill**[2]

IOU *abbr* (accounting/finance)
an abbreviation for *I owe you*. It is written on a note or document specifying the amount borrowed to acknowledge a debt: *I'm sending you an IOU for the money you lent me on Thursday.* ○ *an IOU for £50*

/ˌaɪ əʊ ˈjuː/
note pronounced as individual letters
pl IOUs
⧓ demand, receive, require, write an **IOU**
▶ **debt**

irredeemable securities *noun* (stock exchange)
government bonds or stocks and some debentures that can never be repaid, although they pay interest and can be bought and sold: *The price of irredeemable securities falls when interest rates rise.*

/ˌɪrɪˌdiːməbl sɪˈkjʊərətiz/
note plural noun, used with a plural verb
syn irredeemables
▶ **bond**[1], **debenture, security**

irrevocable letter of credit *noun* (banking/commerce)
▶ **letter of credit**

/ɪˌrevəkəbl ˌletər əv ˈkredɪt/

ISE *abbr* (stock exchange)
International Stock Exchange

/ˌaɪ es ˈiː/
note pronounced as individual letters

issue[1] *noun* (stock exchange)
1 the raising of long-term capital in a company by selling shares to existing shareholders or at an arranged price to selected investors or to the public: *The new share issue proved very popular.*
2 the number of shares that a company offers for sale to the public at any one time: *The issue was divided into shares of £2.40 each.*

/ˈɪʃuː/
pl issues
1 ⧓ a new, an oversubscribed, an undersubscribed **issue**
syn share issue
▶ **allotment, flotation, offer by prospectus, offer for sale, public issue, rights issue, scrip issue, tap issue**

issue[2] *verb*
to give or supply something to someone; to make something available: *Visas can only be issued between 9 am and 4 pm.*

/ˈɪʃuː/
issue, issuing, issued
note transitive verb
⧓ **issue** a certificate, share, visa

issued capital *noun* (stock exchange)
the money that a company raises by the shares it offers for sale: *an issued capital of £2.5 million*

/ˌɪʃuːd ˈkæpɪtl/
note not used with *a* or *an*. No plural and used with a singular verb only.
syn subscribed capital
▶ **capital, unissued capital**

issuing house *noun* (stock exchange/finance)
a financial institution, usually a merchant bank, that sells the shares of a new company to the public: *The new issue of shares was marketed through an issuing house.*

/ˈɪʃuːɪŋ haʊs/
pl issuing houses
⧓ sell through an **issuing house**
▶ **issue**[1]

IT *abbr* (computing/technology)
information technology

/ˌaɪ ˈtiː/
note pronounced as individual letters

itemize *verb* (finance/accounting)
to specify or separate every item on a bill or account or list: *The auditor decided to itemize the account.* ○ *ask for an itemized phone bill*

/ˈaɪtəmaɪz/
itemize, itemizing, itemized
(also **itemise**)
note transitive verb
⧓ **itemize** an account, a bill, a list; an **itemized** account, agenda, bill, list

J. *abbr* (law)
1 judge: *J. Jones* **2** Justice: *Smith J* ○ *Smith and Brown JJ*

pl JJ
note used in written English only

JA *abbr* (banking)
joint account: *The new interest rate affects JA holders.*

note used in written English only

---

janitor *noun*
(*US*) ▶ **caretaker**

/ˈdʒænɪtə(r)/
pl janitors

---

jargon *noun*
specialized or technical words used by a particular group of people and difficult for others to understand: *The article was full of computer jargon.* ○ *She uses so much jargon I can't understand what she means.*

/ˈdʒɑːgən/
note not used with *a* or *an*. No plural and used with a singular verb only.
⋈ advertising, computer, financial, legal, political, scientific **jargon**; to use, write **jargon**

---

jettison *verb* (shipping/insurance)
to throw the cargo of a ship overboard when the ship is in danger: *It was necessary to jettison much of the cargo during the storm.*

/ˈdʒetɪsn/
jettison, jettisoning, jettisoned
note transitive verb
⋈ **jettison** the cargo

---

jingle *noun* (advertising)
a short and simple tune used to advertise a product: *write a jingle for a shampoo advert*

/ˈdʒɪŋgl/
pl jingles
⋈ an advertising, a publicity **jingle**
▶ **slogan**

Jnr *abbr*
junior: *Mr H. Cook Jnr.*

note used in written English only

---

job *noun* (personnel)
1 a position of regular paid work: *She is looking for a new job.* ○ *He has retired from his job as a bank manager.* ○ *He has a good job in computers.* **2** a piece of work or task: *She is paid by the job.* ○ *The computer takes about ten minutes to complete each job.* **3** a function or a responsibility: *It's not his job to tell the sales reps what to do.*

/dʒɒb/
pl jobs
1 ⋈ be out of, give up, have, look for, retire from a **job**; a full-time, part-time, permanent, temporary **job**
▶ **business 1a, occupation, profession, trade[1] 5**
2 ⋈ carry out, complete, finish a **job**

---

job analysis *noun* (management/manufacturing)
a detailed study of a particular task, and its relation to other work done in an organization: *Consultants were brought in to carry out a detailed job analysis to improve productivity.*

/ˈdʒɒb əˌnæləsɪs/
pl job analyses
⋈ to carry out, do a **job analysis**
▶ **analysis**

---

job application *noun*
▶ **application**

/ˈdʒɒb æplɪˌkeɪʃn/

---

jobber *noun* (stock exchange)
▶ **stockjobber**

/ˈdʒɒbə(r)/

---

jobbing *adjective*
of work on small, occasional jobs: *He does jobbing work for a builder.*

/ˈdʒɒbɪŋ/
⧓ a **jobbing** journalist, printer

jobbing production *noun* (industry/manufacturing)
a system of production where items are produced singly or in small numbers: *We are a small firm and most of our machinery is suitable for jobbing production.*

/ˈdʒɒbɪŋ prəˌdʌkʃn/
note not used with *a* or *an*. No plural and used with a singular verb only.
▶ **batch 1, mass production, production 1**

job centre *noun*
(*UK*) a government office that provides information about available jobs and training courses for those who are out of work: *look at the adverts at the local job centre*

/ˈdʒɒb ˌsentə(r)/
pl job centres
(also **Job Centre**)
⧓ go to, visit the **job centre**
▶ **employment agency**

job costing *noun* (industry)
calculating a separate cost for each piece of work in a production process: *Job costing enables us to assess the problem areas in the production process.*

/ˈdʒɒb ˌkɒstɪŋ/
note not used with *a* or *an*. No plural and used with a singular verb only.
▶ **batch costing, costing**

job description *noun* (personnel)
an account of the main aims and tasks of the work done by a particular employee: *Please send for a job description and application form.*

/ˈdʒɒb dɪˌskrɪpʃn/
pl job descriptions
⧓ approve, change, compile, write a **job description**
▶ **job title**

job evaluation *noun* (personnel)
1 examining how much money a job is worth and how much the person doing it should be paid: *Many factors should be taken into account during job evaluation.* ○ *My job evaluation is coming up next week. I hope they decide to pay me more money!* **2** a meeting in which this takes place: *We are carrying out four job evaluations this week.*

/ˈdʒɒb ɪˌvæljuˌeɪʃn/
1 note not used with *a* or *an*. No plural and used with a singular verb only.
⧓ a **job evaluation** panel
2 pl job evaluations
⧓ carry out a **job evaluation**

job holder *noun* (personnel)
the person who has a particular job or position: *The job description must be signed by the job holder.* ○ *The new job holder can decide how to organize the filing system.*

/ˈdʒɒb ˌhəʊldə(r)/
pl job holders
⧓ the current, next, previous **job holder**

job losses *noun* (industrial relations)
positions that have been made redundant: *job losses in the coal industry* ○ *Many job losses are a result of new technology.*

/ˈdʒɒb ˌlɒsɪz/
note plural noun, used with a plural verb
⧓ lead to, result in **job losses**; heavy, serious, severe **job losses**
▶ **natural wastage, redundancy, unemployment**

job lot *noun* (retail)
a group of items sold together: *The house furniture was sold as a job lot.*

/ˌdʒɒb ˈlɒt/
pl job lots

⋈ buy, sell something in/as a **job lot**

▶ **batch, lot 1**

---

job satisfaction *noun* (personnel)
the feeling of achievement and enjoyment a worker gets from a job: *The position is badly paid but it gives lots of job satisfaction.* ○ *As a result of new technology more workers felt there was a lack of job satisfaction.*

/ˈdʒɒb ˌsætɪsˌfækʃn/

note not used with *a* or *an*. No plural and used with a singular verb only.

⋈ a high, low (level of) **job satisfaction**; give, obtain, provide, receive **job satisfaction**

---

job security *noun* (personnel)
a situation where a job is likely to be permanent: *The union is demanding greater job security.*

/ˈdʒɒb sɪˌkjʊərəti/

note not used with *a* or *an*. No plural and used with a singular verb only.

⋈ a high/low level of **job security**

▶ **redundancy**

---

job-sharing *noun* (personnel)
dividing a full-time job for one person between two or more part-time employees: *Since the introduction of job-sharing we have employed a much larger work force.*

/ˈdʒɒb ˌʃeərɪŋ/

note not used with *a* or *an*. No plural and used with a singular verb only.

⋈ introduce, provide opportunities for **job-sharing**

syn work-sharing

---

job specification *noun* (personnel)
▶ **job description**

/ˈdʒɒb ˌspesɪfɪˌkeɪʃn/

pl job specifications

---

job title *noun* (personnel)
the name of a person's job: *My actual job title is departmental manager.* ○ *Please write your name, address and job title on this form.*

/ˈdʒɒb ˌtaɪtl/

pl job titles

⋈ alter, change a **job title**

▶ **job description**

---

joining passenger *noun* (transport)
a person starting an aeroplane journey: *The plane is now boarding for joining passengers.*

/ˌdʒɔɪnɪŋ ˈpæsɪndʒə(r)/

pl joining passengers

▶ **transfer[1] 4, transfer passenger, transit**

---

joint account *noun*
1 (*banking*) a bank account in the names of two of more people: *When we married we put our money into a joint account.* **2** (*stock exchange*) two or more people or companies owning the same shares: *The shares were held in a joint account.* **3** (*accounting*) a financial record of a business or project that is owned or run by two or more people or companies (a JOINT VENTURE): *The books were drawn up as a joint account.*

/ˌdʒɔɪnt əˈkaʊnt/

pl joint accounts

1 abbr JA

⋈ close, have, open, set up a **joint account**

▶ **account[1] 2, bank account**

---

joint and several liability *noun* (law)
a business activity that is set up by a group of people, in which all members of the group are responsible for any debts, etc both as a group and as individuals: *a joint and several liability clause in a contract*

/ˌdʒɔɪnt ənd ˌsevrəl laɪəˈbɪləti/

note not used with *a* or *an*. No plural and used with a singular verb only.

⧓ accept **joint and several liability**

▶ **liability 1**

---

joint investment *noun* (stock exchange)
property, shares or securities owned by more than one person: *To dispose of a joint investment the transfer deed must be signed by all parties.*

/ˌdʒɔɪnt ɪnˈvestmənt/
pl joint investments
⧓ hold, make a **joint investment**
▶ **investment 2**

---

joint owner *noun* (law)
one of two or more people who share ownership of property, land or a business: *The brothers are joint owners of the business.*

/ˌdʒɔɪnt ˈəʊnə/
pl joint owners
⧓ a **joint owner** *of* (something)
syn co-owner

---

joint ownership *noun* (law)
the owning of property, land or a business by two or more people. Each person has the same legal rights as the other(s) and the last surviving person becomes the sole owner: *The freehold of the site is in joint ownership.*

/ˌdʒɔɪnt ˈəʊnəʃɪp/
note not used with *a* or *an*. No plural and used with a singular verb only.
⧓ be in, have **joint ownership**
syn co-ownership

---

joint-stock bank *noun* (banking)
▶ **commercial bank**

/ˈdʒɔɪnt stɒk bæŋk/
abbr JSB

---

joint-stock company *noun* (commerce)
a business formed by a group of people using money provided by them all: *We have pooled our assets and formed a joint-stock company.*

/ˈdʒɔɪnt stɒk ˌkʌmpəni/
pl joint stock companies
⧓ form, set up a **joint stock company**
▶ **company, co-operative**

---

joint supply *noun* (industry/manufacturing)
a production process in which two or more separate commodities are produced: *Milk and butter are produced by joint supply in the dairy industry.*

/ˌdʒɔɪnt səˈplaɪ/
note not used with *a* or *an*. No plural and used with a singular verb only.
syn complementary supply
▶ **supply**[1]

---

joint venture *noun* (commerce)
▶ **venture**

/ˌdʒɔɪnt ˈventʃə(r)/

---

journal *noun*
1 a magazine or newspaper, esp one that is serious and deals with a specialized subject: *the Wall Street Journal* ○ *'Travel Trade Gazette' is a trade journal for the tourism industry.* **2** (*accounting*) a book where business transactions are recorded: *All transactions are to be recorded in the general journal.*

/ˈdʒɜːnl/
pl journals
1 ⧓ edit, produce, publish a **journal**
▶ **house journal, magazine, periodical, trade journal**
2 ⧓ an accounts **journal**; enter, make an entry, record figures, etc in a **journal**
▶ **books, day book**

Jr *abbr*
Junior: *Jr partners* ○ *Mr D. Bannister Jr*

note used in written English only

JSB *abbr* (banking)
joint-stock bank

/ˌdʒeɪ es ˈbiː/
pl JSBs

jt. *abbr*
joint: *jt. account* ○ *jt. venture*

note used in written English only

judge[1] *noun* (law)
a public officer with authority to decide cases in a lawcourt: *The judge sentenced her to three years in prison.* ○ *Judge Woolford*

/dʒʌdʒ/
abbr J.
pl judges

judge[2] *verb*
to decide a case in a lawcourt: *It was the hardest case he had ever had to judge.*

/dʒʌdʒ/
judge, judging, judged
note transitive verb
⋈ **judge** a case

judgment *noun* (law)
a legal or official decision: *The court was asked to reconsider its judgment.*

/ˈdʒʌdʒmənt/
pl judgments
note When the word *judgment* refers to legal matters the 'e' is omitted. When it has a more general meaning the word is spelt *judgement*.
⋈ give, pass, pronounce **judgment**

judgment creditor *noun* (law)
a person, named by a court, to whom any money owed must be repaid: *Payment must be made to the judgment creditor.*

/ˈdʒʌdʒmənt ˌkredɪtə(r)/
pl judgment creditors
⋈ appoint a **judgment creditor**
► **creditor**

judgment debtor *noun* (law)
a person who has been ordered by a court to pay a debt: *The judgment debtor was ordered by the court to pay his debts.*

/ˈdʒʌdʒmənt ˌdetə(r)/
pl judgment debtors
⋈ appoint a **judgment debtor**
► **bankrupt[1], debtor, defaulter**

judgment note *noun* (finance)
a document that enables the holder to have a court order issued against a debtor to make him/her repay money owed: *A judgment note makes a formal lawsuit unnecessary.*

/ˈdʒʌdʒmənt ˌnəʊt/
pl judgment notes
⋈ apply for, issue, obtain a **judgment note**
► **court order, letter of licence**

jump[1] *verb* (stock exchange)
(of amounts, prices, values) to move suddenly upward: *share prices jumped*

/dʒʌmp/
jump, jumping, jumped
note intransitive verb
► **bounce[1]**

jump[2] *noun*
a sudden rise in amount, price or value: *The company's results show a huge jump in profits.* ○ *There was a jump in unemployment figures this month.*

/dʒʌmp/
pl jumps
⋈ a **jump** *in* something
► **bounce[2]**

junior *adjective*
having a low or lower rank in an organization: *She is a junior partner.* ○ *He joined the firm as a junior clerk.*

/ˈdʒuːniə(r)/
abbr Jnr, Jr
⋈ a **junior** clerk, colleague, executive, manager, partner
opp senior

---

junk *noun* (commerce)
1 rubbish; old or unwanted things that are sold cheaply: *Throw away that junk.* ○ *She runs a junk shop.* **2** junk bonds

/dʒʌŋk/
note not used with *a* or *an*. No plural and used with a singular verb only.
⋈ a **junk** dealer, shop, yard

---

junk bond *noun* (stock exchange/finance)
(*esp US*) a bond that has a high rate of interest but is considered to be a very risky investment. It is issued by a company that needs to raise a lot of money quickly to finance a TAKEOVER: *The company issued junk bonds during the takeover.*

/ˈdʒʌŋk ˌbɒnd/
pl junk bonds
⋈ a **junk bond** buyout, deal, dealer, holder, market; buy, deal in, issue, sell **junk bonds**
syn junk

---

junk mail *noun*
unwanted advertising delivered by post: *We are always receiving junk mail.*

/ˈdʒʌŋk meɪl/
note not used with *a* or *an*. No plural and used with a singular verb only.
⋈ deliver, receive, send, throw away **junk mail**
▶ **mail[1] 1**

---

juristic person *noun* (law)
▶ **artificial person**

/dʒʊəˌrɪstɪk ˈpɜːsn/

---

juror *noun* (law)
a member of a jury: *A jury usually consists of twelve jurors.*

/ˈdʒʊərə(r)/
pl jurors
⋈ act as a **juror**

---

jury *noun* (law)
a group of people in a lawcourt, chosen from members of the public, who decide the facts in a case and whether the accused is guilty or not guilty: *The jury found the accused guilty/not guilty.* ○ *The jury is/are still deciding.* ○ *She was called up for jury service* (ie to be a member of a jury).

/ˈdʒʊəri/
pl juries
note used with a singular or a plural verb
⋈ the **jury's** decision, verdict; trial by **jury**
▶ **counsel**

Justice *noun* (law)
(*UK*) the title given to all judges of the High Court: *Mr Justice Richards* ○ *Mrs Justice Green*

/ˈdʒʌstɪs/
abbr J
pl Justices
abbr JJ

K *abbr*
1 (*computing*) kilobyte: *This computer has a thousand K memory.*
2 one thousand: *Her salary is over £20 K.*

/keɪ/
(also **k**)
► **byte, megabyte**

---

keelage *noun* (shipping)
the fee paid by a ship owner to dock in a certain port: *They were unable to dock in that port because keelage was too expensive.*

/ˈkiːlɪdʒ/
note not used with *a* or *an*. No plural and used with a singular verb only.
► **moorage, wharfage**

---

keep *verb*
1 (*commerce*) to own or manage something: *to keep a shop* ○ *She kept a restaurant in the centre of town.* **2** (*sales*) to have available for sale; to have in stock: *We do not keep large sizes.* ○ *I'll have to order it, we don't keep those in stock.* **3** (*sales*) to remain in good condition: *The food must be sold today, it won't keep.*

keep abreast (of something) to stay informed of events, changes, plans, etc: *It is important to keep abreast of technological developments.* ○ *May I come to the meeting? I like to keep abreast of what's going on.*

keep someone on to continue to employ someone: *The company could not afford to keep him on.*

/kiːp/
keep, keeping, kept
1 note transitive verb
⧓ **keep** a pub, shop, restaurant
2 note transitive verb
► **stock**[3]
3 note intransitive verb

---

key[1] *noun* (computing)
the buttons on a computer or typewriter which are pressed to use it: *Press this key to delete the word.* ○ *The keys with arrows on allow you to move text up and down the computer screen.* ○ *The keys on an electric typewriter are much easier to press.*

/kiː/
pl keys
⧓ hold down, press, release a **key**

---

key[2] *verb* (computing)
to use the keys on a computer or word processor: *Please key (in) this letter.* ○ *Have you finished keying that report yet?*

/kiː/
key, keying, keyed
note transitive verb
⧓ **key** in (something), (something) in
► **type**[2]

---

key[3] *adjective*
very important; essential: *This deal will give us a key advantage over foreign competitors.* ○ *The manufacture of electronic equipment is a key industry in Japan.*

/kiː/
⧓ a **key** business, industry, sector

---

keyboard[1] *noun* (computing)
the set of keys on a computer, word processor or typewriter: *He does most of his writing at a keyboard.* ○ *I got fed up with sitting at the keyboard all day.*

/ˈkiːbɔːd/
pl keyboards
⧓ a computer, typewriter **keyboard**
► **cursor, qwerty**

---

keyboard[2] *verb* (computing/office practice)
to do work on a computer or word processor using a keyboard: *Have you finished keyboarding the information?* ○ *We need to get the report keyboarded before the conference.*

/ˈkiːbɔːd/
keyboard, keyboarding, keyboarded
note transitive verb
► **type**[2]

---

keyboarder *noun* (computing/office practice)
a person who does work on a computer or word processor using

/ˈkiːbɔːdə(r)/
pl keyboarders
⧓ work as a **keyboarder**

a keyboard: *employ someone as a keyboarder* ○ *advertise for a keyboarder*

▶ **key[2], audio-typist, copy-typist, shorthand typist, typist**

---

keyed advertisement *noun* (advertising)

an advertisement that has a code printed on its reply coupon identifying the magazine or newspaper where it appeared. The advertiser can then check which magazines are the most useful source of advertising: *The company are placing keyed advertisements to help with market research.*

/ˌkiːd ədˈvɜːtɪsmənt/

pl keyed advertisements

⋈ monitor, place a **keyed advertisement**

▶ **advertisement**

---

key person *noun* (personnel)

an important person in an organization, a project, etc: *We need to send a key person to this conference.* ○ *Who is their key person at the moment?*

/ˌkiː ˈpɜːsn/

pl key people

▶ **king-pin**

---

kickback *noun*

(*informal*) money paid to someone (often illegally) to obtain a favour or to persuade them to join in a business activity: *Most of the government were getting kickbacks from local businessmen.*

/ˈkɪkbæk/

pl kickbacks

⋈ give, receive, take a **kickback**

▶ **bribe[1]**

---

kilobyte *noun* (computing)

1 024 (2^{10}) BYTES used as a measure of computer memory or storage power: *The chip has a 64 kilobyte memory.*

/ˈkɪləbaɪt/

pl kilobytes

abbr K, k

⋈ **kilobyte** memory, storage

---

kiosk *noun* (retail/commerce)

a small shelter for selling goods outside, esp newspapers, tobacco, icecream, etc: *She bought a paper from the kiosk on her way to work.*

/ˈkiːɒsk/

pl kiosks

⋈ a newspaper, tobacco **kiosk**

---

kit *noun*

1 a set of articles, equipment, clothing, etc needed for a specific purpose: *Every workplace should have a first-aid kit.* ○ *We sell wine-making kits that contain everything you need for making your own wine.* **2** (*retail*) a set of parts sold together to be assembled by the buyer: *The furniture is sold in kit form.* ○ *a model aeroplane kit*

/kɪt/

pl kits

2 ⋈ bought, sold as a **kit**; bought, sold in **kits**

▶ **self-assembly**

---

kite *noun* (banking)

(*informal*) a bill of exchange that is signed by someone who pretends to act as a guarantor to help someone to raise money, but whose signature is actually worthless

/kaɪt/

pl kites

▶ **accommodation bill**

---

kite-flying *noun* (banking)

(*informal*) exchanging a worthless bill of exchange (a KITE) at the bank, knowing it will not be paid by the person on whom it is drawn: *Banks must always beware of kite-flying.*

/ˈkaɪt ˌflaɪɪŋ/

note not used with *a* or *an*. No plural and used with a singular verb only.

▶ **discounting, dishonour**

---

kite mark *noun* (quality control)

(*UK*) a sign, shaped like a kite, showing that a product has been approved by the British Standards Institution: *Always look for the kite mark when purchasing expensive goods.*

/ˈkaɪtmɑːk/

pl kite marks

▶ **British Standards Institution, International Standards Organization**

---

kitty *noun* (finance)
a small amount of money collected by a group of people for use in an agreed purpose: *There is no money left in the kitty.* ○ *a telephone kitty*, ie for paying a shared telephone bill

/ˈkɪti/
pl kitties
⋈ put money in, take money out of the **kitty**
► **float²**, **petty cash**

knocking copy *noun* (advertising)
words in an advert that criticize a rival product: *The advert containing knocking copy has been withdrawn.*

/ˈnɒkɪŋ ˌkɒpi/
note not used with *a* or *an*. No plural and used with a singular verb only.
⋈ print, write **knocking copy**
► **copy¹ 2**

knock-for-knock agreement *noun* (insurance)
an agreement between motor insurers not to claim payment for accident damage: *The introduction of a knock-for-knock agreement got rid of much unnecessary admin work.*

/ˌnɒk fə ˈnɒk əˌgriːmənt/
pl knock-for-knock agreements
⋈ make a **knock-for-knock agreement**

knock off *verb*
(*informal*) to stop work: *We usually knock off at 5.30.*

knock something off (*sales*) to take an amount off (the price of something): *The cover of this book is torn. Can you knock something off the price?* ○ *knock five pounds off the original cost*

/ˌnɒk ˈɒf/
note transitive and intransitive verb
⋈ **knock off** work
► **clock off**, **clock on**

knock-out agreement *noun* (commerce)
a secret agreement between dealers not to bid against each other at an auction: *An illegal knock-out agreement accounted for the unusually low prices at the auction.*

/ˈnɒk aʊt əˌgriːmənt/
pl knock-out agreements
⋈ establish, set up a **knock-out agreement**

knot *noun* (shipping)
1 a measure of the speed of a ship or of wind (one nautical mile per hour): *The top speed of the liner was 30 knots.* **2** a measure of the speed of wind: *We had wind gusts of up to 40 knots.*

/nɒt/
pl knots
1 ⋈ cruise at, travel at (a number of **knots**)
2 ⋈ blow at, gust at (a number of **knots**)

know-how *noun*
special knowledge or expertise, esp in planning something new: *It is essential to get someone with the right know-how before we start this project.*

/ˈnəʊhaʊ/
(also **knowhow**)
note not used with *a* or *an*. No plural and used with a singular verb only.
⋈ business, financial, technical **know-how**
► **expertise**

labor union (industrial relations)
(*US*) ▶ **trade union**

/ˈleɪbə ˌjuːniən/

---

labour *noun*
1 physical or mental work done by people: *The building work will require a lot of labour.* ○ *use machines to save on labour costs* **2** the whole group of people who work for a living: *The recession has caused the migration of labour.* ○ *There are an increasing number of young people leaving college and entering the labour market.*

/ˈleɪbə(r)/
(*US* **labor**)
note not used with *a* or *an*. No plural and used with a singular verb only.
▶ **casual, manual [1], work[1]**
2 ⋈ skilled, unskilled **labour**

---

labourer *noun*
a person who does heavy unskilled work: *He tried to find work as a labourer.*

/ˈleɪbərə(r)/
pl labourers
(*US* **laborer**)
⋈ an agricultural, a casual, a manual **labourer**
▶ **artisan, casual, craftsman, manual [1], worker**

---

labour-intensive *adjective* (industry)
needing a lot of people to do the work: *With many people employed at different stages, publishing is a labour-intensive industry.* ○ *Most office work is extremely labour-intensive.*

/ˌleɪbər ɪnˈtensɪv/
(*US* **labor-intensive**)
⋈ a **labour-intensive** industry, method

---

labour relations *noun* (industrial relations)
▶ **industrial relations**

/ˈleɪbə rɪˌleɪʃnz/

---

labour-saving *adjective*
of a machine or process that reduces the amount of work needed to do something: *A washing machine is a labour-saving device.*

/ˈleɪbə ˌseɪvɪŋ/
(*US* **labor-saving**)
⋈ a **labour-saving** device, method, system

LAN *abbr* (computing)
local area network: *The terminal was connected to the LAN.*

/læn/
note pronounced as a word

---

land[1] *noun*
1 (*economics*) ground or soil used for a particular purpose: *fertile agricultural land* **2** (*law*) property in the form of land: *How far does your land extend?*

/lænd/
note not used with *a* or *an*. No plural and used with a singular verb only.
1 ⋈ agricultural, arable, building, farming **land**
▶ **factor of production**
2 ▶ **property 2, real estate**

---

land[2] *verb*
1 (*transport*) to put passengers or cargo onto the land after a voyage: *We landed at Dover.* **2** (of a plane) to touch the earth's surface: *The plane has landed at Heathrow.* **3** (*informal*) to obtain: *She has landed a good new job.*

/lænd/
land, landing, landed
note transitive and intransitive verb

---

land agent *noun*
1 (*commerce*) a person who represents buyers and sellers of land: *The transactions were carried out by a land agent.* **2** (*agriculture*) the manager of a large estate: *Collecting rents is the responsibility of the land agent.*

/ˈlænd ˌeɪdʒənt/
pl land agents
1 ▶ **estate agent**
2 syn estate manager
▶ **agent**

---

land bank *noun*
the amount of land that a developer owns that is waiting to be developed: *The property group has a prime land bank and a strong sales position.*

/ˈlænd bæŋk/
note usually singular
▶ **agricultural bank**

landed *adjective* (import/export)
of the price of exported goods in which the exporter pays for transporting the goods and landing them at the port of destination but not for delivering them to the buyers, warehouse or factory, etc: *All prices quoted are landed.*

/ˈlændɪd/
▶ **free on board**

landing charge *noun* (transport)
a payment that must be made when a cargo arrives at the port of destination: *All landing charges must be paid before unloading.*

/ˈlændɪŋ ˌtʃɑːdʒ/
pl landing charges
⋈ pay a **landing charge**
▶ **light dues**

landing order *noun* (import/export)
(*UK*) a document issued by the Board of Customs and Excise allowing an importer to remove goods from a warehouse: *No goods will be moved without a landing order.*

/ˈlændɪŋ ˌɔːdə(r)/
pl landing orders
⋈ issue, receive a **landing order**
▶ **bond note, order[1] 1**

landlady *noun*
a woman who lets land, a building or part of a building to someone else (a TENANT): *The landlady lives in the same building.*

/ˈlændleɪdi/
pl landladies

landlord *noun*
a man who lets land, a building or part of a building to someone else (a TENANT): *The landlord reserves the right to increase the rent.*

/ˈlændlɔːd/
pl landlords

the Land Registry *noun* (law)
(*UK*) a government department that records information about all property in England and Wales: *When you sell your house you must pay a fee to the Land Registry.*

/ðə ˈlænd ˌredʒɪstri/
⋈ a **Land Registry** fee, office, record

land waiter *noun* (import/export)
(*UK*) a customs officer who examines goods at ports to ensure that all the correct taxes or duties have been charged and paid: *The cargo is about to be examined by a land waiter.*

/ˈlænd ˌweɪtə(r)/
pl land waiters
▶ **Board of Customs and Excise, customs**

language *noun*
1 system of sounds, words, patterns, etc used by humans to communicate: *study language development in young children*
2 language used by a particular group or country: *speak a foreign language* ○ *learn English as a second language* ○ *How many languages do you speak?* **3** the words and expressions used about a particular subject or area: *scientific, technical language* ○ *Some of this legal language is very hard to understand.* **4** (*computing*) system of coded instructions used to produce computer programs

/ˈlæŋgwɪdʒ/
1 note not used with *a* or *an*. No plural and used with a singular verb only.
2 pl languages
▶ **mother tongue**
3 note not used with *a* or *an*. No plural and used with a singular verb only.
4 pl languages
▶ **ALGOL, BASIC, COBOL, FORTRAN, machine language, PASCAL, programming language**

lapse of time *noun* (law)
one of the ways in which a contract may be ended if both parties delay beyond the period specified: *a contract discharged by lapse of time*

/ˌlæps əv ˈtaɪm/
▶ **breach of contract**

laser *noun* (technology)
a device that produces a strong and highly controlled beam of light: *Lasers are used in medicine to treat cancer cells.*

/ˈleɪzə(r)/
pl lasers
⧓ a **laser** beam, light

laser disk *noun* (computing)
a computer disk upon which information is stored and then read by a LASER: *Photographs and documents can be stored on a laser disk.*

/ˈleɪzə dɪsk/
pl laser disks
▶ **disk**

laser printer *noun* (computing)
a computer printer, that produces clear pictures or text using a LASER beam: *The publicity material is very high quality and has been made using a laser printer.*

/ˈleɪzə ˌprɪntə(r)/
pl laser printers
⧓ produced by, use a **laser printer**
▶ **daisywheel, dot matrix printer, letter quality printer**

last in, first out *noun*
1 (*industrial relations*) a situation where the last people to join a company are the first to leave if employers need to reduce staff: *He was dismissed according to the last in, first out principle.*
2 (*accounting/finance*) an accounting method where stock is valued at the price of the latest purchases: *The production costs were calculated on a last in, first out basis.*

/ˌlɑːst ˌɪn ˌfɜːst ˈaʊt/
note not used with *a* or *an*. No plural and used with a singular verb only
abbr LIFO
▶ **first in, first out, stock control**

last trading day *noun* (stock exchange/commerce)
the final day on which trading for a particular delivery period can take place: *The deal was finally transacted on the last trading day.*

/ˌlɑːst ˈtreɪdɪŋ deɪ/
▶ **Account Day, prompt day, settlement day**

lateral integration *noun* (industry)
▶ **horizontal integration**

/ˌlætərəl ɪntɪˈgreɪʃn/

launch[1] *noun* (advertising/commerce)
the introduction of a new product, an idea, a campaign, etc: *Because of production problems the launch had to be postponed.* ○ *a publisher's launch*

/lɔːntʃ/
pl launches
⧓ cancel, delay, get ready for, plan, prepare for a **launch**; a **launch** dinner, party

launch[2] *verb*
1 (*commerce/advertising*) to introduce a new product, an idea, a campaign, etc: *They spent thousands launching the new breakfast cereal.* ○ *launch a publicity campaign* ○ *launch a new magazine*
2 (*stock exchange*) to start a new company: *We have launched our new business on the stock exchange.*

/lɔːntʃ/
launch, launching, launched
note transitive verb
1 ⧓ **launch** a campaign, magazine, product
2 ▶ **float**

launder *verb* (finance)
(*slang*) processing illegally obtained money, eg by paying it into a foreign bank and transferring it to a local bank: *He was convicted of laundering money obtained from the sale of drugs.*

/ˈlɔːndə(r)/
launder, laundering, laundered
note transitive verb
⧓ **launder** money, profits

laundry *noun* (finance)
(*slang*) a bank or other financial organization used to deposit money that is obtained illegally: *The cash was processed in an offshore laundry.*

/ˈlɔːndri/
pl laundries

LAUTRO *abbr* (insurance)
the Life Assurance and Unit Trust Regulatory Organization: *Make sure the firm is a member of Lautro.*

/ˈlaʊtrəʊ/
note pronounced as a word

---

law *noun* (law)
1 a rule established by authority or custom that regulates the behaviour of members of an organization, a community, or a country: *A new law concerning the rights of employees came into force today.* **2** a body of such laws: *The company must act inside the law.* ○ *be on trial in a court of law/a lawcourt* **3** the profession or study of this: *She is studying law/for a law degree.* ○ *He practised law in London for a number of years.* **4** a generally accepted rule: *the law of supply and demand* ○ *the law of gravity*

/lɔː/
1 pl laws
2 note not used with *a* or *an*. No plural and used with a singular verb only.
⋈ civil, criminal, European, international **law**; break, enforce, obey the **law**
▶ **commercial law, company law, lawsuit**
3 note not used with *a* or *an*. No plural and used with a singular verb only.
⋈ **law** college, school
4 pl laws
▶ **law of diminishing returns, law of one price**

---

lawcourt *noun* (law)
▶ **court 1**

/ˈlɔːkɔːt/

---

lawful *adjective* (law)
allowed by the law; legal: *lawful trading*

/ˈlɔːfl/
⋈ a **lawful** practice, trade
opp unlawful

---

law of diminishing returns *noun* (economics)
a belief that, beyond a certain point, as more money and effort are put into something then the amount of profit or productivity no longer increases but is proportionally reduced: *The company's success cannot last, soon the law of diminishing returns will apply.*

/ˌlɔː əv dɪˌmɪnɪʃɪŋ rɪˈtɜːnz/
note not used with *a* or *an*. No plural and used with a singular verb only.
▶ **input, output**

---

law of one price *noun* (economics)
a generally accepted rule that without trade restrictions or transport costs the same goods will sell for the same prices in all countries: *The law of one price is linked to the belief in free trade.*

/ˌlɔː əv ˌwʌn ˈpraɪs/
note not used with *a* or *an*. No plural and used with a singular verb only.

---

law of supply and demand *noun* (economics)
▶ **supply and demand**

/ˌlɔː əv səˌplaɪ ənd dɪˈmɑːnd/
pl laws of supply and demand

---

the Law Society *noun* (law)
(*UK*) the professional organization for solicitors in England and Wales, controlling the education and regulating the standards of the profession: *He is being examined for misconduct by the Law Society.*

/ðə ˈlɔː səˌsaɪəti/

---

lawsuit *noun* (law)
the process of bringing a claim, a dispute, etc before a court of law for settlement: *bring a lawsuit against a drug manufacturer* ○ *a lawsuit between two oil companies*

/ˈlɔːsuːt/
pl lawsuits
⧓ to bring, file a **lawsuit**
► **action**[1]

lawyer *noun* (law)
a person who has studied law and whose job is to give advice on legal matters: *She is training to become a lawyer.*

/ˈlɔːjə(r)/
► **attorney, barrister, solicitor**

lay off *verb* (industry)
to dismiss workers for a period until more work is available: *A quarter of the workforce has been laid off.* ○ *The company has laid off a section of its employees.*

/ˌleɪ ˈɒf/
lay off, laying off, laid off
note transitive verb

lay-off *noun* (industry)
dismissing a worker for a period of time: *There has been an increase in the number of lay-offs this month.* ○ *a two week lay-off*

/ˈleɪ ɒf/
pl lay-offs
⧓ **lay-off** pay

layout
1 (*advertising*) the design of words and pictures in magazines, newspapers, leaflets, etc: *The graphic designer produced a new layout.* **2** (*industry*) the arrangement of the interior of a building: *The factory's layout has been designed for maximum efficiency.* ○ *Can you describe the general layout of the building?*

/ˈleɪ aʊt/
1 pl layouts
⧓ a final, rough **layout**; a magazine, newspaper, page **layout**
2 note usually singular
⧓ an exterior, interior **layout**

lay up *verb* (shipping)
to stop using a ship, a vehicle, a machine because it is damaged or there is no work for it: *The fleet has laid up three of its tankers.*

/ˌleɪ ˈʌp/
lay up, laying up, laid up
note transitive verb

LBO *abbr* (finance)
leveraged buyout: *The company was threatened by an LBO.*

/ˌel biː ˈəʊ/
pl LBOs

LC *abbr* (banking)
letter of credit: *Funds will be paid on receipt of an LC.*

note used in written English only
(also **L/C**, **l.c.**, **l/c**)

LCC *abbr* (commerce)
London Chamber of Commerce: *Our firm is a member of the LCC.*

/ˌel siː ˈsiː/

LCE *abbr* (commerce)
London Commodity Exchange: *She works in the LCE.*

/ˌel siː ˈiː/

LCL *abbr* (transport)
less-than-container (load): *The lorry with a cargo LCL.*

note used in written English only

ld *abbr* (transport)
load

note used in written English only

ldg *abbr*
1 (*transport*) loading: *Switch off engine when ldg.* **2** (*transport*) landing: *Remain seated till after ldg.*

note used in written English only

lead[1] *verb* (industry)
to be the first or in front of others: *We lead the market in software design.*

/li:d/
lead, leading, led
note transitive verb
▶ **market leader**

lead[2] *noun* (insurance)
the group (SYNDICATE) of Lloyd's underwriters chosen to accept the most responsibility for an insurance policy: *The broker tried to get a large syndicate to act as lead.*

/li:d/
pl leads

lead time *noun*
1 (*industry*) the time between placing an order and receiving the product: *The lead time on this item is two months.* **2** (*commerce/advertising*) the time needed for a consumer to make a decision to buy: *Threatening to take something off the market decreases a consumer's lead time.*

/ˈli:d taɪm/
pl lead times
⧓ a long, short **lead time**; decrease, increase, reduce the **lead time**

leaflet *noun* (advertising)
a piece of printed paper, usually folded and free of charge, advertising or providing information about something: *For more information, send for a free leaflet.*

/ˈli:flət/
pl leaflets
⧓ an advertising, a detailed, an explanatory, a publicity **leaflet**; pick up, produce, send for a **leaflet**

leakage *noun* (industry)
1 an amount of liquid lost from a container: *Much of the cargo was lost in leakage.* **2** an allowance made for the loss of liquid in transit: *The delivery will still make a profit even including leakage.*

/ˈli:kɪdʒ/
note not used with *a* or *an*. No plural and used with a singular verb only.
abbr lkge
▶ **ullage, vacuity**

lease[1] *noun* (law)
a written contract by which the owner of land or property gives another the right to use it for a specified period, usually in return for rent: *to grant a 99-year lease* ○ *When does the lease expire?*

/li:s/
pl leases
⧓ to grant, take on, take out a **lease**; a long, short **lease**
▶ **sublease, let[1], reversion, tenancy**

lease[2] *verb* (law)
to grant or obtain the use of property, land, machinery etc for a fixed period: *All company cars are leased from a local garage.* ○ *The offices are leased to an insurance company.*

/li:s/
lease, leasing, leased
note transitive verb
▶ **hire[1], let[2], rent[2]**

lease back *verb* (finance)
to sell property, machinery, etc for cash and then take it back on a LEASE: *They were short of cash so they sold the printing press and then leased it back.* ○ *The company owns a few high street properties that it could sell and lease back.*

/ˌli:s ˈbæk/
lease back, leasing back, leased back
note transitive verb

lease-back *noun* (finance)
an arrangement whereby property, machinery, etc is sold and then taken back on a LEASE: *We took the building back under a lease-back arrangement.*

/ˈli:s bæk/
pl lease-backs
⧓ a **lease-back** arrangement, deal

leasehold *noun* (law)
the right to own and use land for a specified period in return for payment of rent: *We hold the property under leasehold.*

leaseholder a person who has obtained land or property on a lease: *make an agreement with the leaseholder*

/ˈli:shəʊld/
pl leaseholds
⧓ acquire, buy, own, pass on, retain, sell, share the **leasehold**; **leasehold** land, ownership, property, tenure
► **freehold**

---

leave *noun* (personnel)
1 time absent from work or duty: *I can't attend the meeting because I shall be on leave next week.* ○ *She's taking a fortnight's leave.* **2** permission to be away from work: *He was given two days' leave to visit a sick relative.*

annual leave a certain number of days off with pay that an employee is allowed each year: *She has already used all her annual leave.*

compassionate leave days off with pay given to an employee who has suffered some misfortune: *She was given compassionate leave to go to her father's funeral.*

sick leave days off work with pay because of illness: *He took sick leave because he had flu.*

/li:v/
note not used with *a* or *an*. No plural and used with a singular verb only.
⧓ grant, take **leave**; be, go on **leave**
► **day off, holiday, maternity leave, paternity leave, vacation**

---

ledger *noun* (accounting)
a book in which a bank or company records its financial accounts: *write the accounts in the ledger* ○ *make a new entry in the ledger*

ledger clerk a person who writes accounts in the ledger: *be employed as a ledger clerk*

/ˈledʒə(r)/
pl ledgers
⧓ a customer, general, payroll **ledger**
► **bought ledger, nominal ledger, sales ledger**

---

legacy *noun* (law)
money or property left to someone in a will: *She received a substantial legacy from her grandfather on his death.*

/ˈlegəsi/
pl legacies
⧓ inherit, leave, receive a **legacy**
► **bequest, will**

---

legal (law) *adjective*
1 concerning the law: *the legal profession* ○ *seek legal advice*, ie consult a lawyer about something ○ *take legal action against someone*, ie sue or take them to court **2** allowed or required by law; lawful: *Customers have a legal right to demand a replacement or a refund for a faulty product.*

/ˈli:gl/
1 ⧓ **legal** affairs, issues
2 ⧓ a **legal** duty, obligation, requirement, right
opp illegal

---

legal aid *noun* (law)
(*UK*) a government scheme that pays legal fees for people who are poor: *She was able to get legal aid to help with the court case.*

/ˌli:gl ˈeɪd/
note not used with *a* or *an*. No plural and used with a singular verb only.
⧓ apply for, be eligible for, get, grant **legal aid**

---

legal expenses *noun* (law)
money paid to a lawyer for his/her services, esp as the result of a court case: *The court ordered him to pay all legal expenses.*

/ˈli:gl ɪkˌspensɪz/
note plural noun, used with a plural verb
syn costs, legal costs

---

legalize *verb* (law)
to make something legal: *legalize credit card parking meters* ○ *The Ministry of Agriculture has legalized food irradiation.*

/ˈli:gəlaɪz/
legalize, legalizing, legalized

(also **legalise**)
note transitive verb

legal person *noun* (law)
any person who has cetain legal duties or responsibilities, eg to obey the laws of the country in which he/she lives: *be classed as a legal person*

/ˌliːgl ˈpɜːsn/
pl legal persons
▶ **artificial person, natural person**

legal reserve *noun* (law/banking)
the minimum amount of funds that building societies and insurance companies must keep as security: *The building society attempts to keep well above the legal reserve.*

/ˌliːgl rɪˈzɜːv/
note no plural
▶ **reserve**

legal tender *noun* (finance/law)
a form of money that must be accepted if offered as payment: *The old pound note is no longer legal tender.* ○ *1p and 2p coins are accepted as legal tender up to a maximum of 20p.*

/liːgl ˈtendə(r)/
note not used with *a* or *an*. No plural and used with a singular verb only.
▶ **currency 2, tender[1]**

leisure industry *noun* (commerce/industry)
industry concerned with providing goods or services for holiday or spare-time activities: *A shorter working week led to the growth of the leisure industry.* ○ *With my last job as manager of a swimming pool and sports complex I gained experience of the leisure industry.*

/ˈleʒər ɪndəstri/
pl leisure industries
▶ **industry**

lend *verb* (finance/banking)
to give someone a sum of money on the understanding that it will be paid back with interest after a fixed period: *The bank agreed to lend her the money.*

/lend/
lend, lending, lent
note transitive verb
▶ **borrow, loan[2]**

lender *noun* (finance/banking)
▶ **moneylender**

/ˈlendə(r)/

lender of last resort *noun* (banking/finance)
the central bank of a country with responsibility for controlling the country's banking system: *In the UK the Bank of England is the lender of last resort.*

/ˌlendər əv ˌlɑːst rɪˈzɔːt/
note usually singular
⧓ act as **lender of last resort**
▶ **Bank of England, Federal Reserve Bank**

lessee *noun* (law)
a person who holds a piece of land or a building on a LEASE: *The lessee can be evicted for non-payment of rent.*

/leˈsiː/
pl lessees
▶ **tenant**

lessor *noun* (law)
a person who LEASES property or land to someone: *The lessor will not be responsible for any improvements.*

/leˈsɔː(r)/
pl lessors
▶ **landlord, landlady**

less-than-container load *adjective* (law)
of a delivery of goods which shares space in a container with goods belonging to others: *Take care in unloading because this is a less-than-container load.*

/ˌles ðən kənˌteɪnə ˈləʊd/
abbr L.C.L.

let[1] *noun*
a property that someone may use in return for payment of rent: *The classified section of the paper has many short term lets.*

/let/
pl lets
⧓ a long, short **let**
▶ **lease[1]**

let² *verb*
to allow someone to use a house, a room, an office, etc in return for payment of rent: *to let office space in the city centre*

/let/
let, letting, let
note transitive verb
▶ **lease², sublet, rent²**

letterhead *noun* (office practice)
the name and address of a person or an organization printed at the top of personal or office stationery; the part of the letter where this appears: *All necessary contact information is contained in the letterhead.* ○ *Remember to change the address on the letterhead.*

/ˈletəhed/
pl letterheads
⧓ a company **letterhead**
▶ **headed paper, logo**

letter of advice *noun*
1 (*commerce/banking*) a letter sent by the drawer of a bill of exchange advising the drawee that the bill has been drawn: *I sent the company a letter of advice warning them that they should be ready to accept payment.* **2** (*commerce*) a letter from a supplier to a customer giving useful information: *The company sent off letters of advice to all their foreign customers giving addresses of the company's agents abroad.*

/ˌletər əv ədˈvaɪs/
pl letters of advice
⧓ issue, receive, send a **letter of advice**

letter of allotment *noun* (stock exchange)
a letter sent in reply to a request for shares in a company that states how many shares someone has been given (ALLOTTED)

/ˌletər əv əˈlɒtmənt/
pl letters of allotment
⧓ issue, receive, send a **letter of allotment**
syn allotment letter
▶ **allotment, letter of renunciation**

letter of application *noun*
1 (*stock exchange*) a letter from a person asking for a stated number of shares in a company when shares are first issued: *Her letter of application was successful and she became a shareholder.*
2 (*personnel*) a letter written by someone asking for a job, usually in response to an advertisement: *We received over 300 letters of application for the post of sales manager.*

/ˌletər əv æplɪˈkeɪʃn/
pl letters of application
⧓ receive, reply to, send a **letter of application**
▶ **application, letter of regret**

letter of appointment *noun* (management)
a letter from an employer offering someone a job and giving information on pay, hours of work, etc: *Details of his salary and holidays were contained in the letter of appointment.*

/ˌletər əv əˈpɔɪntmənt/
pl letters of appointment
⧓ receive a, send **letter of appointment**
▶ **appointment 2**

letter of attorney *noun* (law)
▶ **power of attorney**

/ˌletər əv əˈtɜːni/

letter of credit *noun* (banking/commerce)
a letter from one bank to another bank, by which a third party, usually a customer, is able to obtain money: *I have arranged for my branch to send a letter of credit to the branch nearest the hotel.*

circular letter of credit a letter of credit which is addressed to all branches, correspondents and agents of the issuing bank: *The issuing branch sent out a circular letter of credit.*

confirmed letter of credit a letter of credit to which the paying bank has added its guarantee that payment will be made against presentation of certain documents: *The*

/ˌletər əv ˈkredɪt/
pl letters of credit
abbr LC, L/C, l.c., l/c
⧓ confirm, issue, receive, send a **letter of credit**
▶ **bank acceptance, bank draft, bank transfer, bill of exchange, credit¹ 3, promissory note, telegraphic transfer**

confirmed letter of credit forced the paying bank to honour the transaction.

direct letter of credit a letter of credit which the issuing bank addresses to one particular branch: *With a direct letter of credit money can be obtained at only one particular source.*

documentary letter of credit a letter of credit to which a number of other documents such as a bill of lading, an insurance certificate, etc have been joined by the exporter to obtain payment from the bank: *Money could not be obtained as the documentary letter of credit did not have an insurance certificate with it.*

irrevocable letter of credit a letter of credit that can only be cancelled with the agreement of the person expecting payment: *He insisted on an irrevocable letter of credit.*

limited letter of credit a circular letter of credit which can only be used in a certain number of places

traveller's letter of credit a document issued by a bank to a traveller whereby the traveller may receive money up to a stated amount from all the bank's agents abroad: *When the traveller's letter of credit is used up it should be sent back to the issuing bank.*

unconfirmed letter of credit a letter of credit in which the issuing bank gives no promise that it will accept bills drawn upon it: *This company will not accept unconfirmed letters of credit.*

---

letter of identification *noun* (commerce/banking)

a letter issued by a bank to a customer who has received a LETTER OF CREDIT ; it contains proof of the customer's identity and a specimen signature: *No circular letters of credit will be accepted without a letter of identification.*

/ˌletər əv aɪˌdentɪfɪˈkeɪʃn/

pl letters of identification

syn letter of indication

⋈ issue a **letter of identification**

---

letter of indemnity *noun*

1 (*commerce*) a letter stating that the organization issuing it will compensate the addressee for a specified loss: *The organization issued a letter of indemnity to all creditors.* **2** (*stock exchange*) a letter asking for a replacement for a lost share certificate and offering to compensate the company for any loss that might occur: *The company has received a letter of indemnity which has been countersigned by the bank.* **3** (*transport/export*) a letter issued by an exporter claiming responsibility for loss or damage to goods during shipment: *With the letter of indemnity the exporter was able to exchange his documents and receive payment.*

/ˌletər əv ɪnˈdemnəti/

pl letters of indemnity

⋈ countersign, issue, receive a **letter of indemnity**

▶ **indemnity**

---

letter of intent *noun*

a formal letter that states the writer's intentions on a particular issue. It is not a promise or contract, but shows that the writer is serious about a certain course of action: *I have sent a letter of intent to the company's solicitors.*

/ˌletər əv ɪnˈtent/

pl letters of intent

⋈ receive, send, write a **letter of intent**

---

letter of licence *noun* (commerce/finance)

a letter from a creditor to a debtor stating that the debtor has a fixed period in which to pay before legal action will be taken: *The letter of licence from our creditors gave us time to find the necessary funds.*

/ˌletər əv ˈlaɪsns/

pl letters of licence

⋈ issue, receive, send a **letter of licence**

▶ **judgment note**

---

letter of lien *noun* (banking/commerce)
a document signed by a debtor allowing a creditor to sell the debtor's property if payment is not made: *The bank asked for a letter of lien as security for the loan.*

/ˌletər əv ˈliːən/
pl letters of lien
⧓ issue, receive, send a **letter of lien**
▶ **lien**

letter of regret *noun* (stock exchange)
a letter from a company stating that an application for an ALLOTMENT from a new issue of shares has been unsuccessful: *The company has had to send letters of regret to hundreds of applicants.*

/ˌletər əv rɪˈgret/
pl letters of regret
⧓ issue, receive, send a **letter of regret**
▶ **letter of application**

letter of renunciation *noun* (stock exchange)
a form on the back of a LETTER OF ALLOTMENT sent to someone who has asked for shares in a company. It must be filled in and sent back if the shares are no longer wanted: *If these shares are not required please use the letter of renunciation on the back.*

/ˌletər əv rɪˌnʌnsiˈeɪʃn/
pl letters of renunciation
⧓ issue, send back a **letter of renunciation**
syn renunciation form

letter quality printer *noun* (computing)
a printer that produces letters with clear dark print that are suitable for business correspondence: *Make sure you use the letter quality printer to print out those letters.*

/ˌletə ˌkwɒləti ˈprɪntə(r)/
pl letter quality printers
▶ **daisywheel, dot matrix printer, laser printer, near letter quality printer**

letters of administration *noun* (law)
(*UK*) a document, issued by a court, that appoints someone to be responsible for the estate of a dead person: *On receipt of the letters of administration she was put in control of the estate.*

/ˌletəz əv ədˌmɪnɪˈstreɪʃn/
note plural noun, used with a plural verb
⧓ grant, receive **letters of administration**

leverage *noun* (finance)
(*US*) ▶ **gearing**

/ˈliːvərɪdʒ/

leveraged buyout *noun* (commerce)
the buying of a company in which a small company borrows money on its own assets and those of the larger company it wants to buy in order to finance the takeover: *We are attempting a leveraged buyout of a much larger competitor.*

/ˌliːvərɪdʒd ˈbaɪaʊt/
pl leveraged buyouts
abbr LBO
⧓ attempt, complete, consider a **leveraged buyout**
▶ **employees' buyout, management buyout**

leveraged currency contract *noun* (finance)
an agreement between an investor and a currency dealer. The investor pays a deposit (a MARGIN) representing, eg 10% of the contract value. If the rate of exchange changes in one direction the investor will make a profit. But if the exchange rate moves in the other direction the deposit will be lost: *We made a leveraged currency contract because we were confident that the dollar would rise against sterling.*

/ˌliːvərɪdʒd ˈkʌrənsi ˌkɒntrækt/
pl leveraged currency contracts
▶ **contract[1], currency 1, foreign exchange market, margin 4**

levy[1] *noun* (tax)
a tax, charge or fine; the act of imposing and collecting it: *Oil spills are to be financed by a levy on oil importers.*

/ˈlevi/
pl levies
⧓ impose a **levy**
▶ **tax[1]**

levy² *verb*

1 (*tax*) to introduce and collect a tax, a charge, etc: *The government has levied a tax on cigarettes.* ○ *They aim to levy price increases for gas and electricity.* **2** (*law*) to seize property by order of a court of law: *The house has been levied by the courts.*

/ˈlevi/

levy, levying, levied

note transitive verb

► **tax²**

---

liability *noun*

1 (*law/finance*) the responsibility to settle a debt or make good a loss or damage: *The company has accepted liability for the damage to the cargo.* **2** (*law/finance*) **liabilities** money owed by a company; a debt: *The company does not have enough money to meet its liabilities.* **3** (*management*) a person or thing that brings loss rather than gain: *An unhappy workforce is a liability.*

/ˌlaɪəˈbɪləti/

1 note not used with *a* or *an*. No plural and used with a singular verb only.

⋈ accept **liability** (*for* something)

► **joint and several liability**

2 pl liabilities

⋈ insurance, pension, tax **liabilities**

► **asset, current liabilities, deferred liabilities, external liabilities, product liability, receivables**

3 note singular noun, used with a singular verb

---

liability insurance *noun* (insurance)

a form of insurance that pays any claims for damages that occur as a result of negligence by the insured person: *I have taken out a liability insurance policy.*

/ˌlaɪəˈbɪləti ɪnˌʃʊərəns/

note not used with *a* or *an*. No plural and used with a singular verb only.

► **product liability insurance**

---

liable *adjective* (law/finance)

1 responsible: *I am liable for the company's debts.* ○ *The bus company was held liable for the accident caused by one of its drivers.* **2** likely to attract: *Inheritances are liable to tax.*

/ˈlaɪəbl/

⋈ be **liable** *for* (something), *to* (something); be held **liable** *for* (something)

LIBOR *abbr* (banking)

London Inter-Bank Offered Rate: *We were offered a loan at one percent over LIBOR.*

/ˈlaɪbɔː(r)/

note pronounced as a word

---

licence *noun* (law)

an official document showing that official permission has been given to own, do or use something: *Applicants must hold a current driving licence.* ○ *The restaurant lost its licence to sell wine and spirits.* ○ *The builder was granted a licence to develop a site outside the town centre.* ○ *The trademark may only be used under licence.*

/ˈlaɪsns/

pl licences

(*US* **license**)

⋈ apply for, grant, issue, lose, obtain a **licence**

► **export licence, import licence, letter of licence, permit¹**

---

license *verb* (law)

to give formal permission for someone to own, do or use something: *The building plans have not yet been licensed.* ○ *Licensed products* (ie ones showing the name of a particular company) *cannot be sold without the manufacturer's permission.*

/ˈlaɪsns/

license, licensing, licensed

note transitive verb

---

licensee *noun* (law)

a person who has been given official permission to own, do or use something: *The brewery has appointed a new licensee to run the pub.*

/ˌlaɪsənˈsiː/

pl licensees

licensor *noun* (law)
a person or organization who grants a licence to someone: *The brewery acts as licensor in appointing a new manager.*

/ˈlaɪsnsə(r)/
pl licensors

---

lien *noun* (law)
the right to hold someone's goods, money or documents and keep them until a debt has been paid: *The bank held a lien on the customer's warehouse.*

general lien the right to hold someone's goods, money or documents as security for all their outstanding debts

particular lien the right to hold someone's goods, money or documents as security for only one particular debt

/ˈliːən/
note no plural
⋈ a shipowner's, solicitor's, warehouse-keeper's **lien**; have, hold a **lien**
▶ **letter of lien**

---

lienee *noun* (law)
a person whose property another person has the right to keep if a debt is unpaid: *The bank consulted the lienee before seizing his property.*

/ˌliːənˈiː/
pl lienees
▶ **lien, lienor**

---

lien on shares *noun* (stock exchange/law)
the right of companies to obtain and sell the shares of any members who owe money: *The company has exerted its lien on shares against all debtors.*

/ˌliːən ɒn ˈʃeəz/
note not used with *a* or *an*. No plural and used with a singular verb only.
▶ **share**

---

lienor *noun* (law)
a person who has the right to keep someone else's property if a debt is unpaid: *The bank acted as lienor in the recovery of the company's debts.*

/ˈliːənə(r)/
pl lienors
▶ **lien, lienee**

---

lieu *noun*
in lieu instead; in exchange for something else: *take a day off in lieu*, ie in exchange for working on a holiday ○ *take a cheque in lieu of cash*

/ljuː/

Life Assurance and Unit Trust Regulatory Organization *noun* (finance/stock exchange)
a SELF-REGULATORY ORGANIZATION that draws up and enforces codes of conduct for the control of life assurance companies and unit trusts

/ˌlaɪf əˌʃʊərəns ənd ˌjuːnɪt ˌtrʌst ˈregjələtri ˌɔːgənaɪˈzeɪʃn/
abbr LAUTRO
⋈ be ruled by, consult, refer to the **Life assurance and Unit Trust Regulatory Organization**
▶ **Financial Intermediaries, Managers and Brokers Association, Investment Management Regulatory Organization, Securities and Futures Authority, Securities and Investment Board, self-regulatory organization**

---

life assured *noun* (insurance)
the person upon whose death a payment is made, eg to a member of the family, according to a life assurance policy: *The life assured in this policy is not actually the owner.*

/ˌlaɪf əˈʃʊəd/
note usually singular
▶ **assurance, insurance**

life-cycle costing *noun* (accounting/industry)
a calculation of the real cost of a machine, including the cost of repairs needed during its working life: *According to the life-cycle costing, the more expensive model will be cheaper in the long run.*

/ˈlaɪf saɪkl ˌkɒstɪŋ/
note usually singular
abbr LCC
⋈ carry out a **life-cycle costing**
▶ **costing**

life estate *noun* (law)
▶ **life interest**

/ˈlaɪf ɪˌsteɪt/

life expectancy *noun* (insurance)
the number of years that a person is likely to live. Life expectancy statistics are used to calculate insurance policies and mortgage rates: *Women have a higher life expectancy than men.* ○ *an average life expectancy of 58 years*

/ˈlaɪf ɪkˌspektənsi/
pl life expectancies
⋈ an average, a long, a short **life expectancy**
▶ **actuarial tables, mortality tables**

life fund *noun* (insurance)
money that is held and invested by an insurance company and used to meet insurance claims: *The insurance company has invested its life fund in a range of securities.*

/ˈlaɪf fʌnd/
pl life funds
▶ **fund[1] 1**

life interest *noun* (law)
the right to own or use land or property or take an income from it that ceases when the owner dies: *She only has a life interest in the estate and her family will not receive payment after her death.*

/ˈlaɪf ɪntrəst/
⋈ have, hold a **life interest**; a **life interest** *in* (something)
syn life estate
▶ **interest 3**

lifestyle *noun* (advertising)
the way people live. Manufacturers, advertisers and designers group people by their lifestyles and target their goods accordingly: *Our new range of convenience foods is aimed at people with a busy but healthy lifestyle.*

/ˈlaɪfstaɪl/
pl lifestyles
(also **life-style**)
⋈ an affluent, a comfortable, a stressful **lifestyle**

life tables *noun* (insurance)
▶ **mortality tables**

/ˈlaɪf ˌteɪblz/

life tenant *noun* (law)
a person who has the right to own, use or take an income from land or property during his/her lifetime: *Rent is to be paid to the life tenant.*

/ˌlaɪf ˈtenənt/
pl life tenants
syn tenant for life
▶ **tenant**

LIFFE *abbr* (finance/stock exchange)
London International Financial Futures and Options Exchange: *Sterling futures started weak on LIFFE, but rallied as the pound recovered its early losses.*

/laɪf, ˈlɪfi/
(also **Liffe**)
note pronounced as a word

LIFO *abbr* (industrial relations)
last in, first out: *The redundancies were made on a LIFO basis.*

/ˈlaɪfəʊ/
note pronounced as a word
▶ **FIFO**

light *adjective*
1 (*shipping/transport*) without cargo: *The plane took off light.* **2** (*stock exchange*) with very little buying and selling: *Trading on today's market was light.* **3** (*commerce*) (of weight) less than the proper amount: *The shopkeeper was fined for giving light weight.*

/laɪt/
2 ▶ **heavy market**

light dues *noun* (shipping)
money collected from ships entering a port: *The ship was unable to enter the port until light dues were paid.*

/ˈlaɪt djuːz/
note plural noun, used with a plural verb
▶ **landing charges**

lighter *noun* (shipping)
a flat-bottomed boat used for carrying cargoes from a ship to dry land: *The cargo was loaded into a lighter and carried to the shore.*

/ˈlaɪtə(r)/
pl lighters
abbr ltr.
▶ **barge**

light industry *noun* (industry)
▶ **industry**

/ˌlaɪt ˈɪndəstri/

Limited *noun* (law/stock exchange)
the word placed after the name of a limited liability company: *Swinburne and Cook Limited.*

/ˈlɪmɪtɪd/
abbr Ltd

limited company *noun* (commerce)
a company whose members are only responsible for its debts up to a limited amount, usually the amount of unpaid shares: *The main reason for forming a limited company is to raise enough capital to run the business.*

/ˌlɪmɪtɪd ˈkʌmpəni/
pl limited companies
⧓ convert to, form, turn into a **limited company**
▶ **company, private limited company, public limited company**

limited letter of credit *noun* (banking/commerce)
▶ **letter of credit**

/ˌlɪmɪtɪd ˌletər əv ˈkredɪt/

limited market *noun* (stock exchange)
▶ **thin market**

/ˌlɪmɪtɪd ˈmɑːkɪt/

limited partner *noun* (management)
▶ **partner**

/ˌlɪmɪtɪd ˈpɑːtnə(r)/

limit order *noun* (stock exchange)
an instruction given by an investor to a stockbroker not to sell above or below a stated price: *The stockbroker has not yet received the client's limit order.*

/ˈlɪmɪt ˌɔːdə(r)/
pl limit orders
syn limit
▶ **day order, good till cancelled order, market order, order[1] 1**

line *noun*
1 a particular business or trade: *What line are you in?* ○ *My brother and I are in the same line of business.* **2** (*commerce*) a particular item sold or made by a business: *We are introducing a new line of video recorders.* ○ *The new lines will be displayed at the front of the shop.* **3** (*stock exchange*) a large quantity of a single security bought by one investor: *The line dealings took place over a long period of time.*

/laɪn/
1, 3 note usually singular
2 pl lines
▶ **above-the-line, assembly line, below-the-line, branch 2, off-line, on line, production line, range 1**

line and staff management *noun* (management)
a system of management in large organizations consisting of line managers and staff managers. The line managers are responsible for the main activities of the company such as manufacturing and sales, while the staff managers control the

/ˌlaɪn ən ˌstɑːf ˈmænɪdʒmənt/
note not used with *a* or *an*. No plural and used with a singular verb only.

support and service areas such as accounting, distribution, and personnel: *As the corporation grew a system of line and staff management was introduced.*

▶ **management**

---

line filling *noun* (industry)
creating new products in an existing range (LINE) to compete with rival companies: *The firm has brought out a variety of different washing machines, line filling in order to corner the market.*

/ˈlaɪn ˌfɪlɪŋ/
note not used with *a* or *an*. No plural and used with a singular verb only.

---

liquid assets *noun* (accounting)
available money or items that can easily be converted into money: *A large proportion of our clients have considerable liquid assets.*

/ˌlɪkwɪd ˈæsets/
note usually plural
syn realizable assets
opp illiquid assets
▶ **asset**

---

liquidate *verb*
1 (*finance/accounting*) to pay a debt: *The firm has liquidated all its debts.* **2** (*accounting*) to sell, to convert to cash: *The company has liquidated its assets.* **3** (*commerce*) to close a company that has stopped trading: *The organization has been liquidated.* ○ *The directors have liquidated the company.*

/ˈlɪkwɪdeɪt/
liquidate, liquidating, liquidated
note transitive verb
2 syn realize
3 ⋈ **liquidate** a business, a company, a firm, an organization
▶ **dissolve, wind up 1**

---

liquidation *noun* (finance/accounting)
the closing of a company that has stopped trading, usually because it has gone bankrupt. Liquidation may be voluntary or compulsory, ie ordered by a court. Any items of value (ASSETS) are assessed and these are sold to pay off the company's debts: *Our firm has gone into liquidation.*

/ˌlɪkwɪˈdeɪʃn/
note not used with *a* or *an*. No plural and used with a singular verb only.
⋈ be put into, go into **liquidation**
▶ **bankruptcy, declaration of solvency, receivership, voluntary liquidation, winding up**

---

liquidator *noun* (law/accounting)
the person appointed by the court to close a company and dispose of its assets: *One of the company directors was appointed liquidator.*

provisional liquidator a person appointed by a court to protect the interests of all parties involved when a company goes into compulsory liquidation: *The court appointed a provisional liquidator.*

/ˈlɪkwɪdeɪtə(r)/
pl liquidators
⋈ appoint a **liquidator**
▶ **administrator 2, official receiver**

---

liquidity *noun*
1 (*finance*) of assets that are easily turned into cash: *The liquidity of the company's assets is a bonus.* ○ *Liquidity is a sign of a safe investment.* **2** (*finance/accounting*) the availability of a company's cash: *We have a problem with the company's low liquidity.*

/lɪˈkwɪdəti/
note not used with *a* or *an*. No plural and used with a singular verb only.

---

liquidity ratio *noun* (banking)
▶ **cash ratio**

/lɪˈkwɪdəti ˌreɪʃiəʊ/

---

list *noun* (commerce)
a document containing information in a particular order: *The suppliers have sent their price list.* ○ *Do you have a list of items in stock?*

/lɪst/
pl lists
▶ **catalogue, checklist, free list, Lloyd's List and Shipping Gazette, mailing list, Stock Exchange Daily Official List, short list**

---

listed company *noun* (stock exchange)
a company whose shares are recorded on the main market of a stock exchange: *The shares are only in listed companies.*

/ˌlɪstɪd ˈkʌmpəni/
pl listed companies
syn quoted company
opp unlisted company
▶ **company, quotation 2**

---

listed securities *noun* (stock exchange)
shares, stocks and equities that are recorded on the official list produced by a stock exchange: *Members of the Stock Exchange only deal in listed securities.*

/ˌlɪstɪd sɪˈkjʊərətiz/
note usually plural
opp unlisted securities
▶ **quoted share, security 1, Stock Exchange Daily Official List**

---

list price *noun* (commerce)
1 the manufacturer's recommended retail price for an article: *The shop was selling goods above the list price.* **2** the price charged by a supplier to a retailer or wholesaler, before any discounts have been taken off: *negotiate a discount of 7% off the list price*

/ˌlɪst ˈpraɪs/
pl list prices
1 ⋈ the manufacturer's **list price**
▶ **manufacturer's recommended price, price[1]**
2 ▶ **retail price, trade price**

---

list renting *noun* (advertising)
giving a list of the names and addresses of potential customers to another organization for a fee. Advertising or marketing information is then sent to the people on the list: *They are an advertising firm which also carries out list-renting for manufacturers.*

/ˈlɪst ˌrentɪŋ/
note not used with *a* or *an*. No plural and used with a singular verb only.
▶ **mailing list**

---

lists closed *noun* (stock exchange)
the time when no more applications for shares in a new share issue are accepted: *I did not submit my application until after lists closed.*

/ˌlɪsts ˈkləʊzd/
note not used with *a* or *an*. No plural and used with a singular verb only.

---

literature *noun* (advertising)
written information about something: *They have sent me all their company literature.* ○ *Advertising literature should be quick and easy to read.*

/ˈlɪtrətʃə(r)/
note not used with *a* or *an*. No plural and used with a singular verb only.
⋈ manufacturer's, official, promotional **literature**
▶ **sales literature**

---

litigant *noun* (law)
a person who is involved in a lawsuit either as the person who has brought a legal action against someone (the PLAINTIFF) or as the person accused (the DEFENDANT): *a litigant in a civil court case*

/ˈlɪtɪɡənt/
pl litigants

---

litigate *verb* (law)
to be involved or contest a claim in a lawsuit: *Both parties agreed to settle their claim out of court rather than litigate.* ○ *litigate a claim against someone for negligence*

/ˈlɪtɪgeɪt/
litigate, litigating, litigated
note transitive and intransitive verb
⋈ **litigate** a claim, an issue, a point

litigation *noun* (law)
1 a lawsuit: *be involved in a litigation* **2** the process of taking legal action: *take a dispute to litigation*

/ˌlɪtɪˈgeɪʃn/
2 pl litigations
1 note not used with *a* or *an*. No plural and used with a singular verb only.
► **action**[1]

live-in *adjective*
living at a place of work: *a live-in caretaker* ○ *It's a live-in job.*

/ˈlɪv ɪn/
⋈ a **live-in** gardener, nanny

livelihood *noun*
a way of earning a living; an income: *The building trade is his livelihood.* ○ *Farmers depend on good weather for their livelihood.*

/ˈlaɪvlihʊd/
note usually singular
► **living, occupation**

livery *noun* (commerce)
(*UK*) distinctive colours or designs used on aircraft, vehicles, products, etc belonging to a particular organization: *The lorry was painted in the company's livery.*

/ˈlɪvəri/
pl liveries
► **logo**

livestock *noun* (agriculture)
live animals kept by farmers as a source of income: *The price of livestock has decreased.* ○ *a mixed farm with grass, livestock and crops*

/ˈlaɪvstɒk/
note not used with *a* or *an*. No plural and used with a singular verb only.
⋈ a **livestock** farmer; breed, feed, keep **livestock**

living *noun*
a means of earning money to buy the things you need: *What do you do for a living?* ○ *earn a living as a journalist*

/ˈlɪvɪŋ/
note usually singular
⋈ earn a **living**
► **cost of living, livelihood, standard of living**

living wage *noun* (personnel)
enough income to pay for the necessities of life: *She is not paid even a living wage.*

/ˌlɪvɪŋ ˈweɪdʒ/
note singular noun, used with a singular verb
⋈ offer, pay, receive a **living wage**
► **wage**

Llds *abbr* (insurance)
Lloyds: *Please consult Llds for the premium.*

note used in written English only

Lloyd's agent *noun* (insurance/shipping)
a representative of Lloyd's situated in a port to carry out Lloyd's insurance business: *The first person to be informed of the wreck was the Lloyd's agent in the port.*

/ˌlɔɪdz ˈeɪdʒənt/
pl Lloyd's agents
► **agent, Lloyd's of London**

Lloyd's associate *noun* (insurance)
a non-member of Lloyd's who needs to visit the Underwriting Room and is made an associate member for this purpose: *He was made a Lloyd's associate for the duration of the visit.*

/ˌlɔɪdz əˈsəʊʃiət/
pl Lloyd's associates
▶ **Lloyd's of London**

Lloyd's List and Shipping Gazette *noun* (insurance)
a daily paper published by Lloyd's giving information about the movement of ships, aircraft accidents, etc: *The necessary information can be found in Lloyd's List and Shipping Gazette.*

/ˌlɔɪdz ˌlɪst ənd ˌʃɪpɪŋ ɡəˈzet/
▶ **Lloyd's of London**

Lloyd's Loading List *noun* (insurance)
a weekly paper published by Lloyd's listing all ships that are, or will be, loading cargoes in British and continental ports: *Exporters are able to find a carrier from Lloyd's loading list.*

/ˌlɔɪdz ˈləʊdɪŋ lɪst/
⧓ consult **Lloyd's Loading List**
▶ **Lloyd's of London**

Lloyd's name *noun* (insurance)
a member of a group (a SYNDICATE) of people at Lloyd's who provide capital for insurance risks underwritten by Lloyd's and who share in the profits or losses: *Many wealthy people seek to be Lloyd's names as an alternative form of investment.*

/ˌlɔɪdz ˈneɪm/
pl Lloyd's names
syn name
▶ **Lloyd's of London**

Lloyd's of London *noun* (insurance)
an association of underwriters and insurance brokers. Lloyd's itself does not accept insurance risks but regulates the activities of its members. The business comes from Lloyd's brokers who are in contact with the public and the insurance is underwritten by syndicates of Lloyd's underwriters who are approached by the brokers, but do not deal directly with the public. ○ *Lloyd's of London deal with all high-risk insurance, but especially marine, aircraft and motor insurance.*

/ˌlɔɪdz əv ˈlʌndən/
syn Lloyd's
abbr Llds
▶ **syndicate, underwriter**

Lloyd's Register of Shipping *noun* (insurance)
an association that sets standards for the maintenance and classification of ships: *Every new ship must be built according to Lloyd's Register of Shipping.*

/ˌlɔɪdz ˌredʒɪstər əv ˈʃɪpɪŋ/
abbr LR
▶ **A1, Lloyd's of London**

Lloyd's Room *noun* (insurance)
the hall of Lloyd's in Lime Street, London where underwriters meet brokers to do business: *Nearly all business is transacted in Lloyd's Room.*

/ˌlɔɪdz ˈrʊm/
▶ **Lloyd's of London, broker, underwriter**

Lloyd's surveyor *noun* (insurance/shipping)
a qualified engineer appointed by Lloyd's to observe the building and repair of ships: *All repair work must be carried out under the eyes of the Lloyd's surveyor.*

/ˌlɔɪdz səˈveɪə(r)/
pl Lloyd's surveyors
▶ **Lloyd's of London, Lloyd's Register of Shipping**

Lloyd's underwriter *noun* (insurance)
a member of Lloyd's of London who examines a risk and works out the premium to be charged for insurance: *She works as a Lloyd's underwriter.*

/ˌlɔɪdz ˈʌndəraɪtə(r)/
pl Lloyd's underwriters
▶ **underwriter**

LME *abbr* (commerce)
London Metal Exchange: *The firm trades at the L.M.E.*

/ˌel em ˈiː/
note pronounced as individual letters

load[1] *noun*
1 (*transport*) a thing that is being carried or to be carried: *The lorry stopped to pick up a load.* **2** (*agriculture*) a measure of corn:

/ləʊd/
pl loads
1 abbr ld, lds

The price of a load has gone up. **3** (*industry*) the amount of work a machine has to do: *a machine load* **4** (*industry*) an amount of weight supported by a structure: *a load-bearing wall*

⋈ a lorry, plane, ship **load**; deliver, pick up, transport a **load**

► **workload**

---

load² *verb*

1 (*distribution*) to put goods into or onto a container: *load cargo onto a ship* ○ *the lorry is still loading* **2** (*computing*) to put data into a computer: *It is necessary to load the program first.*

/ləʊd/

load, loading, loaded

abbr ldg

note transitive and intransitive verb

1 ⋈ **load** a lorry, cargo, ship

2 ⋈ **load** a disk, a program, software; **load** something *onto* a computer

► **input 2**

---

loader *noun* (shipping)

a ship that is taking cargo or passengers on board: *a Pacific loader*

/ˈləʊdə(r)/

pl loaders

► **barge, lighter**

---

loading *noun* (insurance)

an extra sum added to a life assurance premium for management expenses: *This is the total premium excluding loading.*

/ˈləʊdɪŋ/

note not used with *a* or *an*. No plural and used with a singular verb only.

► **back loading, bonus 2, front loading, life assurance, weighting**

---

load line *noun* (shipping)

one of a series of lines painted on the hull of a cargo ship, showing how far it may be immersed in water in different conditions, ie summer or winter, fresh or salt water: *Some of the cargo must be taken off as the ship has sunk below the load line.*

/ˈləʊd laɪn/

pl load lines

syn Plimsoll line

► **water-line**

---

loan¹ *noun* (finance)

something lent, usually money, on the condition it will be paid back after an agreed period with interest: *pay interest on a loan* ○ *ask the bank for a loan/ask for a bank loan*

on loan lent or being borrowed: *This computer isn't mine, it's on loan from the finance department.*

/ləʊn/

pl loans

⋈ arrange, repay, take out a **loan**; a **loan** agreement, repayment

► **back to back loan, bank loan, bridging loan, day-to-day loan, hard loan, personal loan, secured loan, soft loan, syndicated loan, unsecured debenture**

---

loan² *verb* (finance)

to give someone a sum of money on the understanding that it will be paid back with interest after a fixed period: *The bank will loan me the necessary capital.*

/ləʊn/

loan, loaning, loaned

note transitive verb. **Loan** is often used in American English. In British English it is used as a more formal word than **lend**.

⋈ **loaned** *by* (a bank)

► **borrow, lend**

---

loan capital *noun* (finance)
the part of a company's money that is borrowed and has to be repaid at a later date. It is used for the everyday activities of the business: *Loan capital can be repaid when the company has funds.*

/ˈləʊn ˌkæpɪtl/
note not used with *a* or *an*. No plural and used with a singular verb only.
⧓ pay interest on, repay **loan capital**
syn debt capital
▶ **capital, share capital**

loan market *noun* (finance)
the part of the capital market which lends money to governments, finance houses and businesses: *The government has been forced to consult the loan market.*

/ˈləʊn ˌmɑːkɪt/
pl loan markets
⧓ a domestic, foreign **loan market**
▶ **capital market, market[1], money market**

loan note *noun* (stock exchange/finance)
a form of DEBENTURE STOCK where the investor takes a note as opposed to cash to avoid paying tax on the loan immediately: *Loan notes are usually repayable on demand.*

/ˈləʊn nəʊt/
pl loan notes
⧓ a **loan note** scheme

loan shark *noun* (finance)
(*informal*) ▶ **shark**

/ˈləʊn ʃɑːk/

loan stock *noun* (stock exchange)
▶ **debenture stock**

/ˈləʊn stɒk/

loan value *noun* (insurance)
▶ **surrender value**

/ˈləʊn ˌvæljuː/

local area network *noun* (computing)
a system of links between computers, limited to a specific geographical area: *The virus has infected the whole of the local area network.*

/ˌləʊkl ˌeərɪə ˈnetwɜːk/
pl local area networks
abbr LAN
▶ **wide area network, network[1] 2**

local currency *noun* (finance/international trade)
money belonging to a particular country, esp the money of a foreign country with whom a person or company is dealing: *pay in local currency* ○ *What are the goods worth in local currency?* ○ *Credit cards or local currency accepted* ○ *The prices are set in local currencies.*

/ˌləʊkl ˈkʌrənsi/
pl local currencies
⧓ accept, buy, deal in, exchange for **local currency**
▶ **currency 1, foreign exchange**

local time *noun* (transport)
the time in a particular part of the world: *We reach Delhi at 8.30 am local time.*

/ˈləʊkl taɪm/
note singular noun, used with a singular verb
abbr l.t.

lock up *verb* (finance)
to invest money so that it cannot easily be converted to cash: *Most of my capital is locked up in the property market.*

/ˌlɒk ˈʌp/
lock up, locking up, locked up
note transitive verb

loco *adjective*, *adverb* (commerce)
of the price of goods as located in the place specified, excluding any transport and loading charges: *All prices are loco Milan.*

/ˈləʊkəʊ/
⧓ **loco** price

lodge *verb* /lɒdʒ/
lodge, lodging, lodged

1 to live in another person's home and pay rent to do so: *I am lodging with a friend in London.* ○ *We're lodging the trainees with us at the moment.* **2** to present a statement about something formally: *lodge a complaint against the police* **3** place money or important items in a bank, etc for safe keeping: *The documents were lodged with the court until after the appeal.* ○ *lodge money with a bank*

1 ⋈ **lodge** *at, with*
note intransitive and transitive verb
2 note transitive verb
⋈ **lodge** something *against* someone
3 note transitive verb
⋈ **lodge** something *with* someone

---

lodgement fee *noun* (banking) /ˈlɒdʒmənt fiː/

an amount paid by the holder of a cheque when presenting it to a bank for payment: *The lodgement fee on this cheque has not yet been paid.*

pl lodgement fees
► **lodge 3**

---

logo *noun* (advertising) /ˈləʊgəʊ/

a symbol, design or group of letters used on stationery, packing materials, etc to advertise a particular company: *We have redesigned the logo to make it more eye-catching.*

pl logos
⋈ design, display a **logo**
► **brand name, livery, slogan**

---

log off *verb* (computing) /ˌlɒg ˈɒf/
log off, logging off, logged off

to stop work on a computer that is connected to a larger system: *Please ensure you log off when you finish work.* ○ *Have you logged off properly?*

note intransitive verb
syn log out

---

log on *noun* (computing) /ˌlɒg ˈɒn/
log on, logging on, logged on

to start work on a computer that is connected to a larger system: *You need a password to log on.* ○ *Are you logged on?*

note intransitive verb
syn log in

London Chamber of Commerce *noun* (commerce) /ˌlʌndən ˌtʃeɪmbər əv ˈkɒmɜːs/

the largest CHAMBER OF COMMERCE in Britain which aims to improve trading conditions, encourage business and provide business qualifications: *New trade figures were published today by the London Chamber of Commerce.*

abbr LCC
► **chamber of commerce, International Chamber of Commerce**

London FOX *noun* (commerce) /ˌlʌndən ˈfɒks/

the London Futures and Options Exchange. The main market for raw goods imported from tropical countries: *Coffee and cocoa are traded at the London FOX.*

► **actuals, Baltic Exchange, exchange[1] 2, futures market, London International Financial Futures and Options Exchange, London Metal Exchange**

London Gazette *noun* (law/banking) /ˌlʌndən gəˈzet/

an official weekly newspaper giving information about companies: *All information concerning bankruptcies must be published in the London Gazette.*

London Inter-Bank Offered Rate *noun* (banking)
the rate of interest that London banks offer each other: *The interest rate is 1% above the London Inter-Bank Offered Rate.*

/ˌlʌndən ˌɪntəbæŋk ˈɒfəd reɪt/
abbr LIBOR

London International Financial Futures and Options Exchange *noun* (stock exchange)
a financial FUTURES MARKET that deals in futures and option contracts relating to interest rates and exchange rates: *A wide range of futures and options are traded on the London International Financial Futures and Options Exchange.*

/ˌlʌndən ɪntəˌnæʃnəl faɪˌnænʃl ˌfjuːtʃəz ənd ˈɒpʃnz ɪksˌtʃeɪndʒ/
abbr LIFFE
► **actuals, the Baltic Exchange, exchange[1] 2, futures market, London FOX, London Metal Exchange**

London Metal Exchange *noun* (commerce)
the main COMMODITY MARKET in Britain for dealing in metals for which the price is agreed in advance and goods are delivered at a future date: *The London Metal Exchange deals with copper, lead, tin and zinc but not iron.*

/ˌlʌndən ˈmetl ɪksˌtʃeɪndʒ/
abbr LME
► **actuals, the Baltic Exchange, exchange[1] 2, futures market, London Fox, London International Financial Futures and Options Exchange**

London Stock Exchange *noun* (stock exchange)
► **International Stock Exchange**

/ˌlʌndən ˈstɒk ɪksˌtʃeɪndʒ/

long-dated securities *noun* (stock exchange)
► **longs**

/ˌlɒŋ ˌdeɪtɪd sɪˈkjʊərətiz/

long exchange *noun* (banking)
a foreign bill of exchange that will not be ready for payment for 60 or 90 days: *The bill is a long exchange and is not payable yet.*

/ˌlɒŋ ɪksˈtʃeɪndʒ/
pl long exchanges
► **exchange[2] 2**

long position *noun* (stock exchange)
► **bull position**

/ˈlɒŋ pəˌsɪʃn/

longs *noun* (stock exchange)
1 investments such as gilts and other fixed-interest securities that will be repaid in more than 15 years' time: *He has placed his money in longs as a long-term investment.* **2** securities, commodities, currencies, etc held in a bull position

/lɒŋz/
note plural noun, used with a plural verb
1 ⋈ invest in **longs**
syn long-dated securities
► **fixed interest securities, gilts, mediums, shorts 1**
2 ⋈ buy, sell **longs**
► **bull position**

long-term liabilities *noun* (accounting)
► **deferred liabilities**

/ˌlɒŋ tɜːm laɪəˈbɪlətiz/

loro account *noun* (banking)
an account held by a bank with another bank, usually overseas: *credit the loro account of the bank to which funds are being transported*

/ˈlɒrəʊ əˌkaʊnt/
pl loro accounts
► **account[1] 2, nostro account, vostro account**

lorry *noun* (transport)
a large motor vehicle for carrying goods: *The building materials will be transported by lorry.* ○ *deliver a lorry load of sand*

/ˈlɒri/
pl lorries
⧓ an articulated, a container **lorry**; a **lorry** driver

loss *noun*
1 (*accounting/finance*) money lost in a business deal; a financial deficit: *The travel company reported a loss of £4.4 million.* ○ *Small businesses have suffered substantial losses in recent years.* **2** a person or a thing lost; the act of losing something: *The factory closed down with a loss of 500 jobs.* ○ *The company agreed to compensate the employees for loss of earnings.* **3** (*insurance*) damaged or stolen property for which the cost of replacing it is paid by an insurance company: *The marine insurance covers loss or damage due to storms or collision.* ○ *insure against loss*

make a loss to lose money rather than make a profit: *If I reduce the price any more, I'll make a loss.* ○ *He made a loss of £500.*

sell something at a loss to sell something for less money than it cost to buy: *I had to sell the car at a loss to get rid of it quickly.*

/lɒs/
1 pl losses
⧓ make, report, suffer a **loss**
▶ **actual loss, deficit, gain[1], net loss, paper loss, profit[1] 1, realized loss, stop loss, tax loss, terminal loss, trading loss**
2 note singular noun, used with a singular verb
▶ **profit[1] 2**
3 note singular noun, used with a singular verb
▶ **partial loss, total loss**

loss adjuster *noun* (insurance)
the person appointed by an insurance company to assess an insurance claim: *The loss adjuster has produced an independent report on the claim.*

/ˈlɒs əˌdʒʌstə(r)/
pl loss adjusters
⧓ call in a **loss adjuster**
syn loss assessor
▶ **adjust 3, claims assessor**

loss leader *noun* (retail)
a product sold at a loss to encourage trade: *sell a particular brand of coffee cheap as a loss leader* ○ *Shops use loss leaders to attract customers.*

/ˈlɒs ˌliːdə(r)/
pl loss leaders
▶ **brand leader, market leader**

loss ratio *noun* (insurance)
the relationship between the total amount of money (PREMIUMS) received by an insurance company and the total amount paid out in insurance claims during a particular period: *The company requires a loss ratio of 50% to survive.*

/ˈlɒs ˌreɪʃiəʊ/
pl loss ratios
▶ **ratio**

lot *noun*
1 (*commerce*) a particular item or group of items to be sold at an auction: *Lot No 40.* **2** (*US*) a area of land: *a parking lot* ○ *a vacant lot*

/lɒt/
pl lots
▶ **job lot**

lot money *noun* (commerce)
the charge an AUCTIONEER makes for each lot sold: *The figure quoted does not include the auctioneer's lot money.*

/ˈlɒt ˌmʌni/
note singular noun, used with a singular verb
⧓ pay, receive **lot money**

low involvement product *noun* (advertising/retail)
a necessary item that a customer buys regularly and chooses quickly: *Soap powder and toothpaste are low-involvement products.*

/ˌləʊ ɪnˈvɒlvmənt ˌprɒdʌkt/
pl low involvement products
syn low involvement goods
▶ **brand loyalty, fast-moving consumer goods, impulse buying**

low loader *noun* (transport)
a vehicle with a low floor to carry goods under low bridges: *There are several bridges en route so we should hire a low loader.* ○ *The barge, which weighed over 36 tonnes, was taken on a low loader to the shipbuilders for restoration.*

/ˌləʊ ˈləʊdə(r)/
pl low loaders
⧓ drive, hire, use a **low loader**

LR *abbr* (insurance)
Lloyd's Register of Shipping: *Consult L.R. for shipping classifications.*

/ˌel ˈɑː(r)/
▶ **Lloyd's of London**

Ltd *abbr* (commerce)
Limited: *Hart and Russell Ltd.*

note used in written English only

lump sum *noun* (finance/commerce)
an amount of money that is paid at one time: *She was given a lump sum from the pension fund when she retired.* ○ *pay a lump sum into a building society account*

/ˌlʌmp ˈsʌm/
pl lump sums
⧓ invest, pay, provide, receive a **lump sum**
▶ **instalment**

luxury goods *noun* (commerce)
expensive items that are bought from choice and not necessity: *We sell perfumes, cosmetics and other luxury goods.*

/ˈlʌkʃəri ˌgʊdz/
note usually plural
⧓ buy, sell, trade in **luxury goods**; a **luxury goods** firm, manufacturer
▶ **consumer good, goods**

Mm

m *abbr*
1 mile(s): *10m* **2** male: *Please tick m or f.*

note used in written English only

machine *noun* (industry)
a piece of equipment with several moving parts, used for making things or doing a particular kind of work: *We have installed a new printing machine.* ○ *Remember to switch the machine off when you've finished.* ○ *One of the machines has broken down.*

/məˈʃiːn/
pl machines
abbr m/c, mch
⧓ a drilling, fax, welding **machine**; operate, run, switch on/off, turn on/off a **machine**

machine code *noun* (computing)
▶ **machine language**

/məˈʃiːn kəʊd/

machine-down time *noun* (industry)
time when no work is done because a machine has broken down: *Production costs were high because of extensive machine-down time.*

/məˌʃiːn ˈdaʊn taɪm/
note not used with *a* or *an*. No plural and used with a singular verb only.

machine-idle time *noun* (industry)
time when a machine is not used, eg because there are not enough orders or workers: *There was no work for the factory so there was a lot of machine-idle time.*

/məˌʃiːn ˈaɪdl taɪm/
note not used with *a* or *an*. No plural and used with a singular verb only.

machine language *noun* (computing)
a set of codes used in computer programming that are understood directly by a computer: *The program is written in machine language.*

/məˈʃiːn ˌlæŋgwɪdʒ/
pl machine languages
syn machine code
► **ALGOL, BASIC, COBOL, FORTRAN, PASCAL, programming language**

machine operative *noun* (industry)
► **machinist**

/məˈʃiːn ˌɒpərətɪv/

machine operator *noun* (industry)
► **machinist**

/məˈʃiːn ˌɒpəreɪtə(r)/

machine-readable *adjective* (computing)
of information that can be put directly into a computer: *machine-readable price labels on supermarket products* ○ *Is the data in machine-readable form?*

/məˌʃiːn ˈriːdəbl/
⋈ **machine-readable** data, information
► **bar code**

machinery *noun* (technology)
1 machines in general: *invest in new machinery* ○ *printing machinery* **2** the moving parts of a machine: *complex cutting machinery* **3** a system for getting things done: *the machinery of government*

/məˈʃiːnəri/
note not used with *a* or *an*. No plural and used with a singular verb only.
⋈ complex, modern, sophisticated **machinery**
► **plant 1**

machine shop *noun* (industry)
a place where machines are made or repaired: *The old press has been taken to the machine shop for repair.*

/məˈʃiːn ʃɒp/
pl machine shops
► **tool shop, workshop**

machine tool *noun* (industry)
a piece of equipment, that runs on electricity, used to do a particular job: *You need training to work the metal-cutting machine tool.* ○ *a computer-controlled machine tool*

/məˌʃiːn ˈtuːl/
pl machine tools
⋈ use a **machine tool**

machinist *noun* (industry)
a person who is employed to work a machine: *The factory employs ten qualified machinists.*

/məˈʃiːnɪst/
⋈ a skilled **machinist**
syn machine operative, machine operator
► **operative**

macro *noun* (computing)
a code that tells a computer to carry out a set of instructions so that each one does not have to be keyed separately: *set up a macro for instructions that you use frequently*

/ˈmækrəʊ/
pl macros
⋈ key in, set up, type in, use a **macro**

magazine *noun* (advertising)
a type of book with a paper cover that is published every week or month and contains articles, advertisements, photographs and stories by various writers: *a weekly, monthly, quarterly* (ie published every three months) *magazine* ○ *a computer, a women's, a trade, etc magazine* ○ *How often does this magazine come out?*

/ˌmægəˈziːn/
pl magazines
abbr mag
⋈ advertise in, edit, publish, read, write for a **magazine**; a **magazine** article
► **house journal, journal, periodical, trade journal**

magnate *noun* (industry)
a wealthy and important business person: *The newspaper magnate has bought another newspaper.*

/ˈmæɡneɪt/
pl magnates
⋈ a newspaper, an oil, a property, a shipping **magnate**
▶ **tycoon**

mail[1] *noun*
(*esp US*) **1** letters and parcels that have been sent or received by post: *I open my mail when I arrive at the office.* **2** the system for collecting and delivering letters and parcels: *Your letter must have got lost in the mail.* ○ *send a parcel by mail*

/meɪl/
note not used with *a* or *an*. No plural and used with a singular verb only.
1 ⋈ first-class, second-class **mail**; deliver, open, send, sort **mail**
▶ **post**[1] **1, junk mail**
2 ⋈ put a letter, etc in the, send a letter, etc by **mail**
▶ **airmail, direct mail, electronic mail, post**[1] **2, surface mail**

mail[2] *verb*
(*esp US*) to send letters, parcels, etc by post: *Please mail the cheque as soon as possible.*

/meɪl/
mail, mailing, mailed
note transitive verb
▶ **post**[2] **1**

mailing list *noun* (advertising)
a list of names and addresses kept by an organization so that potential customers can be sent information or advertising material: *Shall I put you on our mailing list?*

/ˈmeɪlɪŋ lɪst/
pl mailing lists
⋈ be *on* a **mailing list**
▶ **direct mail, list, mailshot**

mailing machine *noun* (office practice)
a piece of office equipment that automatically seals and stamps envelopes: *The letters have been put into the mailing machine.*

/ˈmeɪlɪŋ məˌʃiːn/
pl mailing machines
⋈ use a **mailing machine**

mail merge *noun* (office practice)
a program on a WORD PROCESSOR that adds names and addresses from a list to lots of copies of the same letter; the action of using this program

/ˈmeɪl mɜːdʒ/
pl mail merges
⋈ do a **mail merge**

mail order *noun* (commerce)
a system of choosing goods from a catalogue or magazine advertisement which are then sent out by post: *Most of the new office furniture was bought by mail order.*

/ˌmeɪl ˈɔːdə(r)/
note not used with *a* or *an*. No plural and used with a singular verb only.
abbr MO
⋈ buy, sell something by **mail order**; a **mail order** brochure, business, catalogue, form
▶ **direct sale, order**[1] **1**

mailshot *noun* (advertising)
advertising material that is sent by post to potential customers; the act of sending this: *The new firm sent out a mailshot to 20 000 people.* ○ *do a series of mailshots*

/ˈmeɪlʃɒt/
pl mailshots
(also **mail shot**)
⋈ do, send out a **mail shot**
▶ **circular, direct mail, mailing list**

main crop *noun* (agriculture)
the principal item grown by a farmer to provide income: *grow wheat as a main crop*

/ˌmeɪn ˈkrɒp/
pl main crops
▶ **cash crop, produce**[1]

mainframe *noun* (computing)
the centre of a computer network to which smaller computers are attached; any large computer system: *There was a fault with the central mainframe.* ○ *Information keyed into computers in offices throughout the country is stored and processed on the mainframe at the company's headquarters.*

/ˈmeɪnfreɪm/
pl mainframes
⋈ a **mainframe** computer
▶ **central processing unit, computer**

main market *noun* (stock exchange)
the primary market for buying and selling equities on the International Stock Exchange. A company that wants to enter this market must show audited trading figures for the last five years and must sell at least 25% of its shares to the public.

/ˌmeɪn ˈmɑːkɪt/
note no plural
⋈ buy, deal, sell, trade on the **main market**
▶ **International Stock Exchange, market**[1]**, third market, unlisted securities market**

maintain *verb*
1 to keep something in good condition or working order: *Are these machines expensive to maintain?* **2** to continue to do or have something; to keep something in existence at the same level, standard, etc: *We need to maintain the quality of our goods but not increase the price.*

/meɪnˈteɪn/
maintain, maintaining, maintained
note transitive verb
1 ⋈ **maintain** a building, car, machine, road, etc
2 ⋈ **maintain** quality, standards

maintenance *noun*
1 keeping something in good condition or working order: *The machines need regular maintenance.* ○ *building, car, machine, road, etc maintenance* **2** keeping something in existence at the same level, standard, etc: *price maintenance* ○ *the maintenance of safety regulations at work*

/ˈmeɪntənəns/
note not used with *a* or *an*. No plural and used with a singular verb only.
1 ⋈ **maintenance** bills, charges, costs, staff, work; regular, routine **maintenance**
▶ **upkeep**

majority interest *noun* (finance)
▶ **controlling interest**

/məˈdʒɒrətɪ ˌɪntrəst/

make[1] *noun* (manufacturing)
the name of the company that produced something; something made by a particular company: *It was an expensive make of computer.* ○ *What make is your car?* ○ *our own make*

/meɪk/
pl makes
⋈ a standard, well-known **make**
▶ **brand**[1]**, model**

make[2] *verb* (industry)
to produce or construct something; to manufacture: *We make components for the aircraft industry.* ○ *What material is it made of?* ○ *made in the UK*

make good to pay for, replace or repair something that has been lost or damaged: *make good a loss* ○ *All cracks in the ceiling will be made good.*

make out to write out something; to complete: *To whom do I make out the cheque?* ○ *Invoices should be made out in triplicate.*

make over to transfer the ownership of something to another person: *The firm was made over to his son.*

/meɪk/
make, making, made
note transitive verb
⋈ **make** something *into* something; **make** something *out of* something
▶ **manufacture**[2]**, produce**[2]

make up to put together; to complete: *The accounts have been made up to the end of the month.* ○ *make up an order*

---

mala fide *adverb* (law)
(*Latin*) dishonestly; intending to deceive: *The deal was conducted mala fide.*

/ˌmælə ˈfaɪdi/
► **bad faith, bona fide, good faith**

---

malfunction[1] *noun*
(*formal*) a failure in a machine; a fault: *The air crash was caused by a malfunction in the flight computer.*

/ˌmælˈfʌŋkʃn/
pl malfunctions
⧓ a technical **malfunction**

---

malfunction[2] *verb* (industry)
(*formal*) (of a machine) to fail to work normally or properly: *The data was incorrectly processed because the computer was malfunctioning yesterday.* ○ *What caused the machine to malfunction?*

/ˌmælˈfʌŋkʃn/
malfunction, malfunctioning, malfunctioned
note intransitive verb

---

man *verb*
to provide workers for something; to operate something: *The factory was manned by experienced workers.* ○ *Who is supposed to be manning the switchboard?*

/mæn/
man, manning, manned
note transitive verb
⧓ **man** something *with* someone
► **staff**[2]

---

manage *verb* (management)
to be in charge or in control of an organization, a department, a project, etc: *She manages our publicity department.* ○ *I manage a small advertising business.* ○ *He manages a team of 15 staff.*

/ˈmænɪdʒ/
manage, managing, managed
note transitive verb
⧓ **manage** a business, factory, shop; **manage** people, staff
► **control**[2], **run**[1] **1**, **supervise**

---

managed currency *noun* (finance)
a currency in which the EXCHANGE RATE is controlled by the government: *The country's central bank buys and sells on the foreign exchange markets to maintain its managed currency.*

/ˌmænɪdʒd ˈkʌrənsi/
note usually singular
⧓ have, maintain a **managed currency**
► **currency**[1]

---

managed fund *noun* (finance)
a fund made up of investments in a wide range of securities, that is managed by a life assurance company to provide low risk investments for the individual investor: *He has put his redundancy pay into a managed fund.*

/ˌmænɪdʒd ˈfʌnd/
pl managed funds
⧓ invest in a **managed fund**
► **fund**[1] **1**, **fund management, investment trust, unit trust**

---

management *noun*
1 (*management*) the control or organization of people, a business, a department of a firm, a project or a process: *financial, information, product, retail, staff management* ○ *The fall in profits was a result of bad management.* ○ *train new managers to develop their management skills* **2** (*management*) the people who control a company: *The management has/have decided to expand the firm.* ○ *The hotel is now under new management.* ○ *employ someone at management level* ○ *negotiations between trade union officials and management*

middle management (*management*) a group of managers each responsible for staff in a particular department who carry out

/ˈmænɪdʒmənt/
abbr mngmt
1 note not used with *a* or *an*. No plural and used with a singular verb only.
⧓ bad, good, poor, skilled, strong **management**
► **fund management, human resource management, line and staff management, personnel management, portfolio management, time**

the policies set by senior management: *provide more training in financial skills for middle management*

senior management (*management*) the highest officers in an organization, including the MANAGING DIRECTOR and other DIRECTORS or EXECUTIVES who make important decisions about company policy: *The decision would have to be made by senior management.* ○ *apply for a senior management position*

management, total quality management

2 note used with a singular or plural verb

⋈ at **management** level; a **management** decision, position, team, trainee

▶ **board 1**

---

management accountant *noun* (accounting)
a person who provides financial information and advice to managers to allow them to organize and develop the business in a profitable way: *regular financial reports prepared by the management accountant*

/ˈmænɪdʒmənt əˌkaʊntənt/

pl management accountants

▶ **accountant, cost accountant, financial accountant**

---

management audit *noun* (management)
an assessment of the work done by the managers of a company by a team of MANAGEMENT CONSULTANTS: *employ an independent consultant to carry out a management audit*

/ˈmænɪdʒmənt ˌɔːdɪt/

pl management audits

⋈ carry out a **management audit**

▶ **audit**

---

management buyout *noun* (management)
the buying of a company, esp one that is going bankrupt or about to be taken over by another company, by its managers who hope to use their knowledge of the company to make it more successful: *The takeover bid was beaten by a £2.6 million management buyout.*

/ˌmænɪdʒmənt ˈbaɪaʊt/

pl management buyouts

abbr MBO

▶ **employees' buyout, leveraged buyout**

---

management by exception *noun* (management)
a way of running an organization where managers concentrate on unexpected costs and events, so that management time is not wasted on planned, routine activities: *Management by exception leaves most of the operation to run as normal.*

/ˌmænɪdʒmənt baɪ ɪkˈsepʃn/

note not used with *a* or *an*. No plural and used with a singular verb only.

⋈ a policy, a system of **management by exception**

---

management by objectives *noun* (management)
a way of directing staff and assessing their work by setting tasks that must be completed within a certain time: *A management by objectives system was introduced to assess productivity.*

/ˌmænɪdʒmənt baɪ əbˈdʒektɪvz/

note not used with *a* or *an*. No plural and used with a singular verb only.

abbr MBO

⋈ a policy, a system of **management by objectives**

---

management consultant *noun* (management)
▶ **consultant**

/ˈmænɪdʒmənt kənˌsʌltənt/

---

management development *noun* (management)
the process of improving the quality and effectiveness of a manager's work by a series of training sessions and short courses: *attend a course in project management as part of a management development programme*

/ˌmænɪdʒmənt dɪˈveləpmənt/

note not used with *a* or *an*. No plural and used with a singular verb only.

⋈ a **management development** activity, program

▶ **development 1**

---

management information system *noun* (computing)
a computer system that allows useful information to be recorded, stored and used by managers without the help of a computer specialist: *Management information systems allow managers to plan production schedules and alter them if necessary.*

/ˌmænɪdʒmənt ɪnfəˈmeɪʃn ˌsɪstəm/
pl management information systems
abbr MIS
⧓ develop, use a **management information system**
▶ **information technology**

manager *noun* (management)
a person who is employed to control, organize and direct part or all of a business or organization: *The company has taken on a new marketing manager.* ○ *an advertising, an export, a factory, a hotel, an office, etc manager* ○ *She is the manager of the accounts department.*

an area manager a person responsible for products, services or staff in a particular country, town or region

department manager (esp in a shop or manufacturing company) a person in control of staff in one section of an organization: *the accounts, electrical, shoe department, etc manager*

deputy manager (esp in a shop or small business) a person in control of staff but under the authority of a manager

product manager a person who is in control of the design and quality of goods made by a company

production manager a person in control of the manufacturing process

rights manager a person who negotiates contracts and fees for buying, selling, distributing or reproducing goods, ideas, designs, etc in another country

/ˈmænɪdʒə(r)/
pl managers
abbr mngr
⧓ a general, line, middle, senior, staff **manager**
▶ **bank manager**, branch manager *under* **branch**, **boss**, **executive**, **foreman**, **sales manager**, **supervisor**, works manager *under* **works**

manageress *noun* (management)
a woman who runs a shop or restaurant: *She started work as a sales assistant in a shoe shop but soon became the manageress.*

/ˌmænɪdʒəˈres/
pl manageresses
note a woman who is in control of a business or part of a firm is called a manager
⧓ a canteen, hotel, restaurant, shop **manageress**

managerial *adjective* (management)
relating to the work of a manager: *employ someone at managerial level* ○ *apply for a managerial position* ○ *take a managerial decision*

/ˌmænəˈdʒɪəriəl/
⧓ **managerial** duties, skills, staff, work

managing director *noun* (management)
a company director who is responsible for the day to day running of a company: *be appointed managing director of a publishing company*

/ˌmænɪdʒɪŋ dɪˈrektə(r)/
pl managing directors
abbr MD, M.D.
⧓ assistant, joint **managing director**
▶ **director**

managing partner *noun* (management)
▶ **partner**

/ˌmænɪdʒɪŋ ˈpɑːtnə(r)/

man-hour *noun* (industry)
the amount of work done by one person in one hour: *The job took 10 man-hours.*

/ˈmæn aʊə(r)/
pl man-hours

manifest *noun* (shipping/transport)
a list of all the cargo or passengers carried by a ship or aircraft: *The manifest was signed by the captain after loading.*

/ˈmænɪfest/
pl manifests
⋈ a flight, passenger, ship's **manifest**
▶ **bill of lading, consignment note, shipping documents**

manning agreement *noun* (industrial relations)
an agreement between managers and workers represented by a union, on how many employees are required for a piece of work: *The dispute was settled when a manning agreement was reached.*

/ˈmænɪŋ əˌgriːmənt/
pl manning agreements
⋈ reach a **manning agreement**

man of business *noun* (law)
a person who has been appointed to act for another in legal matters: *She appointed her solicitor man of business.*

/ˌmæn əv ˈbɪznəs/
pl men of business
syn man of affairs

manpower *noun* (industry)
the number of people working or available for work in a country, a region or a particular industry: *We don't have enough manpower to accept any more orders.* ○ *The introduction of new technology has caused a manpower surplus.*

/ˈmænpaʊə(r)/
note not used with *a* or *an*. No plural and used with a singular verb only.
⋈ a **manpower** deficit, shortage, surplus
▶ **work-force**

manpower planning *noun* (management)
assessing the number of workers needed for a job, taking into account cost, skills, training needs, etc: *A manpower planning report recommended the reduction of the work-force.*

/ˌmænpaʊə ˈplænɪŋ/
note not used with *a* or *an*. No plural and used with a singular verb only.
⋈ carry out **manpower planning**
▶ **planning 1**

manual[1] *adjective* (industry)
done with the hands: *Building a road involves hard manual labour.* ○ *manual labourers employed on a building site*

/ˈmænjuəl/
⋈ a **manual** labourer; **manual** labour, work
▶ **casual, clerical, labour**

manual[2] *noun*
a book of instructions on how to use or repair a machine or carry out a specific task: *If you don't know how to switch on the machine, look it up in the manual.*

training manual a book that gives information about a company and its procedures, usually for new employees: *All new staff are given a training manual which they must read carefully.*

/ˈmænjuəl/
pl manuals
⋈ consult, refer to, use a **manual**; a car, computer, telephone system **manual**
▶ **handbook**

manufacture[1] *noun* (manufacturing)
the making of goods to sell from raw materials: *The company specializes in the manufacture of quality furniture.* ○ *car manufacture*

/ˌmænjəˈfæktʃə(r)/
note not used with *a* or *an*. No plural and used with a singular verb only.
▶ **industry, production**

manufacture[2] *verb* (manufacturing)
to make goods to sell from raw materials: *She works for a firm that manufactures electrical equipment.* ○ *These goods were*

/ˌmænjəˈfæktʃə(r)/
manufacture, manufacturing, manufactured

manufactured in France. ○ *the manufacturing industries*, ie those that make products

note transitive verb
► **make**[2], **produce**[2]

---

manufacturer *noun* (industry/manufacturing)
a person or organization that makes goods from raw materials: *Faulty goods should be returned to the manufacturer.* ○ *a car manufacturer*

/ˌmænjəˈfæktʃərə(r)/
pl manufacturers
⋈ buy from, supplied by the **manufacturer**
► **producer**

---

manufacturer's recommended price *noun* (manufacturing)
the amount that the consumer should pay for a certain product as suggested by the manufacturer. Retailers often charge less to encourage people to buy: *sell goods for less than the manufacturer's recommended price*

/ˌmænjəˌfæktʃərəz ˌrekəmendɪd ˈpraɪs/
note usually singular
abbr MRP, mrp
syn recommended retail price
► **list price 1**, **price**[1]

---

mar. *abbr* (shipping/insurance)
marine: *mar. insce.*

note used in written English only

---

margin *noun*
1 (*retail*) the difference between the cost price and the selling price of goods: *Margins are high because 30% of sales are the company's own brands.* **2** (*stock exchange*) the difference between the buying and selling price of a security: *The market maker placed a large margin on the securities.* **3** (*finance*) the difference between the rate at which money is borrowed by a finance house and the rate at which it is lent to a customer: *a high margin of interest on a car loan* **4** (*stock exchange*) money or securities left with a stockbroker to cover any losses made by the client: *The broker asked the client to increase the margin on a high-risk deal.*

/ˈmɑːdʒɪn/
pl margins
⋈ a high, low **margin**; **margins** fall, increase, rise, soar
► **gross margin**, **profit margin**

---

marginal costing *noun* (manufacturing/accounting)
a way of pricing goods by allowing for only the cost of labour and materials in the sale price: *use marginal costing to calculate the sale price*

/ˌmɑːdʒɪnl ˈkɒstɪŋ/
note not used with *a* or *an*. No plural and used with a singular verb only.
► **absorption costing**, **costing**, **overhead**, **total absorption costing**

---

marine *adjective*
1 (*shipping*) of, near, produced in or by the sea: *marine animals, biology, pollution* **2** (*shipping*) relating to ships, sea trade and navigation: *a marine accident* ○ *marine craft, engineering*

/məˈriːn/
abbr mar.
► **maritime**

---

marine insurance *noun* (shipping/insurance)
a form of INSURANCE for loss or damage to ships and cargo: *The company specializes in marine insurance.*

/məˌriːn ɪnˈʃʊərəns/
note no plural
⋈ a **marine insurance** broker, company
► **abandonment 2**, **average**[1] **3**, **free of all average**, **free of particular average**, **general average**, **Lloyd's of London**, **partial loss**, **running-down clause**, **total loss**, **with average**

---

marine syndicate *noun* (shipping/insurance)
► **syndicate**

/məˌriːn ˈsɪndɪkət/

---

maritime *adjective* (shipping)
1 of, situated or found near the sea: *maritime climate, port, province* **2** relating to ships, sea trade and navigation: *maritime traffic, transport, worker*

/ˈmærɪtaɪm/
► **marine**

---

maritime law *noun* (law/shipping)
a branch of national and international law relating to ships and commercial and navigational rights at sea: *The dumping of cargo is contrary to maritime law.*

/ˌmærɪtaɪm ˈlɔː/
pl maritime laws

---

mark *noun*
► **kite mark, trade mark**

/mɑːk/

---

mark-down *noun* (retail)
a reduction in the price of goods to encourage sales: *All the shops are introducing drastic mark-downs.* ○ *a mark-down price of 15%*

/ˈmɑːk daʊn/
pl mark-downs
► **gross margin, mark-up**

---

mark down *verb* (retail)
to reduce the price of goods to encourage sales: *All the prices in this shop have been marked down by 10%.*

/ˌmɑːk ˈdaʊn/
mark down, marking down, marked down
note transitive verb
► **mark up**

---

marked cheque *noun* (banking)
(*US*) ► **certified cheque**

/ˌmɑːkt ˈtʃek/

---

market[1] *noun* (commerce)
1 a gathering of people for buying and selling; the place where they meet: *a street market* ○ *the stock market* **2** business or trade in the specified item: *the coffee, meat, securities, spice, etc market* ○ *We have cornered the British computer market.* **3** the area, country, section of the population, etc to which goods may be sold: *the foreign, home, teenage, etc market* **4 the market** buyers and sellers: *The market determines what goods are made.* **5** the actual or potential demand for a product: *There's a good market for agricultural machinery here.* **6** the state of trade: *a rising, falling, expanding market*

be in the market for something to look for something to buy (and possibly resell): *She's in the market for antique clocks.*

come on/onto the market (of a product) to start being available for sale: *A new software package has just come on/onto the market.*

flood the market to offer large quantities of certain goods for sale at a low price: *Japanese cameras have flooded the market.*

on the market available to buy: *There are some very powerful microcomputers on the market now.*

play the market 1 to buy and sell stocks and shares on the stock exchange to make a profit **2** to manipulate the state of trade for your own benefit

price yourself/something out of the market to charge such a high price for goods or services that no one wants to buy them

/ˈmɑːkɪt/
abbr mkt
1 pl markets
2, 3, 4, 5, 6 note singular noun, used with a singular verb
► **active market, after market, bear market, black market, bull market, buyer's market, capital market, captive market, commodity market, consumer market, easy market, Euromarket, foreign exchange market, free market, grey market, imperfect market, loan market, main market, money market, open market, perfect market, primary market, secondary market, securities market, sensitive market, spot market, stock exchange, terminal market, thin market, third market, unlisted securities market**

market[2] *verb* (commerce)
to sell or promote products: *The product is being marketed throughout Europe.* ○ *I have marketed the goods to retailers.*

/ˈmɑːkɪt/
market, marketing, marketed
note transitive verb
▶ **promote 1, sell**

marketable *adjective*
1 (*commerce*) able to be sold or used in business: *The goods are cheap and very marketable.* ○ *Typing is a marketable skill.* **2** (*stock exchange*) of securities that can be bought and sold in large quantities on a stock exchange without affecting the price: *Large amounts of marketable securities have been sold.*

/ˈmɑːkɪtəbl/
1 ⋈ a **marketable** commodity, product, skill
▶ **tradeable**

market capitalization *noun* (commerce)
the value of a company calculated by multiplying the number of its issued shares by their MARKET PRICE; a list of these values: *This company has a market capitalization of £315 million.* ○ *Shareholders can look at the latest market capitalization to find out how much their company is worth.*

/ˌmɑːkɪt ˌkæpɪtəlaɪˈzeɪʃn/
(also **market capitalisation**)
note usually singular
⋈ a current, high, low **market capitalization**
syn market valuation

market demand *noun* (economics)
▶ **demand**[1]

/ˌmɑːkɪt dɪˈmɑːnd/

marketeer *noun* (commerce)
a person who supports or trades in a particular market: *a European community marketeer*

/ˌmɑːkɪˈtɪə(r)/
pl marketeers
⋈ a black, city, free **marketeer**

marketer *noun* (commerce)
a person or organization that promotes and sells products and services in a certain market: *The international marketer must be aware of language and cultural differences when deciding how to market a product.* ○ *food marketers*

/ˈmɑːkɪtə(r)/
pl marketers
⋈ global, international, local **marketers**

market forces *noun* (commerce)
factors such as the amount of raw materials and goods available and the amount wanted by customers that influence the price of goods and the way they are distributed and sold: *The price of petrol is influenced by market forces.* ○ *open a state-controlled economy to market forces*

/ˌmɑːkɪt ˈfɔːsɪz/
note usually plural
⋈ **market forces** affect, control, influence (prices, etc)
▶ **demand**[1] **2, supply and demand**

marketing *noun* (advertising/sales)
the actions of identifying, satisfying and increasing the buyer's demand for a company's products; part of a company that deals with this: *She works in marketing.* ○ *How much do we need to spend on marketing?* ○ *High sales figures depend on good marketing techniques.*

/ˈmɑːkɪtɪŋ/
note not used with *a* or *an*. No plural and used with a singular verb only.
⋈ a **marketing** budget, campaign, department, director, manager; **marketing** skills, strategies, techniques
▶ **direct marketing, market**[2]**, market research, merchandising, proactive marketing, reactive marketing, telemarketing, test marketing**

marketing audit *noun* (accounting/advertising/sales)
a detailed inspection of the strengths and weaknesses of the marketing activities of an organization. The results are used to produce a MARKETING PLAN: *The organization has decided to follow the recommendations of the most recent marketing audit.*

/ˈmɑːkɪtɪŋ ˌɔːdɪt/
pl marketing audits
⧓ carry out a **marketing audit**
► **audit**[1], **SWOT analysis**

marketing environment *noun* (marketing)
the combination of factors that affect a company's sales in a particular area or country. These factors include changes in government policy, in people's levels of income, the development of new technology or transport systems and the activity of rival firms: *The company has increased sales because of a favourable marketing environment.* ○ *compare different marketing environments in different countries*

/ˈmɑːkɪtɪŋ ɪnˌvaɪərənmənt/
pl marketing environments
⧓ be affected by, respond to the **marketing environment**

marketing mix *noun* (marketing)
the combination of factors that influence sales and can be controlled by a company. These include product, pricing, promotion and place, often known as the 'four Ps': *We have worked hard to get the right marketing mix for the launch of the new range.*

/ˈmɑːkɪtɪŋ mɪks/
note usually singular
⧓ develop, introduce a **marketing mix**
► **differentiation, undifferentiated marketing**

marketing plan *noun* (marketing)
a detailed report that shows how a company or a department will maintain and improve sales in a certain area. This is done through pricing and promotion, etc (the MARKETING MIX), and by making changes within the company to respond to changes in the market and the activity of rival firms: *draw up a marketing plan for France*

/ˈmɑːkɪtɪŋ plæn/
pl marketing plans
⧓ draw up, prepare, write a **marketing plan**
► **marketing audit, SWOT analysis**

marketing research *noun* (marketing)
► **market research**

/ˈmɑːkɪtɪŋ rɪˌsɜːtʃ, ˈmɑːkɪtɪŋ ˌriːsɜːtʃ/

market leader *noun* (sales)
the company that sells the largest amount of a specific commodity in a particular area; the brand or make of goods that sells the most: *Sony is the market leader in hi-fi equipment.* ○ *The drug Synthroid is the market leader in the treatment of thyroid deficiencies.*

/ˌmɑːkɪt ˈliːdə(r)/
pl market leaders
⧓ become, remain the **market leader**
► **brand leader, loss leader, market share**

market maker *noun* (stock exchange)
a firm that, as a member of the London Stock Exchange, buys and sells securities for a profit. It may act as a BROKER for clients or buy and sell for itself: *Market makers try to predict changes in share prices.* ○ *Market makers have replaced the jobbers who used to buy and sell on the trading floor of the Stock Exchange.*

/ˈmɑːkɪt ˌmeɪkə(r)/
pl market makers
(also **market-maker**)
► **member firm, stockbroker, stockjobber**

market order *noun* (stock exchange)
an order given by an investor to a stockbroker to buy or sell certain securities immediately at the market price: *The private investor issued a market order to the broker.*

/ˈmɑːkɪt ˌɔːdə(r)/
pl market orders
⧓ give, issue, receive a **market order**
► **day order, good till cancelled order, limit order, order**[1] **1**

market-oriented *adjective* (marketing)
of a company that produces goods that it knows will sell because buyers have said that they need them: *We need to be more market-oriented.*

/ˌmaːkɪt ˈɔːrientɪd/
▶ **product-oriented**

---

market penetration *noun* (sales)
the act of obtaining a larger MARKET SHARE by increasing advertising, promotion, etc: *We have changed our packaging to appeal to all age groups in order to obtain maximum market penetration.* ○ *We increased our market penetration by 15% last year.*

/ˌmɑːkɪt ˌpenɪˈtreɪʃn/
note not used with *a* or *an*. No plural and used with a singular verb only.
⧓ an increase, a fall, a rise in **market penetration**

---

market-place *noun* (commerce)
1 an open space in a town where a market is held: *The market-place is always crowded on Saturdays.* **2 the market-place** the situation of buying and selling in business: *Companies must be able to compete in the market-place.* ○ *Petrol prices are determined by the market-place.* ○ *launch a new product into the market-place*

/ˈmɑːkɪt pleɪs/
1 pl market-places
2 note singular noun, used with a singular verb
⧓ a global, an international, a worldwide **market-place**; compete, operate in **the market place**
▶ **market**[1]

---

market price *noun* (commerce)
the price of a raw material, product, service, security, etc that is charged in a free or competitive market: *pay the full market price*, ie without a reduction or discount ○ *He was forced to sell below the current market price to make a quick sale.*

/ˈmɑːkɪt praɪs/
pl market prices
⧓ ask, charge, pay, receive the **market prices**; sell at, sell below the **market price**
▶ **market value, mean price, price**[1]

---

market report *noun* (commerce)
a report, eg in a newspaper or trade journal, about the trading activities of certain companies or of securities on the stock exchange: *The latest market report gives current prices and an indication of possible future trends.*

/ˈmɑːkɪt rɪˌpɔːt/
pl market reports
⧓ compile, prepare, write a **market report**
▶ **marketing plan, report**[1]

---

market research *noun* (marketing)
study carried out by a company before launching a new product, into the needs, lifestyles, incomes, etc of potential buyers and to measure the success of similar products that are already available. It may involve interviewing people in the street or giving away sample products: *carry out market research for a new chocolate bar* ○ *conduct an interview for market research*

market researcher a person who carries out market research

/ˌmɑːkɪt rɪˈsɜːtʃ, ˌmɑːkɪt ˈriːsɜːtʃ/
note not used with *a* or *an*. No plural and used with a singular verb only.
⧓ carry out, do **market research**; a **market research** company, interview, survey
syn marketing research
▶ **attitude research, desk research, motivational research, qualitative market research, quantitative market research, reference group, research**[1]**, telephone research**

---

market segmentation *noun* (marketing)
the division of potential buyers according to age, sex, lifestyle, etc with the aim of designing and promoting goods and services to meet their specific needs: *market segmentation based on levels of income*

/ˌmɑːkɪt ˌsegmenˈteɪʃn/
note not used with *a* or *an*. No plural and used with a singular verb only.

syn segmentation
▶ **differentiation**

---

market share *noun* (sales)
the percentage of the total sales of a product in a particular area or country obtained by one company: *The computer company has a 25% market share.* ○ *The food and drinks company was forced to reduce prices to keep its market share.*

/ˌmɑːkɪt ˈʃeə(r)/
note usually singular
⋈ increase, keep, lose, maintain (your) **market share**
▶ **market leader, value share**

---

market sharing *noun* (commerce)
an agreement between two or more sellers of the same commodity to avoid competition by dividing up the selling area and restricting their activities to one part of it: *The Office of Fair Trading opposes any agreement such as price fixing or market sharing that restricts free competition.*

/ˈmɑːkɪt ˌʃeərɪŋ/
note not used with *a* or *an*. No plural and used with a singular verb only.
⋈ a **market sharing** agreement

---

market trend *noun* (commerce)
a pattern or change in buying and selling activities: *Companies need to produce new products to keep up with market trends.*

/ˌmɑːkɪt ˈtrend/
pl market trends
⋈ follow, forecast, keep up with, predict **market trends**
▶ **trend**

---

market valuation *noun* (commerce)
▶ **market capitalization**

/ˌmɑːkɪt ˌvælju'eɪʃn/

---

market value *noun* (accounting)
the price that could be charged and obtained for a product if it were offered for sale: *Wear and tear has decreased the market value of the machinery.* ○ *To sell it quickly, we had to sell the house for less than its current market value.*

/ˌmɑːkɪt ˈvæljuː/
note usually singular
⋈ decrease, increase, reduce the **market value**
▶ **market price, value[1] 2**

---

mark-up *noun* (retail)
the percentage of the wholesale or cost price added to produce the retail or selling price; an increase in the price of goods: *Some food items are given a 75% mark-up between producer and supermarket.* ○ *a 10% mark-up after the Budget*

/ˈmɑːk ʌp/
pl mark-ups
▶ **gross margin, mark-down**

---

mark up *verb* (retail)
to increase the price of goods; to add a percentage to the cost or wholesale price to produce the retail or selling price: *We marked all the goods up in order to increase profit.* ○ *Prices have been marked up by 10%.*

/ˌmɑːk ˈʌp/
mark up, marking up, marked up
note transitive verb
▶ **mark down**

---

mass media *noun* (advertising)
▶ **media**

/ˌmæs ˈmiːdiə/

---

mass-produce *verb* (manufacturing)
to make large quantities of identical goods, using a fast, mechanized process: *mass-produce cars, fridges, hair-dryers, etc* ○ *It is impossible to mass-produce paper of this quality.*

/ˌmæs prəˈdjuːs/
mass-produce, mass-producing, mass-produced
note transitive verb
▶ **customize, produce[2]**

---

mass-produced *adjective* (manufacturing)
goods that are made in large quantities using a fast, mechanized process: *mass-produced electrical goods* ○ *Cars are mass-produced these days.*

/ˌmæs prəˈdjuːst/

mass production *noun* (manufacturing)
the activity of making large quantities of identical goods usually using a fast mechanized process: *manufacture goods by mass production* ○ *the mass production of cars*

/ˌmæs prəˈdʌkʃn/
note not used with *a* or *an*. No plural and used with a singular verb only.
⧓ **mass production** *of* something
▶ **batch 1, jobbing production, production 1**

master *noun*
1 (*office practice*) the first and clearest version of typed, written, recorded, etc information from which copies can be made: *I will keep the master and distribute photocopies.* ○ *master film, file, tape* **2** a person who is skilled in a particular trade and able to teach others: *a master builder, carpenter, craftsman* **3** (*shipping*) the captain of a merchant ship: *the master of SS Britain*

master's certificate/ticket a qualification given by the British Department of Trade allowing someone to act as a master: *obtain a master's certificate/ticket*

/ˈmɑːstə(r)/
pl masters
1 syn master copy
▶ **carbon copy, copy[1] 1, original, top copy**
3 syn master mariner, ship's master
▶ **mate**

matched bargain *noun* (stock exchange)
a transaction in which a customer who wishes to sell a quantity of securities is paired with another customer who is willing to purchase them: *Rather than use a market maker, the broker arranged a matched bargain.*

/ˌmætʃt ˈbɑːgən/
pl matched bargains
⧓ make a **matched bargain**
▶ **bargain[1]**

mate *noun* (shipping)
an officer on a merchant ship, below the rank of captain or master: *Those jobs are the responsibility of the first mate.*

mate's certificate/ticket a qualification given by the British Department of Trade allowing someone to act as a mate

mate's receipt a temporary document signed by the mate for goods delivered direct to a ship

/meɪt/
pl mates
⧓ first, second **mate**
syn first officer
⧓ a **mate's** certificate, ticket
▶ **master 3**

material *noun* (industry)
a substance or piece of equipment used to make a finished product or to carry out a specific activity: *Iron, steel and oil are materials used in industry.* ○ *cleaning materials*

building materials bricks, timber, sand, etc used for construction work

synthetic materials substances that are made by a chemical process

/məˈtɪəriəl/
note usually plural
⧓ use **materials**
▶ **bill of materials, raw material**

material fact *noun*
1 (*insurance*) any fact that, by law, must be declared by a person applying for insurance: *All material facts must be supplied before the underwriter will accept the risk.* **2** (*stock exchange*) any fact about a company that must, by law, be made known on the issue of a prospectus: *No material facts about the company should be suppressed* **3** (*law*) information given by a witness at a trial, important enough to influence the court's decision: *The witness produced a new material fact.*

/məˌtɪəriəl ˈfækt/
pl material facts
⧓ conceal, hide, produce, provide, supply, suppress a **material fact**

materials buyer *noun* (industry)
the person who buys the materials needed for producing goods in a factory: *It is up to the materials buyer to ensure that raw materials arrive on time.*

/məˈtɪəriəlz ˌbaɪə(r)/
pl materials buyers

syn procurement officer, purchasing officer

▶ **buyer 2**

---

materials control *noun* (industry)

checking that enough materials are available to produce goods, without tying up too much money in unused materials; the section of a company that deals with this: *He is head of materials control and monitors the amount of stock held.*

/məˈtɪəriəlz kənˌtrəʊl/

note not used with *a* or *an*. No plural and used with a singular verb only.

▶ **stock control**

---

materials handling *noun* (industry)

the movement of materials around a factory or from one factory to another so that they are ready when needed to produce goods: *Our materials handling is monitored by computer.*

/məˈtɪəriəlz ˌhændlɪŋ/

note not used with *a* or *an*. No plural and used with a singular verb only.

---

maternity leave *noun* (personnel)

time off work allowed by law to a woman for a period before and after the birth of her child: *She is away on maternity leave.*

/məˈtɜːnəti ˌliːv/

note no plural

⋈ be *on* **maternity leave**

▶ **leave, paternity leave**

---

maternity pay *noun* (personnel)

money allowed by law to a woman who takes time off work for a period before and after the birth of her child. In the UK, money provided by the government is known as State Maternity Pay. Employers may provide more than the minimum amount: *receive 26 weeks' maternity pay*

/məˈtɜːnəti ˌpeɪ/

note no plural

⋈ claim **maternity pay**

syn maternity allowance, maternity benefit

▶ **benefit[1], pay[2]**

---

mature *verb* (banking/commerce)

to become due for payment: *My insurance policy has matured.* ○ *The bill of exchange matures on the 31st of May.*

/məˈtjʊə(r)/

mature, maturing, matured

note intransitive verb

⋈ **mature** *on* (a certain date)

---

maturity *noun* (banking/insurance/stock exchange)

the date on which a bill of exchange, promissory note, insurance policy, debenture or loan stock becomes due for payment or repayment: *The promissory note has passed its maturity.* ○ *What is the maturity date of this debenture certificate?*

/məˈtjʊərəti/

note not used with *a* or *an*. No plural and used with a singular verb only.

⋈ reach **maturity**

syn redemption date

---

max *abbr*

maximum: *max height 10m*

/mæks/

---

maximize *verb*

1 to make something as large as possible: *maximize profit* **2** to make the best use of something: *We must maximize resources.*

/ˈmæksɪmaɪz/

maximize, maximizing, maximized

note transitive verb

(also **maximise**)

opp minimize

---

maximum *noun, adjective*

the largest possible amount, size, price, etc: *a maximum load of 3 tons* ○ *pay the maximum price* ○ *The plane will hold a maximum of 500 passengers.*

/ˈmæksɪməm/

abbr max

note singular noun, used with a singular verb

⋈ **maximum** depth, distance, height, length; reach a **maximum**

opp minimum
▶ **ceiling**

MB *abbr* (computing)
megabyte: *300 MB*

/ˌem ˈbiː/
(also **M**, **Mb**)

MBA *abbr* (management)
Master of Business Administration: *Ms D Cassell MBA* ○ *Where did you do your MBA?*

/ˌem biː ˈeɪ/

MBO *abbr* (management)
1 management by objectives: *a policy of MBO* **2** a management buyout: *We are planning an MBO.*

/ˌem biː ˈəʊ/

MD *abbr*
1 (*management*) managing director: *The MD is on holiday.*
2 (*banking*) memorandum of deposit

/ˌem ˈdiː/
(also **M.D.**)

---

mean *noun*
the middle point between two extremes: *Add up these figures and find the mean.*

/miːn/
note usually singular
⋈ a **mean** figure
▶ **average[1] 1**

---

mean price *noun* (stock exchange)
the price of a security calculated by finding the mid-point between the buying and selling prices: *This week has seen a dramatic increase in the mean price.*

/ˌmiːn ˈpraɪs/
pl mean prices
⋈ calculate, list, report the **mean price**
syn middle price
▶ **market price, price[1]**

---

mechanization *noun* (technology)
the use of machines to do work previously done by people: *mechanization of the food industry*

/ˌmekənaɪˈzeɪʃn/
(also **mechanisation**)
note not used with *a* or *an*. No plural and used with a singular verb only.
▶ **automation, computerization**

---

mechanize *verb* (technology)
to change a process, a factory, etc so that it is run by machines rather than people: *The factory has been completely mechanized.* ○ *a highly mechanized industrial process*

/ˈmekənaɪz/
mechanize, mechanizing, mechanized
note transitive verb
(also **mechanise**)
⋈ **mechanize** a factory, an industry, a process, a system
▶ **automate, computerize**

---

media *noun* (advertising)
the media ways of spreading news and information to the greatest number of people, eg by television, radio or newspapers: *advertised by/on the media* ○ *The event will be given full media coverage.* ○ *The media influence/influences our cultural and political attitudes.*

/ˈmiːdiə/
note plural noun, used with a singular or a plural verb
⋈ **media** advertising, coverage
syn mass media

media analysis *noun* (advertising)
the study of the effectiveness of different kinds of advertising media: *Media analysis indicates that newspaper advertising would be most effective for this product.*

/ˈmiːdiə əˌnæləsɪs/
note not used with *a* or *an*. No plural and used with a singular verb only.
⧓ carry out **media analysis**
syn media research

media planning *noun* (advertising)
choosing where to place an advertisement, eg on television, radio, or in a newspaper, when it appears and how often it is repeated: *We leave all our media planning to the advertising agency.*

/ˈmiːdiə ˌplænɪŋ/
note not used with *a* or *an*. No plural and used with a singular verb only.
⧓ carry out **media planning**
▶ **planning 1**

mediation *noun* (industrial relations)
the action of a third, neutral party, to settle an industrial dispute: *All offers of mediation were rejected.*

/ˌmiːdiˈeɪʃn/
note not used with *a* or *an*. No plural and used with a singular verb only.
▶ **arbitration, industrial dispute**

medical certificate *noun* (management)
a note signed by a doctor stating that a person is unfit for work because of illness or injury: *A medical certificate is required for any absence from work.*

/ˈmedɪkl səˌtɪfɪkət/
pl medical certificates
⧓ issue, provide, require, sign a **medical certificate**
syn doctor's certificate

medium of exchange *noun* (finance)
money, bills, promissory notes, etc that can be used to pay for goods or services: *Credit cards and cheques, rather than cash, are increasingly used as the medium of exchange.*

/ˌmiːdiəm əv ɪksˈtʃeɪndʒ/
note no plural
⧓ use as a **medium of exchange**
▶ **currency 2, exchange[2] 1, money supply, near money**

mediums *noun* (stock exchange)
investments such as gilts and other fixed interest securities that will be repaid in 5 to 15 years' time: *He has put some of his capital into mediums.*

/ˈmiːdiəmz/
note plural noun, used with a plural verb
syn medium-dated securities
▶ **fixed interest securities, gilts, longs, shorts 1**

meet *verb*
1 (**a**) to come together to talk about a particular subject: *Shall we meet on Tuesday to discuss the sales budget?* ○ *I'm meeting him at their Paris office.* ○ *We're meeting with their sales manager tomorrow.* (**b**) to go to a place and wait for someone or something to arrive: *I'll meet you at the airport.* ○ *A car will meet you at the station to take you to our offices.* **2** to pay something: *Can the company meet its debts?* ○ *All costs will be met by the promotions department.* **3** to satisfy a demand, need, etc: *The new product will meet our consumers' needs.*

/miːt/
meet, meeting, met
1 note transitive and intransitive verb
⧓ **meet** *at* (a time or place), *for* (a talk or activity), *in* (a place), *on* (a certain date), *to* (do something), *with* (someone)
2, 3 note transitive verb

meeting *noun*
an organized occasion when a number of people come together to discuss or decide something: *hold a meeting to discuss the latest sales report* ○ *The director has called an urgent meeting. Please make sure all staff in your department attend.*

/ˈmiːtɪŋ/
pl meetings
⧓ arrange, attend, call, cancel, conduct, hold, organize, postpone a **meeting**

▶ **assembly 2, board meeting, business meeting, committee**

---

megabyte *noun* (computing)
1 048 576 (2^{20}), used as a measure of computer memory or storage power: *The main memory has 32 megabytes.*

/ˈmeɡəbaɪt/
abbr M, MB, Mb
pl megabytes
⧓ **megabyte** memory, storage
▶ **byte, kilobyte**

---

member *noun*
1 a person or company that belongs to an organization: *The company is a member of the Association of British Insurers.* ○ *a member of a trade union* **2** (*stock exchange*) a person who owns shares in a company: *Members of a company must be recorded on the register of members.*

/ˈmembə(r)/
pl members
⧓ become a **member** (*of* something)
2 ▶ **shareholder, share register**

---

member bank *noun* (banking)
1 (*UK*) a commercial bank that is a member of the London Bankers' Clearing House: *The central clearing system deals with the circulation of funds for member banks.* **2** (*US*) a commercial bank that is a member of the Federal Reserve System: *The bank has applied to be a member bank.*

/ˌmembə ˈbæŋk/
pl member banks
▶ **bank[1], clearing bank, commercial bank**

---

member firm *noun* (stock exchange)
a firm that buys and sells securities on the International Stock Exchange either on its own behalf or for another investor: *new regulations issued by the stock exchange to its member firms*

/ˌmembə ˈfɜːm/
pl member firms
▶ **market maker, stockbroker, stockjobber**

---

membership *noun*
1 the state of being a member of an organization: *I have applied to renew my membership.* **2** the total members of an organization: *The membership of the union is now over 100 000.* ○ *an organization with a large membership*

/ˈmembəʃɪp/
1 note not used with *a* or *an*. No plural and used with a singular verb only.
⧓ apply for **membership**
2 note used with a singular or a plural verb
⧓ increase, lose, reduce **membership**

---

memo *abbr* (office practice)
memorandum: *A memo has been sent to all departments.*

/ˈmeməʊ/
pl memos
note The abbreviation is often used instead of the full term.

---

memorandum *noun* (office practice)
a short typed or written message sent from one person to another in an organization: *circulate a memorandum to all sales staff*

/ˌmeməˈrændəm/
abbr memo
pl memoranda *or* memorandums
⧓ receive, send, sign, write a **memorandum**

Memorandum of Association *noun* (law)
an official document that, by law, shows that a company exists. It states the name and address of the company, the amount of AUTHORIZED SHARE CAPITAL and how it is divided, a statement of limited liability, ie how its debts will be paid, the purposes for which the company was formed and the goods and services that

/ˌmeməˌrændəm əv əˌsəʊsiˈeɪʃn/
⧓ draw up, sign a **Memorandum of Association**
▶ **Articles of Association**

it deals with: *All essential information is contained in the Memorandum of Association.*

---

memorandum of deposit *noun* (banking)
a document signed by someone who deposits something as security for a loan from a bank: *On signing the memorandum of deposit the bank granted me a loan.*

/ˌmeməˌrændəm əv dɪˈpɒzɪt/
pl memorandums of deposit
abbr MD
▶ **certificate of deposit, deposit[1] 1**

Memorandum of Satisfaction *noun* (law)
a document stating that a mortgage on a property has been repaid: *The Registrar of Companies has received the Memorandum of Satisfaction for the company property.*

/ˌmeməˌrændəm əv ˌsætɪsˈfækʃn/
⋈ issue, sign a **Memorandum of Satisfaction**

---

memory *noun* (computing)
the part of a computer where information is stored and from where it can be retrieved: *The program has been wiped from the memory.* ○ *The data being worked on is stored in the computer's memory.* ○ *There isn't enough memory to open this application.*

/ˈmeməri/
pl memories
⋈ store (data) in the **memory**; a **memory** chip
▶ **storage 2**

---

menu *noun* (computing)
a list of choices and functions that can be performed by a computer program: *Select the word 'save' from the file menu.*

/ˈmenju:/
pl menus
⋈ choose, select *from* the **menu**

MEP *abbr*
Member of the European Parliament: *elect an MEP*

/ˌem i: ˈpi:/

---

mercantile *adjective* (commerce)
of trade and commerce: *The country is trying to protect its mercantile interests.*

/ˈmɜ:kəntaɪl/
⋈ a **mercantile** agent
▶ **commercial**

---

mercantile agent *noun* (commerce)
▶ **factor 1**

/ˌmɜ:kəntaɪl ˈeɪdʒənt/

---

mercantile law *noun* (law)
▶ **commercial law**

/ˌmɜ:kəntaɪl ˈlɔ:/

---

mercantile marine *noun* (shipping)
▶ **merchant navy**

/ˌmɜ:kəntaɪl məˈri:n/

---

merchandise *noun* (commerce)
goods for sale; goods bought and sold: *You are welcome to examine the merchandise before buying.* ○ *Some of the new merchandise will be displayed in the shop window.*

/ˈmɜ:tʃəndaɪz/
note no plural
abbr mdise, mdse
⋈ buy, display, examine, sell **merchandise**; cheap, important, luxury, valuable **merchandise**
▶ **goods**

---

merchandising *noun* (commerce)
buying, selling and promoting goods: *Even with extensive merchandising the goods would not sell.* ○ *give away free samples as part of the merchandising strategy*

/ˈmɜ:tʃəndaɪzɪŋ/
note not used with *a* or *an*. No plural and used with a singular verb only.
⋈ a **merchandising** industry, manager, strategy
▶ **marketing**

merchant *noun* (commerce)
a person or firm that buys goods of a particular type in large quantities; a wholesaler: *buy sand from a builder's merchant*

/ˈmɜːtʃənt/
pl merchants
⧓ a coal, timber, wine **merchant**
▶ **dealer, trader**

---

merchantable quality *noun* (law)
a condition of goods offered for sale that they should be good enough to be used for their intended purpose: *The Sale of Goods Act (1979) states that the goods must be of merchantable quality when you buy them.*

/ˌmɜːtʃəntəbl ˈkwɒləti/
note not used with *a* or *an*. No plural and used with a singular verb only.
⧓ be *of* **merchantable quality**
▶ **quality**

---

merchant bank *noun* (banking)
(*UK*) a bank that specializes in raising capital for industry, accepting bills of exchange, and arranging long-term loans. It advises companies on FLOTATIONS and TAKEOVER BIDS, underwrites new share issues and manages investment portfolios and unit trusts: *The firm has taken advice from a merchant bank on the flotation.* ○ *a loan provided by a merchant bank*

/ˌmɜːtʃənt ˈbæŋk/
pl merchant banks
⧓ a **merchant bank** arranges, provides (a loan)
▶ **bank[1], clearing bank, commercial bank, discount house, private bank**

---

merchant navy *noun* (shipping)
the merchant ships and sailors of a country: *This country has one of the largest merchant navies in the world.*

/ˌmɜːtʃənt ˈneɪvi/
pl merchant navies
syn merchant marine, mercantile marine

---

merge *verb* (stock exchange)
(of two or more companies) to combine, usually to share costs, increase efficiency and avoid competition: *The two insurance companies have agreed to merge.* ○ *merge three businesses into one large group*

/mɜːdʒ/
merge, merging, merged
note transitive and intransitive verb
▶ **amalgamate, take over**

---

merger *noun* (stock exchange)
the combining of two or more organizations, usually to share costs, increase efficiency and avoid competition: *propose a merger of two distribution companies* ○ *arrange a merger between a bank and an insurance company* ○ *The directors of both companies met to discuss the terms of the merger.*

/ˈmɜːdʒə(r)/
pl mergers
⧓ agree to, approve, arrange, propose, take part in, withdraw from a **merger**; a **merger** *between, of* (two or more companies); a **merger** agreement, proposal
opp demerger
▶ **acquisition, City Code on Takeovers and Mergers, Monopolies and Mergers Commission, takeover**

---

merger broker *noun* (finance)
a person or an organization that arranges mergers between companies: *We have a team of solicitors acting as a merger broker on the deal.*

/ˈmɜːdʒə ˌbrəʊkə(r)/
pl merger brokers
⧓ act as a **merger broker**
▶ **broker**

---

meter[1] *noun*
a piece of equipment that measures the amount of gas, water, electricity, time, etc used: *put money in a parking meter* ○ *read an electricity meter*

/ˈmiːtə(r)/
pl meters
⧓ an electricity, a gas, a parking, a water **meter**; read a **meter**

meter² *verb*
to measure something with a meter: *Scientists used to claim that nuclear power would make electricity too cheap to meter.* ○ *metered heating*

/ˈmiːtə(r)/
meter, metering, metered
note transitive verb
⋈ **meter** electricity, gas, water

mfg *abbr* (manufacturing)
manufacturing: *mfg industries*

note used in written English only

microchip *noun* (computing)
► **chip 1**

/ˈmaɪkrəʊtʃɪp/

microcomputer *noun* (computing)
► **personal computer**

/ˈmaɪkrəʊkəmˌpjuːtə(r)/

middleman *noun* (commerce)
a person or organization that buys goods from the producer and sells them to the consumer, for a profit: *buy direct from the manufacturer in order to cut out the middleman*

/ˈmɪdlmæn/
pl middlemen
⋈ act as, go through a **middleman**
► **agent, broker, dealer, factor**

middle price *noun* (stock exchange)
► **mean price**

/ˌmɪdl ˈpraɪs/

mileage *noun* (transport)
1 a distance travelled in miles: *a used car with a low mileage*, ie one that has not been driven many miles **2** the average number of miles that a car will travel on one gallon of petrol: *The car's mileage was around 50 miles per gallon.*

/ˈmaɪlɪdʒ/
note usually singular
⋈ high, low **mileage**

mill *noun* (industry)
a building fitted with machinery for processing materials of different kinds: *wood pulp processed by a paper mill*

/mɪl/
pl mills
⋈ a cotton, flour, paper, **mill**

min *abbr*
1 minimum: *earn £200 per week min* **2** minute: *10 mins*

/mɪn/

mini- *combining form*
very small: *mini-budget* ○ *minibus* ○ *minicomputer*

/ˈmɪni/
► **macro-, micro-**

minimize *verb*
to make something as small as possible: *We must do all that we can to minimize our losses.*

/ˈmɪnɪmaɪz/
minimize, minimizing, minimized
note transitive verb
(also **minimise**)
opp maximize

minimum *noun, adjective*
the smallest possible amount, size, price, etc: *We have done all we can to keep costs to a minimum.* ○ *use a minimum amount of fuel* ○ *pay a minimum charge of £200*

/ˈmɪnɪməm/
note singular noun, used with a singular verb
abbr min
⋈ keep, reduce (something) to a **minimum**
opp maximum

minimum lending rate *noun* (banking)
(*UK*) between 1971 and 1981 the lowest rate of interest at which the BANK OF ENGLAND would lend to discount houses: *The minimum lending rate was reintroduced for one day in 1985.*

/ˌmɪnɪməm ˈlendɪŋ reɪt/
abbr MLR
syn bank rate
▶ **base rate, rate 2**

---

minimum subscription *noun* (finance/commerce)
the smallest amount of money, stated in the PROSPECTUS of a new company, that must be raised if a company is to exist: *The company was easily able to reach the minimum subscription quoted in the prospectus.*

/ˌmɪnɪməm səbˈskrɪpʃn/
note usually singular
⧓ raise, reach the **minimum subscription**
▶ **authorized share capital, issue[1] 2, subscription shares 2**

---

minimum wage *noun* (industrial relations)
the smallest amount an employer may pay an employee by law: *a campaign to introduce a national minimum wage*

/ˌmɪnɪməm ˈweɪdʒ/
pl minimum wages
⧓ earn, introduce, pay a **minimum wage**; a **minimum wage** policy
▶ **wage**

---

minority interest *noun* (stock exchange)
a situation when a person or a company owns shares in a company more than 50% of which is owned by a HOLDING COMPANY. These shareholders receive a share of the profit, but are unable to influence company policy as they will always be outvoted by the holding company: *30% of the company is held by a minority interest.*

/maɪˌnɒrəti ˈɪntrəst/
pl minority interests
⧓ have, hold a **minority interest**
▶ **controlling interest, holding**

---

minority protection *noun* (commerce)
regulations that protect shareholders who have a MINORITY INTEREST in a company from those who hold a CONTROLLING INTEREST, esp when a company goes bankrupt: *The minority shareholders are seeking minority protection while the company is being wound up.*

/maɪˌnɒrəti prəˈtekʃn/
note not used with *a* or *an*. No plural and used with a singular verb only.
⧓ demand, seek **minority protection**

---

minutes *noun* (office practice)
a list or short account of what was said or decided at a business meeting: *start the meeting by reading the minutes of the previous meeting* ○ *take the minutes of a meeting*, ie write down what is said

/ˈmɪnɪts/
note plural noun, used with a plural verb
⧓ go through, read, take the **minutes**

MIS *abbr* (computing)
management information system

/ˌem aɪ ˈes/

---

miscarriage *noun* (transport)
1 (of goods) failure to arrive at or be delivered to the right destination: *The carriers were sued for miscarriage.* **2** transporting goods in an unsuitable way so that they are likely to be lost or damaged: *Many fragile items were broken as a result of miscarriage.*

/ˌmɪsˈkærɪdʒ/
note not used with *a* or *an*. No plural and used with a singular verb only.
▶ **carriage**

---

miscellaneous *adjective*
of various, different types; mixed: *If you don't know what to do with the letter put it in the miscellaneous file.* ○ *a box of miscellaneous items for sale*

/ˌmɪsəˈleɪniəs/
abbr misc
⧓ **miscellaneous** files, goods, items

mission statement *noun* (management)
a statement of the aims, purpose and future activities of an organization: *It is important to prepare a mission statement that can be understood by everyone in the company as well as by the planning team.* ○ *Without a mission statement the company will lack direction.*

/ˈmɪʃn ˌsteɪtmənt/
pl mission statements
⋈ draw up, issue, prepare a **mission statement**
► **business plan, corporate planning, objective**

mixed economy *noun* (economics)
an economy in which some industries are owned by the state and others are owned by individuals and groups of people: *The country appears to have prospered under a mixed economy.*

/ˌmɪkst ɪˈkɒnəmi/
pl mixed economies
► **economy, private sector, public sector**

mkt *abbr* (commerce)
market

note used in written English only

MLR *abbr* (banking)
minimum lending rate

/ˌem el ˈɑː(r)/

MMC *abbr* (stock exchange)
Monopolies and Mergers Commission: *The takeover is being investigated by the MMC.*

/ˌem em ˈsiː/

MO *abbr* (commerce)
mail order

/ˌem ˈəʊ/

model *noun* (industry)
a particular design or type of product: *This is the most popular model in our whole range.* ○ *All this year's new models are displayed at the motor show.*

/ˈmɒdl/
pl models
⋈ a basic, luxury, standard **model**
► **brand[1], make[1]**

modem *noun* (computing)
a device that links a computer system and a telephone line so that information can be sent over long distances from one computer to another: *data transmitted by (a) modem*

/ˈməʊdem/
pl modems
⋈ receive, send, transmit data by **modem**
► **electronic mail, fax[1], telex[1]**

monetarism *noun* (economics)
the theory or practice of controlling a country's MONEY SUPPLY as the main method of stabilizing the economy: *Is the government in favour of monetarism?*

/ˈmʌnɪtərɪzəm/
note not used with *a* or *an*. No plural and used with a singular verb only.
► **money supply**

monetary *adjective* (finance)
relating to money or currency: *the government's monetary policy* ○ *The monetary unit of Japan is the yen.* ○ *What are the benefits of the new computer system in monetary terms?*

/ˈmʌnɪtri/
⋈ **monetary** control, growth, policy, system, value
► **European Monetary System, financial, fiscal**

monetary policy *noun* (finance/economics)
the way in which governments control the economic conditions of a country by increasing or reducing the MONEY SUPPLY: *The government's aim was to keep monetary policy tight.*

/ˈmʌnɪtri ˌpɒləsi/
pl monetary policies
⋈ a loose, tight **monetary policy**
► **monetarism**

monetary system *noun* (finance)
the system used by a country to provide money for public and private use and to control the exchange of its own currency with those of foreign countries: *introduce major changes in the monetary system*

/ˈmʌnɪtri ˌsɪstəm/
pl monetary systems
▶ **European Monetary System, monetarism**

monetary unit *noun* (finance)
the standard form of money in a country: *The lira is the monetary unit of Italy.*

/ˈmʌnɪtri ˌjuːnɪt/
pl monetary units
syn unit of currency
▶ **European Currency Unit**

money *noun* (finance)
a means of payment, esp coins and bank notes, given and accepted in buying and selling: *Our central aim is to make money.*

/ˈmʌni/
note not used with *a* or *an*. No plural and used with a singular verb only.
⧓ borrow, earn, lose, make, save **money**; spending **money**
▶ **active money, allotment money, application money, call money, capital, caution money, cheap money, currency, danger money, dead capital, dear money, easy money, hard currency, hot money, idle money, lot money, near money, option money, salvage money**

money at call and short notice *noun* (banking)
money lent by banks to discount houses, money brokers, the stock exchange and other banks which is repayable on demand, ie at call, or within 14 days, ie at short notice: *Money at call and short notice forms an important part of the bank's liquid assets.*

/ˌmʌni ət ˌkɔːl ənd ˌʃɔːt ˈnəʊtɪs/
note not used with *a* or *an*. No plural and used with a singular verb only.
▶ **accommodation 3, at call, call money**

money broker *noun* (commerce/finance)
a person or an organization that arranges short-term loans between banks, discount houses and dealers in government securities: *The deal was transacted through a money broker who was paid commission.*

/ˈmʌni brəʊkə(r)/
pl money brokers
▶ **broker, money market**

moneylender *noun* (finance)
a person or an organization that lends money and charges interest on the repayments, but not a building society, a bank or an insurance company: *All moneylenders must be registered and carry a licence.*

/ˈmʌni lendə(r)/
pl moneylenders
▶ **interest, loan**

money-maker *noun* (finance)
a person, an organization or a business activity that earns a lot of money: *Your business idea could be a real money-maker.* ○ *Local people have complained that all the profit will go to the money-makers.*

/ˈmʌni ˌmeɪkə(r)/
pl money-makers
▶ **money-spinner**

money market *noun* (finance)
(*UK*) **1** the market in which short-term loans are arranged between banks, the government, discount houses and accepting houses. The main items of exchange are bills of exchange, Treasury bills and trade bills: *Money market rates strengthened as a result of the election.* **2** the foreign exchange market: *Despite the weakness of sterling, money market rates remained fixed at just over 15%.*

/ˈmʌni ˌmɑːkɪt/
pl money markets
⋈ **money market** deals, funds, rates, transactions
► **capital market, loan market, market[1]**
2 ► **foreign exchange market**

money order *noun* (finance)
► **postal order**

/ˈmʌni ˌɔːdə(r)/
abbr MO

money-spinner *noun* (commerce)
(*informal*) something that earns a lot of money: *The book could be a real money-spinner.*

/ˈmʌni ˌspɪnə(r)/
pl money-spinners
► **money-maker**

money supply *noun* (finance/economics)
the total amount of money that exists in the economy of a country: *By restricting the money supply, the government plans to slow down inflation.*

/ˈmʌni səˌplaɪ/
note no plural
⋈ control, increase, reduce the **money supply**
► **medium of exchange**

money wages *noun*
wages expressed in money terms only, without taking inflation into account: *The increase in money wages still falls below the rate of inflation, so it represents a decrease in real wages.*

/ˈmʌni ˌweɪdʒɪz/
note plural noun, used with a plural verb
► **real wages, wage**

monitor[1] *noun* (computing)
a computer terminal consisting of a television screen on which information can be read: *The data was flashed up on the monitor.*

/ˈmɒnɪtə(r)/
pl monitors
⋈ a **monitor** screen
► **screen[1], visual display unit**

monitor[2] *verb*
to observe something closely; to record and test the operation of something: *Factory supervisors assign work and monitor progress.* ○ *I'm responsible for monitoring sales performance.* ○ *At every warehouse computers monitor stock levels and re-order when they fall below a minimum.*

/ˈmɒnɪtə(r)/
monitor, monitoring, monitored
note transitive verb
⋈ **monitor** performance, progress, standards

Monopolies and Mergers Commission *noun* (commerce/law)
(*UK*) a government organization that checks that the supply, manufacture or export of goods is not restricted by an unfair supplier or company: *The Monopolies and Mergers Commission have recommended that the takeover does not take place.*

/məˌnɒpəliz ənd ˈmɜːdʒəz kəˌmɪʃn/
abbr MMC
⋈ refer something to the **Monopolies and Mergers Commission**
► **commission[1] 2, merger, Office of Fair Trading, takeover**

monopoly *noun* (economics)
a situation in which only one person or company produces or sells a particular product: *They have the monopoly on electrical goods in the town.* ○ *gain a monopoly of ore supplies* ○ *The takeover would result in a monopoly against the public interest.*

/məˈnɒpəli/
pl monopolies
⋈ a government, legal, state, virtual **monopoly**; have a **monopoly** *of, on* (something)

bilateral monopoly a situation where there is only one buyer and one seller in a market: *Both buyer and seller are monopolists in a bilateral monopoly.*

commercial monopoly a monopoly where one buyer or supplier is able to fix the price of a commodity: *The buyer is dictating the price in the commercial monopoly.*

public monopoly a monopoly that is owned by the state; usually a public service: *The railways are run as a public monopoly.*

▶ **absolute monopoly, captive market, perfect market**

---

monthly account *noun* (retail)

/ˌmʌnθli əˈkaʊnt/

▶ **budget account 2**

---

moor *verb* (shipping)

/mɔː(r), mʊə(r)/

to attach a ship or boat to a fixed object or to the land with a rope or an anchor: *We'll moor the boat to the riverbank.* ○ *The ship was moored alongside the quay.*

moor, mooring, moored

note transitive and intransitive verb

⧓ **moor** (a ship) *to* something

▶ **berth², dock² 1**

---

moorage *noun* (shipping)

/ˈmɔːrɪdʒ, ˈmʊərɪdʒ/

the fee charged for the use of a MOORING: *Moorage must be paid before the boat can tie up.*

note not used with *a* or *an*. No plural and used with a singular verb only.

⧓ charge, pay **moorage**

▶ **keelage, wharfage**

---

mooring *noun* (shipping)

/ˈmɔːrɪŋ, ˈmʊərɪŋ/

1 a place where boats can be tied up in a harbour: *We have reserved a mooring in the harbour.* **2 moorings** the ropes, anchors, chains, etc used to moor a boat: *The ship loosed its moorings and set sail.*

1 pl moorings

⧓ book, find, hire, reserve a **mooring**

▶ **berth¹ 1**

2 note plural noun, used with a plural verb

⧓ let go, loose the **moorings**

---

moral hazard *noun* (insurance)

/ˌmɒrəl ˈhæzəd/

the incentive to cheat on an insurance policy if there are no penalties for cheating: *The price of an insurance premium has to compensate for moral hazard.*

note usually singular

⧓ allow, compensate for **moral hazard**

---

moratorium *noun* (law)

/ˌmɒrəˈtɔːriəm/

an agreement between a creditor and a debtor to allow extra time for the payment of a debt: *The bank has placed a moratorium on overseas debts.*

pl moratoriums

⧓ announce, declare, impose, introduce, seek a **moratorium**

---

mortality tables *noun* (insurance)

/mɔːˈtæləti ˌteɪblz/

lists of figures that show how many years people of certain ages are likely to live, used to calculate insurance risks: *make a calculation based on mortality tables*

note usually plural

syn life tables

▶ **actuarial tables**

mortgage[1] *noun* (finance/law)
an agreement in which money is lent by a bank or a building society, etc for buying a house or another property. The property acts as the security, ie can be reclaimed by the lender if the mortgage payments are not made; the sum of money lent in this way: *The flat was bought with a £50 000 mortgage.* ○ *take out a 90% mortgage* (ie for 90% of the selling price) *from a building society*

/ˈmɔːɡɪdʒ/
pl mortgages
⋈ apply for, arrange, pay off, repay, take out a **mortgage**; **mortgage** arrears, rates, repayments
► **building society, secured creditor**

---

mortgage[2] *verb* (finance/law)
to take out a loan with a property as security: *She mortgaged her flat to buy the business.*

/ˈmɔːɡɪdʒ/
mortgage, mortgaging, mortgaged
note transitive verb
⋈ **mortgage** a flat, house, property

---

mortgage debenture *noun* (banking/law)
► **secured debenture**

/ˈmɔːɡɪdʒ dɪˌbentʃə(r)/

---

mortgagee *noun* (finance/law)
a person or company that lends money in a mortgage agreement: *The mortgagee has repossessed the property because of non-payment.*

/ˌmɔːɡɪˈdʒiː/
pl mortgagees
► **secured creditor**

---

mortgagor *noun* (finance/law)
a person or company that borrows money in a mortgage agreement: *The mortgagor has defaulted on two consecutive payments.*

/ˌmɔːɡɪˈdʒɔː(r)/
pl mortgagors
(also **mortgager**)

---

mother tongue *noun*
the first language that a person learns to speak as a child: *We need to employ someone who speaks at least two European languages with English as their mother tongue.*

/ˌmʌðə ˈtʌŋ/
note usually singular
syn native language
► **language**

---

motion *noun* (management)
a formal suggestion to be discussed and voted upon at a meeting: *Will anyone second* (ie support) *this motion?* ○ *The motion was passed unanimously* (ie no one voted against it).

/ˈməʊʃn/
pl motions
⋈ oppose, pass, propose a **motion**
► **proposal 1, vote[1]**

---

motivate *verb* (management/personnel)
to make someone act in a certain way by persuasion or reward: *She is excellent at motivating her staff.*

/ˈməʊtɪveɪt/
motivate, motivating, motivated
note transitive verb

---

motivational research *noun* (advertising/marketing)
an examination of why consumers choose one brand before another: *Motivational research has been carried out on our competitors in the market.*

/ˌməʊtɪˌveɪʃnəl rɪˈsɜːtʃ, ˌməʊtɪˌveɪʃnəl ˈriːsɜːtʃ/
note not used with *a* or *an*. No plural and used with a singular verb only.
► **market research**

---

motor insurance *noun* (insurance)
the insurance of a car, the driver and the passengers in case of

/ˈməʊtər ɪnˌʃʊərəns/
note not used with *a* or *an*. No plural and used with a singular verb only.

accident. Drivers have a legal obligation to be covered against third party claims: *Which firm handles your motor insurance?*

► **insurance**

---

mouse *noun* (computing)
a piece of equipment attached to a computer for entering commands without using the keyboard: *With the cursor pointing at the file name, click twice on the mouse to open the file.*

/maʊs/
pl mice
⋈ click on, move, use the **mouse**
► **cursor, keyboard**

---

movables *noun* (law)
property that can be moved or transferred from one place to another, eg money, securities, negotiable instruments, and any personal items of value as opposed to buildings and land: *sell as many movables as possible before going bankrupt*

/ˈmuːvəblz/
note plural noun, used with a plural verb
► **tangible assets**

MP *abbr*
Member of Parliament: *the MP for Leeds Central*

/ˌem ˈpiː/
pl MPs

Mr *abbr*
the title used for a man: *Mr (Thomas) Smith*

/ˈmɪstə(r)/
pl Messrs

MRP *abbr* (manufacturing)
manufacturer's recommended price

/ˌem ɑː ˈpiː/
(also **mrp**)

Mrs *noun*
the title used for a married woman: *Mrs (Mary) Curtis*

/ˈmɪsɪz/

Ms *noun*
the title used for a married or unmarried woman: *Ms (Jane) Dominy*

/mɪz, məz/

---

ms *abbr*
manuscript: *Please return the corrected ms.*

note used in written English only
pl mss

---

multi- *combining form*
many: *multi-cultural* ○ *multi-layered* ○ *a multi-storey car park*

/ˈmʌlti/

---

multilateral *adjective*
of several groups, countries or organizations: *The four countries signed a multilateral trade agreement.* ○ *multilateral trading*

/ˌmʌltiˈlætərəl/
⋈ a **multilateral** agreement, decision, treaty
► **bilateral, unilateral**

---

multinational *noun* (industry)
a very large organization that owns companies in more than one country in order to obtain cheap raw materials and make efficient use of a local workforce: *The firm has been bought out by a major multinational.*

/ˌmʌltiˈnæʃnəl/
pl multinationals
⋈ a **multinational** company, corporation, firm, group
► **conglomerate**

---

multiple pricing *noun* (retail)
giving the same product a different price in different markets: *Multiple pricing means that a lot can be saved on an item if you shop around.*

/ˌmʌltɪpl ˈpraɪsɪŋ/
note not used with *a* or *an*. No plural and used with a singular verb only.
► **differential 2, market segmentation, pricing policy**

multiple taxation *noun* (tax)
► **taxation**

/ˌmʌltɪpl tækˈseɪʃn/

multi-user *adjective* (computing)
of a computer system that can be used by more than one person at once: *install a multi-user computer system*

/ˌmʌlti ˈjuːzə(r)/
⋈ a **multi-user** network, system
► **network**[1] **2**

mutual fund *noun* (stock exchange)
(*US*) ► **unit trust**

/ˌmjuːtʃuəl ˈfʌnd/

mutual insurance company *noun* (insurance)
a type of life insurance company in which there are no shareholders and apart from the money used for running expenses, all profits are distributed to policyholders: *He has a policy with a mutual insurance company.*

/ˌmjuːtʃuəl ɪnˈʃʊərəns ˌkʌmpəni/
pl mutual insurance companies
syn mutual insurance firm
► **insurance**

Nn

naked debenture *noun* (accounting)
► **unsecured debenture**

/ˌneɪkɪd dɪˈbentʃə(r)/

name *noun* (insurance)
► **Lloyd's name**

/neɪm/

narrow market *noun* (stock exchange)
► **thin market**

/ˌnærəʊ ˈmɑːkɪt/

NASDAQ *abbr* (stock exchange)
National Association of Dealers in Securities Automated Quotation

/ˈnæzdæk/

national bank *noun* (banking)
(*US*) a bank, controlled by the central banking organization, (the FEDERAL RESERVE SYSTEM) and used by the public, that can operate in all parts of the country: *The controller of the currency proposed that national banks should hold $8 in capital for each $100 in assets.* ○ *obtain a mortgage from a national bank*

/ˌnæʃnəl ˈbæŋk/
pl national banks
► **commercial bank, Federal Reserve Bank, state bank**

national debt *noun* (economics)
the total amount of money that a government owes as a result of borrowing from within and outside the country: *The government is attempting to reduce the national debt.*

/ˌnæʃnəl ˈdet/
note no plural
⋈ pay off, repay the **national debt**
► **balance of payments, debt, public debts**

National Insurance *noun* (tax)
(UK) a percentage of wages and salaries that employees, employers and the self-employed have to pay towards state sickness, unemployment and retirement payments: *National Insurance is deducted from your salary each month.* ○ *pay £40 per month in National Insurance*

/ˌnæʃnəl ɪnˈʃʊərəns/
abbr NI, N.I.
⋈ pay, qualify for **National Insurance**; **National Insurance** contributions, deductions
► **benefit**[1], **pension**

nationalization *noun* (industry)
the process or result of bringing a company, or different companies in the same industry, under central government control: *propose nationalization of the telephone system*

/ˌnæʃnəlaɪˈzeɪʃn/
(also **nationalisation**)
note not used with *a* or *an*. No plural and used with a singular verb only.
⋈ oppose, propose **nationalization**
▶ **denationalization, privatization**

---

nationalize *verb* (industry)
to bring a company, or different companies in the same industry, under central government control: *The Labour Party in Britain decided to nationalize more industries.* ○ *nationalize the railways, the coal industry, etc* ○ *British Coal is a nationalized industry.*

/ˈnæʃnəlaɪz/
nationalize, nationalizing, nationalized
(also **nationalise**)
note transitive verb
opp privatize
▶ **denationalize, private sector, public sector**

National Savings *noun* (finance)
(*UK*) a system of saving money run by The Post Office: *put money into National Savings* ○ *I'm going to cash one of my National Savings certificates.* ○ *save with the National Savings Bank*

/ˌnæʃnəl ˈseɪvɪŋz/
▶ **savings bank**

---

native language *noun*
▶ **mother tongue**

/ˌneɪtɪv ˈlæŋgwɪdʒ/

---

natural person *noun* (law)
an individual that has legal rights and responsibilities that may be different from that of an organization or from those of a group of people acting together: *be classed as a natural person*

/ˌnætʃrəl ˈpɜːsn/
pl natural persons
▶ **artificial person, legal person**

---

natural wastage *noun* (industrial relations)
the loss of employees because they retire, die or move to a job with another company: *We've calculated that there would be a reduction of about thirty jobs over the next twelve months through natural wastage.*

/ˌnætʃrəl ˈweɪstɪdʒ/
note not used with *a* or *an*. No plural and used with singular verb only.
⋈ process of **natural wastage**
▶ **job losses, redundancy, unemployment, wastage**

NAV *abbr* (accounting)
net asset value

/ˌen eɪ ˈviː/
(also **N.A.V., nav, n.a.v.**)
note pronounced as individual letters

NBV *abbr* (accounting)
net book value

/ˌen biː ˈviː/
(also **nbv**)

---

near letter quality printer *noun* (computing)
a computer printer used for memos and messages sent within a company rather than for important business correspondence: *Is it all right to use the near letter quality printer for these memos?*

/ˌnɪə ˌletə ˌkwɒləti ˈprɪntə(r)/
pl near letter quality printers
abbr NLQ
⋈ use the **near letter quality printer**
▶ **daisywheel, dot matrix printer, laser printer, letter quality printer**

near money *noun* (finance/banking)
an item that can be easily exchanged in the way that money can, although it is not money itself. It includes cheques and postal orders but not banknotes or coins: *calculate the amount of cash and near money*

/ˌnɪə ˈmʌni/
note not used with *a* or *an*. No plural and used with singular verb only.
⧓ liquid, transferable **near money**
syn quasi-money
► **medium of exchange**

---

negative certificate of origin *noun* (shipping)
a document that shows that a product was not made in or imported from a particular country: *Some countries ask shipping companies for a negative certificate of origin to show that items have no connection with a politically opposed country.*

/ˌnegətɪv səˌtɪfɪkət əv ˈɒrɪdʒɪn /
pl negative certificates of origin
⧓ issue, require, show a **negative certificate of origin**
► **certificate of origin**

---

negative income tax *noun* (tax)
(*UK*) payments by the state to people with incomes below those paying standard income tax: *a system of negative income tax*

/ˌnegətɪv ˈɪŋkʌm tæks/
note no plural
abbr NIT
► **income tax, tax**[1]

---

negotiable *adjective*
1 (*management*) that can be changed or decided by discussion: *The terms of the agreement are negotiable.* **2** (*finance*) that can be exchanged for goods, money, etc: *His cheque was not negotiable because it was out of date, and a replacement cheque had to be requested.*

/nɪˈgəʊʃiəbl/
1 ⧓ **negotiable** conditions, rates, terms
syn open to discussion
► **non-negotiable 1, negotiate 1, 2**
2 ► **non-negotiable 2, negotiate 3**

---

negotiable instrument *noun* (finance)
a document that can be exchanged for goods, money, etc: *Cheques, banknotes and bills of exchange are negotiable instruments.* ○ *The travel insurance does not include negotiable instruments of any kind.*

/nɪˌgəʊʃiəbl ˈɪnstrəmənt/
pl negotiable instruments
⧓ hold, possess a **negotiable instrument**
► **bill of exchange, negotiable 2, promissory note**

---

negotiate *verb*
1 to try to reach an agreement through discussion: *We are negotiating with our employers for higher salaries next year.* ○ *The suppliers are refusing to negotiate.* **2** to arrange or settle something in this way: *I'd like to negotiate a discount of 7% off the list price.* ○ *We need to negotiate the terms and conditions of the contract.*
3 (*finance*) to get or give money or goods in exchange for a cheque, share certificates, etc: *This certificate cannot be negotiated.*

/nɪˈgəʊʃieɪt/
negotiate, negotiating, negotiated
1 note intransitive verb
⧓ **negotiate** *with* someone; **negotiate** about, for, over (something)
2 note transitive verb
⧓ **negotiate** a deal, loan, sale, settlement, terms
3 note transitive verb
► **deal**[2]

---

negotiating table *noun*
a meeting where people with different opinions try to come to an agreement: *Both sides still refuse to come to the negotiating table.*

/nɪˈgəʊʃieɪtɪŋ ˌteɪbl/
pl negotiating tables
⧓ discuss, get round, get together

at, sit round the **negotiating table**

---

negotiation *noun*

1 (**a**) the process of trying to reach an agreement through discussion: *The price is not fixed, but is a matter for negotiation.* (**b**) a meeting where this discussion takes place: *An agreement was reached after lengthy negotiations.* **2** (*finance*) the process of exchanging money or goods for a cheque, share certificates, etc: *handle the negotiation of share certificates*

/nɪˌɡəʊʃiˈeɪʃn/

1a note not used with *a* or *an*. No plural and used with a singular verb only.

⧓ a matter for, open to, room for **negotiation**

1b pl negotiations

⧓ break off, carry on, complete, enter into, open, resume **negotiations**

▶ **wage negotiations**

2 note not used with *a* or *an*. No plural and used with a singular verb only.

▶ **negotiable instrument**

---

negotiator *noun*

a person, often representing a particular group or company, involved in discussions that aim to reach an agreement between two sides: *We need a very skilful negotiator for this deal.* ○ *Who will act as negotiator?*

/nɪˈɡəʊʃieɪtə(r)/

pl negotiators

⧓ a skilful, successful, tough **negotiator**

▶ **agent**

---

net[1] *adjective*

1 (of money) remaining after all amounts that are owed DEDUCTIONS have been taken off: *Her net salary last year was $20 000, after paying tax, national insurance and pension contributions.* ○ *He made a profit of £500 net on each sale.* ○ *A year ago the company had a net loss of $4.3 million or 20 cents a share.* **2** (of a weight) without wrapping or packaging: *calculate the net weight of the goods* ○ *How much does it weigh net?* **3** (of a price) fixed: *price £7.50 net* ○ *These are all net prices.* ○ *Are these prices net?*

/net/

1 ⧓ **net** salary, wage

▶ **gross, net loss, net national product, net present value, net profit, net realizable value**

3 (also **nett**)

▶ **net price**

---

net[2] *verb*

to gain as a profit: *National Oil netted twenty-five million last year.*

/net/

net, netting, netted

note transitive verb

---

net asset value *noun* (commerce/finance)

the financial worth of an organization, calculated by adding the number of ASSETS and taking off all its debts (LIABILITIES): *The business was sold for £5 million, only half its net asset value.* ○ *The current net asset value is more than 40p a share.* ○ *The company's net asset value rose by 10.5%.*

/ˌnet ˌæset ˈvælju:/

pl net asset values

abbr NAV, nav

⧓ assess, calculate, quote the **net asset value**

syn asset value

▶ **net book value, value**[1] **2**

---

net asset value per share *noun* (accounting)

the total value of the assets of a company, less the total value of its liabilities, divided by the number of shares issued: *a company with a high net asset value per share* ○ *At the end of the trading period the net asset value per share was 145p.*

/ˌnet ˌæset ˌvælju: pə ˈʃeə(r)/

pl net asset values per share

⧓ a high, low **net asset value per share**

▶ **asset backing, value**[1] **2**

---

net book value *noun* (accounting)
the worth of an asset as recorded in the accounts book of a company, taking into consideration any loss of value because it is old, worn, etc (DEPRECIATION): *The net book value of the company's vehicles was calculated by deducting twenty-five per cent of the purchase value after twelve months.*

/ˌnet ˈbʊk ˌvæljuː/
pl net book values
abbr NBV, nbv
⧓ calculate, record, show the **net book value**
syn net book amount
► **market value, revaluation of assets, value[1] 2**

net income *noun* (accounting)
the amount of money received by a person or an organization in the form of wages, profit or interest after tax has been taken off: *receive a net income of £25 000 a year*

/ˌnet ˈɪŋkʌm/
note usually singular
⧓ an annual, a monthly **net income**
► **gross income, income, take-home pay**

net loss *noun* (accounting)
1 (of money) a total amount lost by a company after tax, etc has been taken off: *The insurance company announced a net loss of $835.7 million in 1991.* **2** the real amount lost after all amounts to be added or taken off have been considered: *Despite the building of a new cigar factory the net loss of jobs is still 1 200.* ○ *During the reorganization there will be no net loss of output.*

/ˌnet ˈlɒs/
pl net losses
► **loss 1, net profit, trading loss**

net national product *noun* (economics)
the amount of money that is available in a country's economy for spending on goods and services. It is the GROSS NATIONAL PRODUCT minus the amount by which resources, machinery, etc lose their value over time.

/ˌnet ˌnæʃnəl ˈprɒdʌkt/
note not used with *a* or *an*. No plural and used with a singular verb only.
abbr NNP
⧓ calculate, contribute to, increase, reduce the **net national product**

net present value *noun* (accounting)
the expected net income from an asset, discounted to the present date, less the initial cost of the asset: *a net present value of £12 million* ○ *A worthwhile project must have a positive net present value.*

/ˌnet ˌpreznt ˈvæljuː/
pl net present values
abbr NPV
⧓ calculate, estimate the **net present value**; a negative, positive **net present value**
► **accounting rate of return, value[1] 2**

net price *noun* (sales)
a fixed price that cannot be reduced: *These are all net price books.*

/ˌnet ˈpraɪs/
pl net prices
(also **nett price**)
⧓ charge, pay a **net price**
► **price[1]**

net profit *noun* (accounting/sales)
the amount of money made from the sale of goods minus the cost of producing, selling and distributing them. Net profit may be calculated before or after an amount has been taken off for tax: *The company's net profit increased by 18% after a tax reduction.* ○ *make a net profit of $20.2 million*

/ˌnet ˈprɒfɪt/
pl net profits
⧓ achieve, earn make a **net profit**; calculate, improve the **net profit**
► **net loss, profit[1], profit and loss account, trading profit**

et realizable value *noun* (accounting)
he amount of money that would be received for an ASSET if it vere sold, after all the costs of the sale have been taken off

/ˌnet ˌrɪəlaɪzəbl ˈvæljuː/
pl net realizable values
abbr NRV
⧓ calculate, estimate the **net realizable value**
▶ **net present value, value[1] 2**

---

etwork[1] *noun*
(**a**) a closely linked group of people, organizations, etc that vork together: *The company operates nationwide through its etwork of agents and contacts.* ○ *an international network of offices nd branches* ○ *a distribution, sales, etc network* (**b**) a complex ystem of roads, railways, telephone lines, etc: *build a rail etwork* ○ *a telecommunications network* **2** (*computing*) a number f computers that are linked together: *They have 250 computers n the network in their main office.*

/ˈnetwɜːk/
pl networks
1 ⧓ construct, create, develop, enlarge, form, set up a **network**
▶ **infrastructure**
2 ⧓ be connected to, be linked to, install, share a **network**: **network** cabling, stations, terminals
▶ **node 1, stand-alone**

---

etwork[2] *verb*
to establish or extend links between people, organizations, etc: *irculating a monthly report is a useful way of networking with ther departments.* **2** (*computing*) to establish or extend links etween computers: *They have recently networked all their omputers.*

/ˈnetwɜːk/
network, networking, networked
1 note intransitive verb
2 note transitive verb

---

et worth *noun* (finance)
he value of a business calculated by subtracting all its debts LIABILITIES) from its items of value (ASSETS): *He is confident that the ompany will be able to increase its net worth.* ○ *The company has a egative net worth. Its liabilities exceed its assets.*

/ˌnet ˈwɜːθ/
note no plural
▶ **net asset value, net book value**

---

ews release *noun* (advertising)
▶ **press release**

/ˈnjuːz rɪˌliːs/

---

ew time buying *noun* (stock exchange/finance)
uying securities on the stock exchange during the last two days f a trading period for settlement in the next period: *There was no vidence of new time buying today.*

/ˌnjuː taɪm ˈbaɪɪŋ/
note not used with *a* or *an*. No plural and used with a singular verb only.
▶ **Account Day, contango**

---

ew York Stock Exchange *noun* (stock exchange)
he main stock exchange in the United States, situated in Wall treet, New York City: *The company was floated on the New York tock Exchange in 1990.*

/ˌnjuː jɔːk ˈstɒk ɪksˌtʃeɪndʒ/
abbr NYSE
⧓ buy, deal, sell, trade on the **New York Stock Exchange**
▶ **International Stock Exchange, stock exchange**

I *abbr* (health and safety)
ational Insurance: *NI payments*

/ˌen ˈaɪ/
(also **N.I.**)

---

ikkei Index *noun* (stock exchange)
he main list of ordinary shares showing price changes on the tock exchange in Tokyo: *The Nikkei Index fell 161.60 to 2376.80.*

/nɪˈkeɪ ˌɪndeks/
⧓ the **Nikkei Index** closed, fell, jumped, rose, sank
▶ **Dow Jones Industrial Average, the Financial**

Times-Stock Exchange 100 Share Index

nil *adjective*
no number or amount: *Profit from overseas sales is expected to be nil.* ○ *We expect to make nil profit on this deal.*
/nɪl/
► **nought**

NIT *abbr* (tax)
negative income tax
/ˌen aɪ ˈtiː/
note pronounced as individual letters

NLQ *abbr* (computing)
1 near letter quality **2** a near letter quality printer: *I hope you are only using that old NLQ for internal memos.*
/ˌen el ˈkjuː/
pl NLQs

NNP *abbr* (economics)
net national product
/ˌen en ˈpiː/

No. *abbr*
number
note used in written English only

no-claims bonus *noun* (insurance)
a reduction in the annual sum (PREMIUM) paid to an insurance company, offered to someone who did not ask for insurance repayments during the previous year: *He lost his no-claims bonus last year after five previous years without a claim.*
/ˌnəʊ ˈkleɪmz ˌbəʊnəs/
pl no-claims bonuses
(also **no claims bonus**)
► **claim**[1] **1, insurance**

node *noun* (computing)
1 a piece of computer equipment (HARDWARE) that links two or more computers to a network: *a node computer* **2** a point in a computer program that provides a link to other items of data: *a data node*
/nəʊd/
pl nodes
⋈ a **node** branch, list, tree
► **network**[1] **2**

nominal *adjective*
relating to an amount of money that is very small but paid because some payment is necessary: *a nominal rent*, ie a rent that is very much below the actual value of the property ○ *He was only charged a nominal amount.*
/ˈnɒmɪnl/
⋈ a **nominal** amount, charge, fee, price; **nominal** pay, value
► **nominal price 1, token charge**

nominal account *noun* (accounting)
the general expenses of a company, eg for heat, light, etc and not amounts relating to named customers and suppliers; the part of a book or computer file (a LEDGER) where these are recorded: *The two largest nominal accounts for that firm are motor expenses, and heat and lighting.* ○ *make an entry in the nominal account*
/ˌnɒmɪnl əˈkaʊnt/
pl nominal accounts
⋈ enter, put (something) in the **nominal account**
syn impersonal account
► **account**[1] **1**

nominal capital *noun* (stock exchange)
► **authorized share capital**
/ˌnɒmɪnl ˈkæpɪtl/

nominal ledger *noun* (accounting)
a book or computer record containing the accounts from which a company prepares its profit and loss figures: *The accounts were entered in the nominal ledger.*
/ˌnɒmɪnl ˈledʒə(r)/
note usually singular
syn impersonal ledger
► **bought ledger, ledger, sales ledger**

nominal partner *noun* (management)
a person whose name is used for the good of the company, eg because he/she is famous, but who is not a legal partner and receives a fee but not a share of the profits

/ˌnɒmɪnl ˈpɑːtnə(r)/
pl nominal partners
▶ **partner**

nominal price *noun*
1 a price that is much lower than the real value of something: *Canteen meals are provided for a nominal price.* **2** (*stock exchange*) the value given to a SHARE when it is first issued: *The Financial Times Ordinary Share Index was quoting those Atlantic Shares at nearly six times their nominal price.*

/ˌnɒmɪnl ˈpraɪs/
pl nominal prices
1, 2 syn nominal value
2 syn face value, par value
▶ **above par, at par, below par, share issue**

nominal yield *noun* (stock exchange)
the amount received from a FIXED-INTEREST SECURITY, expressed as a percentage of its NOMINAL PRICE: *The investment provides a nominal yield of 5%.*

/ˌnɒmɪnl ˈjiːld/
pl nominal yields
⧓ offer, provide, receive a **nominal yield**
▶ **yield**[1]

nominate *verb*
1 (*formal*) to suggest that someone or something should be chosen for a position: *I nominate Mrs Green (for the President).* ○ *I nominate Mr Smith as Chairman.* **2** (*formal*) to choose someone or something for a position or a function: *Mr Baker was nominated by the policyholder as the person who should receive the proceeds of the life assurance policy.* ○ *Your expenses can be paid straight into a bank account nominated by you.*

/ˈnɒmɪneɪt/
nominate, nominating, nominated
note transitive verb
⧓ **nominate** someone/something *as* something, someone/something *for* something
▶ **appoint, vote**[2]

nomination *noun*
1 the process of suggesting or choosing someone for a position: *Nomination should be by letter.* **2** (**a**) the suggestion or choice of someone or something for a position: *My nomination was too late to be considered.* (**b**) the name of the person suggested or chosen for a position: *Here is the list of nominations for members to consider.*

/ˌnɒmɪˈneɪʃn/
1 note not used with *a* or *an*. No plural and used with a singular verb only.
2 pl nominations
⧓ a **nomination** *for* something
▶ **vote**[1]

nominator *noun*
the person who chooses or suggests someone or something for a position: *We need two nominators for each candidate.*

/ˈnɒmɪˌneɪtə(r)/
pl nominators
⧓ act as **nominator**

nominee *noun*
the person who is suggested or chosen for a position: *How many nominees are there?*

/ˌnɒmɪˈniː/
pl nominees
▶ **appointee, candidate**

nominee holding *noun* (stock exchange)
shares that have been bought by one person but have been put in the name of another, often a bank, stockbroker or company: *It is difficult to trace the true owner of a nominee holding.*

/ˌnɒmɪniː ˈhəʊldɪŋ/
pl nominee holdings
syn nominee shareholding
▶ **holding**

non-acceptance *noun* (banking)
the refusal to agree to sign a bill of exchange to say that you promise to pay it

/ˌnɒn əkˈseptəns/
note not used with *a* or *an*. No plural and used with a singular verb only.
▶ **acceptance 2**

non-current liabilities *noun* (accounting) /ˌnɒn ˌkʌrənt ˌlaɪəˈbɪlətiz/
▶ **deferred liabilities**

non-durables *noun* (commerce) /ˌnɒn ˈdjʊərəblz/
▶ **consumer non-durables**

non-negotiable *adjective* /ˌnɒn nɪˈɡəʊʃiəbl/
1 (*management*) that cannot be changed or decided by discussion: *The terms of the contract are non-negotiable.* **2** (*banking*) that cannot be exchanged for money except by the person whose name is written on the document: *The cheque is non-negotiable.*

syn not negotiable
1 ⋈ **non-negotiable** conditions, rates, terms
▶ **negotiable 1, negotiate 1, 2**
2 ⋈ a **non-negotiable** bill of exchange, cheque, share certificate
▶ **negotiable 2, negotiate 3**

nosedive[1] *noun* /ˈnəʊzdaɪv/
a sudden fall: *Prices have taken a nosedive recently.* ○ *Tokyo stock prices went into a nosedive yesterday.*

pl nosedives

nosedive[2] *verb* /ˈnəʊzdaɪv/
to fall suddenly: *Coffee prices nosedived yesterday.*

nosedive, nosediving, nosedived
note intransitive verb

nostro account *noun* (banking) /ˈnɒstrəʊ əˌkaʊnt/
(*UK*) an account which a bank holds with another bank, usually overseas: *The money is held in a nostro account.*

pl nostro accounts
▶ **account**[1] **2, loro account, vostro account**

note *noun* (banking) /nəʊt/
▶ **banknote**

pl notes

notice *noun* /ˈnəʊtɪs/
1 written or printed news or information: *The legal notices are on page 10 of today's newspaper.* ○ *put up a notice on the staff notice-board* **2** a warning (of what will happen): *You may have to fly out to our Tokyo office at short notice* (ie without much warning). ○ *Please give seven days' notice before drawing money out of the account.* ○ *The laboratory will be closed until further notice.* **3** a letter stating that someone is to leave a job at a specified time: *He handed in his notice* (ie announced that he will leave his job). ○ *She was given a month's notice* (ie was told to leave her job in a month).

1 pl notices
⋈ put up, send out a **notice**
2 note not used with *a* or *an*. No plural and used with a singular verb only.
⋈ short, until further **notice**; give **notice**
3 note not used with *a* or *an*. No plural and used with a singular verb only.
⋈ give in, hand in your **notice**

notice of abandonment *noun* (insurance/shipping) /ˌnəʊtɪs əv əˈbændənmənt/
▶ **abandonment**

notify *verb* /ˈnəʊtɪfaɪ/
(*formal*) to inform somebody of something: *Please notify all staff about the meeting.* ○ *You will be notified as soon as the new stock comes in.*

notify, notifying, notified
note transitive verb
⋈ **notify** someone *of* something, someone *about* something

not negotiable *adjective* (banking/management)
▶ **non-negotiable**

/ˌnɒt nɪˈɡəʊʃiəbl/

nought *noun*
the figure 0: *The number of my bank account is seven nought three one four nought six seven (70314067).*

/nɔːt/
pl noughts
▶ **nil**

NPV *noun* (accounting)
net present value

note used in written English only

NRV *noun* (accounting)
net realizable value

note used in written English only

null and void *adjective* (law)
without legal force: *This contract is now null and void.*

/ˌnʌl ənd ˈvɔɪd/
▶ **invalid, void**

nullify *verb* (law)
to make an agreement lose its legal force: *The contract was nullified.* ○ *nullify an agreement*

/ˈnʌlɪfaɪ/
nullify, nullifying, nullified
note transitive verb

number *noun*
symbol or word indicating a quantity of units, used to distinguish, count or label something: *We have not received payment for invoice number 3570.* ○ *The meeting is in room number 22.*

/ˈnʌmbə(r)/
pl numbers
abbr No., no.
⋈ the cheque, file, invoice, order, receipt **number**
▶ **box number, digit, personal identification number, serial number**

Oo

objective *noun* (management)
an aim or target: *Please come to the meeting with a list of specific objectives.* ○ *It is important for us to meet our objectives.* ○ *Our main objective is to cut costs.* ○ *What are your aims and objectives?*

/əbˈdʒektɪv/
pl objectives
⋈ achieve, define, set out an **objective**
▶ **mission statement**

obsolescence *noun* (manufacturing)
the state of being out of date; no longer needed or in use: *Obsolescence is a big problem for companies that rely on computers.*

/ˌɒbsəˈlesns/
note not used with *a* or *an*. No plural and used with a singular verb only.
▶ **planned obsolescence**

obsolescent *adjective* (manufacturing)
out of date; no longer needed or in use: *This washing machine is obsolescent and therefore spare parts are difficult to find.*

/ˌɒbsəˈlesnt/
⋈ become **obsolescent**

occupant *noun*
the person who lives in or has possession of a building or part of it: *Did you know the previous occupants of this house?*

/ˈɒkjəpənt/
pl occupants
⋈ present, previous **occupant**
note Letters to an unnamed person are addressed to 'the

Occupier' not 'the Occupant'.

▶ **occupier, tenant**

---

occupation *noun* (personnel)

a job; employment: *Please write your name, address and occupation on the form.* ○ *What is your present occupation?* ○ *She is a lawyer by occupation.*

/ˌɒkjuˈpeɪʃn/

pl occupations

⋈ a full-time, main, part-time, skilled **occupation**

▶ **business 1 a, livelihood, profession, trade**

---

occupational hazard *noun* (industry/personnel)

a risk or danger associated with a particular job: *Explosions, though they do not happen often, are an occupational hazard for mineworkers.*

/ˌɒkjuˌpeɪʃənl ˈhæzəd/

pl occupational hazards

▶ **danger money**

---

occupier *noun* (law)

a person who has (esp temporary) possession of a building or a piece of land: *The letter was addressed to 'The Occupier, 21 Green Road, Bristol'.*

/ˈɒkjupaɪə(r)/

pl occupiers

⋈ owner **occupier**

▶ **occupant**

ODA *abbr*

Overseas Development Administration

/ˌəʊ diː ˈeɪ/

note pronounced as individual letters

---

odd-even pricing *noun* (sales)

(*UK*) putting a price on an item that has an odd number of pence just below the next pound to make it seem cheaper: *Charging £3.99 instead of £4.00 is an example of odd-even pricing.*

/ˌɒd ˌiːvn ˈpraɪsɪŋ/

note not used with *a* or *an*. No plural and used with a singular verb only.

---

oddment *noun* (sales)

an item that is sold cheaply, usually because it is the last one left from old stock: *sell off a few oddments*

/ˈɒdmənt/

pl oddments

---

offer¹ *noun* (commerce)

1 a thing that is put forward to be accepted or refused: *I cannot accept your offer.* ○ *accept a pay offer of 7%* ○ *The company rejected a serious offer of £5 000 000.* ○ *She turned down the offer of a job.* **2** an amount offered; a bid: *make a cash offer* ○ *The company was forced to increase its offer.* **3** a thing that is put forward at a reduced price or with better conditions than usual: *The offer ends on 31st January.* ○ *The offer is open to account holders only.*

on offer 1 for sale: *look at the goods on offer* **2** for sale at a reduced price: *Washing powder is on offer at the supermarket.*

open to offer(s) willing to consider a price suggested by a buyer: *The price is open to offers.*

under offer (of a building) have a buyer who has made an offer: *The office block is under offer.*

/ˈɒfə(r)/

pl offers

⋈ accept, make, receive, refuse, reject, turn down an **offer**; a share **offer**

▶ **acceptance 1**

3 ⋈ a special **offer**

---

offer² *verb*

to put forward something to be accepted or refused: *I cannot agree to the terms offered.* ○ *We offer a discount for holidays booked in advance.* ○ *Shareholders were offered 18p per share.* ○ *I'm offering you a job overseas.*

/ˈɒfə(r)/

offer, offering, offered

note transitive verb

▶ **accept 1**

---

offer by prospectus *noun* (stock exchange)

a new issue of shares offered to the public with a written

/ˌɒfə baɪ prəˈspektəs/

note no plural

description of the aims, history and financial structure of the company: *The new share issue was made through an offer by prospectus.*

▶ **offer for sale, prospectus**

---

offer document *noun* (stock exchange)
papers sent to the shareholders of a company giving details of a takeover bid: *draw up an offer document*

/ˈɒfə ˌdɒkjəmənt/
pl offer documents
⧓ compile, prepare, send out an **offer document**
▶ **offer for sale**

---

offer for sale *noun* (stock exchange)
a new issue of shares offered to the public through a bank: *The offer for sale was priced at 125p a share.*

/ˌɒfə fə ˈseɪl/
note usually singular
⧓ an **offer for sale** document
▶ **offer by prospectus**

---

offer to purchase *noun* (stock exchange)
▶ **takeover bid**

/ˌɒfə tə ˈpɜːtʃəs/

---

office *noun*
1 (*personnel*) a position of responsibility: *She holds the office of company treasurer.* ○ *The chairman was retained in office.*
2 (*administration*) a building or room where work, esp administrative or clerical takes place: *Let's meet in my office.* ○ *I must phone the office before I leave.* **3** (*administration*) the place where a particular kind of work is done: *You can exchange money at the tourist office.* ○ *He works at the local tax office.* ○ *You need to speak to someone in our main office.*

/ˈɒfɪs/
pl offices
⧓ an **office** block, building, job, worker; **office** equipment, work
3 ⧓ a local, regional **office**
▶ **back office, head office, registered office**

---

office hours *noun* (commerce)
the time during the day when work is done in an office: *Please call during office hours.* ○ *Office hours are between 9 am and 5 pm.* ○ *Ring this number if you need to call outside office hours.*

/ˈɒfɪs ˌaʊəz/
note plural noun, used with a plural verb
▶ **business hours**

Office of Fair Trading *noun* (commerce)
(*UK*) a government department that inspects commercial organizations to protect the public from dishonest and illegal trading: *The Office of Fair Trading will be given more power to enter and search premises if unfair practices are suspected.*

/ˌɒfɪs əv ˌfeə ˈtreɪdɪŋ/
abbr OFT
⧓ apply to, complain to, report to the **Office of Fair Trading**
▶ **the Department of Trade and Industry, fair trading, Monopolies and Mergers Commission, restrictive trade practices, Trading Standards Department**

Official List *noun* (stock exchange)
▶ **Stock Exchange Daily Official List**

/əˌfɪʃl ˈlɪst/

---

official rate *noun* (economics)
the rate of exchange set by a government, or an agency appointed by a government, for a particular foreign currency: *change currency at the official rate*

/əˌfɪʃl ˈreɪt/
pl official rates
⧓ agree, set the **official rate**
▶ **exchange rate, market rate, rate 2**

---

official receiver *noun* (finance)
a person appointed by the government to make the arrangements when a company goes into LIQUIDATION or

/əˌfɪʃl rɪˈsiːvə(r)/
pl official receivers
⧓ appoint, call in, be in the hands of the **official receiver**

becomes bankrupt: *The debts amounted to £108 million despite the efforts of the official receiver to retrieve some of the money.*

syn receiver
▶ **administrator 2, liquidator**

---

official strike *noun* (industrial relations)
▶ **strike**

/əˌfɪʃl ˈstraɪk/

---

off-line *adjective* (computing)
not directly connected to a database or the central part of a computer system: *This terminal is off-line.* ○ *off-line storage of information*

/ˌɒf ˈlaɪn/
▶ **on-line**

---

off-peak *adjective, adverb*
of a time when an item or a service is used less than at other times: *charge an off-peak travel fare* ○ *It is cheaper to travel off-peak.* ○ *Calls are charged at 25p a minute off-peak.* ○ *pay an off-peak tariff for electricity*

/ˌɒf ˈpiːk/
⧓ **off-peak** hours, periods, services, times
▶ **peak**[3]

---

off-season *noun* (commerce/tourism)
of the part of a year when there are fewer tourists or customers: *travel in the off-season* ○ *Summer is the off-season for a ski resort.*

/ˈɒf ˌsiːzn/
note singular noun, used with a singular verb
⧓ an **off-season** resort; **off-season** travel

---

offset *verb* (commerce)
to balance something or compensate for something: *We have offset prices against tax.* ○ *The decline in profits was not offset by increased productivity.*

/ˈɒfset, ɒfˈset/
offset, offsetting, offset
note transitive verb
⧓ **offset** something *by* something
▶ **balance**[2]

---

offshore *adjective*
1 (*industry*) at sea, not far from land: *an offshore oil company* ○ *drilling for oil offshore* **2** (*finance*) (of banks, investment companies, etc) based or registered abroad, usually to avoid tax laws: *keep money in an offshore bank account* ○ *rising investment in offshore operations*

/ˌɒfˈʃɔː(r)/
1 ⧓ **offshore** industry, workers
2 ⧓ **offshore** assets, banking, investment

---

offshore fund *noun* (finance)
a collection of money for investment kept out of a country to avoid tax: *invest in an offshore fund*

/ˈɒfʃɔː ˌfʌnd/
pl offshore funds
▶ **fund**[1] **2, tax haven, umbrella fund**

---

off-the-shelf *adjective* (manufacturing)
designed and made to certain preset standards; ready-made: *an off-the-shelf computer system* ○ *buy something off-the-shelf*

/ˌɒf ðə ˈʃelf/

OFT *abbr* (commerce)
Office of Fair Trading

/ˌəʊ ef ˈtiː/
note pronounced as individual letters

---

on approval *adverb* (retail)
▶ **approval**

/ˌɒn əˈpruːvl/

---

oncost *noun* (industry)
the money needed to produce something that does not change with the quantity produced: *Factory rent is an oncost because it must be paid every year.*

/ˈɒnkɒst/
pl oncosts
note usually plural
▶ **direct cost, fixed cost,**

overhead, unit cost, variable cost

---

on demand *adverb* (banking)
of a bill of exchange that must be paid immediately it is presented for payment: *The bill is payable on demand.*

/ˌɒn dɪˈmɑːnd/
▶ **after date, at sight, bill of exchange, demand[1] 1, sight bill**

---

on-lending *noun* (banking/finance)
lending money that has already been borrowed from elsewhere: *The bank has increased the amount of on-lending.*

/ˈɒn lendɪŋ/
note not used with *a* or *an*. No plural and used with a singular verb only.

---

on-line *adjective* (computing)
connected to a database or the central part of a computer system: *Is the computer on-line at the moment?* ○ *on-line updating of the customer orders database* ○ *We have on-line access to their database.*

/ˌɒnˈ laɪn/
⧓ an **on-line** computer, database, system, terminal
▶ **central processing unit, off-line**

---

o.n.o. *abbr* (sales)
or nearest offer: *Car for sale: £2000 o.n.o.*

/ˌəʊ en ˈəʊ/

---

o.o. *abbr* (retail)
on order: *Your computer is o.o.*

note used in written English only

---

open cheque *noun* (banking)
a cheque that does not have two lines drawn across it (a CROSSED CHEQUE) and can therefore be exchanged for cash at the bank where it was issued: *cash an open cheque* ○ *make out an open cheque to someone*

/ˌəʊpən ˈtʃek/
pl open cheques
⧓ cash, sign, write an **open cheque**
syn uncrossed cheque
▶ **blank cheque, cheque, crossed cheque**

---

open door policy *noun* (import)
a system of importing goods with no or very few restrictions or import duties: *The country has had an open door policy for many years.*

/ˌəʊpən ˈdɔː ˌpɒləsi/
pl open door policies
⧓ operate an **open door policy**
▶ **customs duty, import duty, tariff**

---

open indent *noun* (international trade)
an order given to an overseas agent to buy goods that does not state the name of a particular supplier: *The principal gave his agent an open indent for the goods.*

/ˌəʊpən ˈɪndent/
pl open indents
⧓ give, receive an **open indent**
opp closed indent

---

open market *noun* (commerce)
a situation where there are few or no trading restrictions and prices depend on the amount of goods and the number of buyers available: *compete for buyers on the open market* ○ *Coal prices on the open market are low because of the large amount of coal available.*

/ˌəʊpən ˈmɑːkɪt/
note usually singular
⧓ buy, sell, trade *on* the **open market**
▶ **free market, market[1]**

---

open position *noun* (stock exchange)
a situation in which a dealer has bought commodities, securities or currencies but not yet sold them: *an open position is vulnerable until the position can be closed*

/ˈəʊpən pəˌzɪʃn/
note no plural
▶ **bear position, bull position, hedging, short position**

---

open shop *noun* (industrial relations)
a workplace where the employer may employ workers who are not members of a trade union: *It is a small business and operates an open shop.*

/ˌəʊpən ˈʃɒp/
note no plural
⋈ abolish, establish, form an **open shop**; an **open shop** agreement, policy
► **closed shop**

---

operating loss *noun* (finance)
the net loss made by a company before adding or deducting extraordinary items: *Last year the company made an operating loss of £1.8 million.*

/ˈɒpəreɪtɪŋ ˌlɒs/
pl operating losses
⋈ make an **operating loss**
► **loss 1, trading loss**

---

operating profit *noun* (finance)
the net profit made by a company before adding or deducting extraordinary items: *Rover made an operating profit last year of £67.5 million.*

/ˈɒpəreɪtɪŋ ˌprɒfɪt/
pl operating profits
⋈ make an **operating profit**
► **profit[1], trading profit**

---

operative *noun* (industry)
a worker, esp one who works in a factory: *work as a factory operative* ○ *a machine operative*

/ˈɒpərətɪv/
pl operatives
⋈ a skilled, an unskilled **operative**
► **machinist**

---

oppose *verb*
to disagree with or reject an idea or plan, esp one suggested at a meeting: *The motion was opposed by the sales director.*

/əˈpəʊz/
oppose, opposing, opposed
note transitive verb
⋈ **oppose** an idea, a motion, a plan, proposal, a scheme
opp propose
► **counter**

---

opposer *noun*
a person who disagrees with a suggestion made at a formal meeting: *Do we have an opposer of this motion?*

/əˈpəʊzə(r)/
pl opposers
opp proposer
► **motion**

---

option *noun* (stock exchange)
the right to buy or sell a fixed quantity of a commodity, currency or security on a particular date at a particular price: *Options on securities are traded on the International Stock Exchange.* ○ *buy an option in commodity futures*

/ˈɒpʃn/
pl options
⋈ buy, sell, write, trade an **option**
► **call option, put option, share option, time bargain, time option, traded option**

---

option money *noun* (stock exchange)
the money used to buy an OPTION: *The dealer has paid the option money.*

/ˈɒpʃn ˌmʌni/
note no plural
⋈ pay, put forward the **option money**
► **call money, money**

---

option to purchase *noun* (stock exchange)
a right given to a shareholder to purchase shares in a particular company and at a reduced price: *Major shareholders were given a new option to purchase.*

/ˌɒpʃn tə ˈpɜːtʃəs/
note usually singular
⋈ acquire, give, receive an **option to purchase**

▶ **offer by prospectus, offer for sale, scrip issue**

---

order[1] *noun* (commerce)

/ˈɔːdə(r)/

pl orders

1 a request to make, supply or deliver goods: *receive a major export order* ○ *place an order for a new fax machine* ○ *Orders are up by 5% this month.* ○ *We processed* (ie dealt with) *your order yesterday.* ○ *Please write to confirm your order.* **2** the goods supplied: *Your order has arrived.* ○ *We can supply your order within three weeks.*

in (full) working order (esp of a machine) able to function properly: *The equipment has been thoroughly checked, everything is in full working order now.*

in order 1 in the right position or arrangement: *Please put these files in order.* **2** tidy: *I must put my desk in order before the visitors arrive.*

made to order made according to the customer's particular requirements: *supply made to order goods* ○ *We supply office furniture made to order.*

on order requested but not yet received: *The goods are on order.*

out of order (of a machine) not working: *The photocopier is out of order again.*

⋈ an **order** *for* something; place an **order** *with* someone; a bulk, cash, telephone, written **order**; cancel, confirm an **order**

▶ **back order, day order, good till cancelled order, landing order, limit order, mail order, market order, repeat order, warehouse-keeper's order**

---

order[2] *verb* (commerce)

/ˈɔːdə(r)/

order, ordering, ordered

note transitive verb

to ask for something to be made, supplied or delivered: *The goods were ordered over a month ago.* ○ *order traveller's cheques from a bank*

⋈ **order** something *from* someone

---

order form *noun* (commerce)

/ˈɔːdə fɔːm/

pl order forms

a printed form to be used by a customer requesting goods or a service: *It will save time if you fill in an order form.*

⋈ complete, fill in, process an **order form**

---

ordinary share *noun* (stock exchange)

/ˌɔːdənri ˈʃeə(r)/

pl ordinary shares

a fixed unit of a company's SHARE capital that provides a profit (DIVIDEND) related to the total profits of the company. Owners of ordinary shares have voting rights: *hold ordinary shares in a gas company* ○ *The total dividend per ordinary share was 31p.*

⋈ buy, sell an **ordinary share**; **ordinary share** capital

syn (*US*) common stock

▶ **A share, deferred share, earnings per (ordinary) share, equities, equity capital, security 1, share**

---

organization *noun*

/ˌɔːgənaɪˈzeɪʃn/

(also **organisation**)

1 pl organizations

1 a group of people, departments or institutions that work together: *work for a large manufacturing organization* ○ *The International Chamber of Commerce is the leading world business organization.* ○ *Computers are now being used throughout the organization.* ○ *The use of electronic mail will improve communications within the organization.* **2** the arrangement or control of something: *Each manager is responsible for the organization of his/her own department.* ○ *This project will need careful organization.*

⋈ an industrial, an international, a multinational, a world-wide **organization**; throughout, within an **organization**

▶ **association 1, business 3, company, federation, firm, group, mushroom organization, self-regulatory organization, umbrella organization**

2 note not used with *a* or *an*. No plural and used with a singular verb only.
⧓ careful, detailed, efficient **organization**
▶ **administration, reorganization**

---

original *noun*
the first version of a document from which extra copies are made: *Keep the original and send a photocopy.*

/əˈrɪdʒənl/
pl originals
▶ **carbon copy, copy[1] 1, master 1, top copy**

---

original goods *noun* (industry)
items that are used to produce goods which then have a financial value and can be sold: *land and water are original goods*

/əˌrɪdʒənl ˈgʊdz/
note plural noun, used with a plural verb
⧓ use **original goods**
▶ **raw material**

---

o/s *abbr*
1 (*accounting*) outstanding: *amounts o/s* **2** (*commerce*) out of stock

note used in written English only

---

outbid *verb* (sales)
to offer more money for something than someone else: *He was outbid at the auction.* ○ *She outbid me for the property.*

/ˌaʊtˈbɪd/
outbid, outbidding, outbid
note transitive and intransitive verb
⧓ **outbid** someone *for* something
▶ **bid[2], underbid**

---

outlay *noun* (finance)
spending; the money spent: *an initial outlay of £50 000*

/ˈaʊtleɪ/
note usually singular
⧓ capital **outlay**
▶ **expenditure**

---

outlay account *noun* (accounting)
▶ **appropriation account**

/ˈaʊtleɪ əˌkaʊnt/

---

outlet *noun* (retail)
a shop, etc that sells goods for a particular company: *We have a number of outlets throughout the country.* ○ *The company supplies hotels, restaurants and fast food outlets.*

/ˈaʊtlet/
pl outlets
⧓ a commercial, retail **outlet**
▶ **franchise**

---

out of order *adverb*
▶ **order**

/ˌaʊt əv ˈɔːdə(r)/

---

out of stock *adjective* (sales)
▶ **stock[1]**

/ˌaʊt əv ˈstɒk/
abbr o/s

---

output[1] *noun*
1 (*industry*) the quantity of goods produced by a worker, a machine or an organization: *Factory workers have increased output by 10%.* **2** (*computing*) the information produced by a computer: *improve the quality of computer output*

/ˈaʊtpʊt/
note not used with *a* or *an*. No plural and used with a singular verb only.
1 ⧓ increase, maintain, reduce **output**
▶ **input[1] 1**

2 ⋈ data **output**
▶ **input[1] 2**

output[2] *verb*
1 (*industry*) to produce a quantity of goods in a factory, etc: *output 100 cars in a day* **2** (*computing*) (of a computer) to supply information, results, etc: *The computer will output the data in seconds.*

/ˈaʊtpʊt/
output, outputting, outputted *or* **output**
note transitive verb
▶ **access, input[2]**

outstanding *adjective* (accounting)
unpaid; owed: *There is still an amount outstanding on your account.* ○ *pay off an outstanding debt*

/ˌaʊtˈstændɪŋ/
abbr o/s
⋈ account, amount **outstanding**; an **outstanding** debt

overcharge *verb* (sales)
to charge too high a price for something: *We overcharged him by mistake.* ○ *I was overcharged by £5.* ○ *Don't use that supplier — they always overcharge.*

/ˌəʊvəˈtʃɑːdʒ/
overcharge, overcharging, overcharged
note transitive and intransitive verb
⋈ **overcharge** *by* (an amount)

overdraft *noun* (banking)
a loan made by a bank to a customer so he/she may take out more money than is actually in a bank account: *arrange an overdraft of £500* ○ *I must pay off my overdraft.*

/ˈəʊvədrɑːft/
pl overdrafts
⋈ apply for, arrange, ask for, organize an **overdraft**
▶ **bank loan, debit, in the red**

overdrawn *adjective* (banking)
1 (of an account) with more money taken out than paid or left in: *Interest will be charged if your account goes overdrawn.* ○ *an overdrawn account* **2** (of a person) having an OVERDRAFT: *I'm overdrawn at the bank.*

/ˌəʊvəˈdrɔːn/
⋈ be, go **overdrawn**
▶ **in/into the red**

overhead *noun* (finance/industry)
a regular cost of running a business, eg rent, salaries, heat, light, etc. Overheads are usually divided into fixed costs and variable costs: *We must aim to reduce our overheads.*

/ˈəʊvəhed/
pl overheads
note usually plural
⋈ increase, reduce **overheads**
syn indirect costs, running costs
▶ **expenses 1, fixed cost, oncost, unit cost, variable cost**

overproduce *verb* (agriculture/industry)
to produce more of something than can be sold to make a profit: *Overproduced coffee has depressed market prices.* ○ *A number of countries are overproducing goods.*

/ˌəʊvəprəˈdjuːs/
overproduce, overproducing, overproduced
note transitive verb
▶ **produce[2]**

overproduction *noun* (agriculture/industry)
producing more of something than can be sold to make a profit: *The EC had to legislate against milk overproduction.* ○ *Overproduction at the factory meant that prices had to be reduced.*

/ˌəʊvəprəˈdʌkʃn/
note not used with *a* or *an*. No plural and used with a singular verb only.
▶ **production**

the Overseas Development Administration *noun* (finance)
(*UK*) a UK government department that provides financial and technical aid to developing countries: *The dam was built with funds provided by the Overseas Development Administration.*

/ði ˌəʊvəsiːz dɪˈveləpmənt ədˌmɪnɪˌstreɪʃn/
abbr ODA
▶ **European Bank for Reconstruction and Development, International Bank for Reconstruction and Development, International Development Agency, International Finance Corporation, International Monetary Fund, World Bank**

---

oversold *adjective*
1 (*sales*) having sold more goods, shares, etc than are available: *The new computer system is already oversold.* ○ *The shares are oversold.* **2** (*stock exchange*) of a market where too much has been sold: *The futures market is oversold and prices will start to rise again.*

/ˌəʊvəˈsəʊld/
2 ⧓ an **oversold** market
▶ **undersold**

---

overstaffed *adjective* (personnel)
having more workers than is necessary for the work to be done: *Government departments often seem to be overstaffed and inefficient.* ○ *work in an overstaffed office*

/ˌəʊvəˈstɑːft/
▶ **understaffed**

---

overstock *verb* (sales)
to supply something with too much stock: *The shop was overstocked with unsold goods.*

/ˌəʊvəˈstɒk/
overstock, overstocking, overstocked
note transitive verb
⧓ **overstock** *with* something
▶ **stock**[3]

---

oversubscription *noun* (stock exchange)
a situation where the demand for shares is greater than the number of shares issued: *In cases of oversubscription shareholders will be selected by ballot.* ○ *The offer resulted in an oversubscription of shares.*

/ˌəʊvəsəbˈskrɪpʃn/
note not used with *a* or *an*. No plural and used with a singular verb only.
▶ **issue, subscription shares**

---

overtime *noun* (personnel)
1 work done that is extra to the usual amount: *I did 25 hours overtime last month.* ○ *How much do you get paid for (doing) overtime?* ○ *Union members voted for a ban on overtime.* **2** the amount paid for extra work done; overtime pay: *Do you get paid overtime?* ○ *Overtime is time and a half* (ie if normal pay is £10 per hour, overtime is £15).

/ˈəʊvətaɪm/
note not used with *a* or *an*. No plural and used with a singular verb only.
⧓ **overtime** ban, pay, rates; do, work **overtime**
▶ **double time, time and a half**

---

overtrading *noun* (finance)
a situation where a company tries to produce and sell goods with too little money (CAPITAL): *As a result of overtrading the company went bankrupt.*

/ˌəʊvəˈtreɪdɪŋ/
note not used with *a* or *an*. No plural and used with a singular verb only.
▶ **trading**

---

overvalued *adjective* (stock exchange)
of a security that is too highly priced to attract informed buyers: *The shares were considered to be overvalued.* ○ *The overvalued shares attracted few investors.*

/ˌəʊvəˈvæljuːd/
▶ **value**[1]

own brand *noun* (retail)
a product that is sold under the name of the shop or supplier: *Try our own brand — it's cheaper.* ○ *produce washing powder for a supermarket to sell as their own brand*

/ˌəʊn ˈbrænd/
pl own brands
⧓ **own brand** goods, products, sales
▶ **brand name**

Pp

PA *abbr*
1 (*banking*) personal account **2** (*commerce*) personal assistant: *She works as a PA to the managing director.* **3** (*law*) power of attorney **4** (*insurance*) particular average

/ˌpiː ˈeɪ/
note pronounced as individual letters

p.a. *abbr*
per annum

/ˌpiː ˈeɪ/
note pronounced as individual letters

pack[1] *noun*
a number of things that are offered or sold together: *a pack of six/a six-pack* ○ *We are selling special gift packs for Christmas.* ○ *Each new employee receives an information pack.*

/pæk/
pl packs
⧓ a conference, a gift, an information **pack**

pack[2] *verb*
to put things into containers to be sold or sent somewhere: *Pack these items, will you?* ○ *Goods can be packed and delivered within two days of ordering.*

/pæk/
pack, packing, packed
note transitive and intransitive verb
⧓ **pack** boxes, crates, goods; **pack** into, up

package[1] *noun*
1 a number of things packed tightly together: *This package should be sent by first-class post.* ○ *The package is too big to go through a letter-box.* **2** a group of ideas, suggestions or goods offered or sold together: *She was offered an excellent package of benefits at the interview.* ○ *The computer is sold with a printer and software as part of the package.* ○ *The company has put together a package of pay and working conditions.*

/ˈpækɪdʒ/
pl packages
1 ⧓ a **package** of books, papers
2 ⧓ a compensation, pay, salary, software **package**; offer, put together, sell as a **package**

package[2] *verb* (sales)
to wrap something or put it into a container before it is sold or sent somewhere: *Goods that are attractively packaged sell more quickly.*

/ˈpækɪdʒ/
package, packaging, packaged
note transitive verb
⧓ **package** goods

package deal *noun*
an agreement or offer that includes a number of things which must all be accepted together: *We were offered a package deal on all our stationery for the next year.* ○ *See if you can get a package deal for maintaining the office equipment.*

/ˈpækɪdʒ diːl/
pl package deals
⧓ offer, sell a **package deal**
▶ **deal**[1]

packaging *noun* (advertising)
material used to wrap, contain and protect products; designing and using this material: *The company changed the packaging of its chocolate bars to try to increase sales.* ○ *Consumers are strongly*

/ˈpækɪdʒɪŋ/
note not used with *a* or *an*. No plural and used with a singular verb only.

influenced by (the) packaging. ○ *He owns a number of advertising and packaging companies.*

⧓ attractive, bright, old-fashioned, paper, plastic **packaging**; a **packaging** business, company, design, industry

► **wrapping**

---

packing *noun*

1 the action of putting goods into boxes or parcels for transportation: *The price includes postage and packing.* **2** material used to pack and protect goods: *We need a lot of packing to protect these glasses.*

/ˈpækɪŋ/

note not used with *a* or *an*. No plural and used with a singular verb only.

2 ⧓ paper, plastic, polystyrene **packing**

► **wrapping**

---

paid *adjective*

for which money is given: *Your contract allows you 25 days paid holiday a year.*

/peɪd/

⧓ **paid** holidays, leave

---

paid-up capital *noun* (finance)

the total amount of money that the shareholders of a company have paid to the company for their shares: *The company suffered losses of three million pounds which was more than its paid-up capital.*

/ˌpeɪd ʌp ˈkæpɪtl/

note not used with *a* or *an*. No plural and used with a singular verb only.

syn fully paid capital

► **authorized share capital, called-up capital, capital, issued capital**

---

paid-up policy *noun* (insurance)

a life assurance policy where the policy holder stops paying the premiums before the end of the policy. The amount eventually paid out by the insurance company is adjusted accordingly.

/ˌpeɪd ʌp ˈpɒləsi/

pl paid-up policies

► **insurance**

---

paid-up share *noun* (finance)

a share, of which the value or price it was given when it was first issued (the NOMINAL PRICE) has been paid in full

/ˌpeɪd ʌp ˈʃeə(r)/

pl paid-up shares

► **share**

---

pallet *noun* (distribution/transport)

a large wooden or metal frame on which goods can be stored or easily transported and lifted: *The spare engine parts were delivered on pallets.* ○ *All goods are stored on pallets in the warehouse.*

/ˈpælət/

pl pallets

⧓ a metal, transportation, wooden **pallet**

► **container**

---

panel *noun*

1 a group of people with specialist skills or interests who have been chosen to investigate or provide information on something: *Please consult our panel of carefully chosen experts if you have any problems.* ○ *The panel spent some time researching before coming to any conclusions.* **2** a board linked to a machine where the switches and controls are placed: *The red light on the control panel flashed, indicating danger.* ○ *The switch on the far left of the panel must be turned off.*

/ˈpænl/

pl panels

1 note used with a singular or plural verb

⧓ a **panel** of advisers, experts, judges, scientists; a consumer, representative **panel**

2 ⧓ a control, an instrument **panel**

---

panic buying *noun* (stock exchange/sales)

a rush to buy something because there is a shortage or before the price rises: *The new issue of shares at such a low price resulted in*

/ˌpænɪk ˈbaɪɪŋ/

note not used with *a* or *an*. No plural and used with a singular verb only.

panic buying on the market today. ○ The government stated that there was no need for panic buying as supplies were plentiful.

opp panic selling

panic selling *noun* (stock exchange/sales)
a rush to sell something at any price because there is a surplus or before prices fall: *Panic selling began as soon as the share price showed a sharp fall.*

/ˌpænɪk ˈselɪŋ/
note not used with *a* or *an*. No plural and used with a singular verb only.
opp panic buying

paper *noun*
1 thin material used for writing or printing on: *We need 30 sheets of paper to print this document.* ○ *The company ordered 20 reams of writing paper.* **2** a newspaper: *Have you seen the headlines in today's paper?* **3** an academic or specialist article or essay: *Her paper on the financial implications of 1992 was well received at the banking conference.*
on paper in theory: *It's a wonderful idea on paper, but will it work in practice?*

/ˈpeɪpə(r)/
1 note not used with *a* or *an*. No plural and used with a singular verb only.
⋈ carbon, computer (print-out), fax, headed, recycled, rough, typing **paper**
2 pl papers
⋈ a foreign language, local, national, quality **paper**
3 pl papers
⋈ give, publish, read, write a **paper**
► **papers**

paper loss *noun* (finance)
a loss that appears in a company's accounts, eg an asset that has declined in value, as opposed to a real loss: *The underwriters are carrying a paper loss of around £6 million.*

/ˌpeɪpə ˈlɒs/
pl paper losses
⋈ carry, sustain a **paper loss**
► **actual loss, loss 1**

paper money *noun* (banking)
1 currency in the form of banknotes as opposed to coins or gold **2** banknotes and any other form of paper that can be used as money

/ˌpeɪpə ˈmʌni/
note not used with *a* or *an*. No plural and used with a singular verb only.
1 syn paper currency
► **currency 1, money**
2 ► **bill of exchange, cheque, promissory note**

paper profit *noun* (finance)
a profit that appears in a company's accounts, eg an asset that has increased in value, as opposed to a real profit

/ˌpeɪpə ˈprɒfɪt/
note singular noun, used with a singular verb
⋈ record, register a **paper profit**
► **profit[1] 1**

papers *noun*
1 pieces of paper that have been written or printed on: *He looked through his papers and discovered he'd left the contract in the office.* ○ *Her desk was completely covered in papers.* **2** official documents usually relating to nationality and identity: *The Police stopped him and asked to see his papers.*

/ˈpeɪpəz/
note plural noun, used with a plural verb
2 identity **papers**
► **paper, pass[1], permit[1], visa, work permit**

paperwork *noun*
written work done in an office, such as writing letters or filling in forms: *The paperwork accumulated while I was on holiday.* ○ *My job includes a large amount of paperwork.* ○ *I must get the paperwork done before anything else.*

/ˈpeɪpəwɜːk/
note singular noun, used with a singular verb
⋈ catch up on, get down to the **paperwork**; boring, a lot of,

tedious paperwork
▶ **administration**

---

para *abbr* (commerce)
paragraph

/ˈpærə/
pl paras
note pronounced as a word

---

paragraph *noun*
part of a piece of writing or printed text containing more than one sentence and beginning on a new line: *You'll find the main points of the report in the fourth paragraph.*

/ˈpærəgrɑːf; *US* ˈpærəgræf/
pl paragraphs
abbr para
⋈ begin, end, finish, start a **paragraph**; the concluding, first, introductory, last, new **paragraph**

---

parameter *noun*
fixed limit: *We'll have to work within the parameters of time and cost.* ○ *The financial parameters have already been set.*

/pəˈræmɪtə(r)/
note usually plural
⋈ agree, decide on, define, set the **parameters**; **parameters** of budget, time

---

parent company *noun* (stock exchange)
▶ **holding company**

/ˈpeərənt ˌkʌmpəni/

---

parity *noun*
the state of being equal; equality: *The women working at the factory demanded parity with the men.* ○ *The currencies of both countries are now at parity.*

/ˈpærəti/
note not used with *a* or *an*. No plural and used with a singular verb only.
⋈ achieve, demand, desire **parity**; **parity** *with* something
▶ **equality**

---

parity grid *noun* (economics)
a table that shows the acceptable exchange values (in EUROPEAN CURRENCY UNITS) of a particular currency with each of the other currencies in the European Monetary System

/ˈpærəti grɪd/
pl parity grids
▶ **European Monetary System, Exchange Rate Mechanism**

---

part *noun*
an important piece of a machine: *manufacture car parts* ○ *It's very difficult to get spare parts for these machines nowadays.*

/pɑːt/
pl parts
⋈ a new, spare **part**
▶ **component, replacement 2**

---

part-exchange *noun*
▶ **exchange**[1]

/ˌpɑːt ɪksˈtʃeɪndʒ/

---

partial acceptance *adjective* (banking)
▶ **acceptance**

/ˌpɑːʃl əkˈseptəns/

---

partial loss *adjective* (insurance/shipping)
a situation where only part of a ship or its cargo is damaged and insurance may be claimed for this: *claim insurance for partial loss*

/ˌpɑːʃl ˈlɒs/
abbr P/L
note usually singular
⋈ consider, treat something as a **partial loss**
▶ **abandonment, loss 3, total loss**

---

particular lien *noun* (law)
▶ **lien**

/pəˌtɪkjələ 'li:ən/

---

partner *noun* (management)
one of two or more people who come together to run a business: *She has just joined a top firm of solicitors as a junior partner.* ○ *He was made a partner in the firm.*

general partner a partner who is responsible for the debts of the firm

limited partner a partner who is only responsible for the debts of a firm up to the amount he or she has invested in the firm

managing partner a member of a partnership who has been appointed by the other members to run the firm

/'pɑ:tnə(r)/
pl partners
⋈ become, make (someone) a **partner**; a junior, senior **partner**
▶ **active partner, associate[1] 1, colleague, co-partner, nominal partner, sleeping partner, trading partner**

---

partnership *noun* (law)
an association of two or more people who come together to run a business; being or becoming a partner: *They decided to go into partnership together.* ○ *After only working in the firm for six months, he was delighted to be offered a partnership.*

partnership agreement a document that sets out the rules of the partnership and how the profits will be shared

partnership-at-will a partnership that can be ended at any time by any member if he or she gives notice to the other members

/'pɑ:tnəʃɪp/
pl partnerships
⋈ become, dissolve, form, join a **partnership**; enter, go into **partnership**
▶ **deed of partnership, illegal partnership**

---

part-owner *noun* (law)
▶ **co-owner**

/ˌpɑ:t 'əʊnə(r)/

---

part-payment *noun* (commerce)
a payment of part of a larger sum to be paid later: *make a part-payment after the first delivery of the goods*

/ˌpɑ:t 'peɪmənt/
pl part-payments
⋈ ask for, make, receive a **part-payment**
▶ **deposit[1] 2, instalment, lump sum, payment 2**

---

part-time *adjective, adverb*
for only part of the working day or week: *He's looking for a part-time job.* ○ *She works part-time at the bank.*

/ˌpɑ:t 'taɪm/
⋈ a **part-time** employee, job, worker; **part-time** employment, staff, work
▶ **full-time**

---

party *noun* (law)
1 a person or group of people who take part in a legal agreement or dispute: *Both parties agreed to settle out of court.* **2** any person who signs any kind of legal document: *The other party to the contract has infringed the terms and conditions.*

/'pɑ:ti/
pl parties
⋈ the contracting, opposing **party**
▶ **accommodation party, third party, working party**

---

par value *noun* (stock exchange)
▶ **nominal price**

/'pɑ: ˌvælju:/

PASCAL *noun* (computing)
a language used in computer programming: *a program written in Pascal*

/ˌpæ'skæl/
▶ **ALGOL, BASIC, COBOL, FORTRAN**

pass[1] *noun*
a piece of card, often with a photograph, that allows someone to do something, eg enter a building or travel: *Please show your entry pass at reception.* ○ *Security passes were rigorously checked after the terrorist attack.*

/pɑːs; *US* pæs/
pl passes
⧓ an entry, an official, a security, a travel, a visitor's **pass**; issue, show a **pass**
► **papers 2, permit[1], visa, work permit**

pass[2] *verb*
to approve a bill, law, motion, etc: *The motion was passed after a majority vote in favour.* ○ *The government has passed new legislation concerning health and safety in factories.*

to pass a dividend to pay no dividends in a particular year

/pɑːs; *US* pæs/
pass, passing, passed
note transitive verb
⧓ **pass** a bill, a law, legislation, a motion, a proposal
► **approve**

passbook *noun* (banking)
a book that lists all payments into and withdrawals from a building society or savings bank account: *The amount of interest gained on the savings is shown in the customer's passbook.*

/ˈpɑːsbʊk; *US* ˈpæsbʊk/
pl passbooks
⧓ update a **passbook**
► **bank book, bank statement, paying-in book**

passenger *noun* (transport)
a person who is travelling in a car, bus, train, plane, etc but who is not driving or working on it: *The plane is designed to carry a maximum of 400 passengers.* ○ *The company runs both passenger and freight services.*

/ˈpæsɪndʒə(r)/
pl passengers
⧓ a **passenger** lounge, seat, service; an airline, a coach, a rail **passenger**

password *noun* (computing)
a secret set of characters that are typed into a computer system to allow someone to use it: *Type in the password to access the computer.*

/ˈpɑːswɜːd; *US* ˈpæswɜːd/
pl passwords
⧓ alter, enter, key in, set, use a **password**
syn authorization code

patent[1] *noun* (law)
an official document that gives the holder the sole right to make, use or sell an invention and prevents others from copying it, usually for a fixed period: *The new pain-relieving drug is protected by patent.* ○ *The computer company applied for a patent for its latest software.* ○ *patent medicines*

/ˈpeɪtnt, ˈpætnt/
pl patents
⧓ apply for, grant, obtain, take out a **patent**
► **copyright, intangible asset, intellectual property, royalty, trade mark**

patent[2] *verb* (law)
to obtain an official document that gives the holder the sole right to make, use or sell an invention and prevents others from copying it, usually for a fixed period: *The first hovercraft was patented in 1955.* ○ *The company announced that it had patented a new drug to relieve panic.*

/ˈpeɪtnt, ˈpætnt/
patent, patenting, patented
note transitive verb
⧓ **patent** a design, an invention, a process, a product
► **register[2] 1**

patent office *noun* (law)
a government office that grants patents: *The UK Patent Office keeps a register of all patents granted in the country.* ○ *apply to a patent office*

/ˈpeɪtnt ˌɒfɪs, ˈpætnt ˌɒfɪs/
pl patent offices

paternity leave *noun* (personnel)
time off work given to a male employee who has just become a

/pəˈtɜːnəti liːv/
note no plural
⧓ be *on* **paternity leave**

father: *You are allowed to take five days' paternity leave at any time within one month of the birth.*

▶ **maternity leave, leave**

---

patron *noun*

1 (*commerce*) (*formal*) a regular customer of a business such as a hotel, pub or shop: *The car park is reserved for patrons only.* ○ *As a regular patron, you are entitled to a 10% discount.* **2** a person or company who gives money to a charity or any deserving organization: *a wealthy patron of the arts*

/ˈpeɪtrən/

pl patrons

1 ⋈ a hotel, restaurant **patron**

▶ **customer**

2 ⋈ a **patron** of the arts

▶ **sponsor**

---

pay[1] *verb*

1 to give money to someone for something: *She paid for the goods by cheque.* ○ *There's a discount of 10% if you pay cash.* ○ *He is very well paid.* **2** to give money that is owed to someone: *Have you paid the telephone bill yet?* ○ *The company is paying for its new fax machine in monthly instalments.* **3** to be profitable: *The business was sold because the owners couldn't make it pay.*

pay something back to give money back to a person or an organization that you borrowed from: *You must pay back the loan within three months.* ○ *I'll lend you the money if you promise to pay it back.*

pay off to be successful or profitable: *The deal paid off and we made a lot of money.*

pay someone off to pay someone's wages and dismiss them from a job: *We paid off all the temporary staff at the end of the summer.*

pay something off to pay the whole of a sum of money owed: *It will take years to pay off this loan.* ○ *He finally managed to pay off his debts.*

/peɪ/

pay, paying, paid

note transitive and intransitive verb

1 ⋈ **pay** *for* (something); **pay** *by* cash, cheque, credit card, etc

▶ **unpaid**

---

pay[2] *noun*

money given to an employee by an employer in return for work: *The company offers excellent rates of pay.* ○ *receive an annual pay rise of 6%*

/peɪ/

note not used with *a* or *an*. No plural and used with a singular verb only.

⋈ a **pay** award, increase, rise; **pay** negotiations, talks; holiday, sick **pay**

▶ **back pay, equal pay, maternity pay, performance-related pay, redundancy pay, salary, strike pay, take-home pay, wage**

---

payable *adjective* (banking/finance)

that should or must be paid: *Please make your cheque payable to F. Brown and Sons.* ○ *This bill of exchange is payable on the 13th of October.*

payable in advance that must or may be paid before something is given in exchange for it: *The rent is payable in advance.*

payable on demand that must be paid as soon as it is presented for payment: *The bill of exchange is payable on demand.*

payable to bearer a cheque or bill of exchange that can be signed by the holder and paid to him or her

payable to order a cheque or bill of exchange that must be paid to the person named on the bill

/ˈpeɪəbl/

⋈ *be* payable *to* someone

▶ **accounts payable, bills payable, endorsement**

Pay As You Earn *noun* (tax)
a method of collecting direct taxes in which the employer deducts the amount owed from an employee's weekly or monthly wages and pays it directly to the government

/ˌpeɪ əz juː ˈɜːn/
abbr PAYE
note not used with *a* or *an*. No plural and used with a singular verb only.

payback *noun*
money received as profit after it has been invested in a business activity: *calculate the payback by subtracting the production costs from the selling price* ○ *Most companies these days are looking for a speedy payback.*

payback clause (*banking*) an item in a loan contract setting out the conditions for repaying a loan: *According to the payback clause, £100 is payable on the 5th of every month.*

/ˈpeɪbæk/
note singular noun, used with a singular verb
⋈ calculate, receive a **payback**; delete, include, insert a **payback clause**
► **profit[1] 1**

payback period *noun*
1 (*banking*) the amount of time over which a loan can be repaid: *The payback period for most house mortgages is 25 years.* ○ *The payback period expires on 20th November.* **2** (*commerce*) the amount of time it will take for money invested in a business activity to be returned as profit: *We estimate that the payback period for the new machinery will be 2 years.* ○ *They are counting on a payback period of 5 years.*

/ˈpeɪbæk ˌpɪəriəd/
pl payback periods
1 ⋈ amend, extend, fix a **payback period**
2 ⋈ calculate, estimate a **payback period**; a long, reasonable, short **payback period**

pay-day *noun*
the day when an employee receives his/her wages or salary: *Pay-day in this company is on the 28th of each month.*

/ˈpeɪdeɪ/
note not used with *a* or *an*. No plural and used with a singular verb only.

PAYE *abbr* (tax)
Pay As You Earn

/ˌpiː eɪ waɪ ˈiː/
note pronounced as individual letters

payee *noun* (banking)
the person to whom something is to be paid: *write the name of the payee on a cheque*

/ˌpeɪˈiː/
pl payees
► **account payee, drawee, endorsee**

payer *noun* (banking)
a person or an organization that pays: *He has a reputation for being a rather slow payer.*

/ˈpeɪə(r)/
pl payers
⋈ a good, late, slow **payer**
► **taxpayer**

paying banker *noun* (banking)
the bank stated as responsible for paying a cheque or a bill of exchange

/ˈpeɪɪŋ bæŋkə(r)/
pl paying bankers
► **banker**

paying-in book *noun* (banking)
a book made up of printed forms (PAYING-IN SLIPS), used by the holder of a bank account to record cash or cheques paid into the account: *The bank will automatically send you a new paying-in book.*

/ˌpeɪɪŋ ˈɪn bʊk/
pl paying-in books
⋈ issue a **paying-in book**
► **bank book, passbook**

paying-in slip *noun* (banking)
a printed form used by the holder of a bank account to record

/ˌpeɪɪŋ ˈɪn slɪp/
pl paying-in slips

cash or cheques paid into an account: *Don't forget to fill in the amount of the cheque on the paying-in slip.*

⧓ complete, fill in a **paying-in slip**

syn credit slip, deposit slip

---

payment *noun* (finance)

/ˈpeɪmənt/

abbr payt

1 paying or being paid: *The bill of exchange was presented for payment at the bank.* ○ *We would be grateful for prompt payment of your account.* ○ *What is your method of payment* (ie cash, cheque, letter of credit, etc)*?* **2** an amount of money that is to be paid: *You can repay the loan in 12 monthly payments of £250 each.* ○ *Will you accept £100 as payment for the work?*

payment by results a way of paying people in which the amount of money given depends on the amount of work done or the amount of profit made: *More and more companies are introducing a system of payment by results.*

payment for honour the paying of a bill of exchange after it has been refused for payment (DISHONOURED). This is done to save the honour of the person who has drawn or endorsed the bill of exchange.

payment in advance paying for goods or services before they have been received: *For single orders we expect payment in advance.*

payment in due course the paying of a bill of exchange as soon as it is due for payment

payment in kind payment that is made in goods or services and not in cash

payment on account the paying of money as a deposit

1 note not used with *a* or *an*. No plural and used with a singular verb only.

⧓ accept, receive, refuse **payment**

2 pl payments

⧓ a cash, monthly, quarterly, weekly **payment**; make, receive a **payment**

▶ **balance of payments, down payment, part-payment, progress payment, token payment**

---

payment with order *noun* (commerce)

/ˌpeɪmənt wɪð ˈɔːdə(r)/

▶ **cash with order**

---

pay-off *noun*

/ˈpeɪɒf/

pl pay-offs

(also **payoff**)

(*informal*) **1** a reward or gain: *Look for an investment with a sure pay-off.* **2** the act of paying money to someone, as a bribe; the money paid in this way: *The director was offered a £10 000 pay-off to keep quiet about the takeover.*

1 ⧓ a high, low, sure **pay-off**

▶ **backhander, bribe**

2 ⧓ accept, give, offer, receive a **pay-off**

▶ **trade-off**

---

pay packet *noun* (personnel)

/ˈpeɪ ˌpækɪt/

▶ **wage packet**

---

pay phone *noun*

/ˈpeɪ fəʊn/

pl pay phones

a public telephone that you put money in to use: *Is there a pay phone in this restaurant?*

⧓ put money in, use a **pay phone**

---

payroll *noun* (commerce)

/ˈpeɪrəʊl/

pl payrolls

1 a list of all the people employed by a company, and the amount of money paid to each of them: *She's been on the payroll for nearly 20 years.* ○ *The company has over 2 000 people on its payroll.* **2** the total amount of money paid to the employees of a company: *a weekly payroll of £300 000*

⧓ an annual, a monthly, a weekly **payroll**

---

payroll assistant *noun* (personnel)
▶ **wages clerk**

/ˈpeɪrəʊl əˌsɪstənt/

pay scale *noun* (personnel)
▶ **wage scale**

/ˈpeɪ skeɪl/

pay slip *noun* (personnel)
a piece of paper, given to an employee with his/her weekly or monthly wages, that shows the amount of pay given and any deductions made, eg for income tax: *The pay increase will be shown on your next pay slip.*

/ˈpeɪ slɪp/
pl pay slips
▶ **wage packet**

payt *abbr* (finance)
payment

note used in written English only

PBX *abbr*
private branch exchange

/ˌpiː biː ˈeks/

PC *abbr* (computing)
personal computer

/ˌpiː ˈsiː/

PDR *abbr* (stock exchange)
price-dividend ratio

/ˌpiː diː ˈɑː(r)/
syn P/D ratio

peak[1] *noun*
the highest level, value, rate, etc; the part of a graph that shows this: *Sales were at their peak in December.* ○ *Inflation is believed to have reached its peak.*

/piːk/
pl peaks
⧓ be at, reach a **peak**
▶ **trough**

peak[2] *verb*
to reach the highest level or value: *Interest rates peaked at 11% in the spring.* ○ *The company's sales are expected to peak around Christmas.*

/piːk/
peak, peaking, peaked
note intransitive verb
⧓ inflation, output, prices, productivity, sales **peaked**

peak[3] *adjective*
of a time when an item or service is used the most: *Passengers are advised not to travel during peak hours.* ○ *Telephone calls will be charged at 44p per minute at the peak rate and 33p per minute at other times.*

/piːk/
⧓ **peak** hours, rate, time
▶ **off-peak**

penalty *noun* (law)
1 a punishment for breaking a law: *maximum penalty £100*, eg for dropping litter **2** a sum of money to be paid by a person who breaks a contract: *Any party not abiding by the terms and conditions of this contract will incur a penalty of £500.* **3** a sum of money paid by someone who asks for a loan to be repaid earlier than the agreed date: *A penalty of 90 days' interest is required for early redemption of a loan.*

penalty clause (*law*) a condition in a contract that states the amount of money to be paid by the person who breaks the contract: *The contract contained a penalty clause to ensure that the work was finished on time.*

/ˈpenlti/
pl penalties
⧓ incur, pay the **penalty**

pending[1] *adjective*
waiting to be decided or settled: *Please put those letters in the file marked 'pending'.*

/ˈpendɪŋ/
⋈ a **pending** file, tray

pending[2] *preposition*
while waiting for something; until: *We have the document here, pending your instructions.* ○ *be released on bail, pending a trial*

/ˈpendɪŋ/
⋈ **pending** an appeal, a court case, an inquiry, a trial

penetration *noun* (sales)
▶ **market penetration**

/ˌpenɪˈtreɪʃn/

penny share *noun* (stock exchange)
(*informal*) shares, usually bought from small companies, that have a very low market price: *Penny shares are usually a high risk investment.* ○ *Penny shares costing less than 45p each.*

/ˌpeni ˈʃeə(r)/
pl penny shares
⋈ buy, invest in, sell **penny shares**
▶ **share**

pension *noun* (finance)
a sum of money paid regularly by the State to people above a certain age, and to widowed or disabled people, or by an employer to an employee who has retired: *After working for the company for twenty years, he was offered a good retirement pension.* ○ *She finds it difficult to live on her state pension.* ○ *He was granted a small disablement pension after the accident.*

/ˈpenʃn/
pl pensions
⋈ draw, pay, receive a **pension**; an old-age, a retirement **pension**
▶ **retire, superannuation**

pension fund *noun* (finance)
money collected from employers and employees, or by the State, and invested to provide future pensions: *pension contributions invested by the managers of a pension fund*

/ˈpenʃn ˌfʌnd/
pl pension funds
⋈ invest in, manage a **pension fund**
▶ **fund**[1] **1**

PER *abbr* (stock exchange)
price-earnings ratio

/ˌpi: i: ˈɑ:(r)/
note pronounced as individual letters
syn P/E ratio

per *preposition*
for each: *This will work out at £10 per head.* ○ *How many miles per gallon does your car do?*

/pə(r)/
abbr p.
⋈ **per** gallon, litre, person

per annum *adverb*
(*Latin*) for each year: *The position offers a salary of £25 000 per annum.* ○ *Mortgage interest rates have recently increased to 13% per annum.* ○ *Average profits per annum are in the region of £500 000.*

/pər ˈænəm/
abbr p.a.
note the abbreviation is used more often than the full term

per cent *adjective, adverb*
in or for every hundred: *a 10 per cent increase in price* ○ *There is a 5 per cent delivery charge.*

/pəˈsent/
(also **percent**)
abbr %

percentage *noun*
a rate, number or amount in each hundred: *The figure is expressed as a percentage.* ○ *What percentage of your goods are sold overseas?*

/pəˈsentɪdʒ/
pl percentages
⋈ calculate, estimate a **percentage**

perfecting the sight *noun* (international trade)
▶ **bill of sight**

/pəˌfektɪŋ ðə ˈsaɪt/

perfect market *noun* (economics)
a situation in which there are enough buyers and sellers to prevent prices being controlled by one person or organization and in which companies compete for maximum profit with few government restrictions: *A perfect market rarely exists in real life.*

/ˌpɜːfɪkt ˈmɑːkɪt/
note usually singular
▶ **absolute monopoly, imperfect market, market**[1]**, monopoly**

perfect monopoly *noun* (economics)
▶ **absolute monopoly**

/ˌpɜːfɪkt məˈnɒpəli/

perform *verb*
1 to do a piece of work, a task, etc: *I have to perform a number of very different tasks in my job.* ○ *He performs his job well.* **2** (of a machine, an organization, an invention, etc) to work, or function: *The new drug performed well in tests.* ○ *How will the machine perform in extreme temperatures?*

/pəˈfɔːm/
perform, performing, performed
1 note transitive verb
⋈ **perform** a duty, job, task
2 note intransitive verb
⋈ **perform** badly, well
▶ **work**[2] **2**

performance *noun*
1 doing something: *Care must be taken in the performance of these tasks.* **2** the way something is done, esp how skilfully or efficiently it is done: *Managers are responsible for the performance of their staff.* ○ *How can we improve our sales performance* (ie sell more goods)*?* ○ *The customer was impressed by the machine's performance.*

/pəˈfɔːməns/
note usually singular
1 ⋈ **performance** of a duty, job, task
2 ⋈ a bad, disappointing, good, poor **performance**; economic, financial, industrial, sales, staff **performance**

performance appraisal *noun* (personnel)
▶ **appraisal**

/pəˈfɔːməns əˌpreɪzl/

performance-related pay *noun* (personnel)
pay in which the amount given depends on how well a person has done a job: *More and more companies are adopting a system of performance-related pay.*

/pəˌfɔːməns rɪˌleɪtɪd ˈpeɪ/
note not used with *a* or *an*. No plural and used with a singular verb only.
⋈ a system of **performance-related pay**
▶ **pay**[2]

period *noun*
a length of time: *You can repay the loan over a period of two years/ over a two-year period.* ○ *Sales between April and July this year are 15% up on the same period last year.* ○ *The sales manager is away for the period between the 31st of July and the 24th of August.*

/ˈpɪəriəd/
pl periods
⋈ a **period** *between* (one date, time, etc and another), *of* (a number of days, months, years); the busy, holiday, slack **period**
▶ **accounting period, trial period**

period bill *noun* (banking/commerce)
a bill of exchange that must be paid on a specific date: *a period bill payable on 30 November*

/ˈpɪəriəd bɪl/
pl period bills
syn term bill
▶ **bill of exchange, sight bill, term 2**

periodical *noun*
a magazine that comes out at regular intervals, esp one obtained

/ˌpɪəriˈɒdɪkl/
pl periodicals

from the society that produces it rather than bought from a newsagent: *publish a monthly science periodical*

⋈ a monthly, quarterly, weekly **periodical**; produce, publish, read, subscribe to a **periodical**

► **house journal, journal, magazine, trade journal**

---

period of grace *noun* (commerce)

an extra length of time given to a debtor to repay money owing: *The bank granted him a 30-day period of grace to repay the loan.* ○ *The period of grace expires tomorrow — and the bill must be paid.*

/ˌpɪəriəd əv ˈgreɪs/

pl periods of grace

⋈ allow, grant, extend a **period of grace**

syn grace period

---

peripheral *noun* (computing)

a piece of equipment, such as a printer or keyboard, that is attached to a computer and used to transfer information into and out of it: *The keyboard is a standard peripheral that fits most personal computers.*

/pəˈrɪfərəl/

pl peripherals

syn peripheral device

► **hardware, software, terminal 1**

---

perishables *noun* (commerce)

goods, esp food, that can go bad or decay quickly: *Meat, fish and soft fruit are all perishables.* ○ *The lorry has a refrigerating unit for transporting perishables.*

/ˈperɪʃəblz/

note plural noun, used with a plural verb

⋈ carry, store, transport **perishables**

► **consumer durables**

---

perjure *verb* (law)

to tell a lie, esp in a court of law, after swearing an oath to tell the truth: *The chief witness was prepared to perjure himself to protect the accused.*

/ˈpɜːdʒə(r)/

perjure, perjuring, perjured

note transitive verb

⋈ **perjure** *himself, herself, oneself, yourself*

---

perjury *noun* (law)

1 the act of lying, esp in a court of law, after swearing an oath to tell the truth: *He was convicted of committing perjury during the trial.* ○ *be prosecuted for perjury* **2** a lie, esp in a court of law: *The judge enquired whether his last statement might not be perjury.*

/ˈpɜːdʒəri/

note not used with *a* or *an*. No plural and used with a singular verb only.

1 ⋈ commit **perjury**; **perjury** charges

---

perk *noun* (personnel)

(*informal*) **1** money or goods received in addition to a salary: *He was offered a company car as a perk.* **2** an advantage or benefit of a particular job or position: *One of the perks of the job is being able to work the hours I want.*

/pɜːk/

pl perks

syn perquisite

⋈ be offered something as a **perk**

► **benefit**[1] **2**

---

permanent *adjective*

that is intended to last for a very long time, or for ever: *She is looking for a permanent job.* ○ *As soon as I am settled in Italy, I'll send you my permanent address.* ○ *These changes to working methods are now permanent.*

/ˈpɜːmənənt/

⋈ a **permanent** address, job, position

► **temp**

---

permanent asset *noun* (accounting)

► **capital asset**

/ˌpɜːmənənt ˈæset/

---

permission *noun*
the act of allowing someone to do something: *He gave him permission to borrow the files.* ○ *He was refused permission to publish the document.* ○ *The firm applied for planning permission to extend the factory.*

/pəˈmɪʃn/
note not used with *a* or *an*. No plural and used with a singular verb only.
⋈ ask, give, grant, refuse **permission**; formal, official, written **permission**
► **authority 1 b, planning permission**

permit[1] *noun*
a formal document that allows someone to do something: *You must obtain an entry permit before visiting the site.* ○ *This travel permit expires in 2 weeks.*

/ˈpɜːmɪt/
pl permits
⋈ apply for, grant, issue, obtain, refuse a **permit**; government, travel **permit**.
► **licence, pass**[1]**, visa, work permit**

permit[2] *verb*
to allow: *Only authorized personnel are permitted access to the computer system.* ○ *Smoking is not permitted.*

/pəˈmɪt/
permit, permitting, permitted
note transitive verb
► **authorize**

perpetual inventory *noun* (distribution)
a method of controlling stock in which the movement of each item is recorded, so that the firm always knows the numbers and value of stock remaining in each of its warehouses: *a perpetual inventory system where stock movements are recorded on computers*

/pəˈpetʃuəl ˈɪnvəntri/
note usually singular
⋈ keep a **perpetual inventory**
► **stock control**

perquisite *noun* (personnel)
(*formal*) ► **perk**

/ˈpɜːkwɪzɪt/

personal assistant *noun* (personnel)
a highly-trained secretary who works for an executive or director: *be employed as a personal assistant to the managing director*

/ˌpɜːsənl əˈsɪstənt/
pl personal assistants
abbr PA
► **assistant, clerical assistant, secretary**

personal computer *noun* (computing)
a small computer that fits on a desk and is used at home or in an office to produce letters, tables of figures, etc and store sales, accounting and customer information: *install a personal computer in an office* ○ *use a personal computer to produce graphs of sales figures*

/ˌpɜːsənl kəmˈpjuːtə(r)/
pl personal computers
abbr PC
⋈ use a **personal computer**
syn microcomputer
► **computer, mainframe, word processor**

personal identification number *noun* (banking/computing)
a secret number used by a bank card or credit card holder to take money out of a cashpoint machine, order a bank statement, etc: *key in your personal identification number*

/ˌpɜːsənl aɪˌdentɪfɪˈkeɪʃn ˌnʌmbə(r)/
pl personal identification numbers
abbr PIN
► **cashpoint, credit card**

personal loan *noun* (banking)
a loan given by a bank or building society to an individual. High rates of interest are charged for this kind of loan as no security is

/ˌpɜːsənl ˈləʊn/
pl personal loans
⋈ apply for, issue, pay back, take

required: *take out a personal loan to buy a car* ○ *pay back a personal loan in monthly instalments*

out a **personal loan**

▶ **loan[1]**

---

personal property *noun* (law)

items such as money, shares, personal belongings, but not land or buildings, that can be passed to others on the death of the owner

/ˌpɜːsənl ˈprɒpəti/

note not used with *a* or *an*. No plural and used with a single verb only.

syn personalty

▶ **property, real estate**

---

personalty *noun* (law)

▶ **personal property**

/ˈpɜːsənəlti/

---

personnel *noun* (personnel)

1 the people employed by an organization; the staff: *office, sales, technical, etc personnel* ○ *Training courses are provided for all company personnel.* **2** the department in an organization that recruits and trains employees and deals with their problems: *He was asked to go to personnel for an interview.* ○ *Personnel are arranging courses for selected staff.* ○ *He's worked in personnel for 3 years.*

/ˌpɜːsəˈnel/

1 note plural noun, used with a plural verb

⧓ employ, recruit, train **personnel**

▶ **employee, staff[1], work-force**

2 note not used with *a* or *an*. No plural, but used with a singular or plural verb.

⧓ a **personnel** manager, office

syn personnel department

---

personnel management *noun* (management)

recruiting and training employees and dealing with their problems: *She chose a career in personnel management.* ○ *He works in personnel management.*

/ˌpɜːsənel ˈmænɪdʒmənt/

note not used with *a* or *an*. No plural and used with a singular verb only.

⧓ study, work in **personnel management**

▶ **management 1**

---

petty average *noun* (shipping)

expenses paid by the master of a ship during a voyage

/ˌpeti ˈævərɪdʒ/

note singular noun, used with a singular verb

(also **petit average**)

▶ **average[1] 3**

---

petty cash *noun* (accounting/finance)

a small amount of money kept in an office to pay small expenses: *The company will reimburse you* (ie pay you back) *out of petty cash.*

/ˌpeti ˈkæʃ/

note not used with *a* or *an*. No plural and used with a singular verb only.

⧓ a **petty cash** book, box

▶ **kitty**

---

photocopier *noun* (office practice)

a machine that makes a copy of a document, letter, etc by photographing it: *The photocopier is out of action again.*

/ˈfəʊtəʊkɒpiə(r)/

pl photocopiers

⧓ use a **photocopier**

syn copier

▶ **duplicator**

---

photocopy[1] *noun* (office practice)

a copy of a document, letter, etc that is made by a special machine (a PHOTOCOPIER) that can photograph something

/ˈfəʊtəʊkɒpi/

pl photocopies

⧓ do, make a **photocopy**

quickly: *make a photocopy of the letter* ○ *I need 20 photocopies of the report for the meeting, please.*

▶ **copy¹ 1, duplicate¹, master 1, original**

---

photocopy² *verb* (office practice)
to make a copy of a document, letter, etc using a special machine (a PHOTOCOPIER) that can photograph something quickly: *Please photocopy this report for me.* ○ *Have the minutes of the meeting been photocopied yet?*

/ˈfəʊtəʊkɒpi/
photocopy, photocopying, photcopied
note transitive and intransitive verb
⋈ **photocopy** a document, letter, page, etc
▶ **copy², duplicate² 1**

---

physical capital *noun* (finance)
items such as land, factories and machinery that are used to produce goods and provide services: *By measuring physical capital we can see how far the recession has prevented companies from investing in new equipment.*

/ˌfɪzɪkl ˈkæpɪtl/
note not used with *a* or *an*. No plural and used with a singular verb only.
▶ **capital**

---

physicals *noun* (commerce/stock exchange)
▶ **actuals 1**

/ˈfɪzɪklz/

---

picket¹ *noun* (industrial relations)
an employee, often a member of a trade union, who stands outside an office, a factory, etc to stop other workers from going in to work: *The pickets managed to persuade most of the work-force to turn back.* ○ *Some workers tried to cross the picket line* (ie a line formed by workers on strike).

/ˈpɪkɪt/
pl pickets
▶ **secondary picketing, strike¹, trade union**

---

picket² *verb* (industrial relations)
to stand outside an office or factory, etc and try to stop other workers from going in to work: *Trade union members were picketing outside the factory.* ○ *The offices were being picketed by a third of the work-force.*

/ˈpɪkɪt/
picket, picketing, picketed
note transitive and intransitive verb
⋈ **picket** a factory, an office, workers, a workplace
▶ **strike²**

---

pictogram *noun* (management)
a way of showing figures and statistics on a chart or graph using pictures: *On this pictogram each car represents 1 000 cars sold.*

/ˈpɪktəgræm/
pl pictograms
⋈ draw a **pictogram**
▶ **bar chart, block diagram, chart¹ 1, diagram, flow chart, graph, pie chart**

---

piece rates *noun* (industry)
an amount paid that depends on the amount of work done or the number of goods produced: *Piece rates were introduced at the factory in an attempt to increase production.* ○ *The union condemned piece rates as unfair.*

/ˈpiːs reɪts/
note plural noun, used with a plural verb
⋈ introduce, pay, receive, work for **piece rates**
▶ **rate 1**

---

piece-work *noun* (industry)
work paid for according to the amount done or the number of goods produced: *Piece-work was finally abolished at the factory because it resulted in poor quality goods.*

/ˈpiːs wɜːk/
note not used with *a* or *an*. No plural and used with a singular verb only.
⋈ abolish, introduce **piece-work**

---

pie chart *noun* (management)
a circle divided into sections that represent different amounts, areas, months, etc: *This pie chart shows the sales figures for each of our markets.*

/ˈpaɪ tʃɑːt/
pl pie charts
⋈ draw, produce a **pie chart**
▶ **bar chart, block diagram, chart[1] 1, diagram, flow chart, graph, pictogram**

---

pilot[1] *noun*
1 (*transport*) a person who flies an aircraft: *The pilot was given clearance for an emergency landing.* **2** (*shipping*) a person with a special knowledge of a difficult area of water, who guides ships through it: *The pilot boarded the ship to bring it into the harbour.*

automatic pilot a device in an aircraft or ship to keep it on a set course without human control: *The plane crashed into the sea after flying on automatic pilot for six hours.*

pilot boat a boat used to guide ships into a harbour or through a difficult area of water: *The ship was guided into the harbour by two pilot boats, one on each side.*

/ˈpaɪlət/
pl pilots
1 ⋈ an airline, a helicopter **pilot**
2 ⋈ a harbour, river, sea **pilot**

---

pilot[2] *verb*
1 (*transport/shipping*) to act as a pilot either on an aircraft or on a ship: *The ship was slowly piloted into the harbour.* **2** (*advertising*) to test a product, an idea, etc with a small number of people in a particular area: *pilot a business English language course in a few selected companies*

/ˈpaɪlət/
pilot, piloting, piloted
note transitive verb
1 ⋈ **pilot** an aircraft, a boat, a ship
2 ⋈ **pilot** an idea, a product
▶ **test market[2]**

---

pilot[3] *adjective*
done as an experiment or to test something: *A pilot training scheme for young people was set up last week.* ○ *Pilot research is being undertaken at the university.*

/ˈpaɪlət/
⋈ a **pilot** experiment, project, scheme, study

---

pilotage *noun* (shipping)
the fee paid to a pilot for guiding a ship through difficult waters: *A sum of 250 Finnmarks will cover the pilotage and canal fees.*

/ˈpaɪlətɪdʒ/
note not used with *a* or *an*. No plural and used with a singular verb only.

PIN *abbr* (banking/computing)
personal identification number

/pɪn/

---

pirate[1] *adjective* (law)
(of a book, record, tape, etc) illegally copied: *Pirate editions of the computer software are being sold abroad.*

/ˈpaɪrət/
⋈ a **pirate** copy, edition, tape, video

---

pirate[2] *verb* (law)
to use, copy or sell someone else's work without permission and without having the right to do so: *sell pirated computer games*

/ˈpaɪrət/
pirate, pirating, pirated
note transitive verb
⋈ **pirate** a book, computer software, a record, a tape, a video

---

PL *abbr* (computing)
programming language

/ˌpiː ˈel/

P/L *abbr* (shipping/insurance)
partial loss

note used in written English only

placement *noun*
1 finding and placing somebody in a job: *Students are given work placements with major engineering companies as part of their course.* **2** (*stock exchange*) a method of selling new shares in a company by offering them to selected individuals or organizations who are able to buy in large amounts

/ˈpleɪsmənt/
pl placements
1 ⋈ find, give, offer a **placement**; a job, work **placement**
▶ **position 1, post[1] 3**
2 ▶ **vendor placing**

---

plaintiff *noun* (law)
a person who brings an action against another person (a DEFENDANT) in a court of law: *The plaintiff appealed against the court's decision.*

/ˈpleɪntɪf/
pl plaintiffs
syn complainant
▶ **defendant**

---

plan[1] *noun*
1 an idea or arrangement for doing or achieving something in the future: *The company has no plans to employ more people.* ○ *What is your plan for increasing our overseas sales?* **2** a list, drawing or diagram that shows how something is to be organized: *Before the meeting draw up a plan of what you want to say.* **3** a detailed drawing of part of a town, a building, a room, a machine, etc: *The architect's plans for the new shopping centre have been approved.* ○ *a ground-floor plan of the new offices*

/plæn/
pl plans
1, 2 ⋈ draw up, make, work out a **plan**
▶ **business plan, marketing plan, stowage plan, strategy**
3 ⋈ an architectural, a building, a construction, an office, a town **plan**

---

plan[2] *verb*
1 to decide, organize or prepare for something: *The conference has been planned for 600 people.* ○ *His business trip was very carefully planned.* **2** to intend doing something: *We're planning to arrive at 2 pm.* ○ *She planned to visit all her customers on her trip to Athens.* **3** to make a detailed plan of or for something; to design: *The new office building seems to be badly planned.*

/plæn/
plan, planning, planned
1 note transitive and intransitive verb
⋈ **plan** (something) badly, carefully, in detail, well
2 note transitive and intransitive verb
⋈ **plan** *to* do something
3 note transitive verb
⋈ **plan** a building, an office, a town

---

planned economy *noun* (economics)
a type of ECONOMY that is centrally controlled by a government rather than by the amount of goods available and the amount wanted by customers: *adapt a planned economy to competition and market forces*

/ˌplænd ɪˈkɒnəmi/
pl planned economies
syn command economy
▶ **economy 1, 2, free market, market forces**

---

planned obsolescence *noun*
1 (*manufacturing*) (of a product) being designed to break down or become out of date within a certain length of time, so that people have to buy a new one: *The computer has planned obsolescence.* **2** (*accounting*) the loss in value (DEPRECIATION) of an asset as it becomes older

/ˌplænd ɒbsəˈlesns/
note not used with *a* or *an*. No plural and used with a singular verb only.
syn built-in obsolescence
▶ **obsolescence**

---

planning *noun*
1 making plans or arrangements: *The project requires careful planning.* ○ *hold a planning meeting* **2** the control and design of the growth and development of a town, its buildings, roads, etc, esp by a local government authority: *He works in planning.*

/ˈplænɪŋ/
note not used with a *a* or *an*. No plural and used with a singular verb only.
1 ⋈ careful, detailed **planning**
▶ **aggregate planning,**

corporate planning, manpower planning, media planning

2 ⋈ a **planning** application, department, officer

syn town planning

---

planning permission *noun* (law/industry)
official consent to build on or develop a site given by a local authority: *apply for planning permission to extend a factory*

/ˈplænɪŋ pəˌmɪʃn/

note not used with *a* or *an*. No plural and used with a singular verb only.

⋈ apply for, grant, obtain, refuse, require **planning permission**

---

plant *noun*
1 (*industry*) machinery and equipment used in an industrial or manufacturing process: *The firm has made a huge investment in new plant.* **2** (*industry*) the place where an industrial or manufacturing process is carried out: *A strike at the new manufacturing plant held up production for 2 weeks.*

/plɑːnt; *US* plænt/

1 note not used with *a* or *an*. No plural and used with a singular verb only.

⋈ heavy **plant**

► **machinery**

2 pl plants

⋈ a chemical, an industrial, a power, a processing, a sewage **plant**

► **assembly plant**

---

plc *abbr* (industry)
(*UK*) public limited company

/ˌpiː el ˈsiː/

(also **PLC**)

---

plead *verb* (law)
1 (of a lawyer) to support someone's case in a court of law: *They employed the best lawyer they could to plead their case.* ○ *Who is going to plead for him?* **2** (of someone accused of a crime in a court of law) to say whether you are guilty or not guilty: *He pleaded guilty to the charge.* ○ *How did the prisoner plead?*

/pliːd/

plead, pleading, pleaded

1 note transitive and intransitive verb

⋈ **plead** *for, against* someone; **plead** a case

2 note transitive verb

⋈ **plead** guilty, insanity, not guilty

---

pledge *noun* (finance/law)
something of value given by a borrower to a lender as security for a loan

/pledʒ/

pl pledges

► **collateral, guarantee[1] 3, security 3, unredeemed pledge**

Plimsoll line *noun* (shipping)
► **load line**

/ˈplɪmsəl laɪn/

---

plough back *verb* (finance)
to use the profits made by a business to buy new equipment, etc to improve and expand the business: *All the profits for the year were ploughed back into the business.*

/ˌplaʊ ˈbæk/

plough back, ploughing back, ploughed back

note transitive verb

⋈ **plough back** money, profits

plug[1] *noun* (advertising)
(*informal*) a favourable reference made to a book, record or product, made in public, to make people buy it: *The company's new product was given a good plug on the radio yesterday.*

/plʌg/
pl plugs
⋈ give someone/something a **plug**

plug[2] *verb* (advertising)
(*informal*) to praise a book, record or product in public to make people buy it: *They are really plugging that book on the radio at the moment.*

/plʌg/
plug, plugging, plugged
note transitive verb
⋈ **plug** a book, company, film, product
► **advertise 1, promote 1**

P/N *abbr* (finance)
promissory note

/ˌpiː ˈen/

PO *abbr*
1 post office: *PO Box 500* **2** postal order: *Send a cheque or PO.*

/ˌpiː ˈəʊ/

point *noun*
1 something that is said as part of a discussion; a particular fact, idea or opinion: *I want to raise some important points for discussion at the meeting.* ○ *Point 6 in the agenda deals with the application of profits.* **2** (*banking/finance*) a unit of measure of a rate or an index number, eg an index of share prices: *The FT-share index fell 33.8 points to 17388.* ○ *Since 1985 the growth of consumer spending has exceeded that of income by about 7 percentage points.*

/pɔɪnt/
pl points
1 ⋈ make, raise a **point**
2 ⋈ a decimal, percentage **point**; fall, rise (by a number of) **points**

point of sale *noun* (advertising)
the place where a consumer buys something: *A non-stop video above the counter is used to advertise the goods at the point of sale.*

/ˌpɔɪnt əv ˈseɪl/
pl points of sale
abbr pos
⋈ **point of sale** advertising
► **sale**

poison pill *noun*
(*informal*) a form of defence used by a company to prevent or weaken the effect of an unwanted takeover bid, eg by selling off important assets: *use poison pill tactics to stave off unwelcome takeover bids*

/ˌpɔɪzn ˈpɪl/
pl poison pills
⋈ a **poison pill** defence, option, tactic
► **asset stripping, scorched earth policy**

policy *noun*
a plan of action or statement of ideals: *The shareholders met to discuss policy.* ○ *The firm has implemented a number of drastic cost-cutting policies.* ○ *Only senior management can take policy decisions.* ○ *It is company policy to ensure that all employees receive adequate training for their job.*

/ˈpɒləsi/
pl policies
⋈ develop, discuss, implement (a) **policy**; company, government **policy**; a **policy** decision, document, statement
► **insurance, paid-up policy**

poll *noun*
a way of finding out public opinion by asking a number of people for their views on something: *conduct an opinion poll to find out where local people think the new factory should be built*

/pəʊl/
pl polls
⋈ an opinion, a public opinion **poll**; carry out, conduct a **poll**
► **ballot[1] 1**

pool¹ *noun* (industry)
1 a supply of money, goods or services, used by a particular group of people when needed: *a pool of cars used by the sales staff* **2** a group of people available for work when required: *The typing pool* (ie a group of typists) *deals with general secretarial work from any department.* ○ *recruit staff from a pool of skilled labour*

/puːl/
pl pools
1 ⋈ a **pool** car; a **pool** of capital, funds, resources
2 ⋈ work in a **typing pool**; a **pool** of expertise, labour

---

pool² *verb* (finance)
to put money, resources, etc into a common fund: *They pooled their ideas and came up with an innovative advertising campaign.* ○ *The two companies pooled resources and entered into a joint venture.*

/puːl/
pool, pooling, pooled
note transitive verb
⋈ **pool** funds, ideas, resources

---

portfolio *noun*
1 (*stock exchange*) a group of different investments held by a private investor, or a financial organization: *He manages several portfolios on behalf of a pension fund.* ○ *The company decided to increase its portfolio and bought shares in Smith Ltd.* ○ *pay management fees to the company that manages your portfolio* **2** a large flat case used for carrying papers, documents, etc: *He carried the building plans in a large portfolio.*

/ˌpɔːtˈfəʊliəʊ/
pl portfolios
1 ⋈ analyse, manage a **portfolio**; a balanced, mixed, wide-ranging **portfolio**
2 ⋈ carry a **portfolio**

---

portfolio management *noun* (stock exchange)
the analysis and control of a group of investments with the aim of making the best possible profit with the least possible risk

/ˌpɔːtˈfəʊliəʊ ˌmænɪdʒmənt/
note not used with *a* or *an*. No plural and used with a singular verb only.
▶ **fund management, investment trust, management 1, unit trust**

---

pos *abbr* (retail)
point of sale

/ˌpiː əʊ ˈes/

---

position *noun*
1 paid employment; a job: *He resigned from his position as Managing Director.* ○ *be promoted to a higher position* **2** (*commerce/finance*) situation or circumstances: *We are not in a position to negotiate.* ○ *Our cash position is becoming increasingly precarious.*

/pəˈzɪʃn/
1 pl positions
⋈ advertise, fill, take up a **position**; a **position** *in, with* (a company)
▶ **job 1, placement 1, post¹ 3**
2 note usually singular
⋈ a cash, current, financial, future **position**
▶ **bear position, bull position, long position, open position, short position**

---

post¹ *noun*
1 (*esp UK*) letters and parcels that are collected or delivered: *Has the post come yet this morning?* ○ *I try to open the post as soon as I get to the office.* **2** (*esp UK*) the system for collecting and delivering letters and parcels: *Your letter must have got lost in the post.* ○ *send a parcel by post* **3** a job or position: *He resigned from his post as Chairman.* ○ *It took nearly 6 months to fill the vacant post.* ○ *She was promoted to the post of Sales Manager after only 6 months.* ○ *A new post was created in the advertising department.*

/pəʊst/
1 note singular noun, used with a singular verb
⋈ first-class, second-class **post**; deliver, open, send, sort the **post**
▶ **mail¹ 1**
2 note not used with *a* or *an*. No plural and used with a singular verb only.

⧓ put a letter, etc in the, send a letter, etc by **post**

▶ **mail¹ 2, recorded delivery, registered post**

3 pl posts

⧓ advertise, create, fill, find, take up a **post**; an executive, a junior, a managerial, an overseas, a secretarial, a senior, a vacant **post**

▶ **job 1, placement 1, position 1**

---

post² *verb*

1 (*esp UK*) to send a letter, parcel, etc by post: *The contract must be posted today.* ○ *Could you post these letters for me, please?* **2** to send someone to a particular place of employment: *He will be posted overseas.* ○ *The company has posted her to Germany.* **3** to put someone at a particular place of duty: *Security guards were posted at the entrance to the bank.* **4** to display a notice, etc in a public place: *The names of the successful applicants will be posted up today.*

/pəʊst/

post, posting, posted

note transitive verb

▶ **mail²**

2 ⧓ **post** someone *to* (a place), someone (overseas)

4 ⧓ **post** an advertisement, a bill, a notice

---

postage *noun*

the amount charged for sending something by post: *Does that include postage?* ○ *£2.50 each including postage and packing*

/ˈpəʊstɪdʒ/

note not used with *a* or *an*. No plural and used with a singular verb only.

⧓ **postage** costs, expenses

▶ **post-free**

---

postal *adjective*

1 of the post: *Please write the full postal address of your bank on the form.* **2** sent by post: *Postal applications must be received by 12 December.*

/ˈpəʊstl/

1 ⧓ **postal** collections, delays, districts, services, staff

2 ⧓ **postal** ballot, vote

---

postal order *noun* (finance)

a piece of paper bought from a post office that represents a certain amount of money. It is a safe way of sending money by post and can be exchanged for money by the person named on it.

/ˈpəʊstl ˌɔːdə(r)/

pl postal orders

abbr PO

⧓ buy, cash, post, send a **postal order**

syn money order

▶ **order¹ 1**

---

postcode *noun*

(*UK*) a group of numbers, or letters and numbers, used as part of an address so that letters can be sorted by machine: *Don't forget to use the postcode.* ○ *What is your postcode?*

/ˈpəʊstkəʊd/

pl postcodes

syn postal code, (*US*) zip code

---

post-date *verb*

to put a later date (on a document, letter, cheque, etc) than the date at the time of writing: *He post-dated his cheque so there would be sufficient funds in his account to meet the amount.* ○ *The document was post-dated by three days.*

/ˌpəʊstˈdeɪt/

post-date, post-dating, post-dated

note transitive verb

⧓ **post-date** a bill, cheque, contract, document

▶ **antedate, backdate, date² 1**

---

poster *noun* (advertising)

a large printed picture or notice in a public place, often used to

/ˈpəʊstə(r)/

pl posters

advertise something: *a poster advertising fizzy drinks* ○ *put up advertising posters all over the town*

⧓ a **poster** campaign; display, put up, stick up a **poster**

---

poste restante *noun, adverb*
a place in a post office where letters, parcels, etc can be sent and kept until they are collected by the person they were sent to; sending something in this way: *Send the letter to the poste restante in Padua.* ○ *send the letter poste restante*

/ˌpəʊst ˈrestɑːnt/
▶ **accommodation address, box number 1**

---

post-free *adjective, adverb*
1 carried free of postal charges or with postage already paid: *The goods will be delivered post-free.* **2** (of a price) including the charge for postage: *special offer at £10 post-free*

/ˌpəʊst ˈfriː/
▶ **postage**

---

post office *noun*
1 a place that sells stamps and where letters, parcels, etc can be posted: *buy stamps in a post office* **2 the Post Office** a national organization that is responsible for collecting and delivering letters, parcels, etc: *The Post Office will increase the cost of first-class mail from 24p to 26p.*

/ˈpəʊst ˌɒfɪs/
abbr PO
1 pl post offices
⧓ work at/in a **post office**
2 ⧓ work for the **Post Office**

---

potential[1] *adjective*
that can or may come into existence; possible: *We are making a list of potential clients.* ○ *Is there a potential market in Spain for our products?*

/pəˈtenʃl/
⧓ a **potential** customer, market, problem, risk; **potential** demand, growth, sales, value
▶ **prospective**

---

potential[2] *noun*
the qualities that someone or something has that can be developed: *The junior manager shows a great deal of potential.* ○ *The product has even more potential in export markets.*

/pəˈtenʃl/
note not used with *a* or *an*. No plural and used with a singular verb only.
⧓ have, realize, show **potential**; **potential** *for* development, growth

---

power *noun*
1 (*industry*) energy that is used to do work: *Discuss the benefits and problems of using nuclear power.* ○ *produce electricity from wind power* **2** (*marketing*) control or influence over other people: *The 18 to 20 year old group have a great deal of purchasing power.* ○ *The union has had its bargaining power reduced.* **3** (*law*) the right or authority to do something: *We have the power to stop the deal at any time.*

/ˈpaʊə(r)/
1 note not used with *a* or *an*. No plural and used with a singular verb only.
⧓ electric, gas, hydroelectric, nuclear, wind **power**
▶ **manpower, water power**
2 note not used with *a* or *an*. No plural and used with a singular verb only.
⧓ borrowing, earning, spending **power**
▶ **bargaining power, purchasing power**
3 pl powers
⧓ legal, official **power**
▶ **authority 1**

---

power of attorney *noun* (law)
a legal document giving one person the right to act for another in

/ˌpaʊər əv əˈtɜːni/
pl powers of attorney
abbr PA

legal matters: *Our solicitor has been granted power of attorney over the funds.*

⧓ give, grant someone **power of attorney**

syn letter of attorney

▶ **attorney 1**

---

pp *abbr* (commerce)

(*Latin*) per procurationem; on behalf of or with the authority of someone: *The letter was signed J. Smith and Sons Ltd., pp.* ○ *The contract was signed pp J. Smith and Sons Ltd.*

/ˌpiː ˈpiː/

(also **p.p.**)

note The abbreviation is used more than the full term.

PPI *abbr* (finance)

producer price index

/ˌpiː piː ˈaɪ/

PPP *abbr* (finance)

purchasing power parity

/ˌpiː piː ˈpiː/

PR *abbr* (advertising)

public relations: *She works in PR.* ○ *a PR campaign*

/ˌpiː ˈɑː(r)/

---

practice *noun*

1 (**a**) the work of a professional person, esp a doctor or lawyer: *He has retired from practice.* (**b**) the place where the work is done: *My doctor has a practice in Dean Street.* **2** a repeated exercise done to improve a skill: *An hour's practice every day will soon improve your typing speed.* **3** the actual doing of something; action as opposed to theory: *Now we must put the plan into practice.* ○ *The idea would never work in practice.* **4** a way of doing something: *It is standard practice to pay a deposit with an order.*

/ˈpræktɪs/

1a note not used with *a* or *an*. No plural and used with a singular verb only.

⧓ be *in* **practice**

1b pl practices

⧓ a legal, medical **practice**

2 note not used with *a* or *an*. No plural and used with a singular verb only.

⧓ frequent, regular **practice**

3 note not used with *a* or *an*. No plural and used with a singular verb only.

⧓ put something *into* **practice**

4 note not used with *a* or *an*. No plural and used with a singular verb only.

⧓ bad, good, standard, usual **practice**

▶ **sharp practice, restrictive trade practices**

---

precaution *noun*

care taken in advance to prevent loss or damage: *Staff are asked to keep valuables with them as a precaution against theft.* ○ *The 'no smoking' rule is a fire precaution.*

/prɪˈkɔːʃn/

⧓ fire, safety **precautions**; a **precaution** *against* danger, fire, flood, industrial accident

---

predatory pricing *noun* (commerce/finance)

the pricing of goods and services at a very low level to force out competitors: *The company is using predatory pricing to increase its market share.*

/ˌpredətri ˈpraɪsɪŋ/

note not used with *a* or *an*. No plural and used with a singular verb only.

⧓ use **predatory pricing**

▶ **price war, pricing policy**

---

preference share *noun* (stock exchange)

a fixed unit of a company's share capital that provides a fixed rate

/ˈprefrəns ˌʃeə(r)/

pl preference shares

of interest that must be paid before dividends are paid on ordinary shares and repaid first if the company is liquidated: *These preference shares carry no voting rights.*

⧓ buy, sell a **preference share**

▶ **debenture, equity capital**

---

preferential creditor *noun* (finance)

a creditor whose debt must be paid before others if a company goes into liquidation: *The preferential creditors will meet on Wednesday.*

/ˌprefəˌrenʃl ˈkredɪtə(r)/

pl preferential creditors

⧓ owe (money to), pay, pay off, settle with a **preferential creditor**

▶ **creditor**

---

preliminary *adjective* (management/marketing/sales)

coming before something else that is important; preparatory: *hold a preliminary meeting before the main conference* ○ *Our preliminary inquiries revealed a possible new market.* ○ *The laboratories are doing some preliminary experiments before embarking on the project.*

/prɪˈlɪmɪnəri/

⧓ a **preliminary** discussion, experiment, inquiry, meeting, plan, report; **preliminary** findings, information, negotiations, research, talks

---

premises *noun*

a house or building and the land on which it stands: *The firm is looking for larger premises.* ○ *These goods are made on the premises.*

/ˈpremɪsɪz/

note plural noun, used with a plural verb

⧓ business, commercial, industrial, office **premises**

▶ **property 2**

---

premium *noun*

1 (*insurance*) an insurance premium **2** an extra payment or charge: *A premium of 2% is paid on long-term investments.* ○ *pay a premium for express delivery*

at a premium 1 rare or difficult to obtain and therefore expensive: *Building land in cities is at a premium.* **2** (of a share or security) above the normal value: *These shares are being sold at a premium.*

/ˈpriːmiəm/

pl premiums

▶ **insurance premium**

2 ⧓ charge, pay a **premium**

▶ **acceleration premium**

---

prepaid *adjective, adverb*

paid for in advance: *Please return the questionnaire in the prepaid envelope provided* (ie an envelope that shows that postage has already been paid). ○ *Outward transport costs are prepaid.*

/ˌpriːˈpeɪd/

▶ **pay**

---

present[1] *adjective*

existing or happening now: *How can we increase the present value of the product?* ○ *Who is the present chairman of the company?* ○ *It is difficult for businesses to expand under the present economic climate.*

/ˈpreznt/

▶ **actual, current**

---

present[2] *verb*

1 to show or talk about something: *The management consultants presented their report to the Board of Directors.* ○ *I shall present the results of the market research at the next meeting.* **2** (*banking*) to produce and show a cheque, a bill of exchange, etc for payment: *The cheque was presented for payment on the 9th of June.* ○ *The bill is not due to be presented yet.* **3** to give something to someone, eg at a formal ceremony: *The company was presented with an award for industrial design.*

/prɪˈzent/

present, presenting, presented

note transitive verb

1 ⧓ **present** figures, information, a plan, a proposal, a report, results

▶ **submit**

2 ⧓ **present** a bill of exchange, cheque, promissory note

▶ **accept 3, re-present**

3 ⧓ **present** an award, a certificate, a prize

presentation *noun*
1 (*advertising/commerce*) the act of showing or talking about something: *make a presentation of the end of year sales results* ○ *give a presentation to each of our potential clients* **2** (*finance*) producing and showing a cheque or bill of exchange, etc for payment: *The bill was payable on presentation.*

/ˌprezn'teɪʃn/
1 pl presentations
⋈ arrange, do, give, make, organize a **presentation**; a **presentation** *of* something, *to* someone
2 note not used with *a* or *an*. No plural and used with a singular verb only.
▶ **acceptance 2**

president *noun* (management)
1 (*US*) the chief officer of a company who is responsible for deciding and carrying out company policy: *president of a large steel corporation* **2** (*UK*) a title sometimes given to a former chairman or managing director of a company: *The president still comes to the annual general meeting.*

/'prezɪdənt/
pl presidents
1 syn (*UK*) chairman
2 ▶ **managing director**

press *noun*
1 the Press the journalists who work for newspapers, magazines and the news sections of television and radio; the newspapers, etc produced by them: *The Press were not invited to the conference.* ○ *The freedom of the press must be protected.* ○ *The story was reported in the local press.* **2** the treatment given to someone or something in newspaper, radio, etc reports: *The company has had a lot of bad press since those workers were sacked.*

/pres/
1 note used with a singular or plural verb
⋈ the gutter, local, national, tabloid **press**
2 note singular noun, used with a singular verb
⋈ get, have, receive a good/bad **press**; **press** coverage

press conference *noun*
an interview given to journalists to announce a decision, an achievement, etc: *The chairman announced his resignation at a press conference.*

/'pres ˌkɒnfərəns/
pl press conferences
⋈ hold a **press conference**

press officer *noun* (personnel)
a person employed by an organization to provide information to the PRESS and to answer journalists' questions: *The press officer is trying to improve the public image of the company.*

/'pres ˌɒfɪsə(r)/
pl press officers
⋈ appoint, employ a **press officer**

press release *noun* (advertising)
an official announcement or written information about something given to the PRESS by an organization: *The company will issue a press release giving details of the takeover.*

/'pres rɪˌli:s/
pl press releases
⋈ issue, send out, write a **press release**
syn news release

Prestel *noun* (commerce/finance)
(*UK*) a computerized visual information system operated by British Telecom in the UK. The information is displayed on a personal computer or a television screen. Users can receive news, send messages, buy goods and services, book holidays, etc: *To receive Prestel you need to become a subscriber to the service.* ○ *Prestel is accessed through ordinary telephone lines.*

/'prestel/
⋈ access, book through, receive, subscribe to **Prestel**
▶ **CEEFAX, Teletext, Videotex, viewdata**

pre-tax *adjective* (tax)
before tax has been deducted: *Profits should rise to £10.5m pre-tax.* ○ *The company had a pre-tax deficit of £5.49m in the six months to the end of June.*

/ˌpri: 'tæks/
⋈ a **pre-tax** deficit, income, loss, profit; **pre-tax** earnings
▶ **tax**[1]

pre-testing *noun* (advertising)
showing an advertisement to a sample group of people to see how effective it is: *After pre-testing, the advertising company will analyse public response to the advertisement.*

/ˌpriːˈtestɪŋ/
note not used with *a* or *an*. No plural and used with a singular verb only.
⧓ advertising **pre-testing**; carry out **pre-testing**
▶ **test marketing**

price[1] *noun* (sales)
the amount of money for which something can be bought or sold: *The price for these goods is too high.* ○ *What is the price of petrol now?* ○ *We can't afford to buy the computer at that price.* ○ *a price increase of 10%*

/praɪs/
pl prices
⧓ agree, fix, increase, reduce, set a **price**; a competitive, high, low, maximum, minimum, reasonable **price**; a **price** list, tag
▶ **American Selling Price, asking price, best price, cash price, cost**[1]**, cost price, cut price, intervention price, list price, manufacturer's recommended price, market price, mean price, net price, nominal price, quoted price, retail price, trade price**

price[2] *verb* (sales)
1 to fix the price of something: *These goods are priced too high.* ○ *goods priced at £6.99 each* ○ *Our new range will be competitively priced.* **2** to mark the price on goods in a shop: *The shop assistant priced the goods before putting them on the shelves.*

/praɪs/
price, pricing, priced
note transitive verb
⧓ competitively, highly, moderately, reasonably **priced**
▶ **cost**[2]

price controls *noun* (economics)
government restrictions placed on the price of consumer goods at times of shortage, war, high inflation, etc: *The government promised that its price controls on oil would be removed in six months.*

/ˈpraɪs kənˌtrəʊlz/
note plural noun, used with a plural verb
⧓ abolish, introduce **price controls**
▶ **prices and incomes policy**

price discrimination *noun* (commerce/economics)
the sale of the same product to separate markets at different prices, usually by organizations with a monopoly: *The Office of Fair Trading is investigating price discrimination in the water supply industry.*

/ˈpraɪs dɪskrɪmɪˌneɪʃn/
note not used with *a* or *an*. No plural and used with a singular verb only.
▶ **differentiation, discrimination**

price-dividend ratio *noun* (stock exchange)
the present market price of a company share divided by the dividend per share for the previous year: *The price-dividend ratio will indicate the investment value of the share.*

/ˌpraɪsˈdɪvɪdend ˌreɪʃiəʊ/
pl price-dividend ratios
abbr PDR, P/D ratio
▶ **ratio**

price-earnings ratio *noun* (stock exchange)
the present market price of a company share divided by the earnings per share for the previous year: *The price-earnings ratio indicated rapid growth.*

/ˌpraɪsˈɜːnɪŋz ˌreɪʃiəʊ/
pl price-earnings ratios
▶ **dividend, earnings per share, market price**

abbr PER, P/E ratio
▶ ratio

---

price ex warehouse *noun* (distribution)
the price paid for a product if collected from the warehouse by the purchaser: *All prices shown are price ex warehouse.*

/ˌpraɪs eks ˈweəhaʊs/
note no plural
▶ **retail price, trade price**

---

price-fixing *noun* (sales)
an agreement between traders not to sell goods below a certain price: *Price-fixing keeps prices artificially high.*

/ˈpraɪs ˌfɪksɪŋ/
note not used with *a* or *an*. No plural and used with a singular verb only.
▶ **price ring**

---

price index *noun* (economics)
▶ **Retail Price Index**

/ˈpraɪs ˌɪndeks/

---

price range *noun* (sales)
a group of prices that are close together between two fixed limits: *Do you sell more computers in the lower price range?* ○ *Please send details of any other models in the same price range.*

/ˈpraɪs reɪndʒ/
pl price ranges
⋈ higher, lower, middle **price range**

---

price ring *noun* (commerce)
a group of sellers in the same industry who have agreed to fix a minimum price for a product: *It is illegal to form a price ring.*

/ˈpraɪs rɪŋ/
pl price rings
⋈ form a **price ring**
▶ **price-fixing**

---

prices and incomes policy *noun* (finance)
a system of controlling prices and wage levels, used by a government to reduce inflation and stabilize a country's economy: *The government's prices and incomes policy was deeply resented by both business people and wage earners.*

/ˌpraɪsɪz ənd ˈɪŋkʌmz ˌpɒləsi/
pl prices and incomes policies
▶ **price controls, wage-freeze**

---

price variance *noun* (accounting)
the difference between an estimated cost and the actual cost: *Unexpected increases caused a large price variance.*

/ˈpraɪs ˌveəriəns/
note usually singular
⋈ a large, small **price variance**
▶ **quantity variance, variance**

---

price war *noun* (commerce)
a situation where competing sellers repeatedly reduce their prices in order to attract buyers: *The major oil companies are keen to avoid a price war.*

/ˈpraɪs wɔː(r)/
pl price wars
▶ **predatory pricing**

---

pricing policy *noun* (commerce)
a plan or statement of prices set by an organization for its products and services. The aim is to produce maximum profit while allowing for rival firms and market situations: *The high volume of sales makes the low pricing policy possible.*

/ˈpraɪsɪŋ ˌpɒləsi/
pl pricing policies
⋈ adopt, change, implement, revise a **pricing policy**
▶ **predatory pricing**

---

prima facie *adjective, adverb* (law)
based on first appearances: *There is prima facie evidence suggesting that the company knew about the dishonest dealing.* ○ *Prima facie he is guilty.*

/ˌpraɪmə ˈfeɪʃi/
⋈ **prima facie** evidence, proof; a **prima facie** case, judgement, reason

---

primage *noun* (shipping)
an addition to freight charges intended to ensure extra care in

/ˈpraɪmɪdʒ/
note not used with *a* or *an*. No plural and used with a singular

handling: *The goods were fragile and the shippers charged primage for taking special care.*

verb only.

▶ **charge[1] 1, freight 3**

---

primary industry *noun* (industry)

▶ **industry**

/ˌpraɪməri ˈɪndəstri/

---

primary market *noun* (finance)

the section of the money market where securities are sold for the first time: *A large primary market is needed to finance European industry.*

/ˌpraɪməri ˈmɑːkɪt/

pl primary markets

▶ **market[1], secondary market**

---

primary production *noun* (industry)

the production of crops, crude oil, minerals, ores, timber and other raw materials existing as natural resources: *The manufacturing industry depends on raw materials being made available by primary production.*

/ˌpraɪməri prəˈdʌkʃn/

note not used with *a* or *an*. No plural and used with a singular verb only.

▶ **production, raw materials, secondary production**

---

prime entry book *noun* (accounting)

an account book in which a business's transactions are first recorded: *From the prime entry books, records of transactions are passed on to the ledger accounts.*

/ˌpraɪm ˈentri bʊk/

pl prime entry books

syn book of prime entry

▶ **books, day book, entry 2, journal**

---

prime lending rate *noun* (banking)

(*US*) ▶ **base rate**

/ˌpraɪm ˈlendɪŋ reɪt/

---

prime rate *noun* (banking)

(*US*) ▶ **base rate**

/ˈpraɪm reɪt/

---

prime time *noun* (advertising)

the time of day when the greatest number of people listen to the radio or watch television and when advertising rates are highest: *Prime time on television is usually early evening, ie between 7 and 9 pm.*

/ˈpraɪm taɪm/

note usually singular

⧓ **prime time** advertising, broadcasting

---

principal *noun*

1 a person on whose behalf an agent or a broker acts: *The agent is selling goods on behalf of a principal.* **2** (*finance*) a sum of money lent or invested to earn interest: *Interest will be paid half-yearly and added to the principal unless otherwise required by the depositor.*

/ˈprɪnsəpl/

pl principals

1 ▶ **agent, broker, factor**

⧓ act for, on behalf of a **principal**

2 ⧓ a **principal** sum

---

printer *noun*

1 a person or an organization that prints books, leaflets, etc: *Have the catalogues come back from the printer yet?* ○ *get estimates for printing the advertising leaflets from several different printers*
2 (*computing*) a machine that prints, esp one linked to a computer: *The printer has run out of paper.*

/ˈprɪntə(r)/

pl printers

2 ▶ **daisy-wheel printer, dot matrix printer, laser printer, letter quality printer, near letter quality printer**

---

printout *noun* (computing)

information produced in a printed form from a computer or teleprinter: *Give me a printout of the statistics.* ○ *Is the computer printout clear enough to read?*

/ˈprɪntaʊt/

pl printouts

⧓ computer **printout**

print run *noun*
the number of copies of a magazine, a book, a leaflet, etc printed at one time: *do a print run of 3 000 copies* ○ *a magazine with a very large print run*

/ˈprɪnt rʌn/
pl print runs
⧓ do, increase, reduce a **print run**

priority *noun*
1 the state of being more important than someone or something or of coming before someone or something else: *Instructions from the managing director were given priority.* ○ *The insurance company gave priority to the claims of people made homeless by the disaster.*
2 something that is most important or that must be done before anything else: *Increasing our overseas contacts is a top priority.* ○ *We must decide what the priorities are.*

/praɪˈɒrəti/
1 note not used with *a* or *an*. No plural and used with a singular verb only.
⧓ give something **priority**; give **priority** to something
2 pl priorities
⧓ first, high, main, major, top **priority**; make something a **priority**

private *adjective*
1 belonging to one particular person or group and not to be used by others: *This is private property. You cannot park here.* **2** secret; not to be shared by other people: *The letter was marked 'private'.* **3** with no one else present: *I would like a private interview with the personnel manager.* **4** owned or organized by a person or company and not by the government: *The hotel is run as a private business.*
in private with no one else present: *May I speak to you in private?*

/ˈpraɪvət/
1 ▶ **privatize, public**
2 ▶ **confidential**
4 ⧓ a **private** business, company, firm
▶ **private limited company, private sector**

private bank *noun* (banking)
1 (*US*) a bank owned by one person or a partnership **2** (*informal UK*) a bank not owned by the state: *The money is in a private bank.*
3 a bank that is not a member of a clearing house: *Private banks must use clearing banks as agents.*

/ˌpraɪvət ˈbæŋk/
pl private banks
▶ **bank[1], clearing bank, commercial bank, merchant bank**

private branch exchange *noun*
a telephone exchange that connects internal extension numbers to outside telephone networks: *The calls were routed through a private branch exchange.*

/ˌpraɪvət ˈbrɑːntʃ ɪksˌtʃeɪndʒ/
pl private branch exchanges
abbr PBX

private company *noun* (stock exchange)
▶ **private limited company**

/ˌpraɪvət ˈkʌmpəni/

private enterprise *noun* (economics)
industry and business that is owned by an independent company or individual without being controlled or financed by the government: *Most of the town's leisure facilities are run by private enterprise.*

/ˌpraɪvət ˈentəpraɪz/
note not used with *a* or *an*. No plural and used with a singular verb only.
⧓ attract, encourage, promote **private enterprise**
▶ **enterprise, free enterprise, mixed economy**

private investor *noun* (stock exchange)
a person who invests his/her own money for personal profit and not that of a company: *The share offer was aimed primarily at the private investor.*

/ˌpraɪvət ɪnˈvestə(r)/
pl private investors
⧓ deal with, financed by a **private investor**; the **private investor** market
▶ **investor**

private limited company *noun* (commerce)
a company that may not offer its shares for sale to the public: *A*

/ˌpraɪvət ˌlɪmɪtɪd ˈkʌmpəni/
pl private limited companies

private limited company has the word limited or the initials Ltd after its name.

▶ **limited company, public limited company**

---

private sector *noun* (economics)
the part of a country's economy that is not owned by the government or public corporations, but by independent companies and individuals: *Much of the investment has come from the private sector.* ○ *He left the National Health Service to work for the private sector.*

/ˌpraɪvət ˈsektə(r)/
note singular noun, used with a singular verb
⋈ work for, work in the **private sector**
▶ **corporate sector, public sector, sector**

---

privatization *noun* (industry)
the transfer of a government-controlled company or industry into private ownership: *privatization of the water industry*

/ˌpraɪvətaɪˈzeɪʃn/
(also **privatisation**)
note not used with *a* or *an*. No plural and used with a singular verb only.
⋈ oppose, propose **privatization**
opp nationalization
▶ **denationalization, nationalization**

---

privatize *verb* (industry)
to transfer a state-controlled company or industry into private ownership: *The water industry has now been privatized.* ○ *Many governments are now privatizing their airlines.*

/ˈpraɪvətaɪz/
privatize, privatizing, privatized
(also **privatise**)
note transitive verb
⋈ **privatize** a business, a company, an industry
opp nationalize
▶ **denationalize, private sector, public sector**

PRO *abbr* (advertising)
public relations officer: *We have employed a full-time PRO.*

/ˌpiː ɑːr ˈəʊ/
note pronounced as a individual letters
pl PROs

---

proactive marketing *noun* (marketing)
making people think they need a new product rather than just producing goods that respond to existing needs: *Getting people to include this new health drink in their diet is an example of proactive marketing.*

/ˌprəʊæktɪv ˈmɑːkɪtɪŋ/
note not used with *a* or *an*. No plural and used with a singular verb only.
⋈ carry out **proactive marketing**
▶ **marketing**

---

probationary *adjective*
of a time when someone is being tested to see if they are suitable: *You will be accepted for permanent employment if you complete the three-month probationary period successfully.*

/prəˈbeɪʃnri/
⋈ a **probationary** period, year

---

procedure *noun*
1 the way in which something is done: *It is important to follow the correct safety procedure.* ○ *It is not company procedure to do it this way.* **2** action or series of actions needed to do something: *Obtaining a refund from the company is a complicated procedure.*

/prəˈsiːdʒə(r)/
pl procedures
⋈ correct, normal, standard, usual **procedure**; company, legal **procedure**
▶ **selection procedure**

---

proceedings *noun* (law)
legal action: *Proceedings have been started against the firm.*

/prəˈsiːdɪŋz/
note plural noun, used with a plural verb
⋈ court, legal **proceedings**
▶ **action**[1]

proceeds *noun* (finance)
the money received from selling something: *The proceeds from the sale have been invested.*

/ˈprəʊsiːdz/
note plural noun, used with a plural verb
⋈ gross, net **proceeds**

process[1] *noun* (industry)
the method used to make something: *The company has developed a new fruit preservation process.* ○ *What process do you use to dry the paint so quickly?*

/ˈprəʊses/
pl processes
⋈ an industrial, a manufacturing **process**

process[2] *verb*
1 (*industry*) to change raw materials, food, etc into new products, using machines: *processed cheese* **2** (*administration*) to deal with a document, etc officially: *It will take about two weeks for your order to be processed.* **3** (*computing*) to sort, analyse or present information in a specified way: *The computer will take about an hour to process the data.*

/ˈprəʊses/
process, processing, processed
note transitive verb
1 ⋈ **process** raw materials
2 ⋈ **process** an application, a document, an order
3 ⋈ **process** data, figures, information

procurement officer *noun* (industry)
▶ **materials buyer**

/prəˈkjʊəmənt ˌɒfɪsə(r)/

produce[1] *noun* (agriculture)
food, etc that is grown on a farm and sold: *Many farmers sell their produce directly from the farm.* ○ *transport fresh agricultural produce to market*

/ˈprɒdjuːs/
note not used with *a* or *an*. No plural and used with a singular verb only.
⋈ agricultural, dairy, farm, local **produce**
▶ **cash crop**

produce[2] *verb* (manufacturing)
to make, grow or provide something: *The mine produces 180 000 tonnes of copper per year.* ○ *electronic goods produced in Japan*

/prəˈdjuːs/
produce, producing, produced
note transitive verb
▶ **mass-produce, overproduce, yield**[2]

producer *noun* (industry)
a person, organization or country that makes or grows something: *This country is a major producer of steel.* ○ *Shell is the largest North Sea oil producer.*

/prəˈdjuːsə(r)/
pl producers
⋈ an agricultural, a dairy, an oil, a steel, a timber, a wine **producer**
▶ **middleman**
opp consumer

producer goods *noun* (manufacturing)
▶ **capital goods**

/prəˈdjuːsə gʊdz/

Producer Price Index *noun* (commerce)
a set of figures showing the movement of prices of goods and services purchased and manufactured by industry over a period of time: *The producer price index has decreased since the last quarter.*

/prəˌdju:sə ˈpraɪs ˌɪndeks/
(also **producer price index**)
abbr PPI
syn wholesale price index
▶ **Consumer Price Index, Cost of Living Index, Retail Price Index**

product *noun* (manufacturing)
something that is made to be sold: *We have to find the right product for the market.* ○ *The finished product is destined for export.*

/ˈprɒdʌkt/
pl products
⧓ an agricultural, a chemical, a consumer, a dairy, a household **product**; design, develop, make, manufacture, sell a **product**
▶ **by-product, commodity, end-product, goods, waste product**

product group *noun* (commerce)
a collection of similar items produced by the same organization: *The annual sales plan sets targets for each product group.*

/ˈprɒdʌkt gru:p/
pl product groups
⧓ define, extend, manage a **product group**

production *noun* (manufacturing)
1 the activity of making or growing something: *We must keep the cost of production as low as possible.* ○ *the production of cars, oil, timber, etc* **2** the amount of something that is made or grown: *These new machines will help us to increase production.*

in production being made: *The new car is now in production.*

put something into production to start making something: *When will the new design be put into production?*

/prəˈdʌkʃn/
note not used with *a* or *an*. No plural and used with a singular verb only.
⧓ **production** costs, methods, processes, techniques, workers; increase, reduce **production**
▶ **jobbing production, manufacture[1], mass production, overproduction, primary production, secondary production**

production line *noun* (manufacturing)
a series of stages or processes that an item passes through in a factory to make it into a finished product: *The car has just come off the production line.*

/prəˈdʌkʃn laɪn/
pl production lines
⧓ work on a **production line**
▶ **assembly line**

production manager *noun* (management)
▶ **manager**

/prəˈdʌkʃn ˈmænɪdʒə(r)/

productive *adjective*
that can make or grow something well or in large quantities: *The company wants to sell off its less productive factories.* ○ *productive agricultural land*

/prəˈdʌktɪv/
⧓ a **productive** area, factory; **productive** land
▶ **counter-productive**

productivity *noun* (industry)
the rate or amount produced by a worker, a machine, a factory, etc: *Workers can be paid a productivity bonus.* ○ *Productivity has increased this year.*

/ˌprɒdʌkˈtɪvəti/
note not used with *a* or *an*. No plural and used with a singular verb only.
⧓ high, low **productivity**; increase, raise, reduce **productivity**

productivity agreement *noun* (industrial relations)
an agreement between trade union members and an employer giving workers a specified increase in wages if they increase the number of goods produced: *Both sides have reached a satisfactory productivity agreement.*

/ˌprɒdʌkˈtɪvəti əˌgriːmənt/
pl productivity agreements
⋈ reach, sign a **productivity agreement**

product liability *noun* (law)
a legal requirement that an organization must pay DAMAGES to anyone who is harmed or inconvenienced because their products are faulty: *The pharmaceutical company was sued for product liability.*

/ˌprɒdʌkt laɪəˈbɪləti/
note not used with *a* or *an*. No plural and used with a singular verb only.
⋈ a **product liability** award, claim, lawsuit
► **liability 1**

product-liability insurance *noun* (insurance/law)
an insurance policy taken out by a manufacturer to pay compensation to customers who have suffered because its products were faulty: *The compensation was paid out of the product-liability insurance.*

/ˌprɒdʌkt laɪəˈbɪləti ɪn ˌʃʊərəns/
note not used with *a* or *an*. No plural and used with a singular verb only.
⋈ take out **product-liability insurance**
► **insurance, liability insurance**

product life cycle *noun* (commerce)
the idea that the sale of a product goes through four phases: introduction, growth, maturity and decline: *Fashion goods have a short product life cycle.*

/ˌprɒdʌkt ˈlaɪf ˌsaɪkl/
pl product life cycles
⋈ a long, short **product life cycle**
► **shelf life**

product manager *noun* (management)
► **manager**

/ˌprɒdʌkt ˈmænɪdʒə(r)/

product-oriented *adjective* (marketing)
of a company that produces what it considers to be a good product and then tries to find a market for it: *A product-oriented company does not spend much time on market research.*

/ˈprɒdʌkt ˌɔːriəntɪd/
syn product-led
► **market-oriented**

profession *noun* (personnel)
a job that requires a lot of training and that is respected by other people: *train for the legal profession.*

/prəˈfeʃn/
pl professions
⋈ the accountancy, legal, medical, teaching **profession**
► **business 1 a, job, occupation, trade[1] 5**

profit[1] *noun* (finance)
1 the money gained in a business deal, esp the difference between the amount earned and the amount spent: *We make a profit of 50p on each book we sell.* ○ *The company's pre-tax profits rose from $10.2 million to $17.4 million in the first half year.* ○ *He sold the business at at profit.* **2** financial gain: *Should public transport be run for profit?*

/ˈprɒfɪt/
1 pl profits
⋈ make a **profit**; a drop, a fall, an increase, a rise in **profits**
► **account of profits, accumulated profits, attributable profit, loss 1, net profit, operating profit, paper profit, payback, realized profit, retained profit, total profit, trading**

profit, unappropriated profit

2 note not used with *a* or *an*. No plural and used with a singular verb only.

⋈ do something *for* **profit**

► **gain[1], loss 2**

---

rofit² *verb* (finance)
o make a financial gain: *Building societies profit from the interest hey charge on loans.* ○ *We hope to profit from the sale.*

/ˈprɒfɪt/

profit, profiting, profited

note intransitive verb

⋈ **profit** *from* something

► **gain²**

---

rofitable *adjective* (finance)
hat makes a profit: *make a profitable investment* ○ *This deal should be ighly profitable.*

/ˈprɒfɪtəbl/

⋈ a **profitable** business, company, deal, investment

opp unprofitable

► **cost-effective**

---

rofitability *noun* (finance)
he state of making a profit: *The company could only sustain rofitability by cutting back on research.*

/ˌprɒfɪtəˈbɪləti/

note not used with *a* or *an*. No plural and used with a singular verb only.

⋈ high, low **profitability**

---

rofit and loss account *noun* (accounting)
list of total profits and losses made by a company in its trading ctivities for each year. It usually shows the amount of TURNOVER, he TRADING PROFIT, the total amount of earnings and the total rofit made after tax and interest have been deducted. A tatement of the profit and loss account appears in the company's nnual report: *The profit and loss account shows a trading profit of £186.6 million.*

/ˌprɒfɪt ənd ˈlɒs əˌkaʊnt/

pl profit and loss accounts

syn gain and loss account

► **account[1] 1, accounts 1, appropriation account**

---

rofit centre *noun* (management)
unit within an organization for which a separate account is kept nd which is expected to make a profit: *Targets for performance for ach profit centre in an organization can be established.*

/ˈprɒfɪt ˌsentə(r)/

pl profit centres

⋈ establish, monitor, set up a **profit centre**

---

rofit margin *noun* (commerce)
he difference between the cost of buying or producing something nd the price for which it is sold: *The group had a net profit margin of 30% last year.* ○ *Each product sold will earn a profit margin of 20%.*

/ˈprɒfɪt ˌmɑːdʒɪn/

pl profit margins

⋈ increase, reduce the **profit margin**

► **margin 1**

---

rofit motive *noun* (economics)
he idea that the aim of all business is to create as much wealth as ossible: *It is believed that the profit motive is behind most business entures.*

/ˈprɒfɪt ˌməʊtɪv/

pl profit motives

⋈ be guided by the **profit motive**

---

rofit-sharing *noun* (personnel)
he distribution of the profits of a company among its employees, ither as cash or in shares: *All employees benefit from profit-sharing.*

/ˈprɒfɪt ˌʃeərɪŋ/

note not used with *a* or *an*. No plural and used with a singular verb only.

⋈ a **profit-sharing** scheme

proforma invoice *noun* (commerce)
an invoice that is sent in advance of goods supplied: *send a proforma invoice to a new customer*

/prəʊˌfɔːmə ˈɪnvɔɪs/
pl proforma invoices
⋈ enclose, send a **proforma invoice**
▶ **invoice**[1]

---

program[1] *noun* (computing)
▶ **computer program**

/ˈprəʊgræm/

---

program[2] *verb* (computing)
to write a list of instructions that enables a computer to perform a specific task or function: *The computer has been programmed to do the accounts.* ○ *programmed in high level language*

/ˈprəʊgræm/
program, programming, programmed
note transitive verb
⋈ highly **programmed**
▶ **computer program**

---

programmer *noun* (computing)
▶ **computer programmer**

/ˈprəʊgræmə(r)/

---

programming language *noun* (computing)
a system of coded instructions used to write COMPUTER PROGRAMS that enable a computer to perform specific tasks and functions: *COBOL is a programming language that is relatively easy to learn.*

/ˈprəʊgræmɪŋ ˌlæŋgwɪdʒ/
pl programming languages
abbr PL
▶ **machine language**

---

progress payment *noun* (commerce)
a part of the total payment for work carried out made when a particular stage of the work is completed: *A progress payment will be paid on completion of the foundations of the building.*

/ˈprəʊgres ˌpeɪmənt/
pl progress payments
⋈ give, make, receive a **progress payment**
▶ **payment 2**

---

project *noun*
a business activity; a plan for this: *We are discussing several projects for development.* ○ *The company is working on an engineering project.*

/ˈprɒdʒekt/
pl projects
⋈ a **project** manager, plan; develop, launch, research, work on a **project**

---

promissory note *noun* (finance)
a document in which a person or an organization, such as a bank, promises (on behalf of the buyer) to pay a fixed sum of money on demand or by a certain date, to the person specified (the seller): *The banknote is a form of promissory note.*

/ˈprɒmɪsəri ˌnəʊt/
pl promissory notes
abbr P/N
⋈ pay by, sign, write a **promissory note**
▶ **bill of exchange, negotiable instrument**

---

promote *verb*
1 (*advertising*) to advertise something in order to increase its sales: *The product is being promoted on television and in newspapers.*
2 (*personnel*) to give someone a higher position or more important job: *She worked hard and was soon promoted.* ○ *He was promoted from assistant sales manager to sales manager.*

/prəˈməʊt/
promote, promoting, promoted
note transitive verb
1 ⋈ **promote** (something) actively, heavily, widely
▶ **advertise 1, campaign**[2]**, market**[2]**, plug**[2]**, publicize, sell**
2 ⋈ **promote** someone *to* something
▶ **upgrade**

promoter *noun* (commerce)
a person who organizes or finances something, esp a business or a sporting or leisure activity: *a promoter in the entertainments industry* ○ *The promoter will organize all the advertising for us.*

/prəˈməʊtə(r)/
pl promoters
⋈ a business, an entertainments, a sports **promoter**

---

promotion *noun*
1 (*advertising*) (**a**) advertising or other activity intended to increase the sales of a product: *Television advertising is an expensive but effective method of promotion.* (**b**) an advertising or publicity campaign for a particular product: *We are doing a special promotion of our new range of baby foods.* ○ *We are giving away free pens and T-shirts as part of the promotion.* **2** (*personnel*) (**a**) (the giving or receiving of) a higher position or a more important job: *The job offers a good salary and excellent chances of promotion.* (**b**) an instance of this: *The new job is a promotion for her.*

/prəˈməʊʃn/
1a note not used with *a* or *an*. No plural and used with a singular verb only.
⋈ sales **promotion**
► **campaign[1], sales campaign**
1b pl promotions
⋈ a special **promotion**; do, run a **promotion**
2a note not used with *a* or *an*. No plural and used with a singular verb only.
⋈ be due for, be in line for **promotion**
2b pl promotions
⋈ to get a **promotion**

---

promotional *adjective* (advertising)
of or relating to PROMOTION: *The managing director has cut the promotional budget.* ○ *send promotional leaflets to major customers*

/prəˈməʊʃənl/
⋈ **promotional** literature, material; a **promotional** campaign, tour

---

prompt cash *noun* (commerce)
a condition of payment for goods or services in which payment must be made within a few days (usually not more than 14) of delivery of the goods or the completion of the service: *They sent a demand for prompt cash to the client.*

/ˌprɒmpt ˈkæʃ/
note not used with *a* or *an*. No plural and used with a singular verb only.

---

prompt day *noun* (commerce)
the day on which goods bought at a commodity exchange are due for payment: *The goods will not be delivered before the prompt day.*

/ˈprɒmpt deɪ/
pl prompt days
syn prompt date
► **Account Day, last trading day, settlement day**

---

prompt note *noun* (commerce)
a note sent to a customer as a reminder of payment due: *A prompt note is sent if payment is not received within 14 days of delivery of the goods.*

/ˌprɒmpt ˈnəʊt/
pl prompt notes
⋈ receive, send a **prompt note**

---

proof *noun*
1 (*law*) evidence that shows that something is true or correct: *Do you have any proof that the goods were stolen?* ○ *a document that shows proof of ownership* **2** a copy of printed material produced so that mistakes can be corrected: *He is checking the proofs of our new catalogue.*

/pruːf/
1 note not used with *a* or *an*. No plural and used with a singular verb only.
⋈ legal, official **proof**
► **authentication**
2 pl proofs
⋈ check, correct, read a **proof**; a **proof**-reader; **proof**-reading
► **copy[1] 2**

prop. *abbr*
proprietor: *Prop. Mr P Hart*

/prɒp/

---

property *noun* (law)
1 thing or things owned, whether material or abstract: *Please take care of personal property.* ○ *The box was marked 'private property'.*
2 land and buildings: *invest in property* ○ *The site was bought by a property developer.* **3** a house, factory, etc and the land around it: *buy a property in the south of France*

/ˈprɒpəti/
1 note not used with *a* or *an*. No plural and used with a singular verb only.
⋈ private, public **property**
▶ **intellectual property, personal property**
2 note not used with *a* or *an*. No plural and used with a singular verb only.
⋈ **property** development, speculation
▶ **land[1] 2, premises, real estate**
3 pl properties
⋈ buy, own, rent, sell a **property**

---

proposal *noun*
1 a plan that is suggested; a scheme: *The proposal was rejected by the committee.* ○ *put forward a proposal at the shareholders' meeting*
2 (*insurance*) a printed form that is completed by a person who wants to take out an insurance policy: *The insurer should be able to get all necessary information from the proposal.*

/prəˈpəʊzl/
pl proposals
⋈ accept, put forward, reject a **proposal**
▶ **motion, plan[1] 1**
2 ⋈ complete, fill in a **proposal**
syn proposal form

---

propose *verb*
to suggest something as a possible plan or action: *I proposed a motion at the meeting.*

/prəˈpəʊz/
propose, proposing, proposed
note transitive verb
⋈ **propose** an idea, a motion, a plan, a scheme
opp oppose
▶ **motion, second[1]**

---

proposer *noun*
1 (*insurance*) a person who applies to take out an insurance policy: *The insurance company interviewed the proposer before accepting the policy.* **2** a person who makes a suggestion at a formal meeting: *Do we have a proposer for this motion?*

/prəˈpəʊzə(r)/
pl proposers
2 opp opposer
▶ **motion**

---

proposition *noun* (commerce)
a business arrangement or offer to do or buy something: *He made me a proposition to buy my share of the company.* ○ *To merge the two firms would not be a viable proposition.*

/ˌprɒpəˈzɪʃn/
pl propositions
⋈ an attractive, a business, a financial, a viable, a workable **proposition**

---

proprietary *adjective* (manufacturing)
of a product which is made and owned by a particular company: *You are advised to use only proprietary medicines.*

proprietary name a name of a product or series of products that can only be used by one particular company: *Kodak is a proprietary name for cameras and films.*

/prəˈpraɪətri/
⋈ **proprietary** brands
▶ **brand name, household name, patent, trade name**

---

proprietor *noun*
an owner, esp of a business or hotel: *All complaints should be made to the proprietor.*

/prəˈpraɪətə(r)/
pl proprietors
abbr prop.
⋈ a garage, newspaper, restaurant **proprietor**[1]

prosecute *verb* (law)
to accuse someone of a crime and try to prove it in a court of law: *She was prosecuted for fraud.* ○ *Which of the barristers is prosecuting?*

/ˈprɒsɪkjuːt/
prosecute, prosecuting, prosecuted
note transitive and intransitive verb
⋈ **prosecute** someone *for* something

prosecution *noun* (law)
1 (**a**) accusing someone of a crime and trying to prove it in a court of law: *Failure to pay your parking fine will result in prosecution.* (**b**) an instance of this: *bring a prosecution against someone for theft* **2** a person or group of people who try to prove in a court of law that someone is guilty of a crime: *call a witness for the prosecution*

/ˌprɒsɪˈkjuːʃn/
1a note not used with *a* or *an*. No plural and used with a singular verb only.
1b pl prosecutions
2 note usually singular

prospective *adjective*
possible: *We are interviewing prospective employees this week.* ○ *I have found a prospective buyer for the factory.*

/prəˈspektɪv/
⋈ a **prospective** buyer, client, customer, purchaser
▶ **potential**[1]

prospects *noun*
chances of success: *The country's economic prospects are looking gloomy.* ○ *The job offers a good salary and excellent prospects.*

/ˈprɒspekts/
note plural noun, used with a plural verb
⋈ business, career, economic, job, trading **prospects**

prospectus *noun*
1 (*stock exchange*) a document, leaflet, etc that gives information about a new share issue: *Send for a copy of the share prospectus.* **2** (*advertising*) a small book that gives information about a new company or a commercial venture: *The company has outlined its plans for expansion in its prospectus.*

/prəˈspektəs/
pl prospectuses
⋈ issue, produce, publish a **prospectus**
▶ **offer by prospectus**

protectionism *noun* (international trade)
a system of import controls set up by a government to protect the country's agriculture and industry from foreign competition: *The country has a high level of industrial protectionism.*

/prəˈtekʃənɪzəm/
note not used with *a* or *an*. No plural and used with a singular verb only.
⋈ agricultural, industrial **protectionism**
▶ **anti-dumping, free trade, import restrictions, tariff 1, trade restriction**

prototype *noun* (industry)
the first or original model of something that will be copied or developed: *The prototype has undergone extensive tests.* ○ *Only one prototype was made before the project was abandoned.*

/ˈprəʊtətaɪp/
pl prototypes
⋈ a **prototype** car, machine, model, plane; make a **prototype**

provisional liquidator *noun* (law/accounting)
▶ **liquidator**

/prəˌvɪʒənl ˈlɪkwɪdeɪtə(r)/

proviso *noun* (law)
a condition that is insisted on in a contract before it is accepted: *We agreed to the contract with the proviso that it would be reassessed in two months.*

/prəˈvaɪzəʊ/
pl provisos
⋈ *with* a/the **proviso**
▶ **condition 3**

proxy *noun*
1 the right given to someone to act for someone else: *to vote by proxy* **2** a person who is given the right to act for someone else: *He acted as the managing director's proxy.*

/ˈprɒksi/
1 note not used with *a* or *an*. No plural and used with a singular verb only.
⋈ a **proxy** vote
2 pl proxies
⋈ act as (someone's), appoint a **proxy**

prudence concept *noun* (accounting)
an accounting principle in which expected losses are recorded at the highest possible rather than the lowest possible amount: *Follow the prudence concept when allowing for loss.*

/ˈpru:dns ˌkɒnsept/
note no plural
syn concept of prudence

PS *abbr*
postscript: *There is a PS at the end of the letter.*

/ˌpi: ˈes/

public company *noun* (stock exchange)
▶ **public limited company**

/ˌpʌblɪk ˈkʌmpəni/

public corporation *noun* (industry)
an organization owned by the state and set up to provide a national service or run a nationalized industry: *The British Coal Corporation and the British Broadcasting Corporation are public corporations.*

/ˌpʌblɪk ˌkɔ:pəˈreɪʃn/
pl public corporations
⋈ set up a **public corporation**
▶ **statutory company**

public debts *noun* (public finance)
the money owed by the PUBLIC SECTOR of the economy: *The government has reduced spending in an attempt to reduce public debts.*

/ˌpʌblɪk ˈdets/
note plural noun, used with a plural verb
▶ **debt, national debt**

public deposits *noun* (banking)
the accounts of government departments held in the national bank: *Public deposits are held in the Bank of England.*

/ˌpʌblɪk dɪˈpɒzɪts/
note plural noun, used with a plural verb
▶ **deposit[1] 1**

public examination *noun* (law)
(*UK*) a session in a lawcourt in which a person who is declared bankrupt must meet and explain the situation to creditors and the OFFICIAL RECEIVER: *At the public examination the London Bankruptcy court declared that the debtor would not receive a bankruptcy discharge until he had paid his debts in full.*

/ˌpʌblɪk ɪgˌzæmɪˈneɪʃn/
pl public examinations
⋈ attend, hold a **public examination**
▶ **bankrupt[1]**

public finance *noun* (public finance)
1 raising money for goods and services provided by the government and local authorities: *work in public finance* **2** the money raised or spent in this way: *Most public finance is raised through taxation or borrowing.*

/ˌpʌblɪk ˈfaɪnæns/
1 note not used with *a* or *an*. No plural and used with a singular verb only.
▶ **public spending**
2 pl public finances
▶ **finance[1]**

public finance accountant *noun* (accounting)
a member of the Chartered Institute of Public Finance and Accountancy, who prepares the financial accounts for government agencies, local authorities and nationalized industries: *The local council employed a team of public finance accountants to prepare the accounts.*

/ˌpʌblɪk ˈfaɪnæns əˌkaʊntənt/
pl public finance accountants
⋈ work as a **public finance accountant**
► **accountant**

public holiday *noun* (personnel)
a day, not a Saturday or Sunday, which is a general holiday: *Christmas Day is always a public holiday in the UK.*

/ˌpʌblɪk ˈhɒlədeɪ/
pl public holidays
► **bank holiday, holiday**

public issue *noun* (stock exchange)
a new issue of shares offered to the public through advertisements in newspapers: *a public issue of equity*

/ˌpʌblɪk ˈɪʃuː/
pl public issues
⋈ go on **public issue**
► **issue**[1]**, offer for sale**

publicity *noun* (advertising)
1 (**a**) giving information about something in order to attract people's attention: *The product has sold well considering it was not given much advance publicity.* ○ *launch a publicity campaign* (**b**) a department in an organization that deals with this: *He works in publicity.* **2** notice or attention from the newspapers, television, etc: *The firm tried to avoid adverse publicity about its faulty products.*

/pʌbˈlɪsəti/
note not used with *a* or *an*. No plural and used with a singular verb only.
1 ⋈ a **publicity** agency, budget, campaign, department, manager
► **advertising**
2 ⋈ adverse, bad, favourable, good **publicity**; attract, avoid, seek **publicity**

publicize *verb* (advertising)
to attract the public's attention to something or to give people information about something: *We don't want to publicize the new design until it is finished.* ○ *The company merger has been widely publicized in the national press.*

/ˈpʌblɪsaɪz/
publicize, publicizing, publicized
(also **publicise**)
note transitive verb
⋈ **publicize** (something) well, widely
► **advertise 1, promote 1**

public limited company *noun* (commerce)
a company registered under the Companies Act, that must have an AUTHORIZED SHARE CAPITAL of at least £50 000 and whose shares can be bought on the Stock Exchange: *Public limited companies must use the initials 'plc' in their name.*

/ˌpʌblɪk ˌlɪmɪtɪd ˈkʌmpəni/
abbr PLC, plc
pl public limited companies
⋈ become, be registered as a **public limited company**
► **limited company, private limited company, registered company**

public monopoly *noun* (economics)
► **monopoly**

/pʌblɪk məˈnɒpəli/

public relations *noun* (advertising)
1 the work of presenting a good image of an organization to the public, esp by providing information: *She works in public relations.* **2** the relationship between an organization and the public: *It is important for a company to maintain good public relations.*

/ˌpʌblɪk rɪˈleɪʃnz/
note plural noun, used with a plural verb
abbr PR
⋈ a **public relations** agency, campaign, manager, officer
► **press release**

public sector *noun* (economics)
that part of a country's economy that is owned by the government or public corporations: *The wage settlement applies only to the public sector.* ○ *improve the standards of health care in the public sector*

/ˌpʌblɪk ˈsektə(r)/
note singular noun, used with a singular verb
⋈ work for, work in the **public sector**
► **corporate sector, nationalize, private sector, privatize, sector**

---

public spending *noun* (public finance)
spending by governments and local authorities on public services: *Higher than expected inflation has led to public spending cuts of over £400 million in key areas like railways, schools, hospitals and the environment.*

/ˌpʌblɪk ˈspendɪŋ/
note not used with *a* or *an*. No plural and used with a singular verb only.
⋈ control, cut, increase **public spending**
► **public finance**

---

public warehouse *noun* (import)
a building at or near a port in which goods are stored after being unloaded from or before being loaded onto a ship: *Goods cannot be removed from a public warehouse without a warehouse warrant.*

/ˌpʌblɪk ˈweəhaʊs/
pl public warehouses
► **bonded warehouse, warehouse**

---

public works *noun*
building work, eg of roads, railways, schools, hospitals, etc financed by the government: *The government has increased its spending on industrial development and large-scale public works.* ○ *Public works are often used as a way of reducing unemployment.*

/ˌpʌblɪk ˈwɜːks/
note plural noun, used with a plural verb
⋈ a **public works** programme

---

publish *verb*
1 to prepare and print a book, magazine, etc and make it available to the public: *The dictionary was published by Oxford University Press.* **2** to make something known to the public: *The firm's annual accounts are published at the end of each financial year.*

/ˈpʌblɪʃ/
publish, publishing, published
note transitive verb
⋈ **publish** a book, magazine, newspaper

---

publisher *noun*
a person or an organization that publishes books, magazines, etc: *I sent the article to a publisher of scientic journals.* ○ *His latest novel was rejected by the publisher.*

/ˈpʌblɪʃə(r)/
pl publishers
⋈ a book, magazine, newspaper, periodical **publisher**; accepted, rejected by a **publisher**
► **printer**

---

publishing *noun*
the business of preparing books, magazines, etc to be printed and sold: *I work in publishing.* ○ *the publishing industry*

/ˈpʌblɪʃɪŋ/
note not used with *a* or *an*. No plural and used with a singular verb only.
⋈ book, magazine, newspaper **publishing**; a **publishing** company

---

punter *noun* (sales)
(*informal*) a customer, esp one who is easily persuaded to buy goods and services: *The average punter is more interested in the price than the quality.*

/ˈpʌntə(r)/
pl punters
note the word is often used derogatively
⋈ an average, a general, an ordinary **punter**
► **customer**

purchase[1] *noun*
1 the action of buying something: *What was the date of purchase?* ○ *This receipt is your proof of purchase.* **2** the thing bought: *Choose carefully before making a purchase.*

/ˈpɜːtʃəs/
1 note not used with *a* or *an*. No plural and used with a singular verb only.
⋈ **purchase** price
2 pl purchases
⋈ make a **purchase**; an important, a large, a major **purchase**
▶ **buy**[1], **hire purchase**

purchase[2] *verb*
(*formal*) to buy something: *Faulty goods should be taken back to the shop where they were purchased.* ○ *The factory site was formerly agricultural land purchased from a farmer.*

/ˈpɜːtʃəs/
purchase, purchasing, purchased
note transitive verb
⋈ **purchase** something *at*, *in* (a place), *from* (a person or an organization), *on* (a date)
▶ **buy**[2]

purchase day book *noun* (accounting)
▶ **day book**

/ˌpɜːtʃəs ˈdeɪ bʊk/

purchase ledger *noun* (accounting)
▶ **bought ledger**

/ˈpɜːtʃəs ˌledʒə(r)/

purchaser *noun*
a buyer: *He wanted to sell the house quickly, but was unable to find a purchaser.* ○ *Details of the properties will be sent to prospective purchasers on request.*

/ˈpɜːtʃəsə(r)/
pl purchasers
⋈ a potential, prospective, would-be **purchaser**

purchasing officer *noun* (industry)
▶ **materials buyer**

/ˈpɜːtʃəsɪŋ ˌɒfɪsə(r)/

purchasing power *noun* (economics)
1 the amount of money that a person, an organization or a country has to buy goods and services: *Increased incomes have led to increased purchasing power in the community.* **2** the value of a currency at a particular time: *an increase in the purchasing power of the yen*

/ˈpɜːtʃəsɪŋ ˌpaʊə(r)/
note not used with *a* or *an*. No plural and used with a singular verb only.
1, 2 ⋈ an increase, a reduction in **purchasing power**
2 ⋈ the **purchasing power** of (a currency)
▶ **parity**

pure monopoly *noun* (economics)
▶ **absolute monopoly**

/ˌpjʊə məˈnɒpəli/

put option *noun* (stock exchange)
the right to sell a fixed quantity of a commodity, currency or security at a certain price and on a certain date: *make a put option agreement*

/ˌpʊt ˈɒpʃn/
pl put options
⋈ a **put option** agreement, contract, deal, market
▶ **call option, option, time option, traded option**

pyramid selling *noun* (sales)
a method of selling using a hierarchy of workers. A central distributor sells a FRANCHISE to regional sellers who recruit district distributors who recruit door-to-door salespeople who sell the stock. This system is illegal in the UK: *Pyramid selling tends to benefit the central distributor rather than someone further down the system who might be left with unsellable stock.*

/ˌpɪrəmɪd ˈselɪŋ/
note not used with *a* or *an*. No plural and used with a singular verb only.
▶ **selling**

Qq

QC *abbr* (industry)
quality control

/ˌkjuː ˈsiː/
(also **Q.C.**)

QL *abbr* (computing)
query language: *The program was written in QL.*

/ˌkjuː ˈel/

qlty *abbr*
quality

note used in written English only

qr *abbr*
quarter: *charges for the 1st qr*

note used in written English only

qtr *abbr*
quarter: *sales figures for the first qtr*

note used in written English only

qty *abbr*
quantity

note used in written English only

quadruplicate *noun*
a fourth copy; with four copies

in quadruplicate with four copies: *The invoice will be printed in quadruplicate.*

/kwɒˈdruːplɪkət/
abbr quad
note no plural
▶ **duplicate, triplicate**

qualification *noun*
1 an examination, training or experience that prepares someone for a job or further study; a certificate that shows this: *What professional qualifications do you have?* ○ *Do you have the right qualifications for the job?* ○ *obtain a qualification in computer studies*
2 doing or completing such training: *Qualification takes three years.*

/ˌkwɒlɪfɪˈkeɪʃn/
1 pl qualifications
⋈ get, obtain a **qualification**; an academic, a vocational **qualification**
2 note not used with *a* or *an*. No plural and used with a singular verb only.

qualified acceptance *noun*
(banking/international trade)
an agreement to pay a bill of exchange that depends on certain conditions, eg date, place, etc: *The holder refused to take qualified acceptance.*

/ˌkwɒlɪfaɪd əkˈseptəns/
note not used with *a* or *an*. No plural and used with a singular verb only.
▶ **acceptance 2**

qualified report *noun* (accounting)
a report from an auditor who cannot produce a TRUE AND FAIR VIEW of a company's accounts, eg because information is missing: *It is serious matter if a public limited company receives a qualified report.*

/ˌkwɒlɪfaɪd rɪˈpɔːt/
pl qualified reports
⋈ produce, receive a **qualified report**
▶ **audit, report**[1]

qualify *verb*
to complete training or pass an examination in a specific subject or for a certain job: *qualify as a lawyer* ○ *After qualifying she worked in London.* ○ *a highly-qualified engineer*

/ˈkwɒlɪfaɪ/
qualify, qualifying, qualified
note intransitive verb

---

qualitative market research *noun* (marketing)
the examination of people's attitudes and opinions and how these influence what, where and how much they buy: *carry out qualitative market research by holding group discussions*

/ˌkwɒlɪtətɪv ˌmɑːkɪt rɪˈsɜːtʃ, ˌkwɒlɪtətɪv ˌmɑːkɪt ˈriːsɜːtʃ/
note not used with *a* or *an*. No plural and used with a singular verb only.
► **quantitative market research, market research**

---

quality *noun*
the condition or state of something: *All our goods are of the best quality.* ○ *high quality leather goods* ○ *quality materials*, ie good quality materials

/ˈkwɒləti/
note not used with *a* or *an*. No plural and used with a singular verb only.
abbr qlty
⋈ good, high, poor, top **quality**
► **fair average quality, merchantable quality**

---

quality control *noun* (industry)
checking goods at all stages of the production process to ensure that they are of a good standard: *pass the goods through quality control* ○ *Quality control is an important part of the manufacturing process.*

/ˈkwɒləti kənˌtrəʊl/
note not used with *a* or *an*. No plural and used with a singular verb only.
abbr QC, Q.C.
⋈ a **quality control** system
► **control[1] 1**

---

quantitative market research *noun* (marketing)
a study of the demand for certain products by finding out the number of people who buy or do certain things: *carry out quantitative market research to find out if there is a market for a new leisure centre*

/ˌkwɒntɪtətɪv ˌmɑːkɪt rɪˈsɜːtʃ, ˌkwɒntɪtətɪv ˌmɑːkɪt ˈriːsɜːtʃ/
note not used with *a* or *an*. No plural and used with a singular verb only.
► **qualitative market research, market research**

---

quantity *noun*
an amount or number of items: *It is cheaper to buy goods in large quantities.* ○ *What quantity* (ie how many) *do you require?* ○ *increase the quantity of production*

/ˈkwɒntəti/
pl quantities
abbr qty
⋈ a large, small **quantity**

---

quantity surveyor *noun* (industry)
a person who calculates the cost of materials and labour for a building project: *a report prepared by a quantity surveyor*

/ˈkwɒntəti səˈveɪə(r)/
pl quantity surveyors
⋈ commission, consult a **quantity surveyor**
► **bill of quantities**

---

quantity variance *noun* (accounting)
the difference between an amount sold and the standard amount that should be sold for that price: *We have overspent our budget because of quantity variances in the materials we ordered.*

/ˌkwɒntəti ˈveəriəns/
pl quantity variances
⋈ detect, notice, record a **quantity variance**
► **price variance**

quarantine *noun* (health and safety/shipping)
the isolation of people, animals or things to prevent the spread of disease: *The animal was placed in quarantine in case of rabies.* ○ *a quarantine period of six weeks*

/ˈkwɒrəntiːn/
note usually singular
⧓ place in **quarantine**; **quarantine** regulations, restrictions

quarter *noun*
a period of three months: *Sales have improved this quarter.* ○ *The statement shows all charges for this quarter.*

/ˈkwɔːtə(r)/
pl quarters
abbr qr, qtr
⧓ the first, second, third, fourth **quarter**

quarterly *adjective, adverb*
produced or occurring four times a year: *The financial director presented the quarterly accounts.* ○ *You can arrange to pay monthly or quarterly.* ○ *a quarterly magazine*

/ˈkwɔːtəli/
⧓ a **quarterly** charge, payment, rent

quasi-contract *noun* (law)
an agreement that is legally binding although no formal contract has been made: *establish a verbal agreement as a quasi-contract*

/ˌkweɪzaɪ ˈkɒntrækt/
pl quasi-contracts
▶ **contract[1]**

quasi-money *noun* (banking/finance)
▶ **near money**

/ˌkweɪzaɪ ˈmʌni/

quay *noun* (shipping)
a place in a port where ships can tie up and goods are loaded and unloaded: *The cargo was unloaded at the quay.* ○ *The ship is waiting alongside the quay.*

/kiː/
pl quays
▶ **berth, dock[1], wharf**

query language *noun* (computing)
a computer programming code used to obtain information from a central database: *an instruction written in query language*

/ˈkwɪəri ˌlæŋgwɪdʒ/
note usually singular
abbr QL
▶ **high-level language, low-level language, programming language**

questionnaire *noun* (marketing)
a printed list of questions sent or given to people, esp to find out about their opinions, choices and behaviour: *fill in a questionnaire* ○ *analyse the results of a questionnaire* ○ *We sent out over 1 000 questionnaires but only 300 people replied.*

/ˌkwestʃəˈneə(r)/
pl questionnaires
⧓ reply to, respond to a **questionnaire**
▶ **survey[1] 2**

quot. *abbr* (commerce)
quotation

note used in written English only

quota *noun*
1 a fixed amount that must be produced, done or received: *increase the production quota by using new machines* ○ *The company failed to reach its sales quota.* ○ *supply a full quota of oil* **2** a maximum amount or number of things allowed: *Farmers are protesting because the milk quota has been cut.*

/ˈkwəʊtə/
pl quotas
⧓ increase, raise, reduce a **quota**
▶ **export quota, import quota, sales quota, target[1] 1**

quotation *noun*
1 (*commerce*) a price given for work to be done or a service to be provided: *get a number of quotations from different builders* ○ *a written quotation from a bank of credit services* **2** (*stock exchange*)

/kwəʊˈteɪʃn/
pl quotations
abbr quot.

(**a**) (of a company) the right to have shares that can be bought and sold listed on a recognized stock exchange: *The new company obtained a quotation on the stock market.* (**b**) a quoted price

1 ▶ **estimate[1], quote[1] 1**

2 ⧓ be accepted for, gain, lose, obtain, qualify for a **quotation**

▶ **application for quotation, listed company, Stock Exchange Daily Official List**

---

quote[1] *verb*

1 (*commerce*) to calculate a price for something: *Please quote a price for updating this computer system.* ○ *All prices are quoted in dollars.* ○ *This is the best price I can quote you.* **2** (*stock exchange*) (**a**) to record the name of a company on a stock exchange so that its shares can be bought and sold: *After five years of trading, the company is now quoted on the stock exchange.* (**b**) to give a price for a security on the official list of a stock exchange: *ordinary shares quoted on the stock exchange at 55p a share*

/kwəʊt/

quote, quoting, quoted

note transitive verb

1 ▶ **quotation 1, estimate[2]**

2 ▶ **quotation 2**

---

quote[2] *noun* (commerce)

a price given for work to be done or a service to be provided: *Please give me a quote for repairing the car.* ○ *obtain a number of quotes before going ahead with the work*

/kwəʊt/

pl quotes

▶ **quotation 1, estimate[1]**

---

quoted company *noun* (stock exchange)

▶ **listed company**

/ˌkwəʊtɪd ˈkʌmpəni/

---

quoted price *noun* (stock exchange)

the official price of a security as listed on the stock exchange: *The shares are trading below the quoted price.*

/ˌkwəʊtɪd ˈpraɪs/

pl quoted prices

▶ **listed securities, price[1]**

---

quoted share *noun* (stock exchange)

a share that can be bought and sold on a stock exchange: *a quoted share on the Japanese stock exchange*

/ˌkwəʊtɪd ˈʃeə(r)/

pl quoted shares

▶ **listed securities, quotation 2, share, unquoted share**

---

qwerty *adjective* (computing/office practice)

(*UK*) of a computer or typewriter keyboard where Q-W-E-R-T-Y are the first six letters at the top left: *Does your computer have a qwerty keyboard?*

/ˈkwɜːti/

▶ **keyboard**

Rr

---

racket *noun* (commerce)

(*informal*) a dishonest way of making money: *They were involved in a smuggling racket.* ○ *Police are investigating a gambling racket.*

/ˈrækɪt/

pl rackets

⧓ be in on, be involved in a **racket**

▶ **scam**

---

radiopaging *noun*

a means of contacting people at a distance. The person carries an electronic device (a bleeper) that makes a high-pitched sound when someone calls them. He/she then contacts the caller by telephone: *I hope she is wearing her radiopaging unit.* ○ *We will pass on the message as soon as he responds to the radiopaging call.*

/ˈreɪdiəʊpeɪdʒɪŋ/

note not used with *a* or *an*. No plural and used with a singular verb only.

⧓ a **radiopaging** call, message, unit

---

raider *noun* (stock exchange)
(*informal*) a person or company that buys a large number of shares in another company before making a takeover bid or obtaining control: *The corporate raider acquired 20.2% of the Japanese firm, Koito.*

/ˈreɪdə(r)/
pl raiders
► **dawn raid**

rail *noun* (transport)
the railway; a system of transport using trains to carry passengers or goods: *It is cheaper to send the goods by rail.* ○ *Massive investment is needed to improve the country's road, rail and air systems.*

/reɪl/
note not used with *a* or *an*. No plural and used with a singular verb only.
⋈ a **rail** network, passenger, service, system; **rail** freight, transport, travel
► **free on rail, transport[1] 1**

raise[1] *noun* (personnel)
(*US*) ► **rise**

/reɪz/

raise[2] *verb*
1 to increase or to make higher: *They'll have to raise their offer before we accept.* ○ *We have raised our profit levels by 10%.* **2** to obtain capital, a loan, funds, etc: *They managed to raise sufficient capital to keep the company buoyant.* ○ *The company raised a mortgage to fund the new factory.* **3** to ask people to discuss a subject; bring something up: *She raised the question of overtime payments.* ○ *His sales report raised some valuable points.* ○ *I'm raising the problem of car parking at the next meeting.*

/reɪz/
raise, raising, raised
note transitive verb
1 ⋈ **raise** an offer, a price; **raise** output, productivity, profit, taxation, turnover
2 ⋈ **raise** capital, funds, money; **raise** a loan, mortgage
3 ⋈ **raise** a point, question, subject

rake-off *noun* (finance/commerce)
1 (*informal*) a fee, or a share of the profit: *There was only a small profit left after the parent company had its rake-off.* **2** (*informal*) an illegal fee: *The fraud expert wanted a large rake-off.*

/ˈreɪk ɒf/
pl rake-offs
⋈ expect, pay, receive a **rake-off**
2 ► **bribe**

rally[1] *noun* (stock exchange)
a sudden rise in prices after a period of falling prices or little buying and selling: *a rally in commodity, gilt, share, etc prices* ○ *Share prices had a late rally today.* ○ *Composite insurers led a stock market rally yesterday.*

/ˈræli/
pl rallies
⋈ an early, a late, a market, a share, a stock exchange **rally**; a **rally** *in* (prices), *on* the Stock Exchange; to stage, to sustain a **rally**
► **recovery**

rally[2] *verb* (stock exchange)
to rise suddenly in price after a period of falling prices or little buying and selling activity: *The market is expected to rally when the trade figures are announced.* ○ *The share price rallied on the news of the Chairman's resignation.*

/ˈræli/
rally, rallying, rallied
note intransitive verb
⋈ to **rally** briefly, for a period, sharply, strongly
► **recover 2**

RAM *abbr* (computing)
Random Access Memory

/ræm/
note pronounced as a word

R and D *abbr* (manufacturing)
research and development

/ˌɑːr ənd ˈdiː/
abbr R & D

Random Access Memory *noun* (computing)
the part of a computer memory where information is temporarily stored while the user is working on it. The information can be changed and sorted quickly because the computer does not have to search through each item in order before finding it. The changes will be lost when the machine is turned off unless they are saved onto a hard or a floppy disk: *Random Access Memory works faster than read-only memory.*

/ˌrændəm ˌækses ˈmeməri/
note no plural
abbr RAM, ram
⧓ read to, write to **Random Access Memory**
▶ **direct access, read-only memory, sequential access**

---

range[1] *noun*
1 a collection of similar items: *This is a latest addition to our range of family cars.* ○ *We stock a wide range of video cameras.* ○ *This computer is top of the range* (ie the best of its type). **2** the limits within which something varies: *The salary range is £20 000 to £25 000.* ○ *For this job we are looking for someone within the age range of 25 –35.* ○ *The business has a range of activities from sand extraction to equipment hire.*

/reɪndʒ/
pl ranges
1 ⧓ develop, extend, offer, stock a **range**
1, 2 bottom, top of the **range**
▶ **line 2**

---

range[2] *verb*
to vary or extend between specified limits: *Business courses range in price from a few hundred pounds to thousands of pounds.* ○ *Her previous jobs ranged from editor to publicity manager.* ○ *He has responsibilities ranging from recruitment to employee training.*

/reɪndʒ/
range, ranging, ranged
note intransitive verb
⧓ **range** *between* (two things), *from* (something) *to* (something)

---

rank[1] *noun*
a position in a scale of responsibilty: *You must obtain permission from someone of higher rank.* ○ *The meeting was attended by a number of high-ranking officials.*

pull rank on someone to use your higher position of responsibility to make someone do something, sometimes unfairly: *He tried to pull rank on me to stop me going to the conference.*

/ræŋk/
pl ranks
⧓ a lesser, low, lower, high, higher **rank**

---

rank[2] *verb*
to place in a set order: *Job candidates were ranked in alphabetical order.* ○ *In law, unsecured shares are ranked after secured shares for payment.* ○ *How do you rank her/him as a manager?*

/ræŋk/
rank, ranking, ranked
note transitive verb

---

rate *noun* (commerce/industry)
1 an amount charged or paid for work done or a services provided: *Our rate of charges for van hire is enclosed.* ○ *be paid an hourly rate of £12 per hour* ○ *Your advertising rates are rather high.* ○ *What are the current rates of pay?* **2** (insurance) a measure of an amount, a value or a cost: *a rise in the rate of inflation from 6% to 7%* ○ *a fluctuating rate of exchange between the pound and the dollar*

going rate the usual rate of payment: *He's a good photographer but he charges more than the going rate.*

/reɪt/
pl rates
1 ⧓ current, higher, lower, special, usual **rates**; an annual, a daily, an hourly, a weekly **rate**
▶ **fixed charge, flat rate, hourly rate, piece rates, seasonal rate**
2 ▶ **absenteeism rate, accident frequency rate, annual percentage rate, base rate, discount rate, exchange rate, floating rate, interest rate, minimum lending rate, official rate, standard rate, vacancy rate**

rate of exchange *noun* (banking)
▶ **exchange rate**

/ˌreɪt əv ɪksˈtʃeɪndʒ/

rate of interest *noun* (finance)
▶ **interest rate**

/ˌreɪt əv ˈɪntrest/

rate of return *noun* (finance)
the amount of profit, dividend or interest received from an investment, expressed as a percentage of the original investment: *receive an annual rate of return of 10.3%* ○ *Your capital will earn a good rate of return.*

/ˌreɪt əv rɪˈtɜːn/
pl rates of return
⋈ an average, a good, a high, a low, a minimum, a poor **rate of return**
▶ **accounting rate of return, annual percentage rate, base rate, flat rate, return**[1]

rating *noun*
1 (*advertising*) the estimated audience of a television or radio programme. The rating figure is used to price and promote advertising time: *'News at Ten' has a high rating.* **2** (*insurance*) the cost of an insurance premium based on the risk of loss: *It is an area with a high rating because there is so much car theft.*

/ˈreɪtɪŋ/
pl ratings
⋈ a high, low **rating**
▶ **television rating**

ratio *noun* (finance/commerce/stock exchange)
the relation between two amounts determined by the number of times one contains the other: *work out the ratio between cost of production and the amount of profit received* ○ *The product leads its nearest competitor by a ratio of 3:1.*

/ˈreɪʃiəʊ/
pl ratios
⋈ the **ratio** *of* (something) *to* (something); a high, low **ratio**
▶ **acid test ratio, advances ratio, dividend-price ratio, loss ratio, price-dividend ratio, price-earnings ratio, turnover ratio**

rationalization *noun* (industry)
making changes in an organization in order to increase efficiency: *The number of products has been reduced after a period of rationalization.* ○ *Rationalization often results in job losses.* ○ *The rationalization programme reduced costs considerably.*

/ˌræʃnəlaɪˈzeɪʃn/
note not used with *a* or *an*. No plural and used with a singular verb only.
(also **rationalisation**)
⋈ a period, plan, programme of **rationalization**
▶ **amalgamation, consolidation, integration, merger, reorganization, restructuring**

rationalize *verb* (industry)
to make changes in an organization in order to increase efficiency: *We must rationalize our product process to reduce costs.* ○ *A team of outside consultants are rationalizing our distribution system.*

/ˈræʃnəlaɪz/
rationalize, rationalizing, rationalized
(also **rationalise**)
note transitive verb
⋈ **rationalize** a company, an industry, a process, a system
▶ **amalgamate, consolidate, integrate, merge, reorganize, restructure**

raw material *noun* (manufacturing)
a natural substance, eg copper, wool, coal, used to make

/ˌrɔː məˈtɪəriəl/
pl raw materials

something in an industrial process: *Wood is the raw material used to make paper.* ○ *Company profits were hit by an increase in the price of raw materials.*

⧓ convert, extract, mine, process a **raw material**; an abundance, a lack, a shortage, a source, a supply of **raw materials**

▶ **commodity, material, original goods**

---

re *abbr* (office practice)
with reference to; about; concerning: *Re: your invoice dated 12th January 1992.*

/riː/
note used in formal business letters

---

re- *prefix*
1 again: *readdress* ○ *redo* ○ *resell* **2** to get or give back: *reclaim* ○ *regain* ○ *return*

/riː/

---

react *verb* (stock exchange/finance)
(of share prices and stock markets) to rise or fall in response to a piece of news or market information: *Shares were slow to react to the news of the management buyout.* ○ *The equity market can react in either direction to news of economic improvement.*

/ri'ækt/
react, reacting, reacted
note intransitive verb
⧓ **react** favourably, sharply, slowly, unfavourably

---

readership *noun* (advertising)
the number of people who read a newspaper or magazine, often contrasted with the number of people who actually buy it: *The newspaper has a readership of 10 million.* ○ *Some scientific journals have a very specialist readership.*

/'riːdəʃɪp/
note no plural
⧓ a broad, large, narrow, small, specialist, wide **readership**
▶ **circulation**

---

read-only memory *noun* (computing)
the part of a computer memory that contains information that can be read but not altered. It is used to store programs that allow the machine to carry out specific functions. This information is not lost when the machine is switched off: *The spreadsheet software is part of the read-only memory.*

/ˌriːd ˌəʊnli 'meməri/
note no plural
abbr ROM, rom
▶ **direct access, Random Access Memory, sequential access**

---

ready cash *noun* (commerce/sales)
coins or banknotes available for immediate payment: *You can take these few now if you can pay with ready cash.* ○ *I need some ready cash for the journey.*

/ˌredi 'kæʃ/
note not used with *a* or *an*. No plural and used with a singular verb only.

---

ready-made *adjective, adverb* (sales/manufacturing)
(of goods, esp clothes) made in standard types or sizes and not to suit an individual customer: *Some of our ready-made jackets will be in the sale.* ○ *Most of our garments are ready-made.*

/ˌredi 'meɪd/
⧓ **ready-made** garments, shoes, suits
▶ **customize**

---

real estate *noun* (commerce)
(*US*) land and buildings; the business of buying and selling this: *He owns a lot of real estate in Florida.* ○ *invest in real estate overseas* ○ *She works in real estate in Chicago.*

/'rɪəl ɪˌsteɪt/
note not used with *a* or *an*. No plural and used with a singular verb only.
⧓ buy, develop, invest in, own, sell, work in **real estate**; a **real estate** business, company, developer
syn realty, (*UK*) real property
▶ **estate 1, land[1] 2, personal property**

---

real estate agent *noun*
▶ **estate agent**

/ˈrɪəl ɪˌsteɪt ˌeɪdʒənt/

real investment *noun* (finance/accounting)
the purchase of goods and services for the community, such as hospitals and schools, rather than securities, etc for financial gain; the money used for this: *Spending money on education is (a) real investment.* ○ *It is difficult to raise money for real investment.*

/ˌrɪəl ɪnˈvestmənt/
pl real investments
syn community investment
▶ **investment**

realizable assets *noun* (accounting)
▶ **liquid assets**

/ˌrɪəlaɪzəbl ˈæsets/

realize *verb*
1 (*finance*) to sell something for money: *The sale of the shop realized £150 000.* **2** (*management*) to make something happen; to achieve something: *He was thrilled to realize his franchise scheme.* ○ *It is important to help staff to realize their potential.*

/ˈrɪəlaɪz/
realize, realizing, realized
(also **realise**)
note transitive verb
1 ⋈ **realize** an asset, capital, property
▶ **liquidate, redeem 2**
2 ⋈ **realize** a plan, project, scheme

realized loss *noun* (accounting)
a loss made on the sale of goods or services or other assets: *The company made a realized loss on its investments of $1.06 billion.*

/ˌrɪəlaɪzd ˈlɒs/
pl realized losses
(also **realised loss**)
▶ **loss 1**

realized profit *noun* (accounting)
a gain made on the sale of goods or services or other assets: *The print department made a realized profit of £30 000 in March.*

/ˌrɪəlaɪzd ˈprɒfɪt/
pl realized profits
(also **realised profit**)
▶ **paper profit, profit**[1]

real property *noun*
(*US*) ▶ **real estate**

/ˌrɪəl ˈprɒpəti/

real terms *noun* (economics)
the amount of goods and services a sum of money can buy at a given time taking INFLATION into account: *In real terms, houses are cheaper than they were three years ago because of the housing slump.*

/ˈrɪəl tɜːmz/
note plural noun, used with a plural verb
⋈ assess, calculate, value something *in* **real terms**

realtor *noun*
(*US*) ▶ **estate agent**

/ˈrɪəltə(r)/

realty *noun*
▶ **real estate**

/ˈrɪəlti/

real value *noun* (commerce)
the amount of goods and services, etc that a sum of money can buy at any one time: *The real value of an average weekly wage is decreasing all the time.*

/ˌrɪəl ˈvæljuː/
note no plural
⋈ a decrease, an increase in **real value**
▶ **value**[1] **2**

real wages *noun* (personnel)
the amount of goods and services that can be bought with money earned: *Real wages have fallen by 5% in the last seven years.*

/ˌrɪəl ˈweɪdʒɪz/
note plural noun, used with a plural verb

⧓ a decrease, a drop, a fall, an increase, a rise in **real wages**

▶ **money wages, wage**

---

rebate *noun*

1 (*commerce*) a reduction in the price of a debt or tax; an amount repaid: *Invoices paid within two days will receive a rebate.* ○ *apply for a rent rebate* ○ *He paid too much income tax and received a rebate.* **2** (*banking*) a reduction in a bill of exchange which is paid before the date it is due

/ˈriːbeɪt/

pl rebates

⧓ an income tax, a rent **rebate**; apply for, give, offer, qualify for, receive a **rebate**

▶ **discount**[1], **refund**[1]

---

recall *verb* (commerce)

to ask customers to return a company's product because it does not work or is unsafe: *The electronics group, Amstrad, had to recall thousands of faulty computers.*

/rɪˈkɔːl/

recall, recalling, recalled

note transitive verb

---

receipt *noun* (accounting/sales)

1 a document showing that goods have been paid for: *Keep receipts of everything you spend on the business trip.* ○ *Do you require a receipt for these items?* **2** the act of receiving something: *All invoices are payable within thirty days of receipt.* ○ *The goods were dispatched on receipt of your order.* **3 receipts** the money received by a business: *net receipts of £804 million*

(be) in receipt of something (*formal*) having received something: *We are in receipt of your letter of the 3rd April.*

/rɪˈsiːt/

1 pl receipts

⧓ ask for, file, give, keep, sign a **receipt**

▶ **cash voucher 1**

2 note not used with *a* or *an*. No plural and used with a singular verb only.

⧓ in, on **receipt** (of something)

3 note plural noun, used with a plural verb

⧓ cash, gross, net, tax **receipts**

---

receivables *noun* (accounting)

money that is owed to a business: *an increase in the amount of credit card receivables* ○ *Receivables can be used as security for a loan.*

/rɪˈsiːvəblz/

note plural noun, used with a plural verb

▶ **accounts receivable, debt, liability**

---

receiver *noun*

1 a person who accepts something that has been delivered: *The receiver has complained that the goods were damaged when they arrived.* **2** the part of a telephone that accepts sounds and is held to the ear: *Please replace the receiver after dialling.* **3** (*law*) a person who accepts stolen property: *We cannot trace the goods until we know who the receiver is.*

/rɪˈsiːvə(r)/

pl receivers

1 ▶ **consignee, recipient**

2 ⧓ lift, pick up, replace a **receiver**

▶ **official receiver**

---

receivership *noun* (law)

a situation where an organization has gone bankrupt and is under the control of an OFFICIAL RECEIVER: *The company has been in receivership since March.*

/rɪˈsiːvəʃɪp/

note not used with *a* or *an*. No plural and used with a singular verb only.

⧓ be in, go into **receivership**

▶ **bankruptcy, declaration of solvency, insolvency, liquidation**

---

reception *noun* (office practice)

1 an area in a hotel or office where guests or visitors register or tell the RECEPTIONIST whom they have come to see: *All visitors must report to reception.* ○ *Please ask for me in reception.* **2** a formal

/rɪˈsepʃn/

1 note not used with *a* or *an*. No plural and used with a singular verb only.

⧓ arrive at, call at, check in at,

gathering, usually to welcome someone: *There will be one hundred guests at the reception.*

collect from, go to, meet in, register at **reception**

2 pl receptions

⧓ attend, be invited to a **reception**

---

receptionist *noun*

a person who works in an office or hotel answering the phone, dealing with guests, customers and visitors: *Please tell the receptionist when you arrive.*

/rɪˈsepʃənɪst/

pl receptionists

⧓ a hotel **receptionist**

---

recession *noun* (economics)

a slowing down or fall in business activity. It is usually accompanied by a fall in investment and public spending and a rise in unemployment: *Unemployment rose to three million during the recession.* ○ *Investment is low because of the recession.* ○ *The country has been in recession for a number of years.*

/rɪˈseʃn/

pl recessions

⧓ enter a **recession**; be in **recession**; an economic, an industrial, a property, a trade **recession**

opp boom

► **depressed market, depression, recovery 1, slump[1]**

---

recipient *noun* (office practice)

a person who accepts something, eg a payment, goods delivered, etc: *Ask the recipient to sign the form.*

/rɪˈsɪpiənt/

pl recipients

► **consignee, receiver 1**

---

reciprocal *adjective* (international trade/commerce)

given and received equally from one company, country or person to another: *There was a reciprocal trade agreement between France and Italy.*

/rɪˈsɪprəkl/

⧓ a **reciprocal** agreement, contract

---

reciprocal trading *noun* (commerce)

an arrangement between two companies to buy from and sell to each other: *All the companies in our group have a reciprocal trading agreement.*

/rɪˌsɪprəkl ˈtreɪdɪŋ/

note not used with *a* or *an*. No plural and used with a singular verb only.

⧓ a **reciprocal trading** account, contract, deal

► **trading**

---

reclaim *verb*

to get back something lost or owed: *Reclaim your luggage after passport control.* ○ *If you don't keep up the payments the finance house can reclaim the goods.*

/rɪˈkleɪm/

reclaim, reclaiming, reclaimed

note transitive verb

---

recommended retail price *noun* (retail)

► **manufacturer's recommended price**

/ˌrekəˌmendɪd ˌriːteɪl ˈpraɪs/

abbr RRP, RP

---

record[1] *noun*

1 (*administration*) a written account of something: *The manager keeps a record of daily sales.* **2** the facts that are known; a reputation: *The company had a poor safety record.* **3** the best performance or highest level reached: *Sales for November broke all our previous records.* **4** (*computing*) a unit of related data stored within a computer file: *Each employee has a record on our payroll database.*

/ˈrekɔːd/

pl records

1 ⧓ check, keep, update a **record**

► **records**

2 ⧓ a good, poor, strong **record**

3 ⧓ break, establish, set a **record**

► **track record**

4 ⧓ a customer, an employee, a payroll, a supplier **record**

record² *verb* (administration)
to make a report (usually written) of something that has happened: *record the minutes of a meeting* ○ *The payment of each invoice is recorded on the computer.*

/rɪˈkɔːd/
record, recording, recorded
note transitive verb
⧓ **record** a loss, profit

recorded delivery *noun* (office practice)
(*UK*) a Post Office service in the UK that provides the sender of an inland letter with proof of safe delivery for a fee: *send the parcel by recorded delivery*

/rɪˌkɔːdɪd dɪˈlɪvəri/
pl recorded deliveries
⧓ send (the letter or packet) by, sign for a **recorded delivery**
▶ **post¹ 2, registered post**

records *noun* (administration)
documents or computer files on which information is stored: *Our records show that you have been late every day this week.* ○ *Customers have a right to ask for information stored on their computer records.* ○ *These records must be out of date.*

/ˈrekɔːdz/
note plural noun, used with a plural verb
⧓ file, keep, maintain, see, update **records**
▶ **record¹ 1**

recoup *verb* (finance)
to get back money that has been spent or lost: *We should recoup the cost of a project within a year.* ○ *The company cannot recoup its losses.*

/rɪˈkuːp/
recoup, recouping, recouped
note transitive verb
⧓ **recoup** costs, losses, money
syn recover

recover *verb*
1 (*finance*) to get back something that has been lost, spent or used: *You can recover your expenses for the trip.* ○ *We must try to recover some of these bad debts.* **2** (*stock exchange*) (of market prices) to improve or rise: *Prices have recovered after the fall last week.*

/rɪˈkʌvə(r)/
recover, recovering, recovered
note transitive verb
1 ⧓ **recover** costs, damages, expenses, losses, money
▶ **rally², recoup**

recovery *noun*
1 (*economics*) a rise in the buying and selling of shares or of the economy: *Economic recovery was very slow after the recession.* ○ *The market staged a recovery despite poor trading this morning.*
2 (*law*) the right given by a court of law to get back property or money: *Our legal department has started recovery proceedings.*

/rɪˈkʌvəri/
1 pl recoveries
⧓ a rapid, slow, strong **recovery**; make, stage a **recovery**
▶ **boom, rally¹, recession**
2 note not used with *a* or *an*. No plural and used with a singular verb only.
⧓ debt **recovery**

recruitment *noun* (management/industrial relations)
the process of looking for and choosing new staff for an organization: *She is responsible for the recruitment of new staff.* ○ *We obtain about 30% of our staff from recruitment agencies.*

/rɪˈkruːtmənt/
note not used with *a* or *an*. No plural and used with a singular verb only.
⧓ a **recruitment** agency, interview, officer; staff **recruitment**
▶ **appoint 1, interview¹, selection procedure**

rectify *verb* (accounting)
to put something right: *They will have to rectify the mistakes in these invoices.* ○ *The errors in the cash book have been rectified.*

/ˈrektɪfaɪ/
rectify, rectifying, rectified
note transitive verb
⋈ **rectify** an error, a mistake

recycle *verb* (industry)
to process waste material so that it can be used again: *We collect the aluminium waste and recycle it.* ○ *These products are made from recycled plastic.*

/ˌriːˈsaɪkl/
recycle, recycling, recycled
note transitive verb
▶ **scrap**[1], **waste**[1]

red, in the *adjective*
1 (*banking*) not having money in your bank account; having an overdraft: *I can't afford a holiday, I'm in the red at the moment.* ○ *My account is in the red.* 2 (*accounting*) operating at a loss; having expenditure exceeding income: *The company will end another financial year in the red.*

/ˌɪn ðə ˈred/
⋈ be **in the red**
opp in the black
▶ in debt *under* **debt**

redeem *verb*
1 (*finance*) to pay off a loan or mortgage: *We hope to redeem the mortgage by the end of the year.* 2 (*stock exchange*) to convert shares, bonds, loan stock, etc into money: *You can redeem some of your shares if you need some cash.*

/rɪˈdiːm/
redeem, redeeming, redeemed
note transitive verb
1 ⋈ **redeem** a loan, mortgage
2 ⋈ **redeem** debentures, loan stock, securities, shares, stock
▶ **realize 1**

redeemable preference share *noun* (stock exchange)
a preference share that the company has a right to buy back at any time

/rɪˌdiːməbl ˈprefrəns ʃeə(r)/
pl redeemable preference shares
▶ **preference share**

redemption *noun* (finance/stock exchange)
1 the act of paying off a loan or mortgage: *Is there a penalty for redemption before due date?* 2 the repayment of money saved with a bank or building society or invested in shares, securities, etc: *There is a penalty of 90 days' interest for early redemption.*

/rɪˈdempʃn/
note not used with *a* or *an*. No plural and used with a singular verb only.
1 ⋈ **redemption** of a debt, loan, mortgage; the **redemption** of bonds, securities, shares

redemption date *noun* (finance/stock exchange)
▶ **maturity**

/rɪˈdempʃn deɪt/

redemption yield *noun* (finance/stock exchange)
the amount of income obtained from a fixed interest security, including interest and its repayment value, expressed as a percentage of its current market price: *The debenture issue will produce a redemption yield of 1.6%.*

/rɪˈdempʃn jiːld/
note usually singular
▶ **dividend yield, fixed-interest security, flat yield, yield**

redraft *verb*
to make another rough plan of a document, letter, report, etc: *The plan needs redrafting after the meeting.*

/ˌriːˈdrɑːft; *US* ˌriːˈdræft/
redraft, redrafting, redrafted
note transitive verb
⋈ **redraft** a document, letter, plan, report
▶ **draft**[2]

red tape *noun*
(*informal*) the overuse of official paperwork and regulations: *The project will start as soon as we get through the red tape.* ○ *We will try and cut through the red tape to finish the job.*

/ˌred ˈteɪp/
note not used with *a* or *an*. No plural and used with a singular verb only.
⧓ cut, get through **red tape**
▶ **bureaucracy 2**

---

reduce *verb* (management/sales/retail)
to make an amount, a price, etc smaller or lower: *The accountants have told us to reduce the number of staff at this branch.* ○ *Our costs have been reduced by 15%.*

/rɪˈdjuːs/
reduce, reducing, reduced
note transitive verb
⧓ **reduce** a cost, price, tax

---

reducing-balance method of depreciation *noun*
(accounting)
reducing the value of a fixed asset by the same percentage each year and charging the amount to the profit and loss account: *We use the reducing-balance method of depreciation for our cars.*

/rɪˌdjuːsɪŋ ˌbæləns ˌmeθəd əv dɪˌpriːʃiˈeɪʃn/
note not used with *a* or *an*. No plural and used with a singular verb only.
syn declining-balance method, diminishing-balance method, reducing instalment system
▶ **accelerated depreciation, accumulated depreciation, depreciation, straight line depreciation**

---

redundancy *noun* (management/industrial relations)
1 the loss of a job by an employee because there is no longer any work: *Over 500 steel workers face redundancy.* **2** jobs lost or people dismissed in this way: *The closure will involve 50 redundancies.*

/rɪˈdʌndənsi/
1 note not used with *a* or *an*. No plural and used with a singular verb only.
⧓ accept, face, offer, take **redundancy**
▶ **unfair dismissal, voluntary redundancy**
2 pl redundancies
▶ **job losses, natural wastage, unemployment**

---

redundancy pay *noun* (industrial relations)
a payment made to an employee as compensation for the loss of a job. It is calculated according to the age, length of service and rate of pay of the employee: *receive £5 000 in redundancy pay*

/rɪˈdʌndənsi peɪ/
note not used with *a* or *an*. No plural and used with a singular verb only.
⧓ offer, receive **redundancy pay**
syn severance pay
▶ **compensation, pay**[2]

---

re-exports *noun* (international trade)
goods that are brought into a country and are then exported unchanged: *The value of our re-exports trade has increased.* ○ *Much of the country's convertible currency comes from re-exports.*

/ˌriː ˈekspɔːts/
note plural noun, used with a plural verb
▶ **export**[1]**, import**[1]**, reimports**

---

ref *abbr* (office practice)
reference: *Your ref 3492* ○ *Ref no 371*

/ref/
⧓ Our, Your **ref**

referee *noun*

1 (*management*) a person who writes a report on the character or abilities of someone applying for a job: *This application form asks for the names of three referees.* ○ *I asked my former employer to act as a referee.* 2 (*banking*) a person or organization named on some bills of exchange as a 'referee in case of need' and from whom the holder may demand payment if the bill is dishonoured 3 (*law*) a person appointed to settle a dispute: *An independent referee was called in to settle the dispute.*

/ˌrefəˈriː/
pl referees
1 ⧓ ask for, provide a **referee**; act as a **referee**
► **applicant, reference**
2 ► **bill of exchange**
3 ⧓ appoint, call in a **referee**; act as **referee**
► **arbitrator, industrial dispute**

reference *noun*

1 (*office practice*) numbers and letters that identify a document or a letter: *Our ref: AB987.* ○ *Please quote reference ZK42.*
2 (*management*) a written report on a job applicant's character or ability to do the job: *Mr Smith will give me a reference.*
3 (*commerce*) a report on a company's financial status and reputation: *They need a bank reference before they will give us credit.* ○ *Our new supplier has asked us to give trade references.*

/ˈrefərəns/
1 note usually singular
abbr ref.
⧓ Our, Your **reference**
2 pl references
⧓ ask for, give, supply, write a **reference**
► **testimonial**
3 pl references
⧓ bank, trade **reference**
► **referee**

reference group *noun* (marketing/advertising)

a social group with which consumers identify. Its lifestyle and values can be used in advertising to encourage others to purchase products associated with the group: *an advertisement designed to appeal to a particular reference group*

/ˈrefərəns gruːp/
pl reference groups
► **lifestyle, market research**

refer to drawer *noun* (banking)

words written on a cheque that the bank will not pay, usually because there is not enough money in the account: *This cheque is stamped refer to drawer.*

/rɪˌfɜː tə ˈdrɔːə/
note no plural
► **dishonour 1, drawer, re-present, words and figures do not agree**

refinancing *noun* (finance/stock exchange)

the repaying of money lent with another loan, usually obtained at a lower rate of interest or for a longer period: *Refinancing is needed to pay off major debts.* ○ *arrange (a) refinancing with the bank*

/ˌriːˈfaɪnænsɪŋ/
note no plural
⧓ arrange, organize **refinancing**; a **refinancing** deal

reflate *verb* (economics)

to improve economic conditions in a country by increasing the money supply or reducing taxation or interest rates: *The government is trying to reflate the economy by cutting interest rates.*

/ˌriːˈfleɪt/
reflate, reflating, reflated
note transitive verb
⧓ **reflate** the economy
► **inflation**

reflation *noun* (economics)

government action to improve economic conditions in a country by increasing the money supply or reducing taxation or interest rates: *It is hoped that reflation will encourage public spending.*

/riːˈfleɪʃn/
note not used with *a* or *an*. No plural and used with a singular verb only.
⧓ **reflation** of an economy
► **deflation, disinflation, inflation**

refund[1] *noun* (retail)
money that is given back, usually for faulty or unwanted goods: *She asked for a refund because the goods were damaged.* ○ *bring goods back and get a refund*

/ˈriːfʌnd/
pl refunds
⋈ ask for, be entitled to, offer a **refund**; a full, part **refund**
▶ **discount**[1], **rebate**

refund[2] *verb* (retail)
to give money back to; to repay (a customer): *We can refund your deposit in cases of illness.* ○ *Your expenses will be refunded in full.*

/rɪˈfʌnd, ˈriːfʌnd/
refund, refunding, refunded
note transitive verb
⋈ **refund** a cost, deposit; **refund** expenses, money
▶ **reimburse**

register[1] *noun*
1 an official list of persons, places, things, etc: *a register of local building firms* **2** a book kept at a hotel, an office, etc for guests or visitors to sign to say that they have arrived: *Please sign the hotel register.*

/ˈredʒɪstə(r)/
pl registers
1 ⋈ add (a name) to, enter (a name) in a **register**
2 ⋈ sign, write (a name) in a **register**

register[2] *verb*
1 to write a name, title, etc on an official list: *register the company's new address* ○ *What name was it registered under?* **2** (at a hotel or conference) to sign your name in a book to say that you have arrived: *They registered at the hotel last night.*

/ˈredʒɪstə(r)/
register, registering, registered
note transitive verb
1 ⋈ **register** an address, a company, a name, a property, a ship, a trade mark; **register** *with* an organization
▶ **patent**
2 ⋈ **register** *at* a hotel

registered capital *noun* (stock exchange)
▶ **authorized share capital**

/ˌredʒɪstəd ˈkæpɪtl/

registered company *noun* (stock exchange/law)
(*UK*) a public limited company or a private company registered under the Companies Act: *Marks and Spencer plc is a registered company.*

/ˌredʒɪstəd ˈkʌmpəni/
pl registered companies
▶ **private company, public limited company, Registrar of Companies**

registered office *noun* (law)
(*UK*) the official address of a company where all letters are sent. By law, the Registrar of Companies must be informed of this address: *send a tax bill to the registered office*

/ˌredʒɪstəd ˈɒfɪs/
pl registered offices
▶ **head office, office 2, Registrar of Companies**

registered post *noun*
(*UK*) a UK Post Office service that insures mail for a fee. It is delivered only when the person named on the letter or packet has signed to say they have received it: *It will be safer to send this letter by registered post.*

/ˌredʒɪstəd ˈpəʊst/
note no plural
⋈ send (a letter) by, use **registered post**
▶ **post**[1] **2, recorded delivery**

registered trade mark *noun* (law)
(*UK*) ▶ **trade mark**

/ˌredʒɪstəd ˈtreɪd mɑːk/

register of directors *noun* (law/stock exchange)
(*UK*) a list of directors that every UK company must keep for inspection. It must give the name, address, nationality and occupation of all directors: *be included in the register of directors*

/ˌredʒɪstər əv dəˈrektəz/
note usually singular
► **director, registered office**

register of members *noun* (stock exchange)
► **share register**

/ˌredʒɪstər əv ˈmembəz/

registrar *noun* (law)
(*UK*) a company employee, or an agent acting for a company, who records the transfer of company shares in the share register: *work as a registrar for Lloyd's Bank*

/ˌredʒɪˈstrɑː(r)/
pl registrars
► **share, share register**

Registrar of Companies *noun* (law)
(*UK*) a government official who keeps detailed records of all limited companies in the UK: *notify the Registrar of Companies of a change of address*

/ˌredʒɪˌstrɑːr əv ˈkʌmpəniz/
► **Certificate of Incorporation, registered company, registered office**

registration *noun*
1 the act of being entered on an official list: *Do you have the necessary documents for registration?* **2** the act of signing a register at a hotel or a conference to say that you have arrived: *Registration is followed by coffee and the opening conference speech.*

/ˌredʒɪˈstreɪʃn/
note not used with *a* or *an*. No plural and used with a singular verb only.
⋈ a **registration** card, document, form, number

registration fee *noun*
1 (*stock exchange*) money charged by a company for adding the name of a new share owner to the register: *charge a registration fee* **2** money charged for attendance at a conference, course, etc: *Have you paid your registration fee?*

/ˌredʒɪˈstreɪʃn fiː/
pl registration fees
⋈ charge, pay a **registration fee**

registry *noun* (law)
a place where registers are kept and updated, and where they are usually available for public inspection: *We can check the ownership of the property at the Land Registry.*

/ˈredʒɪstri/
pl registries
► **register**[1] **1, Land Registry**

regret *noun* (stock exchange)
► **letter of regret**

/rɪˈgret/

regular *adjective*
1 (*commerce/manufacturing*) (of goods) standard size or quality: *We stock all the regular sizes.* ○ *We can offer a discount on our regular price for bulk orders.* **2** (*management*) happening at the same time each day, week, month, etc: *hold regular meetings* ○ *run a regular ferry service* ○ *receive a regular update of information* **3** of a person who goes to the same place or uses the same service frequently: *We mustn't lose our regular customers.*

/ˈregjələ(r)/
1 ⋈ a **regular** height, measurement, price, size, weight
2 ⋈ a **regular** bus, ferry, train service, delivery, event, flight, meeting
3 ⋈ client, customer, visitor

regulate *verb* (law)
to control or direct an industry, an organization, etc by rules and restrictions: *The activities of credit card companies are regulated by law.*

/ˈregjəleɪt/
regulate, regulating, regulated
note transitive verb
opp deregulate

regulation *noun* (finance/commerce/management)
1 controlling; making sure that an organization, an event or a service works fairly and well: *The public are demanding tighter regulation of telephone marketing.* ○ *Price regulation might be more difficult after privatization of the water industry.* **2** a rule or a restriction made by an authority: *Make sure the work complies with building regulations.* ○ *The safety regulations state that you must wear goggles and gloves for this work.*

/ˌregjəˈleɪʃn/
1 note not used with *a* or *an*. No plural and used with a singular verb only.
⋈ **regulation** of credit, prices, trade, traffic
opp deregulation
▶ **self-regulatory organization**
2 pl regulations
⋈ building, fire, health, safety, staff **regulations**; comply with **regulations**

---

reimburse *verb* (finance)
to pay back money to someone who has spent or lost it: *Your expenses will be reimbursed in full.* ○ *The customer was reimbursed for the damaged goods.*

/ˌriːɪmˈbɜːs/
reimburse, reimbursing, reimbursed
note transitive verb
⋈ **reimburse** a cost, an expense, a fee; **reimburse** someone *for* (loss or damage)
▶ **refund, repay**

---

reimports *noun* (tax/commerce)
goods that have been exported from a country and are later brought back in: *an increase in the number of reimports*

/ˌriːˈɪmpɔːts/
note plural noun, used with a plural verb
▶ **export[1], import[1], re-exports**

---

reinstate *verb* (industrial relations)
to give back the job or position to someone who was dismissed or moved to a lower position: *The union insisted that sacked staff should be reinstated.* ○ *She was reinstated as department manager.*

/ˌriːɪnˈsteɪt/
reinstate, reinstating, reinstated
note transitive verb
⋈ **reinstate** someone *as* (something), someone *to* (a previous position)

---

reinsurance *noun* (insurance)
the sharing of all or part of a large insurance risk by asking other insurance companies to cover part of it in return for part of the premium: *reduce risk through reinsurance*

/ˌriːɪnˈʃʊərəns/
note not used with *a* or *an*. No plural and used with a singular verb only.
⋈ a **reinsurance** contract, market, policy
▶ **insurance**

---

reinsure *verb* (insurance)
to share an insurance risk with another company, which receives part of the premium: *A risk of this size has to be reinsured.*

/ˌriːɪnˈʃʊə(r)/
reinsure, reinsuring, reinsured
note transitive verb
▶ **insurance**

---

reinsurer *noun* (insurance)
an insurance company that agrees to accept a part of a loss insured by another company: *Lloyd's of London acts as a reinsurer for other insurance companies.*

/ˌriːɪnˈʃʊərə(r)/
pl reinsurers
⋈ act as a **reinsurer**
▶ **insurance company**

---

reject[1] *noun* (retail)
an item that is sold cheaply because it is below the usual

/ˈriːdʒekt/
pl rejects

standard: *The goods were sold as rejects.* ○ *There are plans for a reject china shop in the High Street.*

⧓ **reject** goods, items, products, stock

---

reject² *verb*

1 to refuse to accept something: *He rejected the offer of £350 for the goods.* ○ *The proposal was rejected on the grounds of cost.* ○ *She wanted to know why her job application was rejected.* **2** to put something aside; to throw something away: *Imperfect articles are rejected by our quality control.*

/rɪˈdʒekt/
reject, rejecting, rejected
note transitive verb
1 ⧓ **reject** an application, an offer, a plan, a proposal
2 ⧓ **reject** goods
opp accept

---

relief *noun*

1 someone or something that takes over the work of another: *The relief driver will be here in a minute.* ○ *I have to wait until my relief comes.* ○ *We need a relief bus as this one has broken down.*
2 (*personnel*) the act of taking over a person's work or duties: *I'm due for relief in ten minutes.*

/rɪˈliːf/
1 note no plural
⧓ a **relief** bus, crew, driver, shift
2 note not used with *a* or *an*. No plural and used with a singular verb only.
⧓ be due for **relief**
▶ **tax relief**

---

relocate *verb* (industry)

to move a person or an organization from one place to another; to rebuild a factory, an office, etc in another place: *We're relocating to a rural area.* ○ *Because of the shortage of office space in the city we have to relocate.* ○ *Most of our staff will be relocated.*

/ˌriːləʊˈkeɪt/
relocate, relocating, relocated
note transitive and intransitive verb
⧓ **relocate** a company, a factory, a firm, an office, staff; **relocate** *from, to* (a place)

---

relocation *noun* (industry)

moving a person or an organization from one place to another; rebuilding a factory or an office in another place: *Relocation will take place in August next year.* ○ *Our key staff have been offered relocation expenses.* ○ *The merger will result in relocation.*

/ˌriːləʊˈkeɪʃn/
note not used with *a* or *an*. No plural and used with a singular verb only.
⧓ **relocation** costs, expenses; **relocation** *from, to* (a place)

---

remit¹ *noun* (management)

an important matter that a person or an organization must consider and deal with: *The department's remit is to explore ways to improve the product for export markets.* ○ *Total reorganization of the company is outside our remit.*

/ˈriːmɪt/
note no plural
⧓ fulfil a **remit**; outside, within a **remit**

---

remit² *verb* (finance)

(*formal*) **1** to cancel a debt, tax or payment: *Fees cannot be remitted.* **2** to send money, esp by post: *Please remit the balance without delay.*

/rɪˈmɪt/
remit, remitting, remitted
note transitive verb
1 ⧓ **remit** a debt, deposit, fee, payment, tax
2 ⧓ **remit** a balance, cheque, debt, fee, payment

---

remittance *noun* (finance)

(*formal*) a sum of money sent from one person or place to another: *Please ensure that your remittance reaches us by the end of the month.*

/rɪˈmɪtns/
pl remittances
⧓ post, receive, send a **remittance**

---

remittance slip *noun* (finance/banking)
a printed form sent with an invoice and returned with the payment, giving details of the amount, customer's name, etc: *Please return the remittance slip with your payment.*

/rɪˈmɪtns slɪp/
pl remittance slips
⋈ enclose, return, send a **remittance slip**
▶ **counterfoil**

remunerate *verb* (personnel)
to pay or reward someone for their work: *You will be well remunerated for your work.*

/rɪˈmju:nəreɪt/
remunerate, remunerating, remunerated
note transitive verb
⋈ **remunerate** someone *for* effort, services, work

remuneration *noun* (personnel)
payment for services given; a salary: *She receives excellent remuneration for her work.* ○ *A good director is worth more than his/her remuneration.* ○ *Remuneration depends on performance* (ie salary depends on how well the job is done).

/rɪˌmju:nəˈreɪʃn/
note no plural
⋈ a high, low, poor **remuneration**; accept, receive **remuneration**
▶ **salary, wages**

remunerative *adjective* (finance)
1 (of a business or business activity) profitable: *She turned her hobby into a remunerative business.* **2** (of a job) well paid: *He has a remunerative position with an accountancy firm.*

/rɪˈmju:nərətɪv/
1 ⋈ a **remunerative** business, deal, sale
2 ⋈ a **remunerative** job, position, post; **remunerative** employment

render *verb* (accounting)
to send in (an account) for payment for work done or a service provided: *The account was rendered on the 15th August and is now overdue.* ○ *render an account for £500*

/ˈrendə(r)/
render, rendering, rendered
note transitive verb
⋈ **render** an account
▶ **account rendered**

renew *verb*
to keep something valid for a further period of time; to extend: *I'll ask them to renew the contract.* ○ *The insurance policy was renewed in February.*

/rɪˈnju:/
renew, renewing, renewed
note transitive verb
⋈ **renew** a contract, an insurance policy, a lease, a licence, a subscription

renewal *noun* (insurance)
the act of keeping something functioning or valid for a further period of time: *We recommend renewal rather than repair.* ○ *Please send in your old passport for renewal.*

/rɪˈnju:əl/
note not used with *a* or *an*. No plural and used with a singular verb only.
⋈ **renewal** date, form; due for **renewal**

renewal notice *noun* (insurance)
a note, sometimes in the form of an invoice, from an insurance company asking the insured person to pay the RENEWAL PREMIUM to keep the policy valid: *The renewal notice for the fire insurance has arrived.*

/rɪˈnju:əl ˌnəʊtɪs/
pl renewal notices
⋈ receive, send out a **renewal notice**
▶ **insurance**

renewal premium *noun* (insurance)
a sum of money paid to keep an insurance policy valid, usually for another year: *The renewal premium is more expensive than the last.*

/rɪˈnju:əl ˌpri:miəm/
pl renewal premiums
⋈ pay a **renewal premium**

rent[1] *noun* (finance)
a regular payment for the use of land, or an office, machinery, etc: *City centre rents are very high.* ○ *pay a monthly rent for the use of an office* ○ *owe three months' rent* ○ *The rent is due on the 1st of the month.*

/rent/
pl rents
⧓ an extortionate, high, low, reasonable **rent**; collect, pay, receive **rent**; a **rent** agreement, collector
▶ **lease[1], tenant**

rent[2] *verb* (finance)
to pay money for the use of land, or an office, machinery, etc: *We cannot afford to buy a property so we shall have to rent.* ○ *These machines are rented.* ○ *rent a holiday cottage from an agency*

rent something out to allow someone the use of land, an office, a machine, etc in return for a regular payment: *rent out commercial vehicles*

/rent/
rent, renting, rented
note transitive verb
⧓ **rent** a factory, an office, a piece of land, a property, a shop; rent something *from* someone
▶ **hire[1] 1, lease[2], let[2]**

rental *noun* (finance)
1 the act of renting a car, a telephone, a television, etc: *You have to pay quite a high charge for rental.* **2** money paid for the use of a property, a car, machinery, etc: *Telephone rental charges have risen again.* **3** something that is rented: *an increase in video rentals*

/ˈrentl/
1 note not used with *a* or *an*. No plural and used with a singular verb only.
2 note not used with *a* or *an*. No plural and used with a singular verb only.
⧓ charge, pay **rental**; **rental** charges, costs, fees
3 pl rentals
⧓ telephone, television, video **rentals**
▶ **hire**

renunciation form *noun* (stock exchange)
▶ **letter of renunciation**

/rɪˌnʌnsiˈeɪʃn fɔːm/

reorganization *noun*
1 (*management*) rearrangement of working methods or finance within a company or group of companies: *Payments have been prompt since reorganization.* ○ *Reorganization will mean some redundancies.* **2** (*finance*) an instance of this: *a reorganization of the company into seven new divisions* ○ *a complete reorganization of the management structure*

/riˌɔːɡənaɪˈzeɪʃn/
(also **reorganisation**)
1 note not used with *a* or *an*. No plural and used with a singular verb only.
⧓ a complete, an extensive, a major **reorganization**; **reorganization** *of* a company, a department, a division, an industry
2 note usually singular
▶ **organization 2, restructuring**

rep *abbr* (sales)
(*informal*) representative: *work as a publisher's rep*

/rep/
▶ **sales representative**

repeat order *noun* (sales)
a new request for goods that have been purchased before: *Repeat orders are the mainstay of our business.*

/rɪˌpiːt ˈɔːdə(r)/
pl repeat orders
⧓ encourage, get, receive a **repeat order**
▶ **order[1] 1**

replacement *noun* (industry/personnel)

1 a person who replaces another; a substitute: *The sales manager is leaving so we must find a suitable replacement.* ○ *How much will it cost to train his replacement?* **2** a machine or part of a machine that replaces another; a substitute: *The machine has broken down and we must get a replacement quickly.* ○ *We will give you your money back if we can't find a replacement.* **3** the act of substituting a person or a machine, etc for another: *This old photocopier is due for replacement.*

/rɪˈpleɪsmənt/

1 pl replacements

⋈ advertise for, find, take on a **replacement**

2 pl replacements

⋈ find, look for, obtain, send for a **replacement**; **replacement** costs, parts

3 note not used with *a* or *an*. No plural and used with a singular verb only.

---

reply coupon *noun* (advertising/sales)

a printed form that can be detached from a magazine page, a leaflet, etc and used to ask for advertised goods. The return postage may be paid by the advertiser: *send off a reply coupon for a holiday brochure* ○ *Please use the reply coupon when ordering goods.*

/rɪˈplaɪ ˌkuːpɒn/

pl reply coupons

⋈ complete, fill in, send off, use a **reply coupon**

syn reply slip

► **international reply coupon**

---

repo *abbr* (finance)

repurchase agreement

/ˈriːpəʊ/

---

report[1] *noun* (management)

a written or spoken account of something: *She has to present a progress report on the project.* ○ *The chairman received a confidential report on the reorganization.* ○ *The accountants will have the financial reports ready next week.*

/rɪˈpɔːt/

pl reports

⋈ a confidential, detailed, financial, monthly, newspaper, progress, weekly **report**; draft, draw up, prepare, present, produce, publish, submit, write a **report** (*on* something)

► **account[1] 3, annual report, market report, qualified report, statutory report**

---

report[2] *verb*

1 (*management*) to give a written or spoken account of something: *The sales manager was pleased to report increased sales for the first quarter.* ○ *The lorry driver reported the accident.* ○ *The accountants will report on the cash flow forecast.* **2** (*sales*) to be responsible to another person: *You will have to report to the site foreman.* **3** to go to a specified place: *Report at reception on arrival.*

/rɪˈpɔːt/

report, reporting, reported

1 note transitive and intransitive verb

⋈ **report** *on* (something)

2 note intransitive verb

⋈ **report** *to* (someone)

3 note intransitive verb

⋈ **report** *at* (a place)

---

represent *verb* (management/sales)

to act for or on behalf of someone else: *Our agent represents us in India.* ○ *The shop steward is here to represent the union.* ○ *be represented by a solicitor in court*

/ˌreprɪˈzent/

represent, representing, represented

note transitive verb

⋈ **represent** a client, a company, a party, a person

---

re-present *verb* (banking)

to produce and show a document again, esp a bill of exchange, a cheque or promissory note that was not honoured when previously presented: *Our debtor tells us the cheque will be*

/ˌriːprɪˈzent/

re-present, re-presenting, re-presented

note transitive verb

honoured if we re-present it now. ○ *The bank returned the cheque with the wording 'Refer to drawer. Please re-present'.*

⧓ **re-present** a bill of exchange, cheque, promissory note

▶ **honour, present[2] 2, refer to drawer**

---

representative *noun* (law/finance/management)
1 a person who acts on behalf of another: *My accountant will act as my representative on this matter.* **2** a company which sells goods on behalf of another company: *A. B. Brown Ltd. are our representatives in Scotland.* **3** a person employed by a company to demonstrate and sell goods and services for sale: *Our representative will call next week.*

/ˌreprɪˈzentətɪv/
pl representatives
abbr rep
1 ⧓ act as, send a **representative**
2 ⧓ a foreign, an overseas, a trade **representative**
▶ **agent**
3 ⧓ an overseas, a sales, a trade, a travelling **representative**
▶ **commercial traveller, sales representative**

---

repudiate *verb* (law/finance)
to refuse to pay a debt or honour a contract or agreement: *The company repudiated all debts accrued before the merger.*

/rɪˈpjuːdieɪt/
repudiate, repudiating, repudiated
note transitive verb
⧓ **repudiate** an agreement, a contract, a debt, a document, a statement
▶ **breach of contract**

---

repurchase agreement *noun* (finance/banking)
1 an arrangement in which a security is sold and later bought back at an agreed price and time: *organize a repurchase agreement* **2** (*UK*) an agreement by unit trust managers to buy back unit trusts from a holder: *sign a repurchase agreement*

/riːˈpɜːtʃəs əˌgriːmənt/
pl repurchase agreements
abbr repo
▶ **security 1**

---

require *verb* (management)
(*formal*) **1** to need: *The financial report requires careful study.* ○ *We require a further £5 000 for market research.* **2** to ask for or to command: *You are required by law to have third party insurance.* ○ *Your signature is required on this document.*

/rɪˈkwaɪə(r)/
require, requiring, required
note transitive verb

---

requirement *noun*
something that is needed or asked for by an authority: *This computer system should meet your requirements.* ○ *A second or third language is a requirement for this post.* ○ *Does this equipment meet all safety requirements?*

/rɪˈkwaɪəmənt/
pl requirements
⧓ match, meet a **requirement**; an essential, a legal, a minimum, a safety **requirement**
▶ **condition 2**

---

requisition *noun* (sales)
a written order for materials from a store or shop: *Do you have a requisition number for these goods?*

/ˌrekwɪˈzɪʃn/
pl requisitions
▶ **acquisition 1**

---

research[1] *noun* (industry)
careful study or investigation to collect, find out and test new facts and information: *Our research shows there is a great demand for this product.* ○ *We have been asked to carry out some research into faster and cheaper production methods.* ○ *Many companies can no longer afford to spend much money on research.*

/rɪˈsɜːtʃ, ˈriːsɜːtʃ/
note not used with *a* or *an*. No plural and used with a singular verb only.
⧓ carry out, do **research**; **research** *into* something; the

research indicates, proves, shows; scientific **research**; a **research** department, institute, laboratory, scientist, team, unit, worker

▶ **attitude research, desk research, market research, motivational research, qualitative market research, quantitative market research, telephone research**

---

esearch² *verb* (industry)

o carry out a careful study of something to collect, find out and est information: *We are researching ways of recycling our waste roducts.* ○ *This product was well researched before it was put on the narket.*

/rɪˈsɜːtʃ/

research, researching, researched

note transitive and intransitive verb

⋈ **research** a market, method, product; extensively, fully, well **researched**

▶ **market research**

---

esearch and development *noun* (manufacturing)

he scientific search for new and improved products and nanufacturing processes: *We invest a lot of money in research and evelopment.* ○ *Industry depends on continuing research and evelopment.*

/rɪˌsɜːtʃ ənd dɪˈveləpmənt/

note not used with *a* or *an*. No plural and used with a singular verb only.

abbr R and D, R & D

⋈ a **research and development** department, group, team, unit

▶ **development 1**

---

eserve *noun* (finance)

he capital from a business that is set aside from profit or from hares sold at higher than their original price (NOMINAL PRICE). It orms part of the company's NET ASSETS: *Share capital and other eserves are shown on a company's annual report.*

/rɪˈzɜːv/

pl reserves

▶ **Federal Reserve System, legal reserve**

---

eserve capital *noun* (finance)

hares issued by a company that can only be called upon for ayment when the company is closed down: *call upon reserve apital to pay off the major debts*

/rɪˌzɜːv ˈkæpɪtl/

note no plural

⋈ call upon, use the **reserve capital**

▶ **winding up**

---

eserve currency *noun* (finance/banking)

strong currency kept by governments of other countries to ettle international debts: *use the Deutschmark as a reserve urrency*

/rɪˌzɜːv ˈkʌrənsi/

pl reserve currencies

⋈ hold, keep, use a **reserve currency**

▶ **currency¹**

---

eserve fund *noun* (finance)

rofit put back into a business and used for the purchase of nachinery, etc (ASSETS) and development: *The company has nough in its reserve fund to finance the expansion scheme.*

/rɪˈzɜːv fʌnd/

pl reserve funds

⋈ put money into, take money out of the **reserve fund**

▶ **fund¹ 2, profit, retained profit**

reserve price *noun* (commerce/sales)
the lowest price that a seller will accept for an article that is sold at AUCTION: *The property was withdrawn from sale because it failed to make its reserve price.* ○ *a reserve price of £3 000*

/rɪˈzɜːv praɪs/
pl reserve prices
⋈ achieve, ask, bid above, bid below, reach the **reserve price**

resign *verb* (management/industrial relations)
to give up a job or position: *She has resigned from her post as marketing manager.* ○ *He was asked to resign when the fraud was discovered.*

/rɪˈzaɪn/
resign, resigning, resigned
note transitive and intransitive verb
⋈ be asked, decide, have, offer, threaten to **resign**
▶ **notice 3**

resignation *noun* (management/industrial relations)
the giving up of a job: *She handed in her resignation yesterday.* ○ *His letter of resignation was received this morning.* ○ *Further resignations are expected.*

/ˌrezɪgˈneɪʃn/
pl resignations
⋈ to give, hand in your **resignation**; a letter of **resignation**

resolution *noun* (management)
a decision by members of a company made binding by a formal vote at a meeting: *The resolution was passed at a shareholders' meeting.*

extraordinary resolution a resolution that requires 14 days' notice and the approval of 75% of those voting

ordinary resolution a resolution that requires a majority vote

special resolution a resolution that requires 21 days' notice and the approval of 75% of those voting

/ˌrezəˈluːʃn/
pl resolutions
⋈ give notice of, pass, propose, put forward, vote for a **resolution**

restrict *verb*
to put a limit on something: *restrict the amount of credit given* ○ *The speed limit of heavy goods vehicles is restricted by law.* ○ *Access is restricted to authorized staff only.*

/rɪˈstrɪkt/
restrict, restricting, restricted
note transitive verb
⋈ **restrict** access, borrowing, competition, credit, exports, imports, output, production, spending

restriction *noun*
1 a limit on something: *lift price restrictions on consumer goods* ○ *impose restrictions on importing dangerous chemicals* **2** the act of limiting something: *The importation of alcohol is subject to restriction.*

/rɪˈstrɪkʃn/
1 pl restrictions
⋈ abolish, enforce, impose, lift, raise, remove a **restriction**; currency, trade, travel **restrictions**
2 note not used with *a* or *an*. No plural and used with a singular verb only.

restrictive trade practices *noun* (commerce/law)
agreements between traders that restrict or prevent free competition, eg by controlling prices or the areas where goods may be sold. In the UK, the Restrictive Practices Court will investigate such agreements and allow them to continue only if they are in the public interest: *The government has introduced new legislation on restrictive trade practices.*

/rɪˌstrɪktɪv ˌtreɪd ˈpræktɪsɪz/
note usually plural
⋈ abolish, ban, impose, introduce, lift, remove **restrictive trade practices**
▶ **free trade, Office of Fair**

Trading, single market, third line forcing, trade[1]

---

restructuring *noun* (management)

/ˌriːˈstrʌktʃərɪŋ/

1 major rearrangement of staff, systems or finance within a company or group of companies: *restructuring of the motor industry* ○ *Restructuring resulted in the loss of 500 jobs.* ○ *Because of the recession the company was forced to carry out restructuring.*
2 an instance of this: *The finance division will undergo a restructuring.*

1 note not used with *a* or *an*. No plural and used with a singular verb only.

⧓ complete, extensive, major **restructuring**; **restructuring** costs, plans, proposals

2 note usually singular

⧓ announce, complete, propose a **restructuring**

▶ **reorganization**

---

result¹ *noun*

/rɪˈzʌlt/

the effect or outcome of something: *What was the result of the meeting?* ○ *The market research produced some interesting results.* ○ *This new information could affect the result.*

pl results

⧓ achieve, affect, alter, get, produce, show, sway a **result**

---

result² *verb*

/rɪˈzʌlt/

to occur as the effect or outcome of something: *The grain shortage will result in heavy price increases.* ○ *The company takeover resulted in over 500 redundancies.*

result, resulting, resulted

note intransitive verb

⧓ **result** *in* something

---

results *noun* (accounting/stock exchange)

/rɪˈzʌlts/

the profit or loss made by a company at the end of a trading period: *The board was pleased with the trading results.* ○ *Results are expected to improve in the next financial year.* ○ *announce the end of year results*

note plural noun, used with a plural verb

⧓ annual, company, end of year, financial, half year, sales, trading, yearly **results**; announce, report the **results**; good, improved, poor **results**

▶ **annual report**

---

resume *verb* (management)

/rɪˈzjuːm/

to begin again after a break: *The talks will resume tomorrow.* ○ *They resumed work when new stocks arrived.*

resume, resuming, resumed

note transitive and intransitive verb

⧓ **resume** discussion, negotiations, production, talks, work

▶ **adjourn**

---

résumé *noun* (personnel)

/ˈrezjumeɪ/

(*US*) ▶ **curriculum vitae**

---

retail¹ *noun* (sales)

/ˈriːteɪl/

the sale of goods to the general public, esp in shops: *the retail of consumer goods*

note not used with *a* or *an*. No plural and used with a singular verb only.

▶ **Retail Price Index, wholesale**

---

retail² *adjective, adverb* (sales)

/ˈriːteɪl/

(of a shop, trader, etc) selling to the general public: *The retail*

⧓ a **retail** company, outlet, shop,

trade has suffered during the recession. ○ *The company owns over 1 000 retail outlets throughout the world.* ○ *Did you buy it wholesale or retail?*

store; **retail** goods; the **retail** industry, trade

▶ **retail price, wholesale**

---

retail³ *verb* (sales)

to sell goods to the general public: *These items retail at £5.99.* ○ *We can retail these goods in supermarket chains.*

/ˈriːteɪl/

retail, retailing, retailed

note transitive verb

⋈ **retail** *at, for* (a price); **retail** *in* (a place)

---

retailer *noun* (sales)

a trader, eg a shopkeeper, who buys small quantities of goods from wholesalers to sell to the general public: *a furniture retailer* ○ *a retailer of electrical goods* ○ *Independent retailers are worried about the number of out-of-town supermarkets.*

/ˈriːteɪlə(r)/

pl retailers

⋈ a co-operative, an independent, a large, a small **retailer**

▶ **wholesaler**

---

retail price *noun* (retail)

the money paid for goods by the customer in the shop: *sell goods below the normal retail price*

/ˌriːteɪl ˈpraɪs/

pl retail prices

⋈ normal, recommended **retail price**

▶ **list price, manufacturer's recommended price, price¹, trade price**

Retail Price Index *noun* (finance/economics)

(*UK*) a list, compiled monthly by the Central Statistical Office, of the prices of goods and services in shops bought by average families. The rise and fall of prices on the index is one of the standard measures of the rate of inflation: *This month's Retail Price Index shows a slight rise in the rate of inflation.*

/ˌriːteɪl ˈpraɪs ˌɪndeks/

pl Retail Price Indexes *or* Retail Price Indices

abbr RPI

(also **retail price index**)

▶ **Consumer Price Index, Cost of Living Index, indexation, index-linked, inflation, Producer Price Index**

---

retained profit *noun* (finance/commerce)

part of the annual profit that is not paid out to shareholders as dividend, but reinvested in the company: *Our retained profit will provide capital for the planned growth next year.*

/rɪˌteɪnd ˈprɒfɪt/

note not used with *a* or *an*. No plural and used with a singular verb only.

▶ **profit¹, reserve fund**

---

retire *verb* (personnel)

1 to stop work, esp because of age: *He retired from the bank after 30 years service.* ○ *retire at 65 with a pension* **2** to make an employee stop work, esp because of age: *They retired eight members of staff but did not replace them.*

/rɪˈtaɪə(r)/

retire, retiring, retired

1 note intransitive verb

⋈ **retire** *at* (a certain age); **retire** *from* (a job); **retire** *in* (a number of years)

2 note transitive verb

---

retired bill *noun* (banking)

a bill of exchange that has been withdrawn before its due date, either because it has been paid early or because it has been replaced by a new bill

/rɪˌtaɪəd ˈbɪl/

pl retired bills

▶ **bill of exchange**

---

retirement *noun* (personnel)
the act of stopping work or being asked to stop work and becoming a pensioner: *take early retirement* ○ *The usual age of retirement is 65.*

/rɪˈtaɪəmənt/
note not used with *a* or *an*. No plural and used with a singular verb only.
⋈ **retirement** age; a **retirement** pension; be *in* **retirement**
▶ **pension**

return[1] *noun* (stock exchange)
1 the profit or income from money invested: *These stocks pay a fixed rate of return.* ○ *get a good return on an investment* **2** the profit or income from an investment expressed as a percentage of its cost: *You can expect a 15% return on this sum.* ○ *a future rate of return of 10.5% per annum*

/rɪˈtɜːn/
pl returns
⋈ a good, high, low, poor (rate of) **return**; earn, pay, yield a **return**
▶ **accounting rate of return, annual return, law of diminishing returns, rate of return, returns, tax return,** VAT return *under* **VAT**

return[2] *verb* (sales)
1 to send or take (goods) back to the shop: *These goods have been returned by customers.* **2** to send a cheque back to the bank because the bank refused to pay (HONOUR) it: *The cheque was returned and marked 'refer to drawer'.*

/rɪˈtɜːn/
return, returning, returned
note transitive verb
1 ⋈ **return** damaged, faulty, unsold goods
▶ **refund, sale or return**
2 ▶ **dishonour, refer to drawer**

returnable *adjective* (industry)
that can be returned to its owner, esp containers that can be used again: *There is a deposit paid on these returnable pallets.* ○ *These bottles are non-returnable.*

/rɪˈtɜːnəbl/
⋈ **returnable** bottles, boxes, containers, pallets
opp non-returnable

return on capital *noun* (finance/accounting)
the profits of a business shown as a percentage of total assets less total liabilities: *The return on capital was down slightly at 5.1%.*

/rɪˌtɜːn ɒn ˈkæpɪtl/
note singular noun, used with a singular verb
⋈ a good, high, low, poor **return on capital**
syn return on assets
▶ **capital**

returns *noun* (sales)
1 the profit on a unit of output compared to its cost: *Returns have improved since we installed these computerized machines.* **2** a report of sales, usually daily, weekly or monthly: *These quarterly returns show an improvement in business.* **3** goods sent back to a supplier by a customer because they are unsold or faulty: *These returns were a new line and not popular.*

/rɪˈtɜːnz/
note plural noun, used with a plural verb
1 ⋈ good, high, low, poor **returns**
▶ **law of diminishing returns, return**[1]
2 ⋈ monthly, weekly, yearly **returns**
▶ **annual return**
3 ▶ **sale or return**

Rev. a/c *abbr* (accounting)
revenue account

note used in written English only

revaluation *noun* (finance)
an increase in the value of a currency against other currencies or gold, made by a government with a balance of payments surplus. It results in cheaper imports, but exports are more expensive and less competitive: *The government decided against revaluation.*

/ˌriːvæljuˈeɪʃn/
note not used with *a* or *an*. No plural and used with a singular verb only.
opp devaluation
▶ **exchange rate**

---

revaluation of assets *noun* (accounting)
reassessing a company's assets in terms of their current market value. This is done if the value of the assets has increased or inflation has made them appear unrealistic on the company balance sheet: *The accountant carried out a revaluation of assets.*

/ˌriːvæljuˈeɪʃn əv ˈæsets/
note no plural
⋈ carry out, make a **revaluation of assets**
▶ **net book value**

---

revenue *noun* (finance)
1 money received from the sale of goods or services: *European sales account for 30% of the company's revenue.* ○ *The television company aims to increase its advertising revenue by 5% next year.* **2** money received by a government from taxes: *Cigarette tax is an important source of revenue for the government.*

/ˈrevənjuː/
pl revenues
⋈ increase, provide, raise, reduce **revenue**
1 ▶ **average revenue, income, profit**
2 ▶ **income, Inland Revenue**

---

revenue account *noun* (accounting)
1 the part of a company's accounts where money obtained from the usual trading activity of the company is recorded: *enter figures in the revenue account* **2** an amount of money kept by a government for everyday expenses: *reduce rent arrears in the housing revenue account*

/ˈrevənjuː əˌkaʊnt/
pl revenue accounts
abbr Rev. a/c
note usually singular
▶ **account[1] 1, accounts 1**

---

revenue expenditure *noun* (accounting)
money spent on running a business rather than on land, buildings, machinery (CAPITAL ASSETS): *The revenue expenditure will be written off at the end of this accounting period.*

/ˌrevənjuː ɪkˈspendɪtʃə(r)/
note not used with *a* or *an*. No plural and used with a singular verb only.
▶ **capital expenditure, expenditure, profit and loss account**

---

reverse takeover *noun* (finance/stock exchange)
1 the purchase of a public company by a private company: *There are regulations governing reverse takeovers on the International Stock Exchange.* **2** the purchase of a larger company by a smaller company: *a reverse takeover of a furniture company*

/rɪˌvɜːs ˈteɪkəʊvə(r)/
pl reverse takeovers
▶ **City Code on Takeovers and Mergers, merger, stock exchange, takeover**

---

reversionary annuity *noun* (law/insurance)
an insurance policy paid to a named person after the death of an insured person: *Both husband and wife agreed to take out reversionary annuities.*

/rɪˌvɜːʃənəri əˈnjuːəti/
pl reversionary annuities
⋈ to have, to take out a **reversionary annuity**
▶ **annuity**

---

revolving fund *noun* (finance)
a source of money from which loans are made and then repaid with interest so the fund is maintained and money can continue to be lent: *The work is financed by a revolving fund which gets its revenue from the sale of supplies to other departments.*

/rɪˌvɒlvɪŋ ˈfʌnd/
pl revolving funds
▶ **fund[1] 1**

---

revolving credit *noun* (finance/banking)
a bank credit system that allows someone to take out a loan up to a certain amount at any time. It is automatically renewed when the original debt is paid off: *The bank is offering revolving credit to its long-term customers.*

/rɪˌvɒlvɪŋ ˈkredɪt/
note not used with *a* or *an*. No plural and used with a singular verb only.
⧓ a **revolving credit** account, facility, scheme, system
▶ **bank loan, credit[1] 2, overdraft**

rider *noun* (law/insurance)
an extra clause in a document or contract: *We have added an explanatory rider.*

/ˈraɪdə(r)/
pl riders
⧓ to add, to include a **rider**
▶ **addendum, allonge, annex, appendix**

right *noun* (law)
a legal claim to something or an authority to do something: *The union claims they have a right to strike.* ○ *We are negotiating for exclusive rights to distribute their goods.* ○ *The Consumers' Association safeguards the rights of the consumer.* ○ *Certain shareholders have voting rights in the company.* ○ *There is no right of way across this land.*

/raɪt/
pl rights
⧓ legal, property, trade union, voting **rights**; the **right** to distribute, manufacture, sell (goods); a **right** of access, entry, way
▶ **copyright, intellectual property**

right of action *noun* (law)
the legal authority to bring a case against someone in a court of law: *The creditor has obtained a right of action to recover his debts.*

/ˌraɪt əv ˈækʃn/
note usually singular
▶ **action[1]**

rights issue *noun* (stock exchange)
an offer of new shares made to existing shareholders. Shares are usually offered at a reduced price and can be sold by the shareholders: *The company launched a rights issue to increase funds.* ○ *a one-for-eight rights issue at 50p a share*, ie one share offered for every eight shares already held

/ˈraɪts ˌɪʃuː/
pl rights issues
⧓ announce, launch a **rights issue**
▶ **cum rights, ex-rights, issue[1], scrip issue**

rights letter *noun* (stock exchange)
a document sent to an existing shareholder offering new shares at a reduced price. If the shareholder does not wish to take up the rights, the letter and rights can be sold on the rights market of the stock exchange.

/ˈraɪts ˌletə(r)/
pl rights letters
⧓ receive, sell, take up a **rights letter**

rights manager *noun* (management)
▶ **manager**

/ˈraɪts ˌmænɪdʒə(r)/

riot and civil commotion *noun* (insurance)
a risk not usually covered by insurance policies, unless a special clause has been included: *The broken windows were a result of 'riot and civil commotion' and not covered by the policy.*

/ˌraɪət ənd ˌsɪvl kəˈməʊʃn/
note no plural
▶ **act of God, insurance policy, risk**

rise[1] *noun*
1 an increase; an upward movement: *a rise in the value of the dollar* ○ *Wages were increased to cover the rise in the cost of living.* ○ *There was a rise in unemployment but a shortage of skilled people.*
2 an increase in salary: *She is getting a rise next month.* ○ *Trade union members are asking for a 6% pay rise.*

/raɪz/
note usually singular
1 ⧓ a **rise** in the cost of living, interest rates, prices, productivity, sales, unemployment
2 syn (*US*) raise

⧓ a pay, wage **rise**; ask for, expect, get, need, want a **rise**; a **rise** in salary

---

rise² *verb*

to increase; to move upwards: *Sales have risen by 8% this quarter.* ○ *Prices are rising at an alarming rate.* ○ *West European car sales rose from 1 to 1.5 million.*

/raɪz/

rise, rising, rose, risen

note intransitive verb

⧓ **rise** *by, from, to* (an amount)

---

risk¹ *noun* (insurance)

1 the possibility of loss or damage, esp of money or property: *The property was insured against all risks.* **2** (*stock exchange*) the degree of possibility that an asset may increase or decrease in value: *a high risk investment* ○ *an investment involving a high degree of risk*

at risk 1 in danger of being lost or damaged: *Five thousand jobs are at risk.* ○ *Our new project is at risk because of lack of funds and staff.* **2** (*insurance*) (of goods) likely to be damaged or lost through events already insured against: *The fragile goods were listed as being at risk.*

/rɪsk/

pl risks

⧓ a financial, an insurance **risk**; a high, low **risk**; to run, take a **risk**

---

risk² *verb*

to expose yourself, someone or something to danger, failure or loss: *He risked all his capital in the new business.* ○ *Unless I meet my sales target I risk losing my job.*

/rɪsk/

risk, risking, risked

note transitive verb

---

risk capital *noun* (finance)

▶ **venture capital**

/ˈrɪsk ˌkæpɪtl/

---

rival *noun*

a person or a company that competes with another: *The company is one of our major rivals.* ○ *Unfortunately the contract went to one of our business rivals.*

/ˈraɪvl/

pl rivals

⧓ a **rival** business, company, firm, organization; a close, major, potential **rival**

▶ **competitor**

---

road haulage *noun* (transport)

the transport of heavy loads by lorry: *use road haulage to transport the goods*

/ˈrəʊd ˌhɔːlɪdʒ/

note not used with *a* or *an*. No plural and used with a singular verb only.

⧓ a **road haulage** business, industry

▶ **haulage**

---

robotics *noun* (industry)

(the study of) the use of robots in manufacturing processes

/rəʊˈbɒtɪks/

note singular noun, used with a singular verb

▶ **automation, computerization, cybernetics**

---

rock-bottom *adjective* (commerce)

(*informal*) (of prices, a market or sales) the lowest possible: *That is my lowest offer and a rock-bottom price.* ○ *Car sales reached rock-bottom in January.*

/ˌrɒk ˈbɒtəm/

⧓ reach **rock-bottom**; a **rock-bottom** figure, offer, price

---

rolling stock *noun* (transport)
carriages and wagons used on the railways: *manufacture new rolling stock for the Eurotunnel*

/ˈrəʊlɪŋ stɒk/
note not used with *a* or *an*. No plural and used with a singular verb only.

roll-on roll-off *adjective* (transport)
of a ferry, ship, etc that opens at both ends so that cars and lorries can drive on one end and off at the other: *The roll-on roll-off ferries will have to compete with the Channel Tunnel.*

/rəʊl ˌɒn rəʊl ˈɒf/
abbr RORO
⋈ **roll-on roll-off** cargo vessel, ferry, port facilities, vehicles

ROM *abbr* (computing)
read-only memory

/rɒm/
(also **rom**)
note pronounced as a word.

RORO *abbr* (transport)
roll-on roll-off

/ˈrəʊrəʊ/
note pronounced as a word.

rough *adjective*
1 (of an estimate or calculation) not accurate: *I can give you a rough estimate now, but it may be better to wait for the quotation.*
2 (of a letter or a document) approximate or unfinished: *I'll send you a rough draft of the letter for your comments.*

/rʌf/
1 ⋈ a **rough** calculation, estimate, figure, quote
2 ⋈ a **rough** copy, draft

round figures *noun* (accounting)
(of a number) correct to the nearest 10 or 100: *It will be £2 989, or £3 000 in round figures.* ○ *Give me the sales estimates in round figures.*

/ˌraʊnd ˈfɪgəz/
note plural noun, used with a plural verb
⋈ *in* **round figures**
syn round numbers

route *noun* (transport/shipping)
a way taken or planned from one place to another: *Shipping routes in the channel are very busy.* ○ *Heavy goods vehicles must use an alternative route.* ○ *take the main route north*
en route on the way: *The plane calls at Delhi en route to Hong Kong.*

/ru:t/
pl routes
⋈ an airline, a bus, a plane, a shipping **route**; a busy, main, popular, regular **route**; a **route** *from, to, through, via* (a place)

routine[1] *noun*
a fixed way of doing something: *carry out safety checks according to a strict routine* ○ *This new office equipment will mean a change of routine.*

/ru:ˈti:n/
pl routines
⋈ a daily, set, usual **routine**; follow, stick to a **routine**

routine[2] *adjective*
normal; usual; regular: *We noticed the machine fault during a routine inspection.* ○ *follow a series of routine procedures* ○ *make a number of routine calls to major sales outlets* ○ *The work is routine but it's still important.*

/ru:ˈti:n/
⋈ a **routine** call, check, duty, inspection, task; **routine** work

Royal Mint *noun* (finance)
the organization in the UK that has the sole right to make English coins and bank notes: *coins made by the Royal Mint*

/ˌrɔɪəl ˈmɪnt/

royalty *noun* (finance/law)
1 a sum paid to the owner of a COPYRIGHT or PATENT: *The novelist received a royalty of 8% from the sales of her book.* **2** a sum paid to a landowner for the right to extract oil, coal, etc: *The oil royalties were higher than expected.*

/ˈrɔɪəlti/
pl royalties
⋈ pay, receive **royalties**
▶ **copyright, intellectual property, patent**

RPI *abbr* (finance/economics)
Retail Price Index

/ˌɑː piː ˈaɪ/

RRP *abbr* (retail)
recommended retail price

/ˌɑːr ɑː ˈpiː/
(also **RP**)

run[1] *verb* (management)
1 to control a business, an organization, etc; to manage: *Who runs the firm now?* ○ *He has no idea how to run a successful business.* ○ *The hotel is run by two brothers.* **2** (of a machine) to work or to be in use: *It's cheaper to keep the machines running than to turn them off.* **3** to be in operation or to be valid: *The contract will run for three years.* **4** (*management*) (of a bus, train, etc) to make a regular journey: *The bus to Manchester runs hourly.*

run out of something to use up or finish something: *We've run out of paper.* ○ *The printer has run out of ink.*

/rʌn/
run, running, ran, run
1 note transitive verb
⋈ **run** a business, a company, a firm, an organization, a shop
▶ **control**[1], **manage**
2 note transitive and intransitive verb
⋈ **run** a car, computer, machine, printer
3 note intransitive verb
⋈ a contract, lease **runs**
4 ⋈ irregularly, regularly: **run** *from, to* (a place)

run[2] *noun*
1 (*sales*) a rush to buy a product: *There has been a run on petrol this morning.* **2** (*shipping/transport*) a journey: *This ship has a regular run from Southampton to Saudi.*

/rʌn/
pl runs
⋈ a **run** *from, to* (a place)

running broker *noun* (stock exchange)
a person who acts for buyers and sellers of bills of exchange and who arranges payment of the bills for a fee

/ˌrʌnɪŋ ˈbrəʊkə(r)/
pl running brokers
▶ **agent, bill of exchange, broker**

running costs *noun* (finance/industry)
▶ **overheads**

/ˈrʌnɪŋ kɒsts/

running-down clause *noun* (insurance/shipping)
a condition in a marine insurance policy stating that insurance will be paid if a ship collides with another vessel: *The policy contains a running-down clause.*

/ˌrʌnɪŋ ˈdaʊn klɔːz/
pl running-down clauses
▶ **free of all average, marine insurance**

Ss

sack[1] *noun* (industrial relations)
(*informal*) **the sack** dismissal from a job: *If he is late again he will get the sack.* ○ *She gave them the sack.*

/ðə ˈsæk/
note not used with *a* or *an*. No plural and used with a singular verb only.
⋈ be threatened with, get, give (someone) the **sack**

sack[2] *verb* (industrial relations)
(*informal*) to remove someone from a job: *He was sacked for stealing from company funds.* ○ *I have decided to sack my assistant for incompetence.*

/sæk/
sack, sacking, sacked
note transitive verb
⋈ be **sacked** *by* (someone), *for* (something), *from* (a job)

syn fire

► **dismiss**

SAE *abbr*

stamped addressed envelope

/ˌes eɪ ˈiː/

note pronounced as individual letters

---

safe *noun*

a strong lockable box or cabinet for storing valuable documents, money, etc: *This contract must be kept in the safe.*

/seɪf/

pl safes

⋈ a bank, fireproof, night **safe**

► **strong-room**

---

safe deposit *noun*

a safe or strong, locked room in a bank where valuable documents, jewels, etc can be stored: *I'm going to the bank to put this in (the) safe deposit.* ○ *Most banks provide a safe deposit service.*

/ˈseɪf dɪˌpɒzɪt/

pl safe deposits

⋈ keep, put, store something in (a) **safe deposit**

► **bank deposit, deposit[1]**

---

safe deposit box *noun*

a small lockable box that can be rented to keep documents, money or jewellery safe. It may be kept at a safe deposit: *The will is in my safe deposit box.*

/ˌseɪf dɪˈpɒzɪt bɒks/

pl safe deposit boxes

⋈ lock, rent, unlock, use a **safe deposit box**

► **safe**

---

safety *noun* (health and safety)

not being dangerous or in danger: *We carry out regular safety checks on all our equipment.* ○ *You must take the necessary safety precautions before handling dangerous chemicals.*

/ˈseɪfti/

note not used with *a* or *an*. No plural and used with a singular verb only.

⋈ **safety** checks, levels, limits, margins, measures, precautions, regulations, standards, tests

► **health and safety**

---

salary *noun*

a regular fixed payment for work or services, usually paid monthly by cheque or straight into a bank account: *The starting salary is £15 000 per annum.* ○ *She is much better off since her salary increase.*

/ˈsæləri/

pl salaries

⋈ an annual, a monthly **salary**; a drop, an increase, a rise in **salary**; **a salary** agreement

► **pay[2], wage**

---

sale *noun*

1 selling or being sold; the exchange of items for money: *The cash sale of these goods will help our bank balance.* ○ *the sale of cars, machinery, shares, etc* **2** a time when goods are sold at a lower price than usual: *This stock will be cleared at a reduced price during the summer sales.* ○ *What is the sale price?*

for sale intended to be sold: *Are all these items for sale?* ○ *display only, not for sale*

in the sale among the goods being sold at a cheaper price than usual: *I like this coat but it's not in the sale.*

make a sale to sell something: *Business is bad. I haven't made a sale all week.*

on sale available or ready to be sold: *This magazine is on sale every Thursday.*

/seɪl/

pl sales

1 ► **account sale, bill of sale, cash sale, credit sale, direct sale, point of sale, sales**

2 ⋈ end of season, January, etc, spring, etc **sale(s)**

► **clearance sale, closing down sale**

up for sale (usually of property) available to be bought: *The hotel is up for sale.*

---

sale as seen *noun* (sales)
the sale of goods that have been inspected by the buyer. There is no guarantee of quality or condition by the seller: *The goods are for sale as seen and cannot be returned.*

/ˌseɪl əz ˈsiːn/
note no plural
▶ **sale by description, sale by sample**

---

sale by description *noun* (sales)
goods not seen but sold on the understanding that a true description of their quality and condition is given in the contract of sale: *We must check the goods on arrival as they were for sale by description and must fulfil the contract.*

/ˌseɪl baɪ dəˈskrɪpʃn/
note no plural
▶ **sale as seen, sale by sample**

---

sale by sample *noun* (sales)
goods sold on the understanding that they match the quality and condition of a specimen available for inspection: *These goods are for sale by sample.*

/ˌseɪl baɪ ˈsɑːmpl/
note no plural
▶ **sale as seen, sale by description**

---

sale or return *noun* (sales)
a system where the supplier agrees to take back any goods that a shop has failed to sell. Only the goods that have been sold are paid for: *To test the market for this product it is offered on a sale or return basis.*

/ˌseɪl ɔː rɪˈtɜːn/
note no plural
⧓ offer, take (something) *on* **sale or return**
▶ **return[2] 1, see-safe**

---

sales *noun* (sales)
1 the amount of goods or services sold: *Sales are up/down this month.* ○ *Car sales have decreased because of the recession.* ○ *We had a major sales increase this year.* **2** the activity of selling; part of a company that deals with this: *She works in sales.* ○ *sales staff* ○ *I want to speak to someone in the sales department.*

/seɪlz/
note plural noun, used with a plural verb
1 ⧓ a drop, a fall, an increase, a rise in **sales**
▶ **foreign sales, home sales**
2 ⧓ a **sales** department, manager, team
▶ **telesales**

---

sales analysis *noun* (sales/accounting)
the use of reports and statistics of items sold and where they sell or fail to sell with the aim of increasing future sales: *We cannot tell whether sales of all our products are as high as last year until we have done our sales analysis.*

/ˈseɪlz əˌnæləsɪs/
pl sales analyses
⧓ carry out, conduct, do a **sales analysis**
▶ **analysis**

---

sales campaign *noun* (sales)
a group of organized activities (SALES PROMOTIONS) planned to increase sales, sometimes for a particular product, section of the market or geographical area: *We need to draw up a sales campaign for our Spanish agents.*

/ˈseɪlz kæmˌpeɪn/
pl sales campaigns
⧓ conduct, launch, plan a **sales campaign**
▶ **campaign[1], promotion 1, sales drive**

---

sales conference *noun* (sales)
a meeting of sales representatives, sales managers and other, esp publicity, staff held to discuss past results and future plans: *We are holding our annual sales conference in June this year.*

/ˈseɪlz ˌkɒnfərəns/
pl sales conferences
⧓ attend, hold a **sales conference**
▶ **conference, sales**

---

sales day book *noun* (accounting)
▶ **day book**

/ˌseɪlz ˈdeɪ bʊk/

---

sales drive *noun* (sales)
an organized effort to increase sales: *A sales drive will put us ahead of the competition.* ○ *A major advertising campaign will form part of our sales drive.*

/ˈseɪlz draɪv/
pl sales drives
⋈ launch, mount, organize, plan a **sales drive**
▶ **sales campaign**

---

sales ledger *noun* (accounting)
a book or a computer file in which the money owed or paid to a company for the goods it sells is recorded: *make an entry in the sales ledger*

/ˈseɪlz ˌledʒə(r)/
pl sales ledgers
⋈ a **sales ledger** clerk, department
▶ **bought ledger, ledger, nominal ledger**

---

sales literature *noun* (sales/advertising/marketing)
printed information about a product or a service for possible customers, such as leaflets, brochures or pamphlets: *Please help yourself to our sales literature.* ○ *pick some sales literature from an exhibition stand*

/ˈseɪlz ˌlɪtrətʃə(r)/
note not used with *a* or *an*. No plural and used with a singular verb only.
▶ **literature**

---

salesman, salesperson, saleswoman *noun* (sales)
1 a person who sells goods or services to the public: *The computer saleswoman was very helpful.* ○ *You need to contact the salesperson who dealt with your original order.* **2** a person who calls upon retailers and other potential customers to sell goods or services: *The salesman calls once a month.*

/ˈseɪlzmən, ˈseɪlzˌpɜːsn, ˈseɪlzˌwʊmən/
pl salesmen, salespeople, saleswomen
⋈ an insurance, a travelling **salesman**
▶ **commercial traveller, door-to-door salesman, sales representative**

---

sales manager *noun* (sales)
the person responsible for the sales staff and their work: *The sales manager has called a meeting about the new product range.*

/ˌseɪlz ˈmænɪdʒə(r)/
pl sales managers
⋈ an assistant, a regional, a senior **sales manager**
▶ **manager**

---

salesmanship *noun* (sales)
the skill of persuading customers to buy: *Her/his salesmanship earned her/him very high commission.*

/ˈseɪlzmənʃɪp/
note not used with *a* or *an*. No plural and used with a singular verb only.
⋈ bad, good **salesmanship**

---

sales promotion *noun* (sales)
a group of activities that are intended to improve sales, sometimes including advertising, organizing competitions, providing free gifts and samples. These promotions may form part of a wider SALES CAMPAIGN: *The exhibition is part of our sales promotion.*

/ˈseɪlz prəˌməʊʃn/
pl sales promotions
⋈ carry out, organize, plan a **sales promotion**
▶ **advertising, promotion 1**

---

sales quota *noun* (sales)
the number of items to be sold by a particular salesperson or in a particular area within a given time: *Sales representatives will receive extra commission once the sales quota has been reached.*

/ˈseɪlz ˌkwəʊtə/
pl sales quotas
⋈ exceed, fix, reach a **sales quota**; an annual, a home, a monthly, an overseas **sales quota**
▶ **quota 1, target[1] 1**

---

sales representative *noun* (sales)
a person who sells goods or services by visiting potential buyers, and usually receives a fee (a COMMISSION) for each item sold: *The sales representative will call on Tuesday.*

/ˈseɪlz reprɪˌzentətɪv/
pl sales representatives
abbr sales rep, rep
⋈ work as a **sales representative**
syn trade representative
▶ **commercial traveller, door-to-door salesman, travelling salesman**

---

sales territory *noun* (sales)
a geographical area, section of the market or group of products for which a SALES REPRESENTATIVE is responsible: *The size of my sales territory has recently been increased.*

/ˈseɪlz ˌterətri/
pl sales territories
⋈ be responsible for, look after a **sales territory**

---

salvage[1] *noun*
1 (*shipping*) the rescue of a ship or its cargo: *Salvage of the ship was delayed by the tides.* **2** the rescue of property from fire or flood: *There was sufficient salvage from the fire to send to auction.* **3** cargo or property that has been rescued: *The salvage was inspected and then taken away.*

/ˈsælvɪdʒ/
note not used with *a* or *an*. No plural and used with a singular verb only.
⋈ **salvage** company, goods, tug
▶ **salvage company, salvage money, salvage value**

---

salvage[2] *verb* (shipping)
to save goods or a ship from being destroyed: *The ship will be salvaged when the weather improves.*

/ˈsælvɪdʒ/
salvage, salvaging, salvaged
note transitive verb
⋈ **salvage** cargo, goods, a ship

---

salvage company *noun* (shipping)
an organization that rescues damaged goods and ships for a reward paid by the owners: *A fee has been agreed by the owners and the salvage company.*

/ˈsælvɪdʒ ˌkʌmpəni/
pl salvage companies
syn salvor

---

salvage money *noun* (shipping)
the reward paid by the owners of a rescued ship or goods to the person or organization that saved it/them: *The owners of the ship have no claim on the salvage money, despite their efforts in the rescue.*

/ˈsælvɪdʒ ˌmʌni/
note not used with *a* or *an*. No plural and used with a singular verb only.
syn salvage
⋈ claim, owe, pay **salvage money**

---

salvage value *noun* (shipping/insurance)
the worth of rescued goods, cargo or a ship. It may be claimed by the insurers as part of their settlement.

/ˈsælvɪdʒ ˌvælju:/
note not used with *a* or *an*. No plural and used with a singular verb only.
▶ **partial loss, total loss**

---

sample[1] *noun* (sales/marketing)

1 a single item or part of a whole product that can be looked at to see what the rest is like: *The fabric samples were of good quality, and we are ready to order.* ○ *a sample book/book of samples*, ie of fabrics/paper/designs, etc **2** (*marketing*) a small part of a population taken to represent the whole, usually for MARKET RESEARCH: *A larger sample will give more accurate results.*

/ˈsɑːmpl/
pl samples
⧓ a **sample** of (something); **sample** pack; a random, a representative **sample**; select, take, test, try a **sample**
▶ **free sample, sale by sample**

---

sample[2] *verb*

1 (*sales*) to test a product by taking a small part of it: *We must sample the wine before we leave.* **2** (*marketing*) to ask a small part of the population in order to find out what the rest might think: *We have sampled opinion among the staff about the new working conditions.*

/ˈsɑːmpl/
sample, sampling, sampled
1 note transitive verb
⧓ **sample** food, goods, products
2 ⧓ a **sample** opinion, reaction, response

---

sanction *noun*

a measure taken to force a country to obey international law: *Sanctions were imposed for six months and then lifted.*

/ˈsæŋkʃn/
pl sanctions
⧓ financial, legal, official, political, trade **sanctions**; apply, enforce, impose, lift, maintain, oppose **sanctions**
▶ **ban**[2], **embargo, economic sanctions**

---

sandwich course *noun* (personnel)

a form of training in which time spent at a college alternates with practical work in a company: *attend a three-year sandwich course where the second year is spent with an engineering firm*

/ˈsænwɪdʒ kɔːs/
pl sandwich courses
⧓ attend, be on, run a **sandwich course**
▶ **block release, day release, training**

---

sans recours *adjective, adverb* (law/stock exchange)

▶ **without recourse**

/sænz rɪˈkɔːs/

---

saturate *verb*

to fill something with more than is needed: *The market is saturated with used cars.* ○ *saturate the market with cheap goods*

/ˈsætʃəreɪt/
saturate, saturating, saturated
note transitive verb
⧓ **saturate** (the market) *with* something
▶ **glut**[2]

---

saturation campaign *noun* (advertising/marketing)

the intensive use of mass media in a single advertising drive to make people fully aware of a product or service: *A saturation campaign will help launch this product.*

/ˌsætʃəˈreɪʃn kæmˌpeɪn /
pl saturation campaigns
⧓ conduct, launch, mount, plan a **saturation campaign**
▶ **campaign**[1]

---

saturation point *noun* (marketing)

the level at which a market cannot expand any more and further sales will be limited to replacement needs: *The market has reached saturation point.*

/ˌsætʃəˈreɪʃn pɔɪnt/
note singular noun, used with a singular verb
⧓ achieve, reach **saturation point**

---

save *verb*
/seɪv/
save, saving, saved

1 to keep money for future use; not spend: *They are saving for a holiday.* ○ *New interest rates are encouraging people to save.* **2** to use less; to avoid waste: *to save time* ○ *to save electricity* **3** (*computing*) to store information on a computer hard disk or floppy disk: *Do not forget to save the document before you switch off the machine.* ○ *Work that is not saved is lost when you turn off the computer.*

1 note intransitive verb
⋈ **save** *for* something
2 note transitive verb
⋈ **save** costs, expenditure, expenses, money
3 note transitive verb
⋈ **save** a copy, document, file
▶ **back up**

---

savings account *noun* (banking)
/ˈseɪvɪŋz əˌkaʊnt/
pl savings accounts

an account with a bank or building society for personal savings. The interest is usually higher than that paid on a DEPOSIT ACCOUNT and there may be restrictions on when money can be taken out: *open a savings account with a building society*

⋈ draw money out of, pay money into, withdraw money from a **savings account**
▶ **account[1] 2, bank account, building society, current account 1, deposit account**

---

savings and loan association *noun* (banking)
/ˌseɪvɪŋz ənd ˈləʊn əˌsəʊsiˌeɪʃn/

(*US*) ▶ **building society**

---

savings bank *noun* (banking)
/ˈseɪvɪŋz ˌbæŋk/
pl savings banks

a financial institution that specializes in providing services such as SAVINGS ACCOUNTS as opposed to general banking services: *deposit money in a savings bank*

⋈ put money into, take money out of a **savings bank**
▶ **bank[1]**

---

scab *noun* (industrial relations)
/skæb/

(*informal*) ▶ **blackleg**

---

scam *noun*
/skæm/
pl scams

(*informal*) a dishonest scheme; a case of fraud: *A number of employees were involved in a scam of selling confidential information about the company.*

⋈ be involved in, run, uncover a **scam**
▶ **racket**

---

scarcity value *noun* (sales)
/ˈskeəsəti ˌvælju:/
note not used with *a* or *an*. No plural and used with a singular verb only.

the worth of something that is high when demand is high and supply is low: *When the political situation changes these goods will lose their scarcity value.*

⋈ increase, raise, reduce the **scarcity value**
▶ **value[1] 2**

---

schedule[1] *noun*
/ˈʃedju:l; *US* ˈskedʒu:l/
pl schedules

1 a plan of events or work to be done at or within a certain time: *The majority of flights arrive and depart on schedule* (ie at the expected time). ○ *A factory visit is included on the schedule.* ○ *According to the schedule, she should arrive at 10 am.* ○ *I have a very busy schedule today* (ie lots of things to do). **2** a list, usually added on to a contract or similar document: *Our price schedule is attached.* ○ *The terms and conditions are set out in schedule 1 of this agreement.*

1 ⋈ a busy, heavy, hectic, tight **schedule**; ahead of, behind, on **schedule**; advertising, factory, production, work **schedule**
▶ **deadline, timetable**

2 ⧓ attach, enclose a **schedule**
► **tax schedule**

---

schedule² *verb* (management)
to arrange the time when something will happen: *The plane is scheduled to arrive at 9.24 am.* ○ *Let's schedule the meeting for tomorrow.*

/ˈʃedjuːl; *US* ˈskedʒuːl/
schedule, scheduling, scheduled
note transitive verb
⧓ **schedule** a meeting, project, talk

---

scorched earth policy *noun* (finance)
an extreme method of putting off an unwanted takeover bid. A reversible action, such as borrowing money at very high interest rates, is used to make the balance sheet or profitability seem less attractive.

/ˌskɔːtʃt ˈɜːθ ˌpɒləsi/
pl scorched earth policies
⧓ carry out, use a **scorched earth policy**
► **poison pill, takeover bid**

SCOUT *abbr* (international trade)
Shared Currency Option Under Tender

/skaʊt/
note pronounced as a word

---

scrap¹ *noun* (industry)
waste materials, esp those with some recycling value: *The car was sold for scrap.* ○ *Scrap computer paper fetches a good price.*

/skræp/
note not used with *a* or *an*. No plural and used with a singular verb only.
⧓ **scrap** metal, paper; a **scrap** dealer, merchant, yard
► **recycle, waste¹**

---

scrap² *verb*
to throw away something or stop working on a task: *They had to scrap the old designs.* ○ *We'll have to scrap our plans to move.*

/skræp/
scrap, scrapping, scrapped
note transitive verb
► **waste³**

---

scrap value *noun* (sales)
the worth of an item as waste material to be recycled: *The scrap value of the car was £500.*

/ˈskræp ˌvæljuː/
note singular noun, used with a singular verb
► **value² 2**

---

screen¹ *noun* (computing)
a blank surface on which computer data or television pictures can be shown: *A computer with a large screen is much easier to use.* ○ *I prefer to work on screen* (ie as opposed to writing, designing, etc on paper).

/skriːn/
pl screens
⧓ bring (information) up on, call (information) up on **screen**; a large, small **screen**
► **computer, monitor, visual display unit**

---

screen² *verb*
1 to ensure that a candidate is suitable for a job: *The applications had to be screened by the police.* **2** (*management*) to choose the best new product for development by testing against factors which are known to be successful

/skriːn/
screen, screening, screened
note transitive verb

---

scrip *noun* (stock exchange)
a certificate proving ownership of stocks, shares and bonds

/skrɪp/
pl scrips
⧓ issue, present, receive a **scrip**

scrip issue *noun* (stock exchange)
an issue of free shares given to existing shareholders: *a one-for-eight scrip issue*, ie one free share given for every eight shares already held ○ *a scrip issue of one share for every twenty already held*

/ˈskrɪp ˌɪʃuː/
pl scrip issues
syn (*US*) stock split, bonus issue, capitalization issue, free issue
▶ **ex-scrip, issue**[1], **rights issue**

---

scroll *verb* (computing)
to move text up and down on a computer screen to find the part you want: *If you scroll (through) the text we can look at the next set of data.* ○ *scroll down to the third paragraph*

/skrəʊl/
scroll, scrolling, scrolled
note intransitive verb
⋈ **scroll** data, a document, a file, (through) a text; **scroll** down, up

---

s.d. *abbr* (commerce)
short delivery

/ˌes ˈdiː/

SEAF *abbr* (stock exchange)
Stock Exchange Automatic Exchange Facility

note used in written English only

---

seal[1] *noun* (law)
a piece of paper, metal or wax attached to a document to show it is genuine, or used to close an envelope or parcel to prevent it from being opened by the wrong person: *An official seal is required for this document.* ○ *attach a seal next to the signature*

/siːl/
pl seals
⋈ affix, attach a **seal**

---

seal[2] *verb*
1 to close something in such a way that it can only be torn or broken open: *The contract was sealed in an envelope.* **2** to stamp a document with a seal, or to attach a seal to something

/siːl/
seal, sealing, sealed
note transitive verb
⋈ **seal** a document, letter

SEAQ *abbr* (stock exchange)
Stock Exchange Automated Quotations System

note used in written English only

---

season *noun*
a time of year marked by particular activities or conditions: *The shops are well stocked for the Christmas season.* ○ *take a holiday out of season*, ie when most people do not take their holidays

dead season a quiet time for business: *Those dresses will not sell now as it is a dead season.*

high season a time when business is expected to be good: *It is high season, and you will need to book a hotel room in advance.* ○ *Holiday prices are higher in the peak season.*

/ˈsiːzn/
pl seasons
⋈ autumn, Christmas, holiday, spring, summer, winter **season**

---

seasonal *adjective*
associated with or happening at a particular time of year: *We must control our stock to allow for seasonal demand.* ○ *Many department stores employ seasonal staff at Christmas time.*

/ˈsiːzənl/
⋈ **seasonal** employment, staff, trade, unemployment, work, workers

---

seasonal rate *noun* (advertising)
a variation in prices according to the time of year: *The seasonal rate is too high for us to advertise in the colour supplement.*

/ˌsiːzənl ˈreɪt/
pl seasonal rates
▶ **rate 1**

SEC *abbr* (finance)
Securities and Exchange Commission

/ˌes iː ˈsiː/

---

abbr abbreviation **pl** plural ⋈ collocate (*word often used with the headword*)

second[1] *verb* (management)
to support an idea put forward by somebody else at a meeting: *Will anybody second this motion?*

seconder a person who supports a motion: *The names of the proposer and seconder of this motion must remain secret.*

/ˈsekənd/
second, seconding, seconded
note transitive verb
⋈ **second** a motion, proposal
▶ **oppose, propose**

---

second[2] *verb* (personnel)
to transfer an employee to another organization or a government department for an agreed period of time: *She was seconded to the health authority for one year.* ○ *They seconded him from British Aerospace.*

/sɪˈkɒnd/
second, seconding, seconded
note transitive verb
⋈ **second** someone from/to (something)
▶ **secondment, transfer**[2] **3**

---

secondary data *noun* (advertising/management)
information already collected for one purpose and now used by another researcher for a different project: *We used secondary data obtained from company records.*

/ˌsekəndri ˈdeɪtə/
note not used with *a* or *an*. No plural and used with a singular verb only.
⋈ acquire, make use of, obtain, use **secondary data**

---

secondary industry *noun* (industry)
▶ **industry**

/ˌsekəndri ˈɪn dəstri/

---

secondary market *noun* (stock exchange)
a stock exchange in which existing securities, as opposed to new issues, are traded: *securities traded on the secondary market*

/ˌsekəndri ˈmɑːkɪt/
pl secondary markets
▶ **market**[1]**, primary market**

---

secondary picketing *noun* (industrial relations)
preventing workers not involved in a strike from working or from supplying goods to the organization where the strike is held: *Secondary picketing is now illegal in the UK.*

/ˌsekəndri ˈpɪkɪtɪŋ/
note not used with *a* or *an*. No plural and used with a singular verb only.
⋈ carry out, prevent **secondary picketing**
▶ **picket**[1]**, strike**[1]

---

secondary production *noun* (industry)
the production of goods for sale from raw materials, eg wood, stone and metals: *Car manufacturing is a form of secondary production.*

/ˌsekəndri prəˈdʌkʃn/
note not used with *a* or *an*. No plural and used with a singular verb only.
▶ **primary production, production**

---

secondment *noun* (industrial relations)
a period of time spent with another organization or government department: *He enjoyed his secondment to the Paris branch.* ○ *a six months' secondment*

/sɪˈkɒndmənt/
note usually singular
⋈ on **secondment**
▶ **second, transfer**[1] **3**

---

secretarial *adjective* (administration)
of or relating to the work of a secretary: *apply for a secretarial job*

/ˌsekrəˈteəriəl/
⋈ **secretarial** duties, job, position, skills, staff, work, workers
▶ **clerical**

secretary *noun* (office practice)
an employee who works in an office, usually for another person, and deals with letters, typing, filing, answering the telephone and arranging meetings: *My secretary will make an appointment for you.*

/ˈsekrətri/
pl secretaries
abbr sec.
⧓ personal, private **secretary**
▶ **company secretary, personal assistant**

sector *noun* (economics)
a part of a country's economy: *The agricultural sector in western nations is highly subsidized.*

/ˈsektə(r)/
pl sectors
⧓ agricultural, banking, insurance, manufacturing, retail **sector**
▶ **corporate sector, private sector, public sector**

secured creditor *noun* (banking)
a person who is owed money, but has a legal right to property belonging to the DEBTOR if the money is not repaid

/sɪˌkjʊəd ˈkredɪtə(r)/
pl secured creditors
▶ **creditor, unsecured creditor**

secured debenture *noun* (stock exchange/banking)
a loan made to a company, using the assets of the company as security

/sɪˌkjʊəd dɪˈbentʃə(r)/
pl secured debentures
⧓ hold, issue a **secured debenture**
syn mortgage debenture
▶ **debenture, unsecured debenture**

secured debt *noun* (banking/finance)
an amount of money owed, for which an item of value (an ASSET) has been given in case the money is not repaid

/sɪˌkjʊəd ˈdet/
pl secured debts
⧓ pay back, pay off, repay a **secured debt**
syn secured liability
▶ **bad debt, debt, unsecured debt**

secured loan *noun* (banking)
money that has been lent when an item of value (an ASSET), eg property is used as a guarantee in case the loan is not repaid

/sɪˌkjʊəd ˈləʊn/
pl secured loans
▶ **loan[1], mortgage**

securities *noun* (stock exchange)
▶ **security 1**

/sɪˈkjʊərətiz/

Securities and Futures Authority *noun* (finance/stock exchange)
a SELF-REGULATORY ORGANIZATION that monitors and regulates trading in the securities and futures markets

/sɪˌkjʊərətiz ənd ˈfjuːtʃəz ɔːˌθɒrəti/
abbr SFA
▶ **Financial Intermediaries, Managers and Brokers Regulatory Association, Investment Management Regulatory Organization, Life Assurance and Unit Trust Regulatory Organization, Securities and Investment Board, self-regulatory organization**

Securities and Investment Board *noun* (finance/stock exchange)
(*UK*) an organization that regulates the UK financial markets, makes sure they obey the Financial Services Act (1986) and protects investors from fraud. The Securities and Investment Board is also responsible for a number of SELF-REGULATORY ORGANIZATIONS.

/sɪˌkjʊərətiz ənd ɪnˈvestmənt bɔːd/
abbr SIB
note pronounced as separate letters
▶ **Financial Intermediaries, Managers and Brokers Regulatory Association, Investment Management Regulatory Organization, Life Assurance and Unit Trust Regulatory Organization, Securities and Futures Authority**

Securities Exchange Commission *noun* (stock exchange)
(*US*) an organization in the US that controls and administers the activities of stockbrokers and financial traders. It monitors TAKEOVERS and protects investors from fraud.

/sɪˌkjʊərətiz ɪksˈtʃeɪndʒ kəˌmɪʃn/
abbr SEC
▶ **exchange[1] 2**

---

securities market *noun* (stock exchange)
a place where stocks and shares can be bought and sold; a stock exchange: *The securities market was active today.*

/sɪˈkjʊərətiz ˌmɑːkɪt/
pl securities markets
▶ **market[1], security 1**

---

securitization *noun* (banking/finance/stock exchange)
the issue and trading of securities by large companies as a way of raising money instead of obtaining a bank loan: *Improved technology has increased the use of securitization.*

/sɪˌkjʊərətaɪˈzeɪʃn/
note singular noun, used with a singular verb
▶ **security 1**

---

security *noun*
1 (*stock exchange*) (**a**) an investment or item of financial value (an ASSET), esp a stock, share or debenture, that can be bought and sold on a stock exchange: *a firm dealing in securities* (**b**) a certificate or document proving ownership of one of these **2** something that protects or is protected from loss or attack: *job security* ○ *airport security* ○ *a security van*, ie for transporting money **3** (*finance*) property or an item of financial value (an ASSET) that can be claimed by a person, bank or other organization if a loan is not repaid: *What do you offer as security for this loan?*

/sɪˈkjʊərəti/
1 note usually plural
⋈ buy, deal in, issue, sell, trade in **securities**; a **securities** business, company, dealer, firm, house
▶ **bond, convertible security, debenture, fixed interest security, gilts, listed securities, undated security, unlisted securities**
2 note not used with *a* or *an*. No plural and used with a singular verb only.
⋈ **security** measures, procedures
3 note not used with *a* or *an*. No plural and used with a singular verb only.
▶ **collateral, guarantee[1] 3, surety**

---

security of tenure *noun* (law)
▶ **tenure**

/sɪˌkjʊərəti əv ˈtenjə(r)/

---

seed capital *noun* (management)
money needed for research and development before a new

/ˈsiːd ˌkæpɪtl/
note not used with *a* or *an*. No plural and used with a singular

company is started: *Our seed capital will help us to draw up a business plan.*

verb only.

▶ **capital**

---

segmentation *noun* (marketing)

▶ **market segmentation**

/ˌsegmenˈteɪʃn/

---

selection committee *noun* (personnel)

a group of people appointed to choose someone or something, esp a person for a job: *All the candidates for the new job must be seen by the selection committee.* ○ *The selection committee has/have made their decision.*

/səˈlekʃn kəˌmɪti/

note used with a singular or plural verb

⋈ interviewed, chosen by a **selection committee**

syn selection board, selection panel

▶ **committee**

---

selection procedure *noun* (personnel)

the methods used when choosing someone or something, esp a person for a job: *We try to avoid lengthy selection procedures by using an employment agency.*

/səˈlekʃn prəˌsiːdʒə(r)/

pl selection procedures

▶ **interview[1], recruitment**

---

self *noun* (banking)

word written on a cheque to tell the bank to pay the person who has signed the cheque (the DRAWER)

/self/

note singular noun, used with a singular verb

⋈ pay **self**

---

self-assembly *adjective*

(of furniture) that is bought in parts that have to be fitted together by the buyer: *self-assembly kitchen units*

/ˌself əˈsembli/

⋈ **self-assembly** furniture, units

▶ **kit 2**

---

self-employed *adjective* (personnel)

(relating to) someone who works for her/himself and is not employed by a company: *He is a self-employed plumber.* ○ *She used to work for a design agency, but now she is self-employed.*

/ˌself ɪmˈplɔɪd/

▶ **cottage industry, freelance**

---

self-financing *adjective* (finance)

of a company or project that can produce enough income to pay all its costs and does not need to borrow or receive money from another department, organization or government fund: *Our move into this new market must be self-financing.* ○ *We hope to become self-financing within three years.*

/ˌself faɪˈnænsɪŋ, self ˈfaɪnænsɪŋ/

⋈ a **self-financing** business, company, project

syn auto-financing

---

self-liquidating *adjective*

1 (*banking/finance*) of a loan that is used to finance a project, the profits from which will be used to repay the loan and interest in a short time: *The loan to this company is self-liquidating, and will be repaid when the goods are sold.* **2** (*accounting*) of an asset that will earn its original cost in a fixed period of time: *The new computer will be self-liquidating because it will save us so much time.*
3 (*marketing*) of a free gift offered with a product that is designed to pay for itself and some of the promotional costs: *The free spoon offer is very attractive, and our increased coffee sales should make it self-liquidating.*

/ˌself ˈlɪkwɪdeɪtɪŋ/

3 ▶ **free sample**

---

self-made *adjective*

having become successful, rich, etc by your own work, and not because of inherited wealth or position: *a self-made millionaire*

/ˌself ˈmeɪd/

⋈ a **self-made** man, woman

---

self-regulatory organization *noun* (finance/stock exchange)
(*UK*) one of four associations, who report to the Securities and Investment Board (SIB), whose duty is to draw up and enforce codes of conduct for financial traders. The four self-regulatory organizations are the Financial Intermediaries, Managers and Brokers Regulatory Association (FIMBRA), the Investment Management Regulatory Organization (IMRO), the Life Assurance and Unit Trust Regulatory Organization (LAUTRO), and the Securities and Futures Authority (SFA).

/ˌself ˌregjələtəri ˌɔːgənaɪˈzeɪʃn/
pl self-regulatory organizations
abbr SRO
▶ **Financial Intermediaries, Managers and Brokers Regulatory Association, Investment Management Regulatory Organization, Life Assurance and Unit Trust Regulatory Organization, regulation, Securities and Futures Authority, Securities and Investment Board**

self-service *noun* (retail)
a system of selling where customers serve themselves and pay for the goods when leaving. Used esp in supermarkets and petrol stations: *a self-service canteen* ○ *The nearest petrol station is self-service.*

/ˌselfˈsɜːvɪs/
note no plural
⋈ a **self-service** garage, restaurant, store

self-sufficient *adjective* (economics)
able to produce enough goods or commodities for your own needs: *They are self-sufficient in coal.* ○ *The country used to be self-sufficient.*

/ˌself səˈfɪʃənt/
⋈ a **self-sufficient** community, country, region, state

self-tender *noun* (finance)
a written offer from a company to its shareholders to buy back some or all of its shares: *If our self-tender is successful, it will reduce the chances of a hostile bid and increase our earnings per share.*

/ˌselfˈtendə(r)/
pl self-tenders
⋈ a **self-tender** issue, offer
▶ **tender[1] 1**

sell *verb* (commerce/retail)
1 to give something in exchange for money: *I will sell my car next week.* ○ *She sold her gas shares.* ○ *Shareholders were advised not to sell.* **2** (**a**) to persuade someone to buy something: *Be sure to sell it to the client.* (**b**) to persuade someone of the worth of something: *It won't be easy to sell that idea to the boss.* ○ *At an interview you have to sell yourself* (ie make people think you would be good at the job). **3** to trade in a product: *sell stationery, videos, washing machines* **4** to be bought; to find buyers: *These gifts sell well.*

sell (something) off to sell cheaply items that are unwanted, difficult to sell or expensive to maintain: *sell off old stock* ○ *sell off part of the business/sell part of the business off*

sell out (of something) to sell your whole supply of something: *sell out of tickets, milk, light bulbs*

sell out (to someone/something) to sell all or part of your share in a business: *sell out to a larger firm* ○ *sell out before share prices fall*

sell up to sell a business, property, etc, esp when moving or retiring: *After twenty years in the electronics business he decided to sell up and retire.*

/sel/
sell, selling, sold
1 note transitive and intransitive verb
▶ **buy[2], market[2], undersell, sale**
2 note transitive verb
▶ **hard sell, soft sell**
3 note transitive verb
4 note intransitive verb

seller *noun* (retail/commerce)
1 a person or organization that sells: *The seller might reduce the price.* **2** something that is sold: *The biography was a best seller.*

/ˈselə(r)/
pl sellers
1 ▶ **buyer, vendor**

2 ⋈ a best, big, poor, steady **seller**

---

sellers' market *noun* (commerce/stock exchange)
a situation where certain products are in short supply resulting in high prices: *It was a sellers' market and prices were high.*

/ˌseləz ˈmɑːkɪt/
pl sellers' markets
▶ **buyers' market, easy market, market[1]**

---

selling *noun* (retail/commerce)
the act of finding a buyer or persuading someone to buy something: *He works in selling.*

/ˈselɪŋ/
note not used with *a* or *an*. No plural and used with a singular verb only.
▶ **direct sale, inertia selling, mail order, panic selling, pyramid selling**

---

selling costs *noun* (management/marketing)
the amount of money to be spent when a product or service is sold. It includes the money paid to sales staff, as well as the cost of advertising and promotional material.

/ˈselɪŋ kɒsts/
note usually plural
⋈ high, low **selling costs**
▶ **cost[1]**

---

selling out *noun* (stock exchange)
the selling of securities that have not been paid for by the original buyer. This action is taken by an official broker on the stock exchange, but the original buyer is responsible for the costs incurred.

/ˌselɪŋ ˈaʊt/
note not used with *a* or *an*. No plural and used with a singular verb only.
▶ **buying in**

---

selling short *noun* (stock exchange)
▶ **short selling**

/ˌselɪŋ ˈʃɔːt/

---

sell-out *noun* (retail)
an event for which all the tickets have been sold: *The show was a sell-out.*

/ˈsel aʊt/
note usually singular

---

semi-durable *adjective*
of consumer products that are expected to be replaced in a few years, such as china or small electrical goods

/ˌsemiˈdjʊərəbl/
⋈ **semi-durable** goods, products
▶ **consumer durables**

---

semi-finished *adjective* (manufacturing)
of goods that are only partly made; unfinished: *We receive the semi-finished dresses and put on the final touches ourselves.*

/ˌsemi ˈfɪn ɪʃt/
⋈ **semi-finished** goods, products

---

semi-skilled *adjective* (personnel)
1 of someone who has had some specific training, but less than that of a skilled worker: *Many of our staff are semi-skilled.* ○ *a semi-skilled machine operator* **2** of work suitable for someone of this level of training: *employ somebody for a semi-skilled job*

/ˌsemi ˈskɪld/
⋈ a **semi-skilled** job, labour, worker
▶ **skilled, unskilled**

---

semi-solus *adjective* (advertising)
an advertisement which appears on the same page as another advertisement but is not placed next to it: *We can offer you a semi-solus position on the editorial page.*

/ˌsemi ˈsəʊləs/
▶ **advertisement, solus**

---

senior *adjective*
having a high or higher rank in an organization: *a senior partner in the firm* ○ *a senior managerial position*

/ˈsiːniə/
⋈ **senior** staff; a **senior** editor, manager, partner
opp junior

---

sensitive market *noun* (commerce/stock exchange)
a trading situation that is easily affected by some outside influence such as war, political change or a natural disaster: *The strike by oil rig workers resulted in a sensitive market today.*

/ˌsensətɪv ˈmɑːkɪt/
note usually singular
⋈ encourage, produce, result in a **sensitive market**
▶ **market**[1]

sequential access *noun* (computing)
a system of finding information stored in a computer memory where each item has to be searched through in order until the required information is found: *Sequential access is a much slower way of retrieving information than the random access method.*

/sɪˌkwenʃl ˈækses/
note not used with *a* or *an*. No plural and used with a singular verb only.
▶ **direct access, Random Access Memory**

sequestration *noun* (law)
the taking of property by order of a court of law until ownership of the property is settled, or, in a case of bankruptcy, the property is divided among the creditors: *The union's property is subject to sequestration until the fine is paid.*

/ˌsiːkweˈstreɪʃn/
note not used with *a* or *an*. No plural and used with a singular verb only.
⋈ enforce, order **sequestration**

serial number *noun*
a number in a series that distinguishes an item from others in the same set: *Check the serial numbers on the banknotes against those listed as fakes.*

/ˈsɪəriəl ˌnʌmbə(r)/
pl serial numbers
▶ **bar code**

service *noun* (industry)
1 a system or organization that provides the public with something necessary or useful in daily life: *the postal service* ○ *an international airline service* **2** the job that an organization does: *We provide a number of financial services.* ○ *customer services.* **3** the work or the quality of work done by someone when serving a customer: *Is service included in the bill?* ○ *We provide a fast and good quality service.*

/ˈsɜːvɪs/
pl services
⋈ offer, provide a **service**

service agreement *noun* (management/law)
1 a contract between a company and a senior employee concerning the conditions of employment: *What are the terms and conditions of your service agreement?* **2** an arrangement with a supplier to provide repairs or safety checks for items bought, usually in return for regular payment: *Do you have a service agreement for this washing machine?*

/ˈsɜːvɪs əˌgriːmənt/
pl service agreements
syn service contract
⋈ draw up a **service agreement**
2 ▶ **after-sales service**

service charge *noun*
1 a sum, usually 10% or 15%, added to a bill in a hotel or restaurant for serving customers: *No tip is necessary as a service charge is included.* **2** (*finance*) a fee paid for the arrangement of a loan **3** (*administration*) a fee paid by tenants of a block of flats or offices to cover the cost of repairs, redecorating, etc: *The cost of cleaning is included in the service charge.* **4** a fee paid to a supplier for regular checks, repairs, etc of goods bought: *pay an annual service charge for a central heating system*

/ˈsɜːvɪs tʃɑːdʒ/
pl service charges
1 ▶ **charge**[1] **1**
2 ▶ **fee**
4 ▶ **after-sales service**

service industry *noun* (industry)
an industry that is not concerned with manufactured goods, but provides a service, such as banking, insurance, advertising or catering: *Service industries put on substantial growth during the 1980s.*

/ˈsɜːvɪs ˌɪndəstri/
pl service industries
syn tertiary industry
▶ primary industry, secondary industry *under* **industry**

session *noun* (law/stock exchange)
a meeting, or a period of time spent on one activity: *a court session* ○ *a parliamentary session* ○ *The opening session starts at 10.00 am.* ○ *Share prices rose throughout today's session.*

/ˈseʃn/
pl sessions
⧓ the afternoon, closing, morning, next, opening **session**
► **conference, meeting**

---

set back *verb*
to delay or make something late: *The launch has been set back three weeks because of the strike.*

/ˌset ˈbæk/
set back, setting back, set back
note transitive verb
⧓ **set back** a project

---

set-back *noun*
1 something that delays or stops progress: *Despite a set-back production is on schedule.* ○ *a set-back in the shipbuilding industry* ○ *a set-back for shipbuilders* **2** (*stock exchange*) a fall in prices at a time when they had been rising: *Share prices have risen today despite a set-back earlier this week.*

/ˈsetbæk/
pl set-backs
(also **setback**)
⧓ receive, recover from, suffer a **set-back**

---

set price *noun* (commerce)
► **fixed charge 2**

/ˌset ˈpraɪs/

---

settle *verb*
1 (*accounting*) to pay what is owed: *The account will be settled at the end of the month.* **2** (**a**) (*industrial relations*) to come to an agreement or make a final arrangement about something: *Employers and union members met to try to settle the dispute.* (**b**) (*law*) to come to an agreement over a legal dispute: *The case was settled out of court* (ie privately, before being taken to court).

/ˈsetl/
settle, settling, settled
note transitive and intransitive verb
1 ⧓ **settle** an account, a bill, a charge, a claim, a debt
2a ⧓ **settle** a dispute, strike
2b ⧓ **settle** amicably, out of court

---

settlement *noun*
1 (*accounting*) the payment of an account, debt, bill, etc: *We offer a discount for settlement in cash.* **2** (*stock exchange*) the payment of debts on the stock exchange **3** (*industrial relations*) an agreement between two parties involved in a dispute: *Most union members are happy with the pay settlement.* **4** (*law*) (**a**) the terms on which property or money is given to somebody: *The family met to hear the settlement of the will.* (**b**) the document relating to this: *marriage settlement* (**c**) the money itself: *receive a settlement of £20 000*

/ˈsetlmənt/
1 note not used with *a* or *an*. No plural and used with a singular verb only.
⧓ early **settlement**
2 note not used with *a* or *an*. No plural and used with a singular verb only.
► **Account Day, dues**
3 pl settlements
⧓ an amicable, unfair **settlement**; negotiate, reach, reject, seek a **settlement**; a pay, wage **settlement**
4 pl settlements

---

settlement day *noun* (stock exchange)
the day on which bought stock must be delivered to the buyer and payment made to the seller

/ˈsetlmənt deɪ/
note not used with *a* or *an*. No plural and used with a singular verb only.
► **Account Day, last trading day, prompt day**

severance pay *noun* (industrial relations)
▶ **redundancy pay**

/ˈsevərəns peɪ/

SFA *abbr* (finance/stock exchange)
Securities and Futures Authority

/ˌes ef ˈeɪ/

---

share *noun* (stock exchange)
one of many portions into which a company's capital is divided. The owners of shares become members or shareholders of the company, in which they can vote. They also have a right to part of its profit by payment of a DIVIDEND: *He has shares in British Gas.* ○ *The price of shares rose today on the Stock Exchange.* ○ *fix a price of 240 pence per share*

/ʃeə(r)/
pl shares
⋈ buy, deal in, issue, sell **shares**; hold **shares** in (a company)
▶ **A share, deferred share, dividend per share, earnings per (ordinary) share, equities, lien on shares, net asset value per share, ordinary share, paid-up share, penny share, preference share, share capital, subscription shares, term share, voting share**
syn (*US*) stock

---

share capital *noun* (stock exchange)
the amount of money put into a company by its shareholders when they buy shares and used to buy the items it needs to carry on its activities: *We need to increase our share capital if we want to expand.*

/ˈʃeə ˌkæpɪtl/
note not used with *a* or *an*. No plural and used with a singular verb only.
⋈ enlarge, increase **share capital**
▶ **alteration of share capital, authorized share capital, capital, equity capital, loan capital**

---

share certificate *noun* (stock exchange)
a legal document given to a shareholder to prove that he/she owns shares in a company. It shows the number, class and serial numbers of the shares owned. The document is signed by two directors and the company secretary.

/ˈʃeə səˌtɪfɪkət/
pl share certificates
⋈ hold, issue a **share certificate**
▶ **shareholder**

Shared Currency Option Under Tender *noun* (international trade)
a scheme that allows companies, who hope to obtain a contract to supply goods or services for the same organization or project overseas, to share the risks of dealing in a foreign currency

/ˌʃeəd ˌkʌrənsi ˌɒpʃn ʌndə ˈtendə(r)/
abbr SCOUT
▶ **currency 1, option, tender[1] 1**

---

shareholder *noun* (stock exchange)
a person who owns shares in a company and is, therefore, a member of the company: *Our shareholders will be pleased with this year's figures.*

/ˈʃeəhəʊldə(r)/
pl shareholders
⋈ a controlling, leading, majority, minority **shareholder**
syn (*US*) stockholder
▶ **member 2**

---

share issue *noun* (stock exchange)
▶ **issue[1] 1**

/ˈʃeər ɪʃuː/

share option *noun* (stock exchange)
a right offered to employees, to buy shares in the company where they work at a cheap price: *A share option should increase commitment to the company.*

/ˈʃeər ˌɒpʃn/
pl share options
⋈ offer, take up a **share option**
► **option, traded option**

share register *noun* (stock exchange)
a list of shareholders that every company must keep for inspection. It contains the names and addresses of members and details of the shares they own: *add a name to the share register*

/ˈʃeə ˌredʒɪstə(r)/
pl share registers
syn shareholder's register, register of members
► **Registrar of Companies**

share splitting *noun* (stock exchange)
the division of company shares into a number of smaller units when the price of the original shares is too high for small investors

/ˈʃeə ˌsplɪtɪŋ/
note not used with *a* or *an*. No plural and used with a singular verb only.
syn splitting shares, (*US*) stock splitting
► **share**

shark *noun* (finance)
(*informal*) a person who lends money at a very high rate of interest: *Don't do business with those sharks, unless you can afford to lose money.*

/ʃɑːk/
pl sharks
syn loan shark

sharp practice *noun*
clever business dealings which are not entirely honest: *We suspect there has been some sharp practice, but cannot prove it.*

/ˌʃɑːp ˈpræktɪs/
note not used with *a* or *an*. No plural and used with a singular verb only.
► **practice 4**

shelf life *noun* (commerce/retail)
1 the length of time that goods, esp food items, can be on sale and remain fit for use: *These frozen meals have a shelf life of three months.* **2** the length of time before goods, esp computer items, become out-of-date and people will no longer want them: *The average shelf life for a computer software package is about 18 months.*

/ˈʃelf laɪf/
pl shelf lives
⋈ a long, short **shelf life**
► **product life cycle**

shelf space *noun* (commerce/retail)
the amount of room available for goods to be displayed for sale: *This product is well advertised at the moment and needs more shelf space.* ○ *compete for shelf space in a supermarket*

/ˈʃelf speɪs/
note not used with *a* or *an*. No plural and used with a singular verb only.
⋈ less, more, prominent **shelf space**

shift *noun*
1 (**a**) (*personnel*) the period of time when a number of employees work before being replaced by another group: *He/she works a regular night shift.* (**b**) the employees who are working for that period of time: *The day shift will arrive soon.* **2** a movement or change: *The demand for better fuel economy has meant a shift in the market.* ○ *There has been a shift in our development plans.*

/ʃɪft/
pl shifts
1 ⋈ the afternoon, day, evening, night **shift**; a **shift** system, worker

shipbroker *noun* (shipping)
an agent who arranges contracts, insurance and space on a ship for the transport of cargo (and sometimes passengers) for a fee (BROKERAGE)

/ˈʃɪpbrəʊkə(r)/
pl shipbrokers
► **Baltic Exchange, broker**

shipment *noun* (shipping)
1 the placing of goods on a ship: *Your goods will be ready for shipment on Thursday.* **2** the transport of goods, esp by ship: *Shipment by air would be quicker.* **3** a quantity of goods to be sent together: *This shipment of cars is going to France.* ○ *a furniture shipment*

/ˈʃɪpmənt/
1 note not used with *a* or *an*. No plural and used with a singular verb only.
⋈ due, ready for **shipment**
2 note not used with *a* or *an*. No plural and used with a singular verb only.
⋈ **shipment** charges, costs
3 pl shipments
⋈ a **shipment** of (something)
► **bulk shipment, consignment, drop shipment**

---

shipper *noun* (shipping)
a person or organization that arranges for goods to be sent by sea or air: *The shipper must sign the bill of lading.*

/ˈʃɪpə(r)/
pl shippers
► **shipping and forwarding agent**

---

shipping *noun* (shipping)
1 large boats collectively: *Fog is a danger to shipping.* **2** sending goods, especially by sea: *The cost of shipping these goods is very high.*

merchant shipping (*commerce/shipping*) cargo ships and passenger liners

/ˈʃɪpɪŋ/
note not used with *a* or *an*. No plural and used with a singular verb only.
⋈ **shipping** charges, costs; a **shipping** agent, company

---

shipping and forwarding agent *noun* (shipping)
an organization that arranges for goods to be transported from one country to another by sea, air, rail or road by booking space on the ship or aeroplane, preparing transport and customs documents, and arranging insurance

/ˌʃɪpɪŋ ənd ˈfɔːwədɪŋ ˌeɪdʒənt/
pl shipping and forwarding agents
► **agent, shipbroker, shipper, shipping documents**

---

shipping conference *noun* (shipping)
an association of shipowners whose liners sail the same route. They agree freight and passenger rates, and terms of contract.

/ˈʃɪpɪŋ ˌkɒnfərəns/
pl shipping conferences
syn shipping ring

---

shipping documents *noun* (shipping)
the documents sent by an exporter to the bank or agent in the importer's country. The importer, having paid for the goods, uses the documents to claim the goods at the port and take them through customs. The documents may include a bill of lading, an insurance certificate and, if necessary, a certificate of origin and an export licence.

/ˈʃɪpɪŋ ˌdɒkjəmənts/
note usually plural
syn export documents
► **bill of lading, certificate of origin, consignment note, export licence, way-bill**

---

shipping instructions *noun* (shipping)
a document prepared by an exporter that states how goods are to be transported and delivered

/ˈʃɪpɪŋ ɪn ˌstrʌkʃnz/
note plural noun, used with a plural verb
⋈ according to, include in, refer to, with reference to the **shipping instructions**

ship's certificate of registry *noun* (shipping)
a document that gives details of a ship's country of registration, the owner's name, the amount of cargo and the number of passengers allowed. The certificate must always be available for inspection.

/ˌʃɪps səˌtɪfɪkət əv ˈredʒɪstri/
pl ship's certificates of registry
syn certificate of ownership, ship's register

ship's master *noun* (shipping)
▶ **master 3**

/ˌʃɪps ˈmɑːstə(r)/

ship's papers *noun* (shipping)
the documents that must be available for inspection on every ship. They include the ship's certificate of registry, the bills of lading, the cargo manifest, and, if applicable, the passenger manifest.

/ˌʃɪps ˈpeɪpəz/
note plural noun, used with a plural verb
▶ **bill of lading, manifest, ship's certificate of registry**

shop *noun* (retail)
1 a place where goods are stored and sold: *a bookshop, shoe shop, gift shop, secondhand shop, etc* ○ *The corner shop sells everything you will need.* **2** (*manufacturing*) a place where goods are manufactured or repaired: *workshop* ○ *paint shop* , ie in a factory where cars, etc are painted

open a shop to start selling things in a shop: *We opened a shop in the high street.*

set up shop to start a new business: *She set up shop as a bookseller.*

/ʃɒp/
pl shops
1 syn (*US*) store
⋈ a **shop** front, window; a local, village **shop**
▶ **closed shop, store[1] 2**

shop assistant *noun* (personnel)
▶ **assistant 3**

/ˈʃɒp əˌsɪstənt/

shop-floor *noun*
1 (*manufacturing*) the part of a factory or workshop where goods are made: *Visitors must take care when crossing the shop-floor.*
2 (*industrial relations*) the workers in a factory (as opposed to the management): *We must test opinion on the shop-floor.*

/ˌʃɒp ˈflɔː(r)/
note singular noun, used with a singular verb
1 ⋈ **shop-floor** employees, members, workers

shoplifting *noun* (retail/law)
stealing goods from a shop: *losses due to shoplifting*

/ˈʃɒplɪftɪŋ/
note not used with *a* or *an*. No plural and used with a singular verb only.
⋈ be arrested for, be charged with, be convicted of **shoplifting**; a **shoplifting** charge
▶ **shrinkage**

shop steward *noun* (industrial relations/management)
a trade union official elected by other union members to discuss pay and working conditions with the employer: *Shop stewards are meeting today to discuss a wage increase.*

/ˌʃɒp ˈstjʊəd/
pl shop stewards
⋈ call on, elect, negotiate with a **shop steward**; a **shop steward** at (a chemical plant), in (a factory), for (an engineering union)
▶ **bargain[2] 2, negotiate 1, trade union**

shortage *noun*
a situation where there is not enough of something: *Trains are not running because of staff shortages.* ○ *a shortage of skilled workers*

/ˈʃɔːtɪdʒ/
pl shortages
⋈ a **shortage** of labour, manpower, staff; a food, a fuel, an oil **shortage**
► **glut**[1], **surplus**

short bill *noun* (banking/commerce)
a bill of exchange that must be paid as soon as it is presented for payment or within ten days

/ˌʃɔːt ˈbɪl/
pl short bills
► **sight bill**

short covering *noun* (stock exchange)
the buying of securities or commodities which have been already sold in a SHORT POSITION

/ˈʃɔːt ˌkʌvərɪŋ/
note not used with *a* or *an*. No plural and used with a singular verb only.
► **security 1, short position, shorts, short selling**

short-dated securities *noun* (stock exchange)
► **shorts 1**

/ˌʃɔːt ˌdeɪtɪd sɪˈkjʊərətiz/

short delivery *noun* (commerce)
goods that, on arrival, have fewer items or a lighter weight than stated on the invoice: *Ask the supplier to explain this short delivery.*

/ˌʃɔːt dɪˈlɪvəri/
pl short deliveries
abbr s.d.
⋈ account for, check, complain about, notice, record a **short delivery**

shortfall *noun* (accounting/commerce/management)
an amount missing from an expected total: *There was a shortfall in today's takings.* ○ *a £300 shortfall/a shortfall of £300* ○ *There was a production shortfall of 20 units this week.*

/ˈʃɔːtfɔːl/
pl shortfalls
⋈ a **shortfall** in labour, orders, production, resources, supplies; account for, cover, make up for a **shortfall**
► **adverse balance, deficit, loss 1, trade deficit, windfall**

shorthand *noun* (office practice)
a method of writing rapidly by using special signs to represent words or parts of words: *The minutes of the meeting were taken in shorthand.* ○ *a shorthand speed of 150 words a minute*

/ˈʃɔːthænd/
note not used with *a* or *an*. No plural and used with a singular verb only.
⋈ do, read, write **shorthand**

shorthand typist *noun* (office practice)
a person who can type and read and write SHORTHAND: *Our department needs another shorthand typist.*

/ˌʃɔːthænd ˈtaɪpɪst/
pl shorthand typists
⋈ work as a **shorthand typist**
► **audio-typist, copy-typist, keyboarder, typist**

short list *noun* (management/personnel)
(a list of) a small number of people chosen from many applicants for a job or position from whom the final selection is made: *We need to draw up a short list.* ○ *I was on the short list, but I didn't get the job.*

/ˈʃɔːt lɪst/
pl short lists
(also **shortlist**)
⋈ choose from, compile, draw up, make, select from a **short list**
► **list, selection procedure**

shortlist *verb* (management/industrial relations)
to choose a small number of people from many applicants for a job or position: *He/she was shortlisted for the manager's job.* ○ *shortlisted for interview*

/ˈʃɔːtlɪst/
shortlist, shortlisting, shortlisted
note transitive verb
⋈ **shortlist** someone *for* (a job)

---

short position *noun* (stock exchange)
▶ **bear position**

/ˈʃɔːt pəˌzɪʃn/

---

shorts *noun* (stock exchange)
1 investments such as gilts and other fixed interest securities that can be repaid in less than five years' time: *He has put some of his capital into shorts.* **2** the securities and commodities, etc held in a bear position: *The dealer is selling shorts.*

/ʃɔːts/
note plural noun, used with a plural verb
1 syn short-dated securities
⋈ invest in **shorts**
▶ **fixed interest securities, gilts, longs, mediums**
2 ⋈ buy, sell **shorts**
▶ **bear position**

---

short selling *noun* (stock exchange)
the selling of securities and commodities, etc that a dealer does not actually have, but hopes to obtain before the delivery date at a lower price than agreed in order to make a profit

/ˌʃɔːt ˈselɪŋ/
note not used with *a* or *an*. No plural and used with a singular verb only.
⋈ **short selling** commodities, currencies, securities
syn shorting, selling short
▶ **bear, shorts**

---

short-term *adjective*
of or for a short period of time: *We can take a short-term loan, but the interest will be high.* ○ *These short-term debts must be settled next month.* ○ *The short-term forecast is not very good.*

/ˈʃɔːt tɜːm/
⋈ a **short-term** contract, debt, deposit, forecast, gain, loan; **short-term** capital, interest

---

short-term liabilities *noun* (accounting)
▶ **current liabilities**

/ˌʃɔːt tɜːm laɪəˈbɪlətiz/

---

showroom *noun* (commerce/retail)
a room where goods are displayed for customers to see: *Customers are welcome to visit our showrooms.*

/ˈʃəʊrʊm/
pl showrooms
⋈ a car, a carpet, an electricity, a furniture, a gas **showroom**

---

shrinkage *noun* (retail/commerce/accounting)
the difference between the actual stock and the amount stated in company records. Causes of shrinkage include theft (by employees or customers), goods spoilt during manufacture or delivery, and mistakes made in the invoicing and accounts department: *We lose 5% of our stock through shrinkage.*

/ˈʃrɪŋkɪdʒ/
note not used with *a* or *an*. No plural and used with a singular verb only.
⋈ allow for, because of, due to, through **shrinkage**
▶ **shoplifting**

---

shrink-wrapping *noun* (manufacturing)
▶ **wrapping**

/ˈʃrɪŋk ræpɪŋ/

---

shut-down *noun* (industry)
a time when a factory is closed and work stops, usually for staff holidays: *Our supplier has a shut-down each August.*

/ˈʃʌtdaʊn/
pl shut-downs
⋈ Christmas, holiday, summer, total **shut-down**

SIB *abbr* (stock exchange)
Securities and Investment Board

/ˌes aɪ ˈbiː/
note pronounced as individual letters

SIC *abbr* (manufacturing)
Standard Industrial Classification

/ˌes aɪ ˈsiː/
note pronounced as individual letters

sickness benefit *noun* (insurance)
(*UK*) money paid from a government or private insurance scheme to a person who cannot work because of illness: *I have paid enough National Insurance to claim sickness benefit.*

/ˈsɪknəs ˌbenɪfɪt/
note usually singular
⧓ apply for, claim, pay **sickness benefit**
▶ **benefit**[1] **1**

sideline *noun* (retail/commerce)
work done or goods or services provided in addition to your main activity: *It's really a bookshop, but they do print posters and address labels as a sideline.*

/ˈsaɪdlaɪn /
pl sidelines
⧓ a profitable, useful **sideline**
▶ **by-product, spin-off**

sight bill *noun* (banking)
a bill of exchange that must be paid immediately it is presented for payment: *present a sight bill for payment*

/ˈsaɪt bɪl/
pl sight bills
syn demand bill, sight draft
▶ **after sight, at sight, bill of exchange, short bill**

signatory *noun* (law)
a person who has signed a document and given it his/her approval; an organization or country for whom the document was signed: *The contract needs three signatories.*

/ˈsɪgnətri/
pl signatories
⧓ a **signatory** country, union; an authorized **signatory**

signature *noun*
the name of a person written by him/herself, usually at the end of a letter or document: *Our company cheques need two signatures.*

/ˈsɪgnətʃə(r)/
pl signatures
⧓ await, need, require a **signature**; a forged, valid **signature**

silent partner *noun* (commerce)
▶ **sleeping partner**

/ˌsaɪlənt ˈpɑːtnə(r)/

simulation *noun* (computing/industry)
a model of a real machine, situation or activity used for designing, testing or training purposes: *a computer simulation of our distribution system*

/ˌsɪmjəˈleɪʃn/
pl simulations
⧓ a **simulation** model, program; produce, use (a) **simulation**

single market *noun* (economics)
1 a free trade association with a common currency and unrestricted movement of capital goods and people between countries: *A single market leads to greater economic and monetary integration.* **2 the Single Market** a free trade association between members of the European Community: *the creation of the European Single Market*

/ˌsɪŋgl ˈmɑːkɪt/
note no plural
⧓ create, establish, launch a **single market**
▶ **free trade, market**[1]

sinking fund *noun* (accounting/finance)
money regularly set aside to repay a debt or to replace machinery, etc at a known date in the future: *a company sinking fund*

/ˈsɪŋkɪŋ fʌnd/
pl sinking funds
⧓ put money into, set up, take

money out of a **sinking fund**

▶ **fund[1] 1**

---

sister company *noun* (commerce)
one of two or more organizations that are part of the same group: *Our sister company may share some of the advertising costs with us.*

/ˈsɪstə ˌkʌmpəni/
pl sister companies
▶ **group, holding company, subsidiary company**

---

sister ship clause *noun* (shipping/insurance)
a condition in a marine insurance policy enabling a claim to be made when two ships belonging to the same owner collide

/ˈsɪstə ʃɪp klɔːz/
pl sister ship clauses
⧓ claim under a **sister ship clause**

---

site[1] *noun*
the ground or area on which something is built, or being built: *The garage will be built on a site near the new road.* ○ *The electrician is on the building site.*

on site in the building or area: *Is there an engineer on site?*

/saɪt/
pl sites
⧓ a demolition, a factory, an industrial **site**

---

site[2] *verb*
to place or build something somewhere; to situate: *The main office will be sited near the front entrance.* ○ *site a factory outside the town*

/saɪt/
site, siting, sited
note transitive verb
⧓ conveniently, perfectly **sited**
▶ **situation 3**

---

sitting tenant *noun* (law)
▶ **tenant**

/ˌsɪtɪŋ ˈtenənt/

---

situation *noun*
1 a state of affairs: *Please give me a report on the situation tomorrow.* ○ *Financially, the company is in a very difficult situation.* **2** a job: *She is looking for a situation in advertising.* **3** a location: *Our workshop enjoys a rural situation.*

/ˌsɪtʃuˈeɪʃn/
pl situations
1 ⧓ a financial, legal **situation**; a buoyant, delicate, difficult, strong **situation**
2 ⧓ apply for, look for, seek a **situation**
▶ **position 1, post[1] 3**
3 ⧓ accessible, convenient, urban **situation**
▶ **site**

---

situations vacant *noun* (advertising)
written above job advertisements in a newspaper or magazine: *There is nothing for me under 'Situations Vacant this week.* ○ *put an advert in the situations vacant column*

/ˌsɪtʃuˈeɪʃnz ˈveɪkənt/
note no plural
abbr sits. vac.
⧓ a **situations vacant** column, page, section
▶ **vacant**

---

skilled *adjective*
having or requiring a particular talent or ability: *We need skilled workers for this job.* ○ *a highly skilled job*

/skɪld/
⧓ a **skilled** job, worker, workforce; **skilled** labour
▶ **semi-skilled, unskilled**

---

sleeping partner *noun* (management)
a person who invests money in a business and has a right to a share of the profits, but does not work in it: *a sleeping partner in an electronics company*

/ˌsliːpɪŋ ˈpɑːtnə(r)/
pl sleeping partners
syn silent partner
▶ **active partner, partner**

slogan *noun* (advertising)
a clever and easily remembered phrase or sentence associated with a product or company: *The creative director will devise a slogan for you.* ○ *'Miles Better!' is a good slogan for a petrol company.*

/ˈsləʊgən/
pl slogans
⋈ an advertising **slogan**; commission, devise, invent a **slogan**
► **logo**

slot machine *noun* (retail)
a machine from which small items, such as food or cigarettes can be bought by putting money into a slot: *make a good profit from confectionery slot machines*

/ˈslɒt məˌʃiːn/
pl slot machines
⋈ a cigarette, confectionery, drinks **slot machine**

slump[1] *noun* (economics)
a sudden decline in economic activity, accompanied by a fall in prices; the period when this has happened: *It is difficult to find work during the slump.* ○ *Estate agents are faced with another property slump.*

/slʌmp/
pl slumps
⋈ a price, property **slump**
► **boom**[1], **depressed market, depression, recession**

slump[2] *verb* (sales)
(of trade, prices, business activity) to fall suddenly or heavily: *Share prices slumped by 15p.* ○ *Oil pollution on the beaches has caused tourism to slump.*

/slʌmp/
slump, slumping, slumped
note intransitive verb
⋈ prices, profits, sales **slump**
► **boom**[2]

slush fund *noun* (commerce)
(*informal*) money that is kept for use as a bribe or reward: *There is money in the slush fund for you if you can persuade them to give the contract to us.*

/ˈslʌʃ fʌnd/
pl slush funds
⋈ a discreet, secret **slush fund**
syn slush money
► **bribe**[1]

small ad *noun* (advertising)
(*informal*) ► **classified advertisement**

/ˈsmɔːl æd/

small claims *noun* (law)
(*UK*) a court action involving a small amount of money, esp when a consumer wants a refund for faulty goods from an organization that refuses to pay: *We will try to reclaim this £450 through the small claims court.* ○ *The limit for small claims is £1 000.*

/ˌsmɔːl ˈkleɪmz/
note usually plural
⋈ **small claims** arbitration, case, court, procedures
► **claim**[1]

small print *noun* (insurance/finance)
part of a document, such as a hire purchase agreement or life assurance policy, that is printed in small type and may contain important details that are easy to overlook: *Be sure to read the small print before you sign the agreement.*

/ˈsmɔːl prɪnt/
note singular noun, used with a singular verb
⋈ look at, read, study the **small print**

smuggle *verb* (law)
to take goods secretly and illegally in or out of a country, esp without paying customs duty: *They were caught smuggling foreign currency into the country.* ○ *try to smuggle drugs through customs* ○ *goods smuggled across the border*

/ˈsmʌgl/
smuggle, smuggling, smuggled
note transitive verb
⋈ **smuggle** arms, drugs, tobacco; **smuggle** (goods) into, out of (a country)

smuggler *noun* (law)
a person who takes goods into or out of a country illegally: *Two drug smugglers were arrested at the airport.*

/ˈsmʌɡlə(r)/
pl smugglers
⧓ an arms, a drug **smuggler**

---

social security *noun* (finance)
government payments for people who are sick, unemployed, disabled, retired, etc. The cost is provided by taxes and National Insurance contributions.

/ˌsəʊʃl sɪˈkjʊərəti/
note not used with *a* or *an*. No plural and used with a singular verb only.
⧓ apply for, be eligible for, claim **social security**; **social security** benefits, payments
► **benefit[1] 1, dole, income support, National Insurance**

---

soft commodities *noun* (stock exchange)
goods other than metal, eg cocoa, coffee, grains, potatoes, rubber and sugar, that are traded in the London commodities and futures markets

/ˌsɒft kəˈmɒdətiz/
note usually plural
⧓ deal in, trade in **soft commodities**; **soft commodities** market
syn softs
► **futures**

---

soft loan *noun* (finance)
a loan with a very low rate of interest. It might be made from one country to another, eg through an agency that provides financial help for developing countries, or from a company to an employee: *The soft loan can be repaid in their own currency.*

/ˌsɒft ˈləʊn/
pl soft loans
⧓ make, repay a **soft loan**
► **hard loan, International Development Association, loan[1]**

---

softs *noun* (stock exchange)
(*informal*) ► **soft commodities**

/sɒfts/

---

soft sell *noun* (advertising/sales)
a gentle method of encouraging people to buy things. The seller calmly discusses the qualities of the product in a way that makes the customer feel he/she has chosen, rather than been persuaded, to buy it: *We have more success with a soft sell approach.*

/ˌsɒft ˈsel/
note no plural
⧓ a **soft sell** approach, method
opp hard sell
► **sell 2**

---

software *noun* (computing)
the programs used with a computer: *Our software can cope with a wide range of applications.* ○ *The program was changed to alter the software functions.* ○ *The software specialist will need to change the program.*

/ˈsɒftweə(r)/
note not used with *a* or *an*. No plural and used with a singular verb only.
⧓ desktop publishing, word processing **software**; embedded, function **software**; a **software** dealer, expert, house, specialist, supplier
► **hardware, peripheral**

---

sola *noun* (banking)
a single bill of exchange of which there are no copies

/ˈsəʊlə/
pl solas
syn sola of exchange, sola bill
► **bill of exchange**

---

sole agent *noun* (sales)
an organization that is the only one allowed to sell the products of a particular manufacturer in a specified area: *We have been appointed sole agents for these new washing machines.*

/ˌsəʊl ˈeɪdʒənt/
pl sole agents
⋈ a **sole agent** agreement, contract
▶ **agent,** exclusive distributor *under* **distributor**

sole trader *noun* (commerce)
a person who owns and runs a business, and is the only person responsible for it: *As a sole trader, he is personally liable for any debts that the business has.*

/ˌsəʊl ˈtreɪdə(r)/
pl sole traders
▶ **trader**

solicitor *noun* (law)
a person whose job is to give legal advice, prepare legal documents and speak in the lower courts: *Ask your solicitor for advice before you sign the document.*

/səˈlɪsɪtə(r)/
pl solicitors
⋈ consult, hire a **solicitor**
▶ **attorney, barrister, lawyer**

solus *adjective* (advertising)
of an advertisement or poster that is separated from any competing advertisements or posters, eg is the only one on a page: *a solus position on the front page*

/ˈsəʊləs/
▶ **semi-solus**

solvent *adjective* (finance/accounting)
having enough money to pay your debts; (of a business) having an excess of assets over liabilities: *We can't replace the car fleet and remain solvent.*

/ˈsɒlvənt/
⋈ **a solvent** business, company, firm; keep, remain **solvent**
▶ **insolvent**

source and application of funds *noun* (accounting)
a statement showing the flow of cash in and out of a business. Sources might include trading profits, sales of fixed assets, loans, etc, and typical applications are trading losses, payments of dividends, repayments of loans and purchase of fixed assets, etc: *I have checked the source and application of funds, and borrowings seem to be very high.*

/ˌsɔːs ənd æplɪˌkeɪʃn əv ˈfʌndz/
note no plural
syn (*US*) funds flow statement

spec *abbr* (technology)
specification: *Have you finished the design spec?*

/spek/
pl specs

Special Drawing Rights *noun* (finance/banking)
an international reserve currency system and standard unit of payment for members of the International Monetary Fund. The amount is agreed each year and can be used to settle debts between governments or debts to the International Monetary Fund itself.

/ˌspeʃl ˈdrɔːɪŋ raɪts/
abbr SDRs
▶ **International Monetary Fund, Drawing Rights**

special position *noun* (advertising)
a preferred advertising space in a newspaper or magazine that costs more and must be booked a long time in advance: *The inside cover is a special position, and is booked for the next eight months.*

/ˌspeʃl pəˈzɪʃn/
pl special positions
⋈ book, buy a **special position**
▶ **solus, semi-solus**

specie *noun* (finance/banking)
money in the form of coins and not banknotes: *insist on payment in specie*

/ˈspiːʃi/
note not used with *a* or *an*. No plural and used with a singular verb only.
⋈ in **specie**
▶ **banknote, bullion**

specification *noun* (industry)
a detailed description of a product, process or job: *Is the machine performing to specification?* ○ *Once we have the specifications we can set to work.* ○ *Send for the job specification and see if it is suitable.*

/ˌspesɪfɪˈkeɪʃn/
pl specifications
abbr spec
⋈ alter, check, follow, meet, stick to, work to, write the **specification**; design, safety, technical **specifications**

speculate *verb* (stock exchange)
1 to buy and sell securities, commodities, futures, etc for short-term profit and not as long-term investment: *speculate on the Stock Exchange* **2** to take risks in business in the hope of making a profit: *speculate on a rise in property values*

/ˈspekjuleɪt/
speculate, speculating, speculated
note intransitive verb
⋈ **speculate** *in, on* (something)
► **venture**[2]

speculation *noun* (stock exchange)
1 the buying and selling of securities, commodities, futures, etc for short-term profit and not for long-term investment: *Speculation in coffee futures is keeping prices stable.* **2** (*commerce*) any risky business deal which is for short-term profit: *The land was bought as speculation.*

/ˌspekjuˈleɪʃn/
note not used with *a* or *an*. No plural and used with a singular verb only.
1 ⋈ futures, share, stock exchange **speculation**
2 ► **enterprise 1, venture**[1]

speculator *noun* (stock exchange/commerce)
a person who takes risks on the Stock Exchange or in business in the hope of making a profit when the market price changes: *Speculators were busy buying on the futures market today.*

/ˈspekjuleɪtə(r)/
pl speculators
► **stag**

spin-off *noun* (industry)
something that is produced as a secondary item from a main product or something useful that is discovered unexpectedly while the main product is being made; a by-product: *The building of the Channel Tunnel may produce important spin-offs for the tourist industry.* ○ *Some items of weatherproof clothing now on sale are spin-offs from materials manufactured especially for mountaineering expeditions.*

/ˈspɪn ɒf/
pl spin-offs
⋈ a surprising, useful, valuable, welcome **spin-off**
► **by-product, sideline**

spin off *verb* (stock exchange)
(*US*) to distribute among the shareholders of a leading company in a group the shares of one or more of the subsidiary companies: *The company plans to spin off its television broadcasting subsidiaries.* ○ *a decision to spin off to shareholders most of the company's computer products businesses*

/spɪn ˈɒf/
spin off, spinning off, spun off
note transitive and intransitive verb
► **group, holding company, subsidiary company**

splitting shares *noun* (stock exchange)
► **share splitting**

/ˌsplɪtɪŋ ˈʃeəz/

split trust *noun* (finance)
a trust that provides two types of investment: either an increase in the total amount put in by the investor after a period of time, or a number of regular interest payments: *This split trust offers you a useful regular income, or, if you can wait, a share of the capital gain.*

/ˌsplɪt ˈtrʌst/
pl split trusts
► **trust, unit trust**

sponsor[1] *noun* (advertising)
a person or an organization that pays for a radio or television programme, a sporting or arts event or provides money for research, education or training to gain publicity and public approval: *As sponsors, we hope to gain advertising and prestige from paying for cultural events.* ○ *We need people to act as sponsors.*

/ˈspɒnsə(r)/
pl sponsors
⋈ collect, find a **sponsor**
► **patron 2**

---

sponsor[2] *verb* (advertising)
to pay for a sports, arts or other event; to provide money for research, education or training to gain publicity and public approval: *The music festival was sponsored by the local bank.* ○ *a sponsored exhibition, conference, football match* ○ *sponsor a student through medical college*

/ˈspɒnsə(r)/
sponsor, sponsoring, sponsored
note transitive verb
⋈ agree to **sponsor** (someone/something); **sponsored** *by* (someone/something)

---

sponsorship *noun* (advertising)
money provided for a sports, an arts or other event or for research, education and training by a person or organization, usually to gain advertising or public approval: *The football team received sponsorship from a local computer company.* ○ *£5 000 was raised through sponsorship.*

/ˈspɒnsəʃɪp/
note not used with *a* or *an*. No plural and used with a singular verb only.
⋈ collect, obtain, provide, raise, receive **sponsorship**; a **sponsorship** agreement, deal; business, commercial, industrial **sponsorship**

---

spot cash *noun* (commerce/stock exchange)
payment for goods that are delivered immediately: *receive a spot cash payment*

/ˌspɒt ˈkæʃ/
note not used with *a* or *an*. No plural and used with a singular verb only.
⋈ payment by, request **spot cash**; **spot cash** delivery, payment
► **cash on delivery, spot price**

---

spot goods *noun* (commerce/stock exchange)
goods that are available for immediate delivery, as opposed to futures for which deliveries are arranged for a fixed date in the future

/ˌspɒt ˈgʊdz/
note plural noun, used with a plural verb
► **actuals, futures**

---

spot market *noun* (stock exchange)
the buying and selling of goods, currency or securities that are available for immediate delivery: *They ran out of oil and had to buy on the spot market.*

/ˈspɒt ˌmɑːkɪt/
note usually singular
⋈ buying, selling on the **spot market**
syn cash market
► **futures market, market**[1]

---

spot price *noun* (stock exchange)
the value of an asset that is available for immediate delivery. It is usually lower than the FUTURES price, except when there is a temporary shortage.

/ˈspɒt praɪs/
pl spot prices
► **contango 2, spot cash**

---

spread *noun* (stock exchange)
1 (**a**) the difference between the buying price and the selling price on the Stock Exchange (**b**) the difference between the spot price and the futures price **2** the range of investments in a portfolio: *The broad spread of investments reduces the risk.*

/spred/
pl spreads
2 ⋈ a broad, good, healthy, narrow, safe, specialist, wide, wise **spread**
► **portfolio**

spreadsheet *noun* (computing/accounting)
a computer program that can display and manipulate rows of figures; the display or printout produced by this: *The spreadsheet will help us plan the project.* ○ *print a copy of the spreadsheet*

/ˈspredʃiːt/
pl spreadsheets
⋈ a **spreadsheet** program

squeeze *noun* (finance)
financial limits, eg on salary increases or interest rates, imposed by the government as a way of controlling inflation: *You cannot expect a big pay rise during a pay squeeze.* ○ *The credit squeeze has made it difficult to get a loan.* ○ *Small companies are feeling the squeeze on consumer spending.*

/skwiːz/
note usually singular
⋈ a credit, a dividend, an income, a pay, a price, a wage **squeeze**
▶ **prices and incomes policy**

SRO *abbr* (finance/stock exchange)
self-regulatory organization

/ˌes ɑːr ˈəʊ/
pl SROs

stabilizers *noun* (economics)
the methods used by a government to prevent large fluctuations in prices, production and employment. These include the use of graded income tax and the control of interest rates and government spending and unemployment benefits.

/ˈsteɪbəlaɪzəz/
note plural noun, used with a plural verb

staff[1] *noun* (management/industrial relations)
the workers or employees of an organization: *She is a member of the accounts staff.* ○ *The clerical staff have worked hard on this job.* ○ *How many staff do you have?* ○ *We have a staff of twenty.*

/stɑːf; *US* stæf/
note used with a plural verb
⋈ account, administrative, catering, clerical, counter, industrial, junior, office, permanent, senior, temporary **staff**; **staff** shortages, vacancies; employ, recruit, take on **staff**
▶ **employee, manpower, personnel 1, worker, work-force**

staff[2] *verb* (management/industrial relations)
to provide an organization, a project, etc with employees: *The company is staffed by highly-trained professionals.* ○ *We are understaffed at the moment* (ie more staff are needed).

/stɑːf; *US* stæf/
staff, staffing, staffed
note transitive verb
▶ **employ 1, man**

staffing *noun* (management/industrial relations)
employing a number of people to do a job, run an organization, etc: *Inadequate staffing means that customers have to wait too long for the goods they've ordered.* ○ *Unless we increase staffing levels our rate of production will fall below that of our competitors.*

/ˈstɑːfɪŋ; *US* ˈstæfɪŋ/
note not used with *a* or *an*. No plural and used with a singular verb only.
⋈ **staffing** levels, problems, shortages

staff management *noun* (management)
▶ **line and staff management**

/ˌstɑːfˈmænɪdʒmənt; *US* ˌstæf ˈmænɪdʒmənt/

stag *noun* (stock exchange)
a person who applies for shares with the intention of selling them immediately for profit. If a share offer is oversubscribed, then the market price of the share is higher than its original or issue price, thus providing the stag with a profit.

/stæg/
pl stags
▶ **speculator**

stagflation *noun* (economics)
(*UK informal*) an economy that has a high rate of inflation and a recession at the same time: *Industrial output continued to fall during this period of stagflation.*

/ˌstæɡˈfleɪʃn/
note not used with *a* or *an*. No plural and used with singular verb only.
⧓ a period, time, state of **stagflation**
note formed from *stag*nation and in*flation*
▶ **inflation, recession**

stagnant *adjective* (stock exchange/commerce)
inactive; not increasing or developing: *Trading has been stagnant for the last three months.*

/ˈstæɡnənt/
⧓ a **stagnant** business, economy, market; **stagnant** prices, sales

stake *noun* (commerce/finance)
a sum of money invested in a business: *They have a 25% stake in the business.*

/steɪk/
pl stakes
⧓ acquire, buy, hold, own, sell a **stake**; a large, small **stake**

stale cheque *noun* (banking)
(*UK*) a cheque that is not presented to a bank for payment within six months of being written. It will not be exchanged for money (HONOURED) by the bank and will be returned, marked 'out of date': *The bank has returned a stale cheque.*

/ˌsteɪl ˈtʃek/
pl stale cheques
▶ **cheque**

stamp duty *noun* (tax)
(*UK*) a tax paid on the transfer of land or of stocks and shares to a new owner: *The legal department will arrange to pay the stamp duty on the new site.*

/ˈstæmp ˌdju:ti/
pl stamp duties
▶ **duty 1, transfer duty**

stand *noun*
1 (*retail*) a structure with shelves or tables where goods are displayed in a shop or stall: *Display these hats on the stand near the door.* ○ *a news-stand*, ie where newspapers for sale are displayed
2 (*advertising*) an area where things are displayed or advertised, especially at an exhibition: *be on/have a stand at the trade fair* ○ *You'll find us at stand 42 in the main hall.*

/stænd/
pl stands
⧓ a conference, a display, an exhibition **stand**; erect, put up, set up a **stand**

stand-alone *adjective* (computing)
(of computer equipment) not linked to any other system: *This is a stand-alone machine. It is not compatible with your other machines.*

/ˌstænd əˈləʊn/
⧓ a **stand-alone** computer, machine, system
▶ **network[1] 2**

Standard Industrial Classification *noun* (manufacturing)
a list in which industries and services are coded numerically for reference and research purposes

/ˌstændəd ɪn ˌdʌstriəl klæsɪfɪˈkeɪʃn/
abbr SIC

standardization *noun* (manufacturing/industry)
the process of making things that conform to a fixed size, colour, quality, etc: *Standardization of electrical fittings is essential.* ○ *Standardization reduces the cost of production.*

/ˌstændədaɪˈzeɪʃn/
note not used with *a* or *an*. No plural and used with a singular verb only.
(also **standardisation**)
⧓ **standardization** *of* designs, fittings, measurements, parts, products, sizes, specifications

standardize *verb* (manufacturing/industry)
to make things conform to a fixed size, colour, quality, etc: *standardize the safety regulations in factories* ○ *Paper sizes are usually standardized.*

/ˈstændədaɪz/
standardize, standardizing, standardized
(also **standardise**)
note transitive verb
⋈ **standardize** the colour, quality, size, weight (of something)
▶ **customize**

---

standard of living *noun* (economics)
the level of material comfort and wealth that a person or a community has: *They have a high standard of living and own many luxury goods.* ○ *I hope this new job will give me a better standard of living.*

/ˌstændəd əv ˈlɪvɪŋ/
note usually singular
⋈ a decent, good, high, low, poor, reasonable, satisfactory **standard of living**; improve, raise your **standard of living**
▶ **cost of living, living**

---

standard rate *noun* (tax)
(*UK*) the amount of tax, expressed as a percentage, paid by all taxpayers on the first band of income: *Most people pay the standard rate of income tax.* ○ *a standard rate of 25% or 25p in the pound*

/ˌstændəd ˈreɪt/
pl standard rates
⋈ deduct, pay the **standard rate**
▶ **income tax, rate 2**

---

standing order *noun* (banking)
a customer's instruction to a bank to pay a certain amount to another person or organization at regular intervals: *The rent is paid by standing order.* ○ *fill in a standing order form*, ie to say how much should be paid, to whom and when

/ˌstændɪŋ ˈɔːdə(r)/
pl standing orders
⋈ arrange a, cancel a, pay by **standing order**
syn banker's order, bank order
▶ **direct debit**

---

start-up *adjective* (management)
of money, etc needed to start and develop a new business: *We must include the advertising budget in our start-up costs.*

/ˈstɑːtʌp/
⋈ **start-up** capital, cash, costs; a **start-up** grant, loan
▶ **current capital, venture capital**

---

state bank *noun* (banking)
(*US*) a bank in the US that is governed by state laws rather than by federal laws. Unlike the national banks, state banks do not have to join the Federal Reserve System.

/ˌsteɪt ˈbæŋk/
pl state banks
▶ **commercial bank, Federal Reserve System**

---

statement of account *noun* (accounting)
a list of amounts paid and owed sent from a seller to a buyer, usually on a monthly basis: *Look at the statement of account to see which invoices are outstanding.*

/ˌsteɪtmənt əv əˈkaʊnt/
pl statements of account
⋈ check, file, issue, send a **statement of account**
▶ **account[1] 1**

---

statement of affairs *noun* (law)
a list showing the assets and liabilities of a bankrupt person or company

/ˌsteɪtmənt əv əˈfeəz/
pl statements of affairs
⋈ draw up, issue a **statement of affairs**
▶ **bankrupt[1]**

---

statistics *noun*

1 the collection, classification and use of information in numerical form: *He is studying statistics at university.* **2** the information presented in numerical form: *The statistics show that employment has fallen this year.*

/stəˈtɪstɪks/

1 note singular noun, used with a singular verb

2 note plural noun, used with a plural verb

⧓ economic, government, population **statistics**; analyse, collect, compile, find, present, use **statistics**

---

status inquiry *noun* (finance)

a check on someone's finances to ensure that they have enough money to pay back a loan: *You cannot have credit until we have the results of our status inquiry.*

/ˈsteɪtəs ɪn ˌkwaɪəri/

pl status inquiries

(also **status enquiry**)

⧓ make, request a **status inquiry**

---

statutory books *noun* (law/accounting)

(*UK*) the five books that a limited company is required to keep, showing the company's financial position, listing its members and directors and recording the minutes of directors' meetings: *Details of the directors' shareholdings will be in the statutory books.*

/ˌstætʃətri ˈbʊks/

note plural noun, used with a plural verb

▶ **limited company, registered company**

---

statutory company *noun* (law/finance)

(*UK*) a company that provides a public service, eg one that provides gas or water, formed by special Act of Parliament: *British Telecom and British Gas were formed as statutory companies.*

/ˌstætʃətri ˈkʌmpəni/

pl statutory companies

▶ **company, public sector**

---

statutory meeting *noun* (law)

(*UK*) any meeting required by the Companies Act (1985), esp the annual general meeting of the directors, members and shareholders: *We will need to discuss our share capital at the statutory meeting.*

/ˌstætʃətri ˈmiːtɪŋ/

pl statutory meetings

⧓ arrange, attend, call, hold a **statutory meeting**

▶ **annual general meeting**

---

statutory report *noun* (law)

(*UK*) a report that is required by the Companies Act (1985), esp the annual report: *Be sure the accountants have the statutory report ready in time for the meeting!*

/ˌstætʃətri rɪˈpɔːt/

pl statutory reports

⧓ compile, prepare, print, publish, write a **statutory report**

▶ **annual report, qualified report, report**[1]

---

statutory total income *noun* (tax)

▶ **total income**

/ˌstætʃətri ˌtəʊtl ˈɪŋkʌm/

---

sterling *noun* (finance)

(*UK*) British currency based on the UK pound (the pound sterling): *Do you take sterling?* ○ *Prices were quoted in sterling.* ○ *a sharp rise in the value of sterling on foreign exchange markets*

/ˈstɜːlɪŋ/

abbr stg, ster

note not used with *a* or *an*. No plural and used with a singular verb only.

⧓ accept, invoice in, pay in, quote in, take **sterling**; **sterling** exchange rate, interest rate, investors, sales, traveller's cheques

---

stock[1] *noun* (industry/retail)

1 stocks a supply of raw materials or resources for sale or use: *Grain stocks are high after this year's harvest.* **2** a quantity of goods for sale or distribution in a shop, warehouse, etc: *The shop had its entire stock of televisions stolen.* ○ *Your order can be supplied from stock.*

in stock available for sale in a shop, etc: *The book you wanted is now in stock.*

out of stock not available for sale in a shop, etc: *The colour you wanted is out of stock.* ○ *We're out of stock of size 39 at the moment.*

/stɒk/

1 note plural noun, used with a plural verb

⋈ cereal, coal, food, oil **stocks**

2 note singular noun, used with a singular verb

⋈ new, old **stock**; buy (in), order, replenish **stock**

► **average stock, ex stock**

stock[2] *noun* (stock exchange)

1 (*UK*) a fixed-interest security issued by the government or local authority **2** (*US*) an ordinary share

/stɒk/

pl stocks

1 ► **alpha stocks, assented stock, debenture stock, tap stocks**

2 ► **ordinary share, share**

stock[3] *verb* (retail)

to keep a supply of something (in a shop, etc): *We stock all sizes.* ○ *Do you stock children's clothes?*

/stɒk/

stock, stocking, stocked

note transitive verb

► **keep 2, overstock, stock[1] 2**

stockbroker *noun* (stock exchange)

a person or organization that buys and sells stocks and shares, either by acting as a PRINCIPAL or on behalf of clients in return for a fee (BROKERAGE): *I'll ask my stockbroker to sell these shares for us.*

/ˈstɒkbrəʊkə(r)/

pl stockbrokers

► **stock exchange, market maker**

stock control *noun* (manufacturing/retail)

a system of checking the goods and materials held by a company to ensure that supplies are reordered in time and that goods are not being stolen; the part of an organization where goods are checked: *We have computerized our stock control system.* ○ *She works in stock control.*

/ˈstɒk kənˌtrəʊl/

note not used with *a* or *an*. No plural and used with a singular verb only.

⋈ a **stock control** system; automated, computerized **stock control**

syn inventory control

► **average stock, control[1] 1, first in first out, last in first out, perpetual inventory, stock-taking**

stock exchange *noun* (stock exchange)

a market where stocks and shares are bought and sold under fixed rules, but at prices controlled by supply and demand: *The main international stock exchanges are based in the USA, Japan, and the UK.*

/ˈstɒk ɪksˌtʃeɪndʒ/

pl stock exchanges

abbr S.E., S/E

⋈ **stock exchange** activities, conditions, prices

► **American Stock Exchange, the Financial Times-Stock Exchange 100 Share Index, International Stock Exchange**

Stock Exchange Automatic Exchange Facility *noun* (stock exchange)

a computerized system on the International Stock Exchange that

/ˌstɒk ɪksˌtʃeɪndʒ ɔːtəˌmætɪk ɪksˈtʃeɪndʒ fəˌsɪləti/

abbr SEAF

…utomatically records and completes a transaction

▶ **stock exchange, TALISMAN, TAURUS**

Stock Exchange Automated Quotations System *noun* (stock exchange)
a computerized system on the International Stock Exchange that automatically records and sets the price for securities

/ˌstɒk ɪksˌtʃeɪndʒ ˌɔːtəmeɪtɪd kwəʊˈteɪʃnz ˌsɪstəm/
abbr SEAQ
▶ **stock exchange, TALISMAN, TAURUS, Teletext Output of Price Information by Computer**

the Stock Exchange Daily Official List *noun* (stock exchange)
a detailed record issued by the International Stock Exchange each day, showing prices of shares and securities and details of companies trading on the Stock Exchange: *Details of the day's trading can be found on the Stock Exchange Daily Official List.*

/ðə ˌstɒk ɪksˌtʃeɪndʒ ˌdeɪli əˌfɪʃl ˈlɪst/
syn Daily Official List, Official List
▶ **Stock Exchange**

stockholder *noun* (stock exchange)
(*US*) ▶ **shareholder**

/ˈstɒkhəʊldə(r)/

stock-in-trade *noun* (manufacturing/retail)
the goods or services that a business has for sale at a given time: *The stock-in-trade is shown as an asset on the balance sheet.*

/ˌstɒk ɪnˈtreɪd/
note singular noun, used with a singular verb
syn trading stock, inventory
▶ **first in first out, last in first out, stock[1] 2, stock control, stock turnover**

stockist *noun* (retail)
a dealer or shop that has supplies of a particular item: *The nearest stockist is in Manchester.*

/ˈstɒkɪst/
pl stockists
⧓ the local, nearest, recommended **stockist**
▶ **stock[1] 2, supplier**

stockjobber *noun* (stock exchange)
(*UK*) a dealer who acts as a market maker on the International Stock Exchange, trading with brokers and, since deregulation in 1986, with the general public. Stockjobbers usually specialize in a particular market.

/ˈstɒkˈdʒɒbə(r)/
pl stockjobbers
syn jobber
▶ **market maker, stockbroker**

stock market *noun* (stock exchange)
▶ **stock exchange**

/ˈstɒk ˌmɑːkɪt/

stock market valuation *noun* (stock exchange)
▶ **valuation**

/ˌstɒk mɑːkɪt væljuˈeɪʃn/

stock split *noun* (stock exchange)
(*US*) ▶ **scrip issue**

/ˈstɒk splɪt/

stock splitting *noun* (stock exchange)
(*US*) ▶ **share splitting**

/ˈstɒk ˌsplɪtɪŋ/

stock-taking *noun* (retail/accounting)
the listing, counting and checking of goods held in a warehouse or shop, usually at the end of a financial year: *Stock-taking will probably take three days.* ○ *We are closed for stock-taking next week.*

/ˈstɒk teɪkɪŋ/
note not used with *a* or *an*. No plural and used with a singular verb only.

(also **stocktaking**)
⋈ annual, computerized, daily, monthly, weekly **stock-taking**
▶ **stock control**

---

stock transfer form *noun* (stock exchange)
▶ **transfer form**

/ˌstɒk ˈtrænsfɜː fɔːm/

---

stock turnover *noun* (accounting/retail)
the ratio of the total cost of goods sold in a year and the value of goods held in a shop, etc at any one time. A bread shop has a low stock turnover and small profit margins as almost all items should be sold daily, whereas a jeweller holds high-priced goods for a long time and has a high stock turnover: *The stock turnover is too high, and we need to reduce the amount of stock we keep.*

/ˈstɒk ˌtɜːnəʊvə(r)/
note not used with *a* or *an*. No plural and used with a singular verb only.
⋈ high, low **stock turnover**
syn stock turn
▶ **stock-in-trade, turnover 2**

---

stop loss *noun* (stock exchange)
an instruction given to a broker to sell quickly if the price falls on a particular commodity or security to avoid losing money

/ˌstɒp ˈlɒs/
pl stop losses
⋈ order a **stop loss**
▶ **limit order, loss[1], market order**

---

stoppage *noun* (industrial relations)
an interruption of work, esp because of a strike: *The union called a 24-hour stoppage.* ○ *a stoppage by engineering workers*

/ˈstɒpɪdʒ/
pl stoppages
⋈ call, organize, stage a **stoppage**
▶ **strike[1]**

---

stoppage in transit *noun* (commerce/law)
a situation where a seller who has not been paid can halt a delivery of goods if the buyer goes bankrupt and cannot pay for them

/ˌstɒpɪdʒ ɪn ˈtrænzɪt/
note not used with *a* or *an*. No plural and used with a singular verb only.

---

stopped cheque *noun* (banking)
a cheque that the person who signed it (the DRAWER) has asked a bank not to pay. If such a cheque is paid, the bank must bear the loss: *The bank returned our stopped cheque this morning.*

/ˌstɒpt ˈtʃek/
pl stopped cheques
▶ **cheque**

---

storage *noun*
1 (*manufacturing*) (**a**) the storing of goods: *These goods should be packed carefully for storage.* ○ *What are your storage requirements?* (**b**) the space used or available for this: *Storage is very limited on this site.* ○ *on-site storage* ○ *keep meat in cold storage* (**c**) the cost of storing goods: *pay storage for keeping goods in a warehouse*
2 (*computing*) a facility for keeping information on computer: *We need a disk with an increased storage capacity.* ○ *storage on floppy/hard disk*

/ˈstɔːrɪdʒ/
note not used with *a* or *an*. No plural and used with a singular verb only.
1 ⋈ **storage** capacity, costs, space; long-term, short-term **storage**; a **storage** container, device, shed, site, unit
▶ **warehousing**
2 ⋈ data, disk **storage**
▶ **memory**

---

store[1] *noun* (manufacturing/retail)
1 (**a**) a place where goods are kept: *Put anything that won't fit on the shelves in the store.* (**b**) a quantity of materials kept for when they are needed: *I see you keep a store of paper-clips.* **2** (**a**) (*UK*) a

/stɔː(r)/
pl stores
1 ⋈ a cold, food, grain **store**
▶ **warehouse**

large shop, often with more than one floor, selling lots of different items: *buy something from a London store* ○ *a general store* (**b**) (*esp US*) a shop: *a drugstore*

2 ▶ **chain store, department store**

---

store[2] *verb*

1 (*manufacturing/retail*) to keep things in a warehouse, storeroom, etc for future use: *These must be stored in a dry place.* ○ *store televisions in a warehouse* **2** (*computing*) to keep data for future use: *I'm sure I stored those figures on this disk.*

/stɔ:(r)/

store, storing, stored

note transitive verb

1 ⋈ **store** (something) in, next to, on, on top of, under (something)

2 ⋈ **store** data, information; **store** (something) on computer, on disk

▶ **memory**

---

store audit *noun* (retail)

an examination of what is being purchased in a shop. The audit helps the store to control the stock, but is also useful for marketing and advertising: *The store audit proves that this brand is very popular.*

/ˌstɔ:r ˈɔ:dɪt/

pl store audits

⋈ carry out, complete, do a **store audit**

▶ **audit**[1]

---

store-room *noun* (manufacturing/retail)

▶ **store**[1] **1a**

/ˈstɔ: ru:m/

---

straight line depreciation *noun* (accounting)

a method of calculating depreciation in which the original cost of an item of value (an ASSET) is divided by the number of years it is likely to be used: *Straight line depreciation means the charges are the same each trading period.*

/ˌstreɪt ˌlaɪn dɪˌpri:ʃiˈeɪʃn/

note not used with *a* or *an*. No plural and used with a singular verb only.

▶ **depreciation 1, reducing-balance method of depreciation**

---

strategic planning *noun* (management)

▶ **corporate planning**

/strəˌti:dʒɪk ˈplænɪŋ/

---

strategy *noun* (management)

a plan of future action which, in a company, is usually decided by senior management: *We need to discuss our strategies for expansion.*

/ˈstrætədʒi/

pl strategies

⋈ carry out, develop, draw up, follow, plan, pursue, work out a **strategy**

▶ **plan**[1] **1**

---

streamline *verb* (industry)

to make something more efficient and effective: *We must streamline our production process in order to reduce costs.*

/ˈstri:mlaɪn /

streamline, streamlining, streamlined

note transitive verb

⋈ **streamline** a company, an industry, a method, a process, a system

▶ **amalgamate, consolidate, integrate, merge, rationalize, restructure**

---

street dealing *noun* (stock exchange)

▶ **after-hours dealing**

/ˈstri:t ˌdi:lɪŋ/

street price *noun* (stock exchange)
▶ **after-hours price**

/ˈstriːt praɪs/

strike¹ *noun* (industrial relations)
a time when people protest by refusing to work, usually because they want more money or better working conditions: *The union has called a strike.* ○ *a two-day strike by engineering workers* ○ *a miners', teachers', firemen's, etc strike* ○ *a dock, transport, postal, rail, etc strike* ○ *Two thousand car workers went on strike yesterday.*

all-out strike a strike by all the workers in a particular union, organization or trade: *The union is planning an all-out strike.*

official strike a strike that is organized by and has the approval of a recognized trade union: *An official strike stopped production.*

token strike a short strike, usually used as a warning of further strikes if workers' demands are not met: *The token strike lasted three hours.*

unofficial strike a strike that is called without the approval of a trade union: *The shop steward has called an unofficial strike.*

wildcat strike a strike called at short notice and without trade union agreement: *A wildcat strike will only cause more problems.*

/straɪk/
pl strikes
⋈ be, come out, go on **strike**; take **strike** action
▶ **blackleg, go-slow, industrial action, picket¹, stoppage, trade union, walk-out**

strike² *verb* (industrial relations)
to stop work for a time, usually to persuade employers to provide more money or better working conditions: *Engineering workers are striking for more pay.* ○ *Not all the union members wanted to strike.*

/straɪk/
strike, striking, went on strike
note intransitive verb
⋈ **strike** *against* (something), *for* (something)
▶ **blackleg, picket², walk out**

strikebound *adjective* (industrial relations)
not able to function because of a strike: *The cargo is strikebound in the docks.* ○ *The post office is full of strikebound parcels.*

/ˈstraɪkbaʊnd/
⋈ a **strikebound** cargo, factory, load, lorry, parcel, ship, site

strike-breaker *noun* (industrial relations)
▶ **blackleg**

/ˈstraɪk ˌbreɪkə(r)/

strike pay *noun* (industrial relations)
money paid from union funds to union members during a strike: *They will receive strike pay while funds last.*

/ˈstraɪk peɪ/
note not used with *a* or *an*. No plural and used with a singular verb only.
⋈ draw, give, receive, withdraw **strike pay**
▶ **pay²**

striker *noun* (industrial relations)
a worker who is on strike: *Strikers stopped the lorries from entering the factory gates.*

/ˈstraɪkə(r)/
pl strikers
⋈ an official, unofficial **striker**

strong-room *noun* (banking)
a locked room in a bank where money, valuable documents, etc can be kept with a minimum risk of theft: *Who has keys to the strong-room?*

/ˈstrɒŋ ruːm/
pl strong-rooms
⋈ enter, hold the keys to, keep (something) in a **strong-room**
▶ **safe**

structural unemployment *noun* (economics)
a reduction in the amount of paid work available because of technological changes or poor demand for a product: *South Wales has been hit by structural unemployment in the coal industry as mines close.* ○ *The government plans to introduce retraining schemes to deal with structural unemployment.*

/ˌstrʌktʃərəl ʌnɪmˈplɔɪmənt/
note not used with *a* or *an*. No plural and used with a singular verb only.
▶ **unemployment**

stub *noun*
▶ **counterfoil**

/stʌb/

sub-agent *noun* (retail/marketing)
a person or company employed by or representing an agent: *Our agent doesn't handle all the work himself, but he has a very reliable sub-agent.*

/ˈsʌb eɪdʒənt/
pl sub-agents
▶ **agent**

subcommittee *noun* (management)
a small group of people appointed by a main committee to do a particular area of the committee's work: *The finance subcommittee has/have prepared a report for us.*

/ˈsʌbkəmɪti/
pl subcommittees
note used with a singular or plural verb
⋈ a finance, new developments, planning, staff, etc **subcommittee**; appoint, chair, report to a **subcommittee**
▶ **committee**

subject to *adjective* (law/insurance)
dependent on (the result or conditions of something): *The site is sold subject to contract* (ie if a contract is signed). ○ *The proposals are subject to the director's agreement.*

/ˈsʌbdʒekt tu/
⋈ **subject to** agreement, approval, contract, survey

sublease *noun* (law)
a written agreement given by a tenant to another person allowing him or her the right to use a property on payment of rent: *The solicitor has drawn up a sublease for the first floor office.*

/ˌsʌbˈliːs/
pl subleases
⋈ agree, arrange, draw up, sign a **sublease**
syn underlease
▶ **lease**[1], **tenant**

sublet *verb* (law)
to lease a property which already has a headlease to another tenant: *The shop area below is sublet to an estate agent.*

/ˌsʌbˈlet/
sublet, subletting, sublet
note transitive verb
▶ **lease**[2], **let**[2], **rent**[2], **tenant**

submit *verb* (management)
to give (something) to a person or an organization so that it may be considered or decided upon: *I'd like to submit a design for a new product.* ○ *The sales manager has submitted a report to the managing director.* ○ *Please submit your expense forms monthly.*

/səbˈmɪt/
submit, submitting, submitted
note transitive verb
⋈ **submit** a claim, plan, proposal, report, request, scheme
▶ **present**[2] **1**

subordinate *noun* (personnel)
a person who has a lower or less important position in an organization than someone else: *I'll delegate this work to a subordinate.* ○ *The manager is not getting the best out of his subordinates.*

/səˈbɔːdɪnət/
pl subordinates
⧓ a **subordinate** position, role, status

---

subpoena[1] *noun* (law)
(*Latin*) **1** a legal document that orders a person to appear in a lawcourt: *Mr Green was served with a subpoena by Mrs Desai's lawyers.* **2** a legal document that orders records, files, etc to be brought to a lawcourt for examination

/səˈpiːnə/
pl subpoenas
⧓ ask for, despatch, draw up, issue, request, serve a **subpoena**
▶ **court order, summons**[1]**, writ**

---

subpoena[2] *verb* (law)
(*Latin*) **1** to order a person to appear in a lawcourt: *The prosecution will subpoena her to appear as a witness.* **2** to order records, files, etc to be brought to a lawcourt for examination: *The jury has subpoenaed the company's telephone records.*

/səˈpiːnə/
subpoena, subpoenaing, subpoenaed
note transitive verb
▶ **summons**[2]

---

subscribed capital *noun* (stock exchange)
▶ **issued capital**

/səbˌskraɪbd ˈkæpɪtl/

---

subscriber *noun*
1 a person who pays money regularly (a SUBSCRIPTION) to an organization to receive a magazine, to join a club or society, or to be provided with a service: *Telephone subscribers will receive a bill every three months.* ○ *The journal 'Management Today' increased its subscribers by 20% last year.* **2** (*stock exchange*) a person who buys shares in a new company and signs the MEMORANDUM OF ASSOCIATION: *There were more subscribers than expected for the new share issue.*

/səbˈskraɪbə(r)/
pl subscribers
1 ⧓ existing, new **subscribers**
2 ▶ **shareholder**

---

subscription *noun*
the money paid by someone (a SUBSCRIBER) who regularly receives a magazine, is a member of a club or society, or is provided with a service: *The magazine 'Computer Business' is putting up its subscription this month.* ○ *take out a subscription to a magazine* ○ *I must pay my union subscription this week.*

/səbˈskrɪpʃn/
pl subscriptions
⧓ cancel, increase, pay, put up, raise, take out a **subscription**

---

subscription shares *noun*
1 (*finance*) shares in a building society that are paid for in small regular amounts and provide the highest rate of interest: *Subscription shares can be paid for on a monthly basis.* **2** (*stock exchange*) the first issue of shares bought by subscribers to a company: *The price of the subscription shares proved to be popular.*

/səbˈskrɪpʃn ʃeəz/
note plural noun, used with a plural verb
⧓ buy, invest in **subscription shares**
▶ **issue**[1]**, minimum subscription, oversubscription, share**

---

subsidiary company *noun* (stock exchange)
a company of which at least half the share capital is owned by another company, called a parent or holding company: *There are now five subsidiary companies in the group.* ○ *Each subsidiary company trades under its own name.*

/səbˌsɪdiəri ˈkʌmpəni/
pl subsidiary companies
syn subsidiary
▶ **associate company, group, holding company**

---

subsidy *noun* (finance/economics)
money paid by a government to producers of certain goods, to help them provide low-priced goods without loss to themselves, or to an organization that benefits the public: *The housing association hopes to receive a government subsidy.* ○ *Farmers are unsure who will benefit from the new Common Agricultural Policy subsidies.*

/ˈsʌbsədi/
pl subsidies
abbr sub
⧓ agricultural, arts, farm, food, employment, housing **subsidies**; apply for, benefit from a **subsidy**
▶ **Common Agricultural Policy, intervention price, target price, threshold price**

---

sue *verb* (law)
to take legal action against somebody in a court: *The company is going to sue for damages.* ○ *Tell them we'll sue if the debt isn't paid by the end of the month.* ○ *He's being sued for breach of contract.* ○ *I'm suing him for copying my design.*

/suː/
sue, suing, sued
note transitive and intransitive verb
⧓ **sue** (someone) for damages, libel, negligence, non-payment (of debt, rent, etc)

---

sum insured *noun* (insurance)
the maximum amount that an insurance company will pay when a claim is made. This is agreed in advance in the insurance contract: *The sum insured for permanent disability is £100 000.*

/ˌsʌm ɪnˈʃʊəd/
pl sums insured
⧓ decrease, increase, raise the **sum insured**
▶ **insurance**

---

summarize *verb* (management)
to give (in speech or writing) the main points of something: *Please summarize what was said in the meeting.* ○ *The results of the sales campaign have been summarized in this document.* ○ *summarize a report in 500 words*

/ˈsʌməraɪz/
summarize, summarizing, summarized
(also **summarise**)
note transitive and intransitive verb
⧓ **summarize** an argument, a report, a speech

---

summary *noun* (management)
a short version of something that gives the main points only: *write a summary of the report*

/ˈsʌməri/
pl summaries
⧓ make, present, write a **summary**
▶ **abstract**

---

summary dismissal *noun* (industrial relations)
a sudden end to a person's employment, usually because of serious misconduct or a neglect of duty: *His summary dismissal after the fire was no surprise!*

/ˌsʌməri dɪsˈmɪsl/
pl summary dismissals
▶ **dismissal, unfair dismissal**

---

summons[1] *noun* (law)
(*UK*) an order to attend a court to answer a charge: *receive a summons to attend court* ○ *The summons has been served by a bailiff.*

/ˈsʌmənz/
pl summonses
⧓ issue, receive, serve a **summons**
▶ **court order, injunction, subpoena[1], writ**

---

summons[2] *verb* (law)
to order someone to attend a court to answer a charge: *She was summonsed to appear in court on 25th June.* ○ *The police have summonsed the wrong man.*

/ˈsʌmənz/
summons, summonsing, summonsed
note transitive verb

(also **summon**)

▶ **subpoena**[2]

---

superannuation *noun* (finance/accounting)
money deducted from an employee's salary and repaid with interest when he/she retires: *Their superannuation gives them a comfortable retirement.*

/ˌsuːpərˌænjuˈeɪʃn/

note not used with *a* or *an*. No plural and used with a singular verb only.

⧓ deduct, pay, receive **superannuation**

▶ **pension**

---

supervise *verb* (management/personnel)
to watch someone working or something being done to make sure a job is done properly: *You will have to be supervised until you have finished your training.* ○ *supervise the building work* ○ *We need to employ someone to supervise the canteen.*

/ˈsuːpəvaɪz/

supervise, supervising, supervised

note transitive and intransitive verb

▶ **manage**

---

supervision *noun* (management/personnel)
the process of watching others work to make sure a job is done properly: *She knows what she is doing and can work without supervision.* ○ *For safety, he can only operate the machine under supervision.*

/ˌsuːpəˈvɪʒn/

note not used with *a* or *an*. No plural and used with a singular verb only.

⧓ careful, close, detailed, proper, regular, under, with, without **supervision**

---

supervisor *noun* (management)
a person with authority who watches others work to make sure a job is done properly: *The supervisor will show you how to work the machine.* ○ *You'd better report the problem to your supervisor.*

/ˈsuːpəvaɪzə(r)/

pl supervisors

⧓ a department, an office, a telephone, a warehouse **supervisor**; ask, find, see the **supervisor**

▶ **boss, foreman, manager,** works manager *under* **works**

---

supplier *noun* (manufacturing/retail)
a person or organization that provides necessary goods or services: *You can order the material direct from the supplier.* ○ *Our main suppliers are out of stock at the moment.* ○ *a stationery, gas, furniture, etc supplier* ○ *suppliers of office equipment*

/səˈplaɪə(r)/

pl suppliers

⧓ a chief, a main, a major, a local, an overseas **supplier**; obtain, order (something) from the **supplier**

▶ **distributor, stockist**

---

supply[1] *noun* (manufacturing/retail)
1 providing or being provided: *We need to arrange the supply of office stationery.* ○ *When is your next supply date* (ie when will the goods be sent)*?* **2** the items provided: *order a supply of computer paper* **3** the amount of something that is available to use or buy: *Food supplies are scarce.* ○ *This company needs a supply of highly trained, hard-working people.*

/səˈplaɪ/

1 note not used with *a* or *an*. No plural and used with a singular verb only.

⧓ arrange a **supply**

▶ **excess supply, joint supply**

2 pl supplies

⧓ arrange, obtain, order, receive a **supply**

3 pl supplies

⧓ a limited, a plentiful, a short, an unlimited **supply**

---

supply² *verb* (manufacturing/retail)
to provide a person or an organization with a product or a service: *Please supply six loaves of bread to the canteen.* ○ *I wish they'd supply us with more stationery.*

/sə'plaɪ/
supply, supplying, supplied
note transitive verb

---

supply and demand *noun* (economics)
the amount of goods available and the amount wanted by customers. The relationship between supply and demand influences prices: *If supply and demand are equal, prices remain stable.*

/sə,plaɪ ənd dɪ'mɑ:nd/
note not used with *a* or *an*. No plural and used with a singular verb only.
⋈ a case of, the law of **supply and demand**
▶ **demand¹ 2, glut¹, market forces, shortage**

---

surcharge *noun* (tax)
an extra payment added to the usual amount: *a 20% surcharge on the price of imported goods* ○ *The travel company will not put a surcharge on the price of your holiday.*

/'sɜ:tʃɑ:dʒ/
pl surcharges
⋈ add, impose, pay, put a **surcharge**
▶ **charge¹ 1, service charge**

---

surety *noun* (law/banking)
1 a person who promises to repay a debt for someone else if that person fails to do so: *His mother has agreed to stand surety.*
2 money, property, share certificates, etc kept as a guarantee that a loan will be repaid: *We have the house deeds as surety that the loan will be repaid.* ○ *offer £3 000 as (a) surety*

/'ʃʊərəti/
note usually singular
1 ⋈ act as, stand **surety**
▶ **guarantor**
2 ⋈ deposited, held, left as (a) **surety**
▶ **collateral, guarantee¹ 3, security 3**

---

surface mail *noun* (transport)
the transport of letters and parcels by land and sea: *It is cheaper to send it surface mail.*

/'sɜ:fɪs meɪl/
note not used with *a* or *an*. No plural and used with a singular verb only.
▶ **airmail, mail¹ 2**

---

surplus *noun*
1 (*manufacturing*) an amount that is more than is needed: *Farmers have produced a surplus of milk/a milk surplus.* ○ *These goods are surplus to our requirements.* **2** (*accounting*) the amount of income that is more than expenditure; profit: *This surplus will improve the net value of the business.*

/'sɜ:pləs/
pl surpluses
⋈ make, produce a **surplus**
▶ **glut¹, shortage**
2 opp deficit

---

surrender value *noun* (insurance)
the amount of money an insurance company will pay if a life assurance policy is cancelled before it has run its full term: *The surrender value is low because the policy is only a few years old.*

/sə'rendə ,vælju:/
pl surrender values
abbr s. v.
⋈ calculate, pay, receive the **surrender value**
syn cash surrender value, loan value
▶ **life assurance, value 2**

---

survey¹ *noun*
1 a detailed study (usually followed by a report) of the condition of something: *The government has published a survey of safety conditions in factories.* ○ *A survey of world trade shows that the recession is world-wide.* **2** (*marketing*) a study of people's opinions,

/'sɜ:veɪ/
pl surveys
1 ⋈ carry out, commission, conduct, request a **survey**; a

choices and behaviour, usually made by asking them questions: *The survey will help us with our marketing plan.* ○ *We did a survey to find out what sort of people buy our products.* ○ *The survey showed that most people buy their food from supermarkets.* **3** an examination of the condition of a building, ship, etc, usually requested by someone who wants to buy it: *As a result of the survey we decided not to buy the house.* ○ *The insurance company need to carry out a survey after the fire.* **4** an examination of the area and features of a piece of land, esp to make a map or to prepare for building: *a survey of a plot of land for building*

special survey (*shipping*) a detailed examination of a ship done every four years by Lloyd's surveyors

survey indicates, proves, shows
▶ **report**¹
2 ⧓ a consumer, readership **survey**
▶ **market research**
3 ⧓ a house, an insurance, a mortgage, a property **survey**
4 ⧓ a land **survey**

---

survey² *verb*

1 to study and report on the condition of something: *The government is surveying the training needs of young people.*
2 (*marketing*) to question people to find out about their opinions and behaviour: *Over 50% of the people surveyed said they were not influenced by advertising.* **3** to make a detailed examination of the condition of a building, ship etc: *The house we want to buy is being surveyed tomorrow.* **4** to examine the area and features of a piece of land, esp to make a map or prepare for building: *survey the area between the housing estate and the river*

/səˈveɪ/
survey, surveying, surveyed
1 note transitive verb
▶ **report**²
2 ⧓ **survey** buyers, consumers, people
3 ⧓ **survey** a house, (a) property, a ship
4 ⧓ **survey** an area, land, a site

---

suspense account *noun* (accounting)

a temporary account used to record balances which are needed to correct a mistake or for deals which are not yet finalized: *Money for the French deal has been posted to a suspense account until we are ready to go ahead.*

/səˈspens əˌkaʊnt/
pl suspense accounts
⧓ post to, set up a **suspense account**
▶ **account**¹ **1**

---

suspension *noun* (management/industrial relations)

1 the removal of a person from their work for a time, usually because he/she has done something wrong: *Mr Smith is on suspension until the police have investigated the matter.* **2** stopping something which happens regularly: *Her travel plans have been affected by the suspension of ferries during the bad weather.*

/səˈspenʃn/
note not used with *a* or *an*. No plural and used with a singular verb only.
1 ⧓ be on **suspension**
2 ⧓ a **suspension** *of* deliveries, pay, payments

---

swap *noun* (finance)

the exchange of a product or business asset for another, instead of money

currency swap the exchange of one currency for another on one maturity date, combined with a reverse exchange of the same currencies for a forward maturity date: *We were offered a loan in US dollars at a very low rate but we needed sterling, so we arranged a currency swap.*

interest rate swap the exchange of fixed rate interest payments for floating rate interest payments between two parties: *Our treasurer thinks interest rates are going to rise steeply so we want to arrange a swap on our floating rate loan.*

/swɒp/
pl swaps
(also **swop**)

---

switchboard *noun* (office practice)

equipment for receiving and transferring telephone calls; the staff who use this equipment: *work as a switchboard operator* ○ *Phone (the) switchboard and ask them to take the call.* ○ *Tell switchboard I'll be out all afternoon.*

/ˈswɪtʃbɔːd/
note usually singular
⧓ call, contact, operate, phone (the) **switchboard**

---

switching *noun* (stock exchange)
the process of selling one type of investment and using the money to buy another: *Switching from fixed-interest securities to equity shares is often done.*

/ˈswɪtʃɪŋ/
note not used with *a* or *an*. No plural and used with a singular verb only.

SWOT analysis *noun* (marketing)
SWOT is an abbreviation for strengths, weaknesses, opportunities, threats. In a SWOT analysis, a company identifies its internal strengths and weaknesses and the external opportunities and threats it faces, so that it can be more successful, increase its profits and outdo its competitors. A SWOT analysis often forms part of a MARKETING PLAN: *We'll commission a team of management consultants to do a SWOT analysis.*

/ˈswɒt əˌnæləsɪs/
pl SWOT analyses
⧓ commission, undertake a **SWOT analysis**
► **marketing audit, marketing plan**

syndicate *noun* (industry/finance/stock exchange)
1 a group of people or companies who work together on a project to make money: *An international syndicate will be responsible for building the dam.* ○ *a syndicate of banks* **2** (*insurance*) a number of Lloyd's underwriters who work together as a group. Each LLOYD'S NAME accepts personal responsibility for a risk in return for the some part of the premium. The syndicate tends to specialize in one class of insurance and is run by a manager or agent.

marine syndicate a group of Lloyd's underwriters who specialize in marine insurance: *He is part of a marine syndicate at Lloyd's.*

/ˈsɪndɪkət/
pl syndicates
⧓ belong to, form, join a **syndicate**
1 ► **consortium**
2 ► **Lloyd's of London, underwriter**

syndicated loan *noun* (banking)
a loan made to a large organization by a group of banks where each bank lends an agreed amount

/ˌsɪndɪkeɪtɪd ˈləʊn/
pl syndicated loans
► **loan**[1]

synthetic materials *noun* (industry)
► **material**

/sɪnˌθetɪk məˈtɪəriəlz/

systems analysis *noun* (computing)
identifying the aims, tasks and problems of a company, a department or a project and producing a precise statement of how they can be achieved or improved by the use of computers: *work in systems analysis*

/ˈsɪstəmz əˌnæləsɪs/
note not used with *a* or *an*. No plural and used with a singular verb only.
► **analysis**

systems analyst *noun* (computing)
a person who plans and installs a computer system, provides the programmers with the information they need to write the programs, and trains staff in the use of the system: *We need a systems analyst with experience of graphics software development.*

/ˈsɪstəmz ˌænəlɪst/
pl systems analysts
syn computer analyst
► **analyst**

system software *noun* (computing)
programs supplied with or built into a computer to make the machine itself work, rather than to perform a particular task for the user: *This system software has proved to be very reliable.*

/ˈsɪstəm ˌsɒftweə(r)/
note not used with *a* or *an*. No plural and used with a singular verb only.
► **software**

T, t *abbr*
1 ton(s) or tonne(s) **2** (*commerce/transport*) tare

note used in written English only

---

tab *noun* (office practice)
a setting on a typewriter or word processor that positions text or figures in a column or TABLE as they are typed: *Do you know how to set the tabs on this machine?*

/tæb/
pl tabs
note *tab* is short for *tabulator*, but this word is not often used.
⋈ change, clear, move, position, use the **tab**; **tab** key, positions, settings

---

table *noun* (office practice)
a list of facts and figures systematically arranged, esp in columns: *arrange the figures in a table ○ a table with four columns*

/ˈteɪbl/
pl tables
▶ **chart¹ 1, graph**

---

tabulator *noun* (office practice)
▶ **tab**

/ˈtæbjəleɪtə(r)/

---

tachograph *noun* (transport)
an instrument used esp in a lorry to record the speed and travel time. It shows when lorry drivers have driven too long without a rest: *According to the tachograph, the driver exceeded his distance limit by twenty miles.*

/ˈtækəgrɑːf; *US* ˈtækəgræf/
pl tachographs
⋈ install, read a **tachograph**

---

take *noun* (commerce)
(*US*) the amount of money received by a business or other organization, esp on a specific occasion: *Today's take is a record.*

/teɪk/
note no plural
▶ **takings**

---

take-home pay *noun* (personnel)
the amount of money that a person has left of their wages after tax, national insurance, and any other payments (DEDUCTIONS) have been paid out of them by the employer: *How much do you get in take-home pay? ○ a take-home pay of £300 per week*

/ˈteɪk həʊm peɪ/
note no plural
⋈ a decrease, an increase in **take-home pay**; monthly, weekly **take-home pay**
syn net income
▶ **gross income, net income, pay²**

---

takeover *noun* (finance/stock exchange)
the buying of one company (the TARGET COMPANY) or most of the shares in it, by a person or another company (the BIDDER): *The family will never sell more than 49 per cent of the shares; they don't want any possibility of a takeover. ○ a takeover of a hotel chain ○ an unwelcome takeover by a rival company*

/ˈteɪkəʊvə(r)/
pl takeovers
⋈ a friendly, a hostile, an unfriendly, an unwelcome **takeover**; a **takeover** battle, deal, offer; **takeover** action, plans, talks; agree (to), attempt, fight a **takeover**
▶ **acquisition 2, black knight, City Code on Takeovers and Mergers, dawn raid, grey knight, merger, reverse takeover, takeover bid, target company, white knight**

take over *verb*
1 (*finance/stock exchange*) to buy a company or gain control of it, by buying shares in it from the shareholders: *There are plans to take over the company.* ○ *If we are taken over, there will be redundancies.* **2** (*personnel*) to take control or responsibility for something, esp in place of someone else: *take over as Chairman* ○ *take over responsibility for UK sales* ○ *take over the job of sales manager*

/ˌteɪk ˈəʊvə(r)/
take over, taking over, took over, taken over
1 note transitive verb
⧓ **take over** a business, company, firm
2 note transitive and intransitive verb
⧓ **take over** as, from (someone or something)
▶ **amalgamate, merge**

takeover bid *noun* (stock exchange)
an offer made to the shareholders of a company (the TARGET COMPANY) to buy their shares at a certain price, in order to gain control of it: *The shareholders voted against acceptance of the hostile takeover bid.* ○ *launch a surprise takeover bid*
conditional takeover bid a takeover bid in which the buyer will only buy at the stated price if certain conditions are fulfilled, eg if enough shares can be obtained to ensure control of the company
unconditional takeover bid a takeover bid in which the buyer will pay the stated price for any number of shares with no special conditions

/ˈteɪkəʊvə bɪd/
pl takeover bids
⧓ accept, defeat, launch, make, mount a **takeover bid**; a friendly, a hostile, an unfriendly, an unwelcome, a welcome **takeover bid**
syn offer to purchase
▶ **black knight, grey knight, takeover, target company, white knight**

takings *noun* (sales)
the money received by a business, esp a shop, from sales: *The shop assistant counted the takings at the end of the day.* ○ *Takings were low last week.*

/ˈteɪkɪŋz/
note plural noun, used with a plural verb
⧓ cash, daily, monthly, weekly **takings**; a fall, a rise in **takings**
▶ **take**

TALISMAN *abbr* (stock exchange)
(an acronym for) Transfer Accounting Lodgement for Investors and Stock Management. It is a computerized system for buying and selling securities through a central company (Sepon) for members of the International Stock Exchange of the UK: *Under Talisman the title of each share sold is transferred to Sepon Ltd.* ○ *The Talisman system made buying and selling shares much faster.*

/ˈtælɪzmən/
(also **Talisman**)
note pronounced as a word
⧓ through, under **TALISMAN**
▶ **TAURUS**

tally[1] *noun*
a list of items, eg goods, or amounts of money spent: *You must keep a tally of your expenses.*

/ˈtæli/
pl tallies
⧓ keep a **tally**; a **tally** sheet

tally[2] *verb*
(of figures, stories, etc) to correspond or agree: *These figures don't tally.* ○ *This doesn't tally with the information you gave me earlier.*

/ˈtæli/
tally, tallying, tallied
note intransitive verb
⧓ **tally** *with* (something)

tangible asset *noun* (accounting/finance)
something owned by a person or company that has a material form, eg goods, machines or cash: *The money raised from his tangible assets just about covered his debts.*

/ˌtændʒəbl ˈæsets/
note usually plural
⧓ assess, measure, value **tangible assets**; net **tangible assets**

syn tangibles
▶ **assets, intangible assets, movables**

---

tanker *noun* (transport)
a ship, lorry or railway truck built for transporting liquids in large tanks: *A 5 000 gallon oil tanker caught fire in the North Sea.* ○ *The petrol was transported by tanker.* ○ *a tanker carrying dangerous chemicals*

/ˈtæŋkə(r)/
pl tankers
⋈ a fuel, an oil, a petrol **tanker**

---

tap *noun* (public finance)
a tap stock

long tap a tap stock due to be repaid in more than fifteen years: *This long tap is repayable in twenty years.*

medium tap a tap stock due to be repaid in five to fifteen years

short tap a tap stock due to be repaid in less than five years

/tæp/
pl taps

---

tap issue *noun* (public finance)
the gradual sale of UK government securities, depending on levels of demand at a certain price

/ˈtæp ˌɪʃuː/
pl tap issues
▶ **gilts, issue**[1]

---

tap stocks *noun* (public finance)
UK government securities that are sold gradually by the government when the market price reaches a certain level, rather than all at once: *The government uses the sale of tap stocks to influence interest rates.*

/ˈtæp stɒks/
note usually plural
syn tap
▶ **gilts**

---

tare *noun* (retail/transport)
1 the weight of the container or wrapping in which goods are packed or of the vehicle carrying them: *If you deduct the tare from the gross weight, you get the net weight.* **2** an allowance made for this: *You have to allow for tare.* ○ *the weight including tare*

/teə(r)/
note not used with *a* or *an*. No plural and used with a singular verb only.
abbr T., t.
⋈ allow for, deduct **tare**; **tare** weight
▶ **dead weight**

---

target[1] *noun*
1 (*management*) a goal or result aimed at; an objective: *She has failed to reach her sales target.* ○ *We're setting a higher export target this year.* **2** (*marketing*) a group of people that a product is considered to be especially suitable for. Advertising and marketing is particularly aimed at this group: *Our target is the 50–60 age group.* ○ *The advertising must reach our target market.*

off target not being done at the expected rate; not achieving the expected result: *Production is off target this month.*

on target being done at the expected rate; achieving the expected result: *The building work is still on target.*

/ˈtɑːɡɪt/
pl targets
1 ⋈ exceed, meet, miss, reach, set a **target**; a production, a sales **target**
▶ **quota**
2 ⋈ a **target** group, market

---

target[2] *verb* (marketing)
to aim to sell to a particular group of people, esp by using advertising designed to appeal to the values and interests of this group: *We will target our campaign at young home-buyers.* ○ *These cosmetics are targeted at the teenage market.*

/ˈtɑːɡɪt/
target, targeting, targeted
note transitive verb
⋈ **target** (something) *at* (someone)

---

target company *noun* (finance/stock exchange)
a company that a person or another company tries to buy by

/ˈtɑːɡɪt ˌkʌmpəni/
pl target companies

naking a TAKEOVER BID for it: *The board of the target company is trying to defend the company against the takeover.*

► **takeover**

Target Group Index *noun* (marketing)
(UK) a series of reports made from the results of questionnaires that ask people about a wide range of products made by different companies. The reports can be bought by advertising and market research companies: *The Target Group Index shows that more consumers look for environmentally-friendly products.*

/ˈtɑːgɪt gruːp ˌɪndeks/
abbr TGI
► **market research**

---

target price *noun* (agriculture)
the price set by the European Community under its COMMON AGRICULTURAL POLICY as a reasonable average amount of money for farmers to receive for cereals, meat, poultry, eggs, fruit and vegetables. The community sometimes buys extra stocks of these foods to stop their prices falling too low: *set the target price for wheat*

/ˈtɑːgɪt praɪs/
pl target prices
⧓ agree, fix, set the **target price**; the **target price** for (maize, beef, eggs, etc)
► **intervention price, subsidy, threshold price**

---

tariff *noun*
1 (*tax/import*) an amount that must be paid when particular goods are imported into a country, or occasionally when they are exported: *The EC uses protective tariffs to help its farmers.* ○ *Tariff barriers can make trade difficult.* **2** a list of prices charged for goods or services, eg for rooms or meals in a hotel: *Is room service on the hotel tariff?*

/ˈtærɪf/
pl tariffs
1 ⧓ abolish, impose, lift, pay a **tariff**; **tariff** barriers
► **Board of Customs and Excise, customs 2, General Agreement on Tariffs and Trade**
2 ⧓ daily, weekly **tariff**

---

tariff company *noun* (insurance)
an insurance company that forms an agreement with a number of other insurance companies to charge the same amount (PREMIUM) for each type of insurance policy

/ˈtærɪf ˌkʌmpəni/
pl tariff companies

TAURUS *abbr* (stock exchange)
(an acronym for) Transfer of Automated Registration of Uncertified Stock, a computerized system for members of the International Stock Exchange of the UK for buying and selling securities: *Large organizations can link their own computers into TAURUS.* ○ *TAURUS members can use the system on behalf of other investors.*

/ˈtɔːrəs/
(also **Taurus**)
note pronounced as a word
⧓ operate, use **TAURUS**
► **TALISMAN**

---

tax¹ *noun* (tax)
a sum of money that a government takes from people's incomes, company profits, the sale of goods, etc to be used for public spending: *The government has increased the tax on cigarettes.* ○ *Last year the company paid ten million pounds in tax.*

after tax after tax has been paid: *He earns £12 000 after tax.*

before tax before tax has been paid: *She earns £20 000 before tax.*

set (something) against tax to subtract the cost of producing something from the amount of profit and therefore not pay tax on it: *The car expenses of a business can be set against tax.*

/tæks/
pl taxes
⧓ abolish, cut, impose, levy, pay, raise, reduce, remove (a) **tax**
► **capital gains tax, corporation tax, declaration of income, direct tax, income tax, indirect tax, Inland Revenue, pre-tax, taxation, turnover tax, value added tax**

---

tax² *verb* (tax)
(of a government) to demand a sum of money from a particular source, eg people's incomes, company profits, the sale of goods,

/tæks/
tax, taxing, taxed
note transitive verb

etc to raise money for public spending: *The government always taxes sales of alcohol.* ○ *Some groups of people are heavily taxed.*

⧓ **tax** heavily, lightly, severely

---

taxable income *noun* (tax)
the amount of a person's income on which tax has to be paid: *She has a taxable income of $50 000 per year.*

/ˌtæksəbl ˈɪŋkʌm/
note usually singular
⧓ high, low **taxable income**; a **taxable income** of (an amount per year)
▶ **income tax**

---

tax allowance *noun* (tax)
an amount of money that a person is permitted to earn without paying tax on it: *The level of personal tax allowances has been raised.* ○ *a single person's tax allowance*

/ˈtæks əˌlaʊəns/
pl tax allowances
syn (*US*) tax exemption, tax-free allowance
⧓ **tax allowance** for a single person, etc
▶ **allowance 3, taxable income, tax credit, threshold**

---

tax and price index *noun* (tax/economics)
a measure of how much more taxed income people have to earn in order to compensate for rising prices (INFLATION): *According to the tax and price index, I need a wage rise of £1 500 to keep up with inflation.*

/ˌtæks ənd ˈpraɪs ˌɪndeks/
note usually singular
abbr TPI
⧓ the **tax and price index** reveals, shows; according to the **tax and price index**
▶ **indexation, inflation, Retail Price Index**

---

tax assessor *noun* (tax)
(*US*) ▶ **tax inspector**

/ˈtæks əˌsesə(r)/

---

taxation *noun* (tax)
the system of raising money for public spending: *The government promises to cut taxation.*

multiple taxation the charging of tax by more than two countries on the same income (of a person or an organization): *The organization moved some of its operations from Europe to avoid multiple taxation.*

/tækˈseɪʃn/
note not used with *a* or *an*. No plural and used with a singular verb only.
⧓ abolish, cut, impose, increase, raise, reduce, remove **taxation**
▶ **fiscal, tax¹, tax²**

---

tax avoidance *noun* (tax)
action that is taken in order to pay as little tax as legally possible, eg by making sure that all possible expenses are claimed: *Accountants advise on tax avoidance.*

/ˈtæks əˌvɔɪdəns/
note not used with *a* or *an*. No plural and used with a singular verb only.
▶ **tax evasion**

---

tax base *noun* (tax)
a particular source and amount of money that is taxed, eg a person's taxable income, a company's profits or the sales of a particular item, eg tobacco: *The government aims to broaden its tax base with the aim of stopping tax evasion.*

/ˈtæks beɪs/
note usually singular
⧓ a local, national **tax base**

---

tax bracket *noun* (tax)
a level of income or wealth between a lower and an upper limit, that is taxed at a certain rate. The UK, for example, has two brackets for income, which is taxed at 'basic rate' (25%) or 'higher rate' (40%): *move to a higher tax bracket*

/ˈtæks ˌbrækɪt/
pl tax brackets
⧓ be in the basic rate, bottom, higher rate, top **tax bracket**;

go down, go up, move down, move up a **tax bracket**

tax break *noun* (tax/industry)
a reduction in tax (TAX RELIEF) for certain taxpayers, intended to help a particular group of people or kind of business; eg the government may charge investors in small new companies less tax: *The business expansion scheme provides a good tax break for top rate taxpayers.*

/ˈtæks breɪk/
pl tax breaks
⧓ make the most of, take advantage of a **tax break**
▶ **tax incentive, tax relief**

tax burden *noun* (tax)
the amount of money that a person or an organization loses in tax, either directly or indirectly. The tax burden of VALUE ADDED TAX, for example, falls on the buyers of goods even though the tax is actually paid by traders: *The tax burden of VAT is proportionally greater on the poor than the rich.*

/ˈtæks ˌbɜːdn/
pl tax burdens
⧓ ease, lift, lower, remove, share a **tax burden**; a heavy, light **tax burden**

tax collector *noun* (tax)
a person whose job is to obtain money that is owed to the government in tax: *As a tax collector, she was sometimes involved in bankruptcy cases.*

/ˈtæks kəˌlektə(r)/
pl tax collectors
▶ **Inland Revenue, tax inspector**

tax credit *noun* (tax)
a sum of money that reduces a tax bill because that amount has already been paid in tax. (An investor may receive a tax credit on dividends from shares bought from a company that has already paid tax on them): *receive a tax credit of 20p per share*

/ˈtæks ˌkredɪt/
pl tax credits
syn (*US*) tax offset
⧓ obtain, receive a **tax credit**
▶ **credit[1], tax allowance**

tax deductible *adjective* (tax)
(of an expense, esp a business expense) allowed to be subtracted from profit or income before tax is calculated: *Special work clothing is a tax deductible expense.*

/ˌtæks dɪˈdʌktəbl/
⧓ a **tax deductible** expense; **tax deductible** income
▶ **deductible**

tax evasion *noun* (tax)
illegal action that is taken to reduce the amount of tax paid, eg by giving the taxation authorities false information: *She was jailed for tax evasion.*

/ˈtæks ɪˌveɪʒn/
note not used with *a* or *an*. No plural and used with a singular verb only.
⧓ be charged with, found guilty of **tax evasion**
▶ **tax avoidance**

tax exempt *adjective* (tax)
1 (of a person, organization, etc) free from having to pay tax: *Schools and colleges are usually tax exempt.* **2** (of goods or income) free of tax: *Child benefit payments are tax exempt.*

/ˌtæks ɪgˈzempt/
2 ⧓ **tax exempt** earnings
syn tax free
▶ **deductible**

tax exemption *noun* (tax)
1 (*UK*) the freedom from having to pay tax, given to charities, educational institutions, or to individuals for specific reasons: *The organization claimed tax exemption.* ○ *Tax exemptions from inheritance tax include gifts to a charity or a political party.* **2** (*US*) a tax allowance

/ˌtæks ɪgˈzempʃn/
pl tax exemptions
1 ⧓ **tax exemption** *from* (a particular tax)

Tax Exempt Special Savings Account *noun* (tax)
a UK scheme for saving with a bank or building society for a long period without paying tax on the interest: *Savers with a Tax*

/ˌtæks ɪgˌzempt ˌspeʃl ˈseɪvɪŋz əˌkaʊnt/
abbr Tessa

Exempt Special Savings Account can invest a certain amount per year without paying tax on the interest.

▶ **account[1] 2**

---

tax exile *noun* (tax)

/ˈtæks ˈeksaɪl/

a wealthy person who lives in a country where he/she does not have to pay much tax, in order to avoid taxation at home: *Jersey is full of British tax exiles.*

pl tax exiles

▶ **tax haven**

---

tax form *noun* (tax)

/ˈtæks fɔːm/

▶ **tax return 2**

---

tax-free *adjective* (tax)

/ˌtæks ˈfriː/

(of a gift, earnings, etc) without tax: *My redundancy payment is tax-free.* ○ *receive a tax-free income*

⋈ **tax-free** earnings, income, interest, pay, savings certificates

▶ **duty free, tax allowance, tax exempt**

---

tax-free allowance *noun* (tax)

/ˌtæks friː əˈlaʊəns/

▶ **tax allowance**

---

tax haven *noun* (tax/finance)

/ˈtæks ˌheɪvn/

a country where taxation is very low and therefore attracts investment from foreigners who wish to escape paying tax. Individuals have bank accounts in tax havens without necessarily living there, and companies open offices: *The Bahamas, Monaco and Singapore are tax havens.*

pl tax havens

⋈ hold a bank account, invest in a **tax haven**

▶ **offshore fund, tax exile, tax shelter**

---

tax holiday *noun* (tax/industry)

/ˈtæks ˌhɒlədeɪ/

an agreed period when a company does not pay tax or pays reduced tax. Tax holidays are used to encourage new businesses or the expansion of existing businesses: *The company was given a tax holiday of two years in order to expand its exports.*

pl tax holidays

▶ **holiday**

---

tax incentive *noun* (tax/industry)

/ˈtæks ɪnˌsentɪv/

a reduction in the amount of tax paid in order to encourage people or organizations to carry out certain business or investment activities: *The government should offer tax incentives if it really wants to encourage the recycling of waste.*

pl tax incentives

⋈ introduce, offer, provide a **tax incentive**

▶ **tax break, tax relief**

---

tax inspector *noun* (tax)

/ˈtæks ɪnˌspektə(r)/

a person whose job is to decide how much tax individuals and companies should pay, and to stop people evading tax: *The tax inspector uncovered the accountant's fraud.*

pl tax inspectors

syn (*US*) tax assessor

▶ **tax collector**

---

tax loss *noun* (tax/finance)

/ˈtæks ˌlɒs/

a loss that is declared to the tax office with the aim of reducing the amount of tax paid. The loss may be due to a lack of profit or because the company has spent some of the profit on new machinery, etc: *announce a tax loss of £1.96 m* ○ *set a tax loss against profit*

pl tax losses

⋈ declare, deduct, offset a **tax loss**

▶ **loss 1**

---

tax offset *noun* (tax) /ˈtæks ˌɒfset/

(*US*) tax credit

taxpayer *noun* (tax) /ˈtækspeɪə(r)/

a person or company with enough income or wealth to have to pay tax: *We want to know how the taxpayer's money is being spent.* ○ *What does the Chancellor's Budget mean for the taxpayer?*

pl taxpayers

⧓ a basic rate, a higher rate **taxpayer**

opp non-taxpayer

tax relief *noun* (tax) /ˈtæks rɪˌli:f/

(*UK*) reduction in the amount of tax paid for a particular reason, eg on an amount paid for health insurance: *We are entitled to tax relief on our mortgage.* ○ *The government introduced tax relief for large gifts made to charity.*

note not used with *a* or *an*. No plural and used with a singular verb only.

⧓ claim, get, give, obtain **tax relief**; be eligible for, be entitled to, qualify for **tax relief**; **tax relief** *on* (something)

▶ **depreciation allowance, taxable income, tax allowance, tax exemption**

tax return *noun* (tax) /ˈtæks rɪˌtɜ:n/

1 a statement of a person's income for the past year, including any claims for tax relief. The statement is used by the tax office to calculate the amount of tax to be paid: *Everyone has to make a tax return.* ○ *a tax return for the year 1993-94* **2** the printed form on which a taxpayer's statement is made: *fill in a tax return* ○ *enter (an amount of income, etc) on a tax return* ○ *My tax return has arrived.*

pl tax returns

1 ⧓ make, send in a **tax return**

2 ⧓ complete, fill in a **tax return**; claim (relief), enter (earnings), fill in (earnings) on a **tax return**

syn tax return form, tax form

▶ **declaration of income**

tax schedule *noun* (tax) /ˈtæks ˌʃedju:l/

one of the six categories which the UK tax authorities divide income into in order to assess taxation. They are lettered A to F: *What tax schedule does she come under? If she's self-employed, it must be Schedule D.*

pl tax schedules

⧓ assess under, come under, tax under a **tax schedule**

tax shelter *noun* (tax) /ˈtæks ˌʃeltə(r)/

1 (*US*) a way of avoiding paying tax or of reducing the amount paid, eg by investing in a pension scheme or a loss-making company: *Making a farming loss can be a tax shelter.* **2** (*UK*) a way of using another country's tax laws to reduce the amount of tax paid: *The system in the Netherlands provides a useful tax shelter for some UK companies.*

pl tax shelters

1 ▶ **tax avoidance, tax loss**

2 ▶ **tax haven**

tax threshold *noun* (tax) /ˈtæks ˌθreʃhəʊld/

▶ **threshold**

tax year *noun* (tax) /ˈtæks jɪə(r)/

the period of twelve months, between specified dates, for which the tax owed by a person or an organization is calculated (eg between 6 April and the next 5 April in the UK or between 1 July and 30 June in the USA): *the 1993-94 tax year* ○ *declare what you earn in a tax year*

pl tax years

⧓ the current, next, previous **tax year**

▶ **financial year**

TB *abbr* (accounting) /ˌtiː ˈbiː/
trial balance

tba *abbr* (office practice) /ˌtiː biː ˈeɪ/
1 to be advised **2** to be agreed **3** to be announced

technical *adjective* /ˈteknɪkl/
1 (*technology*) relating to machines, materials and systems that are used in industry and science: *We need to employ more technical staff.* ○ *A number of washing machines were found to have the same technical fault.* **2** (*stock exchange*) relating to the general direction or movement of the price of securities, ie whether their price is gradually rising or falling: *These shares have been rising over the last six months; they're in a strong technical position.*

1 ⋈ a **technical** advance, defect, device, problem; **technical** drawing, knowledge, specifications
► **technological**
2 ⋈ **technical** position, rally

technical author *noun* (technology) /ˌteknɪkl ˈɔːθə(r)/
a person who writes manuals for computers, machinery, etc and provides written information on machine systems and processes: *work as a technical author* ○ *a technical author for a computer company*

pl technical authors
syn technical writer

technical correction *noun* (stock exchange/finance) /ˌteknɪkl kəˈrekʃn/
a rise or fall in the price of a security or currency following an extreme fall or rise to bring it back to its real value: *As a result of a technical correction, your shares rose slightly today after yesterday's fall.*

note usually singular
⋈ a **technical correction** in the market

technological *adjective* (technology) /ˌteknəˈlɒdʒɪkl/
relating to the use and study of scientific methods and mechanical processes: *Because of technological changes, a number of traditional jobs have become obsolete.* ○ *a technological society*

⋈ **technological** advancement, change, development, progress
► **technical**

technology *noun* (technology) /tekˈnɒlədʒi/
1 the activity or study of the use of scientific knowledge and mechanical processes in business, industry, farming, etc: *advances in technology* ○ *It is important to keep up with new technology.* **2** a particular scientific method, mechanical or electrical process used for a particular purpose: *New fuel-burning technologies can reduce the amount of pollution.*

1 note not used with *a* or *an*. No plural and used with a singular verb only.
⋈ computer, information, modern, new **technology**; use **technology**
► **information technology**
2 pl technologies
⋈ agricultural, chemical, food **technologies**

telecommunications *noun* (technology) /ˌtelikəˌmjuːnɪˈkeɪʃnz/
links over long distances by telephone, cable, television, radio and telegraph: *Telecommunications is a growth industry.* ○ *a telecommunications engineer*

note used with a singular or a plural verb
⋈ a **telecommunications** network, service, system; the **telecommunications** industry

telegraphic address *noun* (international trade) /ˌtelɪgræfɪk əˈdres/
a very short business address that is registered with the postal service for use in telegrams and cables. Telegraphic addresses

pl telegraphic addresses
syn cable address

are now used less often than formerly because more companies send messages by TELEX or FAX: *We do still have a telegraphic address, but a fax would be quicker.*

▶ **address[1] 1**

---

telegraphic transfer *noun* (banking/international trade)
a quick way of sending money to someone abroad. The sender's bank cables the money (ie sends an instruction by telegraph for it to be paid) to the bank of the receiver: *payment by telegraphic transfer* ○ *send money by telegraphic transfer*

/ˌtelɪˌɡræfɪk ˈtrænsfɜː(r)/
pl telegraphic transfers
abbr TT
⋈ pay, send by **telegraphic transfer**
syn cable transfer
▶ **bank transfer**

---

telemarketing *noun* (sales)
telling potential customers about a product or service using the telephone: *She works in telemarketing.* ○ *Telemarketing is a successful way of reaching customers directly.*

/ˈteliˌmɑːkɪtɪŋ/
note not used with *a* or *an*. No plural and used with a singular verb only.
▶ **direct marketing, marketing**

---

telephone research *noun* (marketing)
finding out what goods people buy and at what price, etc by talking to them on the telephone. It is a common form of MARKET RESEARCH: *Our telephone research shows that consumers want certain shops to open on Sundays.*

/ˌtelɪfəʊn rɪˈsɜːtʃ, ˌtelɪfəʊn ˈriːsɜːtʃ/
note not used with *a* or *an*. No plural and used with a singular verb only.
⋈ **telephone research** reveals, shows, suggests; find out by **telephone research**
▶ **market research**

---

telephone selling *noun* (sales)
▶ **telesales**

/ˌtelɪfəʊn ˈselɪŋ/

---

teleprinter *noun* (office practice)
a machine that looks like a typewriter, for sending and receiving TELEX messages: *Type the message into the teleprinter.*

/ˈteliprɪn tə(r)/
pl teleprinters
⋈ a **teleprinter** prints (out), receives, sends, transmits; receive (a message) on a **teleprinter**

---

telesales *noun* (sales)
using the telephone to sell goods or services; sales made in this way: *We've increased our telesales this year.* ○ *Telesales is often used for home improvements such as new kitchens, windows, central heating, etc.*

/ˈteliseɪlz/
note used with a singular or a plural verb
⋈ by, through **telesales**
syn telephone selling
▶ **direct mail, direct marketing**

Teletext *noun* (technology)
a system that uses television signals to send out information from a central computer, and makes the information appear on a specially adapted television set: *Can you get Teletext on your television?*

/ˈtelitekst/
note not used with *a* or *an*. No plural and used with singular verb only.
⋈ get, receive, transmit **Teletext**; the **Teletext** service, system
▶ **CEEFAX, Prestel, Videotex, viewdata**

Teletext Output of Price Information by Computer
noun (stock exchange)
a computerized system that provides information about share prices and deals on the International Stock Exchange

/ˌtelitekst ˌaʊtpʊt əv ˌpraɪs ɪnfəˌmeɪʃn baɪ kəmˈpjuːtə(r)/
abbr TOPIC
▶ **Stock Exchange Automated Quotations System**

---

television rating *noun* (marketing)
a measurement of how popular a television programme is, stated as the percentage of television owners who are watching or listening to that particular programme. Advertisers use the results when placing a television advertisement: *This programme has a television rating of 20%.* ○ *television ratings for films, documentaries, independent television, etc*

/ˈtelɪvɪʒn ˌreɪtɪŋ/
pl television ratings
abbr TVR
⋈ **television rating** figures; larger, smaller **television ratings**
▶ **rating 1**

---

telex[1] *noun* (office practice)
1 a way of sending written messages, usually to another country, using the telephone system: *Send the order by telex.* **2** a message sent or received by telex: *The telex is coming through now.* ○ *check today's telexes*

/ˈteleks/
pl telexes
1 ⋈ receive, send (something) by **telex**; a **telex** line, machine, message, operator, system
2 ⋈ receive, send a **telex**; a **telex** comes through, is printed, prints out
▶ **electronic mail, fax**[1], **teleprinter**

---

telex[2] *verb* (office practice)
to send a message using the TELEX system: *Can you telex the order today?* ○ *Telex the New York office to say when I'll arrive.* ○ *He telexed this morning.*

/ˈteleks/
telex, telexing, telexed
note transitive verb
▶ **fax**[2]

---

teller *noun* (banking)
▶ **bank clerk**

/ˈtelə(r)/

---

temp[1] *noun* (personnel)
a temporary employee, esp a temporary secretary, who is employed through a secretarial agency: *We need a temp while my secretary is in hospital.*

/temp/
note The abbreviation *temp* is more commonly used than the full term *temporary*.
⋈ be, work as a **temp**; a **temp** agency

---

temp[2] *verb* (personnel)
to work in temporary jobs, esp as a temporary secretary for a secretarial agency: *I've been temping for a year.* ○ *I temped for Mrs Green while her secretary was on holiday.*

/temp/
temp, temping, temped
note intransitive verb
⋈ **temp** *for* (a person or an organization)

---

temporary assurance *noun* (insurance)
▶ **term assurance**

/ˈtemprəri əˈʃʊərəns/

---

tenancy *noun* (law)
1 the use of land or buildings in return for payment (RENT) to the owner: *tenancy of the property* ○ *a tenancy agreement* **2** the length of time agreed for someone to make use of land or buildings belonging to someone else: *The tenancy expires next year.*

/ˈtenənsi/
1 note not used with *a* or *an*. No plural and used with a singular verb only.
⋈ **tenancy** *of* a flat, a house, an office, etc; the **tenancy** expires, lapses (on a certain date); give

up, hold, renew, surrender a **tenancy**

2 pl tenancies

⧓ life, long-term, short-term, three-year (etc) **tenancy**

▶ **lease[1], rent**

---

tenant *noun* (law)

a person or organization that uses land or a building in return for payment (RENT) to the owner: *Our tenants pay monthly.* ○ *He's a tenant farmer.*

sitting tenant a tenant who has the right to continue to live in a property, or part of it, when it is sold to a new owner: *She bought the house cheap because it had sitting tenants.*

/ˈtenənt/

pl tenants

⧓ a joint, life **tenant**; a **tenant** farmer

▶ **lessee, occupant, rent**

---

tender[1] *noun*

1 (*industry*) a formal offer to supply goods or carry out work for a stated price: *The architect invited tenders from four building firms for the school contract.* **2** (*stock exchange*) a written offer to buy or sell securities, etc at a stated price: *These shares are being sold by tender.* **3** (*shipping*) a boat that is used for taking passengers or goods to or from a larger ship: *The supplies were taken ashore in a tender.*

put (a job, contact, etc) out to tender to ask several firms to estimate in detail what a job will cost: *The building of the new leisure centre was put out to tender.*

win the tender to have an offer to do work accepted: *The most reliable builder won the tender.*

/ˈtendə(r)/

pl tenders

1 ⧓ accept, ask for, invite, make, put in, submit a **tender**

▶ **legal tender, self-tender, Shared Currency Option Under Tender**

---

tender[2] *verb*

1 (*industry*) to make a formal offer to supply goods or carry out work for a stated price: *tender for building an office block* **2** (*stock exchange*) to make a formal offer to buy something, eg securities, at a stated price: *tender for a new issue of shares* **3** (*formal*) to offer or give something formally, esp money: *She tendered a $20 dollar note to pay for the damage.* ○ *He tendered his resignation (to the managing director).*

/ˈtendə(r)/

tender, tendering, tendered

1 note intransitive verb

⧓ **tender** *for* (something); ask, invite someone to **tender** (for something)

2, 3 note transitive verb

---

tenor *noun* (banking)

▶ **term 2**

/ˈtenə(r)/

---

tenure *noun*

1 (*law*) (**a**) the right to use land or a building as agreed with the landlord; the right of tenancy: *He holds the tenure of the office building.* (**b**) the time or condition of this: *a three-year tenure* ○ *a freehold tenure* **2** (**a**) (*personnel*) the holding of a position or office: *She received tenure of the presidency* (**b**) the time or condition of this: *The tenure of the presidency is four years.*

security of tenure the right of a tenant to continue to use land or a building, even if the landlord wishes her/him to leave: *We couldn't get the tenants out of the house because they had security of tenure.*

/ˈtenjə(r)/

1 pl tenures

⧓ freehold, leasehold **tenure**

2 note not used with *a* or *an*. No plural and used with a singular verb only.

⧓ life, lifetime **tenure**

▶ **tenancy**

---

term *noun*

1 a length of time, esp of a formal agreement; period: *a term of twenty years* ○ *a term of office* ○ *a term of a lease* **2** (*banking/*

/tɜːm/

pl terms

2 note often used in combination with the following

insurance) the length of time before a bill of exchange or promissory note becomes due for payment (reaches MATURITY). It is stated on the bill or note: *the term of the bill*

long/short term of or for a long/short period of time: *looking ahead to the long term* ○ *There's no end to the recession in the short term.* ○ *a long/short term agreement*

⧓ a **term** deposit, loan, policy
syn tenor
▶ **period bill, terms**

---

term assurance *noun* (insurance)
a form of LIFE ASSURANCE that only lasts for a fixed time. It is often arranged with a loan and lasts until the date when the loan must be repaid. If the insured person dies after this time no insurance money is paid: *a fifteen-year term assurance* ○ *We have a term assurance policy.*

/ˌtɜːm əˈʃʊərəns/
note not used with *a* or *an*. No plural and used with a singular verb only.
⧓ a **term assurance** policy
syn temporary assurance
▶ **assurance, terminal bonus**

---

term bill *noun* (banking)
▶ **period bill**

/ˈtɜːm bɪl/

---

terminal *noun*
1 (*computing*) the part of a computer used by someone who is putting information in or getting information out of it. The terminal usually consists of a keyboard and a display screen: *The bank has a central mainframe computer, with terminals in all its branches.* **2** (*transport*) an airport building or a dock, etc where passengers arrive or depart, or where goods are loaded or unloaded: *The containers were loaded from the terminal onto the ship.*

/ˈtɜːmɪnl/
pl terminals
⧓ a computer, display, remote **terminal**; sit, work at a **terminal**
▶ **central processing unit, interface, peripheral, workstation**
2 ⧓ an airport, a cargo, a ferry, a freight, an ocean, a passenger **terminal**; a **terminal** building

---

terminal bonus *noun* (insurance)
an extra amount that is added to payments made on a life assurance policy, when the policy reaches its maturity date: *receive a terminal bonus on a life assurance policy*

/ˌtɜːmɪnl ˈbəʊnəs/
pl terminal bonuses
⧓ pay, receive a **terminal bonus**
▶ **bonus, capital sum, life assurance, term assurance**

---

terminal loss *noun* (accounting/tax)
a loss made by a business in the year that it closes down. It may be declared as a TAX LOSS and subtracted from profits of previous years: *We are setting a terminal loss of £10 000 against the last two years' profits.*

/ˌtɜːmɪnl ˈlɒs/
pl terminal losses
⧓ make a **terminal loss**; set a **terminal loss** against profits
▶ **loss 1**

---

terminal market *noun* (commerce)
a market dealing mainly in goods that will be available in the future (FUTURES) rather than goods that are available immediately (ACTUALS). Most terminal markets are outside the countries that produce the goods.

/ˈtɜːmɪnl ˌmɑːkɪt/
pl terminal markets
▶ **commodity market, futures market, market[1], spot market**

---

terms *noun*
1 (*commerce/law*) things that have been formally agreed; conditions offered or accepted: *under the terms of the contract* ○ *We could not agree (on) terms.* ○ *bound by the terms of the agreement* **2** (*accounting/finance*) financial arrangements; payment offered or asked: *What are your terms for car rental?* ○ *We're offering easy terms.* ○ *Our terms are 30 days* (ie before payment is due).

/tɜːmz/
note plural noun, used with a plural verb
1 ⧓ **terms** of employment, sale; **terms** of an agreement, a contract, a lease, a mortgage, an offer; according to, by,

under the **terms** (of the contract, etc)

2 ⋈ investment, loan, payment **terms**; attractive, cash, easy, payment, preferential, settlement, trade **terms**

▶ **real terms**

---

term share *noun* (finance)

a form of building society investment that earns a high rate of interest, but can only be cashed after a certain length of time: *invest in term shares*

/ˈtɜːm ʃeə(r)/

pl term shares

⋈ buy, invest in **term shares**

▶ **share**

---

terms of trade *noun* (economics/international trade)

a measure of the trading success of a country by comparing the prices of its imports with the prices of its exports. If export prices rise faster than import prices, terms of trade are said to improve. A fall in the exchange rate will have an unfavourable effect on the terms of trade: *Economists ask whether the terms of trade are unfavourable for developing countries.*

/ˌtɜːmz əv ˈtreɪd/

note plural noun, used with a plural verb

⋈ adverse, favourable, unfavourable **terms of trade**

▶ **balance of trade, trade**[1]

---

territorial waters *noun* (law/shipping)

the area of sea, usually about twelve miles wide, surrounding and controlled by a country, according to international law. Controls apply to navigation, fishing, customs and health, etc: *Ships are sometimes caught fishing in other countries' territorial waters.*

/ˌterəˌtɔːriəl ˈwɔːtəz/

note plural noun, used with a plural verb

⋈ inside, in violation of, outside, within **territorial waters**

---

tertiary industry *noun* (industry)

▶ **service industry**

/ˌtɜːʃəri ˈɪndəstri/

Tessa *noun* (tax)

(an acronym for) Tax Exempt Special Savings Account: *Do you have a Tessa?* ○ *Are you saving with a Tessa account?*

/ˈtesə/

note pronounced as a word

⋈ take out a **Tessa**; a **Tessa** account

---

testament *noun* (law)

▶ **will**

/ˈtestəmənt/

---

testate *adjective* (law)

having left a legal will at death: *She died testate.*

/ˈtesteɪt/

⋈ a **testate** person

opp intestate

▶ **will**

---

test case *noun* (law)

a lawsuit or other action resulting in a decision that may be used to settle similar cases in the future: *The outcome of these wage talks will be seen as a test case for future pay negotiations.*

/ˈtest keɪs/

pl test cases

⋈ bring, lose, win a **test case**; a **test case** against (someone), for (something); make a **test case** out of (something)

---

testimonial *noun* (personnel)

a written report on a person's character and skills, esp one by a former employer: *When she left, her employer gave her a testimonial that she could use for future job applications.* ○ *I'd be happy to write you a testimonial/write a testimonial for you.*

/ˌtestɪˈməʊniəl/

pl testimonials

⋈ provide, supply, write a **testimonial**; a **testimonial** letter

▶ **reference 2**

testimonial advertising *noun* (advertising)
the use, by advertisers, of famous people to recommend a particular product: *Famous sports personalities often do testimonial advertising for manufacturers of sports equipment.*

/ˌtestɪˌməʊniəl ˈædvətaɪzɪŋ/
note not used with *a* or *an*. No plural and used with a singular verb only.
⋈ do, make use of, use **testimonial advertising**

---

test market[1] *noun* (marketing)
a country, region or small area used to test out a new product before selling it more widely: *We are using Italy as a test market this year.*

/ˈtest ˌmɑːkɪt/
pl test markets
⋈ choose, select, use a **test market**

---

test market[2] *verb* (marketing)
to sell a new product in a small area to find out how consumers react: *We'll test market the washing powder in Manchester.*

/ˈtest ˌmɑːkɪt/
test market, test marketing, test marketed
note transitive verb
▶ **market**[1], **pilot**[2] **2**

---

test marketing *noun* (marketing)
the sale of a new product in a small area to find out how consumers react. The product or advertising can then be changed if necessary before it is more widely sold: *Our test marketing shows that consumers like the fruit flavour better than the mint.*

/ˈtest ˌmɑːkɪtɪŋ/
note not used with *a* or *an*. No plural and used with a singular verb only.
⋈ **test marketing** reveals, shows (that)
▶ **marketing, market research, pre-testing**

TGI *abbr* (marketing)
Target Group Index

/ˌtiː dʒiː ˈaɪ/
note pronounced as individual letters

---

thin *adjective* (stock exchange)
not busy; with little buying and selling: *a thin market* ○ *Trading was thin because of a shortage of stock.*

/θɪn /
⋈ **thin** dealing, trading
▶ **thin market**

---

thin capitalization *noun* (finance/stock exchange)
a situation where a company has very few shares, because it is financed by loans from the holding company. The interest on the loans is then set against tax: *In cases of thin capitalization, some countries may tax the interest on the loan stock.*

/ˌθɪn ˌkæpɪtəlaɪˈzeɪʃn/
note not used with *a* or *an*. No plural and used with a singular verb only.

---

thin market *noun* (stock exchange)
a situation where there is only a limited supply of a particular security available on the stock exchange: *a thin market in Rosehaugh shares*

/ˌθɪn ˈmɑːkɪt/
note usually singular
⋈ buy, sell in a **thin market**
syn limited market, narrow market
▶ **market**[1], **security 1**

---

third line forcing *noun* (commerce/law)
the refusal to sell goods that a customer wants unless he/she also buys something that he/she did not intend to buy. It is usually illegal: *The Office of Fair Trading investigated a case of third line forcing.*

/ˌθɜːd laɪn ˈfɔːsɪŋ/
note not used with *a* or *an*. No plural and used with a singular verb only.
▶ **restrictive trade practices**

---

third market *noun* (stock exchange)

1 (in the UK) one of the trading sections of the International Stock Exchange. It deals in securities that are less strictly listed than for the main market, and are therefore more risky: *invest in the third market* ○ *buy on the third market* **2** (in the USA) the market in which listed securities are bought and sold privately, without using a stock exchange: *I bought the shares from a broker on the third market.*

/ˌθɜːd ˈmɑːkɪt/

note usually singular

1 ⋈ investment in the **third market**; buy, sell on the **third market**

▶ **International Stock Exchange, main market, market[1], unlisted securities market**

2 ⋈ buy, sell on the **third market**

---

third party *noun*

a person who is not one of the two main people involved in an arrangement, a dispute, etc but is affected in some way: *He had to appear in court as a third party in the case.* ○ *Are any third parties affected by this agreement?* ○ *arrange something through a third party*

/ˌθɜːd ˈpɑːti/

pl third parties

⋈ affect, involve a **third party**

▶ **party**

---

third party insurance *noun* (insurance)

a type of insurance that provides compensation for injury or damage to the property of a person (the third party) caused by the insured person: *Employers must hold third party insurance to cover accidents to employees at work.* ○ *You need to produce a third party insurance certificate.*

/ˌθɜːd ˌpɑːti ɪnˈʃʊərəns/

note not used with *a* or *an*. No plural and used with a singular verb only.

⋈ hold, take out **third party insurance**; a **third party insurance** certificate, policy

syn third party cover

▶ **insurance**

---

the third world *noun* (economics)

the developing countries of Africa, Asia and Latin America, esp those which lack the industrial wealth and advanced technology of the western nations

/ðə ˌθɜːd ˈwɜːld/

note no plural

(also **the Third World**)

⋈ sell (goods, etc) in/into/to the **third world**; **third world** countries, culture, debt, development, economies

---

Thirty Share Index *noun* (stock exchange)

the Financial Times Ordinary Share Index: *The Thirty Share Index fell today by three points.*

/ˌθɜːti ˈʃeər ˌɪndeks/

---

threshold *noun*

a level (of pay, tax, etc) which has to be reached before a certain financial arrangement starts to operate: *the threshold of 10% inflation* ○ *a threshold payment*

tax threshold (*tax*) the level of a person's income at which he/she starts paying tax: *Your tax threshold depends on your tax allowances.*

wage threshold (*industrial relations*) the rate of inflation at which a pay increase is given, as agreed in advance between employer and employees: *a wage threshold of 10% inflation*

/ˈθreʃhəʊld/

pl thresholds

⋈ cross, reach, rise above, sink below the **threshold**; a **threshold** for (something); a **threshold** of (10%); **threshold** level, payments

▶ **indexation, tax allowance**

---

threshold agreement *noun* (industrial relations)

an arrangement made between an employer and employees that pay will be increased if inflation reaches a certain level during a particular period: *The union negotiated a threshold agreement to take effect at 10% inflation.*

/ˈθreʃhəʊld əˌgriːmənt/

pl threshold agreements

⋈ a **threshold agreement** comes into effect on, takes effect from (a certain date);

implement, put into effect a **threshold agreement**

▶ **Cost of Living Index, indexation**

---

threshold effect *noun* (advertising)
the way in which the amount of advertising for a product has to reach a certain level before sales begin to increase: *Advertisers have to take the threshold effect into account.*

/ˈθreʃhəʊld ɪˌfekt/
note usually singular
⋈ allow for, take into account the **threshold effect**

---

threshold price *noun* (economics)
the price agreed by the European Community as the minimum price for imported cereals and other farm products: *Threshold prices are fixed by the European Commission.*

/ˈθreʃhəʊld praɪs/
pl threshold prices
⋈ fix, set a **threshold price**
▶ **Common Agricultural Policy, intervention price, subsidy, target price**

---

thrift *noun* (banking/finance)
(*US*) a savings bank or savings and loan association: *The thrifts have increased their interest rates.*

/θrɪft/
pl thrifts
⋈ a **thrift** company, institution; the **thrift** industry
▶ **savings and loan association**

---

throughput *noun* (industry)
the quantity of materials that can be processed, the amount of work that can be done, or the number of customers that can be served in a particular time: *The egg packing department has a throughput of 500 boxes per hour.* ○ *Computerization has increased our throughput of mailings dramatically.* ○ *a throughput of 60 million airline passengers in a year*

/ˈθruːpʊt/
note usually singular
⋈ annual, monthly, weekly **throughput**; increase, reduce **throughput**; **throughput** of (someone or something)

---

tied *adjective*
1 (*retail*) (of a business, eg a public house, petrol station, etc) where the manager must obtain all the goods for sale from one supplier, who is usually the owner: *a tied pub owned by the brewery* **2** (*personnel*) (of a house) available for someone to live in while he/she is working for the owner: *When he retires he will have to leave his tied cottage.*

/taɪd/
1 ⋈ a **tied** outlet, shop
2 ⋈ a **tied** cottage, house

---

tied loan *noun* (finance)
money that is lent to one country by another country on condition that it is spent on goods or services from the country that provided the money: *tied loans to developing countries*

/ˌtaɪd ˈləʊn/
pl tied loans
⋈ accept, make, offer, take (out) a **tied loan**

---

tie up *verb* (finance)
to invest (wealth, capital, etc) in a business, in securities or in material possessions, etc, that are difficult to sell quickly if cash is needed: *The $50 000 she inherited is tied up in her business.*

/ˌtaɪ ˈʌp/
tie up, tying up, tied up
note transitive verb, often used in the passive
⋈ **tie up** capital, money, wealth; **tie up** money *in* something

---

tight money *noun* (economics/finance)
▶ **dear money**

/ˌtaɪt ˈmʌni/

---

till *noun* (commerce)
a machine used in a shop to store money received from sales. Modern tills are operated electronically and record the amount of money received and change given: *The till calculates how much change should be given automatically.*

/tɪl/
pl tills
⧓ put money into, take money out of the **till**; a **till** receipt
syn cash register, cash till

time *noun*
1 a particular moment: *What time do you arrive at the airport?* ○ *We must fix a time for the meeting.* ○ *Now is a good time to buy shares.* **2** a period of hours, days, weeks, months, etc: *It will take a long time to analyse these results.* ○ *Have you got (enough) time to do this?* ○ *I haven't got/I don't have much time.* ○ *The delivery time is about three weeks.*

ahead of time early: *The contract was completed ahead of time.*

behind time late; later than scheduled: *We're behind time with this job.*

be pushed for time (*informal*) to have too little time (to get something done): *I can't talk to you this afternoon — I'm pretty pushed for time.*

in good time early: *He was in good time for the interview.* ○ *She was in good time to park the car before the meeting.*

in time not late; before something is due to happen: *You're just in time for the meeting.* ○ *Am I in time to catch the post?*

make up for lost time to work quickly after a delay in order to get everything done according to the schedule: *Everything's going well again now, so perhaps we can make up for lost time.*

(one) at a time separately; in order: *We'll take the questions one at a time.*

on time not early and not late; at the moment specified: *She was late on Monday but on time for the rest of the week.*

run out of time to have no more time available: *I've run out of time now, but let's meet again next week.*

/taɪm/
1 note usually singular
2 note usually singular
⧓ gain, lose, save, waste **time**; allocate, devote, give **time** to (something); allow, leave **time** for (something); spend **time** on (something)
▶ **access time, down time, flexitime, full time, local time, overtime, part-time, prime time**

time account *noun* (banking)
(*US*) ▶ **deposit account**

/ˈtaɪm əˌkaʊnt/

time and a half *noun* (industrial relations)
an amount paid for extra work done, ie if normal pay is £10 per hour, time and a half is £15 per hour: *I get time and a half for working on Saturdays.*

/ˌtaɪm ənd ə ˈhɑ:f/
note not used with *a* or *an*. No plural and used with a singular verb only.
⧓ get, pay **time and a half**
▶ **double time, overtime**

time and motion study *noun* (management)
a way of finding the cheapest and most efficient way of doing a job, or carrying out a complex process, by making a plan of how long each part of it takes: *A time and motion study is being made of component assembly workers.*

/ˌtaɪm ənd ˈməʊʃn ˌstʌdi/
pl time and motion studies
⧓ carry out, make, undertake a **time and motion study**
▶ **critical path analysis**

time bargain *noun* (stock exchange)
a contract made on a stock exchange for financial investments that will be delivered on a future date

/ˈtaɪm ˌbɑ:gən/
pl time bargains
⧓ make a **time bargain**
▶ **futures, option**

time bill *noun* (banking/international trade)
a bill of exchange that is due to be paid a certain number of days after being drawn or after being presented: *a time bill payable ninety days after presentation*

/ˈtaɪm bɪl/
pl time bills
⋈ a **time bill** payable in (ninety days)
syn time draft
▶ **bill of exchange, short bill, sight bill**

---

time card *noun* (industry)
a card that is marked with the time when an employee arrives or leaves. This is usually done by a machine (a TIME CLOCK). Pay is calculated according to the record on the card: *According to his time card, he's been late on three days this week.*

/ˈtaɪm kɑːd/
pl time cards
⋈ insert, punch, stamp a **time card**; a **time card** records, shows
▶ **clock in/out, time sheet**

---

time charter *noun* (transport)
the hire (CHARTER) of a ship or an aircraft for a particular length of time, rather than for a particular journey. The owners operate the ship or aircraft and are paid expenses as well as the hire: *A time charter was agreed for a monthly rate.* ○ *The tanker is on time charter.*

/ˈtaɪm ˌtʃɑːtə(r)/
pl time charters
▶ **charter[1] 3, charter flight, voyage charter**

---

time clock *noun* (industry)
a machine in a place of work, esp a factory, that records the times when employees arrive or leave by marking special cards (TIME CARDS): *Insert the card into the time clock.*

/ˈtaɪm klɒk/
pl time clocks
syn time recorder
⋈ a **time clock** prints (the time), stamps (the card)

---

time deposit *noun* (banking)
(*US*) ▶ **deposit account**

/ˈtaɪm dɪˌpɒzɪt/
⋈ on **time deposit**

---

time draft *noun* (banking/international trade)
▶ **time bill**

/ˈtaɪm drɑːft; *US* ˈtaɪm dræft/

---

timekeeping *noun* (personnel)
the habit of arriving at work at the right time: *She has a problem with (her) timekeeping.* ○ *bad/good timekeeping*

/ˈtaɪmkiːpɪŋ/
note not used with *a* or *an*. No plural and used with a singular verb only.
(also **time-keeping**)
⋈ bad, good **timekeeping**

---

time limit *noun*
an amount of time within which or by which something must be done: *set a time limit for a job* ○ *The time limit for the project was extended from 10 to 12 weeks.* ○ *We've already gone over the time limit for this meeting.*

/ˈtaɪm ˌlɪmɪt/
pl time limits
(also **time-limit**)
⋈ go over, impose, set a **time limit**
▶ **time-scale**

---

time management *noun* (management)
the skill of using time as efficiently as possible, esp at work: *She works hard but doesn't achieve much — perhaps she needs a course on time management.*

/ˈtaɪm ˌmænɪdʒmənt/
note not used with *a* or *an*. No plural and used with a singular verb only.
⋈ a **time management** course; **time management** skills, techniques
▶ **management 1**

time off *noun* (personnel)
a period when you are not at work because of a holiday, illness, etc: *I need to take some time off. Would a month's unpaid leave be possible?*

/ˌtaɪm ˈɒf/
note not used with *a* or *an*. No plural and used with a singular verb only.
⧓ ask for, take **time off**

time option *noun* (stock exchange)
an agreement to buy or sell goods, currencies, or securities at some time between two future dates, rather than on one particular date: *take up a time option*

/ˈtaɪm ˌɒpʃn/
pl time options
▶ **call option, futures, option, put option, traded option**

time policy *noun* (insurance/shipping)
a form of insurance for ships that lasts for a particular period between one month and one year: *The freighter is insured with a time policy for six months.*

/ˈtaɪm ˌpɒləsi/
pl time policies
⧓ insure (something) with, take out a **time policy**; a **time policy** expires, runs out
▶ **insurance**

time rate *noun* (industrial relations)
payment by the number of hours that a person works, rather than by the number of items that he/she produces: *This job is paid on a time rate.* ○ *He is on a time rate.* ○ *The time rates for this kind of work are usually £10–£12 per hour.*

/ˈtaɪm reɪt/
pl time rates
⧓ get, pay a **time rate**
▶ **hourly rate, job rate, piece rates, rate 1**

time recorder *noun* (personnel)
▶ **time clock**

/ˈtaɪm rɪˌkɔːdə(r)/

time-scale *noun*
the number of days, months, etc, that something lasts for or takes to do: *What is the time-scale for this job?* ○ *Can we finish the project in a shorter time-scale?* ○ *a time-scale of 18 months*

/ˈtaɪm skeɪl/
pl time-scales
(also **time scale**)
⧓ a **time-scale** *of* (a period of time); a **time-scale** *for* (a job)

timeshare *noun* (tourism)
part-ownership of a holiday house which is shared with other co-owners. Each owner of a timeshare uses the property for a certain week, fortnight, etc every year: *We have a timeshare in a house in France every September.* ○ *We have a timeshare in Spain.*

/ˈtaɪmʃeə(r)/
pl timeshares
(also **time-share**)
⧓ a **timeshare** *in* (a property); a **timeshare** contract, development, holiday, operator, property
▶ **share**

timesharing *noun* (computing)
a system of buying or obtaining the use of (programs on) a central computer system for a specified period: *Timesharing allows us to have terminals in our offices all over the country.*

/ˈtaɪmʃeərɪŋ/
note not used with *a* or *an*. No plural and used with a singular verb only.
⧓ a **timesharing** system

time sheet *noun* (personnel)
a printed form for a day or a week on which an employee writes down the number of hours that he/she spends on each job: *Have you filled in your time sheet yet?*

/ˈtaɪmʃiːt/
pl time sheets
(also **time-sheet**)
⧓ complete, fill in a **time sheet**; a daily, weekly **time sheet**
▶ **time card**

timetable *noun*
1 (*transport*) a list showing the times of trains, buses, etc: *consult a railway timetable* **2** a plan of events, meetings, etc: *I have a very busy timetable this week.*

/ˈtaɪmteɪbl/
pl timetables
1 syn (*US*) schedule
⋈ a bus, railway, train **timetable**
▶ **schedule[1] 1**

time zone *noun*
one of 24 segments of the earth between lines of longitude, where the same time is used. Each zone represents one hour: *travel from one time zone to another*

/ˈtaɪm zəʊn/
pl time zones
⋈ across, between **time zones**
▶ **local time**

tip[1] *noun*
a small amount of money (in addition to the normal charge) given to a waiter, taxi-driver, etc to thank him/her: *He gave the taxi driver a tip.*

/tɪp/
pl tips
⋈ give someone a **tip**; give a **tip** *to* someone
▶ **bribe[1], gift 1, gratuity 1**

tip[2] *verb*
to give a small amount of money (in addition to the normal charge) to a waiter, taxi-driver, etc to thank him/her: *Have you tipped the waitress?*

/tɪp/
tip, tipping, tipped
note transitive verb
▶ **bribe[2]**

title *noun* (law)
the legal right of possession of land, a building, goods, etc: *Do you have proof of title?* ○ *She holds the title to the land.*

/ˈtaɪtl/
pl titles
⋈ document, proof of **title**; have, hold the **title** *to* something
▶ **abstract of title**

title deeds *noun* (law)
documents (DEEDS) that prove who the owner of land is. They include documents that transfer the ownership of land and mortgages: *The bank holds our title deeds.*

/ˈtaɪtl diːdz/
note plural noun, used with a plural verb
⋈ have, hold the **title deeds**
▶ **abstract of title, deed, deed of transfer**

TO *abbr* (commerce)
turnover

note used in written English only

token *noun*
a receipt, card, plastic disc, etc that shows that money has been paid for something, and can be exchanged for goods later: *I always give my father book tokens as presents.* ○ *Milk tokens can be left outside the door for the milkman.*

/ˈtəʊkən/
pl tokens
⋈ a book, gift, milk **token**; buy, exchange, give, receive a/the **token**

token charge *noun* (commerce)
a small amount of money charged for goods or services, that is less than their full cost or value: *Pensioners pay only a token charge on city buses, not the full fare.*

/ˌtəʊkən ˈtʃɑːdʒ/
pl token charges
⋈ ask for, make, pay a **token charge**
▶ **nominal**

token payment *noun* (commerce/finance)
a small amount of money paid towards the settlement of a DEBT by a person who owes the money (the DEBTOR), to show his/her intention of paying it back: *Debtors in financial difficulties are advised to make at least token payments to their creditors.*

/ˌtəʊkən ˈpeɪmənt/
pl token payments
⋈ give, make, offer a **token payment**
▶ **payment 2**

token strike *noun* (industrial relations)
▶ **strike**[1]

/ˌtəʊkən ˈstraɪk/

tool shop *noun* (manufacturing)
the department of a factory where special tools and machinery are made: *Have the new designs come out of the tool shop yet?*

/ˈtuːl ʃɒp/
pl tool shops
⧓ make (something) in a **tool shop**
▶ **machine shop, workshop**

top[1] *verb*
to rise above a certain level: *Sales have topped 1 billion for the first time.* ○ *The £13 million bid was topped by another company.*

/tɒp/
top, topping, topped
note transitive verb

top[2] *adjective*
1 best or most important: *We produce top-quality goods* ○ *This item on the agenda must be given top priority.* **2** at the highest level; in the most senior position: *This is a job for top management.* ○ *A public statement was issued by the company's top man.* **3** biggest; conducting the most business: *the top four banks* ○ *The Financial Times Index of the 100 top companies.*

/tɒp/
1 ⧓ **top** grade, priority, quality
2 ⧓ **top** man, management, manager
3 ⧓ **top** banks, businesses, companies, firms

top copy *noun* (office practice)
the first and clearest copy of a document, esp one that is in two or more parts: *Send the original contract back to the author, file the top copy, and give the other copies to the people on the list.*

/ˌtɒp ˈkɒpi/
pl top copies
⧓ file, keep the **top copy**
▶ **carbon copy, copy**[1] **1, master 1, original**

TOPIC *abbr* (stock exchange)
Teletext Output of Price Information by Computer

/ˈtɒpɪk/
note pronounced as a word

tort *noun* (law)
a wrong, eg injury, damage to property, etc for which a person or company can claim compensation (DAMAGES) in a civil court. It does not include a BREACH OF CONTRACT: *be liable in tort for damaging private property*

/tɔːt/
pl torts
⧓ **tort** case, damages, law; be liable in, commit a **tort**

total income *noun* (tax)
all the money that has been paid to a taxpayer from all sources (earnings, profits, rent, etc) on which income tax is calculated: *He declared a total income of £25 000 to the tax authorities.*

/ˌtəʊtl ˈɪŋkʌm/
note usually singular
⧓ a **total income** of (an amount of money)
syn statutory total income
▶ **income, income tax**

total loss *noun* (insurance/shipping)
a situation where a ship or its cargo sinks or is damaged so that the cost of repair is greater than its total value. It is then given up as a total loss in return for an insurance payment: *After the collision damage the ship was written off as a total loss.*

/ˌtəʊtl ˈlɒs/
note usually singular
⧓ consider, treat something as a **total loss**; write something off as a **total loss**
▶ **abandonment, loss 3, partial loss**

total profit *noun* (tax)
all the money that has been paid to a company from all sources, on which the amount of corporation tax is calculated: *They announced total profits for the year of $120 m.*

/ˌtəʊtl ˈprɒfɪt/
pl total profits
⧓ a **total profit** *of* (an amount of money)
▶ **profit**[1]

total quality management *noun* (management)
a system of checking that each department of an organization works in the most efficient way, and that the goods and services it provides are of the best quality: *Under total quality management, we're supposed to answer every letter the same day.*

/ˌtəʊtl ˈkwɒləti ˌmænɪdʒmənt/
note not used with *a* or *an*. No plural and used with a singular verb only.
abbr TQM
⋈ under **total quality management**; a **total quality management** system
▶ **management 1**, **quality control**

tour company *noun* (tourism)
▶ **tour operator**

/ˈtʊə(r) ˌkʌmpəni/

tourism *noun* (tourism)
the industry that provides accommodation, transport, meals, information, entertainment, etc for people who are travelling for pleasure: *A lot of people here earn their living from tourism.*

/ˈtʊərɪzəm/
note not used with *a* or *an*. No plural and used with a singular verb only.
⋈ have a job in, work in **tourism**; develop, encourage, promote **tourism**

tourist-class *adjective, adverb* (transport)
(on ships, aeroplanes, etc) second-class; not paying for the best service and comfort: *tourist-class passengers* ○ *I'm travelling tourist-class.*

/ˈtʊərɪst klɑːs/
⋈ **tourist-class** passengers, travellers; fly, go, travel **tourist-class**
▶ **first-class**

tour operator *noun* (tourism)
a company that organizes travel, accommodation, entertainment, etc for people who are travelling for pleasure: *buy a package holiday from a major tour operator*

/ˈtʊər ˌɒpəreɪtə(r)/
pl tour operators
⋈ a major, package, specialist **tour operator**
syn tour company
▶ **travel agent**

town planning *noun*
▶ **planning 2**

/ˌtaʊn ˈplænɪŋ/

TPI *abbr* (tax)
tax and price index

/ˌtiː piː ˈaɪ/
note pronounced as individual letters

TQM *abbr* (management)
total quality management

/ˌtiː kjuː ˈem/

track record *noun*
the extent to which a person, company, etc, has been successful or reliable in the past: *She established a good track record with her previous company.* ○ *The company has a strong balance sheet and an impressive track record.*

/ˈtræk ˌrekɔːd/
pl track records
⋈ a bad, good, poor **track record**
▶ **record**[1] **2**

trade[1] *noun* (industry)

1 the buying and selling of goods, services, currencies or securities: *Trade between Britain and Japan is increasing.* **2** the buying and selling of particular goods or services: *The tourist trade is the country's main source of income.* ○ *She works in the retail trade.* ○ *a decline in the export trade* **3** the amount of buying and selling that occurs: *Trade is has been rather slow recently.* ○ *Trade is always good over the Christmas period.* **4 the trade** the people or a firm involved in a particular kind of business: *The exhibition opens to the trade today and the public tomorrow.* ○ *This department deals with trade enquiries only.* **5** a job, usually a skilled manual job: *He needs to learn a trade.* ○ *I'm a mechanic by trade.*

domestic/home trade trade between buyers and sellers in the same country: *a growth in domestic trade during the last six months*

foreign/overseas trade trade between buyers/sellers in one country and sellers/buyers in other countries: *The country depends on foreign trade.*

do a good trade in something to sell a large number of items: *We're doing a good trade in computer games.*

in the trade working in a particular kind of business or job: *She knows all about cars, she's in the (motor) trade.*

/treɪd/

1 note not used with *a* or *an*. No plural and used with a singular verb only.

⋈ **trade** *between* (two people, countries, etc), *in* (a certain product), *with* (another person, country, etc)

2 pl trades

⋈ export, import, international, retail, wholesale **trade**

3 note not used with *a* or *an*. No plural and used with a singular verb only.

⋈ **trade** is bad, booming, brisk, declining, picking up, slow

4 note used with a singular or a plural verb

⋈ a **trade** journal

5 pl trades

⋈ learn a **trade**

▶ **balance of trade, business 1, commerce, Department of Trade and Industry, free trade, General Agreement on Tariffs and Trade, restrictive trade practices**

---

trade[2] *verb* (commerce)

1 to buy and sell goods, services or securities: *An increasing number of European firms are trading with Japan.* ○ *The company trades in man-made textiles.* ○ *We've been trading at a loss.* ○ *Securities are traded on a stock exchange.* **2** (of a business) to function; to continue to exist: *The new company trades under the name of Jackson holdings.* ○ *Many companies stopped trading during the recession* (ie have ceased to exist). **3** (*stock exchange*) (of securities) to be bought and sold (at a particular price): *These shares are trading at 115p.*

trade (something) in to return an old item to a dealer as part payment for a new one: *trade in the old photocopier for a new one*

trade (something) off against (something) to agree to one thing on the condition that something else happens: *The workers traded off their right to strike against a big wage increase.*

trade something for something to exchange one item for another: *trade an old car for a new one*

/treɪd/

trade, trading, traded

note transitive and intransitive verb

1 ⋈ **trade** *in* (a particular product), *with* (another person, country, etc); **trade** at a loss, at a profit

2 ⋈ begin, cease, start, stop **trading**; **trade** *under* (a name)

3 ⋈ **trade** *at* (a price)

▶ **deal**[2]

---

tradeable *adjective* (commerce)

able to be bought and sold fairly easily: *deal in tradeable goods*

/ˈtreɪdəbl/

(also **tradable**)

syn marketable

⋈ **tradeable** assets, goods, products, securities

▶ **marketable**

---

tradeable instrument *noun* (finance)

a formal document, eg a BANK DRAFT or PROMISSORY NOTE, that transfers money from one person to another and can be bought

/ˌtreɪdəbl ˈɪnstrəmənt/

pl tradeable instruments

(also **tradable instrument**)

and sold easily. Tradeable instruments can be distributed by large companies to raise finance.

▶ **financial instrument**

---

trade agreement *noun* (international trade)
an arrangement between countries to follow certain rules on pricing, import duties, etc when buying from and selling to each other: *sign a trade agreement with Japan*

bilateral trade agreement a trade agreement between two countries

multilateral trade agreement a trade agreement made by three or more countries

/ˈtreɪd əˌgriːmənt/
pl trade agreements
⋈ draw up, negotiate, set up, sign a **trade agreement**

---

trade association *noun* (management)
an organization of producers or sellers of similar products that provides advice, information and services for its members: *a building trade association*

/ˈtreɪd əsəʊsiˌeɪʃn/
pl trade associations
⋈ be a member of, belong to, join a **trade association**
▶ **association 1, European Free Trade Association**

---

trade bill *noun* (commerce/international trade)
a bill of exchange that is used to pay for goods: *draw up a trade bill*

/ˈtreɪd bɪl/
pl trade bills
⋈ accept, discount, draw, honour, issue a **trade bill**
syn commercial bill
▶ **bank bill, bill of exchange**

---

trade bloc *noun* (international trade)
a group of countries that agree to trade with each other on favourable terms, eg the European Community: *become a member of a trade bloc*

/ˈtreɪd blɒk/
pl trade blocs
⋈ in, outside, within a **trade bloc**
▶ **European Community, European Free Trade Association**

---

trade counter *noun* (commerce)
a part of a factory or warehouse where a retailer can buy goods at reduced (WHOLESALE) prices: *buy discounted goods at a trade counter*

/ˈtreɪd ˌkaʊntə(r)/
pl trade counters

---

trade creditor *noun* (accounting)
a person or business that has supplied goods or services to a company and is owed money for them: *We pay trade creditors within 60 days.*

/ˌtreɪd ˈkredɪtə(r)/
pl trade creditors
⋈ owe (money to), pay, pay off, settle with a **trade creditor**
▶ **creditor**

---

trade deficit *noun* (international trade)
the amount by which the value of a country's imports is greater than the value of its exports: *an annual trade deficit of $20 billion* ○ *cut the trade deficit by reducing imports*

/ˈtreɪd ˌdefɪsɪt/
pl trade deficits
⋈ cut, increase, reduce the **trade deficit**; a falling, rising **trade deficit**
▶ **balance of payments, balance of trade, deficit, loss 1, trade gap, trade surplus**

Trade Descriptions Act *noun* (law)
(*UK*) a law stating that any information given about a product (its size, weight or contents) in advertisements or on packaging, must be true and clear: *be fined under the Trade Descriptions Act*

/ˌtreɪd dɪˈskrɪpʃnz ækt/
⧓ according to, under the **Trade Descriptions Act**
▶ **Office of Fair Trading**

trade directory *noun* (commerce)
a book or DATABASE that contains information about companies and lists them by area, or by the particular product or service they provide: *look for an engineering firm in a trade directory* ○ *Are you listed in the trade directory for this area?*

/ˈtreɪd dɪˌrektəri/
pl trade directories
⧓ a/the **trade directory** advertises, lists (businesses), prints (details), publishes (details); consult, look something up in a **trade directory**

trade discount *noun* (commerce)
an amount that is taken off the normal selling price (RETAIL PRICE) of a product when it is sold by a manufacturer or WHOLESALER to a RETAILER, usually in a large quantity: *The publisher offered the bookseller a trade discount of 35%.*

/ˌtreɪd ˈdɪskaʊnt/
pl trade discounts
⧓ get, give, offer a **trade discount**
▶ **discount[1] 1, retailer, trade counter, trade price, trade terms, wholesaler**

trade dispute *noun* (industrial relations)
▶ **industrial dispute**

/ˈtreɪd dɪˌspjuːt/

traded option *noun* (stock exchange)
a right to buy a commodity or security that can be bought and sold on a stock exchange: *There are traded options in a small number of UK companies.*

/ˌtreɪdɪd ˈɒpʃn/
pl traded options
⧓ buy, sell a **traded option**; the **traded option** market
▶ **call option, option, put option, share option, time option**

trade fair *noun* (industry)
a big exhibition where manufacturers and sellers of similar or related products display their goods, meet customers and each other: *Exhibiting at a trade fair is a good form of publicity.* ○ *have a stand at a major trade fair*

/ˈtreɪd feə(r)/
pl trade fairs
⧓ hold, organize, put on, visit a **trade fair**
▶ **exhibition**

trade figures *noun* (international trade)
the figures showing the value of a country's exports compared with the value of its imports: *The trade figures showed a deficit of $10.24 billion.*

/ˈtreɪd ˌfɪgəz/
note plural noun, used with a plural verb
⧓ announce, produce, release the **trade figures**
▶ **balance of trade, trade deficit**

trade gap *noun* (international trade)
the difference between the value of a country's exports and its imports: *The trade gap continued to widen last month.*

/ˈtreɪd gæp/
pl trade gaps
⧓ a growing, large, narrowing, widening **trade gap**
▶ **trade deficit, trade surplus**

trade investment *noun* (accounting/finance)
money that is invested by one company in another company in the same industry (by making a loan or buying shares) in order to help its own business: *Shares in a retail chain could prove a useful trade investment for a manufacturer.*

/ˌtreɪd ɪnˈvestmənt/
pl trade investments
⧓ make a **trade investment**
▶ **investment**

trade journal *noun* (industry)
a magazine that contains news, articles and advertising connected with a particular industry or business: *'Construction Weekly' is a trade journal for the building industry.*

/ˌtreɪd ˈdʒɜːnl/
pl trade journals
⋈ edit, produce, publish a **trade journal**
syn trade magazine
▶ **house journal, journal, magazine**

trade mark *noun* (marketing/law)
a name or symbol that is used on the products of a particular company. In Britain, trade marks are registered officially and may not be copied by another company: *Our trade mark is known to every consumer in the country.*

/ˈtreɪd mɑːk/
pl trade marks
⋈ a registered **trade mark**
▶ **copyright, intangible asset, intellectual property, patent**

trade name *noun* (marketing/law)
a name that is used by a particular company: *No other company may use this trade name.*

/ˈtreɪd neɪm/
pl trade names
⋈ a registered **trade name**; sell something *under* a **trade name**
▶ **brand name, household name**

trade-off *noun*
a balance between opposing things; a compromise: *a trade-off between increased production and a reduction in quality* ○ *The trade-off for getting a higher pay rise was a loss of flexible working hours.*

/ˈtreɪd ɒf/
pl trade-offs
⋈ a **trade-off** *between* (people or things), *for* (something), *with* (someone)
▶ **bargain, pay-off 2**

trade press *noun* (industry)
any of the newspapers and magazines that are published for a particular trade or industry: *The exhibition was advertised in the trade press.*

/ˌtreɪd ˈpres/
note used with a singular or plural verb
⋈ print, publish, write something in the **trade press**

trade price *noun* (commerce)
a reduced price paid by a retailer when buying goods from a wholesaler or manufacturer. This is the usual retail price minus the TRADE DISCOUNT: *Could you please supply these materials at trade price?*

/ˌtreɪd ˈpraɪs/
pl trade prices
⋈ buy, sell, supply (something) at the **trade price**
syn wholesale price
▶ **price**[1]**, retail price, trade discount, trade terms, wholesale**

trader *noun* (commerce)
a person or an organization that earns money by buying goods and selling them at a profit: *Local traders met to discuss plans for the new shopping centre.* ○ *a trader in leather goods*

/ˈtreɪdə(r)/
pl traders
⋈ a commodity, international, local, retail, street, wholesale **trader**
▶ **dealer, merchant, sole trader**

trade representative *noun* (sales)
▶ **sales representative**

/ˈtreɪd reprɪˌzentətɪv/

trade restriction *noun* (international trade)
an action taken by a government to limit the amount or type of goods imported or exported, usually by introducing taxes and tariffs: *The government imposed trade restrictions on imports.*

/ˈtreɪd rɪˌstrɪkʃn/
pl trade restrictions
⋈ impose, lift, remove **trade restrictions**; a **trade restriction** on (imports, etc)
▶ **cabotage 2, import restrictions, protectionism**

trade secret *noun* (industry)
any piece of knowledge, such as the method of making a product, that a manufacturer does not want other companies to learn: *The recipe is a closely guarded trade secret.*

/ˌtreɪd ˈsiːkrət/
pl trade secrets
⋈ disclose, guard, keep, sell a **trade secret**
▶ **confidentiality agreement**

tradesman, tradesperson, tradeswoman *noun* (retail)
a person who sells goods, esp a shopkeeper: *Local tradespeople say that business is better now.*

/ˈtreɪdzmən, ˈtreɪdzpɜːsn, ˈtreɪdzwʊmən/
pl tradesmen, tradespeople, tradeswomen
▶ **trader**

Trades Union Congress *noun* (industrial relations)
an association of representatives of British trade unions: *The new union is now affiliated to the Trades Union Congress.* ○ *a meeting of the Trades Union Congress*

/ˌtreɪdz ˌjuːniən ˈkɒŋgres/
abbr TUC
⋈ be affiliated to the **Trades Union Congress**; a **Trades Union Congress** leader, meeting, member
▶ **trade union**

trade surplus *noun* (economics)
a situation where a country exports more goods than it imports: *increase imports in order to reduce the trade surplus* ○ *a trade surplus of $79 billion*

/ˌtreɪd ˈsɜːpləs/
pl trade surpluses
⋈ cut, produce, reduce a **trade surplus**; a **trade surplus** *of* (an amount)
▶ **balance of payments, balance of trade, trade deficit, trade gap**

trade terms *noun* (commerce)
a cheaper price offered by a wholesaler to retailers: *We offer reasonable trade terms.*

/ˌtreɪd ˈtɜːmz/
note plural noun, used with a plural verb
⋈ get, give, offer **trade terms**; get, offer, supply (something) at **trade terms**
▶ **trade discount**

trade union *noun* (industrial relations)
an organization of employees working in the same industry, or doing similar jobs, that represents its members in discussions with management, esp about pay and working conditions: *Members of the trade union met their employers to discuss a pay rise.* ○ *Are you a member of a trade union?* ○ *Trade union membership in the company has doubled this year.*

/ˌtreɪd ˈjuːniən/
pl trade unions
abbr TU
(also **trades union**)
⋈ belong to, join, support a **trade union**; a **trade union** leader, member, official
▶ **shop steward**

trading *noun* (commerce/stock exchange)
1 the buying and selling for profit of goods or securities: *At the close of trading, share prices had fallen overall.* **2** the amount of buying and selling done: *Trading was brisk last month.*

/ˈtreɪdɪŋ/
note not used with *a* or *an*. No plural and used with a singular verb only.
⋈ high-street, stock market **trading**
▶ **fair trading, insider trading, Office of Fair Trading, overtrading, reciprocal trading**

trading account *noun* (accounting)
a statement of the money that a business has spent on making or buying goods and of the money received from selling those goods, so that the GROSS PROFIT can be calculated: *The trading account has been drawn up.*

/ˈtreɪdɪŋ əˌkaʊnt/
pl trading accounts
⋈ draw up, present a **trading account**; annual, current, next, quarterly **trading account**
▶ **account[1] 1, profit and loss account**

trading company *noun* (commerce)
a firm that exists to buy and sell goods: *This new trading company imports craft goods from South America and retails them itself.*

/ˈtreɪdɪŋ ˌkʌmpəni/
pl trading companies
⋈ a **trading company** buys, exports, imports, retails, sells

trading conditions *noun* (commerce/international trade)
the financial circumstances in which buying and selling take place, and which influence how much profit is made: *A weak dollar means relatively favourable trading conditions for American exporters.*

/ˈtreɪdɪŋ kənˌdɪʃnz/
note plural noun, used with a plural verb
⋈ adverse, bad, favourable, good, unfavourable **trading conditions**

trading estate *noun* (commerce)
an area, usually on the edge of a town, where factories, warehouses and offices are built: *The company has grown too large for its present building, so it is relocating to a new trading estate.*

/ˈtreɪdɪŋ ɪˌsteɪt/
pl trading estates
syn industrial estate, (US) industrial park
▶ **estate 1**

trading loss *noun* (accounting)
an amount of money lost on the sale of goods because the cost of producing or obtaining them was higher than the amount received from the sale: *During the recession, the company recorded a trading loss for the first time in its existence.*

/ˈtreɪdɪŋ lɒs/
pl trading losses
⋈ make, record, report, turn in a **trading loss**; a **trading loss of** (an amount of money)
syn gross loss
▶ **loss 1, net loss, trading profit**

trading partner *noun* (commerce/international trade)
a company or country that another company or country buys from or sells to: *The company has trading partners in Japan, the Middle East, and the USA.*

/ˈtreɪdɪŋ pɑːtnə(r)/
pl trading partners
⋈ do business with, export to, import from a **trading partner**
▶ **partner**

trading profit *noun* (accounting)
an amount of money received from the sale of goods minus the cost of manufacturing or buying them. The amount is shown on the company's trading account: *Chrysler make $6 000 trading profit on each van they sell.* ○ *a trading profit of £3 million pounds.*

/'treɪdɪŋ ˌprɒfɪt/
pl trading profits
⋈ make, record, report, turn in a **trading profit**; a **tradingprofit** *of* (an amount of money)
syn gross profit
▶ **operating profit, trading loss**

Trading Standards Department *noun* (retail/law)
(*UK*) a local government office that is responsible for protecting the legal rights of people of consumers: *The shop was reported to the Trading Standards Department for selling goods under weight.*

/'treɪdɪŋ ˌstændədz dɪˌpɑ:tmənt/
⋈ report (a shop) to the **Trading Standards Department**; an inspector, officer, official from the **Trading Standards Department**
▶ **the Department of Trade and Industry, Office of Fair Trading**

---

trading stock *noun* (retail)
▶ **stock-in-trade**

/'treɪdɪŋ stɒk/

---

traffic[1] *noun* (commerce/law)
trade, esp in illegal goods: *the drugs traffic* ○ *How do we stop the traffic in pornographic videos?*

/'træfɪk/
note not used with *a* or *an*. No plural and used with a singular verb only.
⋈ **traffic** *between* (people or places), *in* (goods)

---

traffic[2] *verb* (commerce/law)
to buy and sell goods, usually illegal ones: *to traffic in stolen goods* ○ *trafficking arms between terrorist groups*

/'træfɪk/
traffic, trafficking, trafficked
note transitive verb
⋈ **traffic** *between* (people or places), *in* (goods)

---

train *verb*
1 to teach someone to do a job by showing them what to do and directing their work: *We're training a couple of school leavers.* ○ *We train staff in sales techniques.* ○ *We train our staff to deal confidently with clients.* ○ *He's a trained gas fitter.* **2** to learn to do a job: *I'm training as an accountant.* ○ *I'm training for accountancy.* ○ *I'm training to be an accountant.*

/treɪn /
train, training, trained
1 note transitive verb
⋈ **train** *in* (techniques, etc), *to do* (certain things)
2 note intransitive verb
⋈ **train** *as* (an accountant, etc), *for* (a job), *to be* (an accountant, etc)

---

trainee *noun* (management)
a person, usually an employee, who is learning to do a job by having his/her work directed by someone more experienced: *employ a graduate/management trainee* ○ *a trainee accountant/ bricklayer/teacher*

/ˌtreɪ'ni:/
pl trainees
⋈ employ, take on a **trainee**
▶ **apprentice**

---

trainee solicitor *noun* (law)
a person who works in a legal firm for a stated number of years

/ˌtreɪni: sə'lɪsɪtə(r)/
pl trainee solicitors
⋈ take on a **trainee solicitor**

(usually two) while being taught the profession of law: *He was taken on as a trainee solicitor in a London firm.*

note formerly known as an *articled clerk*

---

training *noun* (management)

the process of teaching someone to do a job or of learning to do a job: *On-the-job training is most important.* ○ *We offer hands-on training (courses) in computing.* ○ *There's a one-year training period for this job.*

/ˈtreɪnɪŋ/

note not used with *a* or *an*. No plural and used with a singular verb only.

⋈ industrial, on-the-job, skills, staff, vocational **training**; a **training** centre, course, officer, period, scheme

▶ **apprenticeship, block release, day release, sandwich course**

---

training manual *noun*

▶ **manual**[2]

/ˌtreɪnɪŋ ˌmænjuəl/

---

tranche *noun* (finance)

a part of a loan, a payment, an investment or other large amount of money; an instalment: *The first tranche of the fee will be paid when the contract is signed.* ○ *buy new shares in three tranches*

/trɑːntʃ/

pl tranches

⋈ a **tranche** of capital, money, securities, shares

---

transact *verb*

to carry out a business deal, esp between two people or organizations: *Stockbrokers transact business on behalf of their clients.* ○ *The sale must be transacted by the end of the week.*

/trænˈzækt/

transact, transacting, transacted

note transitive verb

⋈ **transact** affairs, business; **transact** a deal, loan, purchase, sale

---

transaction *noun*

1 the act of doing business or carrying out a business deal: *the transaction of business* **2** a piece of business done; a deal: *He hoped to make a 5% profit on each transaction.* ○ *I have to pay bank charges on all the transactions I make.* ○ *record a transaction in the company accounts*

bear transaction (*stock exchange*) a deal in which a dealer agrees to sell securities at a certain price on a future date, and expects to buy them cheaper beforehand because prices will fall

bull transaction (*stock exchange*) a deal in which a dealer agrees to buy securities at a certain price on a future date, and expects to sell them at a profit afterwards because prices will rise

/trænˈzækʃn/

1 note not used with *a* or *an*. No plural and used with a singular verb only.

2 pl transactions

⋈ carry out, make a **transaction**; a business, commercial, financial **transaction**

▶ **dealings**

---

transactions velocity of circulation *noun* (economics)

the amount of times within a given period that a unit of money forms part of a business deal: *To increase the transactions velocity of circulation consumers must be active.*

/trænˌzækʃnz vəˈlɒsəti əv ˌsɜːkjəˈleɪʃn/

note no plural

⋈ decrease, increase the **transactions velocity of circulation**; a high, low **transactions velocity of circulation**

▶ **circulation 1, income velocity of circulation, velocity of circulation**

ranscribe *verb* (office practice)
o copy a document by writing or typing it; to write down what s spoken: *transcribe a speech made in the House of Commons*

/træn'skraɪb/
transcribe, transcribing, transcribed
note transitive verb
⋈ **transcribe** a document, speech, tape

---

ranscript *noun* (office practice)
written or typed copy of a document or a speech: *Type up a ranscript of the notes, and then I'll edit them.*

/'trænskrɪpt/
pl transcripts
⋈ make, type, type out, type up, write, write out, write up a **transcript** (*of* something)

:ransfer[1] *noun*
(*banking/law*) a change of ownership of money, property, hares, etc: *The transfer of the director's house to his wife was inalized today.* **2** (*banking*) a bank transfer **3** (*industry*) a change of job within the same company or organization: *She has asked or a transfer to the Berlin office.* **4** (*transport*) a change from one ehicle or route to another when travelling: *This is an nnouncement for transfer passenger Mr John Smith.*

/'trænsfɜː(r)/
pl transfers
1 ⋈ a certificate, instrument of **transfer**
▶ **blank transfer, deed of transfer**
2 ⋈ send something *by* **transfer**; a **transfer** document, form
▶ **bank transfer, telegraphic transfer**
3 ⋈ apply for a **transfer**; a **transfer** *between* (two offices, etc), *from* (an office, etc), *to* (another office, etc)
▶ **secondment**
4 ⋈ make a **transfer**; a **transfer** passenger

---

transfer[2] *verb*
(*banking/law*) to change the ownership of money, property, ecurities, etc. from one person or organization (the TRANSFEROR) o another (the TRANSFEREE): *She transferred her house to her laughter.* ○ *Ownership of the shares has been transferred from Mr Smith to his son.* **2** to move something from one place to another: *am transferring my bank account from the city centre branch to one nearer my home.* ○ *This disk is full so the data needs to be transferred o another one.* **3** (*industry*) to change your job or to be moved to new job, usually within the same overall organization: *She was ransferred to the Paris office.* ○ *He transferred from finance to the sales department.* **4** (*transport*) to change from one vehicle or oute to another when travelling: *When you arrive in San Francisco you transfer onto an internal flight to San Diego.*

/træns'fɜː(r)/
transfer, transferring, transferred
1, 2 note transitive verb
3 note transitive and intransitive verb
▶ **second[2]**
4 note intransitive verb
⋈ **transfer** from (a person, place, etc), to (a person, place, etc)

---

transferable *adjective*
hat can be given or sold to, or used by another person: *The icket/document/contract is not transferable.*

/træns'fɜːrəbl/

---

transferable bond *noun* (finance)
a bond that can be given or sold to another person without the company which issued the bond being informed

/træns'fɜːrəbl bɒnd/
pl transferable bonds
⋈ buy, issue, sell a **transferable bond**
▶ **bond**

Transfer Accounting Lodgement for Investors and Stock Management *noun* (stock exchange)
▶ **TALISMAN**

/ˌtrænsfɜːr əˌkaʊntɪŋ ˌlɒdʒmənt fər ɪnˌvestəz ənd ˌstɒk ˈmænɪdʒmənt/

transfer agent *noun* (finance/stock exchange)
(*US*) a person whose job is to keep a record (the TRANSFER REGISTER) of changes of ownership of a company's shares

/ˈtrænsfɜːr ˌeɪdʒənt/
pl transfer agents
⋈ act as, employ a **transfer agent**
▶ **agent, transfer[1] 1, transfer register**

Transfer and Automated Registration of Uncertified Stock *noun* (stock exchange)
▶ **TAURUS**

/ˌtrænsfɜːr ənd ˌɔːtəmeɪtɪd redʒɪˌstreɪʃn əv ʌnˌsɜːtɪfaɪd ˈstɒk/

transfer book *noun* (stock exchange)
▶ **transfer register**

/ˈtrænsfɜː bʊk/

transfer certificate *noun* (finance/stock exchange)
a document from a company stating that it has recorded a change of ownership of some of its shares. The transfer certificate is kept by the new owner (the TRANSFEREE): *Both the original certificate and the transfer certificate are needed as proof of ownership.*

/ˈtrænsfɜː səˌtɪfɪkət/
pl transfer certificates
⋈ issue a **transfer certificate**
▶ **transfer[1] 1**

transfer deed *noun* (finance/stock exchange)
▶ **deed of transfer**

/ˈtrænsfɜː diːd/

transfer duty *noun* (tax)
(*UK*) a tax that is paid when securities are bought and sold. It is paid by the buyers on all securities, except for gilts, new issues and debentures: *You must pay the transfer duty within 30 days of buying the shares.* ○ *Transfer duty is payable within 30 days of buying the shares.*

/ˈtrænsfɜː ˌdjuːti/
pl transfer duties
syn (*US*) transfer tax
⋈ pay **transfer duty**
▶ **duty 1, stamp duty, transfer[1] 1**

transferee *noun* (law/stock exchange)
a person to whom the ownership of property, securities, shares, etc is transferred

/ˌtrænsfɜːrˈiː/
pl transferees
▶ **transfer[1] 1, transferor**

transfer form *noun* (stock exchange)
a standard document used in the UK to change the ownership of securities. The name and address of the buyer (the TRANSFEREE) is written in and the form is signed by the seller: *The buyer was asked to fill in a transfer form*

/ˈtrænsfɜː fɔːm/
pl transfer forms
⋈ fill in, sign a **transfer form**
syn stock transfer form
▶ **transfer[1] 1, transfer deed**

transfer income *noun* (economics/finance)
money received from a government in the form of pensions, unemployment benefits, farming subsidies, etc. It is not payment for goods or services, but is transferred by means of taxation from one group of people to another: *Transfer income is not included in gross national product.*

/ˌtrænsfɜːr ˈɪŋkʌm/
note not used with *a* or *an*. No plural and used with a singular verb only.
syn transfer payment
⋈ calculate, receive, record **transfer income**
▶ **income**

transferor *noun* (law/stock exchange)
the person who transfers the ownership of their property, securities, shares, etc to someone else

/træns'fɜːrə/
pl transferors
▶ **transfer¹ 1, transferee**

transfer passenger *noun* (transport)
an air traveller who changes at an airport from one airline to another one: *Some transfer passengers missed their flights from New York because of the delay in Chicago.*

/'trænsfɜː ˌpæsɪn dʒə(r)/
pl transfer passengers
▶ **joining passenger, transfer¹ 4**

transferred charge call *noun*
a telephone call which is only made if the person receiving the call agrees to pay for it: *The operator said, 'Will you accept a transferred charge call from Edinburgh?'*

/træns,fɜːd ˌtʃɑːdʒ 'kɔːl/
pl transferred charge calls
⋈ accept, ask for, make a **transferred charge call**

transfer register *noun* (stock exchange)
a book in which a change of ownership of a company's shares are recorded: *The transfer register is closed until after the annual general meeting.* ○ *to record transfers in a transfer register*

/'trænsfɜː ˌredʒɪstə(r)/
pl transfer registers
⋈ keep, record (transfers) in a **transfer register**
syn transfer book
▶ **transfer¹ 1, transfer agent**

transfer tax *noun* (tax)
(*US*) ▶ **transfer duty**

/'trænsfɜː tæks/

transhipment *noun* (transport)
the transferring of goods from one form of transport, esp a ship, to another: *There are two transhipments before the goods are delivered at their destination.*

/'trænz'ʃɪpmənt/
pl transhipments
⋈ make a **transhipment**

transit *noun* (transport)
the movement of people or goods from one place to another: *Please arrange transit of the goods.*
in transit on the way from one place to another: *The goods appear to have been lost in transit.*

/'trænzɪt/
note not used with *a* or *an*. No plural and used with a singular verb only.
⋈ damaged, lost in **transit**; a **transit** lounge, passenger, visa

transport¹ *noun* (transport)
1 moving people or goods from one place to another in a vehicle: *What is the best means of transport for getting the goods to Greece?* ○ *Road transport is probably the cheapest.* ○ *How much do you charge for transport?* **2** vehicles used for taking people or goods from one place to another: *Do you have your own transport?* ○ *Will transport be provided?*

/'trænspɔːt/
note not used with *a* or *an*. No plural and used with a singular verb only.
1 ⋈ air, rail, road **transport**; a means, method of **transport**; **transport** charges, costs
2 ⋈ lay on, provide **transport**
syn (*US*) transportation

transport² *verb* (transport)
to move people or goods from one place to another in a vehicle: *It's cheaper to transport goods by road than by rail.* ○ *We're transporting the equipment from New York to Berlin by air.*

/træn'spɔːt/
transport, transporting, transported
note transitive verb
⋈ **transport** *by* air, rail, road, sea, truck
▶ **consign, deliver, despatch², distribute**

transportable *adjective* (transport)
able to be taken from one place to another: *Some fine wines are not easily transportable.*

/træn'spɔːtəbl/
⧓ easily, readily **transportable**

transportation *noun* (distribution)
the movement of goods or people from one place to another; the arrangements made for this: *Does the price include transportation to Australia?* ○ *We will arrange transportation of your order.*

/ˌtrænspɔː'teɪʃn/
note not used with *a* or *an*. No plural and used with a singular verb only.
⧓ arrange **transportation**; **transportation** *of* (goods or people), *to* (a place); a **transportation** system
▶ **carriage 1, delivery, distribution**

Transport International Routier *noun* (transport)
(*French*) a European arrangement for using international documents for sending goods by road. No customs duties are charged on goods crossing the borders of European countries until the goods reach the country of their destination.

/ˌtrænspɔːt ɪn təˌnæʃnəl ˌruːtieɪ/
abbr TIR

travel agent *noun* (tourism)
a person or an organization that arranges travel and accommodation for people going on holiday or on business: *book a holiday through a travel agent* ○ *work as a travel agent*

/'trævl ˌeɪdʒənt/
pl travel agents
⧓ a leading, local **travel agent**
▶ **agent, tour operator**

travel allowance *noun*
money given to an employee to pay for journeys made for business, or to help with the cost of travelling to and from work: *The company has increased my travel allowance.* ○ *a travel allowance of 20p per mile*

/'trævl əˌlaʊəns/
pl travel allowances
⧓ exceed, give, receive, spend a **travel allowance**
▶ **allowance 1**

travel expenses *noun*
money spent by an employee while travelling and staying away from home for business, repaid later by the employer: *Have you claimed last month's travel expenses yet?* ○ *Don't forget to put the cost of the rail fare on your travel expenses.* ○ *All your travel expenses will be covered on this trip.*

/'trævl ɪkˌspensɪz/
note plural noun, used with a plural verb
⧓ claim, cover, repay **travel expenses**
▶ **expenses, travel allowance**

traveller's cheque *noun* (banking)
a cheque for a fixed amount, sold by a bank, that can easily be cashed in foreign countries: *cash a traveller's cheque for $20* ○ *Would you like the traveller's cheques in sterling or in francs?*

/'trævləz tʃek/
pl traveller's cheques
(*US* **traveler's check**)
pl traveler's checks
⧓ cash, issue, sign a **traveller's cheque**
▶ **cheque, eurocheque**

traveller's letter of credit *noun* (banking/commerce)
▶ **letter of credit**

/ˌtrævləz ˌletər əv 'kredɪt/

travelling salesman, salesperson, saleswoman *noun* (sales)
a person who travels around, usually from shop to shop to sell goods and services: *be employed as a travelling salesman* ○ *have frequent visits from travelling salespeople*

/ˌtrævlɪŋ 'seɪlzmən, ˌtrævlɪŋ 'seɪlzpɜːsn, ˌtrævlɪŋ 'seɪlzwʊmən/
pl travelling salesmen, salespeople, saleswomen
⧓ buy from a **travelling salesman**

▶ **commercial traveller, door-to-door salesman, salesman, sales representative**

---

treasurer *noun*
a person who keeps records of the money obtained or spent by an organization, and who is responsible for investing any surplus: *The treasurer will be presenting the accounts at the annual general meeting.*

/ˈtreʒərə(r)/
pl treasurers
⋈ appoint, elect a **treasurer**; act as, become, run for, stand as **treasurer**

---

treasury *noun* (finance)
1 (*UK*) **the Treasury** a government department that controls public finance and spending. The Chancellor of the Exchequer is in charge of the Treasury: *The Treasury and the Bank of England work together in deciding interest rates.* ○ *Treasury officials are said to have advised against cutting income tax.* **2** a public or national supply of money: *receive a grant from the treasury*

/ˈtreʒəri/
note usually singular
⋈ financed by the **Treasury**; **Treasury** figures, funds
▶ **Bank of England, exchequer**

Treasury bill *noun* (public finance)
a bill of exchange issued by the Bank of England, to be repaid within three months, with no interest. Treasury bills are bought by DISCOUNT HOUSES for less than their actual value and then resold: *The discount market tenders for Treasury bills once a week.*

/ˈtreʒəri bɪl/
pl Treasury bills
⋈ discount, issue, tender for a **Treasury bill**
syn finance bill
▶ **bill of exchange, discount house**

Treasury bond *noun* (public finance)
a BOND issued by the US government: *The 30-year Treasury bond yielded a dividend of 8.45%.* ○ *a dealer in Treasury bonds*

/ˈtreʒəri bɒnd/
pl Treasury bonds

---

trend *noun*
a movement in a certain direction; a tendency: *an upward trend in share prices* ○ *a growing trend towards more aggressive takeover bids* ○ *Our course follows recent trends in training techniques.*

/trend/
pl trends
⋈ a downward, a general, a growing, a recent, an upward **trend**; a **trend** away from, in, of, towards (something)
▶ **market trend**

---

trial balance *noun* (accounting)
a way of checking accounts by comparing the total credits with the total debits. The two totals should be the same: *She drew up a trial balance and then went on to prepare the accounts.*

/ˌtraɪəl ˈbæləns/
pl trial balances
abbr TB
⋈ do, draw up, prepare a **trial balance**
▶ **accounts, balance**

---

trial period *noun*
1 (*commerce*) the length of time for which a customer may try out a product before having to pay for it or return it: *You will not be charged if you return the goods within the trial period of seven days.* **2** (*industry*) an agreed length of time that an employee works for before the employer makes the job permanent: *I confirm your appointment as departmental manager, with a three-month trial period.*

/ˈtraɪəl ˌpɪəriəd/
pl trial periods
⋈ inside, outside, within the **trial period**
1 ⋈ allow a **trial period**
2 ⋈ agree on, have a **trial period**

tribunal *noun*
a group of people with the authority to settle certain types of dispute, eg between staff and employees: *The case will be decided by an independent tribunal.* ○ *The employee who was dismissed has appealed to an industrial tribunal.*

/traɪˈbjuːnl/
pl tribunals
⋈ appeal to, refer to, set up, sit on, take a case to a **tribunal**; an industrial, a rent **tribunal**
▶ **the Advisory Conciliation and Arbitration Service, industrial dispute, industrial tribunal**

---

triplicate *noun* (office practice)
in triplicate consisting of the original document and two identical copies: *These forms need to be made out in triplicate.*

/ˈtrɪplɪkət/
note no plural
⋈ copy, invoice, send, submit, type (something) **in triplicate**
▶ **copy[1] 1, duplicate[1], master 1, photocopy[1]**

---

troubleshooter *noun* (industry)
(*informal*) a person whose job is to solve major company problems, eg those caused by industrial disputes, machine faults, bad management, etc: *The company really needs a high-powered troubleshooter for six months or so.*

/ˈtrʌblʃuːtə(r)/
pl troubleshooters
(also **trouble-shooter**)
⋈ employ, find, use a **troubleshooter**; an effective, a high-powered, a successful **troubleshooter**

---

trough *noun* (economics)
a low point or minimum amount of something, esp of business or trade; the part of a graph that shows this: *Since its trough in February the dollar has climbed 21% against the Deutschmark.* ○ *The trough must end soon; there seem to be signs of recovery.*

/trɒf/
pl troughs
⋈ a **trough** ends, lasts
▶ **peak[1]**

---

truck *noun* (transport)
1 a vehicle that is used for transporting goods by road; a lorry: *the goods were transported by truck.* **2** (*UK*) an open railway wagon for transporting goods: *Five coal trucks were derailed yesterday.*

fork-lift truck a vehicle that can carry, raise and lower bundles of goods on metal arms and that can be driven around a warehouse or factory yard

/trʌk/
pl trucks
1 ⋈ send, transport (something) *by* **truck**; drive, fill, load a **truck**; a **truck** driver, load
2 ⋈ a railway **truck**

---

truckage *noun* (transport)
(*US*) **1** the movement of goods by truck: *Truckage costs will be high.* **2** the charge made for transport by truck: *inclusive of truckage*

/ˈtrʌkɪdʒ/
note not used with *a* or *an*. No plural and used with a singular verb only.
⋈ calculate, charge, exclude, include **truckage**; exclusive, inclusive of **truckage**

---

true and fair view *noun* (accounting)
(of company accounts) a record that is accurate and not misleading. Auditors are legally required to check for this: *The accounts have been certified as showing a true and fair view of the company's affairs.*

/ˌtruː ənd ˌfeə ˈvjuː/
note usually singular
⋈ present, show a **true and fair view**; a **true and fair view** of a company's affairs
▶ **accounts, auditor**

---

trunk road *noun* (transport)
(*UK*) a main road; a major route for driving long distances: *The island has one trunk road, linking its two major towns.*

/ˈtrʌŋk rəʊd/
pl trunk roads
⧓ the **trunk road** bypasses, connects, goes through, links; build, construct, drive along, follow, take, use a **trunk road**

---

trust *noun* (finance/law)
an arrangement in which usually two or more people (the TRUSTEES) manage money, property or land for a particular purpose or for another person or group of people (the BENEFICIARIES): *set up a trust for scientific research* ○ *The money is managed as a trust.*

accept a trust to become a trustee

breach of trust the failure of a trustee to manage a trust properly: *When money was discovered to be missing from the pension fund, the trustees were accused of breach of trust.*

in trust being held by trustees for the benefit of another person: *The money he inherits will be held in trust until he is eighteen.*

/trʌst/
pl trusts
⧓ create, establish, manage, set up a **trust**; hold (land, money, property) *in* **trust**
▶ **bequest, charitable trust, endowment, fund, investment trust, split trust, trust fund, unit trust**

---

trust deed *noun* (law)
a formal document that creates a trust. It states the purpose and terms of the trust and the names of the TRUSTEES and BENEFICIARIES: *Under the terms of the trust deed, the trustees can decide how to invest any profit.*

/ˈtrʌst diːd/
pl trust deeds
syn trust instrument
⧓ draw up, sign a **trust deed**
▶ **deed**

---

trustee *noun* (law)
a person who is responsible for managing money, property or land for another person or group of people: *The property will be managed by a board of five trustees.*

/ˌtrʌˈstiː/
pl trustees
⧓ act as, appoint a **trustee**; a board of **trustees**
▶ **fiduciary, trust**

---

trustee in bankruptcy *noun* (law)
a person chosen by the courts to sell the property of a bankrupt person and pay all debts: *The trustee in bankruptcy sold the bankrupt's estate.*

/trʌˌstiː ɪn ˈbæŋkrəpsi/
pl trustees in bankruptcy
syn assignee in bankruptcy
⧓ appoint a **trustee in bankruptcy**
▶ **bankruptcy**

---

trust fund *noun* (law)
the items of value (ASSETS) kept by a trust for the BENEFICIARY of the trust: *The money from the sale of the products is put into a trust fund.*

/ˈtrʌst fʌnd/
pl trust funds
⧓ keep (money) in, put (money) into a **trust fund**
▶ **fund[1] 2**

---

trust instrument *noun* (law)
▶ **trust deed**

/ˈtrʌst ˌɪnstrəmənt/

---

trust receipt *noun* (banking)
a document given to a bank by an importer who has accepted a bill of exchange, but is not able to pay at the time the goods arrive. The bank meanwhile pays the exporter: *A trust receipt covered the unloading of the goods.*

/ˈtrʌst rɪˌsiːt/
pl trust receipts
▶ **bill of exchange**

trust unit *noun* (finance)
a share in a UNIT TRUST: *The price of the trust units is down.*

/ˈtrʌst ˌjuːnɪt/
pl trust units

TS *abbr* (office practice)
typescript: *The corrected TS has been returned.*

note used in written English only

T/S *abbr* (banking)
transhipment: *The goods are for T/S at Liverpool.*

/ˌtiː ˈes/

TT *abbr* (banking/international trade)
telegraphic transfer

/ˌtiː ˈtiː/

TU *abbr* (industrial relations)
trade union: *The local representative of the TU.*

/ˌtiː ˈjuː/
note pronounced as individual letters

TUC *abbr* (industrial relations)
Trades Union Congress: *The TUC met to settle the dispute between two of its members.*

/ˌtiː juː ˈsiː/
note pronounced as individual letters

turnaround *noun* (manufacturing)
(of goods, orders, etc) the process of receiving, processing and sending out again: *What is the turnaround on these goods?* ○ *a seven-day turnaround in providing replacements for faulty goods*

/ˈtɜːnəraʊnd/
note no plural
⧓ **turnaround** time
▶ **turn-round**

turnover *noun*
1 (*accounting*) the total business done by an organization in a given period: *The firm increased its turnover last year.* ○ *an annual turnover of £10 million* ○ *Exports account for 25% of turnover.* **2** (*commerce*) the rate at which stock is sold: *The shop has a rapid turnover.* **3** the rate at which employees join and leave a company: *The company has a very high turnover of staff, perhaps the wages are low.*

/ˈtɜːnəʊvə(r)/
note usually singular
abbr TO
⧓ increase, reduce **turnover**; a fast, high, low, quick, rapid, slow **turnover**
▶ **stock turnover**

turnover ratio *noun* (accounting)
the relationship between the total sales of a business and the value of its land, machinery, etc (CAPITAL ASSETS): *Sales were down resulting in a low turnover ratio.*

/ˈtɜːnəʊvə ˌreɪʃiəʊ/
note usually singular
⧓ a high, low **turnover ratio**
▶ **ratio**

turnover tax *noun* (tax)
tax on the money received from the sale of goods: *The money is set aside for the payment of this year's turnover tax.*

/ˈtɜːnəʊvə tæks/
note no plural
⧓ be charged, pay **turnover tax**
▶ **sales tax, tax**[1]

turn-round *noun* (transport/shipping)
the unloading, refuelling, reloading, etc of a vehicle or ship before it can begin another journey: *A profitable ship must have a quick turn-round.* ○ *a turn-round time of two hours*

/ˈtɜːnraʊnd/
note no plural
⧓ turn-round **time**
▶ **turnaround**

TVR *abbr* (marketing)
television rating

/ˌtiː viː ˈɑː(r)/

tycoon *noun* (industry)
a wealthy and important business person: *a shipping tycoon*

/taɪˈkuːn/
pl tycoons
⧓ a newspaper, an oil, a property, a shipping **tycoon**
▶ **magnate**

type[1] *noun*
letters, words, etc that have been printed or typed: *I can't read this small type.* ○ *Please use bold type for the headings.*

/taɪp/
note usually singular
⧓ bold, italic, small **type**

type[2] *verb* (office practice)
to write something using a typewriter or word processor: *The letter was typed yesterday.* ○ *I need to type up my notes in time for the meeting.* ○ *Could you type out this document for me?*

/taɪp/
type, typing, typed
note transitive and intransitive verb
▶ **key[2], keyboard[2]**

typescript *noun* (office practice)
a document that has been produced on a typewriter: *The typescript is ready to be set by the printer.*

/ˈtaɪpskrɪpt/
pl typescripts
abbr TS

typewriter *noun*
a machine with metal keys that are pressed to produce letters similar to printed ones: *use an electric typewriter*

/ˈtaɪpraɪtə(r)/
pl typewriters
⧓ a **typewriter** keyboard, ribbon
▶ **word processor**

typewritten *adjective* (office practice)
written using a typewriter or a word processor: *A typewritten letter is easier to read than a handwritten one.* ○ *Are your notes typewritten?*

/ˈtaɪprɪtn/
⧓ a **typewritten** document, letter, sheet (of paper)

typing *noun* (office practice)
1 the act of using a typewriter: *I must practise my typing.* ○ *The letter is full of typing errors.* **2** work that must be typed: *There is still a lot of typing to do.*

/ˈtaɪpɪŋ/
note not used with *a* or *an*. No plural and used with a singular verb only.
⧓ accurate, fast **typing**; a **typing** course, error, mistake

typist *noun* (office practice)
a person who types, esp as a job: *work as a typist*

/ˈtaɪpɪst/
pl typists
⧓ an accurate, a fast **typist**
▶ **audio-typist, copy-typist, keyboarder, shorthand typist**

Uu

ullage *noun*
1 (*industry*) the difference between the full capacity of a container and the volume of the contents, ie because of leakage or evaporation: *The heat had caused considerable ullage.* **2** (*import*) the actual contents of a container at the time of importation: *The ullage of each barrel was 5 gallons.* ○ *A 2 tonne ullage.* ○ *What is its ullage?*

/ˈʌlɪdʒ/
note no plural
⧓ large, small **ullage**; **ullage** in (something), of (something)
▶ **leakage, vacuity**

ultimate consumer *noun* (retail)
the person who buys, uses or consumes a product: *The ultimate consumer pays considerably more than the manufacturing price.* ○ *What are the needs of the ultimate consumer?*

/ˌʌltɪmət kənˈsjuːmə(r)/
pl ultimate consumers
⧓ an **ultimate consumer** buys, pays for, requires, uses (a product)
▶ **consumer, end-user 1, producer, manufacturer**

ultimatum *noun*
a demand by one party or country for something to be done by another within a certain period of time, otherwise force or legal action will be used against them: *They have issued an ultimatum.* ○ *Their final ultimatum has been received.*

/ˌʌltɪˈmeɪtəm/
pl ultimatums or ultimata
⧓ deal with, issue, receive, respond to an **ultimatum**; final **ultimatum**
▶ **deadline, final demand**

ultra vires *adjective* (law)
(*Latin*) (of the action of a person, company or government) beyond legal or official powers: *Their action was ultra vires.* ○ *An ultra vires act.*

/ˌʌltrə ˈvaɪriːz/
⧓ **an ultra vires** act, action, agreement

umbrella fund *noun* (international trade/stock exchange)
an offshore fund in a tax haven that invests in other offshore investments: *Her profits were held in an umbrella fund.* ○ *Umbrella funds provide advantageous taxation rates.*

/ʌmˈbrelə fʌnd/
pl umbrella funds
⧓ held in, invest in **an umbrella fund**
▶ **fund[1] 2, offshore fund, tax haven**

umbrella organization *noun* (commerce)
a company, business or institution that includes several smaller ones: *A large umbrella organization.* ○ *An umbrella organization bought her small company.*

/ʌmˈbrelə ˌɔːɡənaɪˌzeɪʃn/
pl umbrella organizations
⧓ an extended, a large **umbrella organization**
▶ **organization 1, group**

umpire *noun* (law/industrial relations/industry)
a person appointed to settle a civil (non-criminal) dispute: *The umpire offered a solution which suited both sides.* ○ *The union wanted to seek the advice of an umpire.*

/ˈʌmpaɪə(r)/
pl umpires
⧓ independent, neutral **umpire**
▶ **arbitrator, mediator, referee 3**

unabsorbed cost *noun* (industry)
the part of the cost of production that is provided by income if output falls below a particular level: *Unabsorbed costs contributed to the company's collapse.* ○ *They could not afford to pay the unabsorbed cost.*

/ˌʌnəbˌsɔːbd ˈkɒst/
pl unabsorbed costs
⧓ incur **unabsorbed costs**
▶ **cost[1]**

unaccounted for *adjective*
missing, without reason or excuse: *Several cheques are unaccounted for.* ○ *We cannot afford funds to go unaccounted for.*

/ˌʌnəˈkaʊntɪd fɔː(r)/
⧓ to be, to go **unaccounted for**; **unaccounted for** funds, income, items
▶ **account[2]**

unanimous *adjective*
of a decision or vote where everyone agrees: *Only a unanimous vote will make her resign.* ○ *reach a unanimous decision*

/juˈnænɪməs/
⧓ a **unanimous** decision, vote

unappropriated profit *noun* (commerce)
profit that has not been used or paid out in dividends: *The unappropriated profit will be carried over to the next financial year.* ○ *Much of last year's takings remains in unappropriated profit.*

/ˌʌnəˌprəʊprieɪtɪd ˈprɒfɪt/
pl unappropriated profits
⋈ to carry over **unappropriated profit**
syn undistributed profit
▶ **profit**[1]**, unissued capital**

unaudited *adjective* (accounting)
of accounts that have not been checked by an auditor: *The accountants would like to see the unaudited accounts.*

/ˌʌnˈɔːdɪtɪd/
⋈ **unaudited** accounts, books, transactions
▶ **audit**[2]**, auditor**

unbalanced *adjective* (accounting)
of a budget or account where expenditure is higher than income, or when the credit total and debit total do not correspond: *The account will be unbalanced until all the figures are returned.*

/ˌʌnˈbælənst/
⋈ **unbalanced** accounts, books
▶ **balance**[1]**, deficit, credit balance, debit balance**

unbundling *noun* (commerce)
selling of subsidiary businesses during the takeover of a large organization: *Unbundling is all that will save the organization.* ○ *unbundling a subsidiary*

/ˌʌnˈbʌndlɪŋ/
note not used with *a* or *an*. No plural and used with a singular verb only.
⋈ **unbundling** a company, a subsidiary
▶ **asset stripping, takeover**

uncashed *adjective*
of a document, esp a cheque, that has not been traded for cash or paid into a bank account: *My salary cheque is uncashed.* ○ *uncashed documents*

/ˌʌnˈkæʃt/
⋈ an **uncashed** cheque, document, security, stock
▶ **cash**[2]

uncertified units *noun* (stock exchange)
a small number of shares that are too low in value to be given a separate certificate: *The uncertified units will be added to the total when they are sold.*

/ʌnˌsɜːtɪfaɪd ˈjuːnɪts/
note plural noun, used with a plural verb
⋈ hold, invest in, sell **uncertified units**
▶ **share certificate**

unconditional *adjective*
with no terms specified; absolute: *The offer received unconditional acceptance.* ○ *He made an unconditional offer.*

/ˌʌnkənˈdɪʃənl/
⋈ an **unconditional** acceptance, bid, offer
▶ **condition**

unconditional takeover bid *noun* (stock exchange)
▶ **takeover bid**

/ˌʌnkənˌdɪʃənl ˈteɪkəʊvə bɪd/

unconfirmed letter of credit *noun*
(banking/commerce) ▶ **letter of credit**

/ˌʌnkənˌfɜːmd ˌletər əv ˈkredɪt/

unconscionable bargain *noun* (law)
an unfair or illegal contract, by which one party takes advantage of another: *They had been the victims of an unconscionable bargain.* ○ *The unconscionable bargain was modified in court.*

/ʌnˌkɒnʃənəbl ˈbɑːgən/
pl unconscionable bargains
⋈ to contract, to draw up, to make an **unconscionable bargain**
syn catching bargain
▶ **illegal contract**

uncrossed cheque *noun* (banking)
▶ **open cheque**

/ˌʌnkrɒst ˈtʃek/

UNCTAD *abbr* (economics)
United Nations Conference on Trade and Development: *They attended a meeting of UNCTAD.*

/ˈʌŋktæd/

undated security *noun* (stock exchange)
a fixed-interest investment which has no specified time-limit for repayment: *Undated securities constitute a long term investment.* ○ *She traded her undated securities.*

/ˌʌndeɪtɪd sɪˈkjʊərəti/
pl undated securities
▶ **security 1**

underbid *verb* (commerce/stock exchange)
to quote less than someone else, eg in a TENDER competition: *We were underbid by another company.* ○ *The organization underbid all their competitors.*

/ˌʌndəˈbɪd/
underbid, underbidding, underbid
note transitive verb
▶ **bid²**, **outbid**

underlease *noun* (law)
▶ **sublease**

/ˈʌndəliːs/

undermentioned *adjective*
of something that appears further down or later on in a document: *Please note the undermentioned statistics.* ○ *The facts are undermentioned.*

/ˌʌndəˈmenʃnd/
⋈ **undermentioned** facts, figures, statistics
▶ **aforementioned**, **undersigned**

undersell *verb*
to sell more cheaply than someone else: *We undersell all our competitors.* ○ *never knowingly undersold*

/ˌʌndəˈsel/
undersell, underselling, undersold
note transitive verb
⋈ **undersell** a competitor
▶ **sell 1**

undersigned *noun*
a person who has signed a letter: *We, the undersigned . . .* ○ *Please contact the undersigned.*

/ˌʌndəˈsaɪnd/
note used with a singular or a plural verb
▶ **undermentioned**

undersold *adjective* (sales)
having sold less goods than are available for sale: *have an undersold stock*

/ˌʌndəˈsəʊld/
opp oversold

understaffed *adjective* (personnel)
not having enough workers for work that has to be done: *I'm sorry your order is late, but we are understaffed at the moment.* ○ *work in an understaffed office*

/ˌʌndəˈstɑːft/
opp overstaffed

undertaking *noun*
1 an activity; a business: *We have embarked upon a commercial undertaking.* **2** (*law*) a legally binding promise: *We require a written undertaking.* ○ *a legal undertaking*

/ˌʌndəˈteɪkɪŋ/
note usually singular
1 ⋈ a commercial, financial **undertaking**
2 ⋈ a legal **undertaking**
▶ **contract¹**

underwrite *verb*
1 (*insurance*) to calculate an insurance risk and work out a suitable premium: *underwrite an insurance policy* **2** (*stock exchange*) to agree to buy up unsold shares when new shares are offered for sale: *underwrite a large part of the new share offer* **3** to bear the cost of something: *underwrite court costs*

/ˌʌndəˈraɪt/
underwrite, underwriting, underwrote, underwritten
1 ⋈ **underwrite** risks
3 ⋈ **underwrite** costs, losses

underwriter *noun*
1 (*insurance*) a person who examines a risk and works out the premium to be charged for insurance: *The underwriter has calculated the risk.* ○ *He is a Lloyd's underwriter.* ○ *a marine underwriter* **2** (*banking/stock exchange*) an organization, eg an ISSUING HOUSE that guarantees to buy a proportion of unsold shares when a new share issue is offered: *The underwriter has guaranteed the flotation.*

/ˈʌndəraɪtə(r)/
pl underwriters
1 abbr U/w
⋈ Lloyd's, marine **underwriter**
▶ **Lloyd's of London**
2 ⋈ financial **underwriter**
▶ **issue**[1]

undifferentiated marketing *noun* (marketing)
the presentation, packaging and distribution of a product, aimed at the widest range of consumers: *The undifferentiated marketing of the product was successful.*

/ʌnˌdɪfəˌrenʃieɪtɪd ˈmɑːkɪtɪŋ/
note not used with *a* or *an*. No plural and used with a singular verb only.
⋈ **undifferentiated marketing** plan, strategy
▶ **differentiation, marketing, marketing mix**

undischarged bankrupt *noun* (commerce)
a person who has been declared bankrupt, ie has unpaid debts, and has not been cleared from such a position: *He has been an undischarged bankrupt since his company collapsed.* ○ *An undischarged bankrupt may not become the director of another company.*

/ˌʌndɪsˌtʃɑːdʒd ˈbæŋkrʌpt/
pl undischarged bankrupts
▶ **bankrupt**[1]

undisclosed factoring *noun* (commerce)
the purchasing of the trade debts of a manufacturer, in which the role of the buyer of the debts (the FACTOR) remains hidden from the debtors: *We used undisclosed factoring to improve our cash-flow without upsetting our customers.*

/ˌʌndɪsˌkləʊzd ˈfæktərɪŋ/
note not used with *a* or *an*. No plural and used with a singular verb only.
⋈ be involved in, carry out **undisclosed factoring**
opp disclosed factoring
▶ **factoring**

undisclosed principal *noun* (commerce)
a person who pays another person (an AGENT or BROKER) to buy or sell for them in order to remain anonymous: *An undisclosed principal was represented by an agent at the auction.* ○ *I am acting as broker for an undisclosed principal.*

/ˌʌndɪsˌkləʊzd ˈprɪnsəpl/
pl undisclosed principals
⋈ act for, represent, stand for an **undisclosed principal**
▶ **principal**

undistributed profit *noun* (commerce)
▶ **unappropriated profit**

/ˌʌndɪˌstrɪbjətɪd ˈprɒfɪt/

unearned income *noun* (tax)
money received from interest or dividends on capital or investments rather than from a salary or business profits: *He lives off his unearned income.*

/ˌʌnɜːnd ˈɪŋkʌm/
note no plural
⋈ be taxed on, calculate, live on **unearned income**
syn investment income
opp earned income
▶ **income**

uneconomic *adjective* (commerce)
of something that loses rather than makes money: *They lost money because of an uneconomic production process.* ○ *It would be uneconomic to employ more staff.*

/ˌʌnˌiːkəˈnɒmɪk, ˌʌnˌekəˈnɒmɪk/
⋈ an **uneconomic** business, industry, process, project
opp economic
▶ **unprofitable**

unemployed[1] *noun*
people with no jobs: *provide more training for the unemployed*

/ˌʌnɪmˈplɔɪd/
note used with a plural verb
⋈ the long-term, short-term **unemployed**
syn jobless

unemployed[2] *adjective*
without a job: *He has been unemployed for over a year.*

/ˌʌnɪmˈplɔɪd/
⋈ **unemployed** people, workers

unemployment *noun*
lack of paid work; unused labour: *The unemployment level has increased this month.* ○ *She receives unemployment benefit.* ○ *Unemployment is a problem during recession.* ○ *Many workers face unemployment.*

seasonal unemployment lack of work that occurs at particular times of the year: *The seasonal unemployment figures are lower in the summer.*

/ˌʌnɪmˈplɔɪmənt/
note not used with *a* or *an*. No plural and used with a singular verb only.
⋈ falling, high, involuntary, level of, long-term, low, rate of, rising **unemployment**; **unemployment** figures
opp employment
▶ **job losses, natural wastage, recession, redundancy, residual unemployment, structural unemployment**

unfair dismissal *noun* (personnel)
1 the removal of an employee from a job without a proper reason: *She was a victim of unfair dismissal.* ○ *The company is being sued for unfair dismissal.* **2** an employee dismissed in this way: *Trade union members are concerned about the increasing number of unfair dismissals.*

/ˌʌnfeə dɪsˈmɪsl/
1 note not used with *a* or *an*. No plural and used with a singular verb only.
⋈ be a victim of, a case of, claim, sue for **unfair dismissal**
2 pl unfair dismissals
syn wrongful dismissal
▶ **dismissal, employment protection, industrial tribunal, sack**

unfavourable balance *noun* (accounting)
▶ **adverse balance**

/ʌnˌfeɪvərəbl ˈbæləns/

unfranked income *noun* (commerce)
money that a company receives from investments on which CORPORATION TAX still has to be paid: *The company has to pay tax on its unfranked income.*

/ˌʌnfræŋkt ˈɪŋkʌm/
note usually singular
⋈ obtain, receive **unfranked income**
▶ **franked income**

unfulfilled *adjective* (law/sales)
of an order or promise that has not yet been supplied or completed: *An unfulfilled contract.* ○ *The order remains unfulfilled.*

/ˌʌnfʊlˈfɪld/
⋈ an **unfulfilled** contract, order, promise

ungeared *adjective* (banking)
having no borrowings: *Her account is ungeared.* ○ *an ungeared balance*

/ʌnˈgɪəd/
⧓ **an ungeared** account, balance
▶ **degearing, gearing, highly geared**

UNIDO *abbr* (international trade)
United Nations Industrial Development Organization: *She is a UNIDO representative.*

/juːˈniːdəʊ/

---

unilateral *adjective*
of or on one side only, ie done by or affecting one person, group, country, etc: *He took a unilateral decision to cancel the contract.*

/ˌjuːnɪˈlætrəl/
⧓ a **unilateral** action, decision, withdrawal
▶ **bilateral, multilateral**

---

union *noun* (industrial relations)
▶ **trade union**

/ˈjuːniən/

---

unique selling proposition *noun* (sales/marketing)
a feature of a product that makes it different from other products and therefore attractive to consumers: *The durability of this car is its unique selling proposition.* ○ *A unique selling proposition gives a product added interest.*

/juːˌniːk ˈselɪŋ prɒpəˌzɪʃn/
pl unique selling propositions
abbr USP
⧓ develop, create, have a **unique selling proposition**

---

unissued capital *noun* (accounting/commerce)
capital that a company has not distributed as shares: *Much of the money remains as unissued capital.* ○ *Unissued capital constitutes much of the company's profits.*

/ˌʌnɪʃuːd ˈkæpɪtl/
note singular noun, used with a singular verb
▶ **capital, issued capital, unappropriated profit**

---

unit *noun*
1 a single product or item: *How many units have been sold?* ○ *Each unit is individually produced.* **2** (*stock exchange*) a share or security: *You can buy a maximum of 100 units.* **3** a group of people working in the same department or on the same project: *a production unit* ○ *a research unit* **4** (*industry*) a building on an industrial estate: *The company is renting a unit on the new industrial estate.* ○ *The workshop is in unit 20.*

/ˈjuːnɪt/
pl units
1, 2 ⧓ buy, sell a **unit**
2 ▶ **unit trust**
4 ⧓ factory **unit**

---

unit cost *noun* (sales/manufacturing)
the cost of producing one item, found by dividing the total production costs by the number of items produced: *Mass production ensures low unit costs.* ○ *The unit cost is high on a limited edition car.*

/ˌjuːnɪt ˈkɒst/
pl unit costs
⧓ decrease, increase, reduce the **unit cost**
▶ **average cost, cost[1], unit price**

United Nations Common Fund for Commodities
noun (economics/international trade)
an organization, established by the United Nations Conference on Trade and Development, to provide finance for the development of commodity markets, ie markets in grain, coffee, wool, cotton, etc: *The United Nations Common Fund for Commodities has funded the purchase of third world commodities.*

/juˌnaɪtɪd ˌneɪʃnz ˌkɒmən ˌfʌnd fə kəˈmɒdətiz/
abbr UNCFC

United Nations Conference on Trade and Development *noun* (economics/international trade)
an organization set up by the United Nations to help third world countries to export goods: *The United Nations Conference on Trade and Development has supplied the finance for the export of commodities to the industrialized countries.*

/juˌnaɪtɪd ˌneɪʃnz ˌkɒnfərəns ɒn ˌtreɪd ənd dɪˈveləpmənt/
abbr UNCTAD

United Nations Industrial Development Organization *noun* (industry/international trade)
an organization set up to help the development of industry in the third world: *The heavy machinery in the sugar processing plant was provided by the United Nations Industrial Development Organization.*

/juˌnaɪtɪd ˌneɪʃnz ɪn ˌdʌstriəl dɪˈveləpmənt ɔːgənaɪˌzeɪʃn/
abbr UNIDO

---

unit of currency *noun* (economics)
▶ **monetary unit**

/ˌjuːnɪt əv ˈkʌrənsi/

---

unit price *noun* (sales/manufacturing)
the price of an item: *Unit price increases with the rarity of the item.*

/ˌjuːnɪt ˈpraɪs/
note usually singular
⋈ decrease, increase in **unit price**
▶ **unit cost**

---

unit trust *noun* (stock exchange)
an organization that manages a fund invested in a wide range of securities. The fund is divided into units, which small investors can buy or sell: *Investing in a unit trust reduces risks for small investors.*

/ˌjuːnɪt ˈtrʌst/
pl unit trusts
⋈ invest in, manage a **unit trust**
syn (*US*) mutual fund
▶ **investment trust, managed fund, portfolio management**

Unit Trust Association *noun* (stock exchange)
an organization that controls the fees and standards of practice for managers of unit trusts to ensure that investors are treated fairly: *The Unit Trust Association is investigating the workings of the unit trust I have invested in.*

/ˌjuːnɪt ˈtrʌst əˌsəʊsiˌeɪʃn/
abbr UTA
▶ **unit trust**

---

unlawful *adjective* (law)
not allowed by law; illegal: *unlawful trading*

/ʌnˈlɔːfl/
⋈ an **unlawful** practice, trade
opp lawful

---

unlisted company *noun* (stock exchange)
a company whose shares are not recorded on the main market of a stock exchange: *buy shares in an unlisted company*

/ʌnˌlɪstɪd ˈkʌmpəni/
pl unlisted companies
syn unquoted company
opp listed company
▶ **company, quotation 2**

---

unlisted securities *noun* (stock exchange)
shares, stocks and equities that are not on an official list produced by a stock exchange: *Unlisted securities carry a high degree of risk.* ○ *The company is small so it has unlisted securities.*

/ˌʌnˌlɪstɪd sɪˈkjʊərətiz/
note usually plural
⋈ issue, trade in **unlisted securities**
opp listed securities
▶ **security 1, Stock Exchange Daily Official List, unquoted shares**

---

unlisted securities market *noun* (stock exchange)
/ˌʌnˌlɪstɪd sɪˈkjʊərətiz ˌmɑːkɪt/
a market established by the International Stock Exchange for the trade in shares of small companies which are not on its official list: *a small company on the unlisted securities market*

note no plural
abbr USM
⋈ trade on the **unlisted securities market**
▶ **International Stock Exchange, main market, market[1], third market**

unofficial strike *noun* (industrial relations)
/ˌʌnəˌfɪʃl ˈstraɪk/
▶ **strike[1]**

unpaid *adjective*
/ˌʌnˈpeɪd/
not paid for; not yet paid (for): *The balance is still unpaid.*

⋈ **unpaid** balance, debts, holiday, invoices, workers
▶ **pay[1] 1**

unprofitable *adjective* (economics)
/ʌnˈprɒfɪtəbl/
of something that does not make money: *The bus company has stopped running the unprofitable routes.* ○ *unprofitable manufacturing methods*

⋈ **an unprofitable** business, industry, shop
opp profitable
▶ **uneconomic**

unquoted company *noun* (stock exchange)
/ˌʌnˌkwəʊtɪd ˈkʌmpəni/
▶ **unlisted company**

unquoted share *noun* (stock exchange)
/ˌʌnˌkwəʊtɪd ˈʃeə(r)/
a share that does not have an official buying and selling price listed by a stock exchange: *He bought unquoted shares belonging to a new venture.*

pl unquoted shares
▶ **quotation 2, quoted share, share, unlisted securities**

unredeemed pledge *noun*
/ˌʌnrɪˌdiːmd ˈpledʒ/
something given as security for a loan which has not been claimed back through the repayment of the loan: *She has not claimed back her unredeemed pledge.*

pl unredeemed pledges
▶ **pledge**

unsecured creditor *noun* (accounting/commerce)
/ˌʌnsɪˌkjʊəd ˈkredɪtəz/
a person who is owed money by an organization, but who is not entitled to specific assets if the money is not repaid or the debtor becomes bankrupt. Unsecured creditors can only claim what is left after other creditors have been paid: *They have paid all but their unsecured creditors.*

pl unsecured creditors
▶ **creditor, secured creditor, unsecured debenture**

unsecured debenture *noun* (accounting/commerce)
/ˌʌnsɪˌkjʊəd dɪˈbentʃə(r)/
a loan taken by a company for which no specific assets have been set aside as security if it is not repaid: *Unsecured debentures usually rely on the reputation of the borrower.*

pl unsecured debentures
syn naked debenture
⋈ to redeem an **unsecured debenture**
▶ **debenture, perpetual debentures, secured debenture, unredeemable securities**

unsecured debt *noun* (finance)
money owed by a company for which no specific assets have been given as security

/ˌʌnsɪˌkjʊəd ˈdet/
pl unsecured debts
⋈ pay back, pay off, repay an **unsecured debt**
► **debt, secured debt**

unskilled *adjective*
not having or requiring a particular talent or ability: *The firm employs unskilled labour.* ○ *Many school leavers are unskilled.*

/ˌʌnˈskɪld/
⋈ **unskilled** labour, workers, workforce
► **skilled, semi-skilled**

unsocial hours *noun* (personnel)
working times which are different from normal office or factory hours: *Hospital and restaurant workers work unsocial hours.* ○ *get paid more money for working unsocial hours*

/ˌʌnsəʊʃl ˈaʊəz/
note usually plural
⋈ do, work **unsocial hours**

unvalued policy *noun* (insurance)
an insurance policy in which the complete sum but not the worth of each item insured is stated in advance. To make a claim the insurer must provide proof of the item's value: *They took out an unvalued policy on their household contents.*

/ˌʌnˌvæljuːd ˈpɒləsi/
pl unvalued policies
⋈ take out an **unvalued policy**
opp valued policy

update[1] *noun*
a piece of information that is added to keep something current: *The sales director asked for an update of our sales figures.* ○ *receive a regular news update*

/ˈʌpdeɪt/
pl updates
⋈ a computer, an information, a news **update**; ask for, get, receive an **update**

update[2] *verb*
to examine or revise something so that it is current: *We are continually updating our computer systems.* ○ *It is essential to update the exchange rate figures.*

/ˌʌpˈdeɪt/
update, updating, updated
note transitive verb
⋈ **update** figures, files, systems

upfront *adjective*
in advance: *They must put half the money upfront.* ○ *We require upfront payments.*

/ˌʌpˈfrʌnt/
⋈ **upfront** money, payments; pay, put (something) **upfront**

upgrade *verb* (personnel)
to promote or increase the importance of a person or a job: *Her position has been upgraded to executive level.* ○ *The company will upgrade me after two years' employment.*

/ˌʌpˈgreɪd/
upgrade, upgrading, upgraded
note transitive verb
⋈ **upgrade** a job, person, position
► **promote 2**

upkeep *noun* (industry/commerce)
the cost of maintaining a building or machine: *An automated factory has a high upkeep.* ○ *Upkeep is a significant part of overheads.*

/ˈʌpkiːp/
note no plural
⋈ high, low **upkeep**; **upkeep** of a building, machinery
► **maintenance**

upmarket *adjective, adverb* (sales)
of something which is expensive, stylish and of good quality, or appeals to wealthy consumers: *The department store sells only upmarket goods.* ○ *The company has gone upmarket.*

/ˌʌpˈmɑːkɪt/
⋈ **upmarket** goods, restaurants, shops; go, move **upmarket**
opp downmarket

upset price *noun* (sales)
the lowest price accepted by a buyer at an auction: *The bidding has not yet reached the upset price.* ○ *The level has fallen below the upset price.*

/ˈʌpset praɪs/
note usually singular
⧓ bid, fall below, reach the **upset price**

up-to-date *adjective*
current or modern: *The organization uses the most up-to-date technology.* ○ *We keep our information up-to-date.*

/ˌʌp tə ˈdeɪt/
(also **up to date**)
⧓ **up-to-date** equipment, system, technology; bring, keep (something) **up-to- date**
▶ **current, date[1], update**

upturn *noun* (sales)
an increase in sales or profit: *The company's annual profits are undergoing an upturn.* ○ *An upturn in sales followed the advertising campaign.*

/ˈʌptɜ:n/
note usually singular
⧓ receive, see, undergo an **upturn**; an **upturn** in profit, sales; an economic, a market **upturn**
opp downturn

usance *noun* (banking/international trade)
the time-limit allowed on the payment of foreign bills of exchange: *A sixty-day usance.*

/ˈju:zəns/
note usually singular
⧓ a **usance** of 30, etc days
▶ **bill of exchange**

user-friendly *adjective*
of something that is easy to use or understand: *These new computer programs are designed to be user-friendly.* ○ *user-friendly technology*

/ˌju:zə ˈfrendli/
⧓ **user-friendly** computers, equipment, programs, software, technology

USM *abbr* (stock exchange)
unlisted securities market: *The USM contains the shares of companies too small for the main market.*

/ˌju: es ˈem/
pl USMs

USP *abbr* (sales)
unique selling proposition: *This new car has no USP.* ○ *A USP must be developed if this product is to sell.*

/ˌju: es ˈpi:/
pl USPs

usury *noun*
the lending of money at high interest rates: *Usury is an uneconomical method of borrowing.*

/ˈju:ʒəri/
note no plural

UTA *abbr* (stock exchange)
Unit Trust Association: *The company is a member of the UTA.* ○ *The UTA is investigating our working practices.*

/ˌju: ti: ˈeɪ/
note pronounced as individual letters

utility *noun*
1 (*economics*) the benefit or satisfaction received by a consumer from a commodity or service: *Water has high utility but low commercial value.* **2** (*industry*) one of the services supplying the public with gas, water, electricity, transport, etc: *They bought shares in one of the utilities.*

/juˈtɪləti/
1 note not used with *a* or *an*. No plural and used with a singular verb only.
⧓ diminishing, marginal, maximise **utility**
2 pl utilities
⧓ public **utilities**; **utility** company, service

utmost good faith *noun* (insurance)
a condition of insurance in which the person taking out a policy must provide all necessary facts and information: *All facts must be supplied in utmost good faith.*

/ˌʌtməʊst gʊd ˈfeɪθ/
note not used with *a* or *an*. No plural and used with a singular verb only.
⋈ in, with **utmost good faith**
► **bad faith, good faith**

U/w *abbr* (insurance)
underwriter: *a marine U/w*

note used in written English only

Vv

VA *abbr* (economics)
value analysis: *The product has undergone VA.*

/ˌviː ˈeɪ/
note pronounced as individual letters

vac. *abbr*
1 vacation: *The office is on Christmas vac.* **2** vacant: *Sit. vac.*, ie situations vacant

/væk/

vacancy *noun*
1 an empty place or room: *The hotel has no vacancies.*
2 (*personnel*) a post to be filled by a new employee: *We have a vacancy for a new promotions manager.*

/ˈveɪkənsi/
pl vacancies
2 ⋈ fill, have a **vacancy**

vacancy rate *noun* (commerce)
the proportion of properties that are unused or unlet at any one time: *There is a 10% vacancy rate at the moment.*

/ˈveɪkənsi reɪt/
pl vacancy rates
⋈ housing, office **vacancy rates**
note usually expressed as a percentage
► **rate 2**

vacant *adjective*
not filled or occupied: *Her retirement has left the position of company manager vacant.* ○ *The new office block is still vacant.*

/ˈveɪkənt/
abbr vac.
⋈ appointments **vacant**; **vacant** positions, posts, premises, sites
► **situations vacant**

vacation *noun*
1 (*personnel*) a holiday or period when people are not working: *a student looking for a vacation job* ○ *Most of the office is on vacation.*
2 (*law*) (*UK*) the period when the courts of law are closed: *The case will have to wait till after the vacation.*

/vəˈkeɪʃn/
pl vacations
abbr vac.
1 ⋈ a **vacation** job, period; **vacation** work
note esp (*US*)
⋈ go away on, have a, take a **vacation**
► **bank holiday, holiday, leave**

vacuity *noun* (import)
(*UK*) the difference between the full capacity of a container and its actual contents: *The vacuity of the barrel is two gallons.*

/vəˈkjuːəti/
note no plural
► **leakage, ullage**

valid *adjective*
legally effective or acceptable; current: *She has a valid passport.* ○ *His driving licence was not valid.* ○ *a valid work permit*

/ˈvælɪd/
⋈ a **valid** contract, document, driving licence, passport, receipt, ticket, will
opp invalid

validate *verb*
to check or certify that something is correct: *His signature was validated by the bank.*

/ˈvælɪdeɪt/
validate, validating, validated
note transitive verb
⋈ **validate** a cheque, document, signature
► **attest, authenticate, certify, witness² 2**

valorization *noun* (finance)
the artificial fixing, usually by a government, of the value or price of something, esp a commodity or currency: *Valorization is necessary to stabilize inflation of the currency.* ○ *Exported commodities have undergone valorization.*

/ˌvælərarˈzeɪʃn/
note not used with *a* or *an*. No plural and used with a singular verb only.
⋈ **valorization** of a commodity, currency; practice, undergo **valorization**
► **revalorization**

valuable *adjective*
1 worth a lot of money: *a valuable work of art* **2** useful or important: *She was a valuable member of the management team.*

/ˈvæljuəbl/
1 ⋈ a **valuable** asset, document
2 ⋈ **valuable** information
opp worthless

valuation *noun* (finance/stock exchange)
1 (**a**) estimating the price of something: *The estate is undergoing valuation.* (**b**) the estimated worth in money of something: *The valuation of £250 000 was well below what we expected.*
2 (**a**) estimating the present worth of the assets of a business: *The company's assets are in valuation.* (**b**) the estimated worth of the assets: *a company valuation of £135*

stock market valuation the value of a company calculated by multiplying the current market price of each share by the total number of shares issued

stock valuation estimating the value of goods not yet sold at the end of an accounting period: *Stock valuation is necessary to draw up a company's balance sheet.*

/ˌvæljuˈeɪʃn/
1a note not used with *a* or *an*. No plural and used with a singular verb only.
1b pl valuations
⋈ a **valuation** fee, report; a house, land, property **valuation**
2a note not used with *a* or *an*. No plural and used with a singular verb only.
2b pl valuations
► **current cost accounting, net asset value**

value¹ *noun*
1 the usefulness or importance of something: *The value of water far exceeds its price.* **2** the worth of something in terms of the money or goods for which it can be exchanged: *The value of sterling has fallen.* ○ *Returned goods can be exchanged for goods of an equivalent value.* ○ *buy goods to the value of £300*

value for money worth the price paid: *The meal was value for money.*

/ˈvælju:/
1 note not used with *a* or *an*. No plural and used with a singular verb only.
2 pl values
⋈ a drop, fall, rise in **value**; of great, high, of little, low **value**
► **book value, face value, holder for value, market value, net asset value, net asset value per share, net book value, net present value, net realizable value,**

par value, real value, salvage value, scarcity value, scrap value, surrender value

---

value² *verb*

to estimate the worth of something: *The house has been valued for the mortgage.* ○ *The jewellery is being valued for insurance.*

/ˈvælju:/
value, valuing, valued
note transitive verb
⧓ **value** a house, property, stock
▶ **devalue, overvalued**

---

value added *noun* (economics/manufacturing)

the worth that is placed on a product by a particular stage in the production process: *Much of the production process is done by hand so there is a high value added.*

/ˌvælju: ˈædɪd/
pl values added
⧓ a decrease in, an increase in, a high, a low **value added**

---

value added statement *noun* (accounting)

a financial document that lists in great detail the income and expenses of a company: *The company asked the bank for a value added statement.*

/ˌvælju: ˈædɪd ˌsteɪtmənt/
pl value added statements
⧓ draft, draw up, receive, send a **value added statement**
▶ **annual report, balance sheet, bank statement, profit and loss account**

---

value added tax *noun* (tax)

a tax charged at 15% of the price of goods and services. It can be charged at each stage of the production process, but can be reclaimed by traders and producers. It is finally paid by the consumer: *The price includes/does not include value added tax.*

/ˌvælju: ˈædɪd tæks/
note no plural. The abbreviation is more commonly used than the full term.
abbr VAT, V.A.T., v.a.t.
⧓ be exempt from, claim, include, pay **value added tax**
▶ **tax¹, ultimate consumer, value added, zero-rated**

---

value analysis *noun* (industry/manufacturing)

studying the manufacture of a product to find out ways of reducing the cost of production without losing quality: *Value analysis reduces the cost of mass-produced goods.*

/ˈvælju: əˌnæləsɪs/
note usually singular
abbr VA
⧓ carry out, conduct a **value analysis**
syn value engineering
▶ **analysis, cost benefit analysis**

---

valued policy *noun* (insurance)

a form of insurance in which the worth of each item insured is agreed in advance: *They have taken out a valued policy on the house contents.*

/ˌvælju:d ˈpɒləsi/
pl valued policies
⧓ to take out a **valued policy**
opp unvalued policy

---

value engineering *noun* (industry/manufacturing)

▶ **value analysis**

/ˈvælju: endʒɪˈnɪərɪŋ/

---

value for money audit *noun* (accounting)

an examination of a non-profit-making organization, esp a government department or charity, to see how effectively it is functioning: *The value for money audit exposed several problems in*

/ˌvælju: fə ˈmʌni ˌɔ:dɪt/
pl value for money audits
⧓ carry out, undertake a **value for money audit**

the organization's workings. ○ *They carried out a value for money audit.*

▶ **audit**[1]

---

valuer *noun* (commerce)
a person who estimates the worth of something, esp land or property: *The house is being examined by the building society valuer.*

/ˈvæljuə(r)/
pl valuers
⧓ a company **valuer**; examined, inspected, seen by a **valuer**
syn (*US*) appraiser
▶ **underwriter**

---

value received *noun* (banking)
the words written on a bill of exchange to show that the bill is a means of payment for goods or services to the value of the bill

/ˌvælju: rɪˈsi:vd/
note not used with *a* or *an*. No plural and used with a singular verb only.
▶ **bill of exchange**

---

value share *noun* (industry/commerce)
the proportion of the market that a particular product has in terms of sales revenue: *It is an established product and has a large value share.*

/ˈvælju: ʃeə(r)/
pl value shares
⧓ decrease in, increase in, large, small **value share**; a product's **value share**
▶ **market share**

---

variable budget *noun* (finance/accounting)
a budget that is not fixed, but varies when necessary: *The project has been allowed a variable budget to accommodate any unforeseeable expenses.*

/ˌveəriəbl ˈbʌdʒɪt/
pl variable budgets
⧓ allocate, allow, give a **variable budget**
syn flexible budget

---

variable cost *noun* (industry)
an amount of money used to produce goods that increases with the quantity made: *Fuel consumption is a variable cost.*

/ˌveəriəbl ˈkɒst/
pl variable costs
⧓ account for, a decrease in, an increase in **variable costs**
▶ **absorption costing, cost**[1]**, fixed cost, oncost, overhead, unit cost**

---

variance *noun* (accounting)
the difference between an estimated and an actual amount: *You must allow for variance in your budget.*

/ˈveəriəns/
note usually singular
⧓ control, reduce **variance**; a large, small **variance**
▶ **budget, price variance, quantity variance**

VAT *noun* (tax)
value added tax: *The price is inclusive of VAT.* ○ *a VAT invoice*

VAT return a statement showing VAT receipts and expenditure: *Don't forget to fill in your VAT return.*

/væt, ˌvi: eɪ ˈti:/
(also **V.A.T.**, **v.a.t.**)
note pronounced as a word or as individual letters.
⧓ including, plus, subject to **VAT**; charge, pay **VAT**
▶ **tax**[1]

VDT *noun* /ˌviː diː ˈtiː/

visual display terminal: *information displayed on the VDT*

VDU *noun* /ˌviː diː ˈjuː/

visual display unit: *She is working at the VDU.*

velocity of circulation *noun* (economics) /vəˌlɒsəti əv ˌsɜːkjəˈleɪʃn/

the average amount of times that a unit of money is passed from person to person in an economy: *A lively economy means a high velocity of circulation.*

note no plural

⧓ decrease, increase the **velocity of circulation**; a high, low **velocity of circulation**

▶ **circulation 1, income velocity of circulation, transactions velocity of circulation**

vendee *noun* (commerce) /ˌvenˈdiː/

▶ **buyer**

vendor *noun* (commerce) /ˈvendə(r), ˌvenˈdɔː/

someone who is selling something, esp a house: *The solicitor was acting on behalf of the vendor during the transaction.*

pl vendors

⧓ a house, market, shop, street **vendor**

▶ **seller**

vendor placing *noun* (commerce/stock exchange) /ˈvendə ˌpleɪsɪŋ/

a deal in which a company agrees to issue new shares to an investor in return for cash in advance: *The organization obtained the necessary cash through vendor placing.*

note not used with *a* or *an*. No plural and used with a singular verb only.

⧓ by, through **vendor placing**

▶ **placement 2, rights issue**

venture[1] *noun* (commerce) /ˈventʃə(r)/

a business or commercial activity in which there may be some risk: *to start a new venture* ○ *His latest venture is in computer software.*

joint venture a business activity in which two or more people or organizations work together: *The two firms formed a joint venture.* ○ *set up a joint venture with a French company*

pl ventures

⧓ a business, commercial, joint, new **venture**; embark on, start, undertake a **venture**

▶ **enterprise 1, speculation 2**

venture[2] *verb* (commerce) /ˈventʃə(r)/

to risk something, esp money, in business: *He ventured all his assets in the new business.*

venture, venturing, ventured

note transitive verb

⧓ **venture** assets, cash, money

▶ **speculate 2**

venture capital *noun* (finance) /ˈventʃə ˌkæpɪtl/

money invested in a company or business for development or expansion. It may provide a good income, but also carries a high risk of loss: *As we cannot get a loan we need to find some venture capital.*

note not used with *a* or *an*. No plural and used with a singular verb only.

⧓ apply for, put up, seek, use **venture capital**; a **venture capital** business, company, firm, group

syn risk capital
▶ capital, start-up

erification of assets *noun* (accounting)
onfirming the existence and calculating the value of a ompany's machinery, capital, etc in order to assess its total vealth: *Verification of assets revealed unexpected results.*

/ˌverɪfɪˌkeɪʃn əv ˈæsets/
note not used with *a* or *an*. No plural and used with a singular verb only.
▶ **asset**

ertical integration *noun* (industry)
situation where two or more organizations that deal with ifferent stages in a production process are combined and ontrolled by one company: *Vertical integration reduces costs and he threat of competition.*

/ˌvɜːtɪkl ɪntɪˈgreɪʃn/
note not used with *a* or *an*. No plural and used with a singular verb only.
▶ **backward integration, diversification, forward integration, horizontal integration, integration**

ice- *prefix* (management)
cting in place of; next in importance to: *The Vice-Chairman is on oliday.*

/vaɪs/
⧓ **vice** -chairman, -chancellor, -president, -principal
▶ **deputy**

ideo conference *noun* (management)
meeting with people who cannot all be together at the same ime using video (television) equipment: *Holding a video onference saves travelling time and expenses.* ○ *A video conference llows you to see and talk to people thousands of miles away.*

/ˈvɪdiəʊ ˌkɒnfrəns/
pl video conferences
⧓ conduct, hold a **video conference**
▶ **audio conference, conference**

ideotex *noun* (computing)
n information system in which computer data is sent via elephone lines and displayed on a television screen: *The data was elayed via Videotex.*

/ˈvɪdiəʊteks/
⧓ by, using, via **Videotex**
▶ **CEEFAX, Prestel, Teletext, viewdata**

iewdata *noun* (computing)
UK) a VIDEOTEX system that uses telephone lines for sending omputer data: *Holiday bookings are made using viewdata.*

/ˈvjuːdeɪtə/
note no plural
⧓ by, using **viewdata**
▶ **CEEFAX, Prestel, Teletext, Videotex**

irus *noun* (computing)
nstructions that are put into a computer program in order to ause errors and destroy information: *a computer program infected y a virus*

/ˈvaɪrəs/
pl viruses
▶ **bug**

isa *noun* (transport)
document or note on a passport, that allows the holder to nter a country: *All foreign visitors require a visa.*

ntry visa a visa that allows the holder to enter a country and stay there permanently or for a stated period: *It is difficult to obtain a permanent entry visa.*

ourist visa a visa that allows the holder to enter a country for a stated period but not to work there: *Only tourist visas are available.*

/ˈviːzə/
pl visas
⧓ apply for, need, obtain, require a **visa**
▶ **papers 2, work permit**

transit visa a visa that allows the holder to spend a short time in a country whilst travelling to another country: *A transit visa is required for overnight stops.*

---

visible balance *noun* (accounting/import/export)
a statement that shows the trade in goods as opposed to services: *An increase in manufacturing has had a healthy effect on the visible balance.*

/ˌvɪzəbl ˈbæləns/
pl visible balances
▶ **balance of trade**

---

visible exports *noun* (international trade)
goods, as opposed to services, that are sold to other countries: *Visible exports have decreased this year.*

/ˌvɪzəbl ˈekspɔːts/
note usually plural
syn visibles
opp invisible exports
▶ **export[1]**

---

visible imports *noun* (import)
goods, as opposed to services, that are bought from other countries: *Foreign technology is a significant visible import.*

/ˌvɪzəbl ˈɪmpɔːts/
note usually plural
syn visibles
opp invisible imports

---

visual control board *noun*
a large board with movable markers used to display and organize information: *The movement of stock was planned using a visual control board.*

/ˌvɪʒuəl kənˈtrəʊl bɔːd/
pl visual control boards
⋈ use a **visual control board**; display, present, show information on a **visual control board**

---

visual display terminal *noun* (computing)
▶ **visual display unit**

/ˌvɪʒuəl dɪˈspleɪ ˌtɜːmɪnl/

---

visual display unit *noun* (computing)
a point of access (including a screen and keyboard) for information stored on computer: *She does most of her work at a visual display unit.* ○ *look something up on the visual display unit*

/ˌvɪʒuəl dɪˈspleɪ ˌjuːnɪt/
pl visual display units
abbr VDU, V.D.U.
syn visual display terminal
⋈ install, use a **visual display unit**
note The abbreviation is more commonly used than the full term.
syn visual display terminal
▶ **display[1] 3, interface, monitor, screen[1]**

---

vocational *adjective* (personnel)
related to training or education for a particular trade or profession: *Doctors must do several years of vocational training.* ○ *a vocational course* , eg typing, accounting, bookkeeping

/vəʊˈkeɪʃənl/
⋈ a **vocational** course, education, qualification
opp non-vocational

---

voice data entry *noun* (computing)
a means of admittance, eg into a building or computer system, using a computer's ability to recognize spoken signals: *The security system uses voice data entry.*

/ˌvɔɪs ˈdeɪtə ˌentri/
note no plural
⋈ a **voice data entry** network, program, system; have, use **voice data entry**
▶ **password**

---

void *adjective* (law)
not legally effective: *The contract is void.* ○ *The document was declared void.*

/vɔɪd/
⧓ to declare something **void**; the cheque, contract, document is **void**
► **null and void**

volume *noun*
1 the space occupied by something, measured in cubic metres (M³) or cubic feet (cu. ft): *The volume of this barrel is 10 m³.* 2 (*commerce*) the total amount of trade that has taken place within a specific period: *The volume of trade between the two countries has decreased.* **3** (*stock exchange*) the total number of shares traded on the stock exchange on a particular day: *Share volume is increasing.* ○ *a growth in stock market volume*

/ˈvɒljuːm/
pl volumes
1 ► **ullage, vacuity**
2 ⧓ **volume** of business, output, sales, trade; sales, trading **volume**
3 ► **turnover 1**

volume business *noun* (commerce)
trade in very large quantities of goods: *The company only trades in volume business.*

/ˈvɒljuːm ˌbɪznəs/
note usually singular
⧓ deal, trade in **volume business**

voluntary arrangement *noun* (finance)
an arrangement made between the members of a company and its creditors, in which the company pays off its debts and manages its financial problems without the need for WINDING UP: *The firms have come to a voluntary arrangement to settle their debts.*

/ˌvɒləntri əˈreɪndʒmənt/
pl voluntary arrangements
⧓ arrive at, come to a **voluntary arrangement**

voluntary liquidation *noun* (finance)
a situation where members of an organization decide to stop trading, to sell off their assets and settle their debts: *The company has decided to take voluntary liquidation.*

/ˌvɒləntri lɪkwɪˈdeɪʃn/
note not used with *a* or *an*. No plural and used with a singular verb only.
► **liquidation**

voluntary redundancy *noun* (personnel)
a situation in which a worker agrees to give up his/her job: *She decided to take voluntary redundancy rather than a cut in pay.*

/ˌvɒləntri rɪˈdʌndənsi/
note not used with *a* or *an*. No plural and used with a singular verb only.
⧓ accept, take **voluntary redundancy**
► **redundancy**

vostro account *noun* (banking)
(*UK*) a bank account held by a foreign bank outside its own country in the currency of the country where the account is held: *our vostro account with Barclays*

/ˈvɒstrəʊ əˈkaʊnt/
pl vostro accounts
► **account¹ 2, loro account, nostro account**

vote¹ *noun*
the formal expression of a choice or opinion; the occasion of this: *The proposal is to be put to the vote.* ○ *Each shareholder has a vote at the annual general meeting.* ○ *win/lose the vote* , ie receive more/less votes than your rivals

/vəʊt/
pl votes
⧓ cast, hold, make a **vote**; a **vote** against, for (someone/something)
► **ballot¹, casting vote, poll**

vote² *verb*
to show your choice or opinion by marking a paper, or raising a hand etc: *He voted against the proposal.* ○ *She has been voted onto the committee.* ○ *vote for a new chairperson* ○ *I was voted chairman.*

/vəʊt/
vote, voting, voted
note transitive and intransitive verb

⧓ **vote** against, for (someone/something)
▶ **ballot**[2]

---

voting rights *noun* (stock exchange/commerce)
the privilege of shareholders to vote at company meetings: *The shareholders have exercised their voting rights.* ○ *Not all shareholders have voting rights.*

/ˈvəʊtɪŋ raɪts/
note usually plural
⧓ exercise **voting rights**

---

voting shares *noun* (stock exchange/commerce)
shares in a company that allow the holder to vote at meetings: *The organization has issued voting shares to all its major shareholders.*

/ˈvəʊtɪŋ ʃeəz/
note usually plural
opp non-voting shares
▶ **share**

---

voucher *noun*
1 (*accounting*) a receipt or written document to show that money has been paid: *The voucher has been supplied by an auditor.* **2** a document that can be exchanged for goods, money or services up to the amount shown: *a petty cash voucher* ○ *a luncheon voucher* ○ *a two-pound voucher/a voucher for two pounds*

/ˈvaʊtʃə(r)/
pl vouchers
2 ⧓ a discount, gift, luncheon **voucher**
▶ **cash voucher, gift voucher**

---

vouching *noun* (accounting)
the responsibility of an auditor or accountant to examine all vouchers, documents and invoices to check company's accounts: *Vouching ensures a correct audit.* ○ *The account's vouching checks the company's balance sheet.*

/ˈvaʊtʃɪŋ/
note not used with *a* or *an*. No plural and used with a singular verb only.
▶ **audit**[1]

---

voyage *noun* (shipping)
a journey made by a ship: *The cargo will be unloaded at the end of the voyage.*

/ˈvɔɪɪdʒ/
pl voyages
⧓ embark on a **voyage**

---

voyage charter *noun* (shipping)
the hire of a ship or cargo space for a number of voyages, rather than for a fixed period of time: *The organization has taken out a voyage charter with the shipping company.*

/ˈvɔɪɪdʒ ˌtʃɑːtə(r)/
pl voyage charters
⧓ agree, take out a **voyage charter**
▶ **charter**[1] **3, time charter**

Ww

WA *abbr* (shipping)
with average

/ˌdʌblju: ˈeɪ/
(also **W.A.**)

---

wage *noun* (personnel)
money paid to a worker for work done: *She is earning a good wage.* ○ *Wages are paid on Fridays.* ○ *a weekly wage of £250*

/weɪdʒ/
pl wages
⧓ decrease, increase, pay, receive **wages**; a gross, net **wage**
▶ **basic wage, fair wage, guaranteed wage, incentive wage, living wage, minimum wage, money wages, pay**[2]**, real wages, remuneration, salary**

wage claim *noun* (industrial relations)
▶ **claim[1] 3**

/ˈweɪdʒ kleɪm/

wage-earner *noun* (personnel)
a person who is paid a weekly wage as opposed to a monthly salary; a person who is paid for the work they do: *The low tax appeals to wage-earners.* ○ *She is the sole wage-earner in that household.*

/ˈweɪdʒ ˌɜːnə(r)/
pl wage-earners
⋈ a low, high **wage-earner**
▶ **salary**

wage-freeze *noun* (industry/economics)
a period during which pay is not allowed to increase: *Productivity decreased during the wage freeze.* ○ *The government imposed a compulsory wage freeze.*

/ˈweɪdʒ friːz/
pl wage freezes
⋈ impose, introduce a **wage freeze**

wage levels *noun* (industry)
rates of pay for different kinds of work: *compare wage levels across the country* ○ *Only 35% of families can afford to buy a house on current wage levels.*

/ˈweɪdʒ levlz/
note plural noun, used with a plural verb
⋈ lower, similar, upper **wage levels**

wage negotiations *noun* (personnel)
discussions between employers and employees about the amount of pay received: *Management met with union leaders for wage negotiations.* ○ *Wage negotiations are continuing.*

/ˈweɪdʒ nɪˌɡəʊʃiˌeɪʃnz/
note plural noun, used with a plural verb
▶ **negotiation 1**

wage packet *noun* (personnel)
1 an envelope containing money earnt by a worker: *You can pick up your wage packet on Friday afternoon.* **2** the real amount of money a worker receives: *The rise means more money in employees' wage packets.*

/ˈweɪdʒ ˌpækɪt/
pl wage packets
⋈ monthly, weekly **wage packet**
syn pay packet

wage policy *noun* (public finance)
government plans and controls for changes in workers' pay: *The government have published their new wage policy.*

/ˈweɪdʒ ˌpɒləsi/
pl wage policies
⋈ implement a **wage policy**
▶ **wage freeze**

wage-price spiral *noun* (economics)
a situation in which inflation encourages demands for higher wages which in turn results in price increases: *The country is trapped in a wage-price spiral.*

/ˌweɪdʒ ˌpraɪs ˈspaɪərəl/
pl wage-price spirals
▶ **cost of living, inflation**

wage scale *noun* (personnel)
a list of rates of pay for different jobs within a company: *The pay rise was made according to the company's wage scale.*

/ˈweɪdʒ skeɪl/
pl wage scales
⋈ adjust, calculate the **wage scale**
syn pay scale

wages clerk *noun* (personnel)
a person in an office who deals with the pay of other employees: *The wages clerk put the money into pay packets.*

/ˈweɪdʒɪz klɑːk/
pl wages clerks
⋈ be employed, work as a **wages clerk**
syn payroll assistant

wages council *noun* (industry)
(*UK*) an organization that states minimum rates of pay in a particular industry: *The wages council has decided on the minimum*

/ˈweɪdʒɪz ˌkaʊnsl/
(also **Wages Council**)
⋈ be advised by, consult the

wage for workers in the motor industry. ○ *the Clothing Manufacturers' Wages Council*

Wages Council

---

wage threshold *noun* (industrial relations)
▶ **threshold**

/ˈweɪdʒ ˌθreʃhəʊld/

---

wagon *noun* (transport)
1 a large road vehicle with four wheels: *drive a container wagon* **2** an open railway truck for transporting goods: *coal wagons* ○ *send goods by wagon*

/ˈwæɡən/
pl wagons
1 ⧓ transport by **wagon**; load, unload a **wagon**
2 syn (*US*) freight car
⧓ a goods, railway **wagon**

---

wagonage *noun* (transport)
1 the movement of goods by wagon: *Wagonage is the main means of transport used by the organization.* **2** the charge made for transport by wagon: *Most of the cost went on wagonage.*

/ˈwæɡənɪdʒ/
note not used with *a* or *an*. No plural and used with a singular verb only.
▶ **waterage**

---

walk-out *noun* (industrial relations)
a strike or stoppage: *Production has been stopped by a walk-out.* ○ *a 24-hour walk-out over pay* ○ *a walk-out by engineering workers*

/ˈwɔːkaʊt/
pl walk-outs
⧓ stage a **walk-out**; an official, unofficial **walk-out**
▶ **go-slow, strike[1], work-to-rule**

---

walk out *verb* (industrial relations)
to strike or stop work: *Unless the employee who was sacked is reinstated the workforce will walk out.* ○ *The entire finance department walked out yesterday.*

/ˌwɔːk ˈaʊt/
walk out, walking out, walked out
note intransitive verb
⧓ the employees, staff, workers, workforce **walked out**
▶ **strike[2]**

Wall Street *noun* (stock exchange)
(*US*) the New York Stock Exchange, named from the street where it is situated; the financial institutions of New York collectively: *Trading is down on Wall St.* ○ *She works in Wall St.*

/ˈwɔːl striːt/
abbr Wall St
⧓ a **Wall Street** bank, employee; **Wall Street** banking, dealing, trading; **Wall Street** prices, securities, shares, stocks; **Wall Street** crashed, dipped, plunged, soared
▶ **Big Board, the City, International Stock Exchange, New York Stock Exchange**

WAN *abbr* (computing)
wide area network: *Information is gathered from a WAN.*

/wæn/
note pronounced as a word

---

warehouse[1] *noun* (distribution)
a large building where goods are kept: *store goods in a warehouse*

/ˈweəhaʊs/
pl warehouses
abbr w'hse
⧓ **warehouse** capacity, space
▶ **bonded warehouse, depot 1, price ex warehouse, public warehouse**

warehouse² *verb* (distribution)

to store goods in a large building: *It will be necessary to warehouse the surplus stock.* ○ *The old stock has been warehoused until the sale.* ○ *the cost of warehousing goods*

/ˈweəhaʊs/
warehouse, warehousing, warehoused
note transitive verb
⧓ **warehouse** commodities, goods, stock
▶ **warehousing**

---

warehouse-keeper *noun* (distribution)

a person responsible for the goods stored in a warehouse: *Stocks can only be obtained from the warehouse-keeper.*

/ˈweəhaʊs ˌkiːpə(r)/
pl warehouse-keepers
syn warehouseman
▶ **warehouse**

---

warehouse-keeper's order *noun* (export/import)

an order from a customs officer to a warehouse-keeper to release goods kept in a warehouse: *The arrival of the warehouse-keeper's order means that the goods can be re-exported.*

/ˌweəhaʊs ˌkiːpəz ˈɔːdə(r)/
pl warehouse-keeper's orders
⧓ issue, receive, send a **warehouse-keeper's order**
▶ **bonded warehouse, order[1] 1, warehouse**

---

warehouse-keeper's receipt *noun* (distribution)

a signed document showing that the goods named on it are stored in a public warehouse: *The goods will not be released without a valid warehouse-keeper's receipt.*

/ˌweəhaʊs ˌkiːpəz rɪˈsiːt/
pl warehouse-keeper's receipts
⧓ issue, provide, sign a **warehouse-keeper's receipt**

---

warehouseman *noun* (distribution)

▶ **warehouse-keeper**

/ˈweəhaʊsmən/

---

warehousing *noun* (distribution)

1 storing goods in a warehouse: *warehousing space* ○ *the warehousing of frozen foods* **2** the control and movement of goods in and out of warehouses: *automated warehousing* ○ *The company also announced the sale of its warehousing operations.*

/ˈweəhaʊzɪŋ/
note not used with *a* or *an*. No plural and used with a singular verb only.
⧓ **warehousing** operations, services, systems
▶ **storage 1**

---

warrant¹ *noun*

1 (*law*) a document that allows someone to do something: *to apply for a warrant* **2** (*commerce*) a document showing that goods have been stored in a warehouse: *A warrant is required to pick up the goods.* **3** (*stock exchange*) an item of financial value that allows the owner to apply for the ordinary shares of a company at a fixed price on a fixed date: *Warrants have been issued to all prospective shareholders.*

distress warrant a document that allows the courts to seize a person's goods to obtain payment: *A distress warrant has been issued to recover unpaid rent.*

search warrant a document signed by a magistrate that allows the police to arrest a person or search a building: *A warrant is required for entry.*

warehouse warrant a document that allows goods to be removed from a warehouse: *Goods may only be claimed on presentation of a warehouse warrant.*

/ˈwɒrənt/
pl warrants
1, 2, 3 ⧓ apply for, issue, receive, require a **warrant**
▶ **guarantee[1] 1**

---

warrant² *verb*
to promise that something is genuine or is in good condition: *All the spare parts are warranted.*

/ˈwɒrənt/
warrant, warranting, warranted
note transitive verb, usually used in the passive tense
▶ **guarantee² 1**

---

warrantee *noun* (commerce/law)
a person to whom a WARRANTY is given: *The warrantee should be aware of all the conditions in the contract.*

/ˌwɒrənˈtiː/
pl warrantees

---

warrant of attachment *noun* (law)
a court order allowing property to be taken, esp for payment of a debt: *No seizure can be made without a warrant of attachment.*

/ˌwɒrənt əv əˈtætʃmənt/
pl warrants of attachment
⋈ issue a **warrant of attachment**

---

warrant of attorney *noun* (law)
a document signed by someone who owes money allowing a lawyer to speak for him/her in court: *sign a warrant of attorney*

/ˌwɒrənt əv əˈtɜːni/
pl warrants of attorney
▶ **judgment debtor**

---

warrantor *noun* (commerce/law)
a person who gives a WARRANTY to someone: *The warrantor will not be held legally responsible if the equipment is misused.*

/ˈwɒrəntɔː(r)/
pl warrantors
⋈ issued by a **warrantor**
▶ **guarantor**

---

warranty *noun*
1 (*commerce/law*) a contract or legal document that promises that something will work, usually for a certain length of time: *The warranty only covers spare parts.* ○ *The washing machine is outside its warranty* (ie the date given on the document has passed). **2** (*insurance*) a condition of an insurance contract that all the information given by the insured person is true. If not, the contract is invalid and insurance money will not be paid: *The policy was in breach of warranty.*

/ˈwɒrənti/
pl warranties
▶ **guarantee¹ 1**

---

wash sale *noun* (stock exchange)
(*US informal*) the illegal sale of certain goods at a high price to pretend that they are in great demand: *The market was artificially inflated by a wash sale.*

/ˈwɒʃ seɪl/
pl wash sales
▶ **black market**

---

wastage *noun*
1 an amount that is wasted: *More raw material is needed because of 10% wastage.* **2** loss through wasting: *Wastage accounts for a significant proportion of potential profits.*

/ˈweɪstɪdʒ/
note not used with *a* or *an*. No plural and used with a singular verb only.
▶ **natural wastage**

---

waste¹ *noun*
1 (*industry*) material produced by a manufacturing process that is unwanted or useless; rubbish: *Toxic waste should be disposed of carefully.* ○ *Many companies try to recycle their industrial waste.*
2 (*commerce*) an inefficient use of time, energy or resources: *That new computer is a waste of money.* ○ *The training weekend was a waste of time.*

/weɪst/
1 note not used with *a* or *an*. No plural and used with a singular verb only.
⋈ dispose of, produce **waste**; **waste** disposal, material

2 note singular noun, used with a singular verb

▶ **recycle, scrap[1]**

---

waste[2] *adjective*

not used: *waste paper* ○ *waste materials*

/weɪst/

---

waste[3] *verb*

to use something inefficiently or to use more of it than is necessary: *to waste money on heating unused offices* ○ *We waste so much time because the machine keeps breaking down.*

/weɪst/

waste, wasting, wasted

note transitive verb

⋈ **waste** energy, money, time

▶ **recycle, scrap[2]**

---

waste product *noun* (industry)

a useless substance produced as a result of a chemical or industrial process: *dispose of toxic waste products*

/ˈweɪst ˌprɒdʌkt/

pl waste products

⋈ dispose of, recycle, throw away a **waste product**

▶ **by-product, end-product, product**

---

wasting asset *noun* (accounting/industry)

an item of value that lasts for a fixed amount of time before it is used up, wears out or becomes out of date: *a wasting asset with a fixed life-span*

/ˌweɪstɪŋ ˈæset/

pl wasting assets

▶ **asset**

---

waterage *noun* (transport/shipping)

1 the transportation of goods by boat, esp on a canal or river: *Waterage provides a slow but useful means of transporting heavy goods.* **2** the charge made for this: *Increases in fuel prices have increased waterage.*

/ˈwɔːtərɪdʒ/

note not used with *a* or *an*. No plural and used with a singular verb only.

⋈ **waterage** charges, costs

▶ **wagonage 2**

---

water-line *noun* (shipping)

the line marking the level of water on the side of a ship: *Most of the cargo is below the water-line.*

/ˈwɔːtəlaɪn /

pl water-lines

⋈ above, below the **water-line**

▶ **load line**

---

waterways *noun* (transport/shipping)

rivers and canals used for transporting goods: *The goods will be distributed via inland waterways.*

/ˈwɔːtərweɪz/

note usually plural

⋈ by, on, via **waterways**; artificial, man-made **waterways**

---

way-bill *noun* (commerce/international trade)

a document that gives information about goods sent, and states whether the buyer or seller is responsible for insurance: *send goods to the address on the way-bill* ○ *Give one copy of the way-bill to the consignor and one to the consignee when the goods arrive.*

/ˈweɪ bɪl/

pl way-bills

abbr WB

(also **waybill**)

⋈ air, rail, road **way-bill**; issue, receive, sign a **way-bill**

▶ **bill of lading, consignment note, manifest, shipping documents**

WB *abbr* (commerce/international trade)
way-bill: *The consignee signed the WB on receipt of the goods.*

/ˌdʌblju: ˈbi:/

w.c. *abbr*
without charge: *The delivery will be made w.c.*

/ˌdʌblju: ˈsi:/

wd *abbr* (commerce/industry)
warranted: *wd 100% pure cotton*

/ˌdʌblju: ˈdi:/
(also **w/d**)

WDA *abbr* (accounting)
writing down allowance: *The depreciation of assets has fallen below the WDA.*

/ˌdʌblju: di: ˈei/
pl WDAs

wealth *noun*
(owning) a large amount of money, goods or property: *He is a man of great wealth.* ○ *wealth based on the tourist trade* ○ *How do you estimate the wealth of a country/a country's wealth?*

/welθ/
note not used with *a* or *an*. No plural and used with a singular verb only.
⋈ agricultural, commercial, economic, financial, industrial **wealth**
▶ **affluence**

wealthy *adjective*
having lots of money, goods or property; rich: *a wealthy businessman, country, lawyer*

/ˈwelθi/
▶ **affluent**

wear and tear *noun* (industry/insurance)
a loss in value of the machinery, vehicles, etc owned by a company because they are old or damaged: *The insurance policy only covers normal wear and tear.* ○ *Wear and tear results in the inevitable depreciation of an asset.*

/ˌweər ən ˈteə(r)/
note not used with *a* or *an*. No plural and used with a singular verb only.
⋈ acceptable, normal levels of **wear and tear**
▶ **depreciation**

weather working days *noun* (personnel/industry)
days on which good weather allows work to be carried out: *During the storm there were very few weather working days.* ○ *Building work was held up by the lack of good weather working days.*

/ˌweðə ˈwɜ:kɪŋ deɪz/
note usually plural

weight *noun*
1 an object of known heaviness, used to weigh other objects: *a 10 kilo weight* ○ *Put more weights on the scale.* **2** a measurement of how heavy something is: *The weight of the van is three tonnes.* ○ *calculate the average weight of the goods* ○ *What is the weight in grams?*

by weight to divide something into units of weight: *Grain is sold by weight.*

/weɪt/
abbr wt.
1 pl weights
2 note usually singular
⋈ gross, net **weight**; an excess, a heavy, a light **weight**
▶ **Inspector of weights and measures**

weighted ballot *noun* (stock exchange)
a vote held if too many people have applied for shares. Shareholders are chosen according to the number of shares they have applied for: *A weighted ballot can be biased towards either the small or large investor.*

/ˌweɪtɪd ˈbælət/
pl weighted ballots
⋈ hold a **weighted ballot**
▶ **ballot**

weighting *noun* (personnel)
(*UK*) extra money paid to people working in a particular (usually expensive) part of the country: *She earns more than me because she gets London weighting.* ○ *The salary is £20 000 plus London weighting.*

/ˈweɪtɪŋ/
note not used with *a* or *an*. No plural and used with a singular verb only.
► **bonus 2, loading**

weight note *noun* (commerce/transport)
a document that states how much a consignment of goods weighed when it was unloaded from a ship: *According to the weight note, this consignment is now under weight.*

/ˈweɪt nəʊt/
pl weight notes
⋈ issue a **weight note**
► **consignment note**

Western European Time *noun*
the name of the time zone for the extreme west of Europe: *All times shown are according to Western European Time.*

/ˌwestən ˌjʊərəˈpiːən taɪm/
abbr WET
⋈ according to **Western European Time**
► **Eastern European Time, Central European Time**
syn Greenwich Mean Time

WET *abbr*
Western European Time: *The time in WET is 10 o'clock.*

/ˈdʌbljuː iː ˈtiː/
note pronounced as individual letters
► **CET, EET, GMT**

wet goods *noun* (commerce)
goods that are liquid and packed in bottles or barrels: *transport wet goods in barrels*

/ˈwet gʊdz/
note plural noun, used with a plural verb
⋈ store, transport **wet goods**
► **dry goods**

wf. *abbr* (shipping)
wharf: *Wf. facilities*

/ˌdʌbljuː ˈef/
(also **whf.**)

wharf *noun* (shipping)
an area of a dock, harbour or port where ships are moored, esp to load or unload goods: *The Customs house is on the wharf.*

/wɔːf/
pl wharves *or* wharfs
abbr wf., whf.
⋈ **wharf** office, workers
► **dock**[1]**, quay**

wharfage *noun* (shipping)
a payment asked for using a WHARF: *Wharfage has been increased to cope with the extra security required.*

/ˈwɔːfɪdʒ/
note not used with *a* or *an*. No plural and used with a singular verb only.
⋈ charge, pay **wharfage**
syn wharf dues
► **keelage, moorage**

wharfinger *noun* (shipping)
the person or firm in charge of the wharf: *Payment must be made to the wharfinger.*

/ˈwɔːfɪndʒə(r)/
pl wharfingers

white-collar worker *noun* (personnel)
a person who works in an office as opposed to one who works in a factory: *The new salary structure only affects white-collar workers.*

/ˌwaɪt ˈkɒlə ˌwɜːkə(r)/
pl white-collar workers
► **artisan, blue-collar worker, craftsman, labourer, manual worker**

white goods *noun* (commerce)
items such as refrigerators and washing machines, so called because they are made of white painted metal: *He works for a white goods dealer.*

/ˈwaɪt gʊdz/
note plural noun, used with a plural verb
⋈ buy, order, sell, trade in **white goods**
▶ **brown goods**

white knight *noun* (stock exchange)
(*informal*) a person or an organization that rescues a company from an unfavourable TAKEOVER BID: *A white knight stepped in and made a better offer.*

/ˌwaɪt ˈnaɪt/
pl white knights
⋈ be in need of, be rescued by, search for a **white knight**
▶ **black knight, grey knight, takeover**

white paper *noun* (law/administration)
(*UK*) an official report by the government on a particular issue: *a white paper on industrial training* ○ *a food safety white paper*

/ˌwaɪt ˈpeɪpə(r)/
pl white papers
(also **White Paper**)
⋈ issue, publish a **white paper**

whizz-kid *noun*
(*slang*) a young person who becomes successful very quickly, esp in business: *Computer whizz-kids seem to be getting younger all the time.*

/ˈwɪzkɪd/
pl whizz-kids
⋈ a business, computer, stock exchange **whizz-kid**

whole-life policy *noun* (insurance)
a form of insurance in which the insured person pays a fixed amount each year, and when he/she dies the insurance company pays a fixed sum to his/her family: *She has just inherited a large sum from her father's whole-life policy.*

/ˌhəʊl ˈlaɪf ˌpɒləsi/
pl whole-life policies
⋈ take out a **whole-life policy**
▶ **life assurance policy**

wholesale *adjective, adverb* (commerce)
connected with buying and selling goods in large quantities from manufacturers: *the wholesale trade* ○ *He buys wholesale and sells retail.*

/ˈhəʊlseɪl/
⋈ a **wholesale** business, company, distributor, market, outlet, price; to buy, sell **wholesale**
▶ in bulk *under* **bulk, retail**

wholesale price *noun* (commerce)
▶ **trade price**

/ˌhəʊlseɪl ˈpraɪs/

wholesale price index *noun* (commerce/finance)
▶ **Producer Price Index**

/ˌhəʊlseɪl ˈpraɪs ˌɪn deks/

wholesaler *noun* (commerce)
a person or an organization that buys large quantities of goods from manufacturers and sells them to retailers who sell directly to the public: *The shopkeeper has gone to the wholesaler to buy new stock.*

/ˈhəʊlseɪlə(r)/
pl wholesalers
▶ **retailer**

w'hse *abbr*
warehouse: *w'hse surplus* ○ *ex w'hse stock*

note used in written English only

wholly owned subsidiary *noun* (commerce)
a company that is completely owned by another: *a wholly owned subsidiary of the insurance company*

/ˌhəʊlli ˌəʊnd səbˈsɪdiəri/
pl wholly owned subsidiaries
⋈ make (a company, a division,

etc) into a **wholly owned subsidiary**

▶ **subsidiary company**

---

wide area network *noun* (computing)

a system of links between computers spread over a large geographical area: *Wide area networks provide efficient transference of information.*

/ˌwaɪd ˌeəriə ˈnetwɜːk/

pl wide area networks

abbr WAN

▶ **local area network, network[1] 2**

---

wildcat *adjective*

(*informal*) **1** (*industrial relations*) of a strike or stoppage that is unofficial and is not supported by a trade union; of a worker who takes part in an unofficial strike: *Employees staged a series of wildcat strikes over pay.* ○ *Wildcat workers called a 24-hour strike.* **2** (*finance*) of a project or a business that is very risky financially: *His new business plan is a wildcat scheme.*

/ˈwaɪldkæt/

1 ⋈ a **wildcat** stoppage, strike, walk-out

▶ **strike[1]**

2 ⋈ a **wildcat** business, enterprise, scheme

---

will *noun* (law)

a legal document that states what should happen to a person's money and property after his/her death: *As she did not make a will, her money will be divided equally between her two children.* ○ *He started a business with the capital his father left him in his will.*

/wɪl/

pl wills

⋈ to make a **will**; leave (money, property, etc) to someone in a **will**

syn testament

▶ **beneficiary, estate 3, executor, legacy**

---

win *verb*

to obtain or achieve something: *They have won a contract worth millions.* ○ *We're winning orders through competitive pricing.*

/wɪn /

win, winning, won

note transitive verb

⋈ **win** a contract, deal

Winchester disk *noun* (computing)

a permanently sealed HARD DISK, used for many microcomputers: *Winchester disks have a high storage capacity.*

/ˈwɪntʃestə(r) dɪsk/

pl Winchester disks

▶ **disk**

---

windfall *noun* (finance)

an unexpected profit, or receipt of money or property: *receive a sudden windfall of £20 000* ○ *make a windfall profit*

/ˈwɪndfɔːl/

pl windfalls

⋈ get, have, receive a **windfall**; a cash, tax-free **windfall**

▶ **shortfall**

---

winding up *noun* (law/stock exchange)

the process of closing a company that has stopped trading, including the sale of its goods and property, and payment of its debts: *The winding up of the company will be announced today.* ○ *The court ordered the winding up of the insurance company.*

voluntary winding up the closing of a company that is agreed by its members and carried out without a court order: *The company members agreed that voluntary winding up was the easiest way to close the company.*

compulsory winding-up order a document issued by a court that orders a company to close: *We have received a compulsory winding-up order so trading has stopped.*

/ˌwaɪndɪŋ ˈʌp/

note not used with *a* or *an*. No plural and used with a singular verb only.

⋈ compulsory, voluntary **winding up**

▶ **liquidation, receivership, reserve capital**

---

winding-up sale *noun* (commerce)
▶ **closing down sale**

/ˌwaɪndɪŋ ˈʌp seɪl/

---

wind up *verb*
1 (*law/stock exchange*) to close a company that has stopped trading: *The court has ordered that the company should be wound up.* ○ *After 100 years in business, the company is winding up.* **2** to end a meeting, a discussion, a talk,etc: *If we all agree, let's wind up the meeting.* ○ *Before I wind up, I'd just like to say one more thing.*

/ˌwaɪnd ˈʌp/
wind up, winding up, wound up
note transitive verb
1 ⋈ **wind up** a business, a company, a firm, an organization
▶ **dissolve, liquidate**
2 ⋈ **wind up** a debate, discussion, meeting, session

---

window-dressing *noun*
1 (*commerce*) the art of arranging goods in a shop window to attract customers: *Good window-dressing has a definite effect on sales.* **2** (*finance*) making a business seem more profitable or efficient than it is: *Window-dressing is an unfair way of attracting customers.*

/ˈwɪndəʊ ˌdresɪŋ/
note not used with *a* or *an*. No plural and used with singular verb only.

WIP *abbr*
work in progress: *Please send me a copy of the WIP report.* ○ *a WIP meeting*

/ˌdʌblju aɪ ˈpiː/
note usually pronounced as individual letters

---

with average *adjective, adverb* (insurance/shipping)
a form of marine insurance that covers damage to a ship or its cargo while at sea: *The policy has been drawn up with average.*

/wɪð ˈævərɪdʒ/
abbr WA
▶ **average[1] 3, free of all average, free of particular average, general average**

---

withdraw *verb*
1 (*banking*) to take money out of a bank account: *She has withdrawn all her savings.* ○ *A fixed sum can be withdrawn each week.* ○ *He withdrew £500 from his account.* **2** to take something back: *They have withdrawn the takeover bid.* ○ *The German company withdrew from negotiations.* ○ *The offer has been withdrawn.* ○ *The faulty goods were withdrawn from sale.*

/wɪðˈdrɔː/
note transitive and intransitive verb
withdraw, withdrawing, withdrew, withdrawn
1 ⋈ **withdraw** cash, money, sums
opp to deposit
▶ **draw 2**
2 ⋈ **withdraw** a bid, an offer, a plan; **withdraw** (something) from sale, from the market
▶ **back out**

---

withdrawal *noun* (banking)
1 removing money from a bank account: *Withdrawals can be made with a week's notice.* **2** an amount of money removed from a bank account: *The statement has not registered the withdrawal.* ○ *a withdrawal of £100*

/wɪðˈdrɔːəl/
pl withdrawals
⋈ to make a **withdrawal**; a cash **withdrawal**; a **withdrawal** in cash
opp deposit

---

without engagement *adjective, adverb* (law)
relating to the price of something when the seller is not legally bound to keep that price: *All prices quoted are without engagement.*

/wɪðˌaʊt ɪnˈɡeɪdʒmənt/
▶ **estimate, quotation**

---

without prejudice *adjective, adverb* (law)
words on a document showing that the information it contains is not legally binding and cannot be used in a court of law: *She made a without prejudice statement.* ○ *The following facts are without prejudice.*

/wɪðˌaʊt ˈpredʒədɪs/

without recourse *adjective, adverb* (law)
words written above a signature on a bill of exchange to show that the holder cannot claim any money from the person who has signed it, if it is not paid by the DRAWEE: *This bill of exchange has been endorsed without recourse.*

/wɪðˌaʊt rɪˈkɔːs/
syn sans recours
▶ **bill of exchange**

with-profits policy *noun* (insurance)
a life assurance policy in which any profit made from investing the insurance payments is added to the original amount insured: *A with-profits policy represents a lucrative form of life assurance.*

/ˌwɪð ˌprɒfɪts ˈpɒləsi/
pl with-profits policies
▶ **interest, dividend**

witness[1] *noun* (law)
a person who sees something being done: *sign a document as/in front of a witness* ○ *We need an independent witness* (ie one who has nothing to gain and who will give an honest opinion). ○ *be called to the court as a witness of the accident*

/ˈwɪtnəs/
pl witnesses
⧓ act as, be, called as, in front of a **witness**

witness[2] *verb*
1 to see something being done: *She witnessed the crime.* **2** (*law*) to sign a document to show that the other signatures are genuine: *I witnessed the signing of the contract.*

/ˈwɪtnəs/
witness, witnessing, witnessed
note transitive verb
1 ⧓ **witness** an act, a crime
2 ⧓ **witness** an agreement, a contract, a signature
▶ **attest, authenticate, certify, validate**

wk. *abbr*
week: *a 10 wk. period*

note used in written English only

w/o *abbr*
without: *Repayment was made w/o interest.*

note used in written English only

w.o.b. *abbr* (shipping/insurance)
washed overboard: *Premiums will not be paid on goods w.o.b.*

note used in written English only

wording *noun* (administration)
the words used to express something; the way something is written: *Did you check the exact wording on the contract?* ○ *You could change the wording to make the meaning clearer.*

/ˈwɜːdɪŋ/
note usually singular
⧓ correct, exact, precise **wording**; the **wording** of a contract, document, report, statement

word-of-mouth advertising *noun* (advertising)
the spread of information about a product by buyers telling other people about it: *It will be a very low key campaign. We shall rely on word-of-mouth advertising.*

/ˌwɜːd əv ˌmaʊθ ˈædvətaɪzɪŋ/
note not used with *a* or *an*. No plural and used with a singular verb only.
⧓ depend on, rely on, use **word-of-mouth advertising**

word processing *noun* (computing)
using a word processor to produce letters, tables, reports, etc: *Word processing has greatly increased our efficiency.* ○ *We need to employ someone with good word processing skills.*

/ˈwɜːd ˌprəʊsesɪŋ/
note not used with *a* or *an*. No plural and used with a singular verb only.
⧓ **word processing** functions, skills, software

word processor *noun* (computing)
a machine with a keyboard and screen, used to produce letters, tables, reports, etc that can be corrected, edited, stored on disks and then printed: *Most of our office typing is now done on a word processor.*

/ˈwɜːd ˌprəʊsesə(r)/
pl word processors
abbr WP
⧓ type something on, use a **word processor**
▶ **computer, typewriter**

words and figures do not agree *noun* (banking)
the words written on a cheque to show that the amount in figures is not the same as the amount in words: *The cheque was returned stamped 'words and figures do not agree'.*

/ˌwɜːdz ənd ˌfɪgəz duː ˌnɒt əˈgriː/
note no plural
▶ **amounts differ**

work[1] *noun*
1 (**a**) what a person does to earn money: *He is looking for work.* ○ *I finish work at 5 pm.* (**b**) the place where you do this: *She is not yet home from work.* ○ *I left my briefcase at work.* **2** something that needs to be done: *There's a lot of work to do.* **3** effort or energy used to produce something: *Most of the work is done by machine.*

/wɜːk/
note not used with *a* or *an*. No plural and used with a singular verb only.
⧓ to do, find, go to, look for **work**; clerical, factory, office **work**
▶ **labour, job, occupation, profession, trade**

work[2] *verb*
1 to do something as a job and receive money for it: *to work as an accountant, an electrician, a secretary, etc* ○ *We are working hard to meet the deadline.* ○ *They work for an engineering company.* ○ *He used to work in the textile industry.* ○ *I work with a team of research scientists.* **2** (of a machine) to function; operate: *Why doesn't this computer work?* ○ *Can you work the new machinery?* ○ *Everything was working when I left last night.*

work something out to calculate something: *work out your monthly expenses*

work to something to follow a plan, a schedule, etc: *We have to work to tight deadlines.*

work towards something to aim to reach or achieve something: *We're working towards a profit of 2 million pounds this year.*

/wɜːk/
work, working, worked
note transitive and intransitive verb
⧓ **work** *as* (something), *at* (something), *at* (a place), *for* (someone), *in* (a place), *with* (someone)
▶ **perform**

workaholic *noun*
a person who works continually and is obsessed with their work: *The managing director is always in the office. He is a real workaholic.*

/ˌwɜːkəˈhɒlɪk/
pl workaholics

worker *noun*
a person who is employed by an organization: *The company has taken on more workers.* ○ *a building, an engineering, a factory, an office, etc worker*

/ˈwɜːkə(r)/
pl workers
▶ **blue-collar worker, casual, manual, white-collar worker**

worker director *noun* (management)
a person who helps to run a company who is a representative of the employees: *She has been elected worker director by both employees and shareholders.*

/ˌwɜːkə(r) dɪˈrektə(r)/
pl worker directors
⋈ appoint, choose, elect a **worker director**
▶ **director**

worker participation *noun* (industry)
a situation where employees are involved in making important decisions in a company, eg by being appointed to the board of directors: *The company has a good reputation for worker participation.*

/ˌwɜːkə pɑːˌtɪsɪˈpeɪʃn/
note not used with *a* or *an*. No plural and used with a singular verb only.
⋈ allow, introduce **worker participation**
syn employee participation

work-force *noun* (personnel)
all the employees in an office or factory: *The strike does not affect the whole work-force.* ○ *We aim to increase/reduce the work-force by 10%.*

/ˈwɜːkfɔːs/
note used with a singular or plural verb
⋈ part of, a section of the **work-force**; the total, whole **work-force**
▶ **manpower, personnel 1, staff**[1]

working *adjective* (industry/personnel)
1 (of people) employed or doing work: *the working population of a country* **2** (of things) functioning correctly or able to function: *produce a working model of a new engineering design*

/ˈwɜːkɪŋ/
2 ⋈ a **working** model

working capital *noun* (finance)
▶ **current capital**

/ˌwɜːkɪŋ ˈkæpɪtl/

working conditions *noun* (industrial relations/industry)
the state of the place where people work: *They have gone on strike for better working conditions.*

/ˈwɜːkɪŋ kənˈdɪʃnz/
note plural noun, used with a plural verb
⋈ good, poor, improved **working conditions**

working day *noun* (industry/personnel)
the part of the day during which work is done; days when work is done: *The unions are campaigning for a shorter working day.* ○ *There are only 28 working days till Christmas* (ie not counting weekends).

/ˌwɜːkɪŋ ˈdeɪ/
pl working days
▶ **day off**

working hours *noun* (commerce)
▶ **business hours**

/ˈwɜːkɪŋ ˌaʊəz/

working party *noun*
a group of experts formed to investigate and solve a problem: *The government has set up a working party to look into the problem.* ○ *The working party has/have finished its/their investigation.*

/ˈwɜːkɪŋ ˌpɑːti/
pl working parties
note used with a singular or plural verb
⋈ form, set up a **working party**; a **working party** advises, decides, recommends, reports
▶ **board, commission**[1] **2 b, committee, council**

work in progress *noun* (accounting)
partly manufactured goods; unfinished work: *The goods are recorded as work in progress in the accounts.*

/ˌwɜːk ɪn ˈprəʊgres/
note not used with *a* or *an*. No plural and used with a singular verb only.
⋈ a **work-in-progress** meeting, report
abbr W.I.P.

workload *noun*
an amount of work that needs to be done by someone: *Better pay would attract more workers and reduce the workload of those already employed.* ○ *Staff in my department cannot cope with their present workload.*

/ˈwɜːkləʊd/
pl workloads
⋈ a heavy, light **workload**; increase, reduce the **workload**
► **load**[1]

workman *noun*
a man who works, esp one who works with his hands: *A gang of workmen have closed the road to carry out repairs.*

/ˈwɜːkmən/
pl workmen
► **worker, labourer**

workmanlike *adjective* (industry)
done with skill or efficiently: *a workmanlike piece of engineering* ○ *The job was done with workmanlike efficiency.*

/ˈwɜːkmənlaɪk/
► **skilled**

workmanship *noun* (industry)
skill in doing something: *Look at the excellent workmanship in this furniture.*

/ˈwɜːkmənʃɪp/
note not used with *a* or *an*. No plural and used with a singular verb only.
⋈ excellent, fine **workmanship**
► **craftsmanship**

work permit *noun* (personnel)
an official document that allows a foreign citizen to work in a country: *He was told to leave because he didn't have a work permit.*

/ˈwɜːk ˌpɜːmɪt/
pl work permits
⋈ apply for, grant, issue, need, refuse a **work permit**
► **papers 2, pass**[1], **permit**[1], **visa**

workplace *noun*
a place where people do their jobs: *The authorities are worried about the increasing number of accidents in the workplace.*

/ˈwɜːkpleɪs/
note usually singular
► **workstation**

works *noun* (industry/manufacturing)
a place of work, esp a factory: *There was an accident at the works.* ○ *The steel works are/is closed for the holidays.*

works manager (*industry/management*) the person in charge of a factory: *The firm have appointed a new works manager.*

/wɜːks/
note used with a singular or plural verb
⋈ a chemical, an engineering, a steel **works**
► **ex works, public works**

work-sharing *noun* (personnel)
► **job-sharing**

/ˈwɜːk ʃeərɪŋ/

workshop *noun* (industry)
a room or building where things are made or repaired: *The company are renting a workshop in the new complex.* ○ *All tools are kept in the workshop.*

/ˈwɜːkʃɒp/
pl workshops
⋈ **workshop** space, staff
► **machine shop, tool shop**

vorkstation *noun* (computing/office practice)
ι desk equipped with a computer, printer, telephone, etc: *I have ;et up a workstation at home.* ○ *a personal workstation linked to a* ·*omputer system*

/ˈwɜːksteɪʃn/
pl workstations
⧓ to set up, to have, to use a **workstation**
▶ **desktop, workplace**

---

vork-to-rule *noun* (industrial relations)
vorking only according to rules agreed between the union and he management as a protest, eg not doing OVERTIME: *A work-to-ule has been called in protest at the unfair working conditions.*

/ˌwɜːk tə ˈruːl/
note singular noun, used with a singular verb
⧓ call, organize a **work-to-rule**
▶ **go-slow, industrial action, walk-out, strike**[1]

---

he World Bank *noun* (banking)
he common name for the central bank, controlled by the United Jations, that lends money to member states. It consists of two ·rganizations, the International Bank for Reconstruction and)evelopment and the International Development Association: *)eveloping countries in the third world have applied to the World 3ank for development grants.*

/ðə ˌwɜːld ˈbæŋk/
⧓ financed by **the World Bank**; a **World Bank** loan
▶ **European Bank for Reconstruction and Development, International Bank for Reconstruction and Development, International Development Association, International Finance Corporation, International Monetary Fund, Overseas Development Administration**

---

vorth[1] *noun*
·alue, esp measured in units of money: *They always try and get heir money's worth.* ○ *Give me £10 worth of petrol.*

/wɜːθ/
note not used with *a* or *an*. No plural and used with a singular verb only.
⧓ net, total **worth**
▶ **value**[1]

---

vorth[2] *adjective*
ιaving a value or a price: *It is not worth the price to repair it.* ○ *The* ·*roperty is worth £125 000.*

/wɜːθ/
note always follows the verb *to be.*

---

vorthless *adjective*
vithout value: *The cheque is worthless unless it is signed.* ○ *vorthless land*

/ˈwɜːθləs/
opp valuable

VP *abbr* (computing/office practice)
vord processor: *She does most of her writing on a WP.*

/ˌdʌbljuː ˈpiː/

VR *abbr* (distribution)
varehouse receipt: *Goods will only be handed over on submission of ι WR.*

/ˌdʌbljuː ˈɑː(r)/

---

vrapping *noun* (manufacturing)
he material used for packing and covering goods: *If we use less vrapping we can cut some of our production costs.*

hrink-wrapping plastic film that fits tightly around something: *shrink-wrapping around cheese, books, etc*

/ˈræpɪŋ/
pl wrappings
⧓ cellophane **wrapping**; **wrapping** paper
▶ **packaging, packing 2**

writ *noun* (law)
a document issued by a court that orders someone to do something: *The court issued a writ to prevent him from seeing his children.*

writ of execution (*law*) a document issued to enforce a court judgement: *The bailiff was carrying a writ of execution.*

writ of delivery (*law*) a document ordering a sheriff to seize certain goods: *Acting on the writ of delivery the sheriff was able to recover goods to the value of the amount stolen.*

writ of summons (*law*) an order issued by the High Court ordering the defendant to appear in court: *She will appear in court when she receives the writ of summons.*

/rɪt/
pl writs
⋈ issue, receive, serve a **writ**
▶ **garnishee order, injunction, subpoena[1], summons**

---

write *verb*
1 to put words and figures onto paper: *I intend to write to the manager.* ○ *The address is written at the top of the letter.*
2 (*insurance*) to accept liability for an insurance contract: *The most active of our underwriters has written a considerable amount of insurance this month.* **3** (*computing*) to introduce new information into the memory of a computer: *The document has been written into the computer.*

/raɪt/
write, writing, written, wrote
note transitive and intransitive verb
1 ⋈ **write** *to* someone; **write** something *down*
2 ▶ **underwriter**

---

write back *verb* (accounting)
to restore the BOOK VALUE of an ASSET that was thought to be valueless: *The customer made a definite promise to pay, so the debt could now be written back.*

/ˌraɪt ˈbæk/
write back, writing back, wrote back, written back
note transitive verb
▶ **write down, write off, write up**

---

write-back *noun* (accounting)
the restoration of the value of an ASSET previously thought to be valueless: *The value of the shares was restored in a write-back.*

/ˈraɪtbæk/
pl write-backs
⋈ **write-back** of a share, of an asset
▶ **write-off, write-down**

---

write down *verb* (accounting)
to reduce an ASSET to a lower value: *The machinery has been written down in the company's books.* ○ *written down value*

/ˌraɪt ˈdaʊn/
write down, writing down, wrote down, written down
note transitive verb
▶ **write back, write off, write up**

---

writedown *noun* (accounting)
recording the value of an ASSET as being lower than before: *The company's assets were severely decreased by the writedown.*

/ˈraɪtdaʊn/
pl writedowns
note transitive verb
▶ **write back, write down, write off**

---

write off *verb*
1 (*accounting*) to reduce the BOOK VALUE of an ASSET to nothing: *The unsuccessful investment had to be written off.* **2** to abandon something because it is so badly damaged that it is worthless or cannot be repaired: *After the storm the cargo was written off.*

/ˌraɪt ˈɒf/
write off, writing off, wrote off, written off
note transitive verb

▶ **write down, write back, write up**

write-off *noun*
a total loss; a reduction of an ASSET: *After the crash the car was a write-off.* ○ *The yearly accounts allow for write-offs.*

/ˈraɪtɒf/
pl write-offs
▶ **write down, write back, write up**

write up *verb* (accounting)
(*US*) to increase the value of an ASSET: *Because the market value of the land and buildings increased their value as assets was written-up.*

/ˌraɪt ˈʌp/
write up, writing up, wrote up, written up
note transitive verb
▶ **write down, write off, write back**

Wtd. *abbr* (commerce/manufacturing)
warranted: *Wtd. 100% pure* ○ *Wtd. machinery*

note used in written English only

W/W *abbr* (commerce/manufacturing)
warehouse warrant: *No retrieval of stored goods without W/W.*

note used in written English only

x *abbr* (office practice)
extension: *x302*

note used in written English only
(also **xtn.**, **extn.**)

x.d. *abbr* (stock exchange)
ex dividend; excluding divided: *x.d. shares*

note used in written English only

xerox[1] *noun* (office practice)
1 a machine that makes copies of letters, documents, etc: *use the xerox machine* ○ *make lots of copies on the xerox* **2** a copy of something produced in this way: *make 50 xeroxes of the document* ○ *The xerox copy is not very clear.*

/ˈzɪərɒks/
pl xeroxes
▶ **photocopier**

xerox[2] *verb* (office practice)
to make a copy of a document, letter etc on a xerox machine: *a xeroxed letter* ○ *I've just finished xeroxing these documents.*

/ˈzɪərɒks/
xerox, xeroxing, xeroxed
note transitive verb
▶ **photocopy**

x-inefficiency *noun* (management)
the amount by which an organization falls below its maximum ability to produce well-made goods by the cheapest and quickest method possible: *The factory was found to have a 25% x-inefficiency.* ○ *x-inefficiency due to bad management*

/ˌeks ˌɪnɪˈfɪʃnsi/
note no plural

xtn. *abbr* (office practice)
extension: *xtn. 216*

note used in written English only

year *noun*
a period of 365 days (366 days in a leap year) or twelve months: *I've worked for this company for three years.* ○ *Prices rose by an average of 5% last year.* ○ *This machine costs £10 000 a year to run.* ○ *an increase in productivity of about 10% per year*

calendar year the period from January 1st to December 31st: *No new jobs will be created this calendar year.*

/jɪə(r)/
pl years
abbr yr
⧓ last, next **year**; the coming, previous **year**
► **accounting period, financial year, tax year**

---

year book *noun* (accounting)
a book produced once a year by an organization, usually giving new or updated information, addresses, events, etc connected with a particular topic: *a copy of the 1991 Writer's and Artist's year book* ○ *Details of the project are recorded in the company's year book.*

/ˈjɪə(r) bʊk/
pl year books
(also **yearbook**)
pl yearbooks
► **handbook**

---

year-end *noun* (accounting)
the end of the FINANCIAL YEAR when a report is made on the accounts of a company: *a 19% improvement in year-end profits* ○ *The company announced a year-end loss of £256 million.* ○ *The latest turnover is £3.2 million, year-end December 1991.*

/ˌjɪər ˈend/
note no plural
► **annual report**

---

yearly *adjective, adverb*
happening every year or once a year: *pay in yearly instalments* ○ *The conference is held yearly.* ○ *a yearly budget of a million pounds* ○ *a half-yearly charge of £500*

/ˈjɪəli/

---

yield[1] *noun*
1 an amount of something that is produced: *The harvest produced a high yield.* ○ *a low milk yield* **2** (*stock exchange*) money received from an investment: *The shares provide a yield of 15%.*

/jiːld/
pl yields
⧓ improve, increase, reduce the **yield**
► **dividend yield, flat yield, gross yield, interest 2, nominal yield, redemption yield**

---

yield[2] *verb*
to produce or provide a product, profit or result: *The shares yielded a high rate of interest.* ○ *New farming methods should not take more from land than it is capable of yielding.*

/jiːld/
yield, yielding, yielded
note transitive verb
► **earn 2, produce[2]**

---

yield curve *noun* (stock exchange)
a curve on a graph that shows the amount of interest obtained from an investment, compared with the time taken for it to be repaid: *High interest securities have a steep yield curve.*

/ˈjiːld kɜːv/
pl yield curves
⧓ plot a **yield curve**

---

yield gap *noun* (stock exchange)
the difference between the amount of interest received from a fixed-interest security and an ordinary share: *The yield gap between the yield on shares and the yield on gilts remains steady.*

/ˈjiːld gæp/
note usually singular
⧓ a large, small **yield gap**

Yours faithfully (office practice)
used above a signature to end a letter that begins, *Dear Sir/Madam* when the person's name is unknown

/ˌjɔːz ˈfeɪθfəli/
▶ **Yours sincerely**

Yours sincerely (office practice)
used above a signature to end a letter that begins with a person's name, eg *Dear Mr/Mrs Smith*

/ˌjɔːz sɪnˈsɪəli/
▶ **Yours faithfully**

yr *abbr*
1 your: *With reference to yr letter of 5th May ...* **2** year: *The applicant must be 18 yrs or over.*

note used in written English only
2 pl yrs

Yrs. *abbr* (office practice)
Yours: *Yrs. sincerely* , ie before a signature on a letter

note used in written English only

Zz

zero[1] *noun*
1 the figure nought: *The code is zero seven zero three.* **2** no quantity; not any: *The sales figures show zero growth.* **3** the point on the scale of an instrument from which a positive or negative quantity can be measured: *Make sure the dial reads zero before you start.* ○ *Set the pointer at zero.*

/ˈzɪərəʊ/
1 pl zeros
2, 3 note not used with *a* or *an*. No plural and used with a singular verb only.

zero[2] *verb*
to set a machine, etc to a zero point: *Zero the timer before we start measuring.*

zero in on (*informal*) to look closely at; focus on: *I'd like you to zero in on these sales figures for a moment.*

/ˈzɪərəʊ/
zero, zeroing, zeroed
note transitive verb

zero inflation *noun* (finance)
inflation at 0%; price stability: *The aim is to achieve zero inflation.*

/ˌzɪərəʊ ɪnˈfleɪʃn/
note not used with *a* or *an*. No plural and used with a singular verb only.
▶ **inflation**

zero-rated *adjective, adverb* (tax)
of an item on which value added tax (VAT) is not charged: *Children's clothes are usually zero-rated.* ○ *zero-rated educational books*

/ˌzɪərəʊ ˈreɪtɪd/
▶ **value added tax**

zip code *noun*
(*US*) ▶ **postcode**

/ˈzɪp kəʊd/

zone *noun*
an area or region with a particular feature or use: *You are now entering an industrial zone.* ○ *Danger zone. Keep out!* ○ *You have to pay more if you travel outside the central zone.*

enterprise zone (*industry*) an area that receives government help to attract business and investment: *encourage building in an enterprise zone*

/zəʊn/
pl zones
▶ free trade zone *under* **free trade-**

economical *adjective* (economics)
careful with money or resources; not wasteful: *The new heating system proved economical to use.* ○ *We are looking for more economical production methods.*

/ˌiːkəˈnɒmɪkl, ˌekəˈnɒmɪkl/ — alternative pronunciation of the headword

⋈ **economical** to run, to use; an **economical** method

---

accepting house *noun* (banking)
an organization, often a merchant bank, that promises to pay a bill of exchange in return for a fee

/əkˈseptɪŋ haʊs/

pl accepting houses

syn (*US*) acceptance bank — American English word with the same meaning as the headword

► **accept 3, acceptance 2, discount house**

---

nationalize *verb* (industry)
to bring a company, or different companies in the same industry, under central government control: *The Labour Party in Britain decided to nationalize more industries.* ○ *nationalize the railways, the coal industry, etc* ○ *British Coal is a nationalized industry.*

/ˈnæʃnəlaɪz/

nationalize, nationalizing, nationalized

(also **nationalise**) — alternative spelling of the headword

note transitive verb

opp privatize

► **denationalize, private sector, public sector**

---

number of headword to show there is more than one headword with the same spelling. **Buy**[1] is a noun, **buy**[2] is a verb. — **buy**[2] *verb* (commerce/retail)
to obtain something by giving money for it; purchase: *buy a ticket, a newspaper, a box of chocolates* ○ *They are planning to buy an American company.* ○ *I have just bought some gas shares.* ○ *Prices are low, it's a good time to buy.*

idiom with its own definition and example — **buy in** to obtain goods or materials for stock or storage: *Our customers are buying in lots of coal for the winter.*

/baɪ/

buy, buying, bought

note usually transitive

► **purchase**[2], **sell**[1] **1**

---

cheque *noun* (banking)
a special printed form filled in and signed by a person (the DRAWER) asking a bank (the DRAWEE) to pay a sum of money to someone (the PAYEE): *The electricity bill may be paid in cash or by cheque.* ○ *write a cheque for £50*

reference to a headword mentioned in a definition — DRAWER

/tʃek/

pl cheques — plural of the headword

(*US* **check**) — different spelling used in American English

⋈ cross, endorse, honour, issue, sign, stop, write a **cheque** — collocates (words commonly used with the headword)

start of collocate section — ⋈